16

SOCIOLOGY: AN INTRODUCTION

SOCIOLOGY
AN INTRODUCTION

RONALD W. SMITH

FREDERICK W. PRESTON

BOTH OF THE UNIVERSITY OF NEVADA, LAS VEGAS

ST. MARTIN'S PRESS
NEW YORK

TO ERIC, KELLEEN, JEANNE, and TERI

Library of Congress Catalog Card Number: 76-28124
Copyright © 1977 by St. Martin's Press, Inc.
All Rights Reserved.
Manufactured in the United States of America.
0987
fedcb
For information, write: St. Martin's Press, Inc.,
175 Fifth Avenue, New York, N.Y. 10010

cover design: Rick Fiala
  Detail from *Death and Life*, painting by Gustav Klimt, 1908 and 1911. Reproduced with permission of Galerie Welz Salzburg.

ISBN: 312-73990-7

ACKNOWLEDGMENTS AND COPYRIGHTS

The authors wish to thank the companies and persons listed below for permission to use material in this book.

TEXTUAL MATERIAL AND TABLES

Excerpt from *The Painted Bird* (The new edition complete and revised with an introduction by the Author) by Jerzy Kosinski, p. 129, copyright by Jerzy Kosinski 1965, 1976. Reprinted by permission of Houghton Mifflin Company and the author.

Excerpts from "Body Ritual Among the Nacirema" by Horace Miner. Reproduced by permission of the American Anthropological Association from the *American Anthropologist* 58(3), 503–505, 1956.

Acknowledgments and copyrights for further textual material and tables and for illustrations continue at the back of the book on page 553, which constitutes an extension of the copyright page.

PREFACE

We have written this introduction to sociology with several goals in mind. The most fundamental of these has been to present a survey that is sociologically sound—a balanced, accurate synthesis of the theories and discoveries of the most perceptive students of human society. A second goal has been to offer our readers a view of sociology as a constantly developing, humanistic discipline that is, at its best, both a science and an art. A third goal has been to make our text not only clearer and more convenient to use but also more immediately interesting for today's students than other texts now available. We do not imagine, of course, that we have achieved all of these goals completely, but we do hope that the product of our efforts will be found useful.

We make no apology for a certain missionary zeal that impels us to try to make our subject appealing. Sociology, in our view, is endlessly fascinating as well as socially valuable, and nothing could please us more than to think that this book had helped to interest some of its readers in pursuing further study in the discipline. At the same time, we recognize that for many students the introductory course will be the first and last in sociology, and we have tried to provide insights and a framework for understanding human society that will enrich our readers' study in other fields and be of permanent value in their lives beyond the college or university.

In accordance with our objectives, there are certain respects in which this book is broader in scope than many others. We have included a chapter on leisure and sport and one on alienation, topics not often given such coverage in introductory texts but topics that are, we believe, important and inherently interesting. We also have a chapter on the future—always a risky subject but one that is very much on the minds of the readers to whom this book is addressed.

A major distinguishing feature of this book is our use of numerous brief excerpts from literature, ranging from Dickens and Balzac to Steinbeck and Vonnegut. Woven into our presentation right alongside quotations from sociologists such as Emile Durkheim, Max Weber, Lester Ward, C. Wright Mills, and Robert Merton (to name but a few), these literary materials are no mere window dressing, no "gimmick"; they are vivid illustrations in dramatic human terms of the sociological imagination at work. They both illustrate and deepen the sociological content. As teachers who live and work in Las Vegas—a laboratory for the sociologist if ever there was one—we have often made effective use of Myron Cohen's charming ethnic humor to illustrate the experience of the immigrant or of Bill Cosby's anecdotes to illuminate the socialization process. Cohen and Cosby are not readily captured on the printed page; but one finds the same kind of impact in F. Scott Fitzgerald's depictions of a society stratified by wealth, or Charles Dickens's description of a delinquent subculture represented by Fagin's "school" of crime, or Shirley Jackson's exploration of cultural determinism in "The Lottery."

We have had a great deal of help in the development of this book. First of all, we thank our students at the University of Nevada in Las Vegas both for their enthusiasm, which has helped us to know when we were on the right track, and for their silent stares (or worse) when we were not. The contribution of Jeanne Preston and Teri Smith, both literary scholars, goes far beyond their suggestion of dozens of literary selections. If our text is, as we think, clearer and more easily read than most, the credit is largely theirs. To the extent that we have fallen short of complete lucidity, they are not to be blamed.

Many of our colleagues have been helpful. We particularly wish to thank Donald Carns, Robert Dodge, Andrea Fontana, James Frey, Rae Horelly, John Horvath, John Irsfeld, Linda Maxwell, Joseph McCullough, Lynn Osborne, Loren Reichert, Rose Richardson, Anthony Schlee III, and John Unrue. We also deeply appreciated the detailed and helpful suggestions of, among others, Charles Allyn of Foothill College; Alan Jensen of California State University, Chico; Florence Karlstrom of Northern Arizona University; James R. McIntosh of Lehigh University; Anthony Walsh of Marquette University; and Jack M. Weller of the University of Kansas.

Editorial assistance has also been of the highest order. Arthur Strimling, Carolyn Eggleston, and Thomas Broadbent of St. Martin's Press and Joy Kryder, Robin Schwartz, and Diane Zach of the University of Nevada have given freely of their talents, patience, and understanding.

Finally, we would very much like to thank each other for the entire experience. Though one name necessarily precedes the other on the cover, there is no primary author of this text. We are equally responsible, and the order in which our names would be listed was decided, very much in the tradition of our city, by the flip of a coin.

Ronald W. Smith
Frederick W. Preston

CONTENTS

INTRODUCTION

1. THE SCIENCE AND ART OF SOCIOLOGY 3

The Meaning and Origins of Sociology 5
Sociology as Science 7
Sociology as Art 9
Humanism 12
The Approach of this Text 13
Summary 14
Key Terms for Review 15
Suggested Readings 15

PART 1 CULTURE AND SOCIALIZATION 17

2. CULTURE 19

Cultural Transmission 20
Nonmaterial Culture 22
   Mores 23, Customs and Folkways 24
Ethnocentrism 25
Cultural Relativism and Cultural Universals 34
Summary 38
Key Terms for Review 38
Suggested Readings 39

3. SOCIALIZATION 41

The Meaning of Socialization 41
Theories of Socialization 49
  Reinforcement Theory 49, Cognitive Theory 52,
  Symbolic Interactionism 52
Variations in Socialization Methods 58
Social Change and Resocialization 60
Summary 61

Key Terms for Review 62
Suggested Readings 62

PART 2 SOCIAL ORGANIZATION 65

4. THE MEANING OF SOCIAL ORGANIZATION 67

Defining Social Organization 68
Norms and Sanctions 70
Status and Role 74
   Types of Statuses 76, Role Performance 79
Deviance and Social Disorganization 84
Summary 91
Key Terms for Review 92
Suggested Readings 92

5. GROUPS 95

Aggregates, Categories, and Groups 96
Types of Groups 98
   Voluntary and Involuntary Groups 98, Open and Closed Groups 99, Large and Small Groups 100, Vertical and Horizontal Groups 100, Majority and Minority Groups 101, In-groups and Out-groups 102, Reference Groups 106
Primary and Secondary Groups 107
Degree of Organization 112
Summary 113
Key Terms for Review 114
Suggested Readings 114

6. BUREAUCRACY 17

Organizations and Bureaucracy 119
The Informal Structure 122
Problem Areas in a Bureaucracy 125
   Bureaucratic Goals and Employee Concerns 125, Goal Displacement 125, Degree of Formal Control 127, Bureaucratic Personality 127, Communication 128, Member Participation 131, Adaptability to Environment 134
Changing Bureaucracies 134
Summary 135
Key Terms for Review 136
Suggested Readings 136

7. STRATIFICATION 139

The Meaning of Stratification 143
Principal Types of Stratification 143
   Caste 143, Estate 144, Class 145
The Structure of Class Society 146
   Economic, Social, and Political Orders 147
The Functional Necessity of Stratification 151
Social Mobility 153
Stratification in American Society 155
   Economic Inequality 155, Status Inequality 157, Power Inequality 161, Vertical Social Mobility 162, Class Consciousness 163
Summary 164
Key Terms for Review 166
Suggested Readings 166

PART 3 INSTITUTIONS 169

8. FAMILY 171

Variations in Family Patterns 171
   Marriage 172, Dominance 176, Residence 176, Descent Privileges 176, Nuclear and Extended Families 177
Functions of the Family 179
   Reproduction 180, Regulation of Sexual Activity 180, Socialization 181, Conferral of Status 183, Provision of Affection and Companionship 185
Family Problems in American Society 185
   Changing Sex Roles 186, Economic Crisis 190, Child-rearing 191, Divorce 192
Nontraditional Family and Marriage Patterns 194
Summary 200
Key Terms for Review 201
Suggested Readings 201

9. RELIGION 205

Defining the Institution 205
The Functions and Dysfunctions of Religion 208
   Priestly Function 208, Prophetic Function 211, Self-Identity Function 212, Buttress Function 214, Age-grading Function 214, Explanation Function 214
Religion and Social Organization 219
   Religion and the Socioeconomic Order 220, Religion and Social Status 220, Religion and Changing

the Social Order 223
Religion and Social Class 223
Magic, Witchcraft, and the Supernatural 226
Summary 227
Key Terms for Review 228
Suggested Readings 229

10. EDUCATION   231

Functions of Education 231
   Transmission of Culture 232, Placement 234,
   Development of New Knowledge 236, Individual
   Development 236
American Values Regarding Education 237
Problems of American Education 239
   Goals of American Education 242, Economic Support for
   Schools 246, Schools and Lower-class Children 251
   The Large, Bureaucratic School 255, Are Students
   Changing? 257
Summary 257
Key Terms for Review 258
Suggested Readings 258

11. POLITICS AND ECONOMICS   261

Conflict and Consensus 262
Power and Authority 264
Politics and Economics in Developing Nations 265
Political Change 267
A World of Postindustrial States 272
   Society and the Threat of Nuclear War 272,
   Ideology 276
Summary 277
Key Terms for Review 278
Suggested Readings 279

PART 4   SOCIAL CHANGE   281

12. SOCIAL CHANGE   283

Explanations for Change 284
   The Theological Explanation 285, The Null
   Explanation 285, Geographic Determinism 285,
   Material Determinism 286, Biological Determinism 286,
   Cultural Determinism 287
The Interaction of Variables 288
Change and Individual Adjustment 293

Summary 298
Key Terms for Review 298
Suggested Readings 299

13. COLLECTIVE BEHAVIOR AND SOCIAL MOVEMENTS 301

Types of Collective Behavior 305
Crowds 305
    Publics 309, Crazes and Fashions 309, Social Movements 310
Explanations of Collective Behavior 310
    Ignorant Mass View 310, Alienated Mass View 311, Value-added Theory 317
Rumor: Communication in Collective Behavior 318
Social Movements 320
    Objectives, Programs, and Ideologies 320, Commitment 321, Stages of Development 323, Kinds of Social Movements 323
Summary 325
Key Terms for Review 326
Suggested Readings 326

PART 5 — PROBLEMS AND ISSUES 329

14. ALIENATION 331

The Concept of Alienation 331
    Powerlessness 331, Meaninglessness 334, Normlessness 335, Isolation 336, Self-estrangement 339, Subjective and Objective Alienation 339
Social Conditions Related to Alienation 342
Alienated Groups in American Society 344
    Industrial Workers 344, Racial and Ethnic Minorities 345, Students 347, The Middle Class 349
Summary 351
Key Terms for Review 352
Suggested Readings 352

15. RACE AND ETHNICITY 355

Interracial and Interethnic Contact 359
    Segregation 359, Stratification 360, Assimilation 360, Pluralism 363, Expulsion 365, Annihilation 367, Amalgamation 367
Race Relations Cycles 372
Power and Race Relations 373

Apartheid in South Africa 373, Stratification in
Hong Kong 376, Segregation in the United States 378
Causes of Prejudice 378
Prospects 380
Summary 383
Key Terms for Review 383
Suggested Readings 384

16. DEVIANCE AND CRIME 387

Explanations for Deviant and Criminal Behavior 389
   Pathology 389, Differential Association 390, Social
   Disorganization 393, Labeling 394, Value Conflict 395
Deviant Behavior and Several of Its Forms 396
   Prostitution 398, Homosexuality 400, Alcoholism 402,
   Mental Illness 406
Crime and Several of Its Forms 408
   Criminal Homicide 409, White-collar Crime 415,
   Organized Crime 417
Summary 421
Key Terms for Review 422
Suggested Readings 422

17. LEISURE AND SPORT 425

The Meaning of Leisure 425
The Meaning and Importance of Sport 427
Why Sports are Popular 429
   The Success of Sports 429, The Comprehensibility of
   Sports 429, The Mystery and Romance of Sports 431,
   Sports and Displacement of Aggression 432, Sports and
   Ethnocentrism 433, The Benefits of Sports 436
Sports and Social Mobility 437
   Early Loss of Income 442, Loss of Public Acclaim 442
The Future of Leisure and Sport 444
Summary 446
Key Terms for Review 446
Suggested Readings 447

18. CITIES AND SUBURBS 449

Urban Growth 451
   Origins of the Modern City 451, Metropolitan Areas
   and the Megalopolis 455
Urban Life 456
Problems of the Central City 462
   Financial Strains 463, Decentralized Government 465,

CONTENTS / xiii

Crime 470, Pollution 472, Mass Transit 473, Ghettos 474
Suburbs 477
Summary 483
Key Terms for Review 484
Suggested Readings 484

19. POPULATION 487

The Population Debate 489
    Malthus: Recognition of the Problem 489, The Neo-Malthusian Position 490, The Marxist Position 492, The Optimists' Position 493
Demographic Data and Terminology 494
    Fecundity Measurement 495, Infant Mortality Measurement 497, Morbidity Measurement 497, Mortality Measurement 497
The Demographic Transition 500
Future Growth 501
Summary 506
Key Terms for Review 506
Suggested Readings 507

EPILOGUE: THE FUTURE 509

Basic Assumptions 509
Predictions and Scenarios 512
    Increasing Culture Lag 512, More Social Control 515
Methods of Social Control 517
    Behavior Modification 517, Electronic Surveillance 520, Centralized Data Systems 522
A Ray of Sunshine 523
Key Terms for Review 525
Suggested Readings 525

NOTES 527

GLOSSARY 539

NAME INDEX 561

SUBJECT INDEX 565

SOCIOLOGY: AN INTRODUCTION

IN THIS CHAPTER

The Meaning and Origins of Sociology   5

Sociology as Science   7

Sociology as Art   9

Humanism   12

The Approach of this Text   13

Summary   14

Key Terms for Review   15

Suggested Readings   15

What is sociology?
Is sociology a science?
What is the relationship between sociology and the arts?

THE SCIENCE AND ART OF SOCIOLOGY

We were once teaching a summer course aboard a posh ocean liner as it made its way around the great circle of the Pacific. During the journey from Sydney to Hong Kong, we were studying data on the population of Hong Kong—how many people live there, their national and ethnic identifications, their average income, and other such information. We thought we knew that British colony very well as we steamed rapidly toward it.

As the ship came within a day of the crown colony, anticipation quickened the leisurely shipboard pace, and we discussed enthusiastically the many bargains offered by this famous trade center. Indeed, we went to sleep the night before arrival dreaming of custom-made dresses and suits, color television sets, and the latest in stereo and quad components.

Dawn revealed the mainland of China. The great ship slowed as it passed through an ever-increasing number of fishing junks and toylike sampans, then stopped in preparation for docking at the marine terminal of Kowloon. We now began to realize the inadequacy of our shipboard knowledge of Hong Kong. We knew the statistics about poverty in the colony, but they came to life for us only when we began to see for ourselves what they represented.

The sampans that were now alongside the ship contained Chinese families begging for food. Even to the untrained eye these families showed unmistakable signs of malnutrition. Toward the outstretched arms of the hungry Chinese we tossed fruit, rolls, and cheese. Suddenly we understood Hong Kong. To us, the crown colony was no longer merely a stopping-off place where the products of cheap labor could be gathered up. Rather, it was a teeming metropolis inhabited by very real people, many of whom lived in conditions of very real poverty.

Our experience of Hong Kong helped us understand more than just the reality of life there, though that was in itself an important understanding.

The sampans and junks of Hong Kong reveal a standard of living well below anything most Westerners can imagine.

Poverty is a way of life for many in Hong Kong. This family has achieved the dream of living in government housing—a 10' × 12' room.

It also gave us some insight into the nature of the subject we were studying—sociology. We could not deny that we had some sociological knowledge of Hong Kong prior to our arrival there. It was a scientific knowledge of statistical data and factual studies of the population. But as we found out, our sociological knowledge was incomplete until we had achieved what we might call an artistic understanding of conditions in Hong Kong: we sensed what life there was like and related to those conditions in a personal way. Our experience convinced us that sociology is both a science and an art. Let us note here that we use the term "art" to refer to a way of perceiving that involves our emotions as well as our intellect and a system of thought that encompasses, rather than excludes, our emotional and sensory perceptions.

In this text we intend to reveal both the scientific and artistic sides of sociology. We will present the concepts, studies, and data of the science of sociology. But we will also furnish, through the works of numerous authors, scenes from literature that help to bring the science to life. We cannot all witness the reality of poverty in Hong Kong or acquire an immediate knowledge of many other sociological phenomena. We should all, however, be able to view the real people behind the concepts and the data that are so impersonal and abstract. First, though, we must set about understanding just what sociology is and how it came to have this dual character as an art and a science.

The Meaning and Origins of Sociology

Although sociology has been studied as an academic discipline for nearly 150 years, it was not well known or accepted by the public until relatively recently. During the 1950s, for instance, sociologists were forever having to explain to neighbors, friends, and relatives that sociologists were not necessarily socialists, that the two words were not the same. Sociologists' attempts to improve social conditions during the 1960s in programs such as Head Start, the Peace Corps, and VISTA somewhat altered the image of the discipline, and now *Time* and *Newsweek* magazines regularly report on sociological research. Yet one still meets more than an occasional blank stare when answering the question "What do you do?" with the response "I am a sociologist."

A concise definition of sociology, at least one that can be agreed upon by most sociologists, has yet to be formulated. Some prefer to emphasize science and are content with the broad definition of sociology as the science of society. Others stress the ideas of change and social process and

It is difficult to understand human beings without seeing them in their own social context. To understand the individuals in this group in Mombasa, Kenya, we need to know something about their culture.

The chanting Masai women pictured here are helping preserve their tribe's traditional culture through ritual and costume.

Auguste Comte, the "father of sociology."

view sociology as the study of human behavior in relationship to other humans—the study of interaction. Still others avoid many of the underlying assumptions of the varying definitions and simply state that sociology is what sociologists do.

For our purposes we shall define *sociology* as the study of human beings within their social contexts. This definition emphasizes that sociology concentrates on learning about interrelationships. Individuals and groups are best understood not as isolated entities, but in relation to other individuals and groups.

In a sense, there have always been students of society interested in investigating the interaction of people in groups to gain insight into the nature of human relationships. But these scholars did not always believe that such insight could be used to help alleviate human suffering and create a better future for humanity. Indeed, many ancient and medieval social philosophers believed that perfection lay in the past not the future. Ancient Jews held the view that humanity had "fallen" and that scholars must look to the past for knowledge and an understanding of the human condition. Later Christian social philosophers inherited the Jewish notion of the Fall and came to believe that earthly perfection was impossible.

Eventually scholars began to consider the possibility of a better life for human beings on earth. Many consider Francis Bacon (1561–1626), lord chancellor of England, the pivotal figure in the development of a progressive world view. He was an advocate of *empiricism*—the practice of relying on observation and experiment to draw conclusions. Through empirical science, Bacon believed, humans could achieve both control over nature and a betterment of their own condition.

With the foundation laid by Bacon, the seventeenth and eighteenth centuries witnessed many inquiries that could be considered sociological. Such thinkers as Goethe, Voltaire, Hobbes, Locke, and Hume dealt with sociological themes. Not until the nineteenth century, however, did sociology as such become a recognized field of study. During the 1830s French social philosopher Auguste Comte (1798–1857) published his *Positive Philosophy*, a statement of belief in a "science of society" and "universal progress."[1] He renamed this "social physics" "sociology," and the discipline had both its name and its "founding father."

Sociology as Science

Early sociologists were enthusiastically optimistic about the new discipline. The success of empiricism and the scientific method was everywhere to be seen. The Industrial Revolution had shown that rigorous thought could bring forth great change. Scholars such as Herbert Spencer (1820–1903) and William Graham Sumner (1840–1910) were quite conservative, however. Sumner felt that the ultimate contribution of sociology would be a recognition that people should not attempt to "better" the human condition. Sociology would reveal natural laws of social interaction and human behavior that would show "misguided" liberals that attempts to bring change were wasted effort.

> *In general it may be said that those whom humanitarians and philanthropists call the weak are the ones through whom the productive and conservative forces of society are wasted. They constantly neutralize and destroy the finest efforts of the wise and industrious, and are a dead-weight on the society in all its struggles to realize any better things.*[2]

But other early sociologists, such as Lester Frank Ward (1841–1913), firmly believed in the direct application of sociological knowledge to the world about them. Ward was almost naively certain that the ability to reason would enable human beings to solve the many persistent problems of society. Upon the discovery of the "canals" of Mars he commented:

> *We may suppose that in Mars the conquest of nature is complete, and that every law and every force of nature has been discovered and utilized. Under such conditions there would seem to be scarcely any limit to the power of the being possessing this knowledge to transform it to his needs. The lesson is that man may also do this.*[3]

As the complexities of human interaction became increasingly obvious, the early euphoria of the field as expressed by Ward gave way to more sophisticated considerations. The University of Chicago's Department of Sociology, under the leadership of Albion W. Small (1850–1926), served as the center for the development of sociology during the first thirty years of this century. One of the early lights of the so-called Chicago school, W. I. Thomas (1863–1947), began to recognize the difficulties that were being encountered by sociologists who used the somewhat simplistic natural science approach in the study of human behavior and interaction. A major difficulty was that human life is far more complex than plant life. In contrast to plants and many animals, humans perceive and define their own position in a social setting. They formulate a *definition of the situation,* a formulation that tends to vary from individual to individual and situation to situation. Whereas a plant presumably does not think about sunlight but simply reacts to it, a human being may interpret and react to sunlight in a variety of ways. Human interaction is necessarily a process—a process of identifying and resolving problems, a process of becoming.

The techniques of investigation in sociology were likewise becoming more complex. New mathematical approaches for dealing with data were developed. Some sociologists believed the complexity of human behavior was matched by the growing complexity and sophistication of sociological inquiry. Others, however, increasingly questioned the assumption that sociology is a science in the sense that physics and biology are sciences.

Discussions over whether or not human behavior differs from all other forms of animal behavior have been a part of sociology from its beginning. During the late 1930s, when sociology finally became accepted in the academic establishment, the question took on new importance. George A. Lundberg (1895–1966), the most famous and articulate spokesman for the school that views sociology as a pure science (like physics), was roundly criticized by Robert M. MacIver (1882–1970), a sociologist who for many years had maintained that human life was unique and that therefore the methods of a science of society must be distinct from those of other sciences. In referring to Lundberg, MacIver intoned:

> *Thus one writer seems to object to our drawing a distinction between the type of causality involved when a paper flies before the wind and that revealed when a man flies from a pursuing crowd . . . the paper knows no fear and the wind no hate, but without fear and hate the man would not fly nor the crowd pursue.*[4]

That particular debate has never been fully resolved, nor can it be. The behavior of human beings is, no doubt, exceedingly complex when compared to that of many other forms of life. Yet even if we accept the notion that human behavior is unique, many of the assumptions of a science of society are still valid. The scientific demands for rigor and careful collec-

In our own society people interact differently depending on the social context in which they find themselves. A block party in a middle-class suburb brings people into friendly contact. Waiting in line for a hurried lunch causes quite different reactions—people stare straight ahead and avoid contact.

tion of data are very much a part of sociology. It is in this sense that almost all scholars agree sociology is a science. Practitioners of the discipline are careful to back their statements about behavior with observations. It is not enough to state that you feel or think that the middle class believes this or that. It is necessary, if you are acting as a scientist, to (1) define what you mean by "the middle class" and (2) describe the procedures you used in collecting and analyzing the data that led you to make a particular statement about the beliefs of that group.

What we are noting here is that science is, in part, a system which requires rigorous and precise definitions as well as empirical (observational) evidence. Utilizing such a system of organized facts, collected in an agreed upon and repeatable manner, sociologists have gathered an impressive amount of information over the years. They can explain what groups tend to behave in certain ways and why. They can demonstrate that much of what is thought to be common sense and "a known fact" may really be nonsensical and factually inaccurate when examined in a scientific manner. The statistical information we were studying on board the ship headed for Hong Kong is just one example of the kind of data sociologists collect. In this book we have attempted to include a great deal of current scientific information, the result of sociologists' research, particularly about contemporary problems and issues.

Sociology as Art

Despite the impressive collection of data sociology has available to it today, MacIver's reservations about the possibility of a science of society are still shared by a number of sociologists. Many feel that sociologists can understand the critical elements in human interaction only by taking the role of the other—by perceiving the world from the point of view of the subject of their investigation. This perspective, of course, does not mean that one must *be* the subject of investigation. To use two analogies from pure science, one does not have to be a molecule to understand the relationships of chemical equations; nor does one have to give birth to understand the processes of birth. Sociologists who emphasize taking the role of the other indicate that obviously it is not necessary to be poor, or an Eskimo, or white, or whatever to understand "what it is like" to be poor, or an Eskimo, or white, or whatever. If that were the case, the only thing we could understand is what we are, and we could only partially understand that since there would be nobody to share our ideas with—other people wouldn't or couldn't understand us either. Clearly what this perspective demands is that we try to understand and appreciate what it is like to be someone else. Such understanding and appreciation are vital to the comprehension of human interaction and critical to an understanding of sociology.

Sociologists who stress taking the role of the other consider their subject more an art than a science. They emphasize the difference between scientific knowledge and artistic understanding. *Knowledge* pertains to what we grasp intellectually—facts. *Understanding* refers to what might be called gut-level acquaintance.

Sociologists Max Weber (1864–1920) and Charles Horton Cooley (1864–1929) give somewhat more eloquent explanations of understanding. Weber called understanding *verstehen* and thought of it as a kind of intuition, something that one knows but may not be able to document or account for scientifically.[5] Cooley referred to understanding as *sympathetic introspection:* a sociologist would come to know his subject by

> *putting himself into intimate contact with various sorts of persons and allowing them to awake in himself a life similar to their own,*

Members of our fast-paced, rapidly changing society would have difficulty imagining the life of Arctic Eskimos. The Eskimo hunters shown here are dragging home huge hunks of flesh cut from a Bowhead whale.

which he afterwards, to the best of his ability, recalls and describes. In this way he is more or less able to understand—always by introspection—children, idiots, criminals, rich and poor, conservative and radical—any phase of human nature not wholly alien to his own.[6]

The sociologist as artist seeks and incorporates into a system of knowledge this kind of understanding—the understanding we achieved that morning in the harbor of Hong Kong.

The distinction between knowledge and understanding is a major difference between sociology as science and sociology as art. In addition, there are important differences in method. Sociologists as scientists are more concerned with certain criteria of formal scientific inquiry. In particular, they feel they must conduct their investigations in such a manner that another person could exactly duplicate, or *replicate*, the process. In other words, if the study were repeated, the results would be similar, just as certain chemical experiments consistently yield the same results.

For example, suppose sociologists using the scientific approach wished to investigate the nature and extent of alcoholism in the United States. They would first gather all existing information and data available on the subject. They might then construct a questionnaire, or questionnaires, designed to collect additional information. The questionnaires would be submitted to a relatively large number of people—alcoholics (including those who have quit drinking), experts in the field, people who work with alcoholics, relatives of alcoholics, and anyone else deemed appropriate. These sociologists would then compile and analyze the responses, carefully specifying each step taken. Thus other sociologists could repeat their study—presumably with the same results.

Sociologists as artists, by contrast, are less concerned with factual data and the ability to have an investigation replicated. In a study on alcoholism, they might utilize literary works, informal interviews, participant observation (the researcher lives among and observes the subjects), and other techniques more geared to feeling as an alcoholic feels than to describing alcoholics. They would not make the assumption that anyone trained in such techniques of investigation could duplicate the process and achieve the same results. However, the sociologist as artist does not ignore the principles of scientific inquiry. Participant observers, for example, take careful notes and record routines as they inhabit and observe the world they are studying—in our example perhaps skid row. The investigator may perceive this world as an artist, but he or she must describe it in an orderly and rigorous manner as a scientist. Still, the assumptions of replication are not necessarily made. As participant observers, you and I might observe and record the same things, but most probably we would not feel and understand them in the same way.

We have emphasized the differences between sociology as science and sociology as art, but in fact both perspectives are needed for full comprehension of the social world. This viewpoint is shared by sociologist Rob-

Sociological data are often collected through attitude polls. How questions are phrased and the way responses are evaluated are crucial aspects of such research.

12 / SOCIOLOGY: AN INTRODUCTION

ert A. Nisbet. He comments that we must never forget that sociology is an art as well as a science, otherwise "we run the risk of losing the science, finding ourselves with a sandheap of empiricism or methodological narcissism, each as far from science as art is from billboard advertisements."[7] In this work we intend to follow the lead of both the scientists and the artists of sociology. And we will utilize the findings and tools of both.

Humanism

Before we start our investigation of sociological topics, one further tradition in human inquiry must be noted—the tradition of *humanism*. The term "humanism" actually refers to a cluster of ideas which together form a cohesive perspective. One aspect of this perspective is the assumption that human beings are able to solve human problems (as opposed to waiting for divine intervention or the functioning of some immutable natural law). This assumption prompts humanist scholars to direct their efforts at identifying, examining, and alleviating such problems. Another aspect of the humanist perspective is the idea that human life should be an end in itself. That is, human beings should always be treated as persons, not as objects or a means to some end. A final critical aspect of humanism is the

Many artists have been concerned with sociological phenomena; this painting by Honoré Daumier is entitled *The Third-Class Carriage*.

Sociologists in the humanist tradition are concerned with alleviating human suffering, captured here by Georges Rouault in "It is hard to live . . ." Plate 12 from *Miserere*, 1922.

related belief that human life is paramount and that it is distinct from all other forms of existence.

In sociology, there are a number of humanists and a rather longstanding humanistic tradition. Most of those who see sociology as an art are humanists, whereas most sociologists who favor the pure science approach are not. C. Wright Mills (1916–1962), a humanist sociologist and a kind of folk hero to many humanist scholars, has given us what stands as the definitive statement for humanist study:

> *It is the political task of the social scientist—as of any liberal educator—continually to translate personal troubles into public issues, and public issues into the terms of their human meaning for a variety of individuals. It is his task to display in his work—and as an educator, in his life as well—this kind of sociological imagination.*[8]

The Approach of This Text

The chapters in this book are centered around concepts (e.g., culture and socialization), institutions (e.g., the family), or problems (e.g., alienation). In all cases we attempt not only to cover the major issues that contemporary sociologists consider important in those areas but also to develop the sociological imagination of the reader. At all times we attempt to integrate the approaches of sociology as art and sociology as science.

Clearly there are particularly appropriate uses for numerical data in the quest for knowledge and understanding, and they are included in a number of instances. Obviously one must use such data or be rather much at the whim of personal experience—what we may call the "my Aunt Gretta theory" of human behavior. This quaint viewpoint is employed when people simply cannot project beyond their own experience. For instance, when told that the highest murder rates in the country are in the South, some would respond with "Well, my Aunt Gretta said that Toledo and St. Louis are really dangerous." Numerical data, properly understood, are much more enlightening than Aunt Gretta.

But we must go beyond numerical data to achieve understanding. We must at times even go beyond the works of sociologists, who, like many other scientists and academicians, are not always trained as writers. The talented author is usually more adept at creating a feeling, capturing a moment, or generating understanding. Therefore, throughout the book, we have included excerpts from various styles and periods of literature both to illustrate ideas and to offer further insight into human behavior.

To give you some idea of literature's great effectiveness in portraying sociological ideas, consider this description of an alcoholic from *Crime and Punishment*, by the Russian novelist Feodor Dostoevsky:

> He was a man of over fifty, of middle height and corpulent build, with grizzled hair and a large bald patch. His face was bloated with continual drinking and his complexion was yellow, even greenish. From between his swollen eyelids his little reddish slits of eyes glittered with animation. But there was something very strange about him; his eyes had an almost rapturous shine, they seemed to hold both intelligence and good sense, but gleams of something like madness showed in them as well.[9]

Now compare Dostoevsky's portrait with this prosaic statement:

> The percentage of alcoholics increases for those over fifty with life expectancy steadily decreasing as numerous alcohol-related bodily dysfunctions increase.

Both passages tell us something about alcoholism, but the picture created by Dostoevsky gives us more insight, a greater involvement, and ultimately more "understanding" of the alcoholic. With the help of great writers, sociological facts can be felt in human terms.

Chapter Summary

Although scholars and intellectuals have long studied societies, sociology as an academic discipline is a very recent phenomenon. Not until the middle of the nineteenth century was a "science of society" recognized. Today, however, sociologists and their work are well known both popularly and academically.

There is not full agreement on a definition of sociology. We define it as the study of human beings within their social contexts. The crucial element of the sociological perspective is that individuals and groups are best understood not as isolated entities, but in relationship to other individuals and groups. Historically, such an understanding has been attempted by utilizing two different approaches, science and art. The two approaches differ in that science seeks a knowledge of facts whereas art attempts an intuitive and personal understanding of the world.

In this text we have sought to benefit from both orientations. We have used the science of sociology in defining precise concepts and relating factual information about groups and individuals. We have utilized the art of sociology by presenting literature that will help bring a more complete understanding of the human experience. Further, we have attempted to write within the framework of humanism, in the belief that scholarship and knowledge serve best when they are directed at the alleviation of human problems.

Key Terms for Review

definition of the situation, p. 8
empiricism, p. 6
humanism, p. 12
knowledge, p. 10
replicate, p. 11

sociology, p. 6
sympathetic introspection, p. 10
taking the role of the other, p. 10
understanding, p. 10
verstehen, p. 10

Suggested Readings

Berger, Peter L. *Invitation to Sociology: A Humanistic Perspective.* Garden City, N.Y.: Doubleday, 1963. Berger presents a popular, readable, and extremely worthwhile introduction to the discipline of sociology. He expands upon the basic introductory statements we have made in this chapter.

Cameron, William Bruce. *Informal Sociology.* New York: Random House, 1963. Like Berger, Cameron has developed an extremely engaging and readable style which enables the reader to understand many sociological issues that are too often submerged in a wave of jargon.

Lundberg, George A. *Can Science Save Us?* New York: David McKay, 1939. Lundberg presents, in what has become one of the classic statements of this orientation, a concise work on the pure science of sociology. Though many fault his stance, few scholars would claim that he was not a most articulate and concerned academician.

Mills, C. Wright. *The Sociological Imagination.* New York: Oxford University Press, 1959. Mills, who has become a kind of folk hero to many younger sociologists, sketches what many feel to be the basic humanist mission of the social sciences. His style is very readable and his passionate concern for humanity is evident throughout this very fine book.

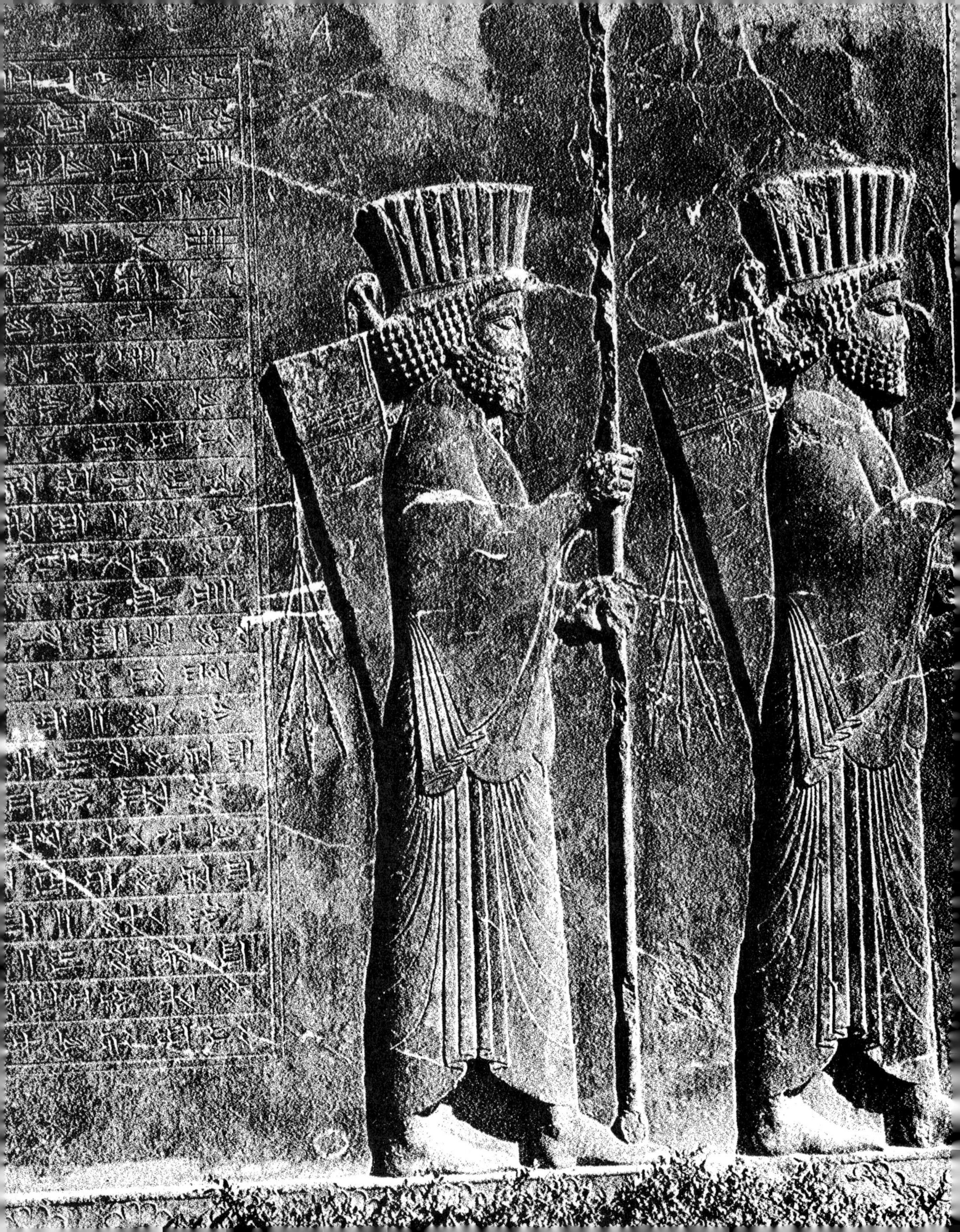

part one

CULTURE AND SOCIALIZATION

Diet and food preparation, recreation, politics, ethics, religious practices, laws, sexual customs, and burial rites vary from society to society. All these distinctive patterns of life—and many more—make up a society's culture. The meaning of culture and the tremendous impact it has on the individual are the major subjects of chapter 2. Chapter 3 examines how we learn culture and become active participants in society. We will discover that individuals learn about their culture from many sources—parents, teachers, friends, television, and movies among them.

IN THIS CHAPTER

Cultural Transmission   20

Nonmaterial Culture   22
    Mores   23
    Customs and folkways   24

Ethnocentrism   25

Cultural Relativism and Cultural Universals   34

Summary   38

Key Terms for Review   38

Suggested Readings   39

What is "culture"?
Are some people more "cultured" than others?
Is it more "cultured" to order une bouteille de Château Lafite-Rothschild than a pint of Pagan Pink Ripple?
Why do some foreigners seem so strange?
Is it inevitable to distrust people and things that are "different"?

CULTURE

When we speak of "culture," many of us think in terms of "cultured" or "refined" individuals. To be cultured, one must be concerned with the finer things in life and act in a properly understated manner. The woman who is at ease with this year's *haute couture* and the development of a Beethoven symphony is cultured, and so is the man who appreciates fine art and knows just which wine to order with a meal. The "cultured" person is the truly educated individual, the connoisseur, the gourmet, the one able to relate the perfectly sophisticated anecdote. A. P. Herbert once characterized this individual as "the kind of person who looks at a sausage and thinks of Picasso."

To social scientists, though, culture is not limited to refinement. To them the San Francisco Opera Company's production of *Tosca* is certainly an example of culture, but so is Forest Lawn Cemetery and a finger lickin' good barrel of Kentucky fried chicken. The ways in which we adapt to our environment are called, collectively, our *culture*. We may, however, make a distinction between *material* and *nonmaterial* culture. Forest Lawn Cemetery is a good example of our material culture, whereas all the ideas which tell us that we should bury people in such a place typify our nonmaterial culture.

Culture and society should not be confused. Sociologists use the term *society* to mean a self-perpetuating group of all ages and both sexes which shares institutions, very often resides within the boundaries of a political state, and shares a culture. In other words, a society is a group of people who have a common culture.

Culture exists because people are able to share creations, pass knowledge from one generation to the next, and thereby change the very conditions for existence. How members of a society transmit, or pass on, their culture and how they understand what they should (ideally) do are subjects we shall consider next.

Cultural Transmission

The question of the uniqueness of *Homo sapiens* has been debated many times over the years. Some argue that humans are neither higher nor lower than any other form of life; to be sure, we are highly complex, but in no genuine sense are we different from, say, baboons. Others, the humanists, maintain that we are indeed unique because of our ability to communicate—our language. Language enables us to conceive of abstractions, think about future occurrences, perceive ourselves mentally, and view ourselves as objects. (See chapter 3 for further discussion of the development of the "self.") It is this last ability that George Herbert Mead (1863–1931) felt makes human beings so special, for only we can stand back and view ourselves much as we view someone else. Because we are able to do this, we stand apart—in our perceptions and ultimately in our behavior—from all other forms of life.[1]

Language does more than allow us to view ourselves as objects. It also enables us to transmit our culture from one generation to the next through oral and written exchange. In saying this, however, we do not wish to imply that language is a mere servant of humanity, carrying pre-formed packages of reality from person to person. In fact, language is a shaper of reality. Benjamin Lee Whorf (1897–1941) was among the first to articulate the proposition that language is a major determinant of human culture, of what we are able to see and do, and therefore of what we consider real. Whorf came to this conclusion after years of careful and systematic

Most of us recognize the "fine arts" as culture, but to sociologists they are simply one aspect of material culture.

Our ever-present hamburger stands are an internationally recognized part of American culture.

To most of us a seal is simply a seal, but this Eskimo hunter would distinguish between a *kassigiak* (black spotted seal) and a *netsiark* (young seal), among others.

evaluation of varying language systems, his most famous work being with American Indian languages, particularly the Hopi. The initial spark of interest in linguistics came to Whorf while he was working as a fire insurance agent. He noticed that workers smoked without apparent concern in areas with empty gasoline barrels but were extremely cautious in areas with full barrels. The difficulty was that the empty barrels were highly combustible, whereas the full ones were relatively safe because they were sealed. This observation fascinated Whorf. "Full" meant dangerous to the workers, and "empty" was interpreted as being safe, despite the fact that the exact opposite was true. This helped Whorf reach the conclusion that language itself is a major factor in determining reality.

Whorf's work, in conjunction with that of anthropologist Edward Sapir (1884–1939), has come to us in the succinct form of the *Sapir-Whorf hypothesis*. The hypothesis states that language directs perceptions; that is, it provides the cultural framework within which we interpret our experiences. A good example of how language provides different frameworks for different cultures can be found in Peter Farb's discussion of the Sapir-Whorf proposal.

> According to the hypothesis, the differences between languages are much more than mere obstacles to communication; they represent basic differences in the "world view" of the various peoples and in what they understand about their environment. The Eskimo can draw upon an inventory of about twenty very precise words for the subtle differences in a snowfall. The best a speaker of English can manage are distinctions between sticky snow, sleet, hail, and ice. Similarly, to most speakers of English, a seal is simply a seal, and

they have only that one word to describe it; if they want to say anything else about the seal, such as its sex or its color, then they have to put an adjective before the word "seal." But the Eskimo has a number of words with which to express various kinds of sealdom: "a young swimming seal," "a male harbor seal," "an old harbor seal," and so forth. A somewhat similar situation exists in English with the word "horse." This animal may be referred to as "chestnut," "bay mare," "stallion," and other names that one would not expect to find in the vocabulary of the horseless Eskimo.[2]

Nonmaterial Culture

A basic concept used in understanding nonmaterial culture is *norm*. When we speak of a norm, we can mean one of two things. In the statistical sense, the term refers to that which is most common, or that which is "normal." But in the sense more frequently of concern to sociologists, a norm means any shared standard of behavior which in turn entails certain expectations of behavior in a given situation.

Although the two aspects of the term are related, clearly they are not the same. That which is normal (most common) is not necessarily that which is normative (a shared expectation). In the United States today, there are numerous examples of differences between that which is normally done and that which is normatively expected. An example known to many college students has to do with changing patterns of sexual behavior. Although sexual relations of a relatively casual sort (i.e., those without deep emotional commitment) have increased since the early 1960s and in certain regions have become common, they are still not considered normative. Many individuals feel compelled to "be in love," even though they are not, in order to have sexual relations since normatively that is what is expected.

Instances of disagreement between normal and normative behavior may occur in any society, and as we will see in a later chapter, social scientists measure the rate of change in a society by how much disagreement there is and how strongly people feel about it. It is enough now for us to recognize that as patterns of behavior change, what one is expected to do does not necessarily change.

Norms, in the sense of shared standards, have great power to motivate behavior. We are aware of both positive and negative *sanctions*, or, as American folk wisdom puts it, the carrot and the stick. When our actions meet normative expectations, we are generally rewarded (or subject to a positive sanction); failure to meet such expectations leads to punishment (negative sanctions).

Not all norms carry the same sanctions because not all norms are of equal importance in a culture. In general, there are three types of norms — mores, customs, and folkways — distinguished by the intensity of feelings they arouse and the consequences that flow from violations of them.

MORES

Virtually any behavior that arouses intense feelings and is subject to extreme consequences comes under the heading of a culture's *mores*. Mores have to do with the basic moral judgments of a society; they are the strongest of the norms. Mores can tell us to do certain things: to love our parents and family, for example. Mores can also tell us not to do certain things: not to kill other human beings, for example.

Within the category of mores, however, there are some that we hold dearer than others. As a result, we tend to condemn violations of these mores more strongly. Thus we would probably be more repelled by someone who barbecued and ate his children than by someone who through neglect allowed them to become sick and die. Still, both individuals would be violating our mores. Both would be immoral (acting against the mores).

William Graham Sumner of Yale, one of the most influential of the early American sociologists, commented on the great power mores have over us. He saw that "the mores can make anything right and prevent the condemnation of anything."[3] But despite the strength of their hold, mores can change, usually slowly, but sometimes dramatically. Moreover, individuals sometimes shift rather quickly from one set of mores to another, generally as a result of group pressures. Jerzy Kosinski movingly illustrates this human ability to shift from one basic assumption to another in his portrayal of the main character in *The Painted Bird*. The dark young lad had learned to despise the Nazi regime, which, in its occupation of Europe, had placed great value on blond, fair-skinned Aryans. His life had been brutally disrupted by the Germans, and his love of the Roman Catholic Church was one of the few sustaining features left to him during the Nazi occupation. Yet, when enough pressure was placed upon him, when new mores were enforced, his belief in himself, in the church and its clergy, and in the evil of the SS all began to disappear.

The officer surveyed me sharply. I felt like a squashed caterpillar oozing in the dust, a creature that could not harm anyone yet aroused loathing and disgust. In the presence of such a resplendent being, armed in all the symbols of might and majesty, I was genuinely ashamed of my appearance. I had nothing against his killing me. I gazed at the ornate clasp of his officer's belt that was exactly at the level of my eyes, and awaited his wise decision.

The courtyard was silent again. The soldiers stood about obediently waiting for what would happen next. I knew my fate was being decided in some manner, but it was a matter of indifference to me. I placed infinite confidence in the decision of the man facing me. I

24 / CULTURE AND SOCIALIZATION

knew that he possessed powers unattainable for ordinary people.

Another quick command rang out. The officer strode off. A soldier shoved me roughly toward the gate. Regretting that the splendid spectacle was over, I walked slowly through the gate and fell straight into the plump arms of the priest, who was waiting outside. He looked even shabbier than before. His cassock was a miserable thing in comparison with the uniform adorned by the death's-head, crossbones, and lightning bolts.[4]

Differences between groups and between individuals can alter the intensity and importance of mores. A group whose mores differ significantly from those of the rest of society shares a *subculture*. The hippies and communes of the 1960s and the Jesus movements of the 1970s are examples of subcultures within our society. Numerous other groups share subcultures, including both the terrifying (the Mafia) and the esoteric (Egyptologists).

Jesus movements have attracted many youthful converts in recent years.

CUSTOMS AND FOLKWAYS

Customs and folkways are two other categories of norms held by society. Though less important to a culture than mores, both have the power to influence behavior.

Customs carry with them less intense feelings than mores, and violations of them are likely to meet with less severe condemnation. If you witness the violation of a custom, you may be revolted, but you would not be morally incensed as you would be if mores were violated. If, for instance, you attended a formal banquet and the person next to you removed his shoes and socks, took a nail clipper from the pocket of his dinner jacket, painstakingly clipped and cleaned his toenails, and then placed the clippings on the butter dish, you might be disgusted, but you would not be morally indignant. Your dinner companion's behavior vio-

The foods we eat and the ways in which we eat are part of our culture.

lated certain specified customs. Norms regarding hygiene, many forms of sexual behavior, and dating are all examples of customs.

The weakest norms, those most often violated and least likely to carry with them intense feelings, are called *folkways*. Whereas the violation of a custom would be likely to evoke feelings of disgust and repulsion, it would be an extremely rare situation where the violation of a folkway would do so. If you had a neighbor who drove a 1958 Ford while you felt embarrassed owning a car over three years old, you might be put off or curious, but you would not be morally indignant nor would you be revolted. Norms regarding styles of dress, politeness, speech, and phrasing are all examples of folkways.

Obviously, there is a wide range of norms, and boundaries between customs and folkways may vary with individuals and with groups. An act that seems revolting to some people may appear merely odd or peculiar to others.

Ethnocentrism

Ethnocentrism is a term coined by Sumner to describe the "view of things in which one's own group is the center of everything and all others are scaled and rated with reference to it."[5] A somewhat more contemporary phrasing defines it as "the tendency of persons to judge other cultures and actors in other social systems by the standards of judgment prevailing in their own."[6] We view the custom of certain Eskimo tribes of leaving old people behind to die as particularly cruel and inhumane, but they no doubt view our own custom of warfare between nations as incredibly crude and barbarous.

We are all ethnocentric, and, as a rule, there is absolutely no way that ethnocentrism can be avoided. But occasionally someone gives us a fresh perspective, and we become aware of the incongruities of our own culture. Horace Miner's classic "Body Ritual Among the Nacirema" makes the importance of perspective embarrassingly clear.

> Nacirema culture is characterized by a highly developed market economy which has evolved in a rich natural habitat. While much of the people's time is devoted to economic pursuits, a large part of the fruits of these labors and a considerable portion of the day are spent in ritual activity. The focus of this activity is the human body, the appearance and health of which loom as a dominant concern in the ethos of the people. While such a concern is certainly not unusual, its ceremonial aspects and associated philosophy are unique.
>
> The fundamental belief underlying the whole system appears to be that the human body is ugly and that its natural tendency is to

debility and disease. Incarcerated in such a body, man's only hope is to avert these characteristics through the use of the powerful influences of ritual and ceremony. Every household has one or more shrines devoted to this purpose. The more powerful individuals in the society have several shrines in their houses and, in fact, the opulence of a house is often referred to in terms of the number of such ritual centers it possesses. Most houses are of wattle and daub construction, but the shrine rooms of the more wealthy are walled with stone. Poorer families imitate the rich by applying pottery plaques to their shrine walls.

While each family has at least one such shrine, the rituals associated with it are not family ceremonies but are private and secret. The rites are normally only discussed with children, and then only during the period when they are being initiated into these mysteries. I was able, however, to establish sufficient rapport with the natives to examine these shrines and to have the rituals described to me.

The focal point of the shrine is a box or chest which is built into the wall. In this chest are kept the many charms and magical potions without which no native believes he could live. These preparations are secured from a variety of specialized practitioners. The most powerful of these are the medicine men, whose assistance must be rewarded with substantial gifts. However, the medicine men do not provide the curative potions for their clients, but decide what the ingredients should be and then write them down in an ancient and secret language. This writing is understood only by the medicine men and by the herbalists who, for another gift, provide the required charm.

The charm is not disposed of after it has served its purpose, but is placed in the charm-box of the household shrine. As these magical materials are specific for certain ills, and the real or imagined maladies of the people are many, the charm-box is usually full to overflowing. The magical packets are so numerous that people forget what their purposes were and fear to use them again. While the natives are very vague on this point, we can only assume that the idea in retaining all the old magical materials is that their presence in the charm-box, before which the body rituals are conducted, will in some way protect the worshipper.

Beneath the charm-box is a small font. Each day every member of the family, in succession, enters the shrine room, bows his head before the charm-box, mingles different sorts of holy water in the font, and proceeds with a brief rite of ablution. The holy waters are secured from the Water Temple of the community, where the priests conduct elaborate ceremonies to make the liquid ritually pure.

In the hierarchy of magical practitioners, and below the medicine men in prestige, are specialists whose designation is best translated "holy-mouth-men." The Nacirema have an almost pathological horror of and fascination with the mouth, the condition of which is believed to have a supernatural influence on all social relationships. Were it not for the rituals of the mouth, they believe that their teeth would fall out, their gums bleed, their jaws shrink, their friends desert them, and their lovers reject them. They also believe that a strong relationship exists between oral and moral characteristics. For example, there is a ritual ablution of the mouth for children which is supposed to improve their moral fiber.

The daily body ritual performed by everyone includes a mouth-rite. Despite the fact that these people are so punctilious about care of the mouth, this rite involves a practice which strikes the uninitiated stranger as revolting. It was reported to me that the ritual consists of inserting a small bundle of hog hairs into the mouth, along with certain magical powders, and then moving the bundle in a highly formalized series of gestures.

In addition to the private mouth-rite, the people seek out a holy-mouth-man once or twice a year. These practitioners have an impressive set of paraphernalia, consisting of a variety of augers, awls, probes, and prods. The use of these objects in the exorcism of the evils of the mouth involves almost unbelievable ritual torture of the client. The holy-mouth-man opens the client's mouth, and using the above mentioned tools, enlarges any holes which decay may have created in the teeth. Magical materials are put into these holes. If there are no naturally occurring holes in the teeth, large sections of one or more teeth are gouged out so that the supernatural substance can be applied. In the client's view, the purpose of these ministrations is to arrest decay and to draw friends. The extremely sacred and traditional character of the rite is evident in the fact that the natives return to the holy-mouth-men year after year, despite the fact that their teeth continue to decay.

It is to be hoped that, when a thorough study of the Nacirema is made, there will be careful inquiry into the personality structure of these people. One has but to watch the gleam in the eye of a holy-mouth-man, as he jabs an awl into an exposed nerve, to suspect that a certain amount of sadism is involved. If this can be established, a very interesting pattern emerges, for most of the population shows definite masochistic tendencies. It was to these that Professor Linton referred in discussing a distinctive part of the daily body ritual which is performed only by men. This part of the rite involves scraping and lacerating the surface of the face with a sharp instrument. Special women's rites are performed only four times each lunar month, but what they lack in frequency is made up for in barbarity. As part of this ceremony, women bake their heads in small ovens for about an hour. The theoretically interesting point is that what seems to be a preponderantly masochistic people have developed sadistic specialists.[7]

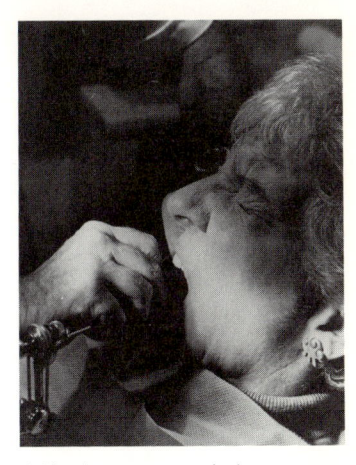

A Nacirema woman being administered to by a "holy-mouth-man."

Ethnocentrism and Our Daily Rituals

All of us are ethnocentric; we tend to assume that our norms are the standards by which behavior should be judged. However, even the routines of daily life that people take very much for granted, such as ways of eating, sleeping, and bathing, vary greatly from one culture to another, as do dress and hair styles.

For Americans, the backyard cookout and regimented school lunches are routine. Knives, forks, and spoons are the accepted utensils for use at the table, and we may eat with our hands only under particular circumstances. In Saudi Arabia, however, it is the norm to eat with one's hand — though it must be the right hand. In Japan, of course, chop sticks are the standard eating utensils, and, as in Saudi Arabia, it is the norm to sit on the floor when eating.

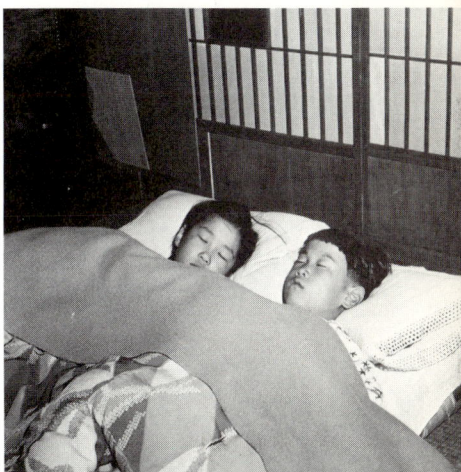

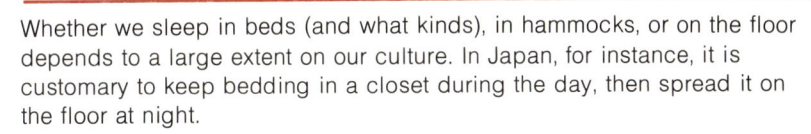

Whether we sleep in beds (and what kinds), in hammocks, or on the floor depends to a large extent on our culture. In Japan, for instance, it is customary to keep bedding in a closet during the day, then spread it on the floor at night.

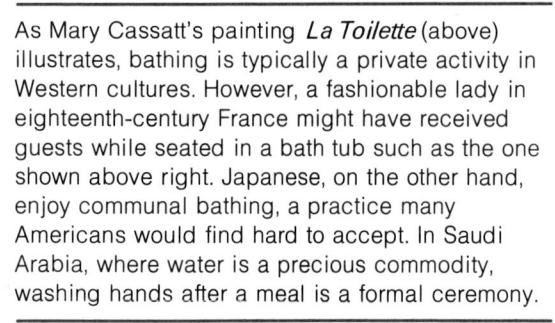

As Mary Cassatt's painting *La Toilette* (above) illustrates, bathing is typically a private activity in Western cultures. However, a fashionable lady in eighteenth-century France might have received guests while seated in a bath tub such as the one shown above right. Japanese, on the other hand, enjoy communal bathing, a practice many Americans would find hard to accept. In Saudi Arabia, where water is a precious commodity, washing hands after a meal is a formal ceremony.

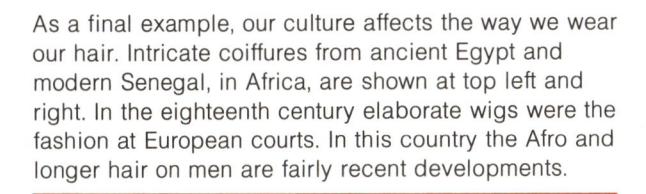

As a final example, our culture affects the way we wear our hair. Intricate coiffures from ancient Egypt and modern Senegal, in Africa, are shown at top left and right. In the eighteenth century elaborate wigs were the fashion at European courts. In this country the Afro and longer hair on men are fairly recent developments.

These Muslims in Afghanistan carefully adhere to the norms for worship within a mosque.

Since we are most familiar with our own culture, we use its norms as a reference point by which to judge other cultures. Even the most sophisticated and well-traveled people tend to rely on certain cultural standards. And although sociologists and cultural anthropologists would seem to be the least likely candidates for ethnocentrism, they too tend to be most comfortable with their original culture. Despite their knowledge of and familiarity with the norms of other cultures, anthropologists and sociologists who live with "different" people—often to study them—find themselves, at least initially, quite disoriented and uncomfortable. They experience what is called *culture shock*; that is, they are unable to adjust immediately to the tremendous differences in viewpoints and behavior that often exist between cultures. It seems fair to conclude, then, that we are all ethnocentric in that we all tend to judge the rest of the world within the framework of our own culture. How could it be otherwise? Our culture is what we know.

Ethnocentrism sometimes leads us to conclude that the norms of our own culture are superior to those of other cultures. It is this assumption that often causes difficulties, as E. M. Forster shows us in his work *A Passage to India*. In a section entitled "The Mosque," Forster introduces us to Aziz, who holds fast to the values of his own culture when they are threatened by contact with another. He feels that Islam is vastly superior to other religions. Islam is, in fact, much more; it is a way of life.

> He had always liked this mosque. It was gracious, and the arrangement pleased him. The courtyard—entered through a ruined gate—contained an ablution-tank of fresh clear water, which was always in motion, being indeed part of a conduit that supplied the city. The courtyard was paved with broken slabs. The covered part of the mosque was deeper than is usual; its effect was that of an English parish church whose side has been taken out. Where he sat, he looked into three arcades whose darkness was illuminated by a small hanging lamp and by the moon. The front—in full moonlight—had the appearance of marble, and the ninety-nine names of God on the frieze stood out black, as the frieze stood out white against the sky. The contest between this dualism and the contention of shadows within pleased Aziz, and he tried to symbolize the whole into some truth of religion or love. A mosque by winning his approval let loose his imagination. The temple of another creed, Hindu, Christian, or Greek, would have bored him and failed to awaken his sense of beauty. Here was Islam, his own country, more than a Faith, more than a battlecry, more, much more . . . Islam, an attitude towards life both exquisite and durable, where his body and his thoughts found their home.[8]

Believing that the British are hopelessly uncouth and ignorant, Aziz assumes that any Britisher would fail to understand the norms relating to the life of Islam. His reaction to the appearance of an Englishwoman in the mosque is therefore instantly negative:

An Englishwoman stepped out into the moonlight. Suddenly he was furiously angry and shouted: "Madam! Madam! Madam!"

"Oh! Oh!" the woman gasped.

"Madam, this is a mosque, you have no right here at all; you should have taken off your shoes; this is a holy place for Moslems."

"I have taken them off."

"You have?"

"I left them at the entrance."

"Then I ask your pardon."

Still startled, the woman moved out, keeping the ablution-tank between them. He called after her, "I am truly sorry for speaking."[9]

It is quite common for people to consider what is not familiar to them inferior. Americans tend to value competition in athletics; those who do not like to compete are thought to be afraid, weak, or inferior. In fact, uncompetitive individuals may simply be "different." In some cases "different" may even mean "better." Consider, for example, the difference between Europeans and Americans in the practice of using dinner utensils. Both Europeans and Americans hold the fork in the left hand and the knife in the right to cut a bite of meat, for instance. Most Americans then put the knife down and transfer the fork to the right hand to eat the bite. Europeans do not switch the fork to the right hand but keep it in the left to bring the bite to the mouth. The American practice is indeed cumbersome, and many, upon first seeing the European style, marvel at its simplicity and efficiency. They do not see it as crude or odd, for simplicity and efficiency are highly admired in our culture.

Table 2–1 indicates that ethnocentrism may lead us to three possible conclusions about folkways and mores that vary significantly from ours. Such norms may be seen as better, worse, or simply different from our own.

Ethnocentrism serves society both positively and negatively or, in sociological terms, is both *eufunctional* and *dysfunctional*. Ethnocentrism is eufunctional when it reinforces societal stability or supports the status quo. Anyone who attacks the status quo may be branded a subversive, as indeed many have been throughout history. Ethnocentrism is also eufunctional when it promotes loyalty and group solidarity. If you assume that your culture is superior, you are very likely to be a strong supporter of the group and, in times of conflict and crisis, will make tremendous sacrifices for the good of the group. The differences in popular support for World War II and the Vietnam War in the United States may be explained, at least in part, by the presence of this feeling of superiority during the earlier war and its absence during the recent conflict. In World War II we were as certain of our morality and the splendid high purpose of Winston

Ethnocentrism sometimes leads to violence. Chinese workers in the nineteenth-century mining camps of Nevada and California often felt this dysfunctional aspect of ethnocentrism.

TABLE 2–1
Three Conclusions from Ethnocentrism

Perspective	Mores: Unhealthy or "deformed" babies are killed at birth.	Folkways: Conversations take place with faces six inches apart.
We may view behavior as worse than our own.	Such practices are beastly, cruel, and inhumane.	It is rude, impolite, and, besides, you'd need a lot of mouthwash.
We may view behavior as different from our own.	With the lack of medical facilities in their society, it is good for them.	It seems quaint. I wonder if they are comfortable doing it?
We may view behavior as better than our own.	With the world population growth and the tremendous emotional strain placed on families by such children, it is a fine idea.	This would be an excellent practice. It would be easier to understand people and it would also be sexy.

Churchill and Dwight Eisenhower as we were of the immorality of our enemies and the dastardliness of Tojo and Hitler. The distinctions between Hanoi and Saigon were seldom quite so clear.

Ethnocentrism can also be dysfunctional to societies. It is dysfunctional whenever it blocks cooperation. On the international level, ethnocentrism has often presented a barrier in the quest for world peace. Within the borders of our own country, it has prevented understanding between people: between classes, ethnic and racial groups, old and young, and so on. Even discussions of ethnocentrism may fail to aid intergroup cooperation and understanding. One of our early attempts to explain ethnocentrism in the classroom ended in disillusionment and failure when a student who had been very attentive commented, "Oh yes, I understand ethnocentrism; the Jews are ethnocentric, always thinking THEY are the best." Evidently, he never considered that such a statement is itself ethnocentric.

Cultural Relativism and Cultural Universals

Cultural relativism maintains that actions and beliefs should be judged within the context of a particular culture. The idea has been a part of the Western heritage for centuries. Indeed, the Sophists of ancient Greece claimed that ethical conduct is relative to a particular context.[10]

When sociologists assert that to understand behavior one must perceive it within its cultural context, they are neither supporting nor denying the existence of standards of right and wrong that hold in all societies. They are simply pointing out that not all societies share the same cultural norms, or give the same weight to certain actions. Belief in cultural relativism is necessary if we are to understand people who live differently than we do. Vast differences in life style may be seen even in the United States, a fact that is warmly illustrated through the childhood experiences of Claude Brown.

When I went home for a visit from Wiltwyck, it seemed like the whole city had changed. I had forgotten all about roaches until I went back home. I had been to that nice old rich white lady's house up in Hyde Park, which wasn't too far from Wiltwyck. She had a big old house that seemed like a whole lot of houses bunched together. The cats who had been up there before said that she used to invite all the cats from Wiltwyck to her house every year and that everybody used to eat until he got sick or just tired of eating. This lady had a real big house; and the first time I went into it, I couldn't understand why she didn't have any roaches in a house that big. I thought they just might have been hiding all the time I was there, but it wasn't like roaches to hide when there were a lot of people around eating food and stuff. That's why Mama didn't like roaches—they were always coming out and showing off when company came.

A mosque in Pakistan. These Muslim worshipers share cultural norms that are sometimes quite different from our own.

I had seen this old rich lady hanging around Wiltwyck a couple of times. I spoke to her the first time I saw her, and she said she was a member of some board or something like that. She started asking me a lot of stupid questions like did I like it up there and things like that. After that, I never had anything to say to her. I knew she was a nice lady, but she seemed to be a little crazy or something, and her voice didn't sound real. It sounded like one of those ladies in the movies. But that was all right, because she wasn't around too much, just once in a while.

I knew that her name was Mrs. Roosevelt and that she used to be married to a cat who was President of the United States. It sure seemed funny to me that the President of the United States would have had time to bother with that crazy-acting old lady. I figured that Dad was right about white people. He would read that paper and say, "White people sure do some damned fool things." I thought that the lady named Mrs. Roosevelt didn't have any roaches in her house because the President used to live there. Roaches didn't want to mess with the President. I said to myself, I bet they come chargin' in here as soon as they find out he's gone . . . Yeah, they're just waitin' to git the news. Roaches are slick like that.[11]

But, though cultural differences exist, even within a society, not all behavior is culturally unique. There is some uniformity, there are some

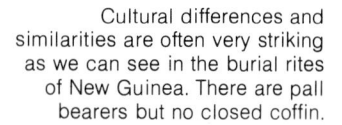

Cultural differences and similarities are often very striking as we can see in the burial rites of New Guinea. There are pall bearers but no closed coffin.

There is a wide variety of ways in which cultural universals are enacted. The informality of an American cookout is quite different from traditional Japanese food preparation.

cultural universals. Sociologists have debated just what those universals are, but most would agree on many, if not all, of the items listed below. This list may be considered "a least common denominator of culture."[12]

CULTURAL UNIVERSALS

age grading	incest taboos
bodily adornment	inheritance rules
calendar	kinship
cooking	language
cooperative labor	law
courtship	luck
division of labor	magic
education	marriage
ethics	meal times
etiquette	modesty
family	mourning
folklore	music
food taboos	puberty customs
funeral rites	religion
games	sexual customs and mores
gestures	tools
hygiene	trade patterns

The content of these universals may vary from culture to culture: not all cultures have the same rules for inheritance or the same cooking patterns, for instance. But all have *some* rules for passing property to offspring and standard ways of preparing foods. Cultural universals are a response to basic human needs.

Chapter Summary

Although culture is commonly thought of as the refinements of gracious and intelligent living, sociologists use the term to refer to all material and nonmaterial adaptations of human beings to their environment. Human beings maintain and transmit their culture chiefly through language. Language, as suggested by the Sapir-Whorf hypothesis, both shapes and is shaped by culture.

The patterns of behavior that are the basis of any culture are enforced by norms. Norms vary in importance—in the intensity of feelings they arouse and the consequences of their violation. Mores are the strongest of the norms and determine a culture's basic morality. Mores are followed in importance by customs and folkways. Like mores, these norms reinforce patterns of behavior, but unlike mores, violations of them meet with less severe condemnation.

All of us are necessarily ethnocentric; that is, we judge other cultures and societies using the norms of our own. Certainly, we all feel somewhat strange in our initial contact with another culture. We experience what is called culture shock. Many of us also assume that our culture is superior to others—that everything and everybody that is different is inferior. But different should not be equated with inferior. Indeed, we may at times see certain norms of another culture as simply different from our own, or even as superior to ours.

There is an incredibly wide range of human behavior, and that which is valued is relative to a particular culture. Nevertheless, there are certain recognized cultural universals that arise in response to basic human needs. The task of sociologists is to explore both cultural differences and cultural universals.

Key Terms for Review

cultural relativism, p. 34
cultural universals, p. 37
culture, p. 19
culture shock, p. 32
customs, p. 24
dysfunctional, p. 33
ethnocentrism, p. 25
eufunctional, p. 33
folkways, p. 25
material culture, p. 19
mores, p. 23
nonmaterial culture, p. 19
norm, p. 22
sanctions, p. 22
Sapir-Whorf hypothesis, p. 21
society, p. 19
subculture, p. 24

Suggested Readings

SOCIOLOGICAL

Castaneda, Carlos. *The Teachings of Don Juan: A Yaqui Way of Knowledge.* New York: Ballantine, 1968. This ethnography, or description of culture, is a brilliantly insightful and illuminating story of the teachings of Don Juan, a Yaqui sorcerer, and his use of hallucinogenic substances. Castaneda's work has enabled many readers to perceive an alternate system of thought, a different world view.

Goldman, Irving. *The Cubeo: Indians of the Northwest Amazon.* Urbana: University of Illinois Press, 1964. From the cultural perspective of the United States, the Cubeo culture represents much that is ideally hoped for but often assumed to be unobtainable. The Cubeo share everything with each other; they are peaceful and thoroughly nonviolent. They have no crime and no enforced labor. The Cubeo seem in many ways to have built a real-life utopia.

Liebow, Elliot. *Tally's Corner.* Boston: Little, Brown, 1967. The subculture of unemployed and marginally employed black men and their streetcorner life in Washington, D.C., is presented in this widely read study. The book is not encumbered by sociological or anthropological jargon, and one is left with a series of profound insights into a world little understood by most Americans.

Mead, George Herbert. *On Social Psychology.* Ed. Anselm L. Strauss. Chicago: University of Chicago Press, 1956. This carefully compiled collection of Mead's work offers the major insights of this seminal scholar.

Sumner, William Graham. *Folkways.* New York: Mentor, 1960; orig. 1906. The work represents Sumner's classic statement on the importance and role of norms in society.

Whorf, Benjamin Lee. *Language, Thought, and Reality.* Ed. John B. Carroll. Cambridge, Mass.: MIT Press, 1956. This well-chosen anthology of Whorf's work contains the studies and verification of the Sapir-Whorf hypothesis.

LITERARY

Kerouac, Jack. *On the Road.* New York: New American Library, 1958. The major fictional figure of the "beat generation," Dean Moriarity, portrays the frenzied and nomadic life of the alienated subculture of beatniks. Like other works of the beat period, this book reveals a very personal search for meaning in a celluloid society.

Swift, Jonathan. *Gulliver's Travels.* Ed. Martin Price. Indianapolis: Bobbs-Merrill, 1963. This epic tale chronicles a series of confrontations with differing cultures, and, at least on one level, it is a marvelous and illuminating study of cultural diversity and culture shock.

Waters, Frank. *The Man Who Killed the Deer.* Chicago: Swallow Press, 1968. Waters presents a sensitive portrait of the Pueblo in this work, seen by many as one of the finest novels on the American Indian.

IN THIS CHAPTER

The Meaning of Socialization   41

Theories of Socialization   49
    Reinforcement theory   49
    Cognitive theory   52
    Symbolic interactionism   52

Variations in Socialization Methods   58

Social Change and Resocialization   60

Summary   61

Key Terms for Review   62

Suggested Readings   62

How do human beings learn?
Are individuals mere reflections of their culture?
How do we develop a self-image?
Do people ever stop learning?

SOCIALIZATION

The Meaning of Socialization

The learning process by which the individual internalizes culture and becomes an active participant in society is called *socialization*.* The process begins at birth and continues throughout life. All of us start life as unsocialized beings—lacking language, unknowledgeable of cultural norms, and incapable of getting along with others—and as we learn we become human in a social sense. No one, however, masters all of a culture or is completely socialized. Indeed, many Americans have never heard of gerrymandering, soul food, bear and bull stock markets, rutabaga, schizophrenia, macrame, taxidermy, smack, kivas, and lox—all aspects of our total culture. Individuals also develop partial and mistaken notions about their culture, although the most obvious misconceptions are those of youths since they have just begun the socialization process.

Samuel Langhorne Clemens, who wrote under the name Mark Twain, relates a number of misconceptions American children have had about their culture:

> Here are some quaint definitions of words. It will be noticed that in all of these instances the sound of the word, or the look of it on paper, has misled the child:
> Capillary, a little caterpillar.
> Equestrian, one who asks questions.
> Parasite, a kind of umbrella.
> . . . Here is one where the phrase "publicans and sinners" has got mixed up in the child's mind with politics, and the result is a definition which takes one in a sudden and unexpected way:
> Republican, a sinner mentioned in the Bible.

---
*For a detailed discussion of the term "socialization" see John A. Clausen, ed., *Socialization and Society* (Boston: Little, Brown, 1968), pp. 18–72.

Upon noticing the woman in the foreground, the observer might giggle, feel disgust or sympathy, or see beauty. Our social and cultural environment influences our perceptions and provides symbolic meanings for fatness as well as thousands of other things in life.

. . . Under the head of "Grammar" the little scholars furnish the following information:

A verb is something to eat.

Every sentence and name of God must begin with a caterpillar.

. . . The chapter on "Mathematics" is full of fruit. From it I take a few samples — mainly in an unripe state.

A straight line is any distance between two places.

Parallel lines are lines that can never meet until they run together.

. . . To proceed with history.

The Indians pursued their warfare by hiding in the bushes and then scalping them.

Abraham Lincoln was born in Wales in 1599.

. . . When the public-school pupil wrestles with the political features of the Great Republic, they throw him sometimes:

A bill becomes a law when the President vetoes it.

The three departments of the government is the President rules the world, the governor rules the State, and the mayor rules the city.

The Constitution of the United States was established to insure domestic hostility.[1]

Obviously, what we become as persons depends a great deal on the culture of the groups surrounding us. Twain illustrates the impact of social environment:

[Young man.] *You keep using that word—training. By it do you particularly mean—*

[Old man.] *Study, instruction, lectures, sermons? That is a part of it—but not a large part. I mean "all" the outside influences. There are a million of them. From the cradle to the grave, during all his waking hours, the human is under training. In the very first rank of his trainers stands "association." It is his human environment which influences his mind and his feelings, furnishes him his ideals, and sets him on his road and keeps him in it. If he leaves that road he will find himself shunned by the people whom he most loves and esteems, and whose approval he most values. He is a chameleon; by the law of his nature he takes the color of his place of resort. The influences about him create his preferences, his aversions, his politics, his tastes, his morals, his religion.*[2]

Are we, however, simply chameleons who automatically change color with our culture as the "old man" says? The answer may at first appear to be yes, especially when we observe people engaged in seemingly bizarre behavior in response to cultural demands. For example, during World War II Japanese Kamikaze pilots flew suicide missions in the name of saving their culture. Shirley Jackson, in her story "The Lottery," shows us how a person will yield to cultural traditions even if it means the murder of a close friend and relative. The story takes place in a small village on the day of the lottery, an annual event during which everyone must draw paper slips from an ominous box.

"We're next," Mrs. Graves said. She watched while Mr. Graves came around from the side of the box, greeted Mr. Summers gravely, and selected a slip of paper from the box. By now, all through the crowd there were men holding the small folded papers in their large hands, turning them over and over nervously.

. . . "They do say," Mr. Adams said to Old Man Warner, who stood next to him, "that over in the north village they're talking of giving up the lottery."

Old Man Warner snorted. "Pack of crazy fools," he said. "Listening to the young folks, nothing's good enough for them. Next thing you know, they'll be wanting to go back to living in caves, nobody work any more, live that way for a while. Used to be a saying about lottery in June, corn be heavy soon. First thing you know, we'd all be eating stewed chickweed and acorns. There's always been a lottery."

. . . Bill Hutchinson reached into the box and felt around, bringing his hand out at last with the slip of paper in it.

The crowd was quiet. A girl whispered, "I hope it's not Nancy," and the sound of the whisper reached the edges of the crowd.

. . . "Tessie," Mr. Summers said. There was a pause, and then Mr. Summers looked at Bill Hutchinson, and Bill unfolded his paper and showed it. It was blank.

"It's Tessie," Mr. Summers said, and his voice was hushed. "Show us her paper, Bill."

Bill Hutchinson went over to his wife and forced the slip of paper out of her hand. It had a black spot on it. . . .

. . . "All right folks," Mr. Summers said. "Let's finish quickly." Although the villagers had forgotten the ritual and lost the original black box, they still remembered to use stones.

The children had stones already, and someone gave little Davy Hutchinson a few pebbles.

. . . Tessie Hutchinson was in the center of a cleared space by now, and she held her hands out desperately as the villagers moved in on her. "It isn't fair," she said. A stone hit her on the side of the head.

Old Man Warner was saying, "Come on, come on, everyone." Steve Adams was in the front of the crowd of villagers, with Mrs. Graves beside him.

"It isn't fair, it isn't right," Mrs. Hutchinson screamed, and then they were upon her.[3]

But *cultural determinism*, the view that behavior is only a reflection of culture, is oversimplified. Although culture influences behavior, it does not stamp us out as carbon copies or exact duplicates of each other. Every person is unique for several reasons. First, each of us in a complex society is exposed to groups whose cultures vary. Some of us are exposed to farmers, Presbyterians, Republicans, Anglos, or Back Bay Bostonians, while others of us learn of life from Southern Baptists, Democrats, blacks, or coal miners. Each person absorbs different views of life, depending on the type and number of subcultures he or she experiences.

Second, each of us learns culture from individuals who have their own unique interpretations of life. Your older brother looks back on the protests and riots of the 1960s as inspiring and hopeful, while your older sister remembers only the fires, looting, and killings.

Third, a culture as complex and varied as that of our own country provides the individual with many conflicting and poorly defined guidelines. For example, there is ample support in America's culture for individuals to be racist and narrowly ethnocentric and, at the same time, to be equalitarian, humanitarian, and democratic. Further, children are often taught the conflicting values of independence ("Stand on your own two feet") and conformity ("Don't rock the boat"). With all these conflicting aspects of culture, the individual must make many personal decisions as to which road to follow.*

Fourth, we must remember that we are all biological creatures and that some of us are taller, stronger, and more mentally capable than others.

---

*A discussion of conflicting values in American culture can be found in Robin Williams, Jr., *American Society: A Sociological Interpretation* (New York: Alfred A. Knopf, 1970), pp. 438–504.

Our biological characteristics make us different from the next person and influence what we become. How many African Pygmies become Olympic high jumpers? How many seven-foot-tall individuals become excellent gymnastic tumblers?

It is important to note here that, although biological factors provide us with the basic materials, it is still culture that directs and gives meaning to these biological traits. Being fat is indeed a biological trait and can inhibit a child from doing well in a physical education class, but it is culture that tells us that doing well in that class is important. Further, American culture says that being overweight is unhealthy; that it is not becoming, particularly for females; and that fat people are supposed to be jolly and talkative. In contrast, ancient Polynesian cultures looked upon being fat as beautiful, particularly among females, because obesity was a symbol of fertility and prosperity.

Human beings are products of both social and biological influences, but it is the former that have the greater impact. Unlike salmon, which without fail make their annual trip to spawn and reproduce, or bears, which automatically hibernate during winter, humans appear to have few biologically inherited and fixed behavior patterns, or *instincts*, and are much

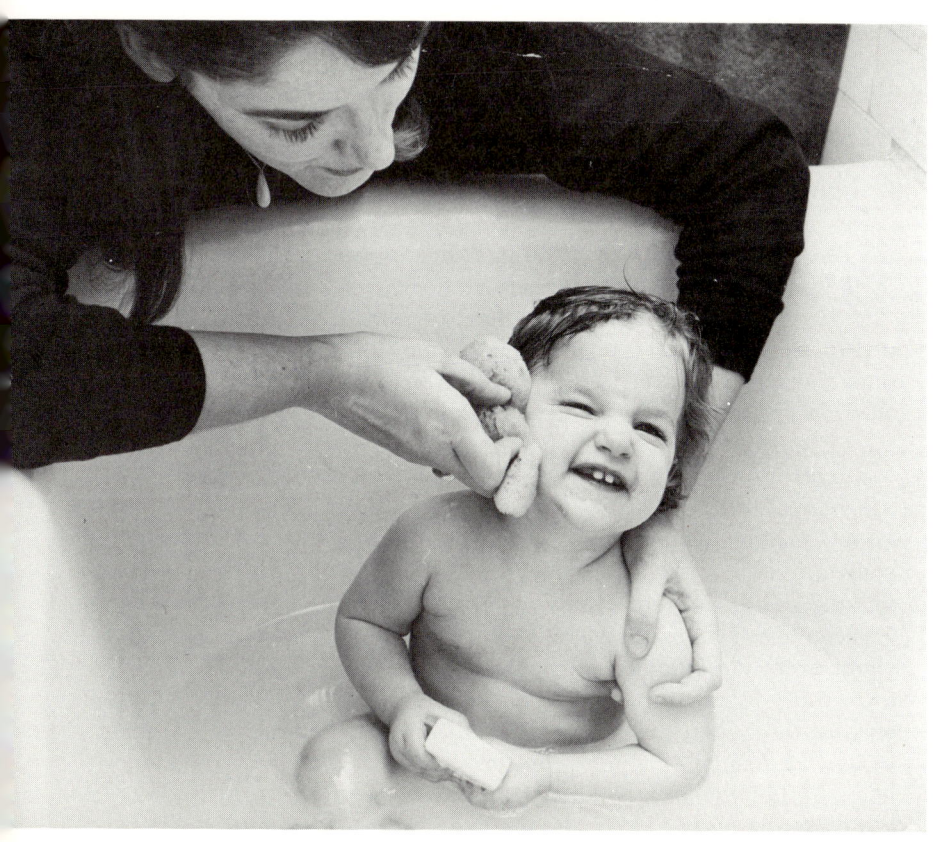

Parents usually play a crucial role in the socialization process, introducing children to many cultural norms. This new arrival in society is learning something about our culture's emphasis on cleanliness.

more dependent for survival on what they learn after birth. Of course, humans have biological drives, such as hunger and thirst, which must be satisfied, but how these drives are satisfied varies from culture to culture. For example, people satisfy the biological drive of sex in a variety of ways. Heterosexuality, homosexuality, voyeurism, masturbation, and pornography all satisfy this drive for different individuals. And, in contrast to other animals, human beings have an enormous capacity for language, feelings, memory, anticipation of the future, and reasoning; all of these attributes help free us from biological constraints. The individual has the unique ability to create and to make a choice.

During childhood our socialization usually centers on the problems of learning proper eating habits, toilet training, hygienic practices, and basic norms regarding sharing, politeness, and honesty. This early and essential preparation for life is called *primary socialization*. Of all the *agents of socialization*, or sources of information about culture, parents tend to play the most important role in teaching these fundamental aspects of life. Because they are usually the first humans we know and because of our extensive contact with them, our parents tend to have an impact upon us even into our adult years. (See chapter 8 for further discussion of the family's role in socialization.) Ernest Hemingway's character Nick Adams, who was thirty-eight years old, still thought a great deal about his father.

> *When he first thought about him it was always the eyes. The big frame, the quick movements, the wide shoulders, the hooked, hawk nose, the beard covering the weak chin, you never thought about — it was always the eyes.*
>
> *. . . They saw much farther and much quicker than the human eye sees and they were the great gift his father had. His father saw as a big-horn ram or as an eagle sees, literally.*
>
> *. . . Like all men with a faculty that surpasses human requirements, his father was very nervous. Then, too, he was sentimental, and, like most sentimental people, he was both cruel and abused. Also, he had much bad luck, and it was not all of it his own. He had died in a trap that he had helped only a little to set.*
>
> *. . . He was very grateful to him for two things: fishing and shooting. His father was as sound on those two things as he was unsound on sex, for instance, and Nick was glad that it had been that way; for some one has to give you your first gun or the opportunity to get it and use it, and you have to live where there is game or fish if you are to learn about them, and now at thirty-eight, he loved to fish and to shoot exactly as much as when he first had gone with his father.*
>
> *. . . His father came back to him in the fall of the year, or in the early spring when there had been jacksnipe on the prairie, or when he saw shocks of corn, or when he saw a lake, or if he ever saw a horse and buggy, or when he saw, or heard, wild geese, or in a duck blind; remembering the time an eagle dropped through the snow to*

Part of the socialization process is internalization of a sex role. Little boys in American society, for example, copy much of the older male's behavior: they dress in typically "masculine" ways and imitate adult male activities.

> strike a canvas-covered decoy, rising, his wings beating, the talons caught in the canvas. His father was with him suddenly, in deserted orchards and in new-plowed fields, in thickets, on small hills, or when going through dead grass, whenever splitting wood or hauling water, by grist mills, cider mills and dams and always with open fires.
>
> . . . Nick loved his father.[4]

Secondary socialization, the learning of more abstract knowledge about life, occurs as we become older. This abstract knowledge may include topics ranging from communism and existentialism to Newtonian mechanics and Oedipal conflict. Sources other than parents—teachers,

Children learn to become active participants in social life from a variety of people, including their peers.

friends, ministers, television, books, newspapers, radio, movies—play the major role in transmitting this information. For example, although parents doubtless play a role in teaching children prejudice toward others, the media also contribute to perpetuating such ideas, as Samuel Langhorne Clemens (Mark Twain) illustrates:

> In San Francisco, the other day, "A well-dressed boy, on his way to Sunday-school, was arrested and thrown into the city prison for stoning Chinamen."
> . . . What had the child's education been? How should he suppose it was wrong to stone a Chinaman?
> . . . He was a "well-dressed" boy, and a Sunday school scholar, and therefore the chances are that his parents were intelligent, well-to-do people, with just enough natural villainy in their composition to make them yearn after the daily papers, and enjoy them; and so this boy had opportunities to learn all through the week how to do right, as well as on Sundays.
> It was in this way that he found out that the great commonwealth of California imposes an unlawful mining-tax upon John the foreigner, and allows Patrick the foreigner to dig gold for nothing—probably because the degraded Mongol is at no expense for whiskey, and the refined Celt cannot exist without it.
> It was in this way that he found out that in many districts of the vast Pacific coast, so strong is the wild, free love of justice in the heart of the people, that whenever any secret and mysterious crime is committed, they say, "Let justice be done, though the heavens fall," and go straightway and swing a Chinaman.

Schools teach students much more than the three Rs. Here immigrant children to the United States during the late 1800s are being taught nationalism and patriotism as they salute the flag.

> ... It was in this way that the boy found out that a Chinaman had no rights that any man was bound to respect; that he had no sorrows that any man was bound to pity; that neither his life nor his liberty was worth the purchase of a penny when a white man needed a scapegoat; that nobody loved Chinamen, nobody befriended them, nobody spared them suffering when it was convenient to inflict it; everybody, individuals, communities, the majesty of the state itself, joined in hating, abusing, and persecuting these humble strangers.
>
> ... Everything conspired to teach him that it was a high and holy thing to stone a Chinaman.[5]

As American culture becomes more specialized and technological, schools and teachers will become increasingly important sources of information. Already most Americans spend twelve years in school, and doctorates require as many as twenty or more years of study. Formal education teaches us the particular skills and attitudes necessary for our jobs, the history of our larger culture and variations within it, and appropriate behavior for us as members of society. (See chapter 10 for further discussion of education's role in socialization.)

Theories of Socialization

Social scientists have offered three major explanations of socialization—reinforcement theory, cognitive theory, and symbolic interactionism. Each of these theories maintains that human behavior is learned from others, rather than being determined biologically. But beyond this general agreement, the theories differ on how and what an individual learns. The disagreement is most obvious between reinforcement theory and the remaining two theories.

REINFORCEMENT THEORY

Reinforcement theorists tend to agree on three assumptions about human beings. The first is that people are guided by *hedonism* in their actions; that is, they seek pleasure, satisfaction, and rewards and avoid pain and punishment in their daily activities. When, at the turn of this century, experimental psychologist E. L. Thorndike made his famous dictum, "Pleasure stamps in; pain stamps out," he was voicing his belief in the principle of hedonism in the learning process. According to a reinforcement theorist, we learn to behave in those ways most pleasurable to us.

The second assumption is that the only way social scientists can understand humans is by observing their behavior, rather than fruitlessly trying to understand states of mind such as perceptions, attitudes, beliefs, and self-images. Reinforcement theorists contend that mental phenomena can never be observed directly and objectively, and that to study them distracts researchers from the crucial environmental factors which determine action.

The third assumption is that people have the ability to associate certain kinds of behavior with particular rewards or punishments. This principle of *associationism* is illustrated by the child who usually blabbers incoherently but one day blurts out, "This is my doggy," to which the parents smile and make encouraging remarks. The child then associates his use of coherent sentence structure with the subsequent approval or reward expressed by his parents.

Reinforcement theorists believe learning is a result of *positive reinforcement*, rewards that may subsequently create certain behaviors, and *negative reinforcement*, punishments that may subsequently eliminate certain kinds of behavior. The individual is seen as an animal that can be conditioned to act in any way if the appropriate rewards and punishments are repeatedly applied. No attention is given to inner feelings or to the individual's ability to imagine and willingness to alter his or her behavior. Humans are simply "reactors," who respond to stimuli, rather than "actors," who create.*

One reinforcement theorist, B. F. Skinner, has gone so far as to suggest that we should create a society whose members would be engineered and controlled by means of reinforcement principles. This society would be more smooth-running and progressive than our present one and would consist of individuals who were happier than those in societies where there is a great deal of freedom. Freedom can be inherently dangerous, according to Skinner, because it exposes the individual to vague, inconsistent, and conflicting guidelines and, hence, a chaotic existence.[6]

Skinner's ideas have been widely criticized. In addition to attacking reinforcement, critics also ask who will be in charge of this conditioning and direct the society Skinner envisions. What is to prevent the conditioners from turning out a nation of robots who serve only their leaders' interests? Totalitarianism could easily result from such programming, as Aldous Huxley so frighteningly portrays in *Brave New World*:

> "Observe," said the Director triumphantly, "observe."
> Books and loud noises, flowers and electric shocks—already in the infant mind these couples were compromisingly linked; and after two hundred repetitions of the same or a similar lesson would be wedded indissolubly. What man has joined, nature is powerless to put asunder.
> "They'll grow up with what the psychologists used to call an 'instinctive' hatred of books and flowers. Reflexes unalterably condi-

---

*For a discussion of reinforcement theory, see Morton Deutsch and Robert M. Krauss, *Theories in Social Psychology* (New York: Basic Books, 1965), pp. 77–125.

Parents, in scolding or punishing a child, hope that such negative reinforcement will lead to more "desirable" behavior in the future.

tioned. They'll be safe from books and botany all their lives." The Director turned to his nurses. "Take them away again."

. . . One of the students held up his hand; and though he could see quite well why you couldn't have lower-caste people wasting the Community's time over books, and that there was always the risk of their reading something which might undesirably decondition one of their reflexes, yet . . . well, he couldn't understand about the flowers. Why go to the trouble of making it psychologically impossible for Deltas to like flowers?

Patiently the D. H. C. explained. If the children were made to scream at the sight of a rose, that was on grounds of high economic policy. Not so very long ago (a century or thereabouts), Gammas, Deltas, even Epsilons, had been conditioned to like flowers—flowers in particular and wild nature in general. The idea was to make them want to be going out into the country at every available opportunity, and so compel them to consume transport.

"And didn't they consume transport?" asked the student.

"Quite a lot," the D. H. C. replied. "But nothing else."

Primroses and landscapes, he pointed out, have one grave defect: they are gratuitous. A love of nature keeps no factories busy. It was decided to abolish the love of nature, but not the tendency to consume transport. For of course it was essential that they should keep on going to the country, even though they hated it. The problem was to find an economically sounder reason for consuming transport than a mere affection for primroses and landscapes. It was duly found.

"We decondition the masses to hate the country," concluded the Director. "But simultaneously we condition them to love all country

sports. At the same time, we see to it that all country sports shall entail the use of elaborate apparatus. So that they consume manufactured articles as well as transport. Hence those electric shocks."
"I see," said the student, and he was silent, lost in admiration.[7]

COGNITIVE THEORY

In contrast to reinforcement theory, *cognitive theory* is concerned with the internal states of the individual. It focuses on how a person perceives, thinks, and chooses. Jean Piaget has examined children's perceptions about rules, punishments, and explanations of behavior and found that children of varying ages reason and solve problems quite differently. For example, younger children have fewer rules and are unwilling or unable to cooperate with others. As they grow older, however, they become less preoccupied with their own point of view, and they begin to agree on rules and see the benefits which can ensue from cooperation. Older children also see that rules are products of mutual consent and that not all rules are absolute and unchangeable. Piaget further observed that older children are better able to understand abstract ideas. While young children tend to define justice as equality—the idea that everyone should receive the same amount and flavor of ice cream—older children tend to view justice as equity—some people may deserve more or less because of extenuating circumstances.

From Piaget's findings we might conclude that socialization is a process of overcoming our self-centered views. We begin to take others into account. It is also a process of developing increasingly abstract reasoning ability. Individuals learn to participate in society and to understand the underlying reasons for cooperation with others.[8]

SYMBOLIC INTERACTIONISM

Of all the theories used to explain socialization, *symbolic interactionism* is given the most attention by sociologists. The theory holds that both the behavior and the internal states of the individual are worthy of study and that individuals are capable of creating their own solutions to life's problems. Although both cognitive theory and symbolic interactionism recognize the importance of internal states, the latter places more emphasis on the role of language in the socialization process. It also focuses on the individual's self-feelings which arise out of his or her interaction with others.

A symbolic interactionist maintains that the symbol is the basis of human communication. A *symbol* is something that stands for something else. In their social interactions, people learn to attach meaning and value to a symbol. For example, when people hear the word "wolf" they are likely to think of more than just a four-legged, hairy animal. They attach a symbolic, or learned, meaning to the word: it is a vicious and bloodthirsty animal, or a misunderstood animal which has been massacred by hunters, or a religious object which should be worshiped. Another example is the simple and often used phrase in our language "I love you," which has many symbolic meanings. It may be used to convey a message of "I want you sexually," "I hope you also love me," "I admire some of your qualities," "I want your protection," or even "I hate you."[9] We also use gestures, like shaking a fist, smiling, pointing, hiding our face, and raising our voice level, as symbols to convey meaning. Although symbols seldom evoke exactly the same meaning from one person to the next, we usually know what is intended. These words and gestures which arouse in another person the ideas and responses that we intend are called *significant symbols*.

Human beings are unique in their mental capacity for storing a huge amount of meanings for objects (wolf, chair, telephone, football) and ideas (freedom, independence, religion, industrialization) which enter their lives and in their ability to create new and different symbols. The difference between ancient and modern meanings of words illustrates human creativity with symbols. The word "lady" once meant breadmaker and now means a woman of quality; "hussy" once meant a housewife and now means a woman of low morals; "deer" meant any small animal and now means a particular animal; and "gossip" meant a godparent and now means a spreader of rumors.[10]

Why is the symbolic interactionist so concerned about language and communication? Simply answered, it is only through language and communication that the individual can learn a culture and become a socialized participant in life. In addition, communication enables a person to develop a self-image.

Two spokesmen of symbolic interactionism, Charles Horton Cooley and George Herbert Mead, have provided more detailed explanations of socialization, emphasizing how self-feelings arise. Cooley maintained that each person develops a *self*, feelings about his or her own identity, through interaction with others. A person may learn that he or she is smart or dull, tall or short, beautiful or ugly, dependent or independent, lovable or obnoxious, coordinated or clumsy, interesting or boring, or whatever. Each person sees himself or herself as an object with distinct psychological and physiological characteristics. It is through interaction with others that we learn who we are. Cooley emphasized this point in his concept of the *looking-glass self*, the notion that the self is a reflection of those with whom the individual comes in contact:

> *Each to each a looking-glass*
> *Reflects the other that doth pass.*

As we see our face, figure, and dress in the glass, and are interested in them because they are ours, and pleased or otherwise with them

As these college students interact with each other, their instructors, and others in society, they continue to develop feelings about their own identity.

according as they do or do not answer to what we should like them to be; so in imagination we perceive in another's mind some thought of appearance, manners, aims, deeds, character, friends, and so on, and are variously affected by it.

A self-idea of this sort seems to have three principal elements: the imagination of our appearance to the other person; the imagination of his judgment of that appearance; and some sort of self-feeling, such as pride or mortification.[11]

Cooley's three principal elements of the looking-glass self can be summarized: If we imagine that others approve of our actions, then we too will likely approve of them. Thus the self is a social product, a result of perceived feedback from other people, and individuals seek approval of their thoughts and behavior from others. Samuel Langhorne Clemens (Mark Twain) notes how important this quest for self-approval is for the individual: "Then perhaps there is something that he loves more than he loves peace—the approval of his neighbors and the public. And perhaps there is something which he dreads more than he dreads pain—the disapproval of his neighbors and the public."[12]

Picture the individual who goes along thinking of himself as charming and witty only to overhear a conversation of "friends" who describe him as an idiotic bore. The person dies a mental death—his rather puffed-up self-concept is deflated because he uses peers as a looking glass. Sherwood Anderson vividly illustrates how painful it can be to fear the rejection of others in his story of a poor, uneducated, nineteen-year-old boy. This youth pretends to be of a higher station in life to impress a well-to-do girl and her friends.

It was a hard jolt for me, one of the bitterest I ever had to face. And it all came about through my own foolishness, too. Even yet sometimes, when I think of it, I want to cry or swear or kick myself. Perhaps, even now, after all this time, there will be a kind of satisfaction in making myself look cheap by telling of it.

. . . I made a fool of myself, that's what I did. I said my name was Walter Mathers from Marietta, Ohio, and then I told all three of them the smashingest lie you ever heard. What I said was that my father owned the horse About Ben Ahem and that he had let him out to this Bob French for racing purposes, because our family was proud and had never gone into racing that way, in our own name, I mean, and Miss Lucy Wessen's eyes were shining, and I went the whole hog.

. . . Lucy Wessen and I was left alone together like on a desert island. Gee if I'd only been on the square or if there had been any way of getting myself on the square. There ain't any Walter Mathers, like I said to her and them, and there hasn't ever been one, but if there was, I bet I'd go to Marietta, Ohio, and shoot him tomorrow.

There I was, big boob that I am. . . . And I was with that girl and she wasn't saying much, and I wasn't saying much either.

. . . Sometimes I hope I have cancer and die. I guess you know what I mean.[13]

George Herbert Mead also maintained that the self was social: "It is not initially there, at birth, but arises in the process of social experience and activity."[14] He divided the self into two parts—the "I" and the "me." Although Mead was vague about the source of the "I," he characterized it as the initial and spontaneous drives and desires that any individual possesses. The "me," however, represents the truly social aspects of the self as it considers the expectations and demands of others. Whereas the "I" is with us at infancy, the "me" takes longer to emerge, because we learn what society expects or demands of us through our interaction with others. According to Mead, the "I" and the "me" are in continual conversation with each other. The "I" advocates immediate and impulsive action, whereas the "me" continually urges a consideration of what "they"—mother, father, friends, community—want the self to be and do.

Mead discussed three stages in the development of the self. The first stage is called *imitation*. The young child simply copies, mimics, or imitates others. For example, a mother will smile at her baby and the baby will smile back, or an older brother will bounce a ball and be copied by a younger sibling. A self has not yet emerged at this stage—the child has not seen himself or herself as a unique social object. The second stage is called *play*. The child pretends to be mother, father, teacher, or others who have been observed and in the process learns what behavior society expects of each of these roles. But the child only plays "at" these roles because he does not fully understand the complex and varying duties and rights of mother, teacher, and so forth. At this stage the child only begins to explore the attitudes of others toward himself. The individual begins mentally to place himself in another's position, or *take the role of others*, to gain their perspective. The "me" part of the self is beginning to develop.

In the third, or *game*, stage, the self becomes more completely developed. When a child plays a game—for example, the game of doctor—he or she learns what is expected not just of the one role, doctor, but also of related roles—nurses and patients. The child learns the attitudes of all the others in the game of doctor. Individuals learn to adjust their behavior to others in this way. Mead's metaphor of a game actually represents what we all must accomplish if we are to become members of society. We must learn to consider the *generalized other*, the total attitudes and expectations of others in society. And the development of the self requires that we internalize and adjust to the attitudes, norms, and beliefs of "those out there."

From our discussion, it is obvious that self-identity and self-feeling can change. We think we know who we are, but then unforeseen events give us self-doubts. Individuals seek self-validation—to know through interaction with others who they are. James Weldon Johnson, a black writer of the early 1900s, describes the crisis of self-meaning for a young boy who learns of his black heritage:

> *The principal came into our room and, after talking to the teacher, for some reason said: "I wish all of the white scholars to stand for a moment." I rose with the others. The teacher looked at me and, calling my name, said: "You sit down for the present, and rise with the others." I did not quite understand her, and questioned: "Ma'm?" . . . I sat down dazed. I saw and heard nothing. When the others were asked to rise, I did not know it. When school was dismissed, I went out in a kind of stupor. A few of the white boys jeered at me, saying: "Oh, you're a nigger too." I heard some black children say: "We knew he was coloured."*
>
> *. . . I took my books and ran into the house. . . . I rushed up into my own little room, shut the door, and went quickly up to where my looking-glass hung on the wall. For an instant I was afraid to look, but when I did, I looked long and earnestly. I had often heard people say to my mother: "What a pretty boy you have!" I was accustomed to hear remarks about my beauty; but now, for the first time, I became conscious of it and recognized it. . . . I ran downstairs and rushed to where my mother was sitting, with a piece of work in her hands. I buried my head in her lap and blurted out: "Mother, mother, tell me, am I a nigger?" . . . There were tears in her eyes and I could see that she was suffering for me. And then it was that I looked at her critically for the first time. I had thought of her in a childish way only as the most beautiful woman in the world; now I looked at her searching for defects. I could see that her skin was almost brown, . . . "No, my darling, you are not a nigger." She went on: "You are as good as anybody; if anyone calls you a nigger, don't notice them."*

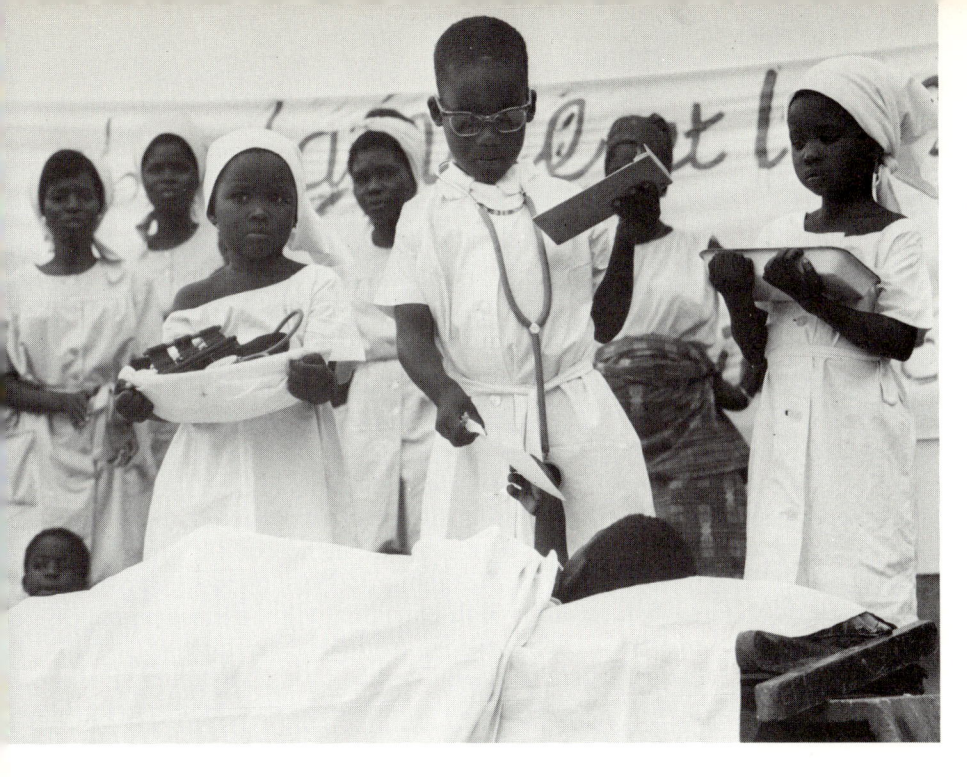

These children are learning about the roles of doctor, nurse, and patient.

But the more she talked, the less I was reassured, and I stopped her by asking: "Well, mother, am I white? Are you white?"

She answered trembling: "No, I am not white, but you—your father is one of the greatest men in the country—the best blood of the South is in you—" This suddenly opened up in my heart a fresh chasm of misgiving and fear, and I almost fiercely demanded: "Who is my father? Where is he?" She stroked my hair and said: "I'll tell you about him some day." I sobbed: "I want to know now." She answered: "No, not now."[15]

Symbolic interactionists disagree as to whether a person has a *core self* —a single, unchanging, coherent view of his or her identity—or *situational selves*—various self-identities that arise as a person interacts with others in unique situations. There is considerable support for the concept of situational selves. An individual may feel and act humble around a physics professor, worldly around a younger brother, and charming around an attractive member of the opposite sex. Each of us may have a repertory of self-feelings and identities, whose importance to us at a particular time depends on our audience.

It seems unlikely that people who become socialized in a complex society like ours can have a single, coherent view of self. American society requires that most individuals interact with a variety of audiences. We are increasingly pressured into playing a number of parts in the course of our lives—mother, wife, student, and club member. The real question each of us must ask is not "Who am I?" but "Who are we?"

Variations in Socialization Methods

Cultures and subcultures vary considerably in their socialization methods. For example, American lower- and working-class parents tend to use techniques of *repressive socialization;* that is, they tend to use punishment to bring about the behavior they desire in their children. They demand that children obey their rules without question and use sanctions like spanking and ridicule when a child disobeys. Two-way communication involving an exchange of ideas between parent and child is often discouraged. Whereas repressive socialization punishes wrong behavior, *participatory socialization* rewards good behavior. Middle-class parents in America tend to utilize the participatory method. Reasoning with the child and praise for proper behavior is emphasized over punishment. Parents motivate children to discover new ideas on their own rather than follow absolute parental commands, and two-way communication is also encouraged.*

The use of repressive and participatory socialization methods varies with occupational groups as well. For example, the socialization of military personnel usually involves repressive methods. New members must obey all commands given from above, and they are ridiculed and assigned undesirable tasks when they do not conform. At the opposite end of the continuum are professionals, such as lawyers, physicians, scientists, and professors; they are given considerable freedom throughout the socialization process that accompanies their occupational pursuits. Unquestionably, professional and graduate schools have rules, sanctions, and supervision for new entrants, but these schools tend to emphasize reward, group participation, and the discovery of new ideas.

After comparing socialization methods in two complex cultures—the Soviet Union and the United States—Urie Bronfenbrenner has criticized the way Americans transmit culture to their children. He found that, although American parents assume responsibility for teaching the infant and very young child, they shirk their responsibility during the child's later years. Socialization is then left almost entirely to the child's friends and the mass media. The result is that children lack close family ties and adult models to guide their behavior. According to Bronfenbrenner, we can only expect more antagonism, violence, alienation, and goalless behavior from American youth because of this pattern.

*Repressive and participatory socialization, as related to social class, are discussed by Urie Bronfenbrenner, "Socialization and Social Class through Time and Space," in *Readings in Social Psychology,* ed. E. E. Maccoby, T. M. Newcomb, and E. L. Hartley (New York: Holt, Rinehart & Winston, 1958), pp. 400–425; and Eleanor E. Maccoby and Patricia K. Gibbs, "Methods of Child Rearing in Two Social Classes," in *Readings in Child Development,* ed. William E. Martin and Celia Burns Stendler (New York: Harcourt Brace Jovanovich, 1954), pp. 380–396.

Repressive socialization methods are sometimes used to instill group norms. In earlier times American teachers thought that "to spare the rod" was "to spoil the child," and today Marine recruits are typically expected to obey orders without question.

In contrast, child-rearing in the Soviet Union is an important responsibility of everyone, including parents, strangers, the child's peers, and teachers. During all the formative years parents maintain extremely close ties with their children. Additionally, the children's social responsibility to friends and family, school, and society in general is emphasized. The result of such socialization is that Soviet children are less aggressive, violent, and rebellious than American children. In brief, they are less antisocial.[16] Some may criticize Soviet society for overcontrolling its members. Still, there are cultural variations in socialization, and Americans might consider other approaches to alleviate social problems.

A typical scene in a park in the Soviet Union, where child-rearing is considered a serious responsibility of parents and all adults.

Wives who pursue their own careers and husbands who take on domestic chores are becoming more and more common in American society, yet these new roles can cause serious resocialization problems for some individuals.

Social Change and Resocialization

As one would expect in a rapidly changing society, Americans face problems that were unknown to earlier generations. Adults are challenged by new ideologies and philosophies and must cope with many different demands on them simultaneously. Americans are also increasingly changing jobs, residences, and life styles; all these changes require *resocialization,* or adoption of a new way of life. To illustrate resocialization more specifically, let us consider a common problem among middle-class females. Traditionally the American female has been directed toward marriage and child-rearing. But what happens after her children are grown and no longer completely dependent on her? Household chores and duties may no longer occupy her time or interests; thus she may decide to pursue a new career to give more meaning to her life. Whether the woman seeking change returns to school, enters the labor force, or participates in civic affairs, she is faced with the problems of learning new skills and coping with new expectations and audiences.

Adults sometimes face extreme resocialization problems when they are transplanted from one society to another. They must learn a new language, eat strange foods, and adjust to other new and unusual aspects of life. Combat veterans and prisoners of war may also face extreme resocialization problems upon their return home. For example, consider the resocialization problems of Shoichi Yokoi, a sergeant in the Japanese Imperial Army during World War II, who, not knowing the war had ended, hid in the jungles on the Pacific island of Guam for almost thirty years. When he finally came out of hiding in 1972, he stated, "We Japanese soldiers were told to prefer death to the disgrace of getting captured alive," "It's all like a dream, and I'm afraid of waking up from it," and "Tell me one thing quick: Is Roosevelt dead?"[17] Prisoners of the war in Vietnam who returned to the United States also had to make some difficult adjustments to the problems they confronted—children on drugs, X-rated movies, long-haired males, divorce, and children who no longer knew them.[18] In these instances, resocialization is traumatic, sometimes resulting in severe psychiatric disorders and suicide. Most of us will likely never face the problems of a returning POW, but we do have to cope with considerable change. Adults are continually learning more about their culture and replacing former ways of life with new ones. (See Chapter 12 for further discussion of the problems individuals face as they attempt to adjust to new situations.)

Chapter Summary

The learning process whereby a person internalizes culture and becomes an active participant in society is called socialization. It is a process which begins at birth and continues throughout life. None of us ever becomes completely socialized or masters all of a culture.

What we become as persons depends largely on the culture around us. Yet we are still unique as individuals because each of us is exposed to different subgroups within a culture, individual interpretations of culture, and conflicting cultural values. Further, to some degree biological traits differentiate us from one another. Primary socialization, the learning of fundamental aspects of life such as what and how to eat, is largely the responsibility of parents. The learning of more abstract cultural knowledge, referred to as secondary socialization, is usually accomplished through contact with peers, teachers, and the mass media.

Theorists disagree about how and what we learn. Reinforcement theorists see the human being as an animal that can be conditioned to act in a certain way through use of rewards and punishments. Cognitive theorists, such as Piaget, see socialization as occurring in developmental stages. The individual eventually learns to overcome his or her self-centeredness and to think more abstractly. Symbolic interactionists emphasize the role of language in the socialization process and the self-feelings which arise out of interaction with others. We develop a self as we internalize and adjust to the attitudes, beliefs, and norms of the generalized other. We are continually seeking approval from others and seeking to know who we are. But as an individual interacts with many audiences and assumes a variety of parts in life, he or she begins to develop not one identity but various self-identities.

Methods of socialization vary among cultures and subcultures. Lower- and working-class parents in America tend to use punishment to reinforce learning, while middle-class parents tend to use rewards. Cultural variation regarding socialization is seen in comparing the United States with the Soviet Union. Soviet culture places more emphasis on family ties and child discipline, with the result that children show less antisocial behavior. Possibly Americans should consider various socialization methods so that they may better deal with their social problems.

As adults, we are continually faced with the task of learning new ways of life, but resocialization can cause numerous adjustment problems. Learning and relearning never end as long as the individual is in interaction with others. In a sense, we are always in a process of becoming.

Key Terms for Review

agents of socialization, p. 46
associationism, p. 50
cognitive theory, p. 52
core self, p. 57
cultural determinism, p. 44
generalized other, p. 56
hedonism, p. 49
"I," p. 55
imitation, play, and game, pp. 55, 56
instincts, p. 45
looking-glass self, p. 53
"me," p. 55
negative reinforcement, p. 50
participatory socialization, p. 58

positive reinforcement, p. 50
primary socialization, p. 46
reinforcement theory, p. 49
repressive socialization, p. 58
resocialization, p. 60
secondary socialization, p. 47
self, p. 53
significant symbols, p. 53
situational selves, p. 57
socialization, p. 41
symbol, p. 52
symbolic interactionism, p. 52
take the role of others, p. 55

Suggested Readings

SOCIOLOGICAL

Bronfenbrenner, Urie. *Two Worlds of Childhood: U.S. and U.S.S.R.* New York: Russell Sage Foundation, 1970. The author compares socialization methods in two complex cultures. In regard to the United States, he predicts that adolescent rebellion and hostility will increase as long as parents shirk their duty of teaching and controlling children.

Clausen, John A., ed. *Socialization and Society.* Boston: Little, Brown, 1968. This is a general survey of sociological, anthropological, and psychological research on socialization. The contributors define basic concepts and discuss theoretical issues.

Danziger, Kurt. *Socialization*. Harmondsworth, Middlesex, Eng.: Penguin, 1971. The author uses a psychological perspective to discuss a wide range of topics including sex-typing, parent-child relationships, personality formation, and extrafamilial influences on the child.

Eisenstadt, S. N. *From Generation to Generation*. New York: Free Press, 1956. Socialization processes and problems during different stages of life are discussed. The author's examination of socialization during adolescence is quite informative.

Gergen, Kenneth. *The Concept of Self*. New York: Holt, Rinehart & Winston, 1971. This short and very readable book deals with the process of self-understanding. The author emphasizes a person's conception of reality and how it affects his or her personal conduct.

Lindesmith, Alfred R., and Anselm L. Strauss. *Social Psychology*. New York: Holt, Rinehart & Winston, 1968. The authors treat the area of social psychology from a symbolic interactionist perspective. The topics of language development, cognitive processes, self-feelings, roles, and socialization are examined.

LITERARY

Golding, William. *Lord of the Flies*. New York: G. P. Putnam's, 1959. In this dramatic novel a group of English schoolboys are stranded on a deserted island. The society that they develop is based on cruelty and savagery. The story makes disturbing conjectures about humans and illustrates the trauma of the resocialization process.

Hemingway, Ernest. "Fathers and Sons." In *The Short Stories of Ernest Hemingway*. New York: Scribner's, 1966. The impact of parents on how we think and what we become is strong. The chief character's goals, preferences, and self-concept reflect much of his boyhood experiences with his father.

Jackson, Shirley. "The Lottery." In *The Best Short Stories of the Modern Age*. Ed. Douglas Angus. Greenwich, Conn.: Fawcett, 1965. Once this short story is read, it is seldom forgotten. Jackson illustrates the tremendous impact of culture on the individual.

Twain, Mark. *Adventures of Huckleberry Finn*. Boston: Houghton Mifflin, 1962. The story of Huck Finn is about the socialization of a young boy. Each day Huck seems to face new problems and adjust to new life styles. Questions regarding religion, racial prejudice, allegiance to parents, and friendship are faced by Huck and most American adolescents.

Twain, Mark. "What Is Man?" In *The Complete Essays of Mark Twain*. Ed. Charles Neider. Garden City, N.Y.: Doubleday, 1963. In this serious and insightful essay an old man and young man discuss how human beings learn and what factors influence behavior. The individual is shown as both a creature and creator of culture.

Wright, Richard. *Native Son*. New York: Harper & Row, 1966. The author vividly portrays the plight of Bigger Thomas, a young black man caught up in an act of violence. The book serves as a warning that ghetto conditions create violent personalities. The idea of cultural determinism is illustrated.

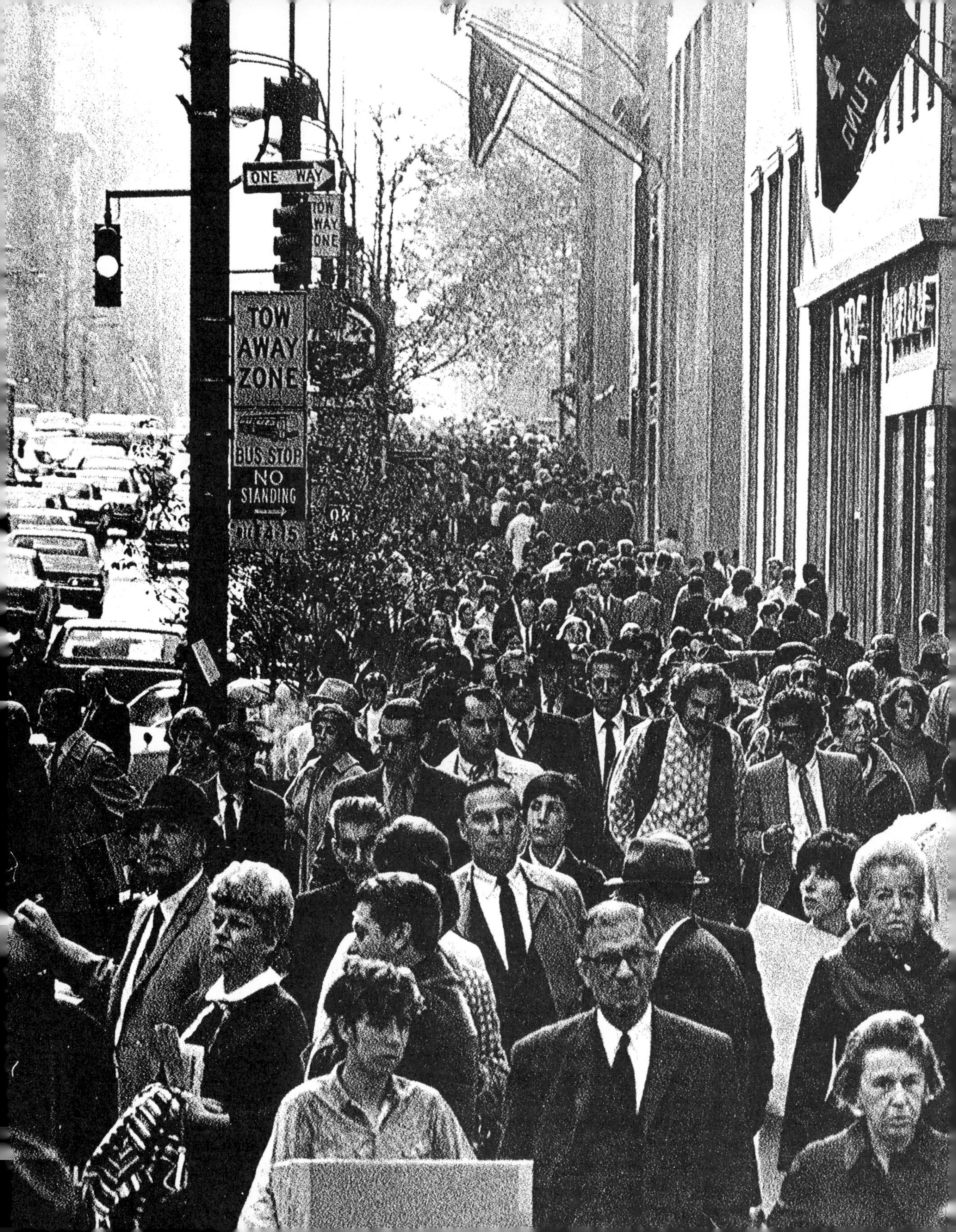
ONE WAY
TOW AWAY ZONE
TOW AWAY ZONE
BUS STOP
NO STANDING

part two

SOCIAL ORGANIZATION

Few would deny that human animals constitute a unique species. We humans are different because we can create and act somewhat idiosyncratically. Still, we are not totally free spirits, for society is orderly and imposes limits on the behavior of its members.

In chapter 4 we will examine the means—norms, sanctions, status, and role expectations—that society utilizes to bring about this order. Our discussion of how life is organized continues in chapter 5 with an examination of the many groups which exist in society. Our behavior is shaped by our membership in groups, and nowhere is this more clearly illustrated than in the bureaucratic organization, treated in chapter 6. Since bureaucracies touch the lives of everyone in complex societies, their problems are of vital concern. Finally, chapter 7 examines social class. We will show there how the status society assigns an individual affects his or her behavior and attitudes about life.

IN THIS CHAPTER

Defining Social Organization   68

Norms and Sanctions   70

Status and Role   74

    Types of statuses   76
    Role performance   79

Deviance and Social Disorganization   84

Summary   91

Key Terms for Review   92

Suggested Readings   92

Are we totally free and independent of the rules and expectations of others? Are we wholly controlled and governed by others? What means do people use to bring about order and control? Would life be chaotic without rules?

THE MEANING OF SOCIAL ORGANIZATION

In his most famous work, *Walden*, Henry David Thoreau, the nineteenth-century American essayist, maintained that an individual can be totally free and independent of others' rules and expectations. Each of us can keep pace to "a different drummer." "Do your own thing," "be a free spirit," or "different strokes for different folks," are contemporary expressions of Thoreau's idea. As appealing as this view is, some have expressed doubts and have proposed an opposite view. Social systems, according to these others, consist of extremely interdependent and coordinated parts, and in such tightly knit systems the actions of individual members are closely controlled and monitored.

The position of most contemporary sociologists on this question is that individuals are neither totally free nor totally controlled. Social systems are to some extent boundary-maintaining; that is, they exert controls that limit human activity. Social behavior is somewhat predictable, and conduct which drifts outside established boundaries is recognized as inappropriate by others. At the same time, however, sociologists today hold that human behavior can vary over an enormous range. Individuals can operate with some leeway within the acceptable boundaries established by others. Further, the boundaries of social systems are never fixed but are always shifting. What is acceptable here and now may be unacceptable in a different place and time, as people continually redefine themselves, others, and situations. In brief, the stance taken by most sociologists is that order is characteristic of social systems, but humans do possess creative potential and can act somewhat idiosyncratically.

Our first and major purpose in this chapter is to examine what sociologists mean when they assert that life is orderly and patterned in a society. We will examine four means which are utilized to bring about this order. Our second purpose is to illustrate some of the choices open to the individual acting within established guidelines. And our third purpose is to look briefly at how behavior outside established boundaries affects social organization.

Defining Social Organization

Scientist Jerome Woolpy and his colleagues studied a pack of timber wolves at the Brookfield Zoo in Chicago from 1960 to 1967. Woolpy reported that the wolves behaved in remarkably patterned and predictable ways. Some members of the pack were more dominant than others; each had rights and duties within the pack; and punishments were applied when rules were disobeyed. Here is how Woolpy describes their behavior:

> *In the typical dominant-submissive interaction, the ranking wolf carries his head erect and his ears forward, his body in a normal position, and his tail straight out and behind him; the deferring submissive animal approaches the dominant with his head down low and his ears back (but not flat against the head), his body wriggling in a crouching walk, and his tail pointed downward and fluttering. The submissive animal will often attempt to get his head beneath the head of the dominant animal and to lick its mouth or muzzle. . . .*
>
> *The separate roles within the pack consist of the dominant, or alpha male, the alpha female, the subordinate males and females, the peripheral males and females, and the juveniles. At some time or other, the alpha male is deferred to by all the other members of the pack. He is the focal point of the "solicitous affection" of the pack; that is, the other members often run up to the alpha male, wag their tails, and paw and lick at him. Frequently, they all gather around him and do this at the same time. This is generally accompanied by howling and is called a "greeting ceremony." He is also the principal guard of the territory and patrols around the periphery of the pack, perhaps looking for intruders. The alpha female is dominant over all the other females and most of the males. She controls the relationships of the rest of the females to the pack. The subordinate males and females, together with the alpha male and female, form the effective nucleus of the pack. The peripheral males and females are kept out of the nucleus as a result of their manifest submissiveness and low rank in the social hierarchy. They are forced to remain at some distance from the nucleus most of the time, although they attempt to participate in pack activities as much as possible.*[1]

Like nonhuman animals, human beings also exhibit *social organization*: they have an orderly way of interacting with one another (or, as some

A symphony orchestra, like any group, functions on the basis of patterned interaction and order: each musician is expected to know his or her part and to follow various rules.

social scientists say, they have a "social structure"). In contrast to other animals, however, humans have far more complex systems of order. Further, humans are usually thought of as unique in their ability to change the order governing their lives.

To illustrate the notion of social organization within human groups, picture yourself at a symphony concert. Prior to the performance you might see some musicians busily tuning their instruments and others chatting or peering at sheet music. The scene appears disorderly. Onto the stage walks the conductor and the musicians become silent. On the down stroke of the conductor's baton what had been a situation of random sounds and actions is now transformed into a symphony pleasing to the ear. The percussion, string, and wind sections work in a coordinated fashion to produce this pleasing sound.

On closer examination, we see that rules are necessary for the musicians. An overanxious flutist who begins his part too soon or a violinist who plays a "sour" note would ruin the composition and probably be criticized by the conductor as well as by fellow musicians. Eventually the flutist might even be dismissed from the group. If we returned to the symphony for several nights, we would begin to realize that each performer largely knows his or her part and what to expect from others. Consider the value of their social organization. If each day the musicians came together at a different time, with different music, and without the correct instruments, the result would surely be chaos.

Social organization can promote stability and predictability in all kinds of groups: an orchestra, two people interacting, a family, a government, the total society. Since human groups could not exist without social organization, the topic is of vital concern to sociologists, and the four means utilized to bring it about—norms, sanctions, status, and roles—must be understood.

Norms and Sanctions

As you will recall from chapter 2, rules, called norms, govern our behavior in social situations. We noted there that three general categories of norms are distinguishable—mores, customs, and folkways—and that these covered everything from morals to etiquette. Consider the following example of the folkways of "gentlemen and ladies" during the 1890s:

VARIETY OF TOILET [COSTUME].

Vary your toilet as much as possible, for fear that idlers and malignant wits, who are always a majority in the world, should amuse themselves by making your dress the description of your person. . . .

A LADY'S POSITION [ON LOVE].

A lady's choice is only negative—that is to say, she may love, but she cannot declare her love; she must wait. . . .

A GENTLEMAN'S POSITION [ON LOVE].

A man may, and he will learn his fate at once, openly declare his passion, and obtain his answer. In this he has great advantage over the lady. Being refused, he may go elsewhere to seek a mate. . . .

DUTIES OF THE WIFE.

On the wife especially devolves the privilege and pleasure of rendering the home happy. . . .
    Remember that your Heavenly Father, who has given you a home to dwell in, requires from you a right performance of its duties. Win your husband, by all gentle appliances, to love religion; but do not, for the sake even of a privilege and a blessing, leave him to spend his evenings alone. . . .

GENERAL RULES FOR BEHAVIOR AT TABLE.

Tea and coffee should never be poured into a saucer. . . .
    If anything unpleasant is found in the food, such as a hair in the bread or a fly in the coffee, remove it without remark. Though your

own appetite be spoiled, it is well not to spoil that of others.

Never, if possible, cough or sneeze at the table. . . .

Never hold your knife and fork upright on each side of your plate while you are talking. . . .

A FILTHY HABIT.

Spitting is a filthy habit, and annoys one in almost every quarter, indoors and out. . . . Smoking is unquestionably so great a pleasure to those accustomed to it, that it must not be condemned, yet the spitting associated with it detracts very much from the enjoyment. No refined person will spit where ladies are present. . . .[2]

Such norms had an influence on the conduct of late nineteenth-century Americans. Of course, not everyone followed these stated norms. Social classes, ethnic groups, and communities differed in their ideas of what was appropriate. Also, although gentlemen and ladies of the 1890s would have followed the preceding table rules in a public setting, they might not have acted so prim and proper in other situations, such as an informal meal with intimate friends. And surely many of the "refined" patterns of behavior described have been abandoned by today's society. Norms, in short, vary with groups, situations, and time.

Sanctions, as we have seen, are those actions of a positive or negative nature that groups use to reinforce their established norms. A smile, a pay raise, a sincere laugh, on the one hand, or a frown, a pay cut, a raised eye-

Some of the most obvious changes in norms in our society since the 1890s concern proper attire and recreation for "ladies and gentlemen."

brow, on the other, are all familiar sanctions to us. When a community defines a norm as important and crucial, it tends to manufacture and utilize severe sanctions to enforce it. A norm which has been rather consistently defined as important in American society concerns child molestation. Those who are apprehended and convicted for such crimes tend to receive both lengthy prison sentences and widespread public condemnation.

Sanctions are used by society to motivate people to act in ways considered right. The power of sanctions to influence one's self-concept and view of the world is well illustrated in Virginia Woolf's story of Mabel and her new dress. It takes only a few gestures by others to inform Mabel of the "unacceptability" of her costume and herself.

> *Mabel had her first serious suspicion that something was wrong as she took her cloak off and Mrs. Barnet, while handing her the mirror and touching the brushes and thus drawing her attention, perhaps rather markedly, to all the appliances for tidying and improving hair, complexion, clothes, which existed on the dressing table, confirmed the suspicion—that it was not right, not quite right, which growing stronger as she went upstairs and springing at her, with conviction as she greeted Clarissa Dalloway, she went straight to the far end of the room, to a shaded corner where a looking-glass hung and looked. No! It was not right. And at once the misery which she always tried to hide, the profound dissatisfaction—the sense she had had, ever since she was a child, of being inferior to other people—set upon her, relentlessly, remorselessly, with an intensity which she could not beat off, as she would when she woke at night at home, by reading Borrow or Scott; for oh these men, oh these women, all were thinking—"What's Mabel wearing? What a fright she looks! What a hideous new dress!"—their eyelids flickering as they came up and then their lids shutting rather tight. It was her own appalling inadequacy; her cowardice; her mean, water-sprinkled blood that depressed her. And at once the whole of the room where, for ever so many hours, she had planned with the little dressmaker how it was to go, seemed sordid, repulsive; and her own drawing-room so shabby, and herself, going out, puffed up with vanity as she touched the letters on the hall table and said: "How dull!" to show off—all this now seemed unutterably silly, paltry, and provincial. All this had been absolutely destroyed, shown up, exploded, the moment she came into Mrs. Dalloway's drawing-room.*[3]

Puritans often punished violations of community norms by putting the offender in the stocks.

PURITAN MORALITY ENFORCED.

We can only guess, but Mabel was probably sufficiently motivated not to wear the dress again, at least around these same people.

Norms can be thought of as either prescriptive or proscriptive. *Prescriptive norms* require specific actions, and *proscriptive norms* prohibit certain behavior. People are required to pay fees while attending a university

The norms of their particular courses, their peer group, the university as a whole, and the larger society all affect the lives of college students such as these.

and to wear clothes in public. People are prohibited from plagiarizing term papers for university courses and from parking their cars by fire hydrants.

Some norms exist throughout an entire society: saying "thank you" when someone does something nice for you and shaking hands upon greeting another person are widely known rules of etiquette in our society. Widely recognized rules are referred to as *communal norms*. In contrast, *associational norms* are rules which are unique to smaller, more defined groups within the society. In a particular college course, for example, a student may be required to pass three exams and write two short research reports, but these rules do not necessarily apply to other courses. Obviously, our lives are shaped by both communal and associational norms.

The decisions that we must make in regard to norms can sometimes be difficult for several reasons. Sometimes disagreement exists over the value of a norm. Some people in our society see marijuana as an evil, dangerous narcotic, while others view it as a source of harmless pleasure. Sometimes a new situation calls into question the applicability of an old norm. Telling a dirty joke at the local bar is usually acceptable, but is it so when your minister or priest is sitting only a few bar stools away? We must, it seems, continually evaluate whether what was once acceptable is still acceptable. At one time Americans considered it immoral to talk of sodomy, bisexuality, and premarital and extramarital sex, but discussion of such behavior is more open today. Additionally, an individual may have to choose between *ideal norms*, those the community says we should follow, and *real norms*, the rules actually followed. Many parents and teachers emphasize to children that cheating is improper, yet many of these adults cheat in filing their income tax returns.

Thus, although norms and sanctions establish some order in social life, society is not perfectly governed by them. Norms may conflict with each other, situations arise where rules are absent or ambiguous, and boundaries between acceptability and unacceptability constantly shift. In a sense, when a person decides on a course of action, he or she is testing the invisible boundaries established by others. Individuals are looking for the boundaries where the lines have been drawn, and they hope their actions in most instances are labeled "appropriate."

Status and Role

The term "status" is often used to mean a position we hold within a group. One may think of a family, for instance, as composed of various positions—father, mother, oldest daughter, youngest son, aunt, grandfather, and so forth. A person's status within a family group gives rise to certain expectations in others. Grandchildren might expect their grandfather to be kind, generous, and paternal, whereas parents might expect their only daughter to study hard and someday become a famous novelist. However, the term "status" implies more than just position. Group members rank positions so that some are superior, some subordinate. For example, children are usually subordinate to parents in a family. *Status* refers to both the position and rank of an individual in a group.

Herman Melville gives us a glimpse of the status of personnel on a nineteenth-century American warship. Each man, from commodore down to seaman, had specific privileges, duties, and rank on the ship.

> Our Commodore was a gallant old man, . . . his presence possessed the strange power of making other people dumb for the time. His appearance on the Quarter-deck seemed to give every officer the lock-jaw.
>
> Another phenomenon about him was the strange manner in which everyone shunned him. At the first sign of those epaulets of his on the weather side of the poop, the officers there congregated invariably shrunk over to leeward, and left him alone. . . .
>
> Turn we now to the second officer in rank, almost supreme, however, in the internal affairs of his ship. Captain Claret was a large, portly man. . . .
>
> The captain's word is law; he never speaks but in the imperative mood. When he stands on his Quarter-deck at sea, he absolutely commands as far as eye can reach. . . .
>
> Next in rank comes the First or Senior Lieutenant, the chief executive officer. . . . By the captain he is held responsible for everything; by that magnate, indeed, he is supposed to be omnipresent; down in the hold, and up aloft, at one and the same time.

He presides at the head of the Ward-room officers' table. . . .

Besides the First Lieutenant, the Ward-room officers include the junior lieutenants, in a frigate six or seven in number, the Sailing-master, Purser, Chaplain, Surgeon, Marine officers, and Midshipmen's Schoolmaster, or "the Professor." . . .

Next in order come the Warrant or Forward officers, consisting of the Boatswain, Gunner, Carpenter, and Sailmaker. Though these worthies sport long coats and wear the anchor-button; yet, in the estimation of the Ward-room officers, they are not, technically speaking, rated gentlemen. The First Lieutenant, Chaplain, or Surgeon, for example, would never dream of inviting them to dinner. In sea parlance, "they come in at the hawse holes;" they have hard hands. . . .

. . . now come the "reefers," otherwise "middies" or midshipmen. These boys are sent to sea, for the purpose of making commodores; . . . The middies live by themselves in the steerage, where, nowadays, they dine off a table, spread with a cloth. They have a castor at dinner; they have some other little boys (selected from the ship's company) to wait upon them. . . .

. . . we come lastly to a set of nondescripts, forming also a "mess" by themselves, apart from the seamen. Into this mess, the usage of a man-of-war thrusts various subordinates—including the master-at-arms, purser's steward, ship's corporals, marine sergeants, and ship's yeomen, forming the first aristocracy above the sailors. . . .

Thus it will be seen, that the dinner-table is the criterion of rank

Traditional family portraits—the father typically standing, the mother often seated with baby in her lap—suggest the status and role of family members. Here we see *The Sargent Family*.

in our man-of-war world. The Commodore dines alone, because he is the only man of his rank in the ship. So too with the Captain; and the Ward-room officers, warrant officers, midshipmen, the master-at-arms' mess, and the common seamen;—all of them, respectively, dine together, because they are, respectively, on a footing of equality.[4]

TYPES OF STATUSES

All of us occupy multiple statuses. An individual may be a female, young adult, student, daughter, sister, wife, mother, part-time clerk, Lutheran, bank depositor, driver, pedestrian, and patient. Of the statuses we hold, some are ascribed and others are achieved. Positions assigned us by society that we virtually cannot change are called *ascribed statuses*. Our sex, place of birth, age, and family affiliation are common examples, and in some societies even rigid social-class position, religion, and occupation are ascribed. For example, a young boy in medieval society could have been expected and compelled to be a carpenter because his father, grandfather, and great-grandfather had all been carpenters.

Achieved statuses are those which individuals can attain through their own choice and effort. An American can become a Republican, Elks Club member, parent, Catholic, electrician, member of the middle class, and high-school graduate.[5] Society ultimately decides which of these statuses should be easier to achieve. In America almost everyone can achieve the status of automobile owner, whereas it is impossible for most of us to become a top executive at General Motors. Americans mistakenly think any education, occupation, and income status can be achieved, particularly if a person works hard enough. Although hard work and resourcefulness may be important for achievement, ascriptive criteria also play an essential part. Compared to males, females have an ascribed status of low regard in reference to intelligence, leadership, and work ability. Consequently, as women attempt to achieve new statuses, they face the persistent expectation of society that women belong in the home.

A member of society can sometimes improve upon his or her status. Such was the case for Frederick Douglass. Born a slave in the South, he escaped his master and became a prominent writer and active spokesman against slavery. In a letter dated September 22, 1848, to his ex-master, Thomas Auld, Douglass tells of his old and new lives:

> I have selected this day on which to address you, because it is the anniversary of my emancipation; and knowing of no better way, I am led to this as the best mode of celebrating that truly important event. Just ten years ago this beautiful September morning, yon bright sun beheld me a slave—a poor, degraded chattel—trembling at the sound of your voice, lamenting that I was a man, and wishing myself a brute. . . .

An individual occupies many statuses, some ascribed and other achieved. Virgil L. Kirk, pictured here, occupies the ascribed statuses of being male, middle aged, and Navajo; at the same time, he has achieved the status of Chief Justice on the Tribal Courts of an Arizona reservation.

> Since I left you, I have had a rich experience. I have occupied stations which I never dreamed of when a slave. Three out of the ten years since I left you, I spent as a common laborer on the wharves of New Bedford, Massachusetts. It was there I earned my first free dollar. It was mine. I could spend it as I pleased. I could buy hams or herring with it, without asking any odds of any body. That was a precious dollar to me. . . .
>
> I met with Wm. Lloyd Garrison, a person of whom you have possibly heard, as he is pretty generally known among slave-holders. He put it into my head that I might make myself serviceable to the cause of the slave by devoting a portion of my time to telling my own sorrows, and those of other slaves which had come under my observation. This was the commencement of a higher state of existence than any to which I had ever aspired. I was thrown into society the most pure, enlightened and benevolent that the country affords. . . .
>
> The transition from degradation to respectability was indeed great, and to get from one to the other without carrying some marks of one's former condition, is truly a difficult matter. I would not have you think that I am now entirely clear of all plantation peculiarities, but my friends here, while they entertain the strongest dislike to them, regard me with that charity to which my past life somewhat entitles me. . . . I can boast of as comfortable a dwelling as your own. I have an industrious and neat companion, and four dear children. . . . These dear children are ours—not to work up into rice, sugar and tobacco, but to watch over, regard, and protect, and to rear them up in the nurture and admonition of the gospel—to train them up in the paths of wisdom and virtue, and, as far as we can to make them useful to the world and to themselves. Oh! sir, a slaveholder never appears to me so completely an agent of hell, as when I think of and look upon my dear children. . . . I remember the chain, the gag, the bloody whip, the death-like gloom overshadowing the broken spirit of the fettered bondman, the appalling liability of his being torn away from wife and children, and sold like a beast in the market. Say not that this is a picture of fancy. You well know that I wear stripes on my back inflicted by your direction. . . .
>
> I am your fellow man, but not your slave,
>
> Frederick Douglass[6]

In complex societies members occupy communal and associational statuses simultaneously. *Communal statuses* are positions known and reacted to by everyone in society. In contrast, *associational statuses* are known only within smaller, more defined groups. For instance, a soldier who wears his uniform is reacted to as a soldier by almost everyone he meets; in this sense he has a communal status. Back at his base, however, he is more than just a soldier. He may have associational status as a private and a mechanic in the motor pool.

At the 1968 Olympics in Mexico City, American medalists Tommie Smith and Juan Carlos departed from usual expectations of Olympic athletes and registered their protest against racial inequality in the United States during the playing of the Star Spangled Banner.

Closely related to the concept of status is that of role. In the play *As You Like It*, William Shakespeare capsulized the meaning of role.

> *All the world's a stage,*
> *And all the men and women merely players:*
> *They have their exits and their entrances;*
> *And one man in his time plays many parts . . .*

Sociologists have used *role* to refer both to the expectations and to the performance of an individual occupying a particular status.

Role as "expectations" means that the person holding the position has certain rights and duties. For example, the role of Olympic skier carries with it numerous expectations. Coaches, fellow team members, and the general public may demand a certain level of technical expertise from the skier. She must practice every day, keep equipment in good condition, dress appropriately, exercise regularly, and maintain a proper diet. And when competing against others, she is expected to conduct herself according to the rules of "good sportsmanship," which, for example, means not throwing tantrums upon losing and not stealing her competitor's favorite skis. The Olympic representative is also afforded rights and preferential treatment. News reporters, autograph seekers, television producers, and ski equipment advertisers will seek out the team member. If they did not, the individual would feel slighted that she was not receiving what her status deserved.

Role as "performance" refers to how the individual actually behaves while occupying a status. Although there are expectations associated with a given position, individuals do not always conform to the wishes of others. One Olympic skier may behave arrogantly by missing practices and breaking training rules, while another may act in an exemplary manner.

ROLE PERFORMANCE

We noted at the beginning of the chapter that a major purpose of our discussion was to illustrate choices open to an individual acting within established guidelines. Although some examples have already been mentioned, to illustrate further the freedom individuals have in performing their roles, we might examine several concepts commonly discussed in sociology. One, called *role set*, refers to the individual's repertoire of performances toward a variety of other people while he or she occupies a given status.[7] A college student may act reserved around his professors, knowledgeable and confident around his parents, who did not attend college, and bored around his fellow students. We adapt our behavior to the persons we confront. We test out a behavior, usually hoping to influence others and to receive feedback from them that our actions are appropriate.*

Further, a person can occupy a status and yet decide to have no commitment to it. Sociologists call this alien situation for the individual *role distance*. The woman who does not want or like children but unexpectedly becomes pregnant and bears triplets would experience role distance. Her personal goals distance her from the status in which she finds herself. In Joseph Heller's popular novel, *Catch-22*, Captain Yossarian, a bomber pilot of the 256th Air Force Squadron, experiences role distance. He feigns an illness in the hospital because he cannot understand why someone would want to be killed or to kill someone else.

But Yossarian couldn't be happy, even though the Texan didn't want him to be, because outside the hospital there was still nothing funny going on. The only thing going on was a war, and no one seemed to notice . . . And when Yossarian tried to remind people, they drew away from him and thought he was crazy. . . .

---

*For a discussion of how people perform their roles, see Erving Goffman, *The Presentation of Self in Everyday Life* (Garden City, N.Y.: Doubleday, 1959).

> *It was a vile and muddy war, and Yossarian could have lived without it—lived forever, perhaps. Only a fraction of his countrymen would give up their lives to win it, and it was not his ambition to be among them. To die or not to die, that was the question. . . . History did not demand Yossarian's premature demise, justice could be satisfied without it, progress did not hinge upon it, victory did not depend on it. That men would die was a matter of necessity; which men would die, though, was a matter of circumstance, and Yossarian was willing to be the victim of anything but circumstance. But that was war. Just about all he could find in its favor was that it paid well and liberated children from the pernicious influence of their parents.*[8]

When we look to others for guidance, we may find disagreement as to how we should perform our roles. Accordingly, we are left with a personal decision and the result may be *role conflict.*

Such a conflict can arise when a person occupies one status for which there are two or more opposing sets of expectations. In Anne Sinclair Mehdevi's essay "A Persian Courtship," an Iranian maiden named Sari is faced with two opposing expectations because of her status as a marriageable female. Her American, English, and youthful Persian friends expect her to choose her own husband, whereas her parents feel that they should arrange her marriage. Sari is caught between two worlds which represent different cultures and times. She initially rejects the parental views about marriage:

> *"I shall never marry a Persian. I'm going to fall in love with a foreigner and I'm going to tell him so and ask him to marry me."* . . .
> *"It's just like tribal days. Sending his parents to my parents! Well, I told my mother long ago that such proposals are out of the question. I'm not a piece of goods to be negotiated about."* She tossed her head and lighted a cigarette.[9]

But the pressure is too strong, and out of guilt she agrees to meet the suitor of her parents' choice. She explains why to a friend, and then we see her shifting attitudes toward her decision:

> *"It's really for Mother's sake. She's miserable when we're not speaking, so we had to start speaking again—that's the only reason I agreed."*
> *"Of course. When will you meet him—this afternoon?"*
> *"Yes. At five. He and his parents are coming."* . . .
> Around four o'clock she had a fit of tears. . . .
> Every once in a while she would make a comment. *"He's a graduate of some American university. That's a good sign."* Or, *"What if his parents don't like me?"* Then she would bite her lip. *"I should*

A clash of cultures can result in role conflict for the individual. Here the sewing machine is symbolic of technology and modernity, while the women's veiled faces represent a traditional, preindustrial way of life.

care," she would say loudly. "I don't care a bit. It's all so horribly old fashioned."

We were still upstairs when we heard a car drive up and stop in front of the garden gate. We heard the car door snap open and then click shut.

Sari jumped up and wrung her hands. "What shall I do?" . . . I watched her with mixed feelings as she trudged reluctantly down the stairs and through the entrance corridor. . . .

I waited upstairs, apprehensive and doubtful, expecting Sari to come scrambling back, bathed in tears. When she didn't after an hour, I tiptoed onto the landing and leaned over the balustrade. I heard sounds of laughter from the living room. . . .

I didn't see Sari again until late the next afternoon. She seemed silent and pensive. "Did you like him?" I asked.

She shrugged. "He's short and chubby."

"What did your parents think of him?"

"Oh, they say it's up to me. Mother wants me to get married. I'm already twenty. She had two children by the time she was twenty. His family is quite rich though not politically important." . . . She glanced up at me obliquely. "That poem of his was nice, wasn't it?"

There was a pause. Then Sari brightened. "I'm getting a car, a white two-seater."

"Oh?"

"It's kind of an engagement present." . . .[10]

A person may also experience role conflict when he or she occupies two or more statuses that have conflicting expectations. Philip Roth describes the dilemma of Nathan Marx, a Jew who is an army sergeant during World War II. Marx's religious status carries with it certain expectations that conflict with those associated with his military status. Jewish soldiers want Marx to defend their right not to eat pork and to protest the army's serving it. In contrast, his commanding officers expect Marx to defend their position, that all soldiers should eat what is prepared or nothing at all and, above all, that soldiers should never complain. Marx is caught in a confrontation between representatives of these two positions—the captain and a Jewish soldier named Grossbart.

"Grossbart, your mama wrote some congressman that we don't feed you right. Do you know that?" the Captain said.

"It was my father, sir. He wrote to Representative Franconi that my religion forbids me to eat certain foods."

"What religion is that, Grossbart?"

"Jewish."

" 'Jewish, sir,' " I said to Grossbart.

"Excuse me, sir. Jewish, sir."

"What have you been living on?" the Captain asked. "You've

been in the Army a month already. You don't look to me like you're falling to pieces."

"I eat because I have to, sir. But Sergeant Marx will testify to the fact that I don't eat one mouthful more than I need to in order to survive."

"Is that so, Marx?" Barrett asked.

"I've never seen Grossbart eat, sir," I said.

"But you heard the rabbi," Grossbart said. "He told us what to do, and I listened."

The Captain looked at me. "Well, Marx?"

"I still don't know what he eats and doesn't eat, sir."

Grossbart raised his arms to plead with me, and it looked for a moment as though he were going to hand me his weapon to hold. "But, Sergeant—"

"Look, Grossbart, just answer the Captain's questions," I said sharply.

Barrett smiled at me, and I resented it. "All right, Grossbart," he said. "What is it you want? The little piece of paper? You want out?"

"No, sir. Only to be allowed to live as a Jew. And for the others, too."

"What others?"

"Fishbein, sir, and Halpern."

"They don't like the way we serve, either?"

"Halpern throws up, sir. I've seen it." . . .

"Marx," the Captain said, "you're a Jewish fella—am I right?"

I played straight man. "Yes, sir."

"How long you been in the Army? Tell this boy."

"Three years and two months."

"A year in combat, Grossbart. Twelve goddam months in combat all through Europe. I admire this man." The Captain snapped a wrist against my chest. "Do you hear him peeping about the food? Do you? I want an answer, Grossbart. Yes or no."

"No, sir."

"And why not? He's a Jewish fella."

"Some things are more important to some Jews than other things to other Jews."

Barrett blew up. "Look, Grossbart. Marx, here, is a good man—a goddam hero. When you were in high school, Sergeant Marx was killing Germans. Who does more for the Jews—you, by throwing up over a lousy piece of sausage, a piece of first-cut meat, or Marx, by killing those Nazi bastards?" . . .[11]

Norms, sanctions, status, and role expectations, then, form a complex network that provides people with guidelines for their behavior. Still, the individual usually has some latitude to behave according to personal interests and desires.

Deviance and Social Disorganization

Thus far, we have been concerned with the means by which society establishes order. Setting boundaries to human conduct involves motivating people to behave in certain expected ways. But, as we have seen, people do not always live up to those expectations. Because violations of social expectations often shed light on the nature of the social order itself, we will consider that topic briefly here. (For further discussion, see chapter 14 and all of part five.)

Violations of society's expectations are numerous. Occasionally, society singles out behavior it considers particularly inappropriate and labels it deviant. *Deviance*, then, refers to that conduct defined by society as unacceptable. Kai T. Erikson has explained the concept of deviance in the following way:

> The term "deviance" refers to conduct which the people of a group consider so dangerous or embarrassing or irritating that they bring special sanctions to bear against the persons who exhibit it. Deviance is not a property inherent in any particular kind of behavior; it is a property conferred upon that behavior by the people who come into direct or indirect contact with it. The only way an observer can tell whether or not a given style of behavior is deviant, then, is to learn something about the standards of the audience which responds to it.
>
> This definition may seem a little awkward in practice, but it has the advantage of bringing a neglected issue into proper focus. When the people of a community decide that it is time to "do something" about the conduct of one of their number, they are involved in a highly intricate process. After all, even the worst miscreant in society conforms most of the time, if only in the sense that he uses the correct silver at dinner, stops obediently at traffic lights, or in a hundred other ways respects the ordinary conventions of his group. And if his fellows elect to bring sanctions against him for the occasions when he does misbehave, they are responding to a few deviant details scattered among a vast array of entirely acceptable conduct. The person who appears in a criminal court and is stamped a "thief" may have spent no more than a passing moment engaged in that activity, and the same can be said for many of the people who pass in review before some agency of control and return from the experience with a deviant label of one sort or another. When the community nominates someone to the deviant class, then, it is sift-

ing a few important details out of the stream of behavior he has emitted and is in effect declaring that these details reflect the kind of person he "really" is. In law as well as in public opinion, the fact that someone has committed a felony or has been known to use narcotics can become the major identifying badge of his person: the very expression "he is a thief" or "he is an addict" seems to provide at once a description of his position in society and a profile of his character.[12]

Deviance has no absolute boundaries. What one group considers deviant another group may not; what may be deviant in one situation may be quite acceptable in another; and what was once deviant may now be seen as totally acceptable.

At first glance, groups appear to define as deviant those acts which could be harmful to their survival. For example, most societies define murder and rape as harmful, and so they impose severe sanctions against those who commit such acts. In reality, however, much behavior that is labeled deviant seems totally unrelated to the survival of a society. For example, prostitution and marijuana smoking certainly do not appear to bear on a society's ultimate survival, although the social sanctions for such behavior can be severe.

The major reason a group defines some acts as deviant and other acts as acceptable lies in the group's traditions, values, and goals. As individuals within a group interact, boundaries are established. When a person tests these boundaries, the group may declare that such testing does not harm its identity, or it may feel its cherished way of life is being threatened. In the latter case, the individual's acts are labeled deviant, and trials, excommunication, ridicule, avoidance, and other boundary-maintaining devices, or sanctions, are employed.

Thus far we have emphasized that deviance represents a break with the social order. But as sociologist Emile Durkheim (1858–1917) recognized, deviance can actually have a positive effect on the social organization of a group. When an individual violates the standards of a community, group members come together to express their intolerance. As a result, their common bonds are affirmed and strengthened.[13]

But social bonds can disintegrate as well, and when this happens, social disorganization results. More formally, *social disorganization* refers to a situation where a group either lacks norms, sanctions, status, and role expectations or these are severely disrupted. The end result is that the group loses control over its members' behavior.

In *The Red Badge of Courage* Stephen Crane offers a good description of social disorganization. In one scene he depicts the total disintegration of an army regiment during a Civil War battle. Instead of showing allegiance to their company and submitting to established guidelines, the youthful, inexperienced Yankee soldiers could think only of personal survival and desertion:

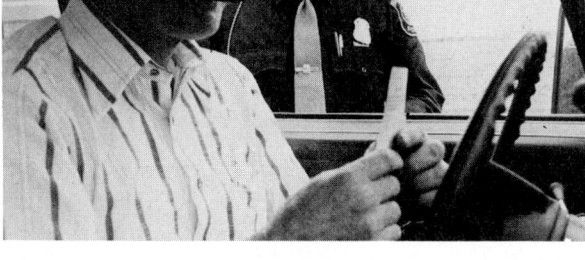

Face-To-Face Interaction

We all play many parts, or roles, in our lives, and in these roles we are subjected to a script—those rules and limits devised by others. Yet role expectations are never completely rigid; they vary in concreteness and consistency. We look to others for guidance in how to play our parts, just as others look to us. As we perform, we are therefore both role-takers and role-makers.

The performance we present contains both verbal and nonverbal communication. To establish, sustain, or alter our image or definition of a situation, we use gestures, body stance, and body positioning.

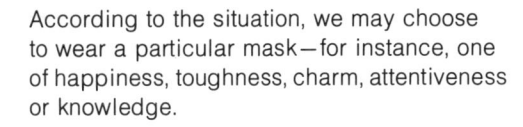

According to the situation, we may choose to wear a particular mask—for instance, one of happiness, toughness, charm, attentiveness or knowledge.

In our performances we also use costumes—uniforms, styles of dress—and props, such as brief cases, gavels, flags, placards, and drinks. Of course, we may choose not to perform in a given role or play a role in an unconventional way. Thus human action is not strictly determined by socio-cultural environment. Life calls forth our ability as interpreters and as actors.

COMPANY

THE SPREAD
OF RED
AMERICAN
PATRIOTS FOR
FREEDOM
10 AVE. "S" B'KLYN
SUPPORT OUR

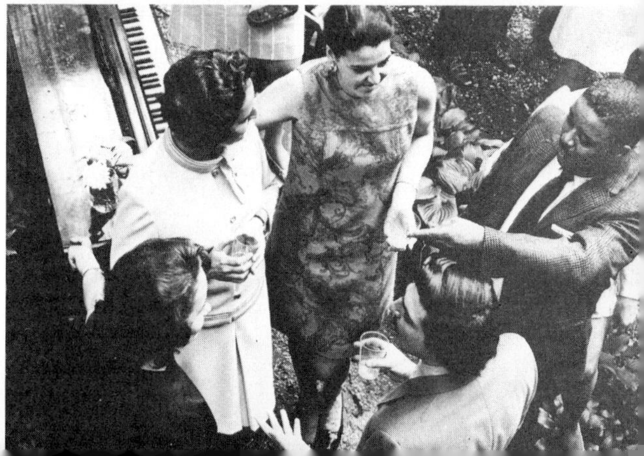

This photo of South Vietnamese civilians and military personnel fleeing from Hue in March 1975 suggests the social disorganization in much of South Vietnam during the closing days of the Vietnam War.

The lieutenant of the youth's company was shot in the hand. . . .

The battle flag in the distance jerked about madly. It seemed to be struggling to free itself from an agony. The billowing smoke was filled with horizontal flashes.

Men running swiftly emerged from it. They grew in numbers until it was seen that the whole command was fleeing. The flag suddenly sank down as if dying. Its motion as it fell was a gesture of despair.

Wild yells came from behind the walls of smoke. A sketch in gray and red dissolved into a moblike body of men who galloped like wild horses. . . .

The new regiment was breathless with horror. "Gawd! Saunder's got crushed!" whispered the man at the youth's elbow. They shrank back and crouched as if compelled to await a flood. . . .

. . . the commander of the brigade, was galloping about bawling. His hat was gone and his clothes were awry. He resembled a man who has come from bed to go to a fire. The hoofs of his horse often threatened the heads of the running men, but they scampered with singular fortune. In this rush they were apparently all deaf and blind. . . .

The battle reflection that shone for an instant in the faces on the mad current made the youth feel that forceful hands from heaven would not have been able to have held him in place if he could have got intelligent control of his legs.

There was an appalling imprint upon these faces. The struggle in the smoke had pictured an exaggeration of itself on the bleached cheeks and in the eyes wild with one desire.

The sight of this stampede exerted a floodlike force that seemed able to drag sticks and stones and men from the ground. They of the reserves had to hold on. They grew pale and firm, and red and quaking.

The youth achieved one little thought in the midst of this chaos. The composite monster which had caused the other troops to flee had not then appeared. He resolved to get a view of it, and then, he thought he might very likely run better than the best of them.[14]

In this case, social disorganization was the result of a disruption and battlefield conditions. Individuals themselves may begin the disorganization process by avoiding, opposing, or arbitrarily changing rules; by applying punishments inappropriately; or by refusing to coordinate their activities with others. A few deviating individuals, however, do not cause social disorganization. Only when a significant number of people continually oppose the organizational foundation of a group is social disorganization likely to result.

Chapter Summary

Groups establish boundaries of acceptability-unacceptability which make life orderly and predictable. Still, individuals can operate with some freedom within established guidelines, especially since the boundaries of a social system are themselves continually changing. Norms, sanctions, status, and role expectations are the major means of bringing about social organization.

Norms are rules which govern behavior in particular situations. They both require and prohibit certain actions. Sanctions are actions that are manufactured and applied to reinforce norms. They can be positive, such as a compliment, or negative, such as ridicule. The group hopes that sanctions will motivate people to act "right." The order that norms and sanctions are supposed to establish is not perfect: sometimes norms conflict, situations emerge where rules are absent or ambiguous, and norms may change over time.

Status refers to both the position and rank of an individual in a group. All of us occupy multiple statuses. Some of the positions we hold are communal, known and reacted to by everyone we meet, while others are associational, known only within smaller, more defined groups. Status may be ascribed on the basis of largely hereditary criteria or achieved through individual choice and effort.

The concept of role refers to both the expectations and the performance of an individual occupying a particular status. Role as "expectations" means that the person occupying a position has certain rights and duties.

Role as "performance" refers to how the individual in the position actually behaves. Role expectations are seldom precisely defined. As a result, we have some freedom in performing our roles. We can adapt our behavior to the status of the persons we confront (role set), or be totally uncommitted to our own status (role distance). We are also given considerable freedom to act in situations where we face the dilemma of two opposing sets of expectancies (role conflict).

Norms, sanctions, status, and role expectations are all socially defined; so is deviance. Groups generally label as deviant any action that threatens their survival or basic traditions. Deviance can have a positive effect on social organization if it serves to strengthen group bonds as group members react to it.

The term "social disorganization" has been used when referring to a situation where group norms, sanctions, status, and role expectations are absent or severely disrupted. The group loses control over its members.

Human beings are a unique species, and the individual can create and perform somewhat idiosyncratically. But the individual is also governed by guidelines established by others. It would seem that social organization is a mechanism of society for averting chaos.

Key Terms for Review

achieved statuses, p. 76
ascribed statuses, p. 76
associational norms, p. 73
associational statuses, p. 77
communal norms, p. 73
communal statuses, p. 77
deviance, p. 84
ideal norms, p. 73
prescriptive norms, p. 72

proscriptive norms, p. 72
real norms, p. 73
role, p. 78
role conflict, p. 80
role distance, p. 79
role set, p. 79
social disorganization, p. 85
social organization, p. 68
status, p. 74

Suggested Readings

SOCIOLOGICAL

Durkheim, Emile. *The Division of Labor in Society.* Trans. George Simpson. Glencoe, Ill.: Free Press, 1933. The work discusses the thesis that crime and all deviance perform positive functions for the society.

Erikson, Kai T. *Wayward Puritans: A Study in the Sociology of Deviance.* New York: John Wiley, 1966. Puritan culture in seventeenth-century New England is examined from the viewpoint of deviance theory. The author illustrates Durkheim's view that every society has a certain amount of deviance and that such deviance helps to maintain the boundaries established by the group.

Goffman, Erving. *The Presentation of Self in Everyday Life.* Garden City, N.Y.: Doubleday, 1959. The author discusses how we perform our roles in everyday life. We vary our performance according to the situation and audience. Further, we defend the "self" as we perform.

Greer, Scott A. *Social Organization.* New York: Random House, 1968. Factors and principles associated with social organization are examined. The author contends that groups assign functions to different people (allocation) and interrelate these functions so that goals can be achieved (integration). Social organization is a continuous process of establishing such cooperation to meet the needs of the group.

Nisbet, Robert. *The Social Bond.* New York: Alfred A. Knopf, 1970. The term "social bond" refers to those cohesive forces which hold society together. Nisbet discusses those aspects of society which explain the social bond: norms, status, roles, groupings, authority, and others.

LITERARY

Malamud, Bernard. *A New Life.* New York: Pocket Books, 1973. The novel illustrates the role conflict experienced by Professor Levin. As a new teacher in Marathon, Cascadia, Levin is confronted with a life style and set of expectations very different from the ones he experienced in New York. The "frontier spirit" and rural climate of his new home are almost too much for him to endure.

Mehdevi, Anne Sinclair. "A Persian Courtship." In Sylvia Z. Brodkin and Elizabeth J. Pearson, eds. *Modern American Essays.* New York: Globe, 1967. This story shows how two opposing sets of expectations can cause role conflict for an individual. A young Persian maiden is torn between two cultures as she faces the issue of marriage.

Roth, Philip. "Defender of the Faith." In *Goodbye Columbus and Five Short Stories.* New York: Modern Library, 1959. The chief character, Marx, is both an army sergeant and Jewish. Others' expectations of Marx come into conflict because of the two roles he occupies.

Updike, John. "A and P." In Richard L. Cherry, Robert J. Conley, and Bernard A. Hirsch, eds. *A Return to Vision.* Boston: Houghton Mifflin, 1971. In this short story two females enter a supermarket in bathing suits, which is unacceptable behavior to the manager. The concepts of role expectations and sanctions are illustrated.

IN THIS CHAPTER

Aggregates, Categories, and Groups   96

Types of Groups   98

    Voluntary and involuntary groups   98
    Open and closed groups   99
    Large and small groups   100
    Vertical and horizontal groups   100
    Majority and minority groups   101
    In-groups and out-groups   102
    Reference groups   106

Primary and Secondary Groups   107

Degree of Organization   112

Summary   113

Key Terms for Review   114

Suggested Readings   114

Can any individual truly live in isolation?
Which better achieves its goals, a small or large group?
Why are we so defensive of our in-groups?
Are human relationships becoming increasingly impersonal and superficial?

GROUPS

No one normally lives in isolation. Even the hermit who lives in a cave, physically apart from the world, still thinks and acts in terms of others. The recluse may feel a certain "glow" when he thinks of the good times he once had with his family. And although he might find it convenient to throw garbage on his cave floor, he would probably not do so because of the manners he has learned from others. Writer George Orwell once witnessed a hanging in Burma. That event made him realize how each individual is tied to others, or is a part of society:

> *It was about forty yards to the gallows. I watched the bare brown back of the prisoner in front of me. He walked clumsily with his bound arms, but quite steadily, with that bobbing gait of the Indian who never straightens his knees. At each step his muscles slid neatly into place, the lock of hair on his scalp danced up and down, his feet printed themselves on the wet gravel. And once, in spite of the men who gripped him by each shoulder, he stepped lightly aside to avoid a puddle on the path.*
>
> *It is curious, but till that moment I had never realized what it means to destroy a healthy, conscious man. When I saw the prisoner step aside to avoid the puddle I saw the mystery. . . . His eyes saw the yellow gravel and the grey walls, and his brain still remembered, foresaw, reasoned—even about puddles. He and we were a party of men walking together, seeing, hearing, feeling, understanding the same world; and in two minutes, with a sudden snap, one of us would be gone—one mind less, one world less.*[1]

We are all members of groups, and these groups perform a multitude of functions for us. They provide us with companionship, experiences, recognition, and security in both a physical and emotional sense. It is certainly understandable why individuals fear ostracism from groups they consider important. Rejection is a punishment few can endure.

Sociology considers the human group its major unit of analysis, and one objective of sociological investigation is to understand the many different types which exist. Groups are studied in terms of their complexity, size, division of labor, communication networks, change, and power over individuals. We will examine several classifications of groups, but first we must see how the term "group" has been variously defined.

Aggregates, Categories, and Groups

Sociologists use the term "group" to describe many kinds of human association. It is occasionally used to mean "a number of individuals gathered together in one place." People in a depot waiting for a train to arrive, pedestrians standing on a street corner waiting for the light to change, or passengers on a jumbo jet bound for London might constitute groups in this first sense of the term. But some scholars maintain that these are not really groups. Instead, each should be called an *aggregate*, a collection of people.

Sometimes group is used to mean "people who share a particular attribute." This definition would cover all welfare recipients, all blue-eyed people, all cancer victims, all residents of New England, all murderers, and all alcoholics, to name just a few. Again, many assert that these are not groups, and that each would more accurately be described as a *category*.

Finally, *group* is used to mean a number of individuals bound together in two ways. First, they interact with one another in some organized fashion. For instance, friends joke and discuss topics with each other on the basis of shared norms, role expectations, and sanctions. Second, group members share a *consciousness of kind*, or a feeling of being bound together by common traits, views, or situations. For example, family members may see themselves as bound together by their blood line and family traditions.

Most sociologists would agree that this last definition of group is the most precise and meaningful. They would also maintain that aggregates can develop into groups. To illustrate, in the fall of 1965 New York City experienced an electrical "blackout." People who had never met and who previously had nothing in common were caught in elevators, office buildings, or subways for hours. Strangers began talking with one another, discussing their lives, and sharing their cigarettes and food as they faced the crisis of darkness and the absence of electric power. A category can also evolve into a group. Americans of Polish ancestry constituted a category on their arrival in the United States during the great period of immigration from eastern Europe. Soon after their arrival, however, many of the new immigrants came together in numerous cultural organizations to discuss

These subway riders form what sociologists refer to as an aggregate—a number of individuals gathered together in one place who have little or no consciousness of kind.

their common problems in their new surroundings. Out of aggregates and categories, groups may emerge wherein people interact and have a consciousness of kind.

Although sociologists generally agree on this definition of the term "group," they also recognize that the word is a common one in the English language, given many diverse meanings. People use the label freely, making little distinction between aggregate, category, and group. And although it is important for sociologists to know the distinctions among the three terms, throughout this book we will follow the more standard usage of group, letting it refer to a wide range of human associations. We will also use it when aggregate or category might be more technically correct, but confusing to the reader.

An aggregate of individuals can develop into a sociologically defined group. Such was the case for these New Yorkers during the massive power failure in 1965.

Types of Groups

VOLUNTARY AND INVOLUNTARY GROUPS

Voluntary groups are those we join through our own choice and effort. Members of American society might conceivably join a political party, church, or occupation. In contrast, *involuntary groups* are those we are forced to join or those that we are automatically members of without choice. Union membership, for example, is sometimes required for maintaining a job, and everyone is automatically a member of sex, age, and racial groups.

It appears rather simple to distinguish a voluntary from an involuntary group. Clearly, becoming a plumber is a matter of choice, at least in the United States, but being middle-aged is not. Sometimes, however, distinguishing these two types of groups is more complicated. When an individual enrolls in a university, is he or she joining a voluntary or involuntary group? Objectively, it would seem that the group is voluntary. But the way in which a particular student perceives his or her group involvement has to be considered too. Indeed, some college students see their situation as one of personal choice and effort. Such was the view of Knute Axelbrod, a character created by Sinclair Lewis. Knute had migrated from Scandinavia to America when he was a child. Like many of us, however, he was soon caught up in a life which differed from his dream.

> As a lad Knute Axelbrod had wished to be a famous scholar, to learn the ease of foreign tongues, the romance of history, to unfold in the graciousness of wise books. When he first came to America he worked in a sawmill all day and studied all evening. He mastered enough book-learning to teach district school for two terms; then, when he was only eighteen, a great-hearted pity for faded little Lena Wesselius moved him to marry her. Gay enough, doubtless, was their hike by prairie schooner to new farmlands, but Knute was promptly caught in a net of poverty and family.[2]

By the time he was sixty-four, Knute's wife had died and his children had left home. He decided to pursue his lifelong dream and attend Yale University. Knute thought that all those who attended universities were eager to acquire knowledge.

> He believed that all college students, except for the wealthy idlers, burned to acquire learning. He pictured Harvard and Yale and Princeton as ancient groves set with marble temples, before which

Personal choice and effort determine membership in voluntary groups, whether the Masons or the Avon Bottle Club.

large groups of Grecian youths talked gently about astronomy and good government. In his picture they never cut classes or ate.[3]

He soon realized, however, that not all students saw their presence at the university as voluntary. Knute's roommate felt coerced to attend so he could obtain a college degree, or "union card," for a good job.

> The roommate was a large-browed soft white grub named Ray Dribble, who had been teaching school in New England and seemed chiefly to desire college training so that he might make more money. . . . Ray Dribble was a hustler.[4]

Knute met many students who felt that society and their parents had forced them to attend college. They saw no alternative in their lives, and as a result they drank a lot of beer and stole street signs rather than study. Some even expressed hatred for books. Clearly, what is defined as a voluntary group by some is an involuntary group to others.

OPEN AND CLOSED GROUPS

An *open group* is one in which virtually anyone can become a member. For example, all but a few can join Weight Watchers. Of course, this group does require something for membership—excess weight and the payment of dues. A *closed group*, however, is much more difficult to join. A clique, for instance, is a select and exclusive group of friends. Outsiders might try for years to become members of a clique before being fully accepted. Some groups, such as elite country clubs and the Mafia, are so exclusive that only a select few can become members. The distinction between open and closed groups is important because it indicates that individuals do not float from one group to another solely according to whim. Groups establish diverse and sometimes stringent criteria for membership.

LARGE AND SMALL GROUPS

The size of a group can affect human relationships. For one thing, group size partially determines whether members achieve their goals. In some cases, small groups are better able to accomplish a stated purpose. Thus, many teachers feel they are better able to reach their goals in a small class since students can receive individualized instruction. And the system of congressional committees—foreign affairs, appropriations, agriculture—is probably preferable to having the entire Congress deliberate every detail of proposed legislation in every field. On the other hand, accomplishing some goals necessitates large groups. An invading army would probably have a better chance for victory with millions of soldiers than with hundreds. And large corporations tend to have more working capital and political influence than small ones.

Group size also tends to influence the kind of human relationships which develop. In small groups people know one another on a personal basis, whereas in large groups they tend to interact on the basis of status. In a small business Joe might be known as a likeable, God-fearing, politically conservative foreman who hates chocolate cookies and loves his wife almost as much as his hobby of fishing. In a large business he might only be known as Mr. Joseph Brown, employee number 756-321-456, foreman in charge of machinery repair.

In contrast to members of small groups, members of large groups tend to have highly differentiated and specialized jobs. In other words, there is a greater division of labor. For example, in a small business consisting of three partners, all may share the tasks of purchasing, production, and sales. If the business were to grow larger and become a corporation, however, each partner might then take responsibility for only a single task.

VERTICAL AND HORIZONTAL GROUPS

A *vertical group* consists of members from all walks of life, while a *horizontal group* consists predominantly of members from one social class. (See chapter 7 for a full discussion of social class.) Horizontal groups occur more frequently than vertical groups in American society. Occupational groups—of physicians, electricians, or garbage collectors, for instance—are composed largely of members from the same social class. So are club, family, and friendship groups. But, though rarer, vertical groups do exist. The ethnic group of Italian-Americans might be considered a vertical group since it consists of upper-, middle-, and lower-class members. Of course, not all ethnic groups span such a wide range of social differences; American Indians, for instance, are overrepresented by working- and lower-class individuals. Churches approach being vertical groups,

Blacks in South Africa constitute a subjugated mass, lacking power to solve even basic problems of housing and sanitation. In this black slum, for example, fresh water is available only from community taps and sanitation facilities are nonexistent.

but even they tend to be composed of members from the same social class. The Episcopalian and Unitarian churches often draw their members from the upper class, while the Baptist and Four Square Gospel religious organizations generally appeal to the working and lower classes. (See chapter 9 for a further discussion of the relation of social class to religion.)

MAJORITY AND MINORITY GROUPS

Most people think of size when they hear the terms "majority group" and "minority group." They assume a majority group has a large number of people and a minority group has only a few people. There are, however, additional considerations about such groups, one being their economic, political, and social power.

Sociologists distinguish four groups when they consider both size and power. First, a *dominant majority* refers to a group of large size that possesses a high degree of power. White Anglo-Saxon Protestants (WASPS) are one such group in American society. Second, a *subjugated mass* refers to a large group that has little power. The blacks of South Africa, who outnumber whites four-to-one yet have little political or economic power, provide a striking example. Third, an *elite group* is small in size, yet it is powerful. The whites of South Africa are the elite group counterpart to the subjugated mass of blacks. And fourth, a *minority* refers to a small group with little power. Chicanos in American society are an example.

These students at the University of South Dakota, who are also all Sioux Indians, have much in common to keep them thinking in terms of "we."

IN-GROUPS AND OUT-GROUPS

An *in-group* is a group with which an individual identifies, one to which he or she belongs and gives allegiance. A person refers to fellow in-group members as "we." "We" are good, important, brave, and intelligent Marines, feminists, Sigma Chis, males, Green Bay Packers, students of Ohio State University, Rotarians, Black Panthers, or whatever. In contrast, an *out-group* is a group to which the individual does not belong and with which he or she does not identify. Out-group members are "they," and "they" are different from us. Obviously, one person's in-group may be another person's out-group and vice versa. James Thurber, in "The Lover and His Lass," illustrates how in-group members tend to view out-group members. His story begins with two parrots watching the love-making of two hippopotamuses.

> *An arrogant gray parrot and his arrogant mate listened, one African afternoon, in disdain and derision, to the love-making of a lover and his lass, who happened to be hippopotamuses.*
>
> *"He calls her snooky-ookums," said Mrs. Gray. "Can you believe that?"*
>
> *"No," said Gray. "I don't see how any male in his right mind could entertain affection for a female that has no more charm than a capsized bathtub."*
>
> *"Capsized bathtub, indeed!" exclaimed Mrs. Gray. "Both of them have the appeal of a coastwise fruit steamer with a cargo of waterlogged basketballs."*
>
> *But it was spring, and the lover and his lass were young and they were oblivious of the scornful comments of their sharp-tongued neighbors, and they continued to bump each other around in the water, happily pushing and pulling, backing and filling, and snort-*

ing and snaffling. . . . To the Grays, however, the bumbling romp of the lover and his lass was hard to comprehend and even harder to tolerate, and for a time they thought of calling A. B. I., or African Bureau of Investigation, on the ground that monolithic love-making by enormous creatures who should have become decent fossils long ago was probably a threat to the security of the jungle. But they decided instead to phone their friends and neighbors and gossip about the shameless pair, and describe them in mocking and monstrous metaphors involving skidding buses on icy streets and overturned moving vans.[5]

Not surprisingly, however, the two hippopotamuses felt much the same way about the love-making of the two parrots.

"Listen to those squawks," wuffled the male hippopotamus.
"What in the world can they see in each other?" gurbled the female hippopotamus.
"I would as soon live with a pair of unoiled garden shears," said her inamoratus.
They called up their friends and neighbors and discussed the incredible fact that a male gray parrot and a female gray parrot could possibly have any sex appeal. It was long after midnight before the hippopotamuses stopped criticizing the Grays and fell asleep.[6]

Throughout our lives we shift our feelings toward both out-groups and in-groups. We may consider a neighboring family haughty and unsocial, then later find that barriers to a friendly relationship can be overcome. Likewise, teenagers may feel a great loyalty to their high school but lose some of this in-group attachment as adults. The individual's shifting allegiance from one group to another is shown in Frank O'Connor's story "My Oedipus Complex." Larry, a young boy, had formed a close bond with his mother while his father was a soldier at war. But when his father returned at the end of the war, Larry suddenly realized that "Daddy" was now the center of his mother's attention.

"Just a moment, Larry!" she said gently.
This was only what she said when we had boring visitors, so I attached no importance to it and went on talking.
"Do be quiet, Larry!" she said impatiently. "Don't you hear me talking to Daddy?"
This was the first time I had heard those ominous words, "talking to Daddy," and I couldn't help feeling that if this was how God answered prayers, he couldn't listen to them very attentively.
"Why are you talking to Daddy?" I asked with as great a show of indifference as I could muster.

While some women identify with the women's liberation movement and see it as their in-group, others find the movement alien and think of it as an out-group.

"Because Daddy and I have business to discuss. Now, don't interrupt again!"...

"You must be quiet while Daddy is reading, Larry," Mother said impatiently.

It was clear that she either genuinely liked talking to Father better than talking to me, or else that he had some terrible hold on her which made her afraid to admit the truth.

"Mummy," I said that night when she was tucking me up, "do you think if I prayed hard God would send Daddy back to the war?"

She seemed to think about that for a moment.

"No, dear," she said with a smile. "I don't think he would."

"Why wouldn't he, Mummy?"

"Because there isn't a war any longer, dear."

"But, Mummy, couldn't God make another war, if he liked?"

"He wouldn't like to, dear. It's not God who makes wars, but bad people."

"Oh!" I said.

I was disappointed about that. I began to think that God wasn't quite what he was cracked up to be.[7]

Larry hated his father, and to make matters worse, his mother quickly brought a baby into the world—Sonny. Now the in-group consisted of three people with Larry still the outsider.

> Sonny arrived in the most appalling hullabaloo—even that much he couldn't do without a fuss—and from the first moment I disliked him. He was a difficult child—so far as I was concerned he was always difficult—and demanded far too much attention. Mother was simply silly about him, and couldn't see when he was only showing off. As company he was worse than useless. He slept all day, and I had to go round the house on tiptoe to avoid waking him. It wasn't any longer a question of not waking Father. The slogan now was "Don't-wake-Sonny!" I couldn't understand why the child wouldn't sleep at the proper time, so whenever Mother's back was turned I woke him. Sometimes to keep him awake I pinched him as well. Mother caught me at it one day and gave me a most unmerciful flaking.[8]

It was not long, however, before Father also experienced the trauma of being rejected.

> One night I woke with a start. There was someone beside me in the bed. For one wild moment I felt sure it must be Mother, having come to her senses and left Father for good, but then I heard Sonny in convulsions in the next room, and Mother saying: "There! There! There!" and I knew it wasn't she. It was Father. He was lying beside me, wide awake, breathing hard and apparently mad as hell.
> After a while it came to me what he was mad about. It was his turn now. After turning me out of the big bed, he had been turned out himself. Mother had no consideration for anyone but that poisonous pup, Sonny. I couldn't help feeling sorry for Father. I had been through it all myself, and even at that age I was magnanimous. I began to stroke him down and say: "There! There!" He wasn't exactly responsive.
> "Aren't you asleep either?" he snarled.
> "Ah, come on and put your arm around us, can't you?" I said, and he did, in a sort of way. Gingerly, I suppose, is how you'd describe it. He was very bony but better than nothing.
> At Christmas he went out of his way to buy me a really nice model railway.[9]

Now it was Mother and Sonny versus Larry and Father, one in-group pitted against the other.

Based on only partial information, in-group members tend to *stereotype*, or categorize, "those others" as being all alike. A common American stereotype of Frenchmen is that they are all carefree, irresponsible wine guzzlers. Frenchmen, on the other hand, often stereotype all Americans as materialistic, exploitive capitalists. In-group bonds combined with stereotypical images have sometimes stirred people to incredible acts of terrorism and violence. The continued conflict between Catholics and Protestants in Northern Ireland is just one example.*

REFERENCE GROUPS

A concept related to the notion of in-group is *reference group*. Sociologists use this term when referring to that group which serves as a point of reference in making comparisons or judgments. A reference group provides us with our basic beliefs and norms, and it is a model for evaluation of self as well as others. The functions that reference groups serve are vividly illustrated in F. Scott Fitzgerald's short story "The Ice Palace." The story begins with the main character, Sally Carrol Happer, leaving her homeland of the South to marry a Yankee. On the final day before heading North, Sally and her fiancé, Harry, walk past a cemetery. Sally expresses a deep affection for those who died for the Confederacy, and, although she is not quite aware of her loyalty and attachment, the reader can easily see that the South will be a difficult reference group for her to leave behind.

> *"These were just men, unimportant evidently or they wouldn't have been 'unknown'; but they died for the most beautiful thing in the world—the dead South. You see,"* she continued, her voice still husky, her eyes glistening with tears, *"people have these dreams they fasten onto things, and I've always grown up with that dream. It was so easy because it was all dead and there weren't any disillusions comin' to me. I've tried in a way to live up to those past standards of noblesse oblige—there's just the last remnants of it, you know, like the roses of an old garden dying all round us—streaks of strange courtliness and chivalry in some of these boys an' stories I used to hear from a Confederate soldier who lived next door, and a few old darkies. Oh, Harry, there was something, there was something! I couldn't ever make you understand, but it was there."*[10]

The South provided Sally with a history, traditions, and goals—a culture—through which she evaluates the conduct of others and herself. For example, upon arrival in the North she perceives nothing but superficial and callous relationships and rushing about, in contrast to the friendliness, warmth, and slow-moving life that she knew in the South. Finally, during a vaudeville performance, Sally realizes that the South is her real reference group—she judges all by Southern standards—and that she must return to her former life.

*A social psychological discussion of stereotyping can be found in David Krech, Richard S. Crutchfield, and Egerton L. Ballachey, *Individual in Society: A Textbook of Social Psychology* (New York: McGraw-Hill, 1962), chap. 2.

That very night at the end of a vaudeville performance the orchestra played "Dixie" and Sally Carrol felt something stronger and more enduring than her tears and smiles of the day brim up inside her. She leaned forward gripping the arms of her chair until her face grew crimson.

"Sort of get you, dear?" whispered Harry.

But she did not hear him. To the spirited throb of the violins and the inspiring beat of the kettle-drums her own old ghosts were marching by and on into the darkness, and as fifes whistled and sighed in the low encore they seemed so nearly out of sight that she could have waved good-by.

> *"Away, away,*
> *Away down South in Dixie!*
> *Away, away,*
> *Away down South in Dixie!" . . .*

"Oh, send somebody—send somebody!" she cried aloud.

Clark Darrow—he would understand; or Joe Ewing; she couldn't be left here to wander forever—to be frozen, heart, body, and soul. This her—this Sally Carrol! Why, she was a happy thing. She was a happy little girl. She liked warmth and summer and Dixie. These things were foreign—foreign. . . .

"Oh, I want to get out of here! I'm going back home. Take me home"—her voice rose to a scream that sent a chill to Harry's heart as he came racing down the next passage—"to-morrow!" she cried with delirious, unrestrained passion—"To-morrow! To-morrow! To-morrow!"[11]

Reference groups may be small or large, intimate or impersonal. And individuals do not have to belong to the group they consider their reference group; they may simply model their behavior after that of members, hoping one day to belong. For example, a teenage girl may aspire to be a "rock" star and so constantly imitate Janis Joplin, Carole King, or Aretha Franklin.*

Primary and Secondary Groups

Sociologist Charles Horton Cooley originally defined a *primary group* as one where members develop close, personal, intimate, and enduring relationships.[12] Family, neighbors, and work associates are examples of such

---

*The concept of reference group is discussed extensively in H. H. Kelly. "Two Functions of Reference Groups," in *Readings in Social Psychology*, ed. G. E. Swanson, T. M. Newcomb, and E. L. Hartley (New York: Henry Holt, 1952); and Robert K. Merton, *Social Theory and Social Structure* (New York: Free Press, 1968), chaps. X and XI.

Colleagues can form a primary group if they interact extensively, share personal as well as work problems, and develop a close relationship.

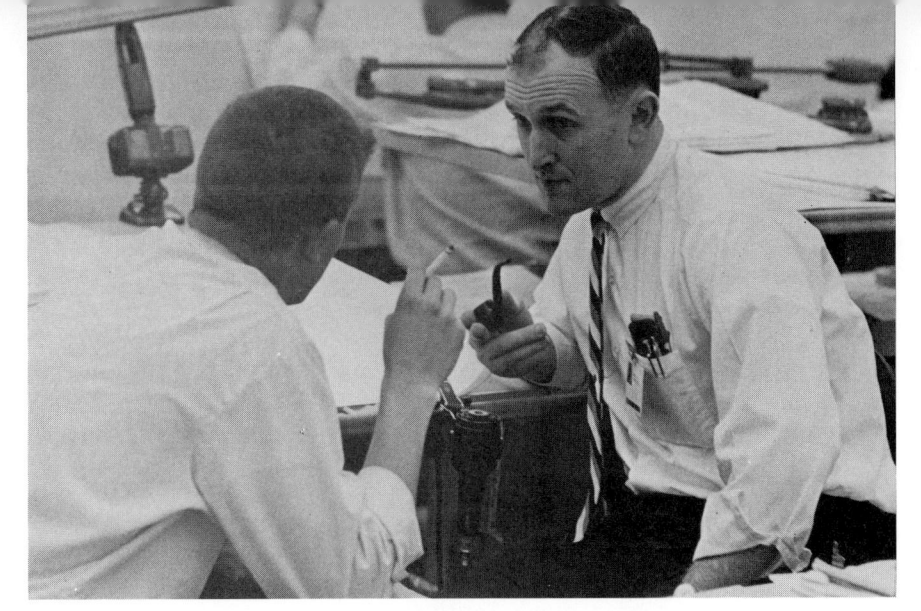

groups. Members know one another well, greatly influence each other, and feel closely related. Alfred Kazin has written about the kitchen of his boyhood home. It is symbolic of his deep affection for his mother and friends, people who once composed a primary group.

The kitchen held our lives together. My mother worked in it all day long, we ate in it almost all meals except the Passover seder, I did my homework and first writing at the kitchen table, and in winter I often had a bed made up for me on three kitchen chairs near the stove. . . .

The kitchen gave a special character to our lives—my mother's character. All my memories of that kitchen are dominated by the nearness of my mother sitting all day long at her sewing machine, by the clacking of the treadle against the linoleum floor, by the patient twist of her right shoulder as she automatically pushed at the wheel with one hand or lifted the foot to free the needle where it had got stuck in a thick piece of material. The kitchen was her life. Year by year as I began to take in her fantastic capacity for labor and her anxious zeal, I realized it was ourselves she kept stitched together. . . .

The kitchen was the great machine that set our lives running; it whirred down a little only on Saturdays and holy days. From my mother's kitchen I gained my first picture of life as a white, overheated, starkly lit workshop redolent with Jewish cooking, crowded with women in housedresses, strewn with fashion magazines, patterns, dress materials, spools of thread—and at whose center, so lashed to her machine that bolts of energy seemed to dance out of her hands and feet as she worked, my mother stamped the treadle hard against the floor, hard, hard, and silently grimly at war, beat out the first rhythm of the world for me. . . .

> *All day long people streamed into our apartment as a matter of course—"customers," upstairs neighbors, downstairs neighbors, women who would stop in for a half-hour's talk, salesmen, relatives, insurance agents. Usually they came in without ringing the bell—everyone knew my mother was always at home. I would hear the front door opening, the wind whistling through our front hall, and then some familiar face would appear in our kitchen with the same bland, matter-of-fact inquiring look: no need to stand on ceremony; my mother and her kitchen were available to everyone all day long.*[13]

Although Kazin's family and friends were cooperative and loving people, not all primary groups are so harmonious. Some primary-group members may act indifferently toward or actually hate each other. Edward Field has written a poem which describes the lack of affection from a cold and callous father. Field looks back on the primary group as a disappointment and sends his father a "bill" for the love which is still owed:

> I am typing up bills for a firm to be sent to their clients.
> It occurs to me that firms are sending bills to my father.
> Who has that way an identity I do not often realize.
> His is a person who buys, owes, and pays,
> Not papa like he is to me.
> His creditors reproach him for not paying on time
> With a bill marked "Please Remit."
> I reproach him for never having shown his love for me
> But only his disapproval.
> He has a debt to me too
> Although I have long since ceased asking him to come across;
> He does not know how and so I do without it.
> But in this impersonal world of business
> He can be communicated with:
> With absolute assurance of being paid
> The boss writes "Send me my money"
> And my father sends it.[14]

We are all members of many primary groups. We engage in personal, confiding relations with our family and with some of our fellow workers, neighbors, and club members. Of course, these close relations can dissolve. Many of us had childhood friends with whom we shared deep, treasured secrets, though today we may not even know where they live.

In addition to the primary groups to which we belong, we are members of a great many *secondary groups*. In these groups individuals act toward one another in rather impersonal, superficial, and utilitarian ways. When we interact with a waiter, mailcarrier, salesperson, or boss at work, we usually do not discuss our bedroom behavior or our spouse's drinking

The woman customer and flower vender shown here probably constituted a secondary group, relating to each other impersonally and for utilitarian ends.

problem. The waiter and the diner, the mailcarrier and the resident, the salesperson and the customer, and the boss and employed worker treat each other merely as categories of people to be dealt with. Personal problems and feelings are unknown or irrelevant to the situation, and actions are directed toward reaching utilitarian objectives, such as ordering a meal, collecting postage due, selling a car, or filling out a business form. In contrast, members of a primary group expect to feel valued and receive satisfaction from one another. Secondary groups, however, can evolve into primary groups. If each week an individual visits the same small restaurant, she may come to know one waiter quite well and eventually the two may form a close relationship.

Historically, societies have been moving toward a greater number of secondary relationships. The German sociologist Ferdinand Tönnies (1855–1936) discussed two kinds of societies. The first, called *Gemeinschaft,* is one where members form a close cohesive unit. Individuals are tied to the community in the sense that they form close associations and share common values and traditions—they have "roots." The second, *Gesellschaft,* is an impersonal society where members are concerned with private rather than community interests. Individuals are quite diverse in values and skills, and they have few common traditions. Tönnies pessimistically predicted that the *Gesellschaft* society would become more pervasive.[15]

Although modern societies are not quite as impersonal as Tönnies predicted, they indeed have alienating features. Anthropologist Oscar

Lewis once reported the conversation of a Puerto Rican describing New York City. The individual's comments illustrate how depersonalized human interaction can become in a *Gesellschaft* society.

> We had been talking of this and that when I asked him, "Have you ever been in New York, Hector?"
>
> "Yes, yes, I've been to New York."
>
> "And what did you think of life there?"
>
> "New York! I want no part of it! Man, do you know what it's like? You get up in a rush, have breakfast in a rush, get to work in a rush, go home in a rush. That's life in New York! Not for me! Never again! Not unless I was crazy.
>
> "Look, I'll explain. The way things are in New York, you'll get nothing there. But nothing! It's different in Puerto Rico. Here, if you're hungry, you come to me and say, 'Man, I'm broke, I've had nothing to eat.' And I'd say, 'Ay Bendito! Poor thing!' And I'd give you some food. No matter what, you wouldn't have to go to bed hungry. Here in Puerto Rico you can make out. But in New York, if you don't have a nickel, or twenty cents, you're worthless, and that's for sure. You don't count. You get swallowed by a horse! . . .
>
> "Let me tell you, boy, New York's a madhouse. You can live twenty years in the same building without ever getting acquainted with your next-door neighbor. Twenty years! My friends here say, 'Oh,

George Tooker's painting *The Subway* (1950) visually represents much of Tönnies's idea of *Gesellschaft* society, in which people would become increasingly rootless, isolated, impersonal, and callous.

New York! It's so pretty, so wonderful, the best!' But if you stop to look at the city, what is it? Nothing but big, big buildings. Just walls and windows.

"Then I explain to my friends about New York in winter. Closed doors, closed windows, no people. If you do see people, you just see them walking. Walking, walking, all the time. You can't stop to talk to them because you are rushing off to work. . . .

"It's easy to get lost there. I've cried like a baby in those New York streets where you can get lost worse than in a jungle. There'll be a lot of people around you, but what do they do when you ask for help? They'll realize you're a rookie and they'll say, 'go that way,' and it'll be the wrong way so you'll get more lost.

"Here in San Juan you can go up to anybody and say, 'Pardon me, where is Cristo Street?' or Tanca Street or any street you want to find and whoever you ask stops and listens. If you happen to ask someone in the car that's going your way he'll say, 'Hop in, I'll take you there.' But not in New York! . . .

"In New York a dog is worth more than a man. Yes, sir, only three things are valued there, dogs, women, and children! As long as you're a minor, you can kill, belong to a gang or steal. No matter what you do, you won't fry, see? Of course, if you're a woman you can get away with anything as long as you live. But if you're a man and over twenty-one and you so much as pick up a stone and aim it at a dog, it means six months in jail. If you hit the dog, it's worse. You can't even defend yourself. Women and dogs can attack you any time and you lose the case, no matter what, Know why? It's the law. That's the way it's written, man. And if you never heard of that law, you're sunk."[16]

One should interpret this conversation with caution. It would be incorrect to conclude, for instance, that a *Gesellschaft* society has no primary relationships. Even though such societies are large, complex, and urban, members form primary groups. Individuals seek out the intimacy and confiding relations that only a primary group can provide. It would also be incorrect to assume that a *Gemeinschaft* society necessarily means peace and solidarity. Historically, small traditional societies, such as Vietnam and Scotland, have experienced much disorganization and violence.

Degree of Organization

Groups in a society are organized to varying degrees. Friends and family members, for example, may have only a few loosely defined and unwritten behavioral guidelines, while other groups have a preponderance of rigid and written rules, expectations, and sanctions to control their members' actions. The best example of a group that has numerous rules and regulations, many of which are formalized and written, is an *organization*. An organization is also known by such terms as formal organization, complex organization, and association. Schools, armies, hospitals, businesses, and government agencies are all organizations, and each is established to achieve a specific goal or goals. For example, most universities are designed to further the goals of effective teaching, community service, and scholarly research. Because organizations have an overwhelming influence on the lives of people in a complex, industrial society, we will discuss their role more extensively in the next chapter.

Chapter Summary

Sociology considers the human group its major unit of analysis. The term "group" commonly refers to a wide range of human associations, although many sociologists contend that to constitute a group individuals must interact with one another in some organized fashion and share a consciousness of kind. By this definition neither aggregates nor categories may be considered groups, though both can evolve into groups. A major task of sociology is to understand the many different types of groups which exist.

A voluntary group is one we join through our own choice and effort, whereas an involuntary group is one we are forced to join or belong to through no choice of our own. Groups have established diverse criteria for membership. Some groups open their doors to almost anyone, but others exclude many types of people. Groups also vary in size. Group size can affect whether or not members reach their goals, the degree of intimacy they achieve, and how they divide their work tasks.

A vertical group contains members from all social classes in society, whereas a horizontal group usually takes in members from only one social class. Horizontal groups are more common than vertical groups in American society. Majority groups and minority groups are generally distinguished by size alone, but they vary as well in how much power they possess. Some majority groups have virtually no power, while some minority groups have a great deal of power.

Each person has in-groups and out-groups. Individuals feel they belong to an in-group and give it their allegiance; out-group members are seen as alien and "all alike." Reference groups provide people with basic beliefs and serve as models for evaluation of self and others. Reference groups can be small or large, intimate or impersonal, and individuals do not have to belong to the group.

In a primary group, members develop close, personal, and intimate relationships. Each of us is at one time a member of many primary groups.

In a secondary group, people interact on an impersonal, superficial, and utilitarian basis. The historical trend has been for societies to move toward more secondary relationships, or, in Tönnies's words, from a *Gemeinschaft* to a *Gesellschaft* type of social organization. However, even in *Gesellschaft* societies, primary relations are still important.

Finally, groups vary in their degree of organization. Some have only a few loosely defined norms, sanctions, statuses, and roles, while others have numerous guidelines, many of which are formalized and written down.

Seventeenth-century poet-essayist John Donne wrote, "No man is an island, entire of itself; every man is a piece of the continent, a part of the main."[17] For the sociologist the meaning of this quote is clear: only if we understand our groups can we understand our history, ourselves, and our social problems, and foresee the future of society.

Key Terms for Review

aggregate, p. 96
category, p. 96
closed group, p. 99
consciousness of kind, p. 96
dominant majority, p. 101
elite group, p. 101
Gemeinschaft, p. 110
Gesellschaft, p. 110
group, p. 96
horizontal group, p. 100
in-group, p. 102
involuntary group, p. 98

minority, p. 101
open group, p. 99
organization, p. 113
out-group, p. 102
primary group, p. 107
reference group, p. 106
secondary group, p. 109
stereotype, p. 105
subjugated mass, p. 101
vertical group, p. 100
voluntary group, p. 98

Suggested Readings

SOCIOLOGICAL   Cooley, Charles Horton. *Social Organization: A Study of the Larger Mind*. New York: Schocken, 1962; orig. 1909. This book was the first to define primary group. The importance of personal, intimate, face-to-face relationships is emphasized.

Homans, George. *The Human Group*. New York: Harcourt Brace Jovanovich, 1950. The author examines both small and large groups. His discussion emphasizes the necessity of small groups and the complexity of primary relationships.

Olmsted, Michael S. *The Small Group.* New York: Random House, 1959. This concise book discusses a wide variety of topics, including primary and secondary groups, classic research involving small groups, and functions of small groups for individuals.

LITERARY

Lewis, Sinclair. *Main Street.* New York: Harcourt Brace Jovanovich, 1920. The author illustrates that even in a small town, a supposedly *Gemeinschaft* society, individuals can live impersonal, distressing lives. Primary relationships and in-group and out-group relations are vividly portrayed.

Miller, Arthur. *Death of a Salesman.* New York: Viking Press, 1967. Almost everyone has heard of the character Willy Loman and his struggle to survive in a *Gesellschaft* society. Unfortunately, even his relationships with wife and children are a disappointment.

O'Connor, Frank. "My Oedipus Complex." In *The Stories of Frank O'Connor.* New York: Alfred A. Knopf, 1950. Rejection by an in-group can be a painful experience. All of us can probably identify with the feelings of the character Larry.

Sartre, Jean-Paul. "The Wall." In Douglas Angus, ed. *The Best Short Stories of the Modern Age.* Greenwich, Conn.: Fawcett, 1965. Pablo Ibbieta, a prisoner of war, has been sentenced to death. His comrades are being tortured and executed, yet Pablo will not reveal the whereabouts of a commando leader. The story illustrates how loyalty to the group and conviction of the rightness of one's cause can help an individual face adversity.

Updike, John. *Couples.* New York: Alfred A. Knopf, 1968. The novel describes the lives of several married couples who are well-to-do Cape Cod residents. Although each couple appears to satisfy the requirements of being a primary group, husband and wife are often competitive and have a superficial relationship. Their combativeness may accurately reflect the interaction of many couples.

IN THIS CHAPTER

Organizations and Bureaucracy   119

The Informal Structure   122

Problem Areas in a Bureaucracy   125

    Bureaucratic goals and employee concerns   125
    Goal displacement   125
    Degree of formal control   127
    Bureaucratic personality   127
    Communication   128
    Member participation   131
    Adaptability to environment   134

Changing Bureaucracies   134

Summary   135

Key Terms for Review   136

Suggested Readings   136

Does the term bureaucracy mean "red tape"? efficiency? a particular type of administrative plan?

Is there more that goes on in an organization than the rule books and memos tell us?

Why are some bureaucrats insecure and unimaginative in their jobs?

Is changing a bureaucracy like fighting a "huge righteous marshmallow"?

BUREAUCRACY

A general manager of a large West Coast corporation thought it would be appropriate and simple enough for his company to order a trade newspaper. The subscription cost was a mere five dollars. Following usual procedure, his secretary sent a memorandum to the company librarian, who, in turn, typed and forwarded a six-part requisition form to the manager of Systems and Procedures, manager of Accounts Payable, and Purchasing Department. It was three weeks before the form was mailed. When the newspaper company did not respond, the corporation sent two additional forms. Eventually, the general manager received a package of "returned" order forms from the newspaper company and a memo which maintained that he was already a subscriber. To say the least, the manager was frustrated with his own staff as well as with the newspaper company because he had never in his life been a subscriber!

> *When the package arrived at my desk today, I sat in a state of shock for ten minutes: A neat four weeks had passed from the inception of the request until the final action. And the final action was Zero. . . .*
>
> *I sit now and wonder who has, in their bulging files, the other five copies missing from this Purchase Order, and I wonder about the mountain of papers for other items, equally as trivial, that are choking the system, stuffing our file cabinets and creating nonproductive expense. The thought staggers my imagination. Saddest of all, since the system and the routine has accomplished its designed purpose, nobody will question it. It will be accepted as the cost of doing business in a large company.*[1]

If high-ranking insiders, such as the general manager, feel pessimistic about the possibilities of changing organizations, imagine the dismay and alienation of those less powerful as they try to bring about change in such groups. Incidents like the one described have helped give bureaucratic organizations a bad name. Nevertheless, such organizations continue to exist and, in fact, play an important part in the lives of nearly everyone in a complex, industrial society. As sociologist Amitai Etzioni put it:

> *We are born in organizations, educated by organizations, and most of us spend much of our lives working for organizations. We spend much of our leisure time paying, playing, and praying in organizations. Most of us will die in organizations, and when the time comes to bury us, the largest organization of all—the state—must grant official permission.*[2]

One might even conjecture that when we die and go to the hereafter, there will be a clerk at the check-in desk who catalogs, numbers, and assigns us to a specific department. Is it possible that this ultimate bureaucracy in the sky could be larger and more complex than such earthly organizations as the AFL-CIO, the American Medical Association, General Motors, or the Pentagon?

Our question suggests a certain irreverence toward bureaucratic organizations, but no one can deny their important role in large industrial societies. A corporation or university could never operate efficiently unless its members' actions were channeled and coordinated by some form of preplanned, formal guidelines. Food could hardly be distributed to millions in society if it were not for bureaucracies. Virtually all Americans

The state unemployment office seems to have become a permanent feature of American society. These organizations are necessary to the survival of many people, yet long lines, extensive paperwork, and callous treatment of clients are common problems these bureaucracies should attempt to alleviate.

are dependent upon these organizations for their schooling, livelihood, goods and services, and other essentials of life.*

Bureaucratic organizations help individuals raise their standard of living and level of accomplishments. If bureaucracies are failing in these tasks—and our example at the beginning suggests that many are—then it is imperative that we know more about their make-up and their specific problems so that we can adjust them to meet our current needs.

Organizations and Bureaucracy

As we noted in the preceding chapter, an *organization* is a group formally designed to achieve a specific goal. Organizations pursue a variety of goals, including making profits (corporations), educating people (schools), protecting society from invaders (armies), treating the sick (hospitals), incarcerating criminals (prisons), assisting the poor (welfare organizations), eliminating pay toilets (Committee to End Pay Toilets in America), and furthering the art of procrastination (Procrastinator's Club of America Incorporated). Depending on one's perspective, some of the goals which organizations pursue are larger and of more consequence to human survival than others.

When we refer to an organization, we mean a group, but *bureaucracy* refers to a type of formal administrative structure or machinery used by an organization to achieve its goals.[3] Max Weber (1864–1920) outlined the distinctive characteristics of bureaucracy as follows:

1. There should be a division of labor. For example, secretaries, purchasing agents, advertisers, machinists, accountants, and other specialists are to work at and master their assigned tasks.
2. There should be a hierarchy of authority. Some individuals should be given more authority than others so that decisions can be made and members' activities can be coordinated. By *authority* we mean the right to issue commands and the expectation that the commands will be followed.
3. Formal rules should be established for members to follow. There may be written rules regarding hours of work, tools to be used, worker absences, style for writing memorandums, type of dress, and frequency of reports. These and other rules are to help bring about predictability.
4. Administrators must remain impersonal and impartial in their relationships with clients. Otherwise, decisions based on favors and personal considerations would create a situation of unequal administrative justice and inefficiency.
5. Organization members should be employed and promoted on the basis of their technical competence. Furthermore, members should be protected

---

*The necessity of bureaucratic organizations in modern society is discussed by Rocco Carzo, Jr., and John N. Yanouzas, *Formal Organization: A Systems Approach* (Homewood, Ill.: The Dorsey Press, 1967), pp. 6–7; and Etzioni, *Modern Organizations*, pp. 1–2.

against arbitrary dismissal so that they can develop a commitment to the organization.[4]

Weber's discussion focused on what sociologists call the formal structure of an organization. The *formal structure* is preplanned and written down, and by-laws, constitutions, charts showing hierarchical authority, performance records, and handbooks of policy and procedure are all mechanisms of this structure. As we will later see, however, what handbooks and charts tell organization members to do and what members actually do are often two different things.

Weber believed that bureaucracy was a superior way to organize people who are attempting to achieve a specific goal. He was reacting in large part to the personal subjugation, nepotism, cruelty, and inefficiency that had characterized organizations prior to and during the very early years of the Industrial Revolution. During this early period people mainly followed rules handed down from one generation to another. Leaders held *traditional authority*—the right to demand certain behavior on the basis that it was the historical, customary thing to do. Individuals also followed rules because of the specific traits of their leaders. They were subject to *charismatic authority*—the ability of certain leaders to command because of their personal qualities.

In contrast, the type of authority pictured in Weber's notion of bureaucracy was to be *rational-legal*. Individuals would behave according to rules, not because of tradition or the charisma of a leader, but because the rules were the most reasonable and efficient means to accomplish organizational goals. Although Weber thought that the individual in a complex, industrial society could survive only if he or she were rational and calculative about reaching goals, he did see the inherent dangers of bureaucracy. Weber feared that the overwhelming order and domination of this administrative machinery might alienate citizens. (For a discussion of Weber's thoughts on bureaucracy and individual alienation, see chapter 13.)

Almost all modern organizations are organized along the lines suggested by Weber. Thus bureaucratically administered organizations are commonly referred to simply as bureaucracies. It is important to note further that Weber was attempting to describe a perfectly bureaucratized organization—yet few, if any, such groups conform totally to his ideal type. Organizations vary in their degree of bureaucratization. For example, they vary in the number of formal rules used to bring about order, the extent of effort expended on administrative problems, the type of hierarchical authority utilized, and so forth.

We should finally note that there are many types of organizations. One classification scheme for distinguishing among them examines the prime beneficiaries of an organization. First, *mutual-benefit organizations*, such as labor unions and fraternal groups, exist to benefit their members. Second, *business concerns*, such as International Telephone and Telegraph

There are many kinds of bureaucratic organizations—among them businesses, political parties, schools, armies, hospitals, and welfare agencies.

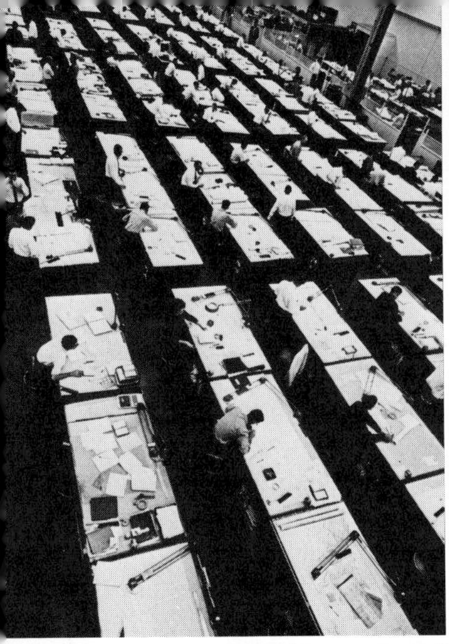

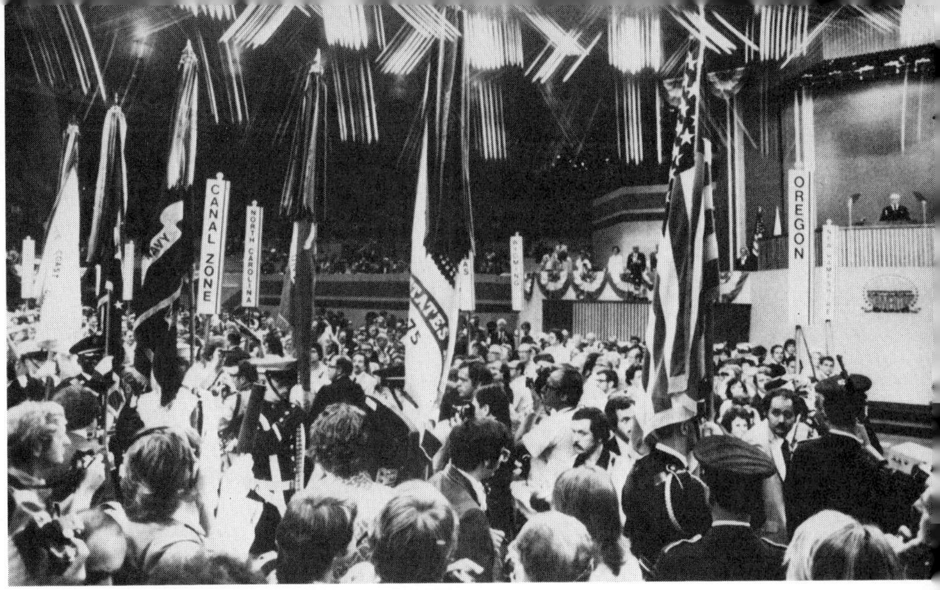
CANAL ZONE
NORTH CAROLINA
OREGON

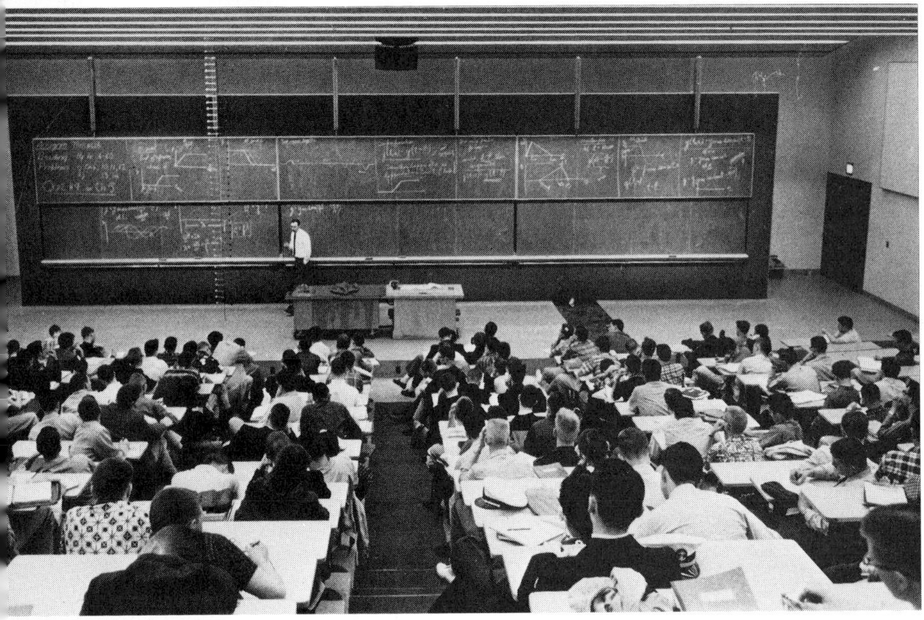

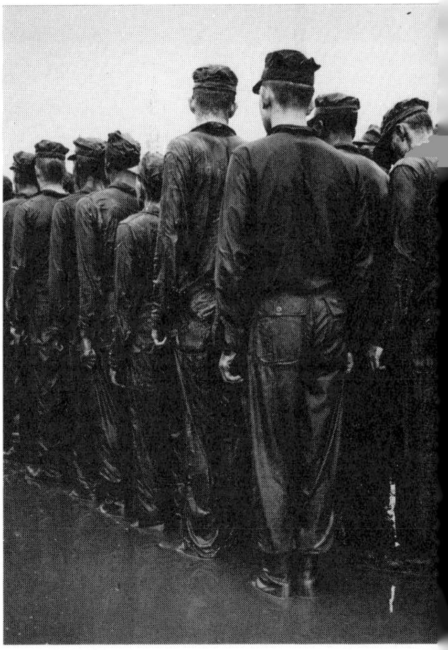

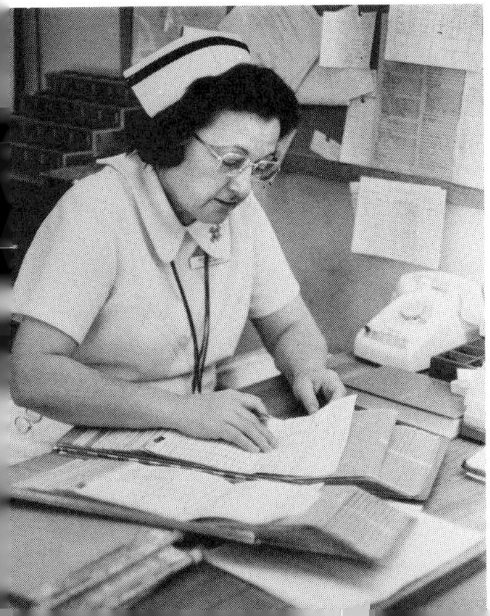

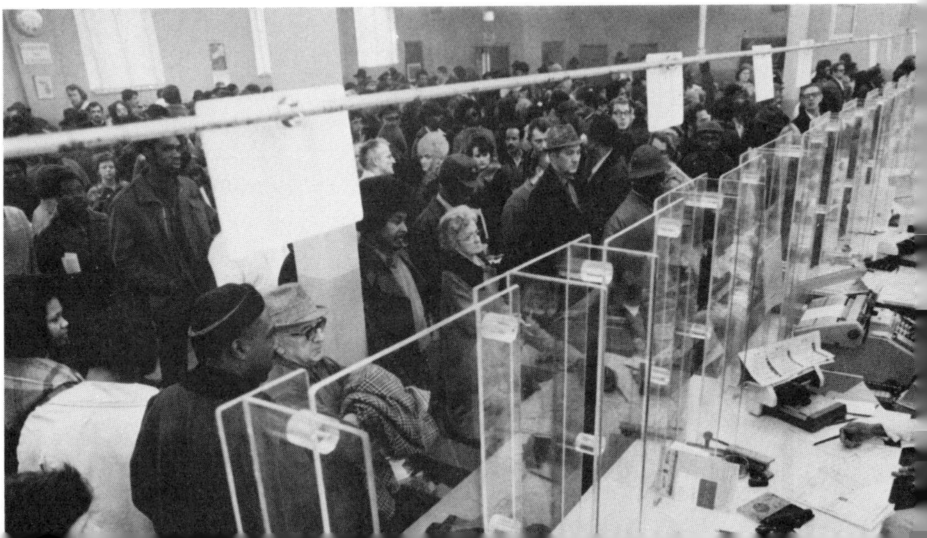

and Standard Oil of California, exist to benefit their owners. Third, *service organizations*, such as mental health clinics and secondary schools, exist to serve their clients. And, fourth, *commonwealth organizations*, such as the U.S. Navy and U.S. Department of Health, Education, and Welfare, exist to benefit the public at large.[5]

Another classification scheme is based on the answers to two questions: (1) What kind of power does an organization use to achieve members' cooperation? (2) What kind of involvement do members have in the organization? One type of organization, the *coercive-alienative organization*, forces members to follow rules and procedures, and as one might expect, members usually become estranged from the organization. A prison is a good example of this type of organization. A second type, the *remunerative-calculative organization*, uses wages or other remunerative rewards to motivate members to comply with its rules. Member involvement is usually of low intensity in the sense of merely working scheduled hours and completing assigned tasks and is based on considerable forethought, caution, and rationality. Businesses are a prime example. A third type, the *normative-moral organization*, uses its own norms and ideology, including rituals, slogans, flags, and leaders, to influence members to abide by its rules. Members usually have an organizational commitment or devotion. Examples are churches, fraternal groups, and some schools.[6]

The Informal Structure

Every organization has an *informal structure* of human relationships in which the members' personal goals, values, and beliefs are important considerations. Elton Mayo and his fellow industrial relations experts have been credited with the "discovery" of the informal structure. Prior to their research, studies in factories during the 1920s had ignored how social relations among workers affect productivity. In the famous Hawthorne Experiment at the Western Electric Company in Cicero, Illinois, Mayo and his researchers learned that workers did not always follow the formal organization's blueprint. They found that friendship ties developed among workers and the resulting social bond enabled informal norms to be enforced. Rules emerged among workers. "Rate-busters," those who worked too much, and "chiselers," those who worked too slowly, were subject to social sanctions by their fellow workers: they were ridiculed and personally avoided. On the other hand, workers who followed the unofficial norms were given high status in the informal network of relationships.[7]

Whereas the formal structure is preplanned, the informal structure develops spontaneously. Further, the informal structure often arises as a reaction to the inadequacies of the formal structure. Erving Goffman, in *Asylums*, provides us with a good example of informal structure when he

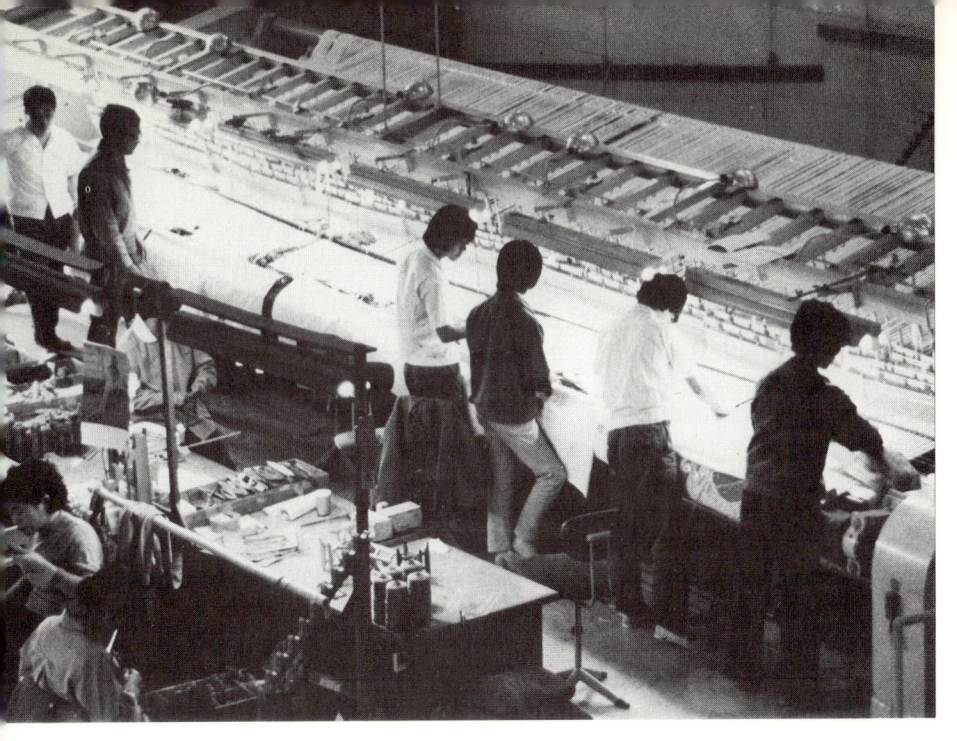

The informal relationships that emerge among workers affect an organization's efficiency. What if these workers decided to slow down the work process? What if there was in informal rule that "rate-busters" were to be condemned?

describes how patients in a mental hospital cope with its impractical and rigid rules. He notes that patients and staff worked out an informal purchasing system:

> In Central Hospital, wards that were relatively far away from the canteen had worked out an informal system of order-placing and delivery. Two or more times a day, those on such a ward—both staff and patients—would make up a list and collect the money needed; a parole patient would then walk over to the canteen to fill the orders, carrying them back in a cigar box that was standard unofficial ward equipment for this purpose.... Stamps, toothpaste, combs, etc., could also be easily bought at the canteen and easily transmitted.[8]

Patients developed informal systems of communication, sometimes taking advantage of established channels to further their own ends:

> Patients made some effort to exploit the established communication system. A patient who had worked in the staff cafeteria, or had friends who did, was sometimes able to use the intramural phone in the kitchen to inform his own ward, some distance away across the campus, that he was not coming in for dinner—a parole patient having the right to skip a meal provided his ward was informed in advance.[9]

There was a unique status hierarchy among patients, and coercive techniques were used by some patients against others:

> *Attendants sometimes joked about the "Svengali" role, pointing to a patient who specialized in the cold use of another, as when, in order to save a good television seat and also get a drink of water one patient in Central Hospital was reported to have used another patient as a seat keeper— putting him in the good chair while getting a drink and pushing him out of it upon return. . . . Open expropriation, blackmail, strong-arm techniques, forced sexual submission— these are methods that can be employed without rationalization as a means of bringing the activities of another into one's own line of action.*[10]

Patients also established a system of buying and selling illicit objects:

> *There was the quite forbidden act of buying and selling liquor, which had been smuggled on to the grounds. Patients claimed that liquor could regularly be had for a price. . . . So, too, it seemed that a few young ladies occasionally prostituted themselves for less than a dollar. . . . A few patients were well-known among fellow inmates and staff for lending money to patients and attendants at relatively high interest, reported to be 25 percent for a short period.*[11]

Another example of informal structure is provided by a rather high-level government bureaucrat who relates five unwritten rules which most civil servants follow in their jobs. The rules are subtle and unarticulated but ever present, commanding, and surely a hindrance to accomplishment of formal goals.

1. Bureaucrats must keep their jobs at all costs. To do this, officials must always appear busy, accomplished best by walking briskly around the office and always looking at papers rather than staring into space. Also, they must remain inconspicuous, which means never wearing new fashions or sporting a hair style that is too long. They should be, in short, just average persons.
2. Bureaucrats must keep their "boss" from being embarrassed. No matter what their assigned responsibilities, their major task is to protect the boss from impertinent demands of outsiders.
3. Bureaucrats should spend all their budgeted funds by the end of the year. After all, not spending budgeted money means that the official mistakenly asked for too much the year before and thus cannot ask for a bigger budget next year. Budgeting within bureaucracies is frequently a source of dismal humor. For example, "former Soviet citizens like to relate the anecdote of the director who interviewed a number of chief accountants for a job. 'How much is two and two?' was his crucial question. 'How much do you need, Comrade Director?' replied one candidate, and he got the job."[12]
4. Bureaucrats should keep alive whatever program they are working on, regardless of whether it is useful or not. Organizational goals are irrelevant; organizational survival and, hence, the bureaucrats' survival are what is important.

5. Bureaucrats should cultivate friendships with influential people and interests outside of government. The friendly and symbiotic relationship between the Department of Defense and various industries or between the Department of Labor and big unions illustrates this practice.[13]

The civil servant's informal code of behavior goes far in explaining much of the inefficiency in government bureaucracies. However, informal relationships are not always a hindrance to the organization's reaching its goals. Members may be so dedicated to their jobs that they are willing to exceed usual work requirements. For example, they may arrive at work two hours early to finish a particular project. Or workers may develop new tools to help them do their job. The informal structure, then, is an integral part of an organization, and it can hinder or help the organization in reaching its official goals.

Problem Areas of a Bureaucracy

Almost everyone carries a personal grudge against bureaucracies. People see them as confusing and frustrating and as a threat to democracy. If bureaucracies are to be changed, we should pinpoint their major problems.

BUREAUCRATIC GOALS AND EMPLOYEE CONCERNS

Administrators, particularly in businesses, frequently make decisions based solely on economic considerations. Cost, profit, and technical efficiency far outweigh employee concerns. If an organization is to reach its goals, however, it cannot ignore the norms, beliefs, and goals of its members. The tasks of producing an item for profit and maintaining good employee relations are interdependent.[14]

GOAL DISPLACEMENT

Goal displacement occurs when an organization or its members substitute for the organization's legitimate goal some other goal for which it was not created.[15] There are many examples of this substitution process. Consider the bureaucrat of long standing who can recite every formal policy and rule in the handbook. He or she may be "obsessed" with obeying rules for their own sake even when procedures not in the handbook might be far more efficient. Such a ritualist has forgotten organizational goals and instead uses rules as ends in themselves.[16]

C. N. Parkinson has also discussed a type of goal-displacing behavior. He asserts that all bureaucrats devise increasingly complicated ways to accomplish tasks. More complicated procedures and paperwork then require more subordinate workers to process the increased workload. Unfortunately, all this additional effort has no connection with accomplishing formal goals.[17]

The bureaucrat's informal code of conduct mentioned earlier provides still another instance of goal displacement. Bureaucrats who subscribe to this code ignore or forget formal goals but ensure their own personal survival. President Harry Truman placed a sign on his desk which read, "The Buck Stops Here." That phrase seldom describes the philosophy of the typical bureaucrat, who tends to be overly cautious and conservative. When faced with a problem or error, many bureaucrats refuse to take responsibility and may instead use the whole organization as a scapegoat. Franz Kafka refers to this refusal to take responsibility and scapegoating by bureaucrats in his novel *The Castle*:

> I don't want any blame to attach to this man, no, not even in your thoughts. It's a working principle of the head bureau that the very possibility of error must be ruled out of account. This ground principle is justified by the consummate organization of the whole authority, and it is necessary if the maximum speed in transacting business is to be attained.[18]

Robert Michels found one other instance of goal displacement worth mentioning here. His examination of European Socialist parties and labor unions led him to conclude that Socialist leaders seldom reflect the demo-

Working at the same task day-in, day-out, whether it be assembling the same parts of a product or typing letters, can be tedious and boring. Allowing workers to switch jobs, try a new work method, or complete a product can sometimes add to workers' personal satisfaction and also increase productivity.

cratic goals their organizations proclaim. Leaders often control the lines of communication and purge young, ambitious challengers to maintain their own authority. Michels's investigations led him to postulate an *iron law of oligarchy,* which maintains that there is a tendency for leadership to become concentrated in a few hands and for leaders to become concerned solely with their own selfish interests.[19] Obviously, when an oligarchy develops in a bureaucracy, organizational goals are likely to suffer.

DEGREE OF FORMAL CONTROL

Bureaucracies face the problem of deciding how much formal control is desirable. Too few rules and procedures may be as harmful as too many. For example, Henry Ford could hardly have organized thousands of untrained and largely immigrant laborers for the mass production of automobiles if he had not imposed a large number of rigid work rules. On the other hand, a long list of rigid rules would surely be ineffective in motivating professionals to produce.

The increased participation of lawyers, medical doctors, scientists, engineers, and other highly educated, specialized workers in bureaucracies has created what some sociologists refer to as a *professional-bureaucratic dilemma.* According to Blau and Scott, the dilemma involves a conflict between professional principles and the principles that govern bureaucracies. They cite four differences between these two sets of principles. First, whereas the bureaucracy expects its members to represent and promote the interests of the organization, a professional is more inclined to represent client interests and emphasize ethical considerations. Second, in contrast to the bureaucratic official, who views authority as resting "on a legal contract backed by formal sanctions," the professional sees authority as "rooted in his acknowledged technical expertness." Third, although the bureaucracy expects its members to comply with the directives it supplies, professionals are likely to be governed by the internalized standards of their own field, such as law, medicine, chemistry, sociology, or psychology. And, fourth, when a disagreement arises, the bureaucrat looks to organizational management for a decision, but a professional refers to his or her colleagues for judgment.[20]

As a result of the conflict between principles, professionals often have a difficult time adjusting to bureaucracies, and work output and morale may decline. We can conclude, therefore, that a control structure which increases the morale and productivity of some members of an organization may have quite the opposite effect on others.

BUREAUCRATIC PERSONALITY

Bureaucratic structure, according to sociologist Robert Merton, affects the character of organization members. Some individuals develop what Merton calls a *bureaucratic personality.* The term describes a

128 / SOCIAL ORGANIZATION

person who is overly concerned with vocational security; formal, impersonal, and harsh in relationships; excessively methodical and disciplined; more concerned with rules than with organizational goals; inflexible and unimaginative in solving problems; and secretive and timid in developing new ideas.[21] Sketches of bureaucrats who possess such traits are common in literature. Kurt Vonnegut, for example, describes the modern American bureaucrat:

Industrial bureaucrats—men who lose things and use the wrong forms and create new forms and demand everything in quintuplicate, and who understand perhaps a third of what is said to them; who habitually give misleading answers in order to gain time in which to think, who make decisions only when forced to, and who then cover their tracks; who make perfectly honest mistakes in addition and subtraction, who call meetings whenever they feel unloved; men who never throw anything away unless they think it could get them fired. A single industrial bureaucrat, if he is sufficiently vital and nervous, should be able to create a ton of meaningless papers a year.[22]

Rather than creating secure and positive-thinking managers, bureaucracies have often produced insecure, timid, and harried officials who feel "behind the eight-ball."

The problem is not peculiar to twentieth-century America. Bureaucratic personalities have existed in other times and other countries. Honoré de Balzac described one such bureaucrat in nineteenth-century France:

Poiret, Jr. had been thirty years in the department. Every action in the poor creature's life was a part of a routine; nature herself is more variable in her revolutions. He always put his things in the same place, laid his pen on the same mark in the grain of the wood, sat down in his place at the same hour, and went to warm himself at the stove at the same minute. . . . His sky is the ceiling, to which his yawns are addressed; his element is dust. . . . the sun scarcely shines into the horrid dens known as public offices; the thinking powers of their occupants are strictly confined to a monotonous round. Their prototype, the millhorse, yawns hideously over such work and cannot stand it for long.[23]

Bureaucracies appear to have changed surprisingly little in a century's time. If bureaucracies are to accomplish their goals in an efficient manner, they must develop a formal structure which allows members to be more problem-solving, flexible, and innovative in their work.

COMMUNICATION

Open communication, the free flow of ideas, is of some importance to the survival of any organization. There is considerable evidence that an open exchange of ideas, criticisms, and advice improves decision-making. For

Better decisions sometimes result when workers of all ranks and positions feel free to share their experience and expertise.

example, as organization members discuss problems with one another, individuals develop the self-confidence to cope with difficult problems. Open communication also allows different people to bring their specific expertise to bear on the problem at hand. Finally, a free flow of communication motivates members to make valuable suggestions and to criticize the ill-considered suggestions of others.

If open communication serves these valuable functions, why, then, is it sometimes absent in bureaucracies? Some have suggested that open communication can be a hindrance to coordinated activity and to efficient and speedy decision-making. Many decisions need to be made and implemented rapidly to ensure an organization's survival, and deliberations by members can delay this process.[24] Undoubtedly, this is true to some extent, though the importance of speed in making decisions is often overrated and the advantages of more input underemphasized.

More often than not, ideas fail to circulate in a bureaucracy not because a free flow would impede efficiency, but because bureaucrats operate in an autocratic fashion and also because they have developed habits of not communicating. Use of the memo is one such habit. Since bureaucrats spend so much time writing and rewriting them, one might conclude that memos must be an effective communication device, but generally this is not the case. Memos frequently are written in bureaucratic jargon, which might include such phrases as "integrated management options," "synchronized logistical programing," and "systematized policy contingency." This jargon is used less to communicate than to hide mistakes or pretend expertise.

Memos can be effective communication devices, but too often they are written unnecessarily, contain nonsensical jargon, and accomplish little other than filling shelves and file cabinets.

Kafka, through his character the mayor, enlightens us about both the meaningless content of some memos and how they are sometimes sent to the wrong department, lost, and even forgotten:

"I can tell you the story even without the papers. We replied with thanks to the order that I've mentioned already, saying that we didn't need a land-surveyor. But this reply doesn't appear to have reached the original department—I'll call it A—but by mistake went to another department, B. So Department A remained without an answer, but unfortunately our full reply didn't reach B either; whether it was that the order itself was not enclosed by us, or whether it got lost on the way—it was certainly not lost in my department, that I can vouch for—in any case all that arrived at Department B was the covering letter, in which was merely noted that the enclosed order, unfortunately an impractical one, was concerned with the engagement of a land-surveyor. Meanwhile Department A was wait-

ing for our answer; they had, of course, made a memorandum of the case, but as, excusably enough, often happens and is bound to happen even under the most efficient handling, our correspondent trusted to the fact that we would answer him, after which he would either summon the Land-Surveyor or else, if need be, write us further about the matter. As a result he never thought of referring to his memorandum, and the whole thing fell into oblivion. But in Department B the covering letter came into the hands of a correspondent famed for his conscientiousness, Sordini by name, an Italian; it is incomprehensible even to me, though I am one of the initiated, why a man of his capacities is left in an almost subordinate position. This Sordini naturally sent us back the unaccompanied covering letter for completion. Now months, if not years, had passed by this time since that first communication from Department A, which is understandable enough, for when—as is the rule—a document goes the proper route, it reaches the department at the outside in a day and is settled that day, but when it once in a while loses its way, then in an organization so efficient as ours its proper destination must be sought for literally with desperation; otherwise it mightn't be found; and then—well, then the search may last really for a long time. Accordingly, when we got Sordini's note we had only a vague memory of the affair; there were only two of us to do the work at that time, Mizzi and myself, the teacher hadn't yet been assigned to us; we only kept copies in the most important instances, so we could only reply in the most vague terms that we knew nothing of this engagement of a land-surveyor and that as far as we knew there was no need for one.

"But"—here the Mayor interrupted himself as if, carried on by his tale, he had gone too far, or as if at least it was possible that he had gone too far, "doesn't the story bore you?"

"No," said K., "it amuses me."

Thereupon the Mayor said: "I'm not telling it to amuse you."

"It only amuses me," said K., "because it gives me an insight into the ludicrous bungling that in certain circumstances may decide the life of a human being."[25]

The habit of not communicating, which the memo reinforces, is an obvious deficiency of bureaucratic systems. Bureaucracies might well reassess the necessity of flooding communication channels with often ineffective messages.

MEMBER PARTICIPATION

How much voice, if any, should members who are not in administrative positions have in making organizational decisions? Do rank-and-file members really want to participate in making decisions? Do managers always have the expertise to make decisions? Answers to these questions vary. Those who follow the *human relations* school of thought maintain that all people want to be self-starting, independent, and responsible. They also contend that precinct workers, students, machinists, nurses, clerks, secretaries, and other such organization members have valuable knowledge which can help managers make correct decisions. Therefore, participation by lower members in decision-making can increase both member morale and organizational efficiency.* In contrast, those who follow the *classical administration* school of thought maintain that rank-and-file members should not participate in decision-making. In their view, although participation may be a worthy goal, it simply will not work. Most members below the administrative level have neither the desire nor the expertise to aid in decision-making. Additionally, these members refuse responsibility, prefer outside direction to independent action, and seek out the safety of uninvolvement.

Robert Townsend, former chairman of the board of Avis Rent-a-Car Corporation, has criticized the classical administration school's perspective of workers. After describing the assumptions of those with this viewpoint, he offers examples of how the assumptions are put into daily practice:

> There's nothing fundamentally wrong with our country except that the leaders of all our major organizations are operating on the wrong assumptions. We're in this mess because for the last two hundred years we've been using the Catholic Church and Caesar's legions as our patterns for creating organizations. And until the last forty or fifty years it made sense. The average churchgoer, soldier, and factory worker was uneducated and dependent on orders from above. And authority carried considerable weight because disobedience brought the death penalty or its equivalent.
>
> From the behavior of people in these early industrial organizations we arrived at the following assumptions, on which all modern organizations are still operating:
>
> 1. People hate work.
> 2. They have to be driven and threatened with punishment to get them to work toward organizational objectives.
> 3. They like security, aren't ambitious, want to be told what to do, dislike responsibility.
>
> You don't think we are operating on these assumptions? Consider:
>
> 1. Office hours nine to five for everybody except the fattest cats at the top. Just a giant cheap time clock. (Are we buying brains or hours?)

---

*The human relations view of employee decision-making is discussed by Chris Argyris, *Personality and Organization* (New York: Harper & Row, 1957) and *Integrating the Individual and the Organization* (New York: John Wiley, 1964).

Despite the sometimes heard managerial claim that all organization members have a significant voice in decision-making, the fact remains that top managers usually hold ultimate power and make the important decisions.

2. *Unilateral promotions. For more money and a bigger title I'm expected to jump at the chance of moving my family to New York City. I run away from the friends and a life style in Denver that have made me and my family happy and effective. (Organization comes first; individuals must sacrifice themselves to its demands.)*
3. *Hundreds of millions of dollars are spent annually "communicating" with employees. The message always boils down to: "Work hard, obey orders. We'll take care of you." (That message is obsolete by fifty years and wasn't very promising then.)*[26]

Sometimes managers who are aware of the problems in the old style of administration but are still unwilling to decentralize decision-making resort to a supervision style called *benevolent autocracy*, which gives rank-and-file members the illusion of participation. Managers who use this style actually make the key decisions and carefully control the actions of subordinates but give an appearance of democracy and concern for those beneath administrative levels.[27]

Strategies like cooptation have also been used to give members a feeling of participation. *Cooptation* is "the process of absorbing new elements into the leadership or policy-determining structure of an organization as a means of averting threats to its stability or existence."[28] During the strikes and riots of the late 1960s, university administrators frequently coopted student activists by appointing them to policy-making committees. This gave the activist leaders a sense of recognition and hope. Later many activists were dismayed to find that the committees were powerless to make significant changes in university policies.

Determining the degree of member participation is a problem facing almost all organizations. The skills and education level of members, the goals and size of the organization, and the larger culture's views on the significance of the individual are all factors which influence how much participation is desirable.

ADAPTABILITY TO ENVIRONMENT

Traditionally, bureaucracies have operated as self-contained systems ignoring the outside world. Yet whether the organization is a university, hospital, government agency, or business, it is dependent on many environmental forces. For instance, an organization might have to consider government policies, laws, sources of economic support, public opinion, competing organizations, and the attitude of skilled labor. Bureaucracies have also failed to adapt quickly to new societal demands. For example, private citizens and public-interest groups have been demanding the development of alternative energy sources to scarce fossil fuels. Nevertheless, it might require several years before existing organizations — whether government bureaucracies or energy-producing firms — redefine their goals to meet these demands; likewise, it might take years for new organizations to emerge that can satisfy these demands.

Open-systems theory has drawn attention to the problem of adaptability to environment. It stresses that all organizations as well as any kind of system must continually receive feedback from the outside world and adapt to ever-changing conditions. The theory maintains that if an organization fails to import needed resources, such as labor, capital, raw materials, and public support, from the environment, it will head toward entropy, or death.*

Changing Bureaucracies

For bureaucracies to meet societal demands, new and sometimes controversial administrative philosophies and programs will have to be implemented. Administrators must view the informal structure as a vital part of the organization, encourage goal achievement rather than goal displacement, devise rules and procedures which take account of the skills and the needs of members, reward flexible and innovative personalities rather than bureaucratic personalities, encourage effective communication, at least consider the possibility of having all organization members participate in decision-making, and be attuned to factors and problems in the outside environment. Although almost everyone would agree with these recommendations, changing a bureaucracy is not an easy task.† Presi-

---

*For a discussion of open-systems theory, see Daniel Katz and Robert L. Kahn, *The Social Psychology of Organizations* (New York: John Wiley, 1966), pp. 14–29.

†The topic of changing bureaucracies is discussed by Warren G. Bennis, *Changing Organizations* (New York: McGraw-Hill, 1966); and Victor A. Thompson, "Bureaucracy and Innovation," *Administrative Science Quarterly,* 10 (1965): 1–20.

dents of the United States have tried to streamline the federal bureaucracy only to find that large departments like Defense firmly oppose change. Unfortunately, the outsider who attacks bureaucracy is generally categorized an unknowledgeable egghead, while the insider who dares to be innovative is derided as a meddler trying to "rock the boat." The difficulty of changing bureaucracies is portrayed in Matthew Dumont's discussion of the federal government:

> It does not respond to the top or the bottom; it does not respond to ideology. It is a great, indestructible mollusk that absorbs kicks and taunts and seductions and does nothing but grow. . . .
> Can you imagine trying to fight a revolution against a huge, righteous marshmallow? Even if you had enough troops not to be suffocated by it, the best you can hope for is to eat it. And, as you all know, you become what you eat. . . . If a revolution harbors the illusion that a reign of terror will purify a bureaucracy of scoundrels and exploiters, it will fail. It matters little whether bureaucrats are Royalists or Republican, Czarist or Bolshevik, Conservative or Liberal, or what have you. It is the built-in forces of life in a bureaucracy that result in the bureaucracy being so indifferent to suffering and aspiration.[29]

Chapter Summary

Bureaucracies touch the lives of everyone in a complex, industrial society. We depend on them for our schooling, livelihood, goods and services, and other essentials of life. Unfortunately, bureaucracies are frequently inefficient and fail to meet the needs of society.

An organization is a group formally designed to achieve a specific goal. Examples are corporations, schools, armies, and hospitals. Bureaucracy refers to the formal administrative machinery used by the organization to achieve its goals. According to Weber, the defining characteristics of bureaucracy are a division of labor, a hierarchy of authority, formal rules, impersonality in administrator-client relations, and employment and promotion based on technical competence. Weber felt that the evils of early organizations would be overcome by bureaucracy. People would no longer follow rules because of tradition or a leader's charisma, but because rules were rational, legal means to accomplish goals efficiently.

What the formal, written rules and procedures tell members of an organization to do and what members actually do may be two different things. Informal relationships among members can greatly affect the organization; they can hinder or help it reach official goals.

Bureaucracies have many problems. First, managers sometimes ignore employee concerns. Second, bureaucracies frequently lose track of the goals they are supposed to pursue, mainly because individual bureaucrats become so concerned with their own survival that they forget the official goals to be accomplished. Third, administrators sometimes err in the degree of control they exert over members: both too much and too little are inefficient. Fourth, bureaucracies unfortunately create insecure, overly formal, methodical, inflexible, and uninnovative workers—the bureaucratic personality. Fifth, a free flow of communication is usually absent in organizations, and memos are often used so as not to communicate. Sixth, managers seldom allow workers who are not in administrative positions to participate in making organizational decisions. The human relations school maintains that member participation is both possible and desirable, though the classical administration school disagrees. Some administrators have used a supervision style called benevolent autocracy and a strategy called cooptation to give lower members a false feeling of participation. And, seventh, many bureaucracies have failed to adapt to the ever-changing conditions of the outside environment. No longer can organizations be run as isolated, self-contained systems.

Unfortunately, too many bureaucracies can be aptly described as uncontrollable monstrosities that eat up valuable resources and fail to meet society's needs. Sadder still is the fact that there is no easy way to change these organizations that affect so much of our lives.

Key Terms for Review

authority, p. 119
benevolent autocracy, p. 133
bureaucracy, p. 119
bureaucratic personality, p. 127
business concerns, p. 120
charismatic authority, p. 120
classical administration, p. 132
coercive-alienative organizations, p. 122
commonwealth organizations, p. 122
cooptation, p. 133
formal structure, p. 120
goal displacement, p. 125
human relations, p. 132

informal structure, p. 122
iron law of oligarchy, p. 127
mutual-benefit organizations, p. 120
normative-moral organizations, p. 122
open-systems theory, p. 134
professional-bureaucratic dilemma, p. 127
rational-legal authority, p. 120
remunerative-calculative organizations, p. 122
service organizations, p. 122
traditional authority, p. 120

Suggested Readings

SOCIOLOGICAL   Blau, Peter M., and Marshall W. Meyer. *Bureaucracy in Modern Society*. New York: Random House, 1956. This excellent book for beginning students covers the general area of bureaucracy. The relationship of bureaucracy to democracy and social change is discussed.

Dumont, Matthew P. "Down the Bureaucracy." *Transaction,* 7 (1970): 10–14. This article discusses, in a humorous but sincere fashion, the bureaucrat's informal code of conduct. The author maintains that bureaucracies can be changed by managers who are concerned with efficient goal achievement.

Etzioni, Amitai. *Modern Organizations.* Englewood Cliffs, N.J.: Prentice-Hall, 1964. This concise and easily understood book discusses the major theories, concepts, and issues pertaining to organizations.

Peter, Laurence, and Raymond Hull. *The Peter Principle.* New York: Bantam, 1970. Excellent examples of bureaucratic incompetence are given. For instance, those workers who most efficiently accomplish organizational goals are given inferior ratings by bureaucratic officials.

Shepard, Jon M., ed. *Organizational Issues in Industrial Society.* Englewood Cliffs, N.J.: Prentice-Hall, 1972. Readings here cover eight controversial areas in the field of organizational behavior, including alternatives to bureaucracy, member participation in decision-making, work incentives, and democratic control structures.

Townsend, Robert. *Up the Organization.* New York: Alfred A. Knopf, 1970. The author gives "down to earth" advice to administrators and students of business on how to increase the efficiency and profitability of business organizations. His suggestions sometimes appear simple and outrageous, but they are certainly worthy of discussion and debate.

Whyte, William. *The Organization Man.* New York: Doubleday, 1957. This book describes how large organizations create bureaucratic personalities and influence the thinking of all of society.

LITERARY

Heller, Joseph. *Catch-22.* New York: Dell, 1967. This bitter but humorous novel illustrates how a bureaucracy, the U.S. Air Force, victimizes an innocent member named Yossarian. "Catch-22" refers to the unwritten loopholes used by authorities to revoke members' rights whenever necessary.

Kafka, Franz. *The Castle.* New York: Alfred A. Knopf, 1956. Kafka voices his fear of bureaucracy in satirical style. Bureaucracy is shown to be puzzling, illogical, nonsensical, and inaccessible. It is a mammoth establishment of documents and procedures which dehumanizes and inhibits a person's artistic talents.

IN THIS CHAPTER

The Meaning of Stratification   143

Principal Types of Stratification   143
    Caste   143
    Estate   144
    Class   145

The Structure of Class Society   146
    Economic, social, and political orders   147

The Functional Necessity of Stratification   151

Social Mobility   153

Stratification in American Society   155
    Economic inequality   155
    Status inequality   157
    Power inequality   161
    Vertical social mobility   162
    Class consciousness   163

Summary   164

Key Terms for Review   166

Suggested Readings   166

Why do societies stratify their members into different social layers?
Does American society have an economic elite? a power elite?
Is it true that any American can go from "rags to riches?"
Will American workers develop a class consciousness and revolt against the rich?

STRATIFICATION

The difference between being in the upper class and being in the lower class can mean the difference between a life of luxury and a dreary existence shortened by malnutrition and disease. In "The Streets—Night" Charles Dickens has given us a distressing picture of the huge gap between rich and poor in nineteenth-century England. The scene is a London street.

> That wretched woman with the infant in her arms, round whose meagre form the remnant of her own scanty shawl is carefully wrapped, has been attempting to sing some popular ballad, in the hope of wringing a few pence from the compassionate passer-by. A brutal laugh at her weak voice is all she has gained. The tears fall thick and fast down her own pale face; the child is cold and hungry, and its half-stifled wailing adds to the misery of its wretched mother, as she moans aloud, and sinks despairingly down, on a cold damp doorstep.
>
> Singing! How few of those who pass such a miserable creature as this, think of the anguish of heart, the sinking of soul and spirit, which the very effort of singing produces. Bitter mockery! Disease, neglect, and starvation, faintly articulating the words of the joyish ditty, that has enlivened your hours of feasting and merriment, God knows how often! It is no subject of jeering. The weak tremulous voice tells a fearful tale of want and famishing; and the feeble singer of this roaring song may turn away, only to die of cold and hunger.
>
> One o'clock! Parties returning from the different theatres foot it through the muddy streets; cabs, hackney-coaches, carriages, and theatre omnibuses, roll swiftly by; watermen with dim dirty lanterns in their hands, and large brass plates upon their breasts, who have been shouting and rushing about for the last two hours, retire to their watering-houses, to solace themselves with the creature comforts of pipes and purl; the half-price pit and box frequenters of the theatres

throng to the different houses of refreshment; and chops, kidneys, rabbits, oysters, stout, cigars, and "goes" innumerable, are served up amidst a noise and confusion of smoking, running, knife-clattering, and waiter-chattering, perfectly indescribable.[1]

In addition to its economic aspect, social class affects us in a multitude of other important ways—manners, the words we use, the beliefs we hold. And members of a social class tend to see their class as normal and often right and best. They may even view other classes as strange and possibly repugnant. In "Sketches and Travels in London" nineteenth-century English author William Makepeace Thackeray described how an upper-class gentleman viewed those beneath him.

They [the lower classes] are not like you indeed. They have not your tastes and feeling: your education and refinements. They would not understand a hundred things which seem perfectly simple to you. They would shock you a hundred times a day by as many deficiencies of politeness, or by outrages upon the Queen's English—by practices entirely harmless, and yet in your eyes actually worse than crimes—they have large hard hands and clumsy feet.[2]

Although class lines were less rigid in England's North American colonies than in the mother country, the gap between rich and poor remained wide. John Singleton Copley's portrait of Mrs. Metcalf Bowler (c. 1763) shows the affluence of the upper class in colonial America.

Is it possible for social classes to be eliminated or, at least, for the economic and social gap between rich and poor to be lessened? Although some thinkers, such as Karl Marx, have maintained that a classless society is possible and, in fact, inevitable, others have been more pessimistic about such a possibility. During the early 1900s social critic and writer George Orwell visited the coal mines of northern England and Wales to observe the plight of the working class. He desperately wanted to do away with the social injustices he witnessed, but he also realized that resolving differences between people from different stations in life would be difficult. Orwell believed that the major hindrance to improving the condition of the masses was the upper-class attitude toward "common" people—an attitude learned during childhood and unlikely to be changed. In *The Road to Wigan Pier,* Orwell writes:

And what is this attitude? An attitude of sniggering superiority punctuated by bursts of vicious hatred. . . . It is no use wasting breath in denouncing this attitude. It is better to consider how it has arisen, and to do that one has got to realise what the working classes look like to those who live among them but have different habits and traditions. . . .

I was very young, not much more than six, when I first became aware of class-distinctions. Before that age my chief heroes had generally been working-class people, because they always seemed to do such interesting things, such as being fishermen and blacksmiths and bricklayers. . . . But it was not long before I was forbidden to

Child labor in a textile mill around 1900. The factory system absorbed even the children of the working class.

play with the plumber's children; they were "common" and I was told to keep away from them. This was snobbish, if you like, but it was also necessary, for middle-class people cannot afford to let their children grow up with vulgar accents. So, very early, the working class ceased to be a race of friendly and wonderful beings and became a race of enemies. We realised that they hated us, but we could never understand why, and naturally we set it down to pure, vicious malignity. To me in my early boyhood, to nearly all children of families like mine, "common" people seemed almost sub-human. They had coarse faces, hideous accents and gross manners, they hated everyone who was not like themselves, and if they got half a chance they would insult you in brutal ways. That was our view of them, and though it was false it was understandable. . . .

But there was another and more serious difficulty. Here you come to the real secret of class-distinctions in the West — the real reason why a European of bourgeois upbringing, even when he calls himself a Communist, cannot without a hard effort think of a working man as his equal. It is summed up in four frightful words which people nowadays are chary of uttering, but which were bandied about quite freely in my childhood. The words were: The lower classes smell.

> *That was what we were taught—the lower classes smell. And here, obviously, you are at an impassable barrier. For no feeling of like or dislike is quite so fundamental as a physical feeling. . . . However well you may wish him, however much you may admire his mind and character, if his breath stinks he is horrible and in your heart of hearts you will hate him. It may not greatly matter if the average middle-class person is brought up to believe that the working classes are ignorant, lazy, drunken, boorish and dishonest; it is when he is brought up to believe that they are dirty that the harm is done. . . . You watched a tramp taking off his boots in a ditch—ugh! It did not seriously occur to you that the tramp might not enjoy having black feet. And even "lower-class" people whom you knew to be quite clean—servants, for instance—were faintly unappetising. The smell of their sweat, the very texture of their skins, were mysteriously different from yours.*[3]

Of course, many would say that Orwell's statement hardly applies to American society. After all, the United States has been described as the land of egalitarian promises! Our society is without kings or nobility. People are supposedly free and equal, capable of achieving a decent economic and social position. Indeed, the gap between rich and poor in American society is far less than that in nineteenth-century European societies and many present-day societies. At the same time, however, we have not reached the ideal of equality and classlessness described by Supreme Court Justice John Marshall Harlan in 1896.

> *In view of the Constitution, in the eye of the law, there is in this country no superior, dominant, ruling class of citizens. There is no caste here. Our Constitution is color blind, and neither knows nor tolerates classes among citizens. . . . The humblest is the peer of the most powerful.*[4]

Class differences exist in our society, and most Americans are keenly aware of them. The welfare poor of Baltimore probably think it absurd and sinful that the beautiful people of Palm Beach have fresh Hawaiian pineapples, mangoes, and papayas flown in for a lavish dinner party. The very rich, on the other hand, may consider many practices of the lower segments of society equally disgusting—watching the Roller Derby, betting on the "numbers," or drinking beer at a neighborhood bar. Every day we hear terms such as the "power structure," the "super rich," "people from the right and wrong side of the tracks," "social climbers," and the "dregs of society"; all of these terms illustrate that Americans know that ours is a multilayered society. No matter that the ideals of equality and classlessness are set forth in the Constitution; we realize that in American society individuals are sorted into categories of high, middle, and low social standing.

The Meaning of Stratification

Every society—whether in Liberia, Canada, Bolivia, Japan, Spain, Yugoslavia, the United States, or the Soviet Union—has a system of *social stratification,* or institutionalized social inequality.* Any important material or symbolic dimension of a society—for example, wealth, education, religion, or family heritage—can serve as the basis for social distinctions. In fact, the bases of stratification vary from society to society. For example, in South Africa race is a primary basis of stratification, whereas in the Soviet Union membership in the Communist party is of primary significance. Local communities within a society may also use different dimensions to categorize people. Consider Mark Twain's statement: "In Boston they ask, How much does he know? In New York, How much is he worth? In Philadelphia, Who were his parents?"[5]

We find that all stratification systems are institutionalized in that they are legitimized, justified, and given stability by the norms, beliefs, and values of the society. In the United States, for example, many people argue that the income tax laws are designed to justify, protect, and perpetuate the wealth of the upper class.

A stratification system is composed of various levels, or *social strata.* A single stratum consists of individuals who have a similar rank in reference to a particular basis of stratification. For example, people who have approximately the same level of income may be viewed as a wealth stratum, and people with approximately the same schooling may be viewed as an education stratum. Sociologists have discovered differences in behavior patterns—for instance, political participation, divorce rates, and child-rearing methods—between strata. They have also found differences in lifetime income, opportunities for formal education, and life span.

Principal Types of Stratification

Stratification systems in all societies tend to approximate one of three types—caste, estate, or class.

CASTE

In a *caste system* individuals born into a particular stratum must remain there for life. For example, a very rigid caste system existed in India until modern times. Although stratification in this society was very complex,

---

*Introductions to the concept of social stratification can be found in Celia S. Heller, ed., *Structured Social Inequality* (London: Macmillan, 1969), pp. 3–4; and Kurt B. Mayer and Walter Buckley, *Class and Society* (New York: Random House, 1970), pp. 5–9.

members were basically divided into five major categories. The Brahmans, the highest caste, ruled society supposedly with divine guidance. The second-ranked caste, Kshatriyas, formed a military aristocracy. The third-ranked caste, Vaisyas, consisted of craftsmen and merchants. The lowest caste, Sudras, were the manual laborers who served the higher castes. Outside of this caste system were the lowliest members of society, the Untouchables, who because they had no caste were excluded from the Hindu spiritual community. Each caste was largely isolated from the others, and there were strong taboos against intermarriage between castes.[6]

ESTATE

A second type of stratification, the *estate system,* is also characterized by clearly distinguished strata. Estate systems most often developed in feudal societies where a person's social position depended upon his relationship to an agricultural economy. The best example of an estate system is found in feudal Europe (800–1400). The highest estate was composed of landowners—the nobility and rulers of society. Of approximately equal standing were the higher ranks of the clergy. Below these two groups were the merchants and craftsmen. At the lowest level of society were

Both in eighteenth-century England and twentieth-century America, the upper classes have used status symbols, such as luxurious and fashionable coaches, as indicators of their worldly success.

The estate system of feudal Europe had clearly distinguished strata based largely on inherited family position.

the peasants and serfs who lived and worked on the estates of the nobility. Each group performed functions for the society that were clearly defined and interrelated. Although feudal societies as a whole were relatively unchanging, occasionally some individuals moved to a new social level. A serf might move into the priesthood, or a wealthy merchant's daughter might marry into the nobility.

CLASS

Whereas caste and estate systems are based on the ascribed criteria of inherited family position, a *class system* emphasizes personal achievement. (See chapter 4 for a discussion of ascribed versus achieved status.) The

United States and Western European nations provide examples of societies with such systems. Within a class system the various strata are called social classes. A *social class* consists of people who are similar usually in their income, wealth, educational background, and occupational prestige. There is frequently, but not always, a smaller economic gap between social classes than between the different castes or estates. For example, those in lower social classes can at times possess some of the symbolically important objects of their society, such as automobiles, televisions, and fashionable clothes. Further, people in a class society have a greater chance to improve upon their social position since they are encouraged to move into new jobs and take advantage of opportunities.

The Structure of Class Society

What forces give rise to social classes? On what bases do modern societies make class distinctions? What is the future of class society? Are members of society conscious of their class position? We find various answers to these questions. One of the most significant interpretations of class society was provided by Karl Marx (1818–1883), whose views may be summarized as follows:

1. *Economic forces give rise to social classes.* The material, or economic, conditions of a society determine the basic institutions and ideologies by which individuals live. Under capitalism, which is characterized by private ownership of property, the stratification system thus comprises two major classes: (a) those who own property and hence control the means of production—the capitalists, or *bourgeoisie*, and (b) those who do not own property—the workers, or wage earners.

2. *There will be a class struggle between owners and workers.* In capitalist society profit that should go to workers is expropriated by the propertied class, and the gap between the have's and the have not's widens. Inevitably, the bourgeoisie and workers become polarized and alienated from each other, and class struggle results. (See chapter 14 for a more detailed discussion of Marx's concept of alienation.)

3. *Workers will be transformed into a proletariat.* A *class-in-itself* refers to an aggregate of individuals who are thrown into a common economic situation. Yet these individuals are unaware of their common position. Such people are said to constitute an *objective class*.

A *class-for-itself* refers to a situation where class members are aware of their common economic position and their role in society. A class consciousness develops among them. Individuals who share a common economic situation and also possess class consciousness constitute a *subjective class*. When class consciousness develops among workers, they are transformed into the *proletariat*. Marx contended that when workers are in conflict with the bourgeoisie, they will eventually become aware of their common interests and develop a political organization to accomplish their goals.

4. *The government is the arm of the capitalists.* The capitalists dominate society not only economically but also politically. The government is run for the bourgeoisie in the sense that it is designed to maintain the status quo, that is, to protect the vested interests of the capitalists. Therefore the proletariat cannot rely on the government to serve its interests.

5. *Revolution will end the class system and a communist society will emerge.* A class-conscious proletariat will eventually overthrow the bourgeoisie. Postcapitalist society will first go through a transitional stage of dictatorship, then move into a new phase called communism.

> *The proletariat will be the nation; and so in the nation there will be no class distinctions and no class struggle. . . . The state will wither away, for the only function of the state is to hold down the exploited class. Since the proletariat will be virtually the total population, and thus cease to be a proletariat, they will need no state.*"[7]*

ECONOMIC, SOCIAL, AND POLITICAL ORDERS

Sociologist Max Weber agreed with some of Marx's assertions concerning class society. He, too, maintained that class society has an *economic order* wherein people are stratified according to their possession of goods and opportunities for income. Similarly, the groups in this stratification order are called social classes. Beyond this point the two theorists disagree, however. Whereas Marx maintained that workers would develop into a class-conscious proletariat and revolt against capitalists, Weber believed that class awareness and revolution may or may not occur. Individuals in an objective class situation may never develop a sense of community and engage in class action.

Additionally, Weber more strongly emphasized the social and political orders in a society and noted that these orders may sometimes exist independently of the economic order. The *social order* is composed of status groups. Members of these groups are stratified not by their income but by the social esteem and honor given them by others. Weber contended that although wealth often confers high status, it does not always guarantee it. For example, members of a very rich family might be snubbed by the aristocracy because they lack refined manners.

The desire to maintain one's status among others is a subject that has been given much attention. In *The Road to Wigan Pier* George Orwell de-

---

*For a detailed discussion of Marxian theory, see T. B. Bottomore and Maxmilien Rubel, eds., *Karl Marx: Selected Writings in Sociology and Social Philosophy* (London: C. A. Watts, 1956); and Ralf Dahrendorf, *Class and Class Conflict in Industrial Society* (Stanford, Calif.: Stanford University Press, 1959).

scribes the English upper-middle class of the late 1800s and shows the importance of manners, opinions, and occupation in determining status.

> *The upper-middle class, which had its heyday in the 'eighties and 'nineties, with Kipling as its poet laureate, was a sort of mound of wreckage left behind when the tide of Victorian prosperity receded. Or perhaps it would be better to change the metaphor and describe it not as a mound but as a layer   the layer of society lying between £2,000 and £300 a year; my own family was not far from the bottom. You notice that I define it in terms of money, because that is always the quickest way of making yourself understood. Nevertheless, the essential point about the English class-system is that it is not entirely explicable in terms of money. . . . Probably there are countries where you can predict a man's opinions of his income, but it is never quite safe to do so in England; you have always got to take his traditions into consideration as well. A naval officer and his grocer very likely have the same income, but they are not equivalent persons. . . .*
>
> *Of course it is obvious now that the upper-middle class is done for. . . . But before the war the upper-middle class, though already none too prosperous, still felt sure of itself.*
>
> *Before the war you were either a gentleman or not a gentleman, and if you were a gentleman you struggled to behave as such, whatever your income might be. . . . Probably the distinguishing mark of the upper-middle class was that its traditions were not to any extent commercial, but mainly military, official, and professional. People in this class owned no land, but they felt that they were landowners in the sight of God and kept up a semi-aristocratic outlook by going into the professions and the fighting services rather than into trade. . . . To belong to this class when you were at the £400 a year level was a queer business, for it meant that your gentility was almost purely theoretical. You lived, so to speak, at two levels simultaneously. Theoretically you knew all about servants and how to tip them, although in practice you had one or, at most, two resident servants. Theoretically you knew how to wear your clothes and how to order a dinner, although in practice you could never afford to go to a decent tailor or a decent restaurant. . . . Practically the whole family income goes in keeping up the appearances.*[8]

In Weber's *political order* people are stratified according to the power they possess to influence the course of society. The groups in this order, called parties, tend to be well organized and aimed toward specific goals. A party may represent the interests of one or more classes or status groups as they attempt to influence each other and government policies. To gain and exercise power parties may use violence or more subtle methods, such as propaganda, hired lobbyists, and political payoffs.[9]

Wealth, status, and power are often closely related. At Yale College in the 1800s, for example, the sons of the wealthy were educated for such prestigious professions as law and theology.

Weber illustrated that an individual or group can be in a high stratum in one order and in lower strata of the other orders. Thus a person may have high status in the view of others without possessing wealth or power. Or an individual may be very wealthy but not have power or honor.

Alternatively, we see in "The Diamond as Big as the Ritz," a short story by F. Scott Fitzgerald, that people can possess consistent amounts of wealth, status, and power. The main character, John, is invited by a school chum, Percy, to visit his family. John quickly discovers that his friend's family is the "richest" in the world. In fact, the family château is built on a mountain of solid diamond!

> "Percy, Percy—before you go, I want to apologize."
> "For what?"
> "For doubting you when you said you had a diamond as big as the Ritz-Carlton Hotel."
> Percy smiled.
> "I thought you didn't believe me. It's that mountain, you know."
> "What mountain?"
> "The mountain the château rests on. It's not very big for a mountain. But except about fifty feet of sod and gravel on top it's solid diamond. One diamond, one cubic mile without a flaw. Aren't you listening? Say—". . .
>
> By the end of a fortnight he had estimated that the diamond in the mountain was approximately equal in quantity to all the rest of the diamonds known to exist in the world. There was no valuing it by any regular computation, however, for it was one solid diamond— and if it were offered for sale not only would the bottom fall out of

the market, but also, if the value should vary with its size in the usual arithmetical progression, there would not be enough gold in the world to buy a tenth part of it. . . .

He was, in one sense, the richest man that ever lived.[10]

Not surprisingly, John is awed by the wealth of Percy's family, and he immediately looks upon possessing such treasures as an honor. In John's eyes, the family has the highest "status" in the world. Fitzgerald writes:

"I was reading in the World Almanac," began John, "that there was one man in America with an income of over five million a year and four men with incomes of over three million a year, and—"

"Oh, they're nothing," Percy's mouth was a half-moon of scorn. "Catch-penny capitalists, financial small-fry, petty merchants and money-lenders. My father could buy them out and not know he'd done it."

"But how does he—"

"Why haven't they put down his income tax? Because he doesn't pay any. At least he pays a little one—but he doesn't pay any on his real income."

"He must be very rich," said John simply. "I'm glad. I like very rich people.

"The richer a fella is, the better I like him."[11]

It is only a short while before John realizes that the family is also the most "powerful" in the world. The father and grandfather had manipulated and corrupted officials so that outsiders could not discover the mountain made of diamond. As Fitzgerald puts it:

"Are we in Canada?"

"We are not. We're in the middle of the Montana Rockies. But you are now on the only five square miles of land in the country that's never been surveyed."

"Why hasn't it? Did they forget it?"

"No," said Percy, grinning, "they tried to do it three times. The first time my grandfather corrupted a whole department of the State survey; the second time he had the official maps of the United States tinkered with—that held them for fifteen years. The last time was harder. My father fixed it so that their compasses were in the strongest magnetic field ever artificially set up. He had a whole set of surveying instruments made with a slight defection that would allow for this territory not to appear, and he substituted them for the ones that were to be used. Then he had a river deflected and he had what looked like a village built up on its banks—so that they'd see it, and think it was a town ten miles farther up the valley."[12]

The Functional Necessity of Stratification

Why is it that all societies have stratification systems? Although there is no answer on which all sociologists would agree, some have maintained that stratification is necessary for human survival—that if we did not stratify people into particular ranks, important societal jobs would never be accomplished. The views of sociologists Kingsley Davis and Wilbert E. Moore clearly illustrate this perspective. Their argument may be summarized as follows:

1. Certain positions are more important for a society's survival than others and require special skills. In most societies the occupations of ruler, teacher, physician, and priest are considered vital.
2. Only a select few in society have the "talent" (intelligence, energy, and leadership ability) to perform in these more important positions.
3. To convert these talents into usable skills involves both training (extensive education) and sacrifice (loss of time and money).
4. To motivate talented people to endure training and sacrifice, society must give these individuals additional rewards. The rewards given to people are of three types—sustenance and comfort (high income, company cars, big homes), humor and diversion (vacations and leisure time), and self-respect and ego-expansion (large offices and status titles).
5. Social inequality, which involves some strata receiving more societal rewards than others, is thus both inevitable and essential. It is the means by which society can "insure that the most important positions are conscientiously filled by the most qualified persons."[13]

The view of stratification that Davis and Moore present is a form of *functional theory*, which holds that social phenomena are best understood in terms of how they function or contribute to other parts of the social system or the entire system. Thus Davis and Moore maintain that stratification contributes to the larger society by insuring that important jobs are accomplished. For example, an assembly-line worker receives lesser rewards than a company president because the worker's services are presumably less critical to the society's survival than those of the company president.

While functional theory offers one answer to the question of why societies have stratification systems, conflict theory offers another. *Conflict theory* asserts that stratification exists because those who already possess extensive property and income—the upper classes—simply wish to protect and perpetuate their positions. In a sense, the rich and powerful are the creators and exploiters of institutionalized social inequality. Whereas functional theory views society as a group whose members work together

Although training and education are needed for certain important positions in society, it may be argued that attending an exclusive university is hardly a "sacrifice."

harmoniously, conflict theory asserts that the masses are dissatisfied with their condition. Society is seen as an arena wherein people and groups compete for rewards.

One conflict theorist, Melvin M. Tumin, has responded quite specifically to the Davis-Moore stratification thesis. He contends that many possible meanings can be given to the notion of "functionally important positions" in society. In the long run, garbage collectors and electricians may be just as important to the survival of a society as doctors and lawyers. What a society must concern itself with is adequate motivation for all its members. Tumin then goes on to challenge the idea that only a select few have the talent to perform important jobs. Surely, much talent is never discovered in rigidly stratified societies because those in the lower levels have been deprived of opportunities to develop fully. How many potential Albert Einsteins have gone undiscovered because they were members of the lower strata?

Tumin maintains that members of the higher strata are merely offering a rationalization for their own privileged position when they say that the "talented" undergo much "training and sacrifice."[14] It is certainly not a sacrifice for an upper-class person to attend exclusive prep schools and universities. The satisfying conditions that accompany such a situation—personal prestige and contact with influential people, for instance—far outweigh any so-called sacrifice.

Tumin also asserts that money and status are not the only ways of motivating people. Conceivably, societies could utilize concepts such as "service to others," "personal satisfaction," or "duty to society" to ensure that people accomplish important work tasks. He is aware that these motivational schemes may seem idealistic, but he argues that they are theoretically possible.

Finally, Tumin maintains that stratification negatively affects the thinking of lower-class members. Poor people can become so frustrated that they feel helpless to improve their condition. And members at the bottom of the social ladder can develop negative self-images and feelings of suspicion, hostility, and disloyalty toward the larger society.

Obviously, Tumin sees several dysfunctional aspects to stratification.[15] And he has made some compelling arguments against the rigid functionalist interpretation of stratification.

Several facts about American life indicate that a functional explanation of stratification does not accurately describe our society. For example, the theory assumes that everyone has an equal opportunity to achieve a high-status position in society; of course, such is not the case in the United States. Accidents of birth often contribute to giving some individuals greater opportunity to become corporation executives, United States senators, or medical doctors—all highly valued positions. The functional theory of stratification further assumes that a quality education is available to all citizens, but again it is quite apparent that there is considerable inequality in the American educational system. A ghetto child rarely receives as good an education as a child from an exclusive part of town. (See chapter 10 for a discussion of the inequality of schooling in the United States and reasons for it.) Additionally, functionalists seem to assume that society is open and that members attain positions on the basis of achievement, but in American society race, sex, and other factors certainly influence a person's chances for a reasonably satisfying life.

Social Mobility

Horizontal social mobility refers to movement by individuals or groups from one position to another in society which does not involve a shift into a higher or lower stratum. For example, in American society horizontal social mobility occurs when a Baptist becomes a Methodist or an electrician becomes a carpenter. Shifting takes place, but society does not consider the individual's or group's new position as deserving of a higher or lower rank.

Of greater importance to the sociologist than horizontal movements in society are movements up or down the social ladder. This would occur, for instance, when a tenant farmer inherits a large sum of money or an investor loses all her money in an economic depression. Movement of individuals or groups into either a higher or a lower stratum of society is called *vertical social mobility*. In Western societies the desire of members of the lower and middle classes to move to a higher station in life has sometimes led them to act in rather bizarre ways. For example, in "London Recreations" Charles Dickens describes how many middle-class people in eighteenth-century England imitated the upper class with the hope that they too would become aristocratic.

These poor people in Colombia, South America, have little chance of moving to a higher social standing. There are few occupational opportunities, and lack of skills and education inhibit upward mobility.

The wish of persons in the humbler classes of life to ape the manners and customs of those whom fortune has placed above them, is often the subject of remark, and not unfrequently of complaint. The inclination may, and no doubt does, exist to a great extent, among the small gentility — the would-be aristocrats — of the middle classes. Tradesmen and clerks, with fashionable novel-reading families, and circulating-library-subscribing daughters, get up small assemblies in humble imitation of Almack's, and promenade the dingy "large room" of some second-rate hotel with as much complacency as the enviable few who are privileged to exhibit their magnificence in that

exclusive haunt of fashion and foolery. Aspiring young ladies, who read flaming accounts of some "fancy fair in high life," suddenly grow desperately charitable; visions of admiration and matrimony float before their eyes . . .[16]

When people move up or down the social scale, they may travel through one or many strata. Individuals who increase their yearly income from $10,000 to $30,000 obviously do not move up as many strata as those who increase their yearly income from $10,000 to $300,000. Acquiring wealth and property is the major means of moving up in modern societies, but other channels are open. Entering an occupation with high honor (Supreme Court justice), receiving a Ph.D. degree, or marrying into an aristocratic family are a few such channels.

Very little vertical social mobility is possible in a *closed society*. Colombia and India provide examples of such societies. In contrast, an *open society* allows for greater vertical social mobility. However, even in open societies people cannot move from one stratum to another without resistance. Every society has established criteria — which might be proper manners, family lineage, education, or racial affiliation — that must be satisfied before people can move to a higher social level.

Most open societies tend to be highly industrialized. As societies industrialize, new skills are demanded and occupations are created that were previously unnecessary. New occupations mean more opportunities for wage earners: manual laborers can become semi-skilled factory workers, for example. Additionally, urbanization contributes to vertical social mobility because ascriptive criteria become less important in the anonymity of the city. People become achievement oriented, competitive, and status-striving. In industrial societies governments also begin to narrow the range of inequality by providing unemployment benefits, welfare programs, and old-age and health insurance. In brief, many factors in modern society tend to stimulate upward social mobility.[17]

Stratification in American Society

ECONOMIC INEQUALITY

The bulk of corporate stock in the United States, approximately 60 to 80 percent, is owned by less than 1 percent of the population.* In addition, the top 20 percent of American families receive about 41 percent of all the

*See Gerhard Lenski, *Power and Privilege: A Theory of Social Stratification* (New York: McGraw-Hill, 1966), for a discussion of status inconsistency.

Poverty is strikingly evident in many of our central cities. Slum dwellers are crowded into inadequate, often unsafe housing, from which there is little escape besides sitting on the front steps or playing in the street, and the search for a job is frequently in vain.

available income, a huge and disproportionate share of earnings compared with the rest of the society.[18] These income distribution figures have changed very little since World War II. Many contend, moreoever, that these figures do not adequately represent the real income of the wealthiest people in America. The rich are said to have much more income than is publicly known since they illegally use expense accounts, fail to declare gifts, and employ shrewd lawyers to find tax loopholes.*
In the United States, then, wealth is unequally distributed and an economic elite exists at the top of society.

It is an unfortunate irony that in the wealthiest nation that has ever existed, poverty is a fact of life for many. Of the 25.5 million Americans that the government says are now impoverished, certain groups seem to be particularly hard hit.[19] For example, the poverty rate for blacks is three times higher than that for whites.[20] Old people also make up a large segment of the poor. Retirement plans and Social Security benefits seldom provide enough income for an adequate living. In addition, husbandless women with children and physically disabled people are frequently victims of poverty.

Many middle- and upper-class individuals contend that laziness is the major reason why people are poor. That explanation is unsupported,

*See Gabriel Kolko, *Wealth and Power* in *America* (New York: Praeger, 1962) for a discussion of the practices used by the rich to avoid taxes.

however, since most poor people either lack the education, skills, and abilities necessary for good jobs or cannot work because of physical impairment or old age. Only a major redistribution of wealth will eliminate poverty in the United States. But a drastic restructuring of society is not likely in the near future since well-to-do Americans have a vested interest in maintaining the status quo.

STATUS INEQUALITY

Most of us seek status, prestige, honor, or esteem from our companions. In a story entitled "Being Refined," William Saroyan describes how his relatives, new immigrants to America, tried to win the respect of their new associates:

> Being refined is a very nice thing, and I have had some happy times noticing refinement in the members of my family, most of whom, especially those who were born in the old country, in Bitlis, finally learned that vocal modulation, for instance, constituted one of the many signs of being refined. Shouting was all right in the family, but out among Americans and people like that it was always a good idea to modulate the voice, at least until you found out that the Americans themselves weren't very refined. . . .

Another good sign of being refined was to look at a painting and not have your mouth hanging open in wonder because the fruit on the plate seemed so real you wanted to reach out and take some, which was pretty much the way paintings were appreciated by the immigrants who had only recently arrived in America.

Still another good idea was not to ask priests difficult questions about God, or biology, or about a stick becoming a snake, or a body of water dividing itself so that there would be a dry road running through it, or a dead man coming to life. Asking such questions really didn't demonstrate that you were an intelligent man, or that you had safely emerged from the Dark Ages, or that you knew how to think for yourself; all it seemed to do was make refined people look at you sideways, cockeyed-like, by which they meant that you must be some sort of unrefined person.[21]

Many factors combine to determine the status an individual holds in society—education, occupation, income, and racial and ethnic affiliation, among others. For most individuals, these factors are linked in an expected way. Thus one would presume a corporation executive (holding a high-prestige occupation) to be college educated (have a high-level education). Some individuals, however, experience *status inconsistency*, which occurs when there is some disparity among the factors that determine a person's rank in society. The black doctor in America, for example, may experience status inconsistency since his occupational group is highly respected by society, but his racial affiliation is considered undesirable by some. Inconsistencies of status can be a source of considerable strain for the individual and have been linked to alcoholism, drug abuse, and suicide.*

Occupation is probably the most important component of status for most Americans. Upon first meeting people and exchanging greetings, we usually ask, "What do you do?" After the response, depending on the attributes and prestige of the person's occupation, we may act humble, intelligent, disrespectful, or fearful. Americans have tended to agree in their ratings of the prestige of occupations, and these views are consistent over time.

In two studies conducted by the National Opinion Research Center, ninety occupations were rated for their prestige by a national sample. The results, given in Table 7-1, show that the ratings in 1947 and 1963 were much the same. One of the few changes was that scientific occupations increased in prestige, a fact that may indicate the growing significance of "science" to Americans. It may also be inferred from the table that various factors influence our ranking of occupations. We often think that economic reward is the only factor affecting the esteem given to occupations,

---

*Both Robert J. Lampman, *The Share of Top Wealth-Holders in National Wealth, 1922–1956* (Princeton, N.J.: Princeton University Press, 1962), and G. William Domhoff, "The Power Elite," *The Center Magazine*, 3 (March 1970), give evidence supporting these figures.

TABLE 7-1
Occupational Prestige Ratings, 1963 and 1947

Occupation	1963 Score	1947 Score	Occupation	1963 Score	1947 Score
U.S. Supreme Court Justice	94	96	Newspaper columnist	73	74
Physician	93	93	Policeman	72	67
Nuclear physicist	92	86	Reporter on a daily newspaper	71	71
Scientist	92	89	Radio announcer	70	75
Government scientist	91	88	Bookkeeper	70	68
State governor	91	93	Tenant farmer—one who owns livestock and machinery and manages the farm	69	68
Cabinet member in the Federal Gov't.	90	92			
College professor	90	89			
U.S. Representative in Congress	90	89	Insurance agent	69	68
Chemist	89	86	Carpenter	68	65
Lawyer	89	86	Manager of a small store in a city	67	69
Diplomat in U.S. Foreign Service	89	92	A local official of a labor union	67	62
Dentist	88	86	Mail carrier	66	66
Architect	88	86	Railroad conductor	66	67
County judge	88	87	Traveling salesman for a wholesale concern	66	68
Psychologist	87	85			
Minister	87	87	Plumber	65	63
Member of the board of directors of a large corporation	87	86	Automobile repairman	64	63
			Playground director	63	67
Mayor of a large city	87	90	Barber	63	59
Priest	86	86	Machine operator in a factory	63	60
Head of a dept. in state government	86	87	Owner-operator of a lunch stand	63	62
Civil engineer	86	84	Corporal in the regular army	62	60
Airline pilot	86	83	Garage mechanic	62	62
Banker	85	88	Truck driver	59	54
Biologist	85	81	Fisherman who owns his own boat	58	58
Sociologist	83	82	Clerk in a store	56	58
Instructor in public schools	82	79	Milk route man	56	54
Captain in the regular army	82	80	Streetcar motorman	56	58
Accountant for a large business	81	81	Lumberjack	55	53
Public school teacher	81	78	Restaurant cook	55	54
Owner of a factory that employs about 100 people	80	82	Singer in a nightclub	54	52
			Filling station attendant	51	52
Building contractor	80	79	Dockworker	50	47
Artist who paints pictures that are exhibited in galleries	78	83	Railroad section hand	50	48
			Night watchman	50	47
Musician in a symphony orchestra	78	81	Coal miner	50	49
Author of novels	78	80	Restaurant waiter	49	48
Economist	78	79	Taxi driver	49	49
Official of an international labor union	77	75	Farm hand	48	50
			Janitor	48	44
Railroad engineer	76	76	Bartender	48	44
Electrician	76	73	Clothes presser in a laundry	45	46

Continued

SOURCE: Robert W. Hodge, Paul M. Siegel, and Peter H. Rossi, "Occupational Prestige in the United States: 1925–1963," *American Journal of Sociology*, 70 (November 1964): 286–302.

TABLE 7-1 Continued

Occupation	1963 Score	1947 Score	Occupation	1963 Score	1947 Score
County agricultural agent	76	77	Soda fountain clerk	44	45
Owner-operator of a printing shop	75	74	Share-cropper—one who owns no livestock or equipment and does not manage farm	42	40
Trained machinist	75	73			
Farm owner and operator	74	76			
Undertaker	74	72	Garbage collector	39	35
Welfare worker for a city government	74	73	Street sweeper	36	34
			Shoe shiner	34	33
			Average	71	70

but education, responsibility, cleanliness of work, power over others, and aesthetic aspects also influence prestige ratings. The seventeenth-ranked occupation of minister is one illustration of a job that is rated high because of factors other than income.

Many studies have examined prestige in small American communities.* The results indicate that most Americans tend to use the same or similar criteria to rank others. Researchers usually discovered an upper-upper prestige group, its members distinguished by aristocratic family lineage, wealth, proper manners, and homes in the best part of town. Ranked below this group was a lower-upper prestige group with even more wealth than the upper-upper group but lacking aristocratic family heritage. Members of the lower-upper group were considered *nouveau riche* (a French phrase referring to individuals with newly acquired wealth but without noble family heritage) and seldom associated with the community elite. The remaining residents were generally ranked on the basis of occupation and related factors. They had less prestigious jobs than members of the two upper groups, were less wealthy and well educated, and lived in less desirable neighborhoods. The lowest-ranked members of the community were not only poor but usually considered immoral.

Although these studies give us some indication of how Americans rank one another, we should be cautious in assuming that *all* people agree on

*These studies include Robert and Helen Lynd, *Middletown* (New York: Harcourt, Brace, 1929) and *Middletown in Transition* (New York: Harcourt, Brace, 1937). Other studies describe "Yankee City" (Newburyport, Mass.): W. L. Warner and P. L. Lunt, *The Social Life of a Modern Community* (New Haven, Conn.: Yale University Press, 1941) and *The Status System of a Modern Community* (New Haven, Conn.: Yale University Press, 1942); W. L. Warner and Leo Srole, *The Social Systems of American Ethnic Groups* (New Haven, Conn.: Yale University Press, 1945); and W. L. Warner and J. O. Low, *The Social System of a Modern Factory* (New Haven, Conn.: Yale University Press, 1947). Some describe "Jonesville," "Elmstown," "Hometown," or "Prairie City" (Morris, Ill.): W. L. Warner, R. J. Havighurst, and M. L. Loeb, *Who Shall Be Educated* (New York: Harper, 1944); W. L. Warner and Associates, *Democracy in Jonesville* (New York: Harper, 1949); W. L. Warner, M. Meeker, and K. Eels, *Social Class in America* (Chicago: Science Research Associates, 1949). Finally, James West, *Plainville, U.S.A.* (New York: Columbia University Press, 1945), and A. B. Hollingshead, *Elmstown Youth* (New York: John Wiley, 1949), are further studies.

what criteria determine prestige. Racial, political, religious, educational, and geographical subcultures can differ in the emphasis they place on what is important and deserving of honor.

POWER INEQUALITY

Pluralist theory maintains that power in American society is equally distributed among many diverse organized interest groups, sometimes called veto groups because of this distribution of power. Business associations, organized racial and ethnic groups, labor unions, farmers, religions, and other groups maneuver and pressure each other to protect and advance their particular interests. These groups, which supposedly represent the will of the masses, in a sense check one another's power so that no one group dominates the entire society.[22]

Many have criticized the pluralist view of power, most notably C. Wright Mills. According to Mills, one group in American society, a *power elite*, dominates and controls the major aspects of life. This elite is composed of select business people, politicians, and military leaders. These individuals have similar backgrounds, views about the world, and vested interests to maintain. They shape the entire society by deciding on broad and important policies, such as interest rates on loans, levels of production and employment, international trade agreements, income tax laws, military commitments, and so on, while the trivial issues are left to others.*

Mills described the power elite as an inner circle or an interlocking directorate that exists at the top of society. Below this elite is a middle level of interest groups with power over minor issues. At the lowest level of society are the unorganized masses, who have no power. According to Mills, members of the power elite continue to increase their influence over society and to manipulate the masses. Members are so powerful that they can no longer be held accountable for their decisions.[23]

Mills's thesis has considerable support, but the debate between the two views, pluralist theory versus the power elite thesis, will not be resolved in the near future.† Citizens will continue to see national power in terms of their preconceived notions of American politics. An active member of the National Farmers Organization, National Council of Christians and Jews, or Young Democrats may feel that she can eventually change the direction of society, while the apathetic citizen, saturated with news of political wheeling and dealing, may feel, "What's the use of trying since the big boys will do what they want anyway." (See chapter 11 for additional discussion of decision-making in American society.)

---

*For a comparison of pluralist power theory and power elite theory, see William Kornhauser, "Power Elite or Veto Groups?" in *Class, Status, and Power*, Bendix and Lipset, eds., pp. 210–218.

†Both Floyd Hunter, *Top Leadership, U.S.A.* (Chapel Hill: University of North Carolina Press, 1959), and G. William Domhoff, *Who Rules America?* (Englewood Cliffs, N.J.: Prentice-Hall, 1967), support the power elite view of American society.

VERTICAL SOCIAL MOBILITY

Studies of *intergenerational mobility* provide clues about the amount and direction of vertical social mobility in the United States. These studies have compared the occupations of fathers and their sons at similar career points in their lives. The findings indicate that there is substantial mobility in our society and that more of it is upward than downward.[24] Although this information could be interpreted to mean that anyone can go from "rags to riches," we should take care not to reach a hasty and false conclusion.

First, consider that the rate of mobility in American society is actually no higher than that in most other industrialized societies. Seymour Lipset and Hans Zetterberg found mobility rates to be approximately the same in West Germany, Sweden, Japan, France, Switzerland, Great Britain, and the United States.[25]

Second, opportunities for occupational improvement are good mainly for members of the middle class. Because of the socioeconomic standing of their families, middle-class individuals are the recipients of more and better education, which is the major factor enabling Americans to advance in their careers.[26] In contrast, members of the lower class are inhibited in career advancement not only by their lack of education but also by the many hurdles and subsequent frustrations they encounter repeatedly in everyday life. Herbert Gans discovered that lower-class individuals think of work as boring, undesirable, and transitory — something to be engaged in only to avoid poverty. He further found that they are action- or thrill-seeking, have short-term goals, and are motivated toward neither formal education nor job success.[27] Such outlooks are understandable when one considers that most poor neighborhoods are burdened by inadequate schools, insufficient jobs, and other dehumanizing conditions.

Third, when children in this country do improve on the occupational status of their parents, they usually move no higher than one stratum. Contrary to popular belief, seldom does the son or daughter of an unskilled worker become a medical doctor, lawyer, or other professional.

Fourth, people tend to think only about those who move up the occupational ladder and forget that some also move down that ladder. A general economic slowdown or an oversupply of labor in a particular industry can suddenly plunge many workers into lower-paying jobs.

Evidently, the rags-to-riches belief is unfounded as a general principle. The stories of Horatio Alger, the nineteenth-century writer whose characters always went from poverty to success by hard work plus a bit of luck, would not ring true in contemporary American society.

Some groups in American society have had virtually no chance for upward mobility. David Matza suggests that such groups include racial or ethnic minorities for whom poverty has become a way of life, new immi-

STRATIFICATION / 163

Although some members of American society, such as Abraham Lincoln (shown here), have moved from poverty to fame, the notion that any citizen can reach the top — be it fame or fortune — is generally unfounded.

grants without funds and work skills, skid-row alcoholics and drug addicts, and physically handicapped and elderly individuals who cannot escape their impoverishment. Members of these groups are plagued by high rates of unemployment, divorce, desertion, mental illness, illegitimate children, and criminal arrests and convictions. They have been left behind by the rest of society and, unfortunately, lack any real chance to escape their situation. It appears that there is a class of people in the United States who are truly outsiders to the workings of modern industrial life.[28]

CLASS CONSCIOUSNESS

According to Marx, workers under capitalism eventually develop a class consciousness. John Steinbeck in *The Grapes of Wrath* shows us how Americans might develop such an awareness. He portrays this development as the movement from "I" to "we":

The two men squat on their hams and the women and children listen. Here is the node, you who hate change and fear revolution. Keep these two squatting men apart; make them hate, fear, suspect each other. Here is the anlage of the thing you fear. This is the zygote. For here "I lost my land" is changed; a cell is split and from its splitting grows the thing you hate—"We lost our land." The danger is here, for two men are not as lonely and perplexed as one. And from this first "we" there grows a still more dangerous thing: "I have a little food" plus "I have none," the thing is on its way, the movement has direction. Only a little multiplication now, and this land, this tractor are ours. . . . This is the beginning—from "I" to "we."[29]

Middle- and working-class Americans have demonstrated little or none of the class consciousness Steinbeck described. Few realize their common economic interests and political powerlessness, and few regard the rich and super-rich as an enemy class. There are many reasons for this lack of awareness. First, members of the middle class and to a lesser extent those in the lower classes have been able to possess some material objects. For example, blue-collar workers may have low-status jobs, but frequently their pay or credit rating is high enough to allow them to purchase such items as boats, furs, and sports cars. Possession of these material objects tends to obscure class lines. Second, the major political parties seldom try to identify solely with the interests of one class. The Democratic and Republican parties seek support from all levels of society and attempt to represent the interests of various groups. Third, American society is extremely heterogeneous, that is, composed of many diverse groups. Blacks, Navajos, Appalachian whites, Catholics, Southerners, farmers, auto workers, and others often have different interests and views. The differences among these groups inhibit the development of class awareness. Fourth, individualism is highly valued in our society. Seldom are societal problems and institutions seen as the cause of a person's failure. The combination of all these factors makes it appear unlikely that class consciousness will develop among lower- and middle-class workers or that a class-based revolution will occur in the near future.

Chapter Summary

Every society has a system of social stratification, or institutionalized social inequality. Different societies base their stratification systems on different dimensions, but occupation, education, wealth, religion, and family heritage are frequently important. The norms, beliefs, and values of a society legitimize, justify, and give stability to its stratification system.

There are three major types of stratification systems. Caste systems consist of strata arranged in a fixed order of superiority-inferiority, and individuals born into one stratum must remain there for life. Estate systems, with a land-based economy, also have somewhat fixed strata, but individuals have more opportunity to move into another stratum. A class system emphasizes personal achievement. Each of its strata, called social classes, usually consists of members with approximately equal income, education, and occupational prestige.

In the debate over class society, Marx argued that economic forces give rise to social classes and that class struggle is inevitable. In contrast, Weber maintained that people are stratified according to status and power as well as economic well-being. Weber's contention that workers might not develop a class consciousness was also in disagreement with Marx.

There is no answer on which all sociologists would agree as to why all societies are stratified. Functional theorists such as Davis and Moore argue that stratification is necessary to the survival of a society. If social classes did not exist, important societal jobs would not be accomplished. Conflict theorists such as Tumin assert that stratification exists because the wealthy desire to protect their material interests. Consequently, they exploit the masses.

Vertical social mobility occurs when people move either to a higher or lower stratum in society. Acquiring more income, moving into a prestigious occupation, achieving more education, and marrying into a higher social class are possible channels for upward movement. An open society experiences a considerable amount of vertical social mobility, while a closed society does not.

In American society there is considerable income inequality. At the top of society is an economic elite and at the bottom are millions of impoverished citizens. Those most affected by poverty include blacks, old people, husbandless women with dependent children, and the disabled. Considerable status inequality also exists in American society. We assign different prestige to our associates according to their occupation, education, family lineage, and wealth. Finally, power also appears to be unequally distributed in American society. According to C. Wright Mills, a power elite—composed of select business people, military officials, and politicians—makes the broad policy decisions affecting us all. Pluralists, on the other hand, disagree and maintain that major decisions affecting society are decided by diverse veto groups—business associations, farmers, labor unions, racial and ethnic groups, and so on. According to pluralists, power is equally balanced among these groups so that no single group dominates decision-making.

The existence of such inequalities belies the notion that any American can go from "rags to riches." In fact, only members of the middle class have a good chance of moving to a higher position in life, and when they do move up the social ladder, it is usually only one stratum. In addition, many Americans are downwardly mobile during periods of economic slowdown. And, undoubtedly, some groups, such as new immigrants without funds and work skills, have virtually no chance for upward mobility.

Despite the existence of inequalities, little class consciousness has developed among American workers, and a class-based revolution is unlikely. Class lines between rich and poor can sometimes be difficult to distinguish. Additionally, the structure of our major political parties, the heterogeneity of our society, and the belief in individualism are factors that inhibit the development of class awareness.

In the late 1800s Victorian poet Matthew Arnold stated: "Inequality has the natural and necessary effect, under the present circumstances, of materializing our upper class, vulgarizing our middle class, and brutalizing our lower class."[30] Many would maintain that his statement describes much about twentieth-century America.

Key Terms for Review

bourgeoisie, p. 146
caste system, p. 143
class consciousness, p. 146
class-for-itself, p. 146
class-in-itself, p. 146
class system, p. 145
closed society, p. 155
conflict theory, p. 151
economic order, p. 147
estate system, p. 144
functional theory, p. 151
horizontal social mobility, p. 153
intergenerational mobility, p. 162

objective class, p. 146
open society, p. 155
pluralist theory, p. 161
political order, p. 148
power elite, p. 161
proletariat, 146
social class, p. 146
social order, p. 147
social strata, p. 143
social stratification, p. 143
status inconsistency, p. 158
subjective class, p. 146
vertical social mobility, p. 153

Suggested Readings

SOCIOLOGICAL

Bendix, Reinhard, and Seymour Martin Lipset. *Class, Status, and Power*. New York: Free Press, 1966. This anthology includes many excellent readings. The contributions cover theories of stratification, the functionalist debate, stratification in other societies, power and status relations, life chances and life styles, social mobility, and unresolved issues in stratification.

Dahrendorf, Ralf. *Class and Class Conflict in Industrial Society*. Stanford, Calif.: Stanford University Press, 1959. The author gives an excellent analysis of Marx's class theory. He also discusses his own theory of stratification and applies it to postcapitalist society.

Lopreato, Joseph, and Lionel S. Lewis. *Social Stratification: A Reader*. New York: Harper & Row, 1974. This volume emphasizes the areas of power, class consciousness, and social mobility. Particular attention is given to the theoretical statements of Karl Marx and the issue of social class and race.

LITERARY

Crane, Stephen. "An Experiment in Luxury." In Thomas A. Gullason, ed. *The Complete Short Stories and Sketches of Stephen Crane*, pp. 147–154. Garden City, N.Y.: Doubleday, 1963. The character in this short story finds that the rich are not unhappy and anxiety-ridden, as some people are led to believe. He discovers that wealth opens many doors and provides liberty for its possessors.

Fitzgerald, F. Scott. *The Great Gatsby*. New York: Scribner's, 1925. The novel is often considered Fitzgerald's best. Gatsby was a poor boy who made it rich but was never secure in his new status. The character displays the anxieties associated with a newly acquired status and the "on the make" mentality of many individuals.

Lewis, Sinclair. *Babbitt*. New York: Harcourt, Brace, 1922. Written with wit and sarcasm, the novel attacks the conformity, shallowness, and pettiness of middle-class America. Lewis aptly describes the status-striving and status frustration of the middle class.

Sinclair, Upton. *The Jungle*. New York: Signet, 1973; orig. 1906. This work is a powerful muckraking novel describing lower-class life in the Chicago stockyards during the early 1900s. The poverty, disease, depravity, and despair of the lower classes are brought to life.

Steinbeck, John. *The Grapes of Wrath*. New York: Bantam, 1970. The author writes an exciting and melodramatic novel about dispossessed Americans during the Great Depression. His vivid descriptions illustrate the frustrations of lower-class members.

Wharton, Edith. *The Age of Innocence*. New York: Modern Library, 1948. The moral decline of the aristocratic upper class and the abrasive practices of the new industrialists are described in this novel.

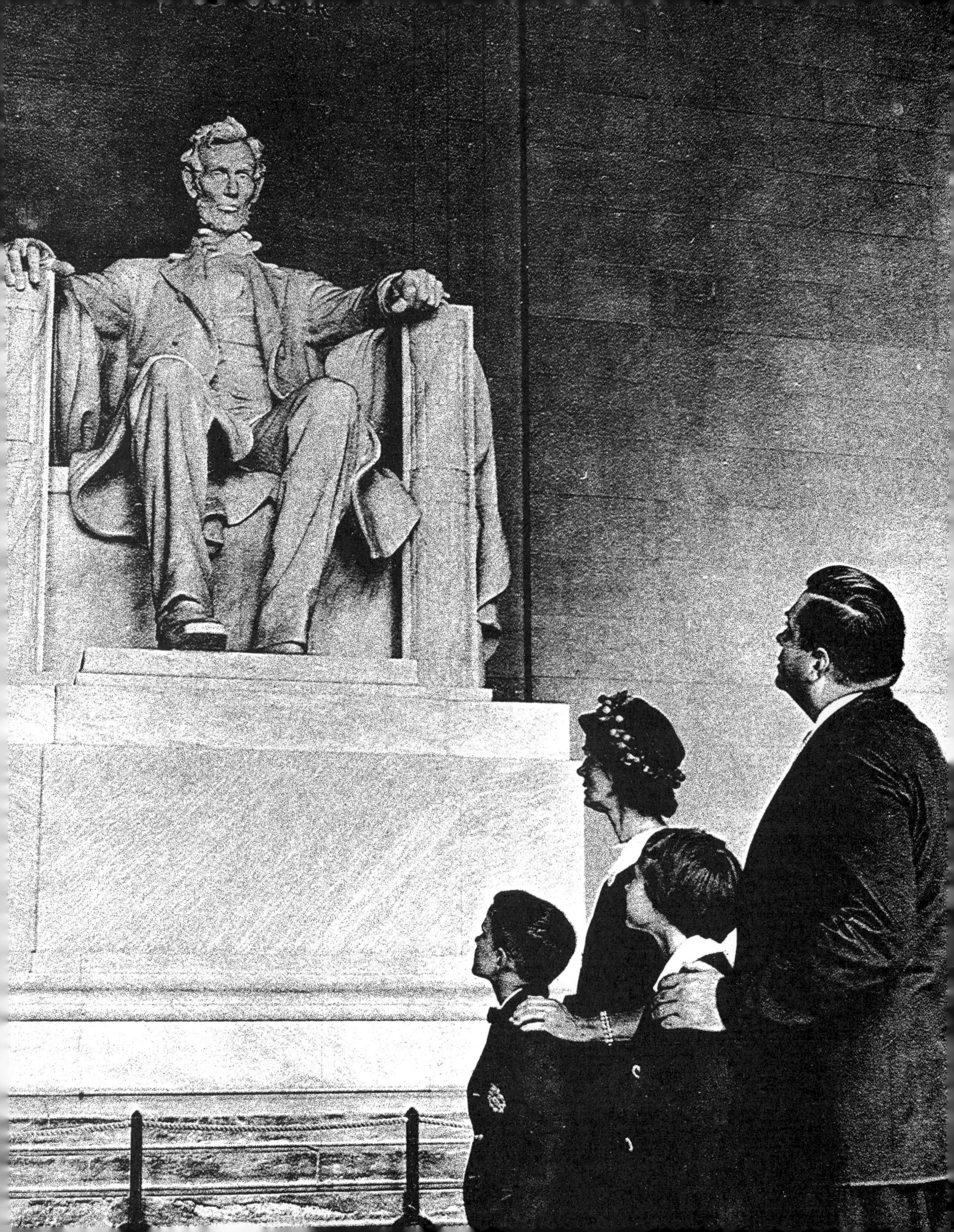

part three

INSTITUTIONS

Institutions develop as ways of dealing with a society's concerns. For example, the institution of the family helps us deal with the problems of reproduction and child-rearing. We also face the task of teaching skills and values to new members of society; the educational institution fills this need. The matter of governing people is handled by the governmental, or political, institution. The institution of religion exists to aid our understanding of the mysteries of life, the unknown and supernatural. And an economic institution is needed to organize the production, distribution, and consumption of goods and services.

An *institution* is an established, relatively enduring, and organized set of procedures that enables a society to solve one or more of its major problems.* Although a university is commonly referred to as an institution, it is more aptly described as an organization with official goals, positions, and rules. All the schools, educational policies and procedures, and teaching topics, styles, and methods within a society make up its educational institution.

Institutions consist of norms. The American political institution, in part, tells people to participate in their democracy by casting a ballot on election day, and our family institution expects that a marriage will include only one husband and one wife at a time. Sanctions arise to enforce these norms. "Stuffing" the ballot box and bigamy are not only frowned upon but condemned by law.

Institutions change with time and vary from society to society. As new problems arise, institutions tend to adapt, though the speed, degree, and direction of this change is always problematic. Many people condemn institutions for lagging behind contemporary realities. The outcry of "God is dead" during the late 1960s illustrates the views of some about one institution. Certain institutions that exist in some societies are absent from others. However, all societies have some form of five basic institutions—family, religion, education, government (or polity), and economy. These institutions are examined in chapters 8, 9, 10, and 11.

*This definition is based on a discussion by R. M. MacIver and Charles H. Page, *Society: An Introductory Analysis* (New York: Holt, Rinehart & Winston, 1962), pp. 15–16.

169

IN THIS CHAPTER

Variations in Family Patterns   171

    Marriage   172
    Dominance   176
    Residence   176
    Descent privileges   176
    Nuclear and extended families   177

Functions of the Family   179

    Reproduction   180
    Regulation of sexual activity   180
    Socialization   181
    Conferral of status   183
    Provision of affection and companionship   185

Family Problems in American Society   185

    Changing sex roles   186
    Economic crisis   190
    Child-rearing   191
    Divorce   192

Nontraditional Family and Marriage Patterns   194

Summary   200

Key Terms for Review   201

Suggested Readings   201

Is the family a dying institution?
Are families around the world pretty much the same?
Have American parents shirked their responsibility toward their children?
Will "communes," "open marriage," and "swinging" replace the traditional family?

FAMILY

Sociologists have always taken special interest in the family institution. This interest is due to the wide variations in family life found throughout the world and the fact that the institution performs crucial functions for both the individual and society. In modern industrial societies the family faces many problems that invite special study, and people today are experimenting with new family and marriage patterns. These developments heighten sociologists' interest in the institution. Variations in family living, the functions of the family, the problems of the modern family, and nontraditional family and marriage patterns are the topics we will explore in this chapter.

Variations in Family Patterns

A *family* is a social group which usually consists of members who are related either through "blood" ties or marriage. Family members are also bound together by legal, moral, and economic rights and duties. Most of us actually belong to two different kinds of family groups during our life. The *family of orientation* in the group in which we are born and reared, and the *family of procreation* is the group we establish when we marry and have children of our own.

Family patterns vary enormously around the world. The Tungus of northwest Asia quiet a baby by tickling its genitals, and the Aborigines of Australia show their reverence for dead relatives by preserving them through a smoking process. Also, among the Tiwi of northern Australia there is never an unmarried female. At birth a female baby is given in marriage, and if her husband dies, she is assigned to a new male. Because of our own ethnocentrism, we may consider such family patterns bizarre or immoral. But, from the viewpoint of those in other societies, the traditional American practice of stigmatizing the illegitimate child may seem equally strange and unacceptable. An examination of family variations will lead us to question our ethnocentric viewpoint and help us to understand family patterns in American society.

MARRIAGE

A systematic discussion of variations in family patterns should begin with a definition of marriage. The cynical and humorous Ambrose Bierce defined marriage as "a community consisting of a master, a mistress, and two slaves, making in all two."[1] Although some sociologists might agree with this view, most approach the relationship in a more scholarly fashion. In the sociological sense, *marriage* is a socially approved sexual and economic relationship between male and female. Obviously, in all societies men and women may engage in sexual acts without incurring economic obligations and may develop economic ties without sex, but a husband and wife are expected to share both sex and economic responsibilities. Additionally, in the eyes of society a husband and wife constitute a legitimate and permanent group and are expected to live together and procreate.

In American society an individual is to be married to only one person at a time. This pattern is called *monogamy*. In fact, most present-day societies practice monogamy, as was shown in George Peter Murdock's study of 200 societies.[2]

In contrast to monogamy, *polygamy* refers to the practice of having several mates at one time. Although many societies have encouraged polygamy as an ideal, few have actually practiced it. Economic considerations account for the infrequency of plural marriages. The wealthy tend to be the only members of a society able to support more than one mate. However, an increasing number of Americans practice *serial monogamy*, a pattern in which the individual has one, two, or more mates during a lifetime, but always one at a time. Several factors account for the increasing frequency of this pattern, including the ease of obtaining a legal divorce and the social acceptability of remarriage.

Polygamy may be further divided into three subtypes. In *cenogamy*, or group marriage, several men and several women form a marriage relationship with one another. This pattern is discouraged in virtually all societies and is rarely found. In *polyandry* one woman is married to two or more men at the same time. This practice is also uncommon, but the Toda of southern India provide one example. When a Toda woman marries a man, she also becomes the wife of all his brothers. Here polyandry results from the shortage of Toda women caused by the institutionalized practice of female infanticide. Finally, in *polygyny*, the most common form of polygamy, one male is married to two or more females at the same time. Since the Islamic religion allows a man to have several wives at one time,

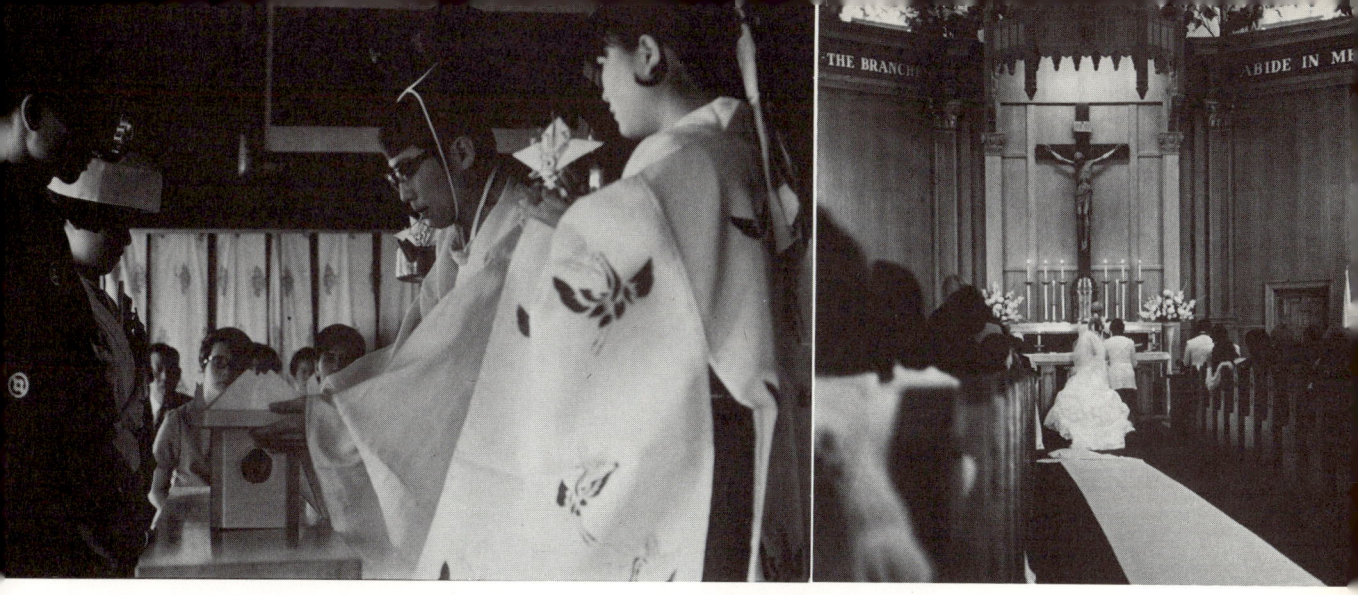

Traditional Shinto and Christian wedding ceremonies. Marriage rites symbolize a legitimate and permanent union between male and female, particularly in sexual and economic matters.

Muslims practice polygyny. Also, Brigham Young, one of the founders of the Mormon church, believed in polygyny and had numerous wives. Although polygyny was officially banned by the Mormons in 1890, one estimate maintains that 35,000 heretical church members in the United States and Mexico still practice that marriage pattern.[3]

In polygyny each wife usually holds a rank in the family and has specific duties to perform, such as cooking, housecleaning, or child-rearing. In *The Adventurous History of Hsi Men and His Six Wives*, Chin P'ng Mei provides a glimpse of the rank and duties of several wives in one such family in sixteenth-century China.

> *Although Moon Lady held first rank among Hsi Men's five wives, her delicate health usually prevented her from fulfilling the obligations imposed by her rank. When visits were to be paid, Li Kiao, the Second Wife, usually took her place. It was Li Kiao, Lady Sunflower, who managed the household budget. Snowblossom, the Fourth Wife, supervised the kitchen and the staff of servants.*[4]

The author also tells a revealing story about a squabble that arose among the wives as they competed for their husband's approval. We see the sources of tension that might exist within a family practicing polygyny.

> *Hsi Men once more spent the night with his favorite, Gold Lotus. In a generous mood, he promised to go immediately after breakfast to the Temple Market to buy Gold Lotus some pearls. When he told Spring Plum to fetch breakfast from the kitchen—ordering lotus-seed tarts and silver carp soup—the little girl suddenly refused. She absolutely would not go to the kitchen.*

174 / INSTITUTIONS

This typical Mormon family (1870s) included a husband, two wives, and numerous children.

Gold Lotus explained to Hsi Men: "There is someone in the kitchen who says I induced the little one to let you have your way with her, which proves that my love for you is mere hypocrisy. This person is trying to strike at me by reviling others. You had better not send the little one to the kitchen. Send Autumn Aster instead."

"Who is this person?"

"The question is superfluous. All the cooking pots in the kitchen are witnesses."

Hsi Men sent Autumn Aster to the kitchen. A long time passed.

"Go and see where that creature is loitering. She must be waiting to watch the grass grow."

Unwillingly Spring Plum obeyed. She found Autumn Aster standing in the kitchen, waiting.

"You naughty girl!" Spring Plum scolded her. . . .

She seized Autumn Aster by the ear, and dragged her out of the kitchen. "I have much more reason to complain of you, you insolent creature!" Snowblossom angrily shouted after her.

"Whether you complain or don't complain, it's all the same to me!" Spring Plum called back. "But you won't succeed in sowing dissension in this house!"

And she rushed off in a fury. Yellow with rage, she dragged Autumn Aster before her mistress.

"What is the matter?" Gold Lotus inquired.

"Ask her! When I came into the kitchen, she was standing about looking on. The other was taking as long to prepare a little breakfast as it takes to make doughnuts. When I told her that the master was in a hurry for his breakfast, that wretch burst out and called me a slave wench, and made other ugly personal remarks, even insulting our master! She seems to think the kitchen is intended for scolding and back-biting instead of for cooking."

"What did I tell you?" cried Gold Lotus, turning to Hsi Men. "We ought not to have sent Spring Plum to the kitchen. That woman tries to quarrel with everybody. She insinuates that Spring Plum and I have appropriated you for ourselves, and won't let you out of our bedchamber. To endure such insults from that woman!"

Her words produced the desired effect. Hsi Men angrily rushed into the kitchen, and kicked Snowblossom repeatedly. . . . Moon Lady, who was having her hair dressed, heard the disturbance in the kitchen, and sent her maid, Little Jewel, to learn the cause of the trouble. Little Jewel came back with the story. . . .

Snowblossom could not get over the treatment she had suffered, and as soon as Hsi Men left the house she went to Moon Lady to vindicate herself. She did not suspect that Gold Lotus was creeping after her, or that she hid herself under the window, where she could overhear everything that Snowblossom said to Moon Lady and to Sunflower, who was also in the room.

"You have no idea what this man-crazy woman, who has monopolized Hsi Men, says and does behind our backs," Gold Lotus heard her declare. "One doesn't blame a woman for carrying on all night with her husband once in a while. But this woman simply can't exist without a man. People like that are capable of anything. Didn't she get rid of her first husband by poisoning him?". . .

Gold Lotus walked in. Looking steadily at her enemy, she began:

"Suppose I really had poisoned my first husband, then you shouldn't have allowed Master Hsi Men to receive me into his household. You would then have reason to complain that I prevent him from enjoying himself with you. . . . But I can go, if you wish; I can simply ask him to give me a letter of divorcement when he comes home."

"I don't really understand what you two have against each other," Moon Lady intervened. "But in any case, if you were all a little more sparing of words, everything would go smoothly."[5]

Society gives us rules as to whom we can marry and not marry. In the preceding selection Hsi Men was a rich man, and for a master to marry a servant or a member of the lower class was unthinkable. All his wives were from a "proper" station in life. Marrying within groups specified by society as acceptable is called *endogamy*. Americans are encouraged to marry someone with a similar class standing and the same religion, and there is strong pressure for whites to marry whites and for blacks to marry blacks. Sometimes endogamous rules are codified into laws. As late as the 1960s, for example, several states had statutes forbidding interracial marriage. In contrast, rules concerning *exogamy* tell us to marry outside a specific group. In the United States these rules apply in particular to close relatives. A son cannot marry his mother, and a brother and sister cannot marry each other. Americans have both endogamous and exogamous rules governing marriage.

DOMINANCE

In our story of the polygynous Chinese family, the most dominant member was unmistakably Hsi Men. In a *patriarchal family* the husband has more power in making decisions, and the wife has little influence except in some aspects of child-rearing. In most societies families are patriarchal, yet there are exceptions. For example, families in Navajo society have traditionally been *matriarchal,* or female-dominated.

In an *equalitarian family* the husband and wife share responsibility and power equally. Economic and family decisions are made jointly. This family pattern is a recent historical development and is found in urban, industrial societies which stress the importance of individualism and personal growth. The American family has traditionally been patriarchal, but the equalitarian relationship is becoming more accepted.

RESIDENCE

Where newlyweds reside varies from society to society. Murdock found four different residential patterns. In a culture with a *patrilocal* residence pattern, a newlywed couple lives with the husband's parents. Where a *matrilocal* pattern prevails, the couple resides with the wife's parents. Under a *bilocal* pattern the couple lives with either the husband's or the wife's parents. And a *neolocal* pattern leaves the husband and wife free to choose a residence away from their parents.

Marital residence can influence family relationships. For example, if a wife lives with her husband's family, she is sometimes treated as a stranger and she tends to have less control over her children. Of course, a husband who lives with his wife's parents faces the same situation. A neolocal pattern generally allows the new family privacy and room for independent development. However, family crises—the death of a member, child-rearing problems, or divorce—must often be met without assistance from close relations. The neolocal pattern is characteristic of American families.

DESCENT PRIVILEGES

Descent privileges are of crucial importance in some societies. They may determine inheritance, authority, or the right of participation in rituals and ceremonies. In the case of *patrilineal descent,* privileges are passed through the male line. As an illustration, an American male inherits and keeps his father's last name, while a female usually inherits her father's last name then assumes her husband's. *Matrilineal descent* occurs when privileges are passed through the female line. The matrilineal pattern exists in an extreme form among the Nayar of India. The wife's family is the basic domestic unit and is solely responsible for the socialization of children. The married couple lives together for three days only. After this brief period, the wife's children are fathered by her lovers.[6]

In the United States, despite the patrilineal custom concerning names, descent privileges are passed through both the male and female lines. Children are seen as belonging to both their mother's and father's families and may inherit privileges from both. This dual descent pattern is called *bilateral descent*.

NUCLEAR AND EXTENDED FAMILIES

Our earlier definition of family can be expanded by distinguishing between the nuclear and the extended unit. When Americans think of family, they picture a husband, wife, and dependent children, all probably living in the same place. Together these members form a *nuclear family*. In contrast, the *extended family* consists of a husband and wife, their children, and such other members as grandparents, brothers and sisters, aunts and uncles, and cousins. Sometimes these members all live together and sometimes not, but they are at least geographically close.

The extended family tends to be more prevalent in societies or segments of societies which face adverse living conditions.[7] In many lower-class American families, for example, relatives cooperate with one another when problems arise. They may provide numerous services, such as lending money to an uncle who is "down and out," helping a brother move his furniture, or counseling a distraught nephew. The extended family is essentially an aid to survival.

In *Black Spring* Henry Miller gives a vivid description of his extended family. He tells us about the peculiarities of several relatives and also reveals that he is quite alienated from his family.

> *However, always merry and bright! If it was before the war and the thermometer down to zero or below, if it happened to be Thanksgiving Day, or New Year's or a birthday, or just any old excuse to get together, then off we'd trot, the whole family, to join the other freaks who made up the living family tree. It always seemed astounding to me how jolly they were in our family despite the calamities that were always threatening. Jolly in spite of everything. There was cancer, dropsy, cirrhosis of the liver, insanity, thievery, mendacity, buggery, incest, paralysis, tapeworms, abortions, triplets, idiots,*

Although the nuclear family predominates in American society, extended family units continue to exist. This Vermont farm family includes husband, wife, dependent children, and grandparents.

drunkards, ne'er-do-wells, fanatics, sailors, tailors, watchmakers, scarlet fever, whooping cough, meningitis, running ears, chorea, stutterers, jailbirds, dreamers, storytellers, bartenders. . . . in the sink Crazy George is trying to scratch his neck with an empty sleeve. New Martini, the ne'er-do-well, is fiddling with the phonograph, his wife Carrie is guzzling it from the tin growler. The brats are down stairs in the stable playing stinkfinger in the dark. In the street, where the shanties begin, the kids are making a sliding-pond. It's blue everywhere, with cold and smoke and snow. Tante Melia is sitting in a corner fingering a rosary. Uncle Ned is repairing a harness. The three grandfathers and the two great-grandfathers are huddled near the stove talking about the Franco-Prussian war. Crazy George is lapping up the dregs. The women are getting closer together, their voices low, their tongues clacking. Everything fits together like a jigsaw puzzle—faces, voices, gestures, bodies.[8]

When tragedy befalls a relative in an extended family, one member generally takes on or is given the responsibility of assisting. Henry Miller describes his unfortunate Aunt Mele and tells how his cowardly and insensitive relatives assigned him the task of escorting her to an asylum. Again, from *Black Spring:*

And then Mele sitting there in the corner—she was another case. She was queer even as a child. So was the mother, for that matter. It was too bad that Paul had died. Paul was Mele's husband. Yes, everything would have been all right if that woman from Hamburg hadn't shown up and corrupted Paul. What could Mele do against a clever woman like that—against a shrewd strumpet! Something would have to be done about Mele. It was getting dangerous to have her around. Just the other day they caught her sitting on the stove. Fortunately the fire was low. But supposing she took it into her head to set fire to the house—when they were all asleep? . . .

And now I'm going to tell you what those bastards said to me . . .

They said—Henry, you take her to the asylum tomorrow. And don't tell them that we can afford to pay for her.

Fine! Always merry and bright! The next morning we boarded the trolley together and we rode out into the country. If Mele asked where we were going I was to say—"To visit Aunt Monica." But Mele didn't ask any questions. She sat quietly beside me and pointed to the cows now and then. She saw blue cows and green ones. She knew their names. She asked what happened to the moon in the daytime. And did I have a piece of liverwurst by any chance?

During the journey I wept—I couldn't help it. When people are too good in this world they have to be put under lock and key. There's something wrong with people who are too good. . . .

Walking down the gravel path towards the big gates Mele becomes uneasy. Even a puppy knows when it is being carried to a pond to be drowned. Mele is trembling now. At the gate they are waiting for us. The gate yawns. Mele is on the inside, I am on the outside. They are trying to coax her along. They are gentle with her now. They speak to her so gently. But Mele is terror-stricken. She turns and runs towards the gate. I am still standing there. She puts her arms through the bars and clutches my neck. I kiss her tenderly on the forehead. Gently I unlock her arms. The others are going to take her again. I can't bear seeing that. I must go. . . . I sobbed as I had never sobbed since I was a child. Meanwhile they were giving Mele a bath and putting her into regulation dress, . . .[9]

In practice, then, family life in the United States can be generally described as monogamous, both endogamous and exogamous, patriarchal but becoming more equalitarian, neolocal, bilateral, and nuclear. But, of course, there are social-class, racial, ethnic, and religious variations in these patterns.

Functions of the Family

In a rural society the family often performs an economic function. Each member has work duties—plowing the fields, milking the cows, hunting, sewing, canning vegetables—which he or she performs to ensure the over-

Grant Wood's painting *American Gothic* (1930) captures the flavor of traditional, rural America, in which the patriarchal family played a most important role.

all well-being of the family. The family is an economic unit, and survival depends on the work output of each person. In such a society the family often plays a major role in teaching religion as well. For example, frequent prayer and reading of the Bible were relatively common practices in the pioneer family of American history. And in a rural society some education, though minimal, is also provided in the home. The three "Rs"— readin', 'ritin', and 'rithmetic—plus farm-related skills were taught to children by older family members in pioneer America. Finally, recreation is largely a family affair in such a society, for example, the picnics, games, sewing bees, and similar activities of pioneer Americans.

In modern, complex, industrial societies, the family unit no longer has primary responsibility for performing these economic, religious, educational, and recreational functions. Economic activities are now largely carried on outside the home, and frequently only one member of the family, the head of the household, provides the family's financial support. Also, although some religion may be taught by parents, most of this function has been taken over by the churches. Further, schools—elementary, secondary, and college—have almost totally assumed the educational function. And, finally, recreation is less and less a home-centered affair as individual members seek entertainment on their own.

No doubt the family in urban, industrial society has given over many of its traditional functions to other institutions. Does this mean that the modern family is dying? Obviously not. The family remains an important institution, and an examination of its present-day functions for the individual and society will reveal why it persists and will continue to exist.

REPRODUCTION

Although parenthood does not have to be limited to marital partners, all societies look to the legally constituted family to produce children and simultaneously condemn child-bearing outside of marriage. Undoubtedly, the family has been chosen to fulfill the reproduction function because it is through this group that a child has the best chance to survive. Human beings are almost totally dependent both physically and psychologically during youth, and the lengthy socialization process required for living cannot be left to chance. The family provides for individual needs and ensures an orderly and continual performance of an important societal process.

REGULATION OF SEXUAL ACTIVITY

A society helps the individual deal with sex by establishing rules to regulate sexual activity. Marriage is always defined as the primary, though not the only, place where sexual needs are to be met.

Social norms limit sexual conduct in a variety of ways. For example,

Parents perform important functions for children, such as caring for physical needs, transmitting culture, and providing an intimate relationship.

incest, or sexual intercourse between closely related persons such as a parent and child, is forbidden everywhere today.[10] Explanations for the universality of the incest taboo range from the belief that incest would create chaos in the family by arousing sexual jealousies to the idea that incest would confuse family roles and disrupt socialization. It would be difficult, for example, for a mother to be both a disciplinarian and a lover to her son.

Norms governing marriage limit sexual activity by indicating that husband and wife should engage in sex only with each other. In most societies extramarital relations are discouraged, although the norm forbidding adultery is never completely adhered to or enforced.

SOCIALIZATION

The family is an important agent of cultural transmission. Older family members, who obviously know much of the ways of the larger culture, teach children what is desirable and undesirable, proper and improper, true and false, and so on. In fact, of all the sources of information, none has such an enduring impact on the child as the family. (See chapter 3 for further discussion of the family's role in childhood socialization.)

Parental influence is shown in a selection from *Memoirs of a Dutiful Daughter* by Simone de Beauvoir. She looks back on her early family experiences, particularly her relationship with her mother, with some pain. She despised being taught that her role in life should be that of "wife and mother," and she resented the illogic of parents' demands. Still, she admits that her "essential self still belonged to them as much as to me." She felt it her duty to obey.

By being born into this family, these six children have been assigned a wide range of statuses —nationality, racial affiliation, social class, religion, to mention several.

I had lost the sense of security childhood gives, and nothing had come to take its place. My parents' authority remained inflexible, but as my critical sense developed I began to rebel against it more and more. I couldn't see the point of visits, family dinners, and all those tiresome social duties which my parents considered obligatory. Their replies, "It's your duty" or "that just isn't done," didn't satisfy me at all. My mother's eternal solicitude began to weigh me down. She had her own "ideas" which she did not attempt to justify, and her decisions often seemed to me quite arbitrary. We had a violent argument about a missal which I wanted to give my sister for her First Communion; I wanted to choose one bound in pale fawn leather, like those which the majority of my schoolmates had; Mama thought that one with a blue cloth cover would do just as well. I protested that the money in my money box was for me to do what I liked with; . . . But in the end I had to give in, with rage in my heart, vowing never to forgive her for what I considered to be an abuse of her power over me. . . . I had the habit of obedience, and I believed that, on the whole, God expected me to be dutiful: the conflict that threatened to set me against my mother did not break out; but I was uneasily aware of its underlying presence. My mother's whole education and upbringing had convinced her that for a woman the greatest thing was to become the mother of a family; she couldn't play this part unless I played the dutiful daughter. . . .

My real rival was my mother. I dreamed of having a more intimate relationship with my father; but even on the rare occasions when we found ourselves alone together we talked as if she were there with us. When there was an argument, if I had appealed to my father, he would have said: "Do what your mother tells you!" I only once tried to get him on my side. He had taken us to the races at Auteuil; the course was black with people, it was hot, there was nothing happening, and I was bored; finally the horses were off; the people rushed toward the barriers, and their backs hid the track from my view. My father had hired folding chairs for us and I wanted to stand on mine to get a better view. "No!" said my mother, who detested crowds and had been irritated by all the pushing and shoving. I insisted that I should be allowed to stand on my folding chair. "When I say no, I mean no!" my mother declared. As she was looking after my sister, I turned to my father and cried furiously: "Mama is being ridiculous! Why can't I stand on my folding chair?" He simply lifted his shoulder in an embarrassed silence, and refused to take part in the argument. . . . I no longer believed in my father's absolute infallibility. Yet my parents still had the power to make me feel guilty; I accepted their verdicts while at the same time I looked upon my self with different eyes than theirs. My essential self still belonged to them as much as to me.[11]

As we read the excerpt from de Beauvoir, we suspect that at some point she experienced considerable stress in defining her goals in life. Certainly, in making decisions regarding schooling, marriage, and occupation, many of us find ourselves torn between the expectations of members of our family and those of other socializing agents, such as teachers and peers.

CONFERRAL OF STATUS

By reason of being born into a particular family, we inherit many statuses. We may be white, Protestant, and middle-class, or Puerto Rican, Catholic, and lower-class, for example. At a later point in life, however, we may conceivably change at least some of these statuses. (The concepts of ascribed and achieved status are discussed in chapter 4.)

The statuses conferred on us because of our family ties may limit the opportunities we have in life. For example, in English society around the turn of the century, family background was of vital importance when an aristocrat contemplated marriage. Oscar Wilde, in his satire of the English upper classes, *The Importance of Being Earnest*, relates a conversation between a young man asking for a debutante's hand in marriage and the girl's mother, Lady Bracknell. The young man's "inferior" family heritage creates a serious problem for the mother.

LADY BRACKNELL.   *Are your parents living?*
JACK.   *I have lost both my parents.*

LADY BRACKNELL. Both? . . . That seems like carelessness. Who was your father? He was evidently a man of some wealth. Was he born in what the Radical papers call the purple of commerce, or did he rise from the ranks of the aristocracy?

JACK. I am afraid I really don't know. The fact is, Lady Bracknell, I said I had lost my parents. It would be nearer the truth to say that my parents seem to have lost me . . . I don't actually know who I am by birth. I was . . . well, I was found.

LADY BRACKNELL. Found!

JACK. The late Mr. Thomas Cardew, an old gentleman of a very charitable and kindly disposition, found me, and gave me the name of Worthing, because he happened to have a first-class ticket for Worthing in his pocket at the time. Worthing is a place in Sussex. It is a seaside resort.

LADY BRACKNELL. Where did the charitable gentleman who had a first-class ticket for this seaside resort find you?

JACK (gravely). In a hand-bag.

LADY BRACKNELL. A hand-bag?

JACK (very seriously). Yes, Lady Bracknell. I was in a hand-bag — a somewhat large, black leather hand-bag, with handles to it — an ordinary hand-bag in fact.

LADY BRACKNELL. In what locality did this Mr. James, or Thomas, Cardew come across this hand-bag?

JACK. In the cloak-room at Victoria Station. It was given to him in mistake for his own.

LADY BRACKNELL. The cloak-room at Victoria Station?

JACK. Yes. The Brighton line.

LADY BRACKNELL. The line is immaterial. Mr. Worthing, I confess I feel somewhat bewildered by what you have just told me. To be born, or at any rate bred, in a hand-bag, whether it had handles or not, seems to me to display a contempt for the ordinary decencies of family life that remind one of the worst excesses of the French Revolution. And I presume you know what that unfortunate movement led to? As for the particular locality in which the hand-bag was found, a cloak-room at a railway station might serve to conceal a social indiscretion — has probably, indeed, been used for that purpose before now — but it could hardly be regarded as an assured basis for a recognized position in good society.

JACK. May I ask you then what you would advise me to do? I need hardly say I would do anything in the world to ensure Gwendolen's happiness.

LADY BRACKNELL. I would strongly advise you, Mr. Worthing, to try and acquire some relations as soon as possible, and to make a definite effort to produce at any rate one parent, of either sex, before the season is quite over.

JACK. Well, I don't see how I could possibly manage to do that. I can produce the hand-bag at any moment. It is in my dressing-room at home. I really think that should satisfy you, Lady Bracknell.

LADY BRACKNELL. Me, sir! What has it to do with me? You can hardly imagine that I and Lord Bracknell would dream of allowing our only daughter—a girl brought up with the utmost care—to marry into a cloak-room, and form an alliance with a parcel? Good morning, Mr. Worthing! (Lady Bracknell sweeps out in majestic indignation.)[12]

Status conferral is thus another important function of the family. From our families we acquire at birth a place in life—a class position, nationality, clan membership, religion, and so forth.

PROVISION OF AFFECTION AND COMPANIONSHIP

All of us need contact with others and affection throughout our lives. Children who have not received warmth and affection from others frequently are unsure of their identities and develop negative self-images. Adults, too, need intimate relations, particularly in a society in which impersonal and transient relations are common. The companionship that family members offer enables the individual to cope with life. The family can give a person a sense of positive identity, permanence, and security, for in that group ideas are shared on a most intimate level. We must remember, of course, that the family is only one of many groups that can provide intimacy, and that not all families have harmonious relationships.

Family Problems in American Society

Views on marriage sometimes differ widely. Martin Luther had this to say about the institution: "There is no more lovely, friendly and charming relationship, communion or company than a good marriage."[13] Robert Louis Stevenson saw marriage in a rather different light: "Marriage is like life in this—that it is a field of battle, and not a bed of roses."[14]

For most people marriage and family life are neither all heaven nor all hell—they are a mixture of both. Yet few would deny that the American family is beset by numerous crises and that these crises have affected and will continue to affect family life. An examination of the problems of the American family will give insight into the institution's future—a future which will witness considerable change.

CHANGING SEX ROLES

In recent years the American woman has gained greater economic self-sufficiency and has begun to reassess her goals in life. In 1973 there were 35 million working women in this country, making up almost 40 percent of the labor force. Almost three out of five working women were married and living with their husbands. And of the 13 million mothers in the labor force, 4.8 million had children under six years of age.[15] Figure 8–1 illustrates the growing percentage of married women in the 20–44 age range (those most likely to have dependent children) in the labor force since 1960.

We can safely conclude that "working woman" and "working wife" are now commonplace roles, although at one time they were not acceptable to most of American society. Earlier in our history women were barred from voting and owning property, and for a woman to work outside the home was considered irresponsible and sinful. The increased number of females now in the labor market is the result of several factors: (1) an expanding economy has created more jobs, (2) both single and married women need to work to achieve financial independence and a suitable standard of living, and (3) a continuous effort since the 1800s by women's rights movements has succeeded somewhat in lessening sex discrimination.

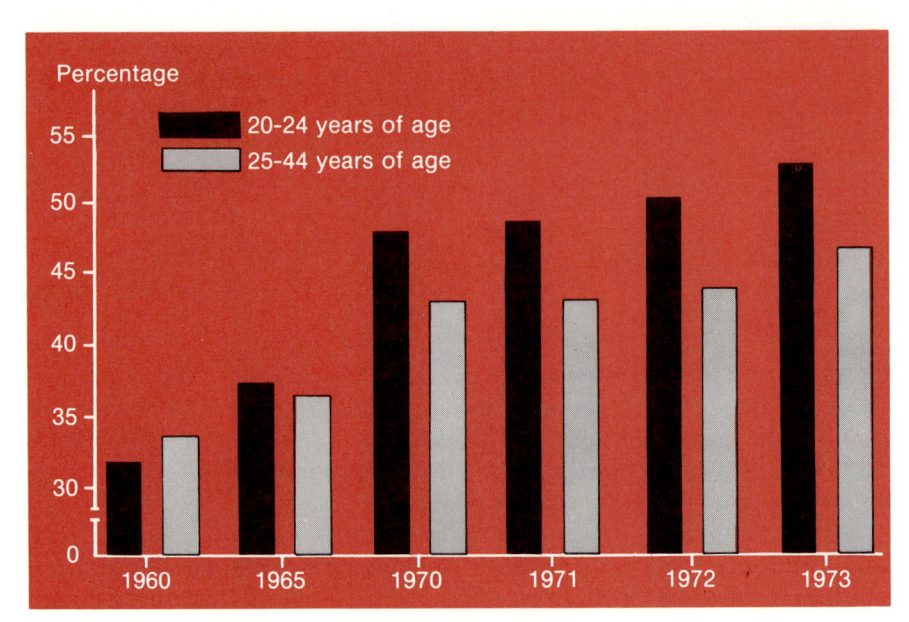

FIGURE 8–1 Increasing Percentage of Married Women (living with husband) between 20 and 44 Years of Age in the U.S. Labor Force, 1960–1973
SOURCE: U.S. Bureau of the Census, *Statistical Abstract of the United States: 1974* (Washington, D.C., 1974), p. 338.

The picture has not been totally pleasant, however, for the working woman. Overall, females are given lower-paying, less prestigious jobs than males; furthermore, they are promoted less frequently and have higher unemployment rates. For example, the Department of Labor reported that in 1973 the average women worker earned less than three-fifths the salary of the average man, even when both worked full-time, year round. In addition, women held mainly clerical, service, and factory jobs with only 15 percent classified as professional and technical workers (see Figure 8–2). Yet the average female worker is slightly better educated than the average male worker.[16] Finally, another source notes that, contrary to popular belief, the pay gap between men and women is actually widening.[17] This second-class citizenship is the result of both discrimination and the traditional belief held by both sexes that a woman is "by nature" suited to be solely a mother, wife, and sex partner.

The view of women as submissive, unintelligent, sexual playmates is well illustrated by the ancient Roman writer Ovid. He gives instructions to the female of his day on how she can better advertise her qualities to the male. One wonders if such advice might not just as readily be found today in certain popular women's magazines.

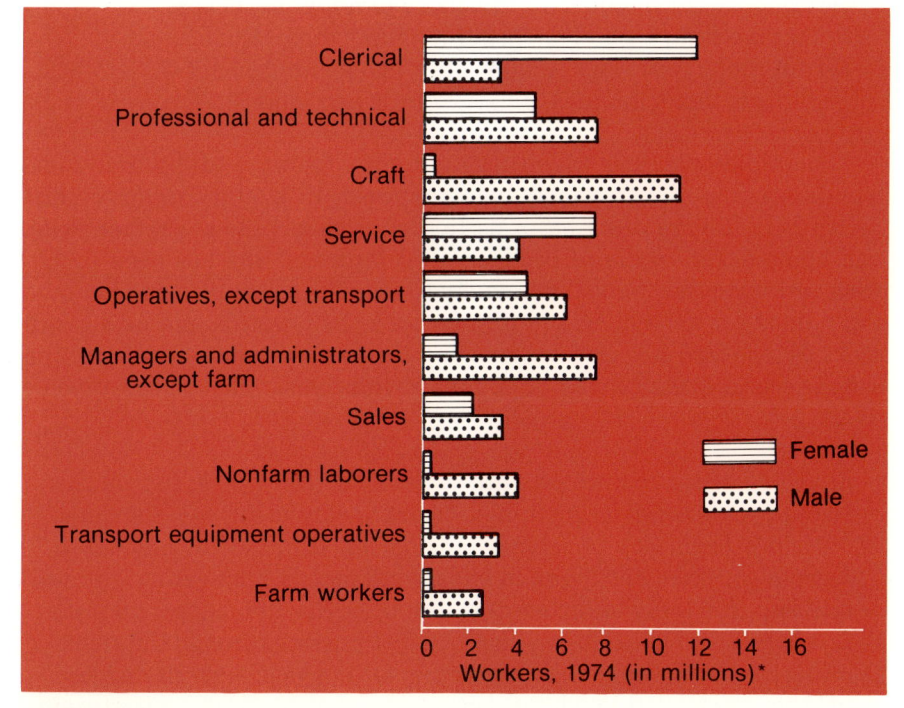

FIGURE 8–2 Employment in Major Occupational Groups, by Sex

SOURCE: Adapted from U.S. Department of Labor, Bureau of Labor Statistics, *Occupational Outlook Handbook, 1976–77 Edition* (Washington, D.C., 1976), Bulletin 1875, p. 16.

*Includes self-employed and unpaid family workers.

Although women make up a large share of the labor force, their jobs are often the less prestigious ones—clerical, secretarial, and so on—rather than managerial.

> *Faults of the face or physique call for attempts at disguise.*
> *If you are short, sit down, lest standing, you seem to be sitting,*
> *Little as you may be, stretch out full length on your couch.*
> *Even here, if you fear some critic might notice your stature,*
> *See that a cover is thrown, hide yourself under a spread.*
> *If you're the lanky type, wear somewhat billowy garments,*
> *Loosely let the robe fall from the shoulders down.*
> *If you're inclined to be dark, white is an absolute must.*
> *Let an ugly foot hide in a snow-covered sandal.*
> *If your ankles are thick, don't be unlacing your shoes.*
> *Do your collarbones show? Then wear a clasp at each shoulder.*
> *Have you a bust too flat? Bandages ought to fix that.*
> *If your fingers are fat, or your fingernails brittle and ugly,*
> *Watch what you do when you talk; don't wave your hands in the air.*
> *Eat a lozenge or two if you think your breath is offensive,*
> *If you have something to say, speak from some distance away.*
> *If a tooth is too black or too large, or the least bit uneven,*
> *Pay no attention to jokes; laughter might give you away.*
> *Who would believe it? The girls must learn to govern their laughter.*
> *Even in this respect tact is required, and control.*
> *Do not open the mouth too wide, like a braying she-jackass,*
> *Show your dimples and teeth, hardly much more than a smile.*
> *Do not shake your sides or slap your thigh in amusement—*
> *Feminine, that's the idea; giggle or titter, no more.*[18]

The dehumanization which results from adherence to the traditional female sex role is increasingly being exposed. In *Up the Sandbox* Anne Richardson Roiphe describes a particular woman's life as mother, wife, and homemaker—a life of drudgery and dullness. She has been socialized, and in a sense forced, by society to accept roles opposed to her own aspirations for herself. She is torn between two worlds and as a result seeks escape into her private fantasies. Toward the end of the selection Roiphe sees a distant ray of hope for a revolutionary change in women's lives.

> *Elizabeth has come to me with a demand that I push her on the swing. I am tired of doing things. I want to stay in my own thoughts, but she's beginning to whine, sensing my withdrawal, and I will have to go, since discipline in one's work means subjugating whims and impulses, self, to higher plans. I will be disciplined, get up from this bench and go to the swings, my feet passing through the steam rising from the cement. I am a guru, an Indian yogi. I can sit on a bed of nails and walk through fire, because I can concentrate on God and exclude all other sensations. No, I cannot concentrate on God. I find when I try I only brood about myself. Elizabeth, I am coming to the swings. . . .*

I push Elizabeth on the swing and she kicks her feet in pleasure. Her small brown sandals are scuffed and in need of a polishing they will never get. I'm perspiring from the activity and there are wet dark circles under the armholes of my cotton dress. I think of Elizabeth lying on a bed some many years from now, a boy, a man, awkwardly spreading her legs apart, touching her, and she, not knowing how to stop, how to prevent the vacuum from sucking her up, will lie passive and be consumed, and as I think of the heat and sensation of her body rolling on the sheets, in sex, in labor, in illness and in death, I feel a great exhaustion, a fatigue of certain defeat — that's all that can possibly come of the days I spend in the park expecting secretly the playground concrete to crack and wild orchids to push their way up to the sunlight, and lizards to dash between the slide and the swing, and nature to change back to an Eden before the apple, where Paul and I can live without erosion in perpetual beauty.

I know that we have been condemned to a simple life of increasing compromises. I know that minor hatreds and petty resentments will come more and more between us. Paul, Elizabeth, Peter, the new baby and I will grow closer and closer in memories of days that promised more than they gave and love that offers everything and then like a mirage disappears as we get closer. But what else can I do but listen to myself as I prepare chicken in wine sauce for the friends we will have to dinner tomorrow night, read Elizabeth a book about Raggedy Ann and how she got her candy heart that says "I love you" sewed right into the middle of her chest — what else can I do but tell Paul that I have not given up all hope for a revolution that will not be corrupt . . . a barricade can still be erected behind which saints may stand? I must believe evolution is not complete. I'll take Peter to the five and dime and buy him a stuffed elephant like the one he wanted to take from the carriage parked next to ours.[19]

The current women's liberation movement has attempted to convince society that females should receive equal treatment — in employment, education, and political life — and that people must redefine the traditional female role. Why should women have to sacrifice their careers for marriage and a family? Why should child care be the responsibility of the mother and not the father?*

Although complete equality of the sexes does not exist, some changes have gradually come about. Accordingly, American males have been forced to question their historical roles. The married man who cooks dinner, cleans house, and watches the children is no longer an oddity. Both men and women are increasingly looking toward marriage as a relationship based on companionship and mutual sexual fulfillment. Because of

---
*For a discussion of the problems facing the American woman in terms of equality, see Betty Roszak and Theodore Roszak, eds., *Masculine-Feminine: Readings in Sexual Mythology and the Liberation of Women* (New York: Harper & Row, 1970).

changing sex roles, many individuals are now working within the framework of new expectations.

ECONOMIC CRISIS

The American family now spends more on consumer purchases than at any other time in this nation's history. The owning of houses, lawn mowers, freezers, trash compactors, and automobiles is common, and credit devices such as Master Charge, BankAmericard, and the Sears installment plan help keep consumption by the middle-class American family at a high level. Lower-class families, however, cannot afford as high a level of consumption and, in fact, in times of inflation and unemployment have difficulty maintaining a minimal standard of living. Middle-class families as well face economic difficulty as increased taxes and inflation devalue the real worth of their income. While lower-class families may experience absolute deprivation, middle-class families often experience frustration because of relative deprivation — the feeling that they deserve more.

Economic problems can take a great toll of family goals and relationships. The wife may be forced to seek full-time employment, and older children may have to postpone a college education to pursue a job. Time away from the home may increase, and worry, anxiety, and arguments over money matters may become intense. In the short story "Dark Eye" Harry Mark Petrakis has given us a look at what complete economic despair can do to the thinking of a man and his family. The story is told by a son about his father. The father was once a Greek *Karaghiozis*, a puppetmaster, but such a profession had no place in America, his new home. The father's unemployment led to his loss of self-identity and pride and to a strained relationship among all the family members.

> *My father must have come to America thinking that in a new country of myriad opportunities, he would be able to practice his craft. But the children who had never seen a Karaghiozis had other allegiances to Laurel and Hardy, Buster Keaton and baseball. And their parents were too involved with the artifacts of home and the rigors of business to bother with an old-country art. . . .*
>
> *He never performed the Karaghiozis in public again. In the years that followed, he kept the cardboard figures of the players, perhaps twenty-five or thirty of them, in a footlocker at the rear of his closet. Sometimes, when he was drunk, he would pull out the footlocker, open it and sit down on the floor beside it. He would bring out the mad Karaghiozis and all his companions. . . .*
>
> *My father lost his job in the grocery, worked for a while in a laundry and then lost that job as well. During this period, my mother took work as a waitress to pay our rent and food. When he could not find money on which to drink, my father spent his time brooding. . . .*

His last hope had fled and he seemed more furiously bent on his own destruction. His credit was dried up at the taverns on our street and he made futile pilgrimages to other neighborhoods. When he could not bully or steal money from my mother or my cousin Frosos, he begged and borrowed from friends and strangers along the street. Abandoning all efforts to find any kind of work, he whirled in a wind of drunken despair.

Any redeeming memory I had of him, any bond of blood remaining between us was demolished in the blustering, whining, raging moments when he cursed fate, the misfortune of his marriage, the madness that made him leave the old country. And in his frenzy his voice altered, becoming shrill and hoarse, taunting and pleading, demanding and denouncing, as if all the myriad tongues of the Karaghiozis players were crying through his lips.

My mother suffered as he suffered, . . .

Once, only once, did I condemn my father to my mother. . . . I whispered a wish to my mother that he might die.

She had never struck me before, but she beat me then. She beat me savagely with a belt while I screamed in shock and pain.

"Listen to me," she said, her face white and her eyes like knives. "Say such a thing again and I'll have the flesh hot from your back. In the old country your father was an artist, a great Karaghiozis. They came from villages a hundred miles away to see him perform. Now nobody cares for his skill and he rages and drinks to forget his grief and loss. Do you think a man whose soul is being torn apart can help himself? We can only love him and have faith in him. He has nothing else."

But I could not understand, and for turning my mother against me, for the beating she gave me, I hated him more.[20]

In short, economic insecurity and frustrations in financial matters can have a profound effect on a family. An economic crisis can damage self-images, warp family relationships, and even lead to disintegration of the family.

CHILD-REARING

The child-rearing methods of the American family have come under considerable fire. Many critics blame parents for exerting too much pressure on children to conform and for stifling children's imagination and sense of independence. With quite the opposite view, Urie Bronfenbrenner contends that Americans have shirked their responsibility to socialize children. Adults live in their complex and hurried worlds separate and isolated from children. They are not involved with the activities of children and give children little or no responsibility within the family. As a result, childhood socialization is left to peers and the mass media, sources which frequently do not inculcate values that the parents themselves would approve. According to Bronfenbrenner, our confused and alienated young people are, in large part, an outgrowth of the fragmented family.[21]

(Additional discussion of Bronfenbrenner's criticism of American socialization methods is found in chapter 3.)

DIVORCE

Almost one out of three marriages in the United States today ends in divorce. Some interpret this high divorce rate as a sign that the family is no longer performing important functions, and thus marriages are more readily dissolved. Others condemn Americans for no longer defining marriage as sacred and permanent. In contrast, there are those who see divorce as a potentially positive act. The husband, wife, and children might all lead happier lives after a divorce, particularly if continuing the marriage would mean constant battling and disruption.

The underlying reasons for divorce are numerous. The husband and wife may disagree on who should make family decisions, on whether the wife should pursue a career, on child-rearing methods, or on what life style is desirable for the family. In this last regard, one researcher found that many couples divorced because the wife was dissatisfied with her husband's job and income-earning ability.[22]

Saul Bellow, in *Seize the Day*, dramatizes several factors which may bring about divorce. In a phone conversation between a husband and wife who have separated, we find intense disagreement over what roles each partner should play in the family. Tommy maintains that Margaret should get a job to help make ends meet, particularly since he supported her through college. However, Margaret believes her place is in the home so she can bring up the children. Margaret also feels that Tommy is a child, a dreamer, who has not performed well in his breadwinner role. He tries to explain his difficulties:

> "I've had some bad luck. As a matter of fact, it's been so bad that I don't know where I am. I couldn't tell you what day of the week this is. I can't think straight. I'd better not even try. This has been one of those days, Margaret. May I never live to go through another like it. I mean that with all my heart. So I'm not going to try to do any thinking today. Tomorrow I'm going to see some guys. One is a sales manager. The other is in television. But not to act," he hastily added. "On the business end."
>
> "That's just some more of your talk, Tommy," she said. "You ought to patch things up with Rojax Corporation. They'd take you back. You've got to stop thinking like a youngster."
>
> "What do you mean?"
>
> "Well," she said, measured and unbending, remorselessly unbending, "you still think like a youngster. But you can't do that any

more. Every other day you want to make a new start. But in eighteen years you'll be eligible for retirement. Nobody wants to hire a new man of your age."

"I know. But listen, you don't have to sound so hard. I can't get on my knees to them. And really you don't have to sound so hard. I haven't done you so much harm."

"Tommy, I have to chase you and ask you for money that you owe us, and I hate it."

She hated also to be told that her voice was hard.

"I'm making an effort to control myself," she told him. . . .

"Rojax take me back? I'd have to crawl back. They don't need me. After so many years I should have got stock in the firm. How can I support the three of you, and live myself, on half the territory? And why should I even try when you won't lift a finger to help. I sent you back to school, didn't I? At that time you said—"

His voice was rising. She did not like that and intercepted him. "You misunderstood me," she said.

"You must realize you're killing me. You can't be as blind as all that. Thou shalt not kill! Don't you remember that?"

She said, "You're just raving now. When you calm down it'll be different. I have great confidence in your earning ability."

"Margaret, you don't grasp the situation. You'll have to get a job."

"Absolutely not. I'm not going to have two young children running loose."

"They're not babies," Tommy said. "Tommy is fourteen. Paulie is going to be ten."

"Look," Margaret said in her deliberate manner. "We can't continue this conversation if you're going to yell so, Tommy. They're at a dangerous age. There are teenaged gangs—the parents working, or the families broken up."

Once again she was reminding him that it was he who had left her. She had the bringing up of the children as her burden, while he must expect to pay the price of his freedom.

Freedom! he thought with consuming bitterness. Ashes in his mouth, not freedom. Give me my children. For they are mine too.

Can you be the woman I lived with? he started to say. Have you forgotten that we slept so long together? Must you now deal with me like this, and have no mercy?

He would be better off with Margaret again than he was today. This was what she wanted to make him feel, and she drove it home. "Are you in misery?" she was saying. "But you have deserved it." And he could not return to her any more than he could beg Rojax to take him back. If it cost him his life, he could not. Margaret had ruined him with Olive. She hit him and hit him, beat him, battered him, wanted to beat the very life out of him. . . .

He begged her, "Margaret, go easy on me. You ought to. I'm at the *end of my rope and feel that I'm suffocating. . . . You've got to let me breathe. If I should keel over, what then? And it's something I can never understand about you. How you can treat someone like this whom you lived with so long. Who gave you the best of himself. Who tried. Who loved you."* Merely to pronounce the word "love" made him tremble. . . .

"I'll get a divorce if it's the last thing I do," he swore.[23]

In this conversation, we can also see the personal trauma which can result when two adults engage in battle. There is no understanding, sympathy, or affection. And, indeed, most divorces create extreme emotional strains. A divorced person may experience a sense of failure, be rejected by old friends, and use the children as go-betweens or even as a weapon when quarrels develop. The postdivorce adjustment process is long and difficult.*

Nontraditional Family and Marriage Patterns

During the 1960s and early 1970s new and sometimes radically different family and marriage patterns emerged in American society. In one alternative family pattern, the *commune*, a small number of artists, religious worshipers, ex-drug users, or political idealists ban together to dissociate themselves from what they consider a corrupt society. Members tend to be antibureaucratic, antimaterialistic, and anti-Puritanical in sexual matters. The day-to-day operating principle of the commune is that duties and resources are to be shared by all members.[24] Also, children are usually seen as belonging to the group, and all adults are therefore expected to play a role in their physical care and socialization.

Members of a commune often pair off, and these couples tend to form rather long-term relationships. Free love, or totally unregulated sexual activity, seldom occurs. Apparently, sexual competition and conflict result when no order is imposed on sexual activity.

Another new pattern, called *open marriage*, is based on complete equality between husband and wife. Family responsibilities, such as economic support, household work, and child care, are assigned in a flexible manner to both marriage partners. Because traditional marriage is seen as too restraining, both husband and wife have the freedom to look outside the family for intellectual, emotional, and sexual expression. The goal of

---

*See William J. Goode, *After Divorce* (New York: Free Press, 1956) for a discussion of problems divorced people face.

A nontraditional wedding and a commune in New Mexico. Because new and different marriage and family patterns have been tried, some mistakenly believe the institution of the family is dying.

open marriage—to maintain a meaningful relationship within marriage while simultaneously allowing for extramarital relationships—is a difficult one to accomplish. The Puritanical belief in the unacceptability of sex outside marriage is still widely held by Americans. Additionally, many individuals may experience feelings of rejection and jealousy in such an arrangement.*

Swinging, where two or more married couples mutually decide to switch partners or engage in group sex, has also gained some popularity in recent years. Couples become involved with swinging for a variety of reasons. They may simply want alternative sex partners outside marriage; they may desire to expand upon an already joyous emotional and affectional relationship with another couple; or one partner may want to swing and the other partner agree to it to salvage the marriage. Philosophically, those committed to swinging stress treating males and females as peers and allowing the group to operate democratically. Members are expected to be honest in their views and responsive to others' desires and goals.[25]

*Nena O'Neill and George O'Neill, *Open Marriage: A New Life Style for Couples* (New York: Avon, 1972), discuss and advocate open marriage.

Changing Sex Roles

To be the ideal American woman has usually meant being a wife, mother, and housekeeper. Moreover, physical attractiveness has often been emphasized over intelligence. Females have traditionally been thought of as helpless, illogical, and emotional and, accordingly, unable to compete in a "man's" world. A woman who worked was expected to pursue a limited career in some "feminine" occupation—elementary school teacher, for instance. In many ways women have been the "second sex." As for the "first sex," the ideal male has usually been seen as strong, silent, and unemotional—master of women and leader of men.

Changes are occurring, however, in both of these traditional sex roles. Women are increasingly moving into scientific, technical, and physically demanding jobs, as well as professions such as law and medicine. And some are assuming prominent positions in politics, as illustrated by the influential Democratic congresswoman from Texas, Barbara Jordan (bottom left).

The "weaker" sex has begun to organize to fight sex discrimination in hiring, stop harrassment of the female in criminal cases involving rape and prostitution, and end the use of sex-biased books and materials in public schools. Aggressiveness, historically taboo behavior for a female, is being exhibited more frequently. Females have entered male-dominated sports like basketball, baseball, soccer, and even boxing. And advertisements that exploit the stereotype of the woman as a sex object are being condemned.

Men, too, are changing their traditional attitudes in growing numbers. Many are reassessing cherished beliefs about marriage, the home, and the world of work. Roles are being modified so that the male often finds himself cooking, cleaning house, caring for children, and working with or for a woman in his job.

However, change is a slow and difficult process because sex roles are deeply imbedded in societal values and institutions. At this point, the historic male-female images are crumbling, but they have certainly not collapsed.

Commune living, open marriage, and swinging are attempts to deal with the problems of the traditional family, but it is doubtful that these new patterns will be quickly adopted by society. Only a few people have thus far been attracted to these new forms, and some participants have, in fact, encountered severe problems in adjusting to their new life styles.

Chapter Summary

There is a seemingly endless variety of family patterns. Most societies practice monogamy, which allows a person to marry only one other person at a time; however, polygamy, or the practice of having several mates, is permitted by a few groups. Social rules governing endogamy — marriage within groups specified as acceptable — and exogamy — marriage outside defined groups — also vary. Additionally, some families are male-dominated, or patriarchal; others are female-dominated, or matriarchal; and still others, equalitarian families, are governed in a democratic fashion. Residence patterns, too, vary: under a patrilocal pattern the couple lives with the husband's parents; in a matrilocal pattern the couple resides with the wife's parents; a bilocal pattern means the couple can live with either set of parents; and a neolocal pattern allows the couple to live completely apart from parents. Moreover, the way certain privileges are passed down varies from society to society. Privileges may pass through the male or female lines (patrilineal and matrilineal descent) or through both lines (bilateral descent). Finally, the nuclear family, consisting of husband, wife, and dependent children, is of major importance in some societies, while the extended family, consisting of husband, wife, children, grandparents, uncles and aunts, cousins, and so on, is important and even necessary for subsistence or survival in other societies.

In practice, family life in America is monogamous, both endogamous and exogamous, patriarchal but becoming more equalitarian, neolocal, bilateral, and nuclear. We should remember, however, that there are variations in these patterns caused by differences in social class, race, ethnic background, and religion.

The family institution in urban, industrial society no longer has as much responsibility as it once had in performing economic, religious, educational, and recreational functions. The family persists in modern society, however, because it performs other crucial functions — in the areas of reproduction, regulation of sexual activity, socialization of children, conferral of status on family members, and the provision of affection and companionship.

The American family is now beset by numerous crises. Changing sex roles have forced both females and males to reassess their involvement in family life as well as their personal goals. Family relationships have been altered and seriously damaged under conditions of economic crisis. Critics have attacked the traditional family for its child-rearing methods, claiming both that it exerts too much control over a child's life and that it does not exercise enough responsibility for a child's socialization. Divorce is another crisis because of the personal conflict which results and the difficult postdivorce adjustment process.

Some American couples are experimenting with new and different family and marriage patterns, such as communes, open marriage, and swinging. These alternatives to traditional marriage have so far not been widely accepted by members of society.

The statement that the family is dying is probably an inaccurate one if it is taken to mean that the institution will completely dissolve. The family, like any institution, will persist as long as it solves problems for the individual and society. If, on the other hand, the statement means that the institution as we now know it is under strain and will likely change in the future, then it is surely correct.

Key Terms for Review

- bilateral descent, p. 177
- bilocal, p. 176
- cenogamy, p. 172
- commune, p. 194
- endogamy, p. 175
- equalitarian family, p. 176
- exogamy, p. 176
- extended family, p. 177
- family, p. 171
- family of orientation, p. 171
- family of procreation, p. 171
- incest, p. 181
- institution, p. 169
- marriage, p. 172
- matriarchal family, p. 176
- matrilineal descent, p. 177
- matrilocal, p. 176
- monogamy, p. 172
- neolocal, p. 176
- nuclear family, p. 177
- open marriage, p. 194
- patriarchal family, p. 176
- patrilineal descent, p. 176
- patrilocal, p. 176
- polygamy, p. 172
- polyandry, p. 172
- polygyny, p. 172
- serial monogamy, p. 172
- swinging, p. 195

Suggested Readings

SOCIOLOGICAL

Cuber, John, and Peggy Haroff. *Sex and the Significant Americans: A Study of Sexual Behavior Among the Affluent.* New York: Penguin, 1965. The researchers interviewed 437 affluent married people. Some individuals were found to be resigned to a disappointing marital relationship, while others had an intense emotional relationship based on sharing and togetherness.

Goode, William J. *World Revolution and Family Patterns*. New York: Free Press, 1963. The author examines family institutions in various cultures. He is largely concerned with the impact of industrialization and urbanization on family structures and functions.

Gordon, Michael, ed. *The American Family in Social-Historical Perspective*. New York: St. Martin's Press, 1973. The social history of the American family from the colonial era to recent times is examined. Selections cover topics such as male-female roles and relationships, childhood and youth, sex behavior, and marriage trends.

Komarovsky, Mirra. *Blue Collar Marriage*. New York: Random House, 1962. The working-class marriage is researched and contrasted with the middle-class marriage.

O'Neill, Nena, and George O'Neill. *Open Marriage: A New Life Style for Couples*. New York: Avon, 1972. The authors see "open marriage" as an option that solves some of the problems of the traditional marriage. This new form of marriage might work particularly well in societies which stress equality and self-fulfillment, and which provide numerous opportunities for outside relationships.

Skolnick, Arlene. *The Intimate Environment: Exploring Marriage and the Family*. Boston: Little, Brown, 1973. The author contends that the nuclear family is particularly susceptible to strains and disruptions. For example, the small family unit of father, mother, and children means that emotional relationships are intense; as a result, angry, neglectful, or missing parents have considerable ill-effects on the child. In contrast, the traditional family usually consisted of many relatives. Children had many emotional relationships and felt more psychologically secure.

Sussman, Marvin B., ed. *Sourcebook in Marriage and the Family*. Boston: Houghton Mifflin, 1974. This anthology contains thirty-six articles on the sociology of the family. The section on nontraditional family forms in the 1970s is particularly informative.

LITERARY

Albee, Edward. *Who's Afraid of Virginia Woolf*. New York: Pocket Books, 1964. The author of this highly dramatic play unfolds a story of a love-hate relationship between a husband and wife. The action centers on a series of "games" the husband and wife play. The games reveal a life of misery and despair each leads.

De Beauvoir, Simone. *Memoirs of a Dutiful Daughter*. Trans. James Kirkup. Cleveland: World Publishing, 1959. The author describes her life as a dutiful daughter until one day she rebels. Like so many children, she experienced guilt when the thought of disobeying parents entered her mind.

Roiphe, Anne Richardson. *Up the Sandbox*. New York: Simon & Schuster, 1970. The principal character of the story gives the reader an inside look at her dull life, which centers on fulfilling the role of mother and housewife. Although outsiders react to her only in her traditional female sex role, the reader gains a sense of her as a person with intellect, curiosity, fantasies, and desires.

Roth, Philip. *Portnoy's Complaint*. New York: Random House, 1969. In a bizarre, profane, and humorous style, the author vividly illustrates the overcontrol of parents. The mother-child relationship is one the author remembers with defiance.

Tavuchis, Nicholas, and William J. Goode, eds. *The Family Through Literature*. New York: McGraw-Hill, 1975. Selections from Tolstoy, Thackeray, Malamud, Shakespeare, Hemingway, Huxley, Twain, and many other writers are included in this anthology on the family. Topics covered include sex and love relations, parental concerns, family disorganization, and sex roles. Several of the selections included in the book were used in the present chapter.

Updike, John. *Couples*. New York: Alfred A. Knopf, 1968. Well-to-do suburban couples may appear to "have it made," but the problems of such couples can be numerous. Updike describes the lack of understanding and affection between husbands and wives as they devote their lives to material objects and to their children.

IN THIS CHAPTER

Defining the Institution   205

The Functions and Dysfunctions of Religion   208

    Priestly function   208
    Prophetic function   211
    Self-identity function   212
    Buttress function   214
    Age-grading function   214
    Explanation function   214

Religion and Social Organization   219

    Religion and the socioeconomic order   220
    Religion and social status   220
    Religion and changing the social order   223

Religion and Social Class   223

Magic, Witchcraft, and the Supernatural   226

Summary   227

Key Terms for Review   228

Suggested Readings   229

Does religion destroy human initiative?
Has religion become irrelevant as a force in human affairs?
Why does religion seem to be so important?
Are magic, religion, and astrology all superstitions?

RELIGION

Although religion, like all our institutions, has changed, it continues as a very real and major force in the lives of people throughout the world. In the United States today, regardless of declining attendance and sagging church incomes, most data suggest that we remain a nation of believers. The religious revolution of the late 1960s and early 1970s, which saw the rise of cults and sects such as the Krishnamurti, Jesus People, Divine Light Mission, and World Unification Church, represents a major revitalization of religiosity and spirituality among the young. The assertion that "God is dead" is evidently not true, at least for a large part of the American population.

Defining the Institution

Most people in the United States consider themselves to be members of a religion. Indeed, fewer than 3 percent (according to the Census Bureau's 1973 report) responded to the question "What is your religious faith?" with the answer "none."[1] Yet the incredible growth in the importance of science and empiricism during the past century has caused many people to regard religion as a *superstition*, an irrational belief. That perception is undoubtedly accurate in some instances. Religion, dealing as it does with areas not subject to scientific demonstration, has attracted some eccentric people espousing often engagingly bizarre beliefs. Ambrose Bierce had these people and others in mind when he defined the institution as "a goodly tree, in which all the foul birds of the air have made their nest."[2]

The human desire to explain that which is not easily or rationally explainable has kept many an exploitative charlatan in business. Such individuals are thought to possess great supernatural powers, though in fact they have none. Their power over people is frequently immense. James Thurber's "The Owl Who Was God" is an allegory about a religious charlatan.

> Once upon a starless midnight there was an owl who sat on the branch of an oak tree. Two ground moles tried to slip quietly by, unnoticed. "You!" said the owl. "Who?" they quavered, in fear and astonishment, for they could not believe it was possible for anyone to see them in that darkness. "You two!" said the owl. The moles hurried away and told the other creatures of the field and forest that the owl was the greatest and wisest of all animals because he could answer any question. "I'll see about that," said a secretary bird, and he called on the owl one night when it was very dark. "How many claws am I holding up?" said the secretary bird. "Two," said the owl, and that was right. "Can you give me another expression for 'that is to say' or 'namely'?" asked the secretary bird. "To wit," said the owl. "Why does a lover call on his love?" asked the secretary bird. "To woo," said the owl.
>
> The secretary bird hastened back to the other creatures and reported that the owl was indeed the greatest and wisest animal in the world because he could see in the dark and because he could answer any question. "Can he see in the daytime too?" asked a red fox. "Yes" answered a dormouse and a French poodle. "Can he see in the daytime too?" All the other creatures laughed loudly at this silly question, and they set upon the red fox and his friends and drove them out of the region. Then they sent a messenger to the owl and asked him to be their leader.
>
> When the owl appeared among the animals it was high noon and the sun was shining brightly. He walked very slowly, which gave him an appearance of great dignity, and he peered about him with large, staring eyes, which gave him an air of great importance. "He's God!" screamed a Plymouth Rock hen. And the others took up the cry. "He's God!" So they followed him wherever he went and when he began to bump into things they began to bump into things, too. Finally he came to a concrete highway and he started up the middle of it and all the other creatures followed him. Presently, a hawk, who was acting as outrider, observed a truck coming at them at fifty miles an hour, and he reported to the secretary bird and the secretary bird reported to the owl. "There's danger ahead," said the secretary bird. "To wit?" said the owl. The secretary bird told him. "Aren't you afraid?" he asked. "Who?" said the owl calmly, for he could not see the truck. "He's God!" cried all the creatures again, and they were still crying "He's God!" when the truck hit them and ran them down. Some of the animals were merely injured, but most of them, including the owl, were killed. Moral: You can fool too many of the people too much of the time.[3]

Charlatans aside, religion persists in the face of scientific "evidence" that either fails to support some religious tenets or even appears to negate them. Yet, though religion has always been present and has often been a prominent human institution, it is a difficult one to define. Part of the problem is that religion includes a wide variety of practices, both current and historical. Still, at least one working definition of the phenomenon, that of Emile Durkheim, remains useful. He found *religion* to be "a unified system of beliefs and practices relative to sacred things, uniting into a single moral community all those who adhere to those beliefs and practices."[4] The very center of Durkheim's definition of religion is the word "sacred." But what does that word encompass? According to Durkheim, we can apply the term "sacred" to a wide variety of things, even a rock or a piece of wood:

> *But by sacred things one must not understand simply those personal beings which are called gods or spirits; a rock, a tree, a spring, a pebble, a piece of wood, a house, in a word, anything can be sacred. A rite can have this character; in fact, the rite does not exist which does not have it to a certain degree. There are words, expressions and formulae which can be pronounced only by the mouths of consecrated persons; there are gestures and movements which everybody cannot perform. The circle of sacred objects cannot be determined, then, once for all. Its extent varies infinitely, according to the different religions. That is how Buddhism is a religion: in default of gods, it admits the existence of sacred things, namely the four noble truths and the practices derived from them.*[5]

Durkheim is saying that what is sacred, or religious, is determined within a particular cultural context. Anything that people in a society consider to be sacred and celebrate in recognized rites becomes so. Religion, then, rests on beliefs, sacred things, prescribed rites, and officially consecrated individuals to celebrate those rites.

A quite different view of religion is provided by the functionalists. (See chapter 7 for a discussion of their general views.) They believe that religion is an attempt to transcend the tedium of everyday life; that is, it involves "a belief in and a response to some kind of beyond."[6] Kingsley Davis, in particular, emphasizes the "beyond" aspect of the institution. Thus, whereas Durkheim concentrated on the social basis (rites and sanctified leaders) of the sacred, Davis proposes that sacred objects represent not social beliefs but "the unseen world which gives the actor a source and final justification for his group ends—ends that he shares with other members of society."[7]

Both views of religion, Durkheim's and Davis's, can be quite helpful both in categorizing and understanding human behavior. But to fully understand the institution of religion, we also need to know what purposes, or functions, it serves.

Chicomecoatl, goddess of maize (corn), watched over the agricultural production of the powerful Aztec nation.

Vishnu, in Hindu tradition, descends from his transcendental state to preserve the world when it is threatened with destruction.

The Functions and Dysfunctions of Religion

Many sociologists maintain that if religion were pure superstition, the institution probably would not have endured as long as it has. The fact that religion has persisted may be explained by the functions it performs for society and the individual. Sociologists have distinguished six such functions, although there is some disagreement whether certain of these functions might better be considered dysfunctions that serve to harm rather than aid society's general well-being.

PRIESTLY FUNCTION

Religion performs what may be termed a *priestly function;* that is, it supports the existing culture of a society by making its norms sacred. Just as a priest has the power to sanctify objects and individuals, so religion has

Most religions have officially consecrated individuals to celebrate prescribed rites, for example, the various orders of the Roman Catholic Church. (The Jesuit priest at right is leading a folk mass.)

the power to make sacred those rules by which a society governs itself. In this way religion acts as a stabilizing influence, reinforces group rather than individual goals, and helps curb social deviance.

Karl Marx considered this function of religion particularly objectionable, as his statement "Religion is the opiate of the people" indicates. When religion raises social norms to the status of inviolable rules, it is acting to support the status quo. Religion, according to Marx, thus deterred individuals from overthrowing "all those conditions in which man is an abased, enslaved, abandoned, contemptible being."[8] In other words, it functioned to support the harsh conditions of class exploitation.

There is ample support for Marx's view that religion, in its priestly function, has been used to support social inequalities. The rich have often used religious ideas to justify their wealth. For example, the founder of Standard Oil, John D. Rockefeller, stated that "The good lord gave me my money," and the clergyman of banking magnate J. P. Morgan commented that "Godliness is in league with riches; it is only to the moral man that wealth comes. Material prosperity makes the nation sweeter, more joyous, more unselfish, more Christlike."[9] Moreover, religion's message to the poor has often been to accept conditions as they are. One former slave, for example, recalled his religious upbringing thus:

They had preaching one Sunday for white folks and one Sunday for black folks. They used the same preacher there, but some colored preachers would come on the place at times and preach under the trees down at the quarters. They said the white preacher would say, "You may get to the kitchen of heaven if you obey your master, if you don't steal, if you don't tell stories," etc.[10]

Indeed, the idea that life after death will bring a final change, that "the meek will inherit the kingdom," encourages support of the existing order. Of course, while those who are deprived tend to think the established order will change after death and deliverance, those who have power and a preferential position tend to perceive life after death as very much the same as it is on earth. As Arna Bontemps writes in *The Black Experience*:

In the early twenties the poet Countee Cullen recalled the genesis of a provocative quatrain he had written. It involved a personal story—perhaps a parable. An elegant white woman was visiting a black church in the ghetto. Young Cullen had been a confirmed Sunday school boy, and the church happened to be one in which his foster parent was a minister.

The boy did not know, or possibly didn't remember, the circumstances that brought the visitor into their midst with such éclat that day, nor how it happened that she was invited, or volunteered, to teach a class of restless and inattentive youngsters, including himself. Nevertheless, for him the occasion was somehow embalmed.

In its priestly function, religion acts as a conservative force.

When she realized that she was not getting complete attention, the visiting teacher resorted to a device she must have considered suitable. She began telling a dream she said she recently had experienced. She had been in heaven, as it seemed, and she went on to describe the beauties she had seen. These were right out of the scriptures, of course: streets paved with gold, rainbow walls, pearly gates, children petting lions and sheep at the same time, milk and honey flowing.

She had exhausted the narrative when a young Harlem imp raised his hand to ask a question. She paused, smiling, but the smile soon disappeared. The boy wanted to know whether or not she had seen any colored people up there. Not wanting to lie, and not wanting to discourage him either, she finally confessed that she had not seen any, but she quickly added for his comfort that this may have been because she had neglected to look into the kitchens.

Needless to say, a member of the class who had remained silent, Countee Cullen himself, went to his room in the parsonage and wrote what he thought might serve as a suitable epitaph for this visiting teacher's headstone:

> *She even thinks that up in heaven*
> *Her class lies late and snores,*
> *While poor black cherubs rise at seven*
> *To do celestial chores.*[11]

In its priestly function, therefore, religion supports the existing social structure and encourages both the privileged and the dispossessed to accept the status quo.

PROPHETIC FUNCTION

A quite different aspect of religion is its power to inspire great change. It can enable individuals to transcend social forces—to act in ways other than those prescribed by the social order. This function of religion is termed the *prophetic*. Religion serves a prophetic function when it provides a basis for judging the standards and values of a society to be in error. God's laws are seen as independent of and superior to the laws of man. Joan of Arc, Mohandas Gandhi, Sir Thomas More, and Jesus of Nazareth all died upholding spiritual beliefs that were not those of the social order in which they lived.

In the 1960s we witnessed numerous examples of the prophetic function of religion in our own society: the deeply religious Cesar Chavez, who established the United Farm Workers' union; the inspiring and articulate Martin Luther King, Jr., who used his religious ideals to attack the prevailing racist social order; the nonviolent demonstrators who opposed what they felt to be unjust laws in our society. These inspired bearers of change in the 1960s were preceded by a long line of prophetic martyrs.

The belief in the existence of divine laws superior to human laws—a belief so strong that it is beyond reasoning and, perhaps more importantly, beyond intimidation by civil authorities—gives power to the prophetic function. If individuals are so firm in their beliefs that the threat of death is not an intimidation, their power and independence are extraordinary and are often perceived as springing from a supernatural source. For example, Nat Turner, leader of the famous slave revolt, felt himself called by God to go forth and destroy the oppressors of his people.

> *And on the 12th of May, 1828, I heard a loud noise in the heavens, and the spirit instantly appeared to me and said the Serpent was loosened, and Christ had laid down the yoke he had borne for the sins of men, and that I should take it on and fight against the Serpent, for the time was fast approaching when the first should be last and the last should be first.*[12]

The prophetic function of religion, then, is quite the opposite of the priestly function. Religion, in its prophetic function, provides individuals with an unshakable foundation for social criticism.

Quaker protests against the Vietnam War were but one example of the prophetic function of religion during the 1960s.

SELF-IDENTITY FUNCTION

A third function of religion is its role in giving individuals a sense of *self-identity*. Religion may suggest to people that they are not worthless or almost meaningless creatures randomly placed in an endless universe, but rather divinely inspired beings capable of achieving the highest good. Religion is one of the most powerful of the institutional agents of socialization. It can give individuals a profound and positive self-identity, one that enables them to cope effectively with the many doubts and indignities of everyday life.

Sometimes, though, religion instills a self-identity not through a strong positive experience but through debilitating fear. Sinclair Lewis's Elmer Gantry, in the novel of the same name, is the prototype of the evangelist who uses hellfire and brimstone to bring about religious socialization. Typical of his style is the following:

> "You have laughed now. You have sung. You have been merry. But what came ye forth into the wilderness for to see? Merely laughter? I want you to stop a moment now and think just how long it is since you have realized that any night death may demand your souls, and that then, laughter or no laughter, unless you have found the peace of God, unless you have accepted Christ Jesus as your savior, you may with no chance of last-minute repentance be hurled into horrible and shrieking and appalling eternal torture!"[13]

Failure to follow what others consider the path of righteousness may also cause a person to be judged hopelessly wicked and evil. Young Jane Eyre in Charlotte Bronte's novel was thus condemned to bear such guilt by that very pious lay preacher Mr. Brocklehurst:

> "Do you say your prayers night and morning?"
> "Yes, sir."
> "Do you read your Bible?"
> "Sometimes."
> "With pleasure? Are you fond of it?"
> "I like Revelations, and the book of Daniel, and Genesis and Samuel, and a little bit of Exodus, and some parts of Kings and Chronicles and Job and Jonah."
> "And the Psalms? I hope you like them?"
> "No, sir."
> "No? it's, shocking! I have a little boy, younger than you, who knows six psalms by heart; and when you ask him which he would rather have, a gingerbread-nut to eat, or a verse of a Psalm to learn, he says: 'Oh! the verse of a Psalm! angels sing Psalms'; says he, 'I wish to be a little angel here below'; he then gets two nuts in recompense for his infant piety."
> "Psalms are not interesting," I remarked.
> "That proves you have a wicked heart; and you must pray to God to change it; to give you a new and clean one; to take away your heart of stone and give you a heart of flesh."[14]

Persons convinced of their own essential wickedness can suffer extreme personal difficulties. In this sense, the self-identity function religion performs can be harmful. As Kingsley Davis noted:

> Like other medicines it [religion] can sometimes make worse the very thing it seeks to remedy. Innumerable are the psychoses and neuroses that have a religious content. The supraempirical world is so elastic, so susceptible to manipulation by the imagination, that the disordered mind can seize upon it to spin itself into almost any kind of bizarre pattern.[15]

The self-identity function of religion is of course not always debilitating or personally destructive. Indeed, religion in this role sometimes serves as a liberating and integrating force. This is well illustrated in the success of Alcoholics Anonymous (A.A.) in bringing sobriety to seemingly hopeless alcoholics. A.A.'s "program of recovery" is based primarily on "twelve steps of recovery," with "spiritual growth" and "God as we understood him" as their foundation. The A.A. relabeling process, the basis of which is the substitution of a positive and spiritual self-identity for one of guilt and drunkenness, has been unequaled by other alcoholism treatment programs.[16]

BUTTRESS FUNCTION

Religion serves another function, which can be termed its *buttress function*, when it provides support, reconciliation, and consolation to individuals during times of personal and social crisis. Some sociologists see this function of religion as one that is sorely needed in a troubled society. Thus, according to Thomas O'Dea, "Men need emotional support in the face of uncertainty, consolation when confronted with disappointment and anxiety—religion provides important emotional aid in the face of these elements of the human condition."[17] Other sociologists, such as Kingsley Davis, disagree, maintaining that when human beings use religion in this fashion, as a "prop," they are really refusing to face their problems squarely.[18]

Regardless of the conflicting views of sociologists, the buttress provided by religion can be magnificent. Coretta King, who displayed great strength following the assassination of her husband, Martin Luther King, Jr., in April 1968, later commented that her belief in God had provided such personal strength, and that her religion had given her much "support, consolation, and reconciliation."

AGE-GRADING FUNCTION

The *age-grading function* of religion serves to formalize and make sacred the maturation process. Religion provides rites and sacred ceremonies that mark points of passage from one level of responsibility to another. The bar mitzvah—the sacred ceremony of the Jews admitting a boy as an adult member of the Jewish community, most often at the age of thirteen—is one of the better-known examples of such rites. The confirmation ceremony of the Roman Catholic and Anglican churches provides a similar point of demarcation. Most societies have such ceremonies, which serve to mark new levels of status and responsibility.

EXPLANATION FUNCTION

Another function of religion is that of providing some sort of *explanation* for what is commonly thought of as beyond ordinary understanding. Some sociologists view religion in much the same way as Hans Reichenbach does in *The Rise of Scientific Philosophy*.[19] Briefly, Reichenbach finds religion to be a superstitious explanation for those things which could not historically and cannot now be explained by "natural" laws. Much of what we now know to be subject to natural law was once, not very long ago, attributed to supernatural forces. Thus lightning was once thought of as a display of anger by the gods; today we know it to be simply an electrical discharge.

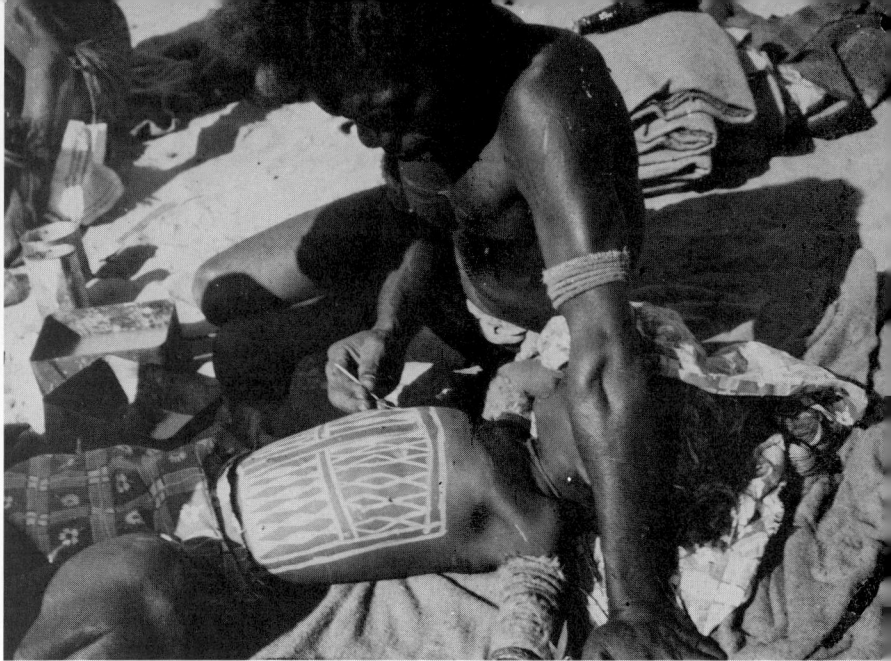

The age-grading function of religion is seen here in the bar mitzvah of a Jewish boy and the ritual painting of a young Australian Aborigine prior to a circumcision ceremony.

The boundary between science and religion is never quite clear and is forever changing. It is subject to social forces and shifting belief systems as well as to new empirical information. This may be seen in the classic exchange between Clarence Darrow and William Jennings Bryan during the 1925 "monkey trial" of John T. Scopes for teaching evolution in the public schools of Dayton, Tennessee. As Irving Stone dramatizes it in "The Scopes Evolution Case":

"You have given considerable study to the Bible, haven't you, Mr. Bryan?" he asked quietly.

"Yes, I have," replied Bryan. "I have studied the Bible for about fifty years."

Clarence Darrow (left) and William Jennings Bryan (right) debated the explanatory function of religion during the "monkey trial" in Dayton, Tennessee, in 1925.

"Do you claim that everything in the Bible should be literally interpreted?"

"I believe everything in the Bible should be accepted as it is given there; some of the Bible is given illustratively. For instance: 'Ye are the salt of the earth.' I would not insist that man was actually salt or that he had flesh of salt, but it is used in the sense of salt as saving God's people."

"When you read that the whale swallowed Jonah, how do you literally interpret that?"

"When I read that a big fish swallowed Jonah, I believe it, and I believe in a God who can make a whale and can make a man and make them both do what he pleases. One miracle is just as easy to believe as another."

"You mean just as hard?" smiled Darrow.

"It is hard to believe for you, but easy for me," replied Bryan.

After a brief flare-up by Stewart on the grounds that Darrow's questions were argumentative Darrow continued. "Do you believe Joshua made the sun stand still?" he asked Bryan.

"I believe what the Bible says," answered Bryan doggedly.

"I suppose you mean that the earth stood still?"

"I don't know. I am talking about the Bible now. I accept the Bible absolutely."

"Do you believe at that time the entire sun went around the earth?"

"No, I believe the earth goes around the sun."

"Do you believe that the men who wrote it thought that the day could be lengthened or that the sun could be stopped?"

"I believe what they wrote was inspired by the Almighty, and He may have used language that could be understood at that time—instead of language that could not be understood until Darrow was born."

There was laughter and applause in the courtyard. Bryan beamed. Darrow stood quietly by, expressionless.

"Now, Mr. Bryan, have you ever pondered what would have happened to the earth if it stood still suddenly?"

"No."

"Don't you know it would have been converted into a molten mass of matter?"

"You believe the story of the flood to be a literal interpretation?" Darrow now asked.

"Yes, sir," replied Bryan.

"When was that flood?"

"I would not attempt to fix the day."

"But what do you think the Bible itself says? Don't you know how it was arrived at?"

"I never made a calculation."

"What do you think?"
"I do not think about things I don't think about."
"Do you think about things you do think about?"
"Well, sometimes."

Once again there was laughter in the courtyard, but this time it was derisive laughter turned against William Jennings Bryan. He did not like it. He turned to glare at the spectators. Russell D. Owen reports that "Bryan was calmly contemptuous of this intellectual upstart as he answered the first questions, but he became restless under Darrow's relentless prodding and finally lost all control of his temper." When Attorney General Stewart objected to Darrow's cross-examination his own witness Bryan replied, "These gentlemen did not come here to try this case. They came here to try revealed religion. I am here to defend it, and they can ask me any questions they please."

This answer drew sharp applause. Darrow commented acidly, "Great applause from the bleachers."

"From those who you call yokels," declared Bryan.

"I never called them yokels."

"That is the ignorance of Tennessee, the bigotry," mocked Bryan.

"You mean who are applauding you?" grinned Darrow.

"Those are the people whom you insult."

"You insult every man of science and learning in the world because he does not believe in your fool religion!" retorted Darrow.[20]

Just what is being explained by religion is subject to change. Most of us could not state with the certainty of Darrow that Bryan's religion was foolishness. Indeed, many brilliant theologians suggest that something similar to the fundamentalist interpretation of the beginning of life may be much closer to truth than are more scientific explanations. Others see the biblical explanation as a poetical interpretation. Whatever the viewpoint. it is obvious that religious explanations of natural phenomena are subject to extra-religious pressures.

At times, in viewing the world around them, people question the explanations offered by religion. Mark Twain's heroine Bessie, in "Little Bessie Would Assist Providence," was just such a seeker of truth, questioning her mother's grasp of the ways of God.

Little Bessie was nearly three years old. She was a good child, and not shallow, not frivolous, but meditative and thoughtful, and much given to thinking out the reasons of things and trying to make them harmonize with results. One day she said:

"Mama, why is there so much pain and sorrow and suffering? What is it all for?"

"It is for our good, my child. In His wisdom and mercy, the Lord sends us these afflictions to discipline us and make us better."

"Is it He that sends them?"

"Yes."

"Does He send all of them, mama?"

"Yes, dear, all of them. None of them comes by accident; He alone sends them, and always out of love for us, and to make us better."

"Isn't it strange?"

"Strange? Why, no, I have never thought of it in that way. I have not heard anyone call it strange before. It has always seemed natural and right to me, and wise and most kindly and merciful."

"Who first thought of it like that, mama? Was it you?"

"Oh no, child, I was taught it."

"Who taught you so, mama?"

"Why, really, I don't know—I can't remember. My mother, I suppose; or the preacher. But it's a thing that everybody knows."

"Well, anyway, it does seem strange. Did He give Billy Norris the typhus?"

"Yes."

"What for?"

"Why, to discipline him and make him good."

"But he died, mama, and so it couldn't make him good."

"Well, then, I suppose it was for some other reason. We know it was a good reason whatever it was."

"What do you think it was, mama?"

"Oh, you ask so many questions! I think it was to discipline his parents."

"Well, then, it wasn't fair, mama. Why should his life be taken away for their sake, when he wasn't doing anything?"

"Oh, I don't know! I only know it was for a good and wise and merciful reason."

"What reason, mama?"

"I think—I think—well, it was a judgement; it was to punish them for some sin they had committed."

"But he was the one that was punished, mama. Was that right?"

"Certainly, certainly. He does nothing that isn't right and wise and merciful. You can't understand these things now, dear, but when you are grown up you will understand them, and then you will see that they are just and wise."

After a pause:

"Did He make the roof fall in on the stranger that was trying to save the crippled old woman from the fire, mama?"

"Yes, my child. Wait! Don't ask me why, because I don't know. I only know it was to discipline some one, or be a judgement upon somebody, or to show His power."

"That drunken man that struck a pitchfork into Mrs. Welch's baby when—"

"Never mind about it, you needn't go into particulars; it was to discipline the child—that much is certain anyway."

"Mama, Mr. Burgess said in his sermon that billions of little creatures are sent into us to give us cholera, and typhoid, and lockjaw, and more than a thousand other sicknesses and—mama, does He send them?"

"Oh, certainly, child, certainly. Of course."

"What for?"

"Oh, to discipline us. Haven't I told you so, over and over again?"

"It's awful cruel, mama! And silly! and if I—"

"Hush, oh hush! Do you want to bring the lightning?"

"You know the lightning did come last week, mama, and struck the new church, and burnt it down. Was it to discipline the church?"

(Wearily) "Oh, I suppose so."

"But it killed a hog that wasn't doing anything. Was it to discipline the hog, mama?"

"Dear child, don't you want to run out and play for a while? If you would like to—"

"Mama, only think! Mr. Hollister says there isn't a bird, or fish, or reptile, or any other animal that hasn't got an enemy that Providence has sent to bite it and chase it and pester it and kill it and suck its blood and discipline it and make it good and religious. Is that true, mother—because if it is true why did Mr. Hollister laugh at it?"

"That Mr. Hollister is a scandalous person, and I don't want you to listen to anything he says."

"Why, mama, he is very interesting, and I think he tries to be good. He says the wasps catch spiders and cram them down into their nests in the ground—alive, mama!—and there they live and suffer days and days and days, and the hungry little wasps chewing their legs and gnawing into their bellies all the time, to make them good and religious and praise God for His infinite mercies. I think Mr. Hollister is just lovely, and ever so kind; for when I asked him if he would treat a spider like that he said he hoped to be damned if he would; and then he —Dear mama, have you fainted! I will run and bring help! Now this comes of staying in town this hot weather."[21]

For some people, such as Bryan, religion continues to explain aspects of the world long after empirical data suggest a more scientific explanation. For others, like little Bessie, religion is never a fully satisfying explanation for much of anything.

Religion and Social Organization

Since the time of Marx's dismissal of religion as a dangerous perverter of truth and Durkheim's celebration of it as humanity's highest cultural good, sociologists have investigated this complex and powerful institution. Their studies have revealed a variety of aspects relating the institution to social organization. We will briefly examine several of the most prominent investigations.

RELIGION AND THE SOCIOECONOMIC ORDER

In 1904 Max Weber published his now classic *The Protestant Ethic and the Spirit of Capitalism*. This work was primarily an investigation of the relationship of religion to the economic and social orders. At the time Weber undertook his study of religion, many sociologists agreed with Marx's tenet of economic determinism, which maintained that all social institutions (including religion) are determined by or result from economic factors. Thus Catholicism arose from the economic structure of feudalism and Protestantism from the economic structure of capitalism.

Weber turned Marx's analysis around. He demonstrated that religion can have a determining effect on the economic structure. Thus the Protestant religion encouraged people to value thrift, hard work, and sobriety. According to Weber, it was the people's belief in this *Protestant ethic* that provided the conditions in which capitalism could grow. In this case at least, religion was as important as material forces in determining the social order of a people.[22]

RELIGION AND SOCIAL STATUS

Another classic analysis of religious life, Liston Pope's *Millhands and Preachers* (1942), explores the relationship among religious beliefs, social class, and perceptions of the social order. Marx, Weber, and Durkheim all gave these factors consideration, at least indirectly, and these factors are considered in the six functions of religion that we have just discussed. It was Pope, however, who gave a detailed account of how the poor compensate for their lack of social status by emphasizing their religious status.

In *Millhands and Preachers* Pope demonstrated that the millworkers were bound together by their religious sect and had become a family of believers. Their religion gave them a sense of community, a sense of being supported under very trying living conditions. But most importantly, the religion of the millhands told them that they were better than the owners of the mills, that in the eyes of God they, not the wealthy, were the superior people.

Pope's study also makes distinct the dichotomy of *church* and *sect*.

The Sect	The Church (denomination)
1. Composed primarily of the poor and propertyless.	1. Composed primarily of the affluent and property owners.
2. On the cultural fringes of the community.	2. At the cultural center of the community.

3. Noted for renunciation of or indifference to the prevailing culture and social order; noncooperation with or ridicule of established churches.
4. Religion is personal, self-centered, and based on highly emotional individual experiences of the "gospel." A moral community excluding unworthy members.
5. Membership is voluntary, confessional; principal concern is with adults.
6. Emphasis is on evangelism, conversion, and emotional experiences.
7. Ministry is nonspecialized, unprofessionalized, and part-time (often composed of members of the congregation); participation by members in services and administration is high.
8. Psychology is one of persecution; stress is placed on a fu-

3. Noted for active affirmation or at least acceptance of the prevailing sociopolitical and economic order; cooperation with other established churches.
4. Religion is culture-centered, based on rational understanding of both biblical and denominational teaching. A social institution that embraces all who are socially compatible with it.
5. Membership is based on rites or social prerequisites; equal concern with adults and children of members.
6. Emphasis is on religious education, liturgy, catechism, and ritualistic incantations.
7. Ministry is specialized, highly educated, and full-time; delegated responsibility is to a comparatively small percentage of the membership.
8. Psychology is one of success and dominance; primary in-

The baptismal ceremony of many sects—both historically and today—stresses and formalizes adult entry into the group.

The priestly function of established churches is reflected in their socialization of children through involvement in rituals and ceremonies.

ture in the next world and emphasis on preparation for death.
9. Strict biblical standards adhered to, though particular interpretations vary.
10. Worship services marked by fervor and spontaneous expression of religious feelings; hymns tend to be in the form of folk music and ballads.

terest in worldly future and emphasis on successful worldly life.
9. General cultural standards adhered to.
10. Worship services have a fixed, highly traditional order and are marked by restraint, passive listening to sermons; regular services held at fixed intervals; use of slow, often stately hymns frequently originating in a remote liturgical past.[23]

As with virtually all dichotomies, the distinction between church and sect is based on ideal types, and in reality most religious groups tend to fall somewhere in between the extremes of church and sect. Clearly, sects tend to be more prophetic (challenging the status quo), while churches are priestly (defending it). Religious movements, like other collective movements, often begin with a small group headed by a charismatic leader, then pass through stages of change until they become highly bureaucratized. In this way the sect becomes a church.

The charismatic leader in religion is the prophet, and early Christianity, which stood in opposition to the established social order, had a prophet (Jesus), lay leadership, and many of the other characteristics of a sect. The teachings of Jesus are now subject to a wide range of interpretation. Christian sects still perceive Jesus as something of an antiestablishment revolutionary, whereas in the eyes of established churches, Jesus appears rather more conservative. In other words, the teachings of Jesus are interpreted according to the position of those doing the interpreting.

In Sinclair Lewis's *Elmer Gantry*, the main character addresses the question of the actual meaning of the teachings of Jesus.

> "What did he teach? One place in the Sermon on the Mount he advises—let me get my Bible—here it is: 'Let your light so shine before men that they may see your good works and glorify your Father which is in heaven,' and then five minutes later he is saying, 'Take heed that ye do not your alms before men, to be seen of them, otherwise ye have no reward of your Father which is in heaven.' That's an absolute contradiction, in the one document which is the charter of the whole Christian Church. Oh, I know you can reconcile them, Phil. That's the whole aim of the ministerial training: to teach us to reconcile contradictions by saying that one of them doesn't mean what it means—and it's always a good stunt to throw in 'You'd understand it if you'd only read it in the original Greek'!
>
> "There's just one thing that does stand out clearly and uncontra-

dicted in Jesus' teaching. He advocated a system of economics whereby no one saved money or stored up wheat or did anything but live like a tramp. If this teaching of his had been accepted, the world would have starved in twenty years after his death!"[24]

RELIGION AND CHANGING THE SOCIAL ORDER

Over time, a religion may vary in the function it exercises. Sometimes a religion, stressing its priestly function, gives passive assent to the status quo; at other times it may serve a distinctly prophetic function. This variation over time can be seen in the religion of the Plains Indians of the 1800s.

At that time, the Cheyenne, Pawnee, Sioux, and Arapaho tribes engaged in what sociologists refer to as *nativistic* and *revivalistic* movements. These were attempts by the Indians to restore the traditional native social order and drive the invaders from their territory. The Plains Indians hoped to accomplish their purpose by revival of a religious ceremony known as the *Ghost Dance*, from which the revivalist movement took its name. The Ghost Dance movement taught that through performance of this ritual dance Indians could make themselves immune to white men's bullets. Eventually, the whites would be destroyed in a great holocaust, and a world inhabited by the lost buffalo herds and ghosts of the dead would follow their demise.[25]

The Indian defeat at Wounded Knee in 1890 put an end to the Ghost Dance movement and thereby to the prophetic functioning of the Plains Indians' religion. In place of the Ghost Dance there arose the much more passive and priestly *Peyote cult*, which was primarily concerned with the search for accommodation and peace through the use of a form of cactus known as the peyote button. The priestly function of the Plains Indians' religion was now dominant.

One may argue the merits of the Ghost Dance as opposed to the Peyote cult.[26] The American Indian Movement (AIM) and other groups advocating social change would probably insist that the religious-political Ghost Dance was a much healthier form of religious expression. More passive seekers of spiritual growth, such as the followers of Carlos Castaneda, would maintain that the Peyote cult represented a superior religious form. In any case, the Indians themselves had little choice in 1890. The more priestly and accommodating cult was their only alternative.

Religion and Social Class

Different religions serve varying needs; they appeal to members of different social classes and support a diversity of world views. Table 9–1 gives a general profile — education, occupation, income, and so on — of American

Protestants (three denominations), Catholics, and Jews. For example, under education, we see that 24 percent of all Methodists are college educated, compared with 47 percent of all Episcopalians.

In the United States Protestant denominations have adherents in all social classes, with class distinctions appearing in various congregations and parishes. Yet correlations between social status and denominations exist. Episcopalians, Unitarians, Congregationalists, and Presbyterians tend to be upper and upper-middle class, while Baptists and Disciples of Christ are more often lower-middle and working class. There is a strong tendency for members of the lower classes to associate themselves with sects rather than established churches. The various Pentecostal and Holiness sects, which exhibit virtually all the characteristics of the ideal type of sect presented in the list on page 220, draw heavily from the lower classes.

Roman Catholicism has adherents from all social classes, although in this country there is a concentration of membership in the lower-middle and working classes. Internal distinctions within the Catholic church tend to be along ethnic lines. Most urban areas have Italian, Irish, Polish, Spanish, and other ethnic parishes. The ethnic cleavages that were so important to the immigrants to the United States of the late nineteenth and early twentieth centuries remain associated with the Catholic parish, which is still a community focal point.

Judaism in the United States tends to have class distinctions within the religion, although, like Protestantism, it has adherents from all social classes. Related to the pattern of upward mobility for Jews in the United States has been a movement away from Orthodoxy to Conservative and Reform Judaism. The higher the education and the better the income, the greater is the probability that a Jew will be a member of a Reform or Conservative congregation rather than an Orthodox one. The older Orthodox beliefs give way to the more cosmopolitan views of later and more educated generations.

Ethnographic and extensive research surveys over a rather long period of time indicate that religion tends to support and maintain social stratification in the United States. Despite the continuing Christian emphasis on individual autonomy and the divine worth of the person, religion is, finally, a group phenomenon.

This characteristic, the tendency of religion to draw together people from similar backgrounds and with similar ideas, is apparent in the Jesus movement of the 1970s. The adherents are primarily youthful dropouts who are refugees from the political activism and drug subcultures of the 1960s. They have concluded that major social issues such as racism, power conflicts, war, poverty, and drug abuse are ultimately issues of personal morality.[27] The Jesus movement supports and maintains this belief. The movement tends to antagonize both sects and traditional Christian churches by its use of such devices as "up-beat" advertising. Gone are the days of early Christianity when the outline of a fish drawn in the sand

TABLE 9–1
Profiles of American Religions (by percent)

Characteristics	Protestants Total	Methodists	Episcopalians	Baptists	Catholics	Jews
Percentage of population	65	14	3	21	26	3
EDUCATION						
College	22	24	47	12	21	42
High school	52	55	42	54	57	42
Grade school	26	21	12	34	23	16
OCCUPATION						
Professional and business	20	22	38	14	22	40
Clerical and sales	12	12	12	10	12	22
Farmers	8	8	1	8	3	1
Manual	40	38	25	49	45	16
INCOME						
$15,000+	12	13	32	6	15	30
$10,000–$14,999	22	23	25	18	27	26
$7,000–$9,999	20	20	15	20	23	16
$5,000–$6,999	17	17	10	20	5	11
$3,000–$4,999	15	14	7	19	10	9
Under $3,000	13	12	10	16	9	7
COMMUNITY SIZE						
1,000,000+	12	10	20	11	31	66
500,000–999,999	10	9	18	9	18	14
50,000–499,999	22	21	25	22	26	14
2,500–49,999	18	19	16	18	10	3
Under 2,500 (rural)	37	41	22	39	14	1
POLITICS						
Republican	33	35	44	21	19	6
Democrat	39	36	32	52	52	63
Independent	26	26	23	25	27	29

SOURCE: Gallup Opinion Index, *Religion in America, 1971*. Report no. 70, April 1971, p. 57.

signified a fellow believer; now it is "Honk If You Love Jesus" emblazoned in bold bright colors on bumperstickers.

Such dashes of the advertising age, though, are joined with a very traditional personal asceticism. Jesus people emphasize temperance, moderation, and a rejection of material goods. Table 9–2a shows the decline in premarital sex and the use of alcohol, tobacco, and drugs by people who joined the Jesus movement. Table 9–2b illustrates the changes in political self-characterization brought about by joining the Jesus movement. The dramatic increase in the number of people characterizing themselves politically as "nothing, don't care" reflects the movement's belief that personal morality is more important than politics in contemporary society.

TABLE 9–2a

Sex, Use of Alcohol, Tobacco, and Drugs Before and After Joining Christ Commune (first visit)

	Before	After
Premarital sex	76	5
Alcohol	75	1
Tobacco	59	2
Drugs	79	0

TABLE 9–2b

Political Self-Characterization Before and After Joining Christ Commune (first visit)

Characterize Self As	Before	After	Change
Conservative	8	6	−25%
Moderate	6	5	−17
Liberal	19	1	−95
Radical	23	3	−87
Nothing, don't care	27	71	+163

SOURCE: Mary White Harder, James T. Richardson, and Robert B. Simmonds, "Jesus People," *Psychology Today*, December 1972, p. 110.

Magic, Witchcraft, and the Supernatural

Despite our everyday reliance on scientific ways of thinking and sophisticated technology, numerous unconventional religions and a belief in the supernatural continue to thrive. In the United States today, 175,000 full- and part-time astrologers do an annual business estimated at $200 million. Various forms of *scrying* (seeing or perceiving the future) continue to hold the confidence of many of our contemporaries, who consult fortunetellers using crystal balls, tea leaves, the palm of one's hand, or a smooth surface of water to predict the future. While the *diviners*, those practicing the art or science of scrying, may only perceive the future, *sorcerers* are thought to be able to control it. The objectives of such "mystics" are sometimes quite worldly, as in the case of the Italian sorcerer who put the "evil eye" on the opponents of his favorite soccer team.[28]

Although many of us tend to think of good and wicked witches only in the context of *The Wizard of Oz*, a substantial number of people take witchcraft quite seriously. In fact, the faith and seriousness believers in witchcraft attach to the practice of the supernatural arts often exceed the commitment of those professing more standard religions. The British witch-diviner Sybil Leek, who now lives in Las Vegas, contends that it is only through the efforts of good witches such as herself that much evil in the world is averted. If it were not for their work, she states, the forces of black magic would control life.

Despite the large number of people and the great amount of money involved in occult practices, most modern societies find such practices unacceptable. Indeed, most industrialized societies consider them superstitious holdovers from more primitive times. Magic is seen as the "science" of the less-developed countries and peoples. Only a preliterate tribal group would cope with the world through such means.

Magic and superstition in our own society tend to be centered in very closed subcultures known as *cults,* whose practices and membership are quite secret. When occult practices are openly displayed—as in the case of numerology, astrology, or common superstitions, such as lucky numbers, black cats, and breaking mirrors—those who are sophisticated and educated are constrained by contemporary norms to treat these practices in a glib manner. But the existence of such practices and the success of recent books like *The Secret Life of Plants, The Bermuda Triangle,* and *Chariots of the Gods?* strongly suggest that a good many people consider the "nonstandard" science of the supernatural something other than the carryings-on of lunatics and the naive.

Chapter Summary

Religion as a social institution is characterized by its universality, its rituals, its sacredness, and its persistence. In an age marked by trust in empirical science, the continuing presence of religion as a stable force in the day-to-day lives of individuals may seem strange to some. Yet an examination of the major social functions that religion performs reveals that the institution continues to serve a variety of vital roles in contemporary society. It is a major force both for personal and societal change and for stability. Religion can console us and give us strength in times of personal difficulty or national crisis, and it can inspire us to bring about change both in ourselves and society.

Aspects of the Jesus movement include "up-beat" advertising, joyous expressions of faith, and personal asceticism.

Sybil Leek, one of the most famous contemporary witches.

Most scholars now recognize that religion is a determinant as well as a reflection of social structure. Weber's work on the Protestant ethic marked a rejection of the more extreme forms of Marxist orthodoxy. The Marxist interpretation of religion, however, remains basic to sociological inquiry. For example, sociologists continue to find a strong correlation between social class and different forms of religion. Religion among the lower classes usually takes the form of sects, which emphasize the prophetic function (challenging the status quo). Among the upper and middle classes, churches, which tend to emphasize the priestly function (reinforcing the status quo), are the dominant religious form. Historically, a group's religion tends to change with changes in the group itself. The shift of the Plains Indians from the Ghost Dance to the Peyote cult is one example.

The major American religions reflect both the class outlook and status of their membership. Religion still plays a major role in this country, though most often a passive one (a priestly role). The most recent change in the institution of religion in this country is the rise of numerous mystical cults and the Jesus movement among the young.

Finally, unconventional forms of religion—the occult, the magical, and the supernatural—continue to be present to a surprising degree. Practices that are usually thought of as being part of a preliterate culture command a considerable following in the "advanced" nations as well.

Key Terms for Review

age-grading function, p. 214
buttress function, p. 214
church, p. 220
cult, p. 227
diviners, p. 226
explanation function, p. 214

RELIGION / 229

Ghost Dance, p. 223
nativistic movement, p. 223
Peyote cult, p. 223
priestly function, p. 208
prophetic function, p. 211
Protestant ethic, p. 220
religion, p. 207
revivalistic movement, p. 223
sacred, p. 207
sect, p. 220
scrying, p. 226
self-identity function, p. 212
sorcerers, p. 226
superstition, p. 205

Suggested Readings

SOCIOLOGICAL

Lenski, Gerhard. *The Religious Factor.* Garden City, N.Y.: Doubleday, 1961. This widely acclaimed and insightful study is based on survey research data collected in Detroit. Lenski examines the role and importance of religion in contemporary American urban society. Religion is viewed in the context of standard sociological categories, such as race and ethnicity, social class, and education.

O'Dea, Thomas F. *The Sociology of Religion.* Englewood Cliffs, N.J.: Prentice-Hall, 1966. O'Dea's concise review of the dominant themes in the sociological study of religion is an extremely useful introduction to the area. This work is part of the "Foundations of Modern Sociology" series.

Pope, Liston. *Millhands and Preachers.* New Haven, Conn.: Yale University Press, 1942. This is Pope's now classic exploration of how the small religious sects of the millhands assist in compensating for their demeaning and degrading life. The study is a well-researched and well-written portrayal of the interaction between religion and social status.

Yinger, J. Milton. *Religion, Society, and the Individual.* New York: Macmillan, 1957. This is a sound and thorough examination of religion in society. Yinger's sociological and philosophic grasp of the issues makes this one of the best presentations currently available.

LITERARY

Lawrence, Jerome, and Robert E. Lee. *Inherit the Wind.* New York: Bantam, 1964. The confrontation between somewhat glib rationalism in the person of Clarence Darrow and the old-time Bible Belt religion of William Jennings Bryan is presented in this best-selling account of the Scopes trial.

Lewis, Sinclair. *Elmer Gantry.* New York: Harcourt, Brace, 1927. The very human and often conniving Elmer Gantry has served many Americans as the twentieth-century prototype of the hellfire preacher. Gantry takes us through the very old battle of spirit and flesh, with flesh usually winning out.

Short, Robert L. *The Gospel According to Peanuts.* Richmond: John Knox Press, 1964. This is a highly sophisticated and amusing presentation of the Scriptures and their implications, employing the cartoons of Charles Schulz. One comes away from Short's work with a new understanding of popular culture and the realization that Schulz, who is an active lay preacher, often thrusts religion into the comic sections of daily newspapers.

IN THIS CHAPTER

Functions of Education   231

    Transmission of culture   232
    Placement   234
    Development of new knowledge   236
    Individual development   236

American Values Regarding Education   237

Problems of American Education   239

    Goals of American education   242
    Economic support for schools   246
    Schools and lower-class children   251
    The large, bureaucratic school   255
    Are students changing?   257

Summary   257

Key Terms for Review   258

Suggested Readings   258

10

Do Americans think that all education is good?
Do people expect too much from schools?
Should schools teach academic knowledge or vocational training? facts or morality?
Should schools justify the status quo or advocate change?
Is formal education insensitive toward poor and minority-group students? Are testing procedures culturally biased and racist?

EDUCATION

In *Pudd'nhead Wilson* Mark Twain offers a pithy comment on the importance of education: "Training is everything. The peach was once a bitter almond; cauliflower is nothing but cabbage with a college education."[1] All societies face the task of transforming their newborn — in Twain's analogy, "bitter almonds" or "cabbages" — into culture-possessing individuals. In a preliterate society this socialization process rests almost entirely with parents and relatives, who educate children in practically all aspects of life. But in modern societies education increasingly takes place in organizations. Elementary and secondary schools, colleges, and universities are now charged with the responsibility for education, and teaching is a formal, planned activity.

Formal education in the United States is an immensely large undertaking. As of 1973 approximately 59 million students, from three to thirty-four years of age, attended about 120,000 schools. Over $89 billion, or 7.7 percent of the gross national product, was spent in support of schools. And persons twenty-five years of age and older had completed, on the average, 12.3 years of formal education.[2] Additionally, more people are pursuing four-year college degrees than ever before (see Figure 10–1), and some people spend still more time in universities working toward graduate degrees.

An institution of such importance in American society deserves further study. The functions of education, the expectations that Americans have of their educational system, and the problems that many schools are encountering will be the topics of investigation in this chapter.

Functions of Education

Education, like all institutions, helps a society solve its problems. We will begin our discussion of education by examining how it does this — how it functions to serve the individual and society.

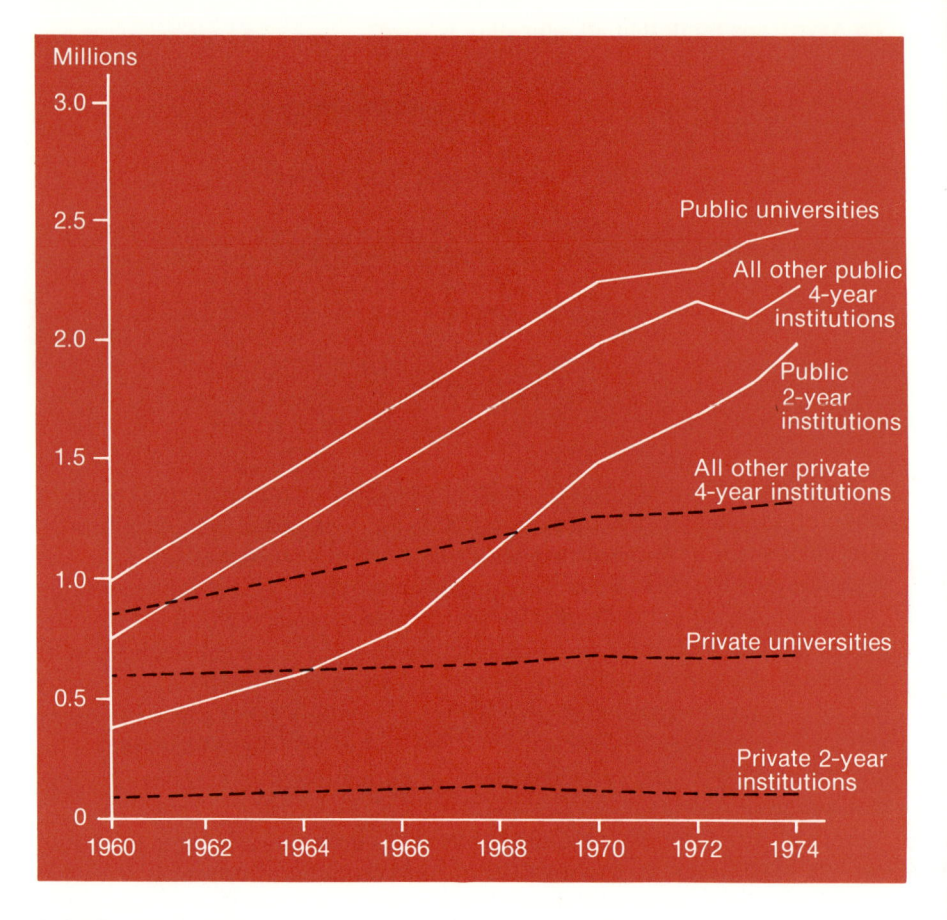

FIGURE 10-1   Enrollment in Higher Education, 1960–1974
SOURCE: Adapted from U.S. Department of Heath, Education, and Welfare, *The Condition of Education, 1976 Edition: A Statistical Report on the Condition of Education in the United States* (Washington, D.C., 1976), p. 17.

TRANSMISSION OF CULTURE

Elementary and secondary schools provide us with fundamental information, such as basic reading and math skills, so that we can make our way through a highly complicated world of income tax forms, applications, written instructions, and reports. Joseph C. Pattison in "How to Write an 'F' Paper," illustrates in a "backward" way the basic rules our culture follows in formal writing. As an English teacher and agent of socialization, he gives "advice" to students on how to write an "F" paper. His facetious approach leads us to suspect that many instructors are cynical about their students' ability to learn such vital rules.

> Writing an "F" paper is admittedly not an easy task, but one can learn to do it by grasp of the principles to use. The thirteen below, if

practiced at all diligently, should lead any student to that fortune in his writing.

Obscure the ideas:

1. Select a topic that is big enough to let you wander around the main idea without ever being forced to state it precisely. . . .

2. Pad! Pad! Pad! Do not develop your ideas. Simply restate them in safe, spongy generalizations . . .

3. Disorganize your discussion. For example, if you are using the time order to present your material, keep the reader alert by making a jump from the past to the present only to spring back into the past preparatory to a leap into the future preceding a return hop into the present just before the finish of the point about the past. . . .

4. Begin a new paragraph every sentence or two. . . .

Mangle the sentences:

5. Fill all the areas of your sentences with deadwood. . . .

6. Using fragments and run-on or comma-spliced sentences. . . .

7. Your sentence order invert for statement of the least important matters. . . .

8. You, in the introduction, body, and conclusion of your paper, to show that you can contrive ornate, graceful sentences, should use involution. . . .

Slovenize the diction:

9. Add the popular "-wise" and "-ize" endings to words. . . .

10. Use vague words in place of precise ones. . . .

11. Employ lengthy Latinate locutions wherever possible. Shun the simplicity of style that comes from apt use of short, old, familiar words, especially those of Anglo-Saxon origin. . . .

12. Inject humor into your writing by using the wrong word occasionally. Write "then" when you mean "than." . . .

13. Find a "tried and true" phrase to use to clinch a point. It will have a comfortingly folksy sound for the reader. . . .

Well, too ensconce this whole business in a nutshell, you, above all, an erudite discourse on nothing in the field of your topic should pen. Thereby gaining the reader's credence in what you say.

Suggestion-wise, one last thing: File-ize this list for handy reference the next time you a paper write.[3]

The information taught to elementary and high school students, however, goes beyond basic skills. Schools also transmit cultural values and norms regarding good citizenship, cheating, fighting, chewing gum, lying, cursing, and body cleanliness. Many of us can remember the time when our third-grade teacher was more concerned with our slouching at our desks or the degree of respect we showed for the flag than our ability to multiply and divide.

Colleges, universities, and occasionally some high schools build upon

Much early schooling is concerned with transmitting ideal cultural values, such as honesty, trust, and concern for others.

fundamental information and teach specialized knowledge. And as our society becomes more technically complex, schools and teachers at all levels will play an increasingly important role in transmitting specialized information.

PLACEMENT

Teachers, counselors, and school administrators have been given the right and, in fact, the obligation by society to test and evaluate students. Accordingly, some students will be labeled "bright and intelligent," while others will be regarded as "slow and backward." Such labels can have a profound impact on the student's future. For example, a student labeled "shiftless and not very bright" by school representatives may find many future routes closed. In high school he or she might be advised to take vocational training courses rather than college preparatory courses in mathematics. Personal recommendations for future jobs are also likely to reflect the negative label.

James Herndon, in *How to Survive in Your Native Land*, discusses the process that schools and teachers use to sort out "successful" students and "failures."

> Winning is never permanent. You may be a winner in the first grade, but by the fourth you may be losing. The rites of passive of the

school go on and on. Each year it is circumcision time all over again; obviously you may weep for what has been hacked off by the time you are thirty-five and have a Ph.D.

How does the school make certain that it will have winners and losers? Well, obviously by giving grades. If you give A's, you must also give F's. Without the rest of the grades, the A is meaningless. Even a B is less good than an A — in short, every kid who does not get an A is failing and losing to some extent. The median on the bell curve is not a median, it is not an average, it is not a norm, not to the school and not to the kids in the school. It is a losing sign, a failure, and a hex. You must be way out there on the right-hand edge where the curve approaches the base line. But it is the nature of bell curves that most everyone cannot be there.

But even if the school abandons grades and IQ and achievement testing it will still produce losers aplenty and winners. The fundamental act of the American public school is to deal with children in groups. Once it has a group of children of any age, it decides what those children will be expected to do, and then the teacher, as representative of the school, tells the children all at once. The children hear it, and when they hear it they know whether they can do it or not. Some of the children will already know how to do it. They will win.[4]

Herndon is surely correct that grades and IQ scores are the major devices used today to sort out and place individuals into jobs and positions. But many people are asking whether these devices are valid indicators of a person's true worth and potential. Test items on which grades and IQ scores are based can be illogical, vague, and culture-bound. Does an IQ

Schools are expected to evaluate students and channel them into appropriate programs — academic or vocational. However, the devices used to place students, mainly grades and IQ scores, have come under considerable criticism.

score mean potential to learn, as most think, or is it merely a crude indicator of what has already been achieved by an individual in particular areas of academic knowledge? The evidence suggests that this latter explanation is more accurate and goes far to discredit the common interpretation of IQ scores. Yet these scores continue to have weight in our culture in determining who will receive training for high-status jobs.

Besides limiting job opportunities, low grades and IQ scores can also harm individuals psychologically. Those labeled losers may develop negative self-concepts and actually resign themselves to lesser goals than they might otherwise accomplish. Such persons experience the phenomenon of the *self-fulfilling prophecy*—they become what they believe themselves to be. Thus a negative self-image (the person is taught to think of himself as a loser) may contribute to personal failure. Of course, self-fulfilling prophecies can also work in the opposite direction: a positive self-image may motivate a person toward greater accomplishments.[5]

Despite the deficiencies in current methods of testing and grading and the destructive effects of incorrectly labeling students, the educational system will be expected to continue the placement function. Given the necessity of performing this function, educators will hopefully become more sensitive to the impact of labels and the criteria on which labels are based.

DEVELOPMENT OF NEW KNOWLEDGE

Part of the "American dream" is a belief in progress, and new knowledge is sometimes, but certainly not always, related to progress. Our society relies heavily on its educational institution, particularly colleges and universities, to develop new knowledge. University researchers are awarded government, business, and foundation grants to conduct a wide variety of studies ranging from the discovery of new energy sources to the development of new ways to make organizations efficient. Ideally, academicians are supposed to test and question existing information and search for new knowledge to improve the quality of life in our society.

Although universities have been the source of many new ideas, some people criticize professors for spending too much time doing research and neglecting their teaching duties. Scholars defend themselves by maintaining that research and teaching are complementary. Engaging in research stimulates the instructor to provide information for the student in the classroom. The debate over university goals is likely to continue.

INDIVIDUAL DEVELOPMENT

Education functions to provide individuals with skills, knowledge, and official titles (e.g., M.D., B.A., Ph.D., LL.D.) to aid their upward social mobility. It has been shown that one's lifetime earnings are directly re-

In the 1800s the spelling bee was a common method of encouraging Americans to learn to read and write, skills needed in a complex society.

lated to the amount of schooling one has. Based on the value of the dollar in 1972, the average lifetime income of males who start work at age eighteen and have a high school degree is estimated at $479,000. Males with one to three years of college, however, will earn an average of $543,000 in their lifetime, and those with four or more years of college will, on average, accumulate $758,000.[6] Formal education allows a person to enter more prestigious occupations and gives greater opportunity for job mobility and advancement.

American Values Regarding Education

The massive size of formal education in the United States is, in part, a result of our society's extensive economic and professional specialization. But specialization is only one of the factors accounting for millions of students and billions of dollars spent to support their education. Our emphasis on education is also a result of our cultural values.

One value held by virtually all Americans is that education is our major hope for a better life. Many see education as crucial to this nation's freedom, for only through an informed electorate can we preserve democracy. James Bryant Conant, while president of Harvard University, echoed this general feeling:

The primary concern of American education today is not the development of the appreciation of the "good life" in young gentlemen born to the purple.... Our purpose is to cultivate in the largest possible number of our future citizens an appreciation of both the responsibilities and the benefits which come to them because they are Americans and free.[7]

Education is also seen as the major hope for a better life because it provides individuals with a chance for upward social mobility. All citizens of the United States have the right to equal opportunity in schooling so that they can achieve success, but unfortunately the ideal of equality in education has never been reached, as we will discuss shortly.

We must caution, however, that Americans do not believe that all education is "good." In some communities teachers might have been called traitors and fired for discussing the irony that thousands of American draft resisters still living in Canada were unable to return to their homes while thousands of Vietnamese refugees were welcomed to the United States during 1975. Also, until recently sex education, religion, and communism were generally considered taboo subjects in the public schools. Moreover, a person with too much education is often eyed with suspicion. Unfortunately, American society has always experienced some *anti-intellectualism*—the belief that individuals with too much schooling are impractical dreamers and cannot be trusted.[8] In the view of many people, too much education tends to produce mad scientists who, given the chance, would manipulate the masses toward evil ends.

Many Americans value especially education that is practical in a short-run, visibly productive way. These people believe that the purpose of education is to help the individual find a job, achieve a promotion, or become a better citizen. They see abstract, theoretical topics, such as Kantian philosophy and theories of penal reform, as intellectual exercises that are inapplicable to the "real" world. Those who dissent from this view hold that we should explore all topics since any knowledge is valuable and important to humankind.

Many Americans also believe that education should teach individuals the importance of work and competition. Americans have been described as adhering to what Max Weber called the Protestant ethic, which, as we noted in the last chapter, encourages people to be self-disciplined, competitive, and hard working in order to gain worldly, economic success.[9] Our society does indeed stress the virtues of hard work and intense competition. These values have become deeply embedded in American education, and teachers place great emphasis on them. Unfortunately, competition has been overly stressed by some students and has come to mean the ruthless pursuit of high grades rather than the search for knowledge and self-fulfillment.

Finally, Americans value formal education for the social conformity it can produce. Particularly during the elementary and high school years, students are taught to give allegiance to their country and its flag, and to obey societal laws in general. Students are supposed to accept uncritically the goals, teaching methods, and rules of their school.

Education helps weld together our heterogeneous society. Children from diverse backgrounds are taught basically the same language, cultural values, mathematics, biology, and so forth.

The emphasis on conformity is, however, contradictory to another American value—the belief that people should "stand on their own two feet" and "think for themselves." Individuals are said to have dignity and worth as well as responsibility for their own actions. What we find here is a value conflict: both social conformity and individualism are seen to be needed for the society's survival.

Problems of American Education

Few people would question that American education faces serious problems today. Probably no other novel better sensitizes a reader to the problems of modern education than Bel Kaufman's *Up the Down Staircase*. The story tells of the joys and sorrows of Sylvia Barrett, a teacher beginning her high school teaching career in the New York City school system. Many of her concerns and frustrations are seen in the postscripts of notes she wrote to fellow teachers.

> *P. S. Did you know that according to the Board of Education's estimate it would cost the city $8 million to reduce the size of classes "by a single child" throughout the city? . . .*
>
> *P. S. Did you know that only 21% of New York City's budget goes for education, compared with as much as 70% in small communities? . . .*
>
> *P. S. Did you know that out of the 77,000 dropouts in New York City 90% are Negroes and Puerto Ricans?*[10]

Sylvia Barrett's student suggestion box was continually filled to overflowing. The suggestions, some humorous and others deadly serious and heartbreaking, illustrate many of the students' problems with teachers, school, and parents. Students dropped these notes into the box:

> *What I learned in English is to doodle. It's such a boring subject I just sat and doodled the hours away. Sometimes I wore sunglasses in class to sleep.*
>
> Doodlebug

. . .

Don't think you'll get off so easy just because you speak nice and you don't seem scarred of us, last term we had a man teacher and we made him cry.

Yr. E̶m̶e̶n̶y̶ Enemy

. . .

Everybody is always picking on me because of prejudice and that goes for everybody. Mr. Machabe realy has it in for me just because I am color. I have allready fill a complain to Dr. Clark.

Edward Williams, Esq.

. . .

I want to thank you for giving me your time after school, for encouraging me to write, for trying. But with 40 others in the class, whose problems are so different, I realize how little you can do, and I feel we are both wasted.

Elizabeth Ellis

. . .

I know school is supposed to help me with my life, but so far it didn't.

Rusty

. . .

The more time in school the less time to make $.

Dropout

. . .

Federal Lunches are Lousy.

Eater

. . .

I'm getting behine because school goes to fast for me to retain the work. Maybe if they go more slower with the readings?

Repeter

. . .

When in Miss Lewis' class a pupil finds it necessary to visit the men's room he is often denied that priviledge.

Sophomore

. . .

I wrote the same identical book report for two different English teachers I had last term. One gave me 91 and the other 72 on the same identical paper. Go figure it out![11]

Are driver education programs such as this an expensive "frill" that schools could eliminate, or should more schools have such programs?

Letters from parents to Sylvia Barrett indicate the frustrations teachers experience in educating children. For example, some parents undermined the effort of teachers and showed little concern about their child's learning.

Dear Miss Barret,

It's not my son's (Lou) fault he failed spelling, he comes from a broken home. When he gets bad marks it only discourages him more and he starts cutting up. He's getting too big for the other kids in his class, so all the teachers said they'll pass him on. After all, it's only spelling.

Mrs. Bess Martin[12]

Overcrowding, understaffing, insufficient supplies, inefficiency, racial prejudice, student boredom, high dropout rates, and teacher incompetency are just a few of the many problems facing formal education today. Although it may be an exaggeration to say that the school walls are completely falling down, those walls are indeed crumbling and cracking. The problems facing American education should be closely examined.

GOALS OF AMERICAN EDUCATION

When the typical citizen is asked, "What should schools teach?" that person is likely to be momentarily puzzled but then may glibly state that schools should teach "facts and information." School "experts" are likely to give the same vague response, although they may disguise their lack of an answer with educational jargon.

Jacques Barzun, in his insightful book *Teacher in America*, attempts to understand the goals of American education. After asking what citizens expect of their schools, he arrives at a twofold conclusion: everybody wants something different and people expect far too much.

> *Apparently Education is to do everything that the rest of the world leaves undone. . . . An influential critic, head of a large university, wants education to generate a classless society; another asks that education root out racial intolerance (in the third or the ninth grade, I wonder?); still another requires that college courses be designed to improve labor relations. One man, otherwise sane, thinks the solution of the housing problem has bogged down—in the schools; and another proposes to make the future householders happy married couples—through the schools. . . .*
>
> *Then there are the hundreds of specialists in endless "vocations" who want Education to turn out practiced engineers, affable hotelkeepers, and finished literary artists. . . .*
>
> *No one in his senses would affirm that Schooling is the hope of the world. But to say this is to show up the folly of perpetually confusing Education with the work of the schools; the folly of believing against all evidence that by taking boys and girls for a few hours each day between the ages of seven and twenty-one, our teachers can "turn out" all the human products that we like to fancy when we are disgusted with ourselves and our neighbors. It is like believing that brushing the teeth is the key to health. No ritual by itself will guarantee anything. . . . Free compulsory "education" is a great thing, an indispensable thing, but it will not make the City of God out of Public School No. 26.*[13]

Granted that our schools cannot accomplish every social purpose, what can we reasonably expect them to work for? There is no general agree-

Although the situation is changing somewhat today, vocational training programs have typically fostered traditional male-female roles. Girls have been taught to cook and sew or become beauticians, for example, while boys have learned woodworking and similar "masculine" skills.

ment. Debate over for what, and for whom, formal education exists centers on three major issues.

Academic Knowledge versus Vocational Training. A major debate rages in our society over whether schools should be teaching academic knowledge or providing vocational training. *Academic knowledge* refers to education that teaches a person to think, understand, question, and reason. The goal is accomplished by study of the fine arts, humanities, social sciences, and physical and biological sciences. In contrast, *vocational training* refers to education aimed at imparting specialized skills for particular jobs. Instruction is less concerned with fostering general knowledge and an ability to understand the world than with providing occupational skills and on-the-job experience. Police science, dentistry, fire science, nursing, hotel management, office administration, and cosmetology are generally thought of as vocational-training programs.

There is a clear demand for both academic knowledge and vocational training in our society. Few education systems, however, have the student demand or the resources and personnel to provide extensive, quality education in both orientations. Thus there is conflict within academia, particularly in secondary schools and institutions of higher learning, over which orientation should be given priority.

Elite versus the Masses. A second debate over goals concerns whether schools should teach only a select few, the "bright" elite, or everyone who wishes to enter the classroom, the masses. Until the late 1800s education in the United States was directed primarily toward the upper and upper-middle classes. Most secondary schools were private academies that prepared students for the universities, where they learned a profession, such as law, theology, or medicine. Education was for "gentlemen" and was a

In marked contrast to today, schoolmasters once used stern discipline and corporal punishment to instill cultural norms.

means to maintain status. At the turn of the century, however, the need for both a skilled labor force and a literate population which could participate in political affairs led to the growth of public schools. Mass education had arrived.

Some Americans question whether mass education is working. They argue that although schools are raising the level of skills of many individuals, the quality of education has gone down. Many instructors in introductory courses in state colleges would agree. They maintain that a large class consisting of students with a wide range of intellectual abilities forces them to dilute class material. Jacques Barzun, in *Teacher in America*, echoes this educational elitist stance by discussing a question most teachers in state-supported schools face: Which level student should I teach? Barzun shows little sympathy for the unmotivated student or the slow learner.

If every college were in a position to replace the lower half of its student body with a group equal in caliber to its present upper half, one of the great dilemmas of college teaching would vanish. For among teachers, there is a professional meaning to the question, "Whom shall we teach?" That meaning is, Shall I work upon the top students in the group before me or spend most of my time whipping up the laggards? . . . In a normal class, the break comes somewhat below the median. A student of "C" grade is either a good man not working or a really poor bet. This is sufficiently recognized whenever a "screening" for putting students on probation takes place; and in pedagogical literature, the "average" student forms the subject of innumerable attempts to raise or rouse him. This is the man I should prefer to call "subaverage," in the belief that if we really tapped the best talents in the country, the average would be of astonishingly good quality. But so far the only schemes proposed for coping with him consist either in segregation by means of placement tests, or in designing special courses, slower paced or somehow diluted. . . .

Beyond the line that separates the educable from the rest lies a wasteland that would require vast irrigation and incubator nursing of each weakly plant to turn into a flowering plain. The sluggish minds are stunted, timid, rooted in resentments, and paralyzed by a laziness which is not of the body merely, but of the emotions. They are not so much hopeless for teaching as themselves without hope of learning, and if no fairness of form or skill of hand redeems them in their own eyes, they are indeed the disinherited. . . . We must teach those who can learn, having first found them wherever they may be and cleared the path that leads to the campus.[14]

One solution suggested for the elite versus the masses dilemma is to have diverse types of schools, some designed for mass participation and others directed toward the intellectual elite. Unfortunately, where different types of schools now operate, socioeconomic status rather than academic potential usually determines who will attend the elite schools. Another suggestion is for society to increase not only the financial rewards but also the prestige of blue-collar occupations, thereby lessening societal pressure for individuals to enter college and pursue such already overcrowded professions as law and teaching. Americans seem to be quite unwilling, however, to change their rather unfavorable image of blue-collar occupations. (See Table 7–1 in chapter 7 for status rankings of ninety occupations.)

Status Quo versus Change. A third debate over educational goals involves the question of whether schools should teach existing, conservative ideas, thus perpetuating the status quo, or teach new ideas and advocate social change. Jules Henry, in an article entitled "American Schoolrooms: Learning the Nightmare," contends that American society is no different from any other in wanting its schools to stress tradition and stability. Although we may give lip service to creativity and independent thinking, most educators, representing the larger society, do not want creative types who dare to question basic cultural norms and who attempt to foster social disorganization. Jules Henry states the problem as follows:

> *Another learning problem inherent in the human condition is this: We must conserve culture while changing it, we must always be more sure of surviving than of adapting. Whenever a new idea appears, our first concern as animals must be that it does not kill us; then, and only then, can we look at it from other points of view. In general, primitive people solved this problem simply by walling their children off from new possibilities by educational methods that, largely through fear, so narrowed the perceptual sphere that nontraditional ways of viewing the world became unthinkable.*
>
> *The function of education has never been to free the mind and the spirit of man, but to bind them. To the end that the mind and the spirits of his children should never escape, Homo sapiens has wanted acquiescence, not originality, from his offspring. It is natural that this should be so, for where every man is unique there is no society, and where there is no society there can be no man. Contemporary American educators think they want creative children, yet it is an open question as to what they expect these children to create. If all through school the young were provoked to question the Ten Commandments, the sanctity of revealed religion, the foundations of patriotism, the profit motive, the two-party system, monogamy, the laws of incest, and so on, we would have more creativity than we could handle. In teaching our children to accept fundamentals of social relationships and religious beliefs without question we follow the ancient highways of the human race.*[15]

The debate over whether schools should seek to conserve or reform cultural values surfaced during the university turmoil of the 1960s. The Students for a Democratic Society (SDS) maintained that universities should be used as instruments of social change to solve such problems as poverty, racism, and war. At this same time resistance to almost any sort of change was particularly strong among the dominant political, military, and business interests.

Debates over educational goals are actually debates over the future course of society. In *Crisis in the Classroom* Charles E. Silberman tells of a legendary conversation between an imprisoned rabbi and a chief of police in regard to God's question "Where art thou?" Silberman implies that American society cannot answer this question and thus there is a crisis in the classroom. He makes a plea for citizens and educators not to throw up their hands in despair over the task before them.

> *Legend has it that Rabbi Schneur Zalman, one of the great Hasidic rabbis of the late eighteenth and early nineteenth centuries, was imprisoned in St. Petersburg on false charges. While awaiting trial, he was visited by the chief of police, a thoughtful man. Struck by the quiet majesty of the rabbi's appearance and demeanor, the official engaged him in conversation, asking a number of questions that had puzzled him in reading the Scriptures. Their discussion turned to the story of the Garden of Eden. Why was it, the official asked, that a God who was all-knowing had to call out when Adam was hiding and ask him, "Where art thou?"*
>
> *"You do not understand the meaning of the question," the rabbi answered. "This is a question God asks of every man in every generation. After all your wanderings, after all your efforts, after all your years, O man, where art thou?"*
>
> *It is a question asked of societies as well as of individuals. One is almost afraid to ask it of this society at this moment in time; the crisis in the classroom is but one aspect of the larger crisis of American society as a whole, a crisis whose resolution is problematical at best. It does no good, however, to throw up our hands at the enormity of the task; we must take hold of it where we can, for the time for failure is long since passed.*[16]

ECONOMIC SUPPORT FOR SCHOOLS

Children who attend a Palm Beach or Beverly Hills school are provided with some of the best teachers, curriculums, facilities, and supplies available in our society, while in Harlem, Watts, and other lower-class communities, children are faced with the worst school conditions in the nation. Some education systems have more than ample economic support while others are in financial ruins because school financing is largely a local matter. Over half the monies contributed to public education are from

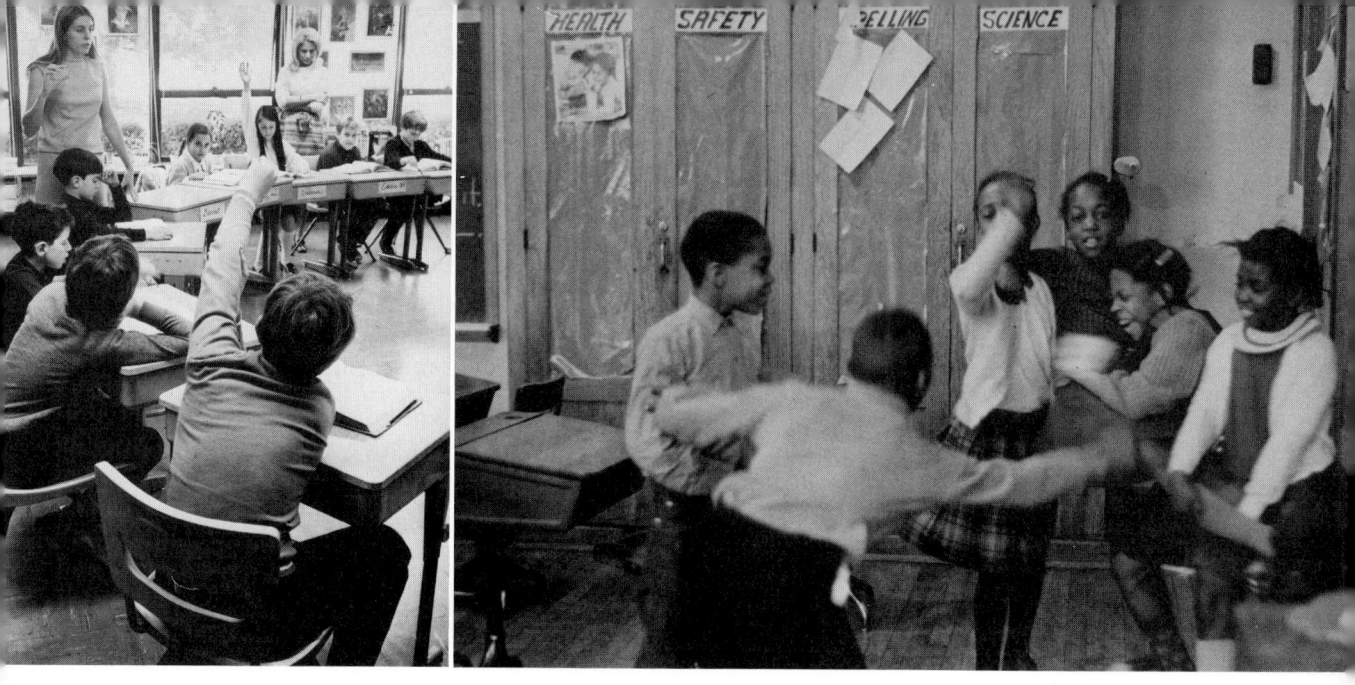

Schools in middle- and upper-class neighborhoods usually have well-trained teachers, teacher assistants, and new equipment and furnishings, whereas schools in lower-class areas are often poorly equipped and staffed.

local funds, and more than 80 percent of such funds come from property taxes.[17] States, too, vary widely in terms of money spent on education. For example, Alabama, a state with a large share of poor people, spends an average of only $716 per student per year, while Illinois spends $1,228.[18] Figure 10–2 compares public and private school enrollments from 1960 to 1974; Figure 10–3 shows public and private school expenditures for the same period.

Jonathan Kozol, a former elementary teacher on the south side of Boston, gave an assignment to his students asking them to describe their school. These responses, which delineate a ghetto school environment where learning is nearly impossible, are from his book *Death at an Early Age*, a most appropriate title:

> "In my school," began a paper that was handed back to me a few days later, "I see dirty boards and I see papers on the floor. I see an old browken window with a sign on it saying, Do not unlock this window are browken. And I see cracks in the walls and I see old books with ink poured all over them and I see old painting hanging on the walls. I see old alfurbet letter hanging on one nail on the wall. I see a dirty fire exit I see a old closet with supplys for the class. I see pigons flying all over the school. I see old freght trains throgh the fence of the school yard. I see pictures of contryies hanging on the wall and I see desks with wrighting all over the top of the desks and insited of the desk.". . .
>
> A little girl wrote this: "I can see old cars with gas in it and there is always people lighting fires old regrigartor an wood glass that comes from the old cars old trees and trash old weeds and people

put there old chairs in there an flat tires and one thing there is up there is wood that you can make dog houses and there are beautiful flowers and there are dead dogs and cats."...

This was one more: "I see pictures in my school. I see picture of Spain and a pictures of Portofino and a pictures of Chicago. I see arithmetic paper a spellings paper. I see a star chart. I see the flag of our Amerrica. The room is dirty.... The auditorium dirty the seats are dusty. The light in the auditorium is brok. The curtains in the auditorium are ragged they took the curtains down because they was so ragged. The bathroom is dirty sometime the toilet is very hard. The cellar is dirty the hold school is dirty sometime.... The flowers are dry every thing in my school is so so dirty."[19]

There are many variables in addition to physical environment that account for the substandard performance of children in ghetto schools, but the environment described above certainly does not help the learning process. Further, the ghetto school environment not only affects students; it also frustrates the most well-intentioned and humanitarian teachers, until many resign themselves to the impossibility of success or change.

Unequal school resources are largely a result of class distinctions which exist throughout our society. Wealthy neighborhoods provide a sufficient amount of money for their schools, while poor neighborhoods are unable to do so. Those in decision-making positions—the wealthy—have been condemned for not working to change unjust educational con-

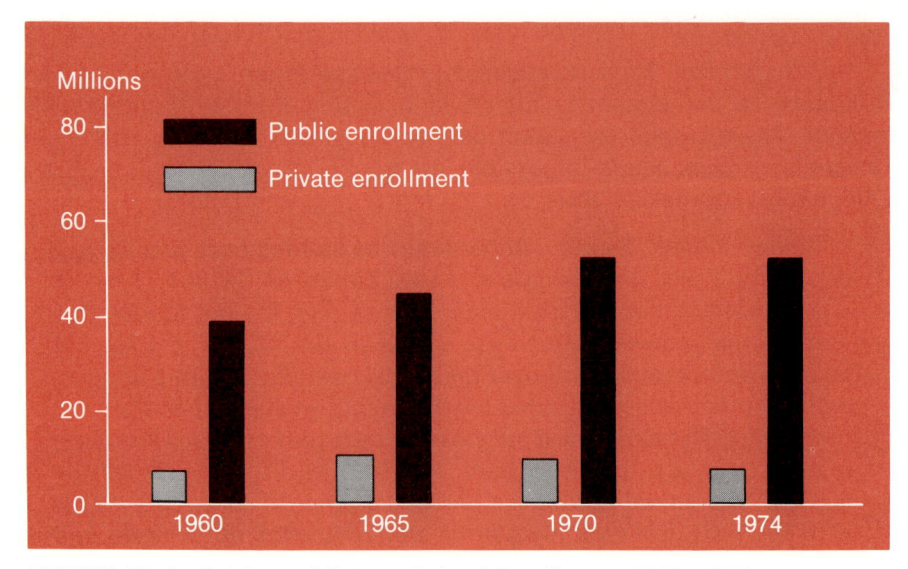

FIGURE 10–2 Public and Private School Enrollment, 1960–1974

SOURCE: Adapted from U.S. Bureau of the Census, *Statistical Abstract of the United States: 1975* (Washington, D.C., 1975), p. 109.

ditions. In his more recent book, *Free Schools,* Kozol makes such a condemnation. He contends that rich and poor will have to instruct one another, to raise each other's consciousness of problems, before change can occur.

> *However far the journey and however many turnpike tolls we pay, however high the spruce or pine that grow around the sunny meadows in which we live and dream and seek to educate our children, it is still one nation. It is not one thing in Lebanon, New Hampshire: one thing in the heart of Harlem. No more is it one thing in Roxbury or Watts, one thing in Williamsburg or Canyon, California. The passive, tranquil, and protected lives white people lead depend on strongly armed police, well-demarcated ghettos. While children starve and others walk the city streets in fear on Monday afternoon, the privileged young people in the Free Schools of Vermont shuttle their handlooms back and forth and speak of love and of "organic processes." They do "their thing." Their thing is sun and good food and fresh water and good doctors and delightful, old, and battered eighteenth-century houses, and a box of baby turtles; somebody else's thing may be starvation, broken glass, unheated rooms, and rats inside the bed with newborn children. The beautiful children do not wish cold rooms or broken glass, starvation, rats or fear for anybody; nor will they stake one hour of the sunlit morning, or sacrifice one moment of the golden afternoon, to take a hand in altering*

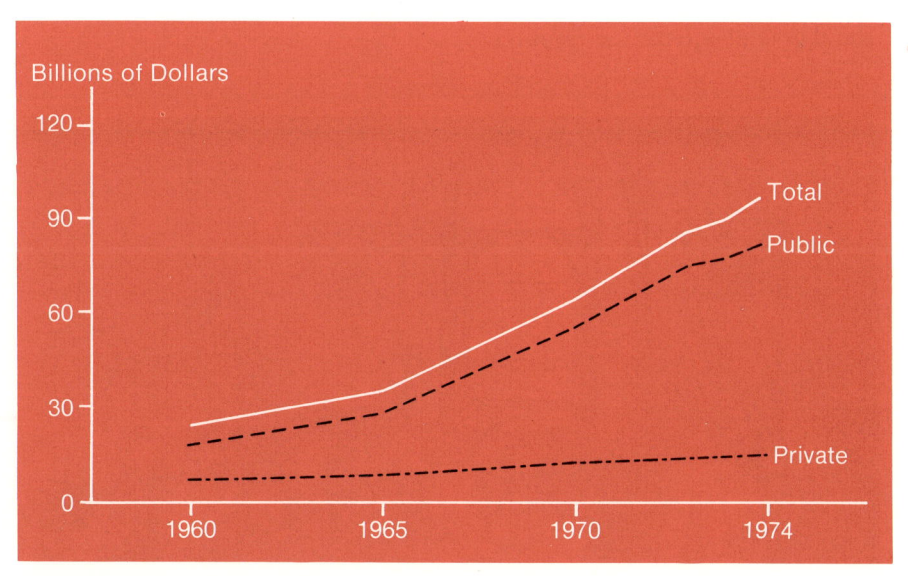

FIGURE 10–3 Public and Private School Expenditures, 1960–1974

SOURCE: Adapted from U.S. Bureau of the Census, *Statistical Abstract of the United States: 1975* (Washington, D.C., 1975), p. 109.

the unjust terms of a society in which these things are possible. . . .

The basic point that I am trying to establish in this book is the distinction between the life-style "revolution" of rich people, which transpires at all times within the safe and nonpolitical context of the white, the whimsical, the privileged, the not-in-need, and the real-life revolution of those who are in great pain or in grave danger—whether they might be black or white or Spanish-speaking—and who, as a consequence, are locked into a nonstop struggle for survival. The first pertains to individual transformations, better relations between those who are already given access to the proceeds of an unjust and unequal social order, a more inspiring and more meaningful experience of what life has to offer to those who have already all they need for physical health and for material well-being; the second, to matters of power, cash, oppression, exploitation, confrontation and control. I do not propose that serious young white men and women ought to abdicate their principles of personal and inward liberation in the face of middle-class traditions or conventional social expectations. I do propose, however, that the way to forge or to empower an important, ethical or political upheaval in the consciousness of those who are the mothers, fathers, sisters, brothers of poor children is not through imposition but through the slow and gradual process of reciprocal instruction.[20]

Many would say that Kozol's idea of "consciousness raising" may be well intentioned, but that institutional changes, such as government programs to redistribute school funds, are what are really needed to bring about greater equality in resources.

Inadequate school facilities in poor neighborhoods are hardly a recent development. Note the overcrowding in this classroom on New York City's Lower East Side in the 1880s—and also the open gas jets aloft.

SCHOOLS AND LOWER-CLASS CHILDREN

When educators are confronted by children from lower-class families, special problems arise. We will now examine two such problems—language differences and teacher-student status differences. We will also look at attempts that are being made in order to equalize educational opportunities.

The Language Development Problem. An important question for teachers and school administrators is, How do lower-class children differ from the larger society in language development?

Some teachers maintain that children from lower-class families generally suffer a *developmental lag;* that is, they have not reached the degree of skill in manipulating language attained by other children of their age, though with instruction they can reach that level. Thus an elementary school child who says "they mine" is performing like a preschool middle-class child and, with time, will insert a verb into his or her speech pattern. Teachers who hold this view assume that developmental lag arises because lower-class parents have failed to provide their children with the language stimulation, such as asking questions and encouraging conversation, that middle-class parents give their children.

This view may underestimate the language development of lower-class children. Such children may indeed have a highly developed sense of language, but current tests are designed to demonstrate the skills of the middle-class child alone.[21] The culture bias which can exist in testing is vividly shown in the so-called "Chitling Test" developed by Adrian Dove.[22] The typical white middle-class child could also be shown to be suffering a "developmental lag" if the following sample questions were used, since they were designed with the black ghetto child in mind.

1. A "handkerchief head" is: (a) a cool cat, (b) a porter, (c) an Uncle Tom, (d) a hoddi, (e) a preacher.
2. Which word is most out of place here? (a) splib, (b) blood, (c) gray, (d) spook, (e) black.
3. A "gas head" is a person who has a: (a) fast-moving car, (b) stable of "lace," (c) "process," (d) habit of stealing cars, (e) long jail record for arson.
4. If a pimp is up tight with a woman who gets state aid, what does he mean when he talks about "Mother's Day"? (a) second Sunday in May, (b) third Sunday in June, (c) first of every month, (d) none of these, (e) first and fifteenth of every month.
5. What are the "Dixie Hummingbirds"? (a) part of the KKK, (b) a swamp disease, (c) a modern gospel group, (d) a Mississippi Negro paramilitary group, (e) deacons.

Answers: 1. (c), 2. (c), 3. (c), 4. (e), 5. (c).

Somewhat related to the developmental lag theory is the *cumulative deficit* thesis. Those who subscribe to this thesis also maintain that lower-class children generally fail to learn "acceptable" language at home, but, more pessimistically, they claim such children will never be able to catch up. Not only will lower-class children become increasingly unable to speak and write in complex, abstract ways, but their cognitive, or thinking, ability will also be increasingly impaired.

Like the developmental lag theory, the cumulative deficit thesis assumes that cognitive ability can have only one meaning—those ways of thinking exhibited by members of the middle class. Is there any basis for saying that middle-class ways of thinking and speaking are superior to lower-class ways?

Those who hold the *difference theory* of language development say "no." They maintain that individuals from different social classes (which often involves different racial groups) should simply use the dialect they have been taught. Poor and minority group students may indeed be deficient when judged against the larger society, but not when judged against their own subcultures. Advocates of this view contend that the dominant society should understand and accept different language patterns.*

Opponents of the difference theory complain that it is unrealistic and harmful not to change the language patterns of lower-class children to that of the middle class. After all, teachers speak and textbooks are written in middle-class English, and for lower-class individuals to be successful in jobs will require some conformity to the dominant language pattern.

Educators have come to no firm conclusion on which theory it would be best to pursue. Probably few would consent to following the cumulative deficit theory because that would be viewed as fatalistic and opposed to the society's belief that hard work brings success. But a choice still has to be made between treating children for language deficiency (developmental lag theory) and allowing them free rein on how to express themselves (difference theory).

Teacher-Student Status Differences. Teachers working in ghetto schools also frequently face the problem of how to reach students whose values and life style are different from their own. Middle-class educators have often been insensitive to the needs of poor and minority-group children. Jonathan Kozol, in *Death at an Early Age,* describes one such teacher in his Boston school. This teacher's insensitivity stifled students' interests and creativity.

> *The Art Teacher's most common technique for art instruction was to pass out mimeographed designs and then to have the pupils fill*

---

*See Lawrence S. Wrightsman, *Social Psychology in the Seventies* (Monterey, Calif.: Brooks/Cole, 1972), chap. 8 for a detailed discussion of the cumulative deficit and difference views. Also, a number of linguists have concluded that nonstandard black English in many ways constitutes a distinct and unique language pattern. See Marvin D. Loflin, "Negro Nonstandard and Standard English: Same or Different Deep Structure?" *Orbis,* 18 (1969): 74–91.

Puerto Rican, Cuban, Mexican, and other non-English-speaking students in the United States face the problem of learning a new language.

them in according to a dictated or suggested color plan. An alternate approach was to stick up on the wall or on the blackboard some of the drawings on a particular subject that had been done in the previous years by predominantly white classes. These drawings, neat and ordered and very uniform, would be the models for our children. The art lesson, in effect, would be to copy what had been done before, and the neatest and most accurate reproductions of the original drawings would be the ones that would win the highest approval from the teacher. None of the new drawings, the Art Teacher would tell me frequently, was comparable to the work that had been done in former times, but at least the children in the class could try to copy good examples. The fact that they were being asked to copy something in which they could not believe because it was not of them and did not in any way correspond to their own interests did not occur to the Art Teacher, or if it did occur she did not say it. Like a number of other teachers at my school and in other schools of the same nature, she possessed a remarkable self-defense apparatus, and anything that seriously threatened to disturb her point of view could be effectively denied.[23]

Middle-class biases can be harmful in other ways. Educators have been known to prejudge students on the basis of racial stereotypes rather than seeking to determine each child's intellectual ability. Black Muslim leader Malcolm X described in his autobiography the stereotyped treatment he received during adolescence from an English teacher. Although the teacher, Mr. Ostrowski, was an excellent instructor in nouns, verbs, and adjectives, his white, middle-class background greatly affected the kind of advice he gave to blacks. The teacher expected little of Malcolm and suggested that he be "realistic" in choosing his occupation.

> Somehow, I happened to be alone in the classroom with Mr. Ostrowski, my English teacher. He was a tall, rather reddish white man and he had a thick mustache. I had gotten some of my best marks under him, and he had always made me feel that he liked me. He was, as I have mentioned, a natural-born "advisor," about what you ought to read, to do, or think—about any and everything. We used to make unkind jokes about him: why was he teaching in Mason instead of somewhere else, getting for himself some of the "success in life" that he kept telling us how to get?
>
> I know that he probably meant well in what he happened to advise me that day. I doubt that he meant any harm. It was just in his nature as an American white man. I was one of his top students, one of the school's top students—but all he could see for me was the kind of future "in your place" that almost all white people see for black people.
>
> He told me, "Malcolm, you ought to be thinking about a career. Have you been giving it thought?"
>
> The truth is, I hadn't. I never have figured out why I told him, "Well, yes, sir, I've been thinking I'd like to be a lawyer." Lansing certainly had no Negro lawyers—or doctors either—in those days, to hold up an image I might have aspired to. All I really knew for certain was that a lawyer didn't wash dishes, as I was doing.
>
> Mr. Ostrowski looked surprised, I remember, and leaned back in his chair and clasped his hands behind his head. He kind of half-smiled and said, "Malcolm, one of life's first needs is for us to be realistic. Don't misunderstand me, now. We all here like you, you know that. But you've got to be realistic about being a nigger. A lawyer—that's no realistic goal for a nigger. You need to think about something you *can* be. You're good with your hands—making things. Everybody admires your carpentry shop work. Why don't you plan on carpentry? People like you as a person—you'd get all kinds of work."
>
> The more I thought afterwards about what he said, the more uneasy it made me. It just kept treading around in my mind.
>
> What made it really begin to disturb me was Mr. Ostrowski's advice to others in my class—all of them white. Most of them had told him they were planning to become farmers, like their parents—to one day take over their family farms. But those who wanted to strike out on their own, to try something new, he had encouraged. Some, mostly girls, wanted to be teachers. A few wanted other professions, such as one boy who wanted to become a county agent; another, a veterinarian; and one girl wanted to be a nurse. They all reported

that Mr. Ostrowski had encouraged whatever they had wanted. Yet nearly none of them had earned marks equal to mine.[24]

Equalizing Educational Opportunities. The language problem and the problem of status differences between students and teachers are but two of the difficulties modern schools face in dealing with lower-class children. Such problems, if unmet, can destroy the American ideal of equal educational opportunity for all members of society. But solutions to the problem of inequality in education are being sought, and some programs to improve the situation have been tried.

Two main approaches have been used in the effort to equalize educational opportunities. The first approach, *compensatory education*, attempts to help children in the lower class compensate for their presumed cultural deprivation. As an example, the Head Start program gives disadvantaged children preschool training to help them catch up with middle-class children in school-related abilities. The program's success in academic terms has been less than expected, in part because the children's home and neighborhood environment remains unchanged.

The second approach, busing, aims at ending segregated schooling by sending students from one neighborhood to another. Busing is an explosive issue, particularly among white suburbanites who resent sending their children to predominantly black and presumably inferior schools and who also resist the importing of children from different racial and social-class groups into their neighborhood schools. They contend that the quality of their children's education will surely go down and that racial turmoil will be inevitable.

THE LARGE, BUREAUCRATIC SCHOOL

Although one could hardly advocate a return to the one-room schoolhouse and the teacher who taught all grades and subjects, it does appear that many present-day educational problems are related to the size and complexity of modern schools and the fact that they must be administered in a bureaucratic fashion. Sylvia Barrett, the young teacher in Bel Kaufman's *Up the Down Staircase*, was hardly a fan of certain bureaucratic aspects of her school, but an experienced teacher eventually gave Sylvia the real meanings of the nonsensical jargon used by school administrators:

"Keep on file in numerical order" means throw in wastebasket. You'll soon learn the language. "Let it be a challenge to you" means you're stuck with it; "interpersonal relationships" is a fight between kids; "ancillary civic agencies for supportive discipline" means call the cops; "Language Arts Dept." is the English office; "literature based on child's reading level and experiential background" means that's all they've got in the Book Room; "nonacademic-minded" is a delinquent; and "It has come to my attention" means you're in trouble.[25]

One illustration of the seemingly endless clerical duties and forms demanded by school officials is Sylvia Barrett's reminder list for her homeroom period:

FILL OUT ATTENDANCE SHEETS
SEND OUT ABSENTEE CARDS
MAKE OUT TRANSCRIPTS FOR TRANSFERS
MAKE OUT 3 SETS OF STUDENTS' PROGRAM CARDS (YELLOW) FROM MASTER PROGRAM CARD (BLUE), ALPHABETIZE AND SEND TO 201
MAKE OUT 5 COPIES OF TEACHER'S PROGRAM CARD (WHITE) AND SEND TO 211 . . .
FILL OUT AGE-LEVEL REPORTS
ANNOUNCE AND POST ASSEMBLY SCHEDULE AND ASSIGN ROWS IN AUDITORIUM
ANNOUNCE AND POST FIRE, SHELTER AND DISPERSAL DRILLS REGULATIONS
CHECK LAST TERM'S BOOK AND DENTAL BLACKLISTS
CHECK LIBRARY BLACKLIST
FILL OUT CONDITION OF ROOM REPORT . . .
SALUTE FLAG (ONLY FOR NON-ASSEMBLY OF Y2 SECTIONS)
POINT OUT THE NATURE AND FUNCTION OF HOMEROOM: LITERALLY, A ROOM THAT IS A HOME, WHERE STUDENTS WILL FIND A FRIENDLY ATMOSPHERE AND GUIDANCE[26]

There are several problems that can be linked to the large, bureaucratized school. First, because of huge enrollments, test scores and grades—rather than in-depth knowledge of a student's family background, problems, motivations, and other personal characteristics—become the major means for labeling the student and determining his or her future. Second, the increased impersonality of teacher-student relationships means that students, particularly the deprived ones, cannot receive the personal counseling and reinforcement for a positive self-image or the exposure to "acceptable" role models that they need. Third, official rules are difficult to change when new problems arise, and these rules also tend to overcontrol the behavior of school personnel. Fourth, teachers and students often feel powerless to alter school conditions and so become apathetic about solving problems. (See chapter 14 for further discussion of students' feelings of powerlessness and isolation in reference to their schools.) And, fifth, teachers and particularly administrators can become bureaucratic personalities—insecure, overly protective of their jobs, narrowly specialized, increasingly less concerned with teaching, and inflexible in their daily behavior. (See chapter 6 for a discussion of problems in bureaucratic organizations.)

ARE STUDENTS CHANGING?

Since the conservative McCarthy era of the late 1940s and early 1950s, students, particularly those in universities, have increasingly questioned educational goals, course content, and teaching methods. Beginning with the violent protests of the 1960s, students have expressed a desire to participate in restructuring formal education. This drive to gain influence in shaping educational programs lost momentum in the early 1970s as students became either apathetic about the possibility of change or more interested in their own private lives. Still, today's students feel more at ease about challenging school policies than did their counterparts a generation earlier, and the complaint can still be heard that courses and instruction lack relevance. Although "relevancy" is variously defined, the term has increasingly come to mean job-related, practical, and useful education. Whether formal education can or should meet the needs of students remains an unanswered question.

Chapter Summary

Formal education performs vital functions for both society and the individual. Schools and teachers transmit culture—skills, values, and specialized knowledge—to the young; sort out and place people into jobs and positions; develop new ideas and inventions; and provide people with official titles and the necessary training for upward social mobility.

The growth and popularity of education in the United States is a result of both the need for specialized labor and the values of our society. Americans see education as the major promise for a better life—as a way to preserve democracy and as a vehicle for self-improvement. Additionally, Americans tend to think education should be practical or useful in the short-run; should stress the importance of work and competition; and should teach children the value of conformity (though Americans also profess an attachment to individualism).

There is heated debate in this country over what educational goals should be pursued. Some maintain that academic knowledge should be taught, while others stress the importance of vocational training, or specialized skills for particular jobs. Another debate exists over whether schools should concentrate on providing a quality education for only a few elite individuals or spread educational resources to reach the masses. Many contend that mass education has failed. Finally, there is disagreement as to whether schools should perpetuate the status quo by teaching existing, conservative ideas or teach new ideas and advocate change.

Lack of agreement on goals is only one of the problems schools face. Another crucial problem is inadequate economic support. Overcrowding, understaffing, and inadequate facilities can seriously affect the learning process. The teaching of lower-class children presents special problems. These children differ from middle-class children in their language patterns, and there is disagreement between those who wish to change "deficient" language usage to meet the standards of the larger society and those who contend that the dominant society should understand and accept different language patterns. The problem of teacher insensitivity to poor and minority-group students because of middle-class bias is also a serious one that schools must come to terms with if they are to provide equal educational opportunities for all.

Other concerns in education today include the problems associated with the large, bureaucratic school and the issue of adjusting formal education to meet the changing needs and interests of students. Although the school walls have not yet fallen down, education in American society is in a state of crisis.

Key Terms for Review

academic knowledge, p. 243
anti-intellectualism, p. 238
compensatory education, p. 255
cumulative deficit theory, p. 252

developmental lag theory, p. 251
difference theory, p. 252
self-fulfilling prophecy, p. 236
vocational training, p. 243

Suggested Readings

SOCIOLOGICAL

Brim, Orville. *Sociology and the Field of Education.* New York: Russell Sage Foundation, 1962. The author gives a concise sociological analysis of the goals and social organization of formal education.

Caplow, Theodore, and Reece J. McGee. *The Academic Marketplace.* New York: Basic Books, 1958. The problems and politics of being a university professor are discussed. Hiring, firing, promotion, tenure, and "publish or perish" are the major topics examined.

Clark, Burton. *Educating the Expert Society*. San Francisco: Chandler, 1962. As a society experiences industrialization and population growth, its education system changes. Education becomes more massive, bureaucratic, and concerned with teaching specialized knowledge and skills. It also assumes a more active role in cultural affairs.

Coleman, James. *The Adolescent Society*. New York: Free Press, 1961. This in-depth study of ten high schools found that each school contained a unique subculture which molded adolescents' views on academic achievement, popular heroes, sports, and other concerns.

Sexton, P. *The American School: A Sociological Analysis*. Englewood Cliffs, N.J.: Prentice-Hall, 1967. This brief summary of issues in the sociology of education is a good introductory source for the student.

LITERARY

Barzun, Jacques. *Teacher in America*. Boston: Little, Brown, 1945. The author describes the goals and problems of education, emphasizing in particular the state of affairs in universities. He offers us his many ideas for change.

Herndon, James. *How to Survive in Your Native Land*. New York: Simon & Schuster, 1971. A teacher reflects upon his satisfying and alienating experiences with students. The episodes described in the book illustrate the ill effects of many educational policies and approaches.

Kaufman, Bel. *Up the Down Staircase*. Englewood Cliffs, N.J.: Prentice-Hall, 1964. Problems of education are illustrated both in a humorous and serious fashion in this novel. The protagonist, Sylvia Barrett, faces unmotivated students, bungling school officials, and unconcerned parents.

Kolb, Ken. *Getting Straight*. New York: Bantam, 1970. This entertaining novel describes a graduate student's search for meaning in life. The "relevance" of education courses and instruction is seriously questioned.

Kozol, Jonathan. *Death at an Early Age*. New York: Bantam, 1970. The author unleashes a scathing attack on the insensitive and racist practices of the Boston public school system. His major thesis is that existing educational approaches have caused the spiritual and psychological death of many students.

———. *Free Schools*. New York: Bantam, 1972. More and more adults in poor, urban neighborhoods have started "free schools" as alternatives to typical public education. Kozol conceives of the free school as small, privately supported, and neighborhood-created. And, most important, he sees it as sensitive to the needs of poor and minority-group children.

IN THIS CHAPTER

Conflict and Consensus   262

Power and Authority   264

Politics and Economics in Developing Nations   265

Political Change   267

A World of Postindustrial States   272
- Society and the threat of nuclear war   272
- Ideology   276

Summary   277

Key Terms for Review   278

Suggested Readings   279

How important are individual personality traits in determining the course of political events?

Are political decisions simply considerations of power?

What will happen to the Third World?

Have nuclear weapons made war out of date?

What is the role of political ideology in determining what we think about the world?

11

POLITICS AND ECONOMICS

Since the Watergate affair, it is very tempting to characterize American politics much as Ambrose Bierce did: "A means of livelihood affected by the more degraded portion of our criminal classes."[1] The definition betrays a view of politics that holds individual personalities important in determining the course of political events. Thus Watergate might be seen as the result of "peculiarities" in the personality of Richard Nixon. Such an explanation would be given credence by the assessment offered by former President Harry S Truman prior to Watergate: "Nixon is a shifty-eyed, goddamn liar, and people know it."[2]

But for the most part, the sociological study of politics, usually called *political sociology*, does not focus on individuals' aberrations. Sociologists studying politics have only passing interest in personalities. Their inquiries are much more likely to concentrate on the nature of political power, the ways major political and economic decisions are made (both within and outside of government bodies), and the differences that exist in the political socialization and ideologies of different social classes. Many students of political sociology are more likely to agree with Bierce's second definition of politics: "A strife of interests masquerading as a contest of principles. The conduct of public affairs for private advantage."[3]

Actually, political sociologists use the term "politics" to refer to those processes people use to resolve conflicts between private interests and the common good that occur within the institutional framework of government. Thus a society's political institution, or politics, is, like other institutions, a means of dealing with societal problems. In this chapter we will examine theories about the role of politics in society, the uses of power and authority, the relationship between politics and economics, types of political change, and certain aspects of modern, postindustrial states.

Conflict and Consensus

Sociologists have presented a wide variety of theories to explain the role of politics in society. Two explanations, conflict theory and consensus theory, offer totally opposite assumptions about what creates social order, how it is maintained, and what motivates members of any given society or group. The following list summarizes the differences between the two theories.

CONFLICT THEORY	CONSENSUS THEORY
1. Society is established by group conflict.	1. Society is integrated and interdependent.
2. Individual and group action stems from perceived interests.	2. Individual and group action stems from values and norms.
3. Conflict is inherent in social relationships.	3. Balance, equilibrium, and shared power are the norm in social relationships.
4. Conflict is ubiquitous.	4. Balance is ubiquitous.
5. Society is basically unstable.	5. Society is basically stable.
6. Social change is constant and results from specific and inherent conflicts in the social structure.	6. Social change is usually quite slow and most often results from shifts and imperfections in the socialization process.
7. Social control is the result of force.	7. Social control is the result of members' voluntarily adhering to norms and values.

Conflict theorists assume that human beings are for the most part quite selfish and that chaos and strife are both common and natural. Consensus theorists, on the other hand, suggest that human beings are not necessarily selfish and that chaos and disorder are neither common nor natural. Kurt Vonnegut, Jr., in his preface to *Slaughterhouse-Five*, deals with one aspect of the debate—whether or not warfare is inevitable:

> Over the years, people I've met have often asked me what I'm working on, and I've usually replied that the main thing was a book about Dresden.
>
> I said that to Harrison Starr, the movie-maker, one time, and he raised his eyebrows and inquired, "Is it an anti-war book?"
>
> "Yes," I said. "I guess."
>
> "You know what I say to people when I hear they're writing anti-war books?"
>
> "No. What do you say, Harrison Starr?"
>
> "I say, 'Why don't you write an anti-glacier book instead?'"

England's once powerful House of Lords. Formal governing bodies are only one of several major focal points for sociologists studying political institutions.

What he meant, of course, was that there would always be wars, that they were as easy to stop as glaciers. I believe that, too.[4]

In this instance both Vonnegut and Harrison Starr subscribe to conflict theory: both see war (conflict) as inevitable.

Many sociologists and social theorists have followed the conflict tradition. Karl Marx, who assumed that all of history had been a constant series of changes and confrontations, was one of the major architects of conflict theory. In the *Communist Manifesto* Marx and Frederick Engels wrote:

The history of all hitherto existing society is the history of class struggles.

Freeman and slave, patrician and plebeian, lord and serf, guildmaster and journeyman, in a word, oppressor and oppressed, stood in constant opposition to one another, carried on an uninterrupted, now hidden, now open fight, a fight that each time ended, either in a revolutionary reconstitution of society at large, or in the common ruin of the contending classes.[5]

One must be careful in categorizing Marx, however, since he did not believe that warfare would continue forever. With the coming of communism and the resolution of class struggle, there would emerge a stable society, very much like that consensus theorists envision, in which there would be little need for the use of force.

Many American sociologists and political scientists have viewed societies using the assumptions of consensus theory. Without indulging in his blatant chauvinism (touting the glory of the British empire), scholars of the consensus perspective are in essential agreement with Prime Minister Benjamin Disraeli's concept of an integrated and interdependent society:

> I mean the splendor of the Crown, the lustre of the peerage, the privileges of the Commons, the rights of the poor. I mean the harmonious union, that magnificent concord of all interests, of all classes, on which our national greatness and prosperity depends.[6]

Conflict theorists, then, view the political arena as a battleground on which are waged inevitable and constant struggles for power and dominance. Consensus theorists, on the other hand, tend to see politics as the focal point of an overall system of accomodation and compromise.

Power and Authority

The focal point of most scholarly inquiries into government is power and its uses. In the popular mind political power conjures up visions of Boss Tweed and Tammany Hall, cigar smoke and a thick bluish haze, and phone calls at 3:00 A.M. Political decision-making is seen as exercised by power brokers whose only true allegiance is to colleagues who also wield power. Recent presidential administrations have done little to change this popular stereotype. The "black book" of Lyndon Johnson and the private back entrance that Richard Nixon added to the oval office would seem appropriate details in portraying the intricacies of power politics.

To discuss power thoroughly, however, one must move beyond stereotypes and come to a fairly clear agreement on terminology. But debates among social scientists over the proper definition of power have been numerous, longstanding, and often tedious. Still, much, although not all, of the difficulty is resolved by distinguishing between power and authority.

Power is the ability of groups or individuals to assert themselves—sometimes, but not always—in opposition to the desires of others. Some scholars have defined power more rigidly by arguing that it necessarily involves overcoming another's will. Max Weber defined power (*Macht*, in German) as "the probability that one actor within a social relationship will be in a position to carry out his own will despite resistance, regardless of the basis on which this probability rests."[7] Contemporary political scientists such as Robert Dahl and Nelson Polsby seem to prefer Weber's definition of power, maintaining that decisions made without any opposition are not indicative of power. Advocates of a broader definition of power, such as the one we employ, suggest that many decisions are made without opposition precisely because of the great power decision makers wield. Indeed, powerful decision makers are even able to determine what issues reach the point at which decisions have to be made.

Authority is distinguished from power in that it refers to agreed-upon relationships. *Authority* is a recognized or legitimate relationship of domination and subjugation. For example, when a decision is made through legitimate, recognized channels of government in this country, the carrying out of that decision falls within the realm of authority. The differences between various types of authority—charismatic, traditional, and rational-legal—were discussed in chapter 6 and require no further explanation here.

To return to the case of the Watergate affair, one could say that the Nixon administration so clearly violated norms defining authority that it abused its power. Or, as conflict theorists might say, members of the administration of Richard Nixon did not have sufficient power to overcome the resistance that resulted from their violations of norms.

Thomas Nast's revealing caricature of Boss Tweed, the notorious leader of New York's Tammany Hall and archetype of contemporary power bosses.

Politics and Economics in Developing Nations

Whereas a society's political institution functions to resolve conflicts between private interests and the common good, its economic institution serves to control the use of resources and organize the production and distribution of goods and services. Quite obviously, the political and economic spheres overlap.

The inevitable link between politics and economics is most obvious in processes of development that Third World (generally unindustrialized) nations experience. Gabriel A. Almond and Seymour Martin Lipset see a relation between economic growth and an increase in political participation. According to both, as countries grow economically (as shown by such economic indicators as gross national product and per capita income), they become more democratic.[8] Daniel Lerner's highly respected study of modernization in the Middle East reached very similar conclusions, although Lerner was less willing to state that more democracy accompanies economic growth. He did, however, suggest that as individuals' share of the economic pie grows, so does their participation in governing themselves.[9]

Of course, other factors besides economic growth could account for the growth of political participation. One study demonstrated that the intro-

Building a modern industrial state is often a long and painful process. Here women in Ghana carry water for use in making bricks for a model home.

duction of transistor radios in Third World countries encouraged people to express themselves publicly and participate in elections. Thus the introduction of technology, whether or not accompanied by economic growth, may be the key factor in increasing self-government.[10]

There are other ties between politics and economics that can be seen by studying the development of Third World countries. Many political scientists hold that there is a link between the diversity of industries and the degree of democracy in a country. Many Third World nations have depended on one major industry, whether light manufacturing, agriculture, or mining. One example is what used to be called the "banana republics"— underdeveloped Central American countries economically dependent upon the production of bananas. Moreover, ownership of the major indus-

Dependence on one major industry or export crop—for example, bananas in some Central American countries—presents problems for many Third World nations.

try in such countries has often been foreign. (For instance, the United Fruit Company, a United States firm, has dominated the banana industry in Central America.) Leaders of these countries, with few if any alternate sources of power of their own, have had to depend on foreign business interests for money and support. In such cases, democracy suffers, leaders vie with one another to gain the backing of foreign interests, and political instability—revolutions and guerrilla warfare—results.

Ultimately, developing countries move toward true nationhood, and their citizens develop a national consciousness. People begin to identify themselves not as members of a tribe or particular group, but as citizens of a state. However, there are great variations in this movement toward nationhood—when it occurs, how it is brought about, what type of government is adopted. While Lipset and others believe that the move results in more democracy, Irving Louis Horowitz has suggested that, in order for economic growth to occur, governments may have to become less democratic and limit the freedom of their people.[11] Predictions, at this point, are most difficult.

Political Change

A society's political institution, like its other institutions, is subject to change. The change may be slow or rapid, legitimate or nonlegitimate. Table 11–1 categorizes major types of political change according to their speed and legitimacy.

TABLE 11–1
Types of Political Change

Rate of Change	Nonlegitimate	Legitimate
slow	coup d'état	electoral process (continuous)
rapid	revolution	electoral process (truncated)

The American value system tends to support relatively slow, legitimate change, and there is a strong, widespread belief in stability and the electoral process. Despite sudden and often unexpected changes at the presidential level over the past fifteen years—the assassination of Kennedy, the pressured decision of Johnson not to run, and the forced resignation of Nixon—the role of chief executive has not been significantly altered. However abrupt the change in officeholders, the governmental structure has remained intact. The system continues to be one of rational-legal authority, run by laws held by the people to be reasonable and just. This system has enjoyed remarkable stability.

The continuous and stable electoral process of the United States is, however, hardly universal. While such a system tends to prevail in West-

Adolf Hitler, shown here addressing the Reichstag (German parliament) in 1940, combined both power and authority in instituting momentous changes in Nazi Germany.

ern — or Westernized — industrialized nations, alternative systems do exist. The Soviet Union, for example, grounds much of its stability on *totalitarianism*, a political system that maintains governmental surveillance and control over virtually all aspects of the lives of citizens.

The second form of relatively slow political change occurs by means of a *coup d'état*. Although a coup is defined as "a sudden and forcible seizure of power by a political faction in defiance of normal constitutional processes,"[12] it seldom results in rapid political change. Instead, it simply marks a change in political elites as one ruling clique replaces another without much actual change in the system. The coup d'état is quite common in developing Third World countries, where there are numerous political factions whose power is untempered by traditional or rational-legal authority.

A coup, as we have stated, is the rapid and forceful seizure of power which results in little real political change. By contrast, seemingly stable electoral processes may sometimes yield relatively rapid change, change that often terminates the electoral process entirely. The totalitarian regime of Adolf Hitler in Germany began in such a manner. Hitler and the Nazi party won power in Germany through a legitimate election, but they abolished elections soon after Hitler became chancellor in 1933.

Revolutions, by definition, are nonlegitimate and bring about far-reaching and sometimes cataclysmic change. They are nonlegitimate, of course, from the perspective of the existing system. But participants and observers often view them as both legitimate and necessary. As Aimé Césaire writes:

> This attitude, this behavior, this shackled life caught in the noose of shame and disaster rebels, hates itself, struggles, howls, and, my God, others ask: "What can you do about it?"

"Start something!"
"Start what?"
"The only thing in the world that's worth the effort of starting: The end of the world, by God!"[13]

The changes brought about by such a wrenching shift as revolution are magnified on the interpersonal level. True revolutionaries must be willing to sacrifice themselves for the cause. The idea of change is greater than the idea of self. For many who live through times of rapid change, however, such times are very confusing; in these instances, the breakdown of social norms often creates a sense of rootlessness in people. In Charles Dickens's *A Tale of Two Cities,* an innocent young seamstress is caught in the turmoil of the French Revolution. Indiscriminately imprisoned with members of the French nobility by the revolutionary authorities, she finds it difficult to comprehend her role in the great upheaval of the revolution. Here, she confronts her fellow prisoner, the aristocratic Evrémonde:

A very few moments after that, a young woman, with a slight girlish form, a sweet spare face in which there was no vestige of colour, and large widely opened patient eyes, rose from the seat where he had observed her sitting, and came to speak to him.

"Citizen Evrémonde," she said, touching him with her cold hand. "I am a poor seamstress, who was with you in La Force [prison]."

He murmured for answer: "True. I forget what you were accused of?"

"Plots. Though the just Heaven knows I am innocent of any. Is it

The French Revolution of 1789 frightened ruling classes throughout Europe. This is a depiction of the storming of the Bastille, the prison in Paris that had become a symbol of monarchical tyranny.

> likely? Who would think of plotting with a poor little weak creature like me?"
>
> The forlorn smile with which she said it, so touched him, that tears started from his eyes.
>
> "I am not afraid to die, Citizen Evrémonde, but I have done nothing. I am not unwilling to die, if the Republic which is to do so much good to us poor, will profit by my death; but I do not know how that can be, Citizen Evrémonde. Such a poor weak little creature!"
>
> As the last thing on earth that his heart was to warm and soften to, it warmed and softened to this pitiable girl.[14]

For many commentators and scholars a true revolution, one that brings about real and lasting social change, has never existed, and for some it is an impossibility. Those within the conflict tradition, for instance, believe that no ultimate revolutionary utopia is possible, only the continuous replacement by force of one social order by another, each successive order as unjust as the last. Such have been the conclusions of Milovan Djilas (a leading Yugoslav Communist party and government official until 1954) in viewing the results of the Russian Revolution of 1917. For Djilas the huge government bureaucracy of industrial communism is also a hardened exploiter.[15]

The idea that force and use of power are inevitable and that all humanity is finally corruptible was at the center of the world view of Willy Stark (Robert Penn Warren's name for the real-life political figure Huey Long in his novel *All the King's Men*).

> It all began, as I have said, when the Boss [Willy Stark], sitting in the black Cadillac which sped through the night, said to me (to Me who was what Jack Burden, the student of history, had grown up to be), "There is always something."
>
> And I said, "Maybe not on the Judge."
>
> And he said, "Man is conceived in sin and born in corruption and he passeth from the stink of the didie to the stench of the shroud. There is always something."
>
> The black Cadillac made its humming sound through the night and the tires sang on the slab and the black fields streaked with mist swept by. Sugar-Boy was hunched over the wheel, which looked too big for him, and the Boss sat straight up, up there in the front seat. I could see the black mass of his head against the tunnel of light down which we raced. Then I dozed off.
>
> It was the stopping of the car that woke me up. I realized that we were back at the Stark place. I crawled out of the car. The Boss was already out, standing in the yard, just inside the gate in the starlight; Sugar-Boy was locking the car doors.
>
> When I went into the yard, the Boss said, "Sugar-Boy is going to sleep on the couch downstairs, but there's a cot made up for you

upstairs, second door on the left at the head of the stairs. You better get some shut-eye, for tomorrow you start digging for what the Judge dropped."

"It will be a long dig," I said.

"Look here," he said, "if you don't want to do it you don't have to. I can always pay somebody else. Or do you want a raise?"

"No, I don't want a raise," I said.

"I am raising you a hundred a month, whether you want it or not."

"Give it to the church," I said. "If I wanted money, I could think of easier ways to make it than the way I make it with you."

"So you work for me because you love me," the Boss said.

"I don't know why I work for you, but it's not because I love you. And not for money."

"No," he said, standing there in the dark, "you don't know why you work for me. But I know," he said, and laughed.

Sugar-Boy came into the yard, said good night, and went on to the house.

"Why?" I asked.

"Boy," he said, "you work for me because I'm the way I am and you're the way you are. It is an arrangement founded on the nature of things."

"That's a hell of a fine explanation."

"It's not an explanation," he said, and laughed again. "There ain't any explanations. Not of anything. All you can do is point at the nature of things. If you are smart enough to see 'em."[16]

Stark appears to be the ultimate conflict theorist. Power is its own justification and nothing else matters.

Senator Huey Long of Louisiana, known as the "Kingfish," was a colorful and powerful figure in American politics during the 1930s. Long served as the model for the character Willy Stark in *All the King's Men*.

A World of Postindustrial States

Since World War II the advanced nations of the world have entered a period of postindustrialism. A *postindustrial socioeconomic system* is one which has moved from a production-centered economy to a service-centered economy, that is, from a concentration on the production of goods (cars, television sets, typewriters) to a concentration on the provision of services (education, health care, transportation).[17] Obviously the world's leading nation-states still produce an enormous number of goods ranging from disposable diapers to highly sophisticated weaponry. But what is crucial has been the acceleration in the service sector of the economies of these nations. The producer has been supplanted by the manager; the material product has been increasingly replaced by the idea; ideas and knowledge are now more important than muscle and diligence in these nations' economies.

Postindustrial socioeconomic systems are dominated by *technocrats*, narrowly specialized "experts" whose skill and knowledge are seen as important to the governmental decision-making process. Engineers, computer scientists, automation experts, and highly specialized scholars are increasingly called upon to advise legislators and are being placed at the center of the decision-making process. Legislators, with only occasional exceptions, are often unable to do more than follow the advice placed before them by these experts.

The postindustrial world has also witnessed tremendous growth in the number and power of multinational corporations. Many government leaders feel that these corporations pose a threat to their nations' sovereignty. And, indeed, multinational corporations have long presented themselves as major forces in international politics. Yet until quite recently many scholars were reluctant to suggest that multinational corporations actively undermined national governments. Revelations about the involvement of International Telephone and Telegraph (ITT) in the overthrow of the Allende government in Chile in 1973 have decisively ended such reluctance.*

SOCIETY AND THE THREAT OF NUCLEAR WAR

The postindustrial world lives under the threat of nuclear annihilation. Contemporary arsenals held by the United States and the Soviet Union to maintain the "balance of terror" are capable of destroying every man, woman, and child now living. And the growing number of nuclear powers

---

*For an account of ITT's role in the fall of the Allende government, see Anthony Sampson, *The Sovereign State of ITT* (Greenwich, Conn.: Fawcett, 1974).

Representatives of Saudi Arabia at a 1975 OPEC (Organization of Petroleum Exporting Countries) conference. Oil plays a role in international politics as well as economics.

appears to many to increase the possibility that eventually such weapons will be used.

If nuclear warfare were to occur, just how might the final moments begin? We can only guess. They could come with the malfunctioning of some sophisticated gadgetry. Eugene Burdick and Harvey Wheeler, in their novel *Fail-Safe*, give us a chilling account of how just such an accident could occur.

> "There is nothing further to report, Mr. President," General Bogan said. Colonel Cascio was staring straight at the Big Board. "Group 6 is about two hundred and sixty miles past Fail-Safe and continuing on what is apparently an attack course."
>
> "Do you know what happened to them?" the President's voice asked.
>
> "No, sir, we do not," General Bogan said. "There is a chance, an outside chance, that they made a navigational error and will swing back."
>
> "Have they ever made a navigational error that big before?" the President asked crisply.
>
> "No, sir," General Bogan said. "But when you're traveling over 1,500 miles an hour, a little error can throw you a long distance off."
>
> "Let's rule that one out," the President said. "Why haven't you been able to raise them yet by radio?"
>
> "We don't know for sure, Mr. President," General Bogan said. "We have tried them on all frequencies and can't make contact."

"Why?" the President broke in, his voice impatient.

"First, there might be natural meteorological disturbances, and our weather people say there is a big electrical storm just behind the Vindicators," General Bogan said. "Secondly, the Russians might be jamming our radio reception—"

"Why the hell would they do that?" the President asked.

"I don't know," General Bogan said, paused, and then went on. He spoke slowly, his voice unconvincing. "There is a remote possibility that their Fail-Safe black boxes might be giving them a 'go' signal and that Russian jamming is preventing our verbal Positive Control system from operating."

"Is that possible?" the President said sharply.

General Bogan paused. Then his voice gained confidence. "No, Mr. President, the odds against both systems failing at the same time are so high I think that is impossible," General Bogan said. He was aware that Colonel Cascio was watching him. He felt an undefined and nagging discomfort. "Almost impossible."

"All right," the President said. "Now if we do regain radio contact will they respond to a direct order from me to return?"

"They will answer, sir," General Bogan said, "providing we can reach them by radio within the next five minutes." Then he paused. "However, if after that time their black boxes still tell them to 'go' they are under orders not to turn back even if someone who sounds like you orders them back. You can see the reason for that. The enemy could easily abort a real attack just by having someone around who could make a good imitation of your voice. Those people in the Vindicators have to obey the Fail-Safe mechanism. They can't rely on voice transmissions."

Something like a sigh came over the speaker.

"All right, let me sum up," the President said. "For reasons which are unknown to us Group 6 has flown past its Fail-Safe point and right now seems to be on an attack course toward Russia. We can't raise them by radio, but there's an outside chance that we may later. What is their target?"

"Moscow," General Bogan said bluntly.[18]

Perhaps even more frightening than a malfunction, nuclear war could come because of an assumption that our technology is much more sophisticated than it actually is. In *The Warfare State* Fred Cook describes an alarming incident that took place in 1960.

On one occasion in the spring of 1960, a group of Air Force officers at an Atlantic seaboard missile base were sitting down to dinner when they happened to glance out a window and saw a sight that chilled them with horror. A nuclear-armed Bomarc missile, on its launching pad, had begun to spout fumes from its tail pipe. The *officers rushed to the launching site, yanked off wires and threw switches. With only a few split seconds of leeway, they managed to stop the unpremeditated flight of the Bomarc. But what had impelled the electronically controlled "brain" of the great missile to decide to take off on a flight of its own? This question, despite months of investigation, was never fully answered. One theory was that radio signals from passing police cars might have merged with the impulses from a radio station to form an accidental pattern that fed a fire order into Bomarc's sensitive electronic brain.*[19]

Awareness that the entire world may at any moment witness the ultimate horror of nuclear destruction seems to force us all to use a kind of mass psychological defense mechanism. Although we know that destruction is conceivably imminent, we go about our daily routines, concerned not with international power politics, but with day-to-day survival, *Rolling Stone*, and the upcoming basketball season.

This seeming lack of concern over the possibility of a nuclear Armageddon is related to Marx's notion of false consciousness, although Marx was describing not balance-of-terror politics but class conflict when he introduced the concept. For Marx, *false consciousness* referred to the inability of the disenfranchised and powerless proletariat to recognize that they were being exploited in the capitalist system. Many of the exploited masses even seemed to agree with the ideology that their oppressors had generated, whatever it happened to be at the time.

Today, false consciousness encompasses a new and even more horrifying dimension—it enables us to envision nuclear war as either (1) some-

The Communist ideology of Mao Tse-tung (at center in this 1962 photograph) brought radical changes to Chinese society.

thing that is beyond our control and thus something we should avoid thinking about, or (2) something that can be dealt with rationally. Although most individuals assume the first form of contemporary false consciousness, many of our more creative minds tend toward the latter, perhaps thinking along the lines suggested more than a decade ago by the imaginative leader of the Hudson Institute, Herman Kahn.

Kahn has suggested in both *On Escalation* and *On Thermonuclear War* that the incredible technology of modern warfare has made war neither inevitable nor outdated, but has simply increased the options of strategists. Whereas thousands of years ago the cave dweller's only option when feeling threatened or aggressive was to bash someone over the head with a club, today's technology allows us, according to Kahn, a series of forty-four options, ranging from conventional warfare to total nuclear war. The truly amazing aspect of Kahn's suggestions is that they seem not only plausible but eminently rational as well. One comes away from reading his works believing that although nuclear warfare may not be inevitable, nuclear weapons have given us all a marvelous range of options.[20]

IDEOLOGY

Ideology refers to a pattern of beliefs, which may or may not be factual, that serves to simplify and explain complex social phenomena. In this century ideologies—fascism, communism, capitalism—have had a profound effect on societies and on international relations.

The impact of an ideology can be well conveyed by satire. In *The Pooh Perplex*, for instance, Frederick Crews discusses the characters in A. A. Milne's classic *Winnie the Pooh* from the point of view of a Marxist ideologist.

> *Scarcely less central a symbolic character than Rabbit is Owl, the pedantic plutocrat who resides at "The Chestnuts, an old-world residence of great charm, which was grander than anybody else's." A spelling champion and a master of flowery, empty rhetoric, Owl is the necessary handservant to the raw acquisitive passion of Rabbit, which badly needs to be cloaked in grandiosities. The friendship of these two intellectual thugs is a perfect representation of the true role of "scholarship" in bourgeois-industrial society: the end purpose of Owl's obscure learning is to spread a veil of confusion over the doings of the fat cats, to cow the humble into submission before the graven idols of "objective truth" and the "Western tradition," and to rob the proletariat of its power to protest. What could be more meaningful than the fact that Owl has stolen the very tail from the back of Eeyore, the most downcast, bounced-upon member of society, and has converted it to his doorbell? When Pooh comes to retrieve it he is not so much as offered a lick of honey. Rabbit, the industrial manager, at least understood that one must give a*

subsistence, in exchange for the worker's largely unpaid toil, but Owl, the "pure" scholar who professes to be innocent of the ways of the world, excuses himself from even this much elementary compassion. The trahison des clercs is the correct name for this sort of thing.

We should beware, however, of thinking that the symbolic roles of Milne's characters remain absolutely static from one fable to the next. If the meaning is always essentially the same, the way of embodying it changes rather capriciously. Thus Pooh, who represents the workers' cause in the examples above, is cast as a wildcatting capitalist in the Heffalump chapter. He and Piglet, joint partners in the imperialistic venture of bringing back a live Heffalump (subjecting and exploiting colonial peoples), fall out over the question of who is to supply the capital (acorns or honey to set the trap) and who is to do the manual labor of pit-digging. The solution, naturally, is that the smaller and weaker Piglet is issued a shovel and put to work. Shepard's drawing of Piglet-as-miner, looking upward with mixed fatigue and resentment as the exacting supervisor Pooh arrives with the honey, is touching enough, one would think, to soften the heart of a Father Coughlin or a Joseph Kennedy. Pooh himself has been too loyal to his leisure-class environment (A. A. Milne's household) even to carry out the minimal duties of the capitalist properly: he has consumed most of the capital en route. Thus, of course, there ensues a general shortage of funds, which is still nothing in comparison with the hardship that will follow when it is discovered that Heffalumps do not even exist (i.e. that there never was a sufficient labor force in the subjected land to make the unnecessary product for the conspicuous consumption of an already bloated market).[21]

So, given the power of an ideological perspective, even our old, trusted, and bumbling friend Pooh may become a hated enemy of the people.

An ideology may distort reality beyond any recognizable form. It can cause people to see others—different classes, other nationalities—as enemies when no real cause for enmity exists. In such instances an ideology can serve as an extremely powerful force either to promote or retard change in a social system. We can expect that ideologies will continue to play a significant role in the postindustrial world.

Chapter Summary

Political sociologists have offered two opposite explanations of how social order arises—conflict theory and consensus theory. The former stresses conflict and change as the center of political life, while the latter stresses cooperation and stability. There is also disagreement among sociologists on the nature of political power. Some claim that power involves the exercise of one's will over the opposition of others in society; others maintain that the truly powerful often arrange to have their will carried out without arousing opposition. Whatever definition is accepted, power must be distinguished from authority, which is an agreed-upon, legitimate relationship of domination and subjugation.

The political and economic institutions of a society are closely related, as can be seen especially by an examination of developing Third World nations. Studies have shown that economic development is usually accompanied by political change. Some sociologists maintain that there is a necessary connection between economic growth and an increase in democracy, though others disagree. Third World countries have been slow to develop economically. Many still depend on one industry—often foreign owned or controlled—which can also hinder their political development. As a result, many Third World nations are in a constant state of political turmoil.

Most political change in Third World countries occurs by means of coups, which usually succeed only in replacing one elite with another. In the United States and other Western industrialized nations, political change usually occurs slowly through the electoral process. The electoral process can bring about rapid political change, but democracy may suffer as a result (as was the case in Nazi Germany). The most rapid, widespread, and disruptive changes in the social order occur through revolutions.

Today most of the advanced nations of the world have postindustrial economies, which rest on the provision of services more than the production of goods. In the postindustrial world two forces wield a great deal of power—narrowly specialized technocrats and multinational conglomerates. Many see both as a threat to democracy, as are the sophisticated weapons systems that are also a product of this age. Though nuclear technology threatens the obliteration of the world, sophisticated rationales have been worked out which enable us all either to ignore these ever-present means of our destruction or to think that the weapons are fine and liberating things. Ideologies continue to be a powerful force in the postindustrial world and are capable of promoting or retarding change in a social system as well as generating dissension among nations.

Key Terms for Review

authority, p. 265
conflict theory, p. 262
consensus theory, p. 262

coup d'état, p. 268
false consciousness, p. 275
ideology, p. 276

Macht, p. 264
political sociology, p. 261
postindustrial socioeconomic
  system, p. 272

power, p. 264
revolution, p. 268
technocrat, p. 272
totalitarianism, p. 267–268

Suggested Readings

SOCIOLOGICAL

Bendix, Reinhard, ed. *State and Society.* Boston: Little, Brown, 1968. This anthology enjoys a continuing reputation as a leading collection of sound and sophisticated articles encompassing a variety of theoretical and applied academic perspectives on political sociology.

Boorstin, Daniel. *The Sociology of the Absurd or: The Application of Professor X.* New York: Simon & Schuster, 1970. Boorstin explores the political and ideological absurdities involved in the academic relationship with the corporate state. His sardonic humor makes the work both interesting and insightful.

Eells, Richard, ed. *Global Corporations.* New York: Free Press, 1976. Eells offers a fine collection of essays which examine the growing force of international corporate power.

Mills, C. Wright. *Power, Politics and People.* New York: Oxford University Press, 1963. The work is a fine collection of the essays of one of the most noted conflict theorists. Mills's perspective and insights remain fresh and useful years after his death.

Yankelovich, Daniel. *The New Morality.* New York: McGraw-Hill, 1974. This is a fine recent survey of American attitudes and opinions covering a range of public policy issues. Yankelovich offers sound data with equally sound interpretations.

LITERARY

Mailer, Norman. *The Armies of the Night.* New York: Signet, 1968. Mailer presents his own perspective on the major political movement of the 1960s: the "armies" of youth who formed around the central issue of the Vietnam War.

Vonnegut, Kurt, Jr. *Slaughterhouse-Five.* New York: Dell, 1974. In Vonnegut's unique style, this account of Billy Pilgrim and his life after the bombing of Dresden is a mixture of dark humor, fantasy, and insight.

Warren, Robert Penn. *All the King's Men.* New York: Bantam, 1973; orig. 1946. This classic study of the world of Huey Long in the character of Willy Stark and the popular movement that brought him to a position of immense political power remains a fine fictional window on the world of political motivation.

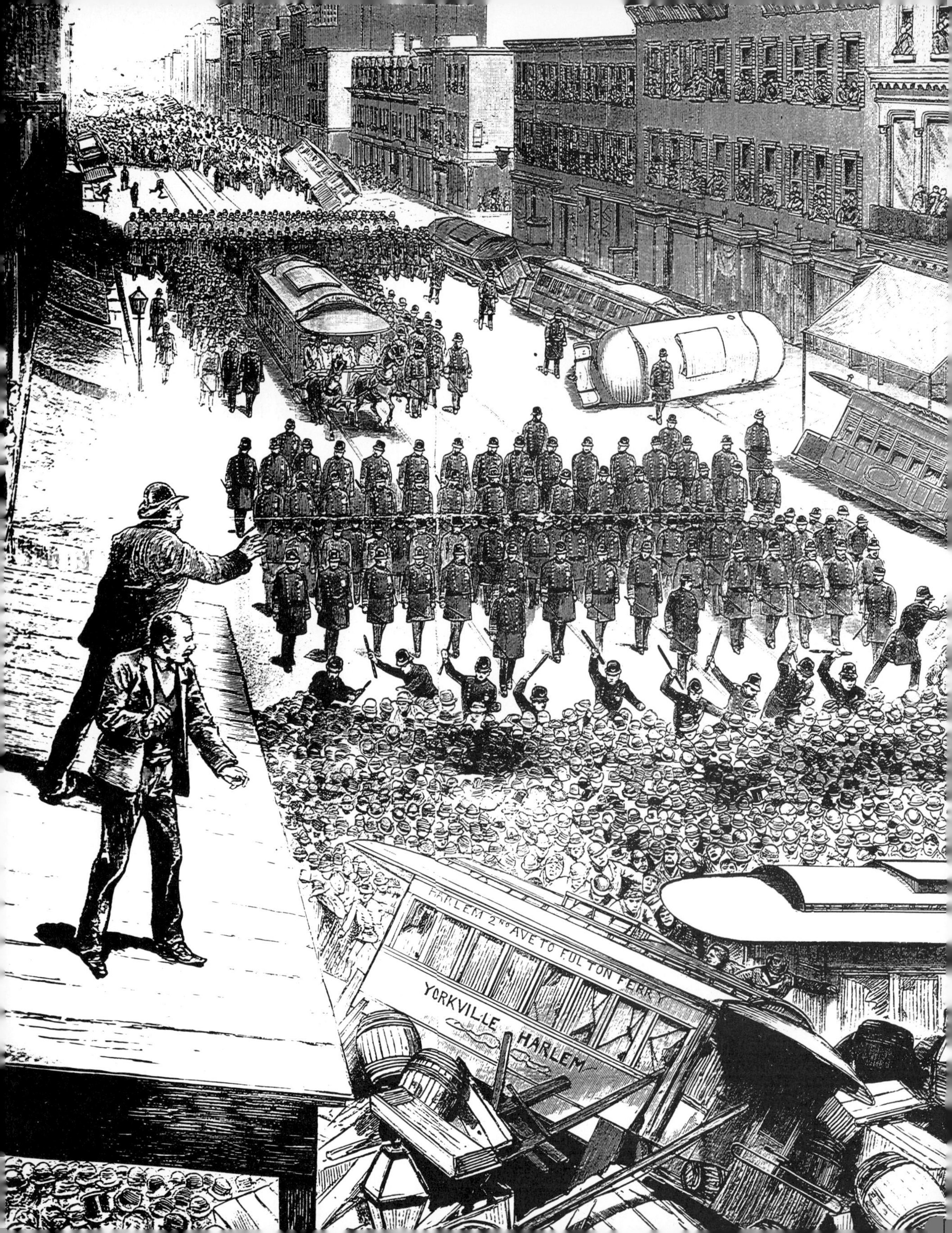
HARLEM 2ND AVE TO FULTON FERRY
YORKVILLE HARLEM

part four

SOCIAL CHANGE

Although social change has always been characteristic of societies, today it occurs more quickly than it previously did. Transience has become a fact of life for nearly everyone in today's complex societies. In chapter 12 we examine the factors contributing to social change and the effects of accelerating social change on the individual. In chapter 13 we discuss crowds, publics, crazes, fashions, and social movements—indicative of the strains and problems that may exist in a society—and point out that collective behavior can produce sweeping social change. No one would doubt that movements such as Christianity, women's liberation, and black civil rights have greatly affected the course of history.

IN THIS CHAPTER

Explanations for Change   284

    The theological explanation   285
    The null explanation   285
    Geographic determinism   285
    Material determinism   286
    Biological determinism   286
    Cultural determinism   287

The Interaction of Variables   288

Change and Individual Adjustment   293

Summary   298

Key Terms for Review   298

Suggested Readings   299

Was the pace of change slower in the "old days"?
What factors help bring about social change?
Will we be able to cope with the accelerating pace of change?
What are the problems associated with change?

12

SOCIAL CHANGE

The sometimes devastating and always disorienting effects of social change are ever present and are something we all experience. Most of us first encounter the rigors of change as we move from one social world to another or from one set of expectations and norms to another. For example, a high school football star might find it difficult to adjust to the new demands of college sports and a student body perhaps less impressed with his ability to run through walls of flesh. Sometimes we learn to cope with what our new world expects of us, and sometimes we do not. However, we must also cope with change even when we are not entering a new social world. This is because society itself is changing.

Social change refers to a significant shift in the material and nonmaterial culture of a society. The critical word here is "significant"; minor alterations in cultural life do not constitute what sociologists term social change. Quite obviously all societies change, but some of this represents slow—or routine—change. Sociologists are much more interested in rapid change within a society. For instance, changes in the material and nonmaterial culture of Japan over the past century have interested sociologists a great deal more than changes in the culture of New Guinea because the former have been far more rapid and dramatic.

Within a century Japan was transformed from an isolated agrarian country into a highly industrialized world power. This period also witnessed the deification of the emperor by the state religion, Shintoism, the rising influence of the military in national government, overseas aggression, total defeat in World War II (with obvious consequences for militarism and emperor worship), and a return to prosperity in the postwar years. Thus virtually every aspect of Japanese society—economic, religious, political, social—underwent significant change in a relatively brief period of time. How these rapid changes were brought about and their effects on individuals and groups in Japanese society have long fascinated sociologists.

Commodore Perry meeting Japan's imperial commissioners. In the 1850s Japan opened its doors to the West and embarked on a period of extremely rapid change.

The social change that has accompanied industrialization in the United States has also fostered sociological inquiries—and widespread anxieties as well. When Henry Ford made available his "basic black" Model A Fords, he had a noticeable impact on various aspects of our nonmaterial culture. For instance, one could certainly be more innovative in courtship as a result of the introduction of the automobile. As we might expect, enthusiasm for the newly created range of freedom was hardly universal. The norms specifying and delineating courtship behavior were not yet ready for the phenomenon of the rumble seat.

In this chapter we will be concerned with several aspects of social change: the various explanations that have been offered for change, the variables affecting change, and the impact of change on individuals and society.

Explanations for Change

A variety of reasons have been offered throughout history to explain why social change occurs. Contemporary sociologists do not give the same weight to all of these theories; in fact, they discount some altogether. But it is worthwhile looking into all of them before discussing which are most helpful in furthering our understanding of the phenomenon of social change.

THE THEOLOGICAL EXPLANATION

Throughout much of history, most people have accepted a *theological explanation* for change. God is seen as the prime mover, the source of change. He may bestow great gifts upon the world (for example, cause a society to become rich and powerful) or, if offended, may bring final devastation. Most religious leaders still support this theological explanation of change. They may possess differing ideas of God—some seeing Him as a wrathful punisher of evil, others as a patient source of mercy—but all present the common theme that "all things are possible to God."[1] God is the source of our power and the shaper of all things.

THE NULL EXPLANATION

A second way of accounting for social change, sometimes proposed in jest but ultimately a very serious assertion, is referred to as the *null explanation*. Those who propose this explanation maintain that either (1) there is no cause or reason for change, it simply happens; or (2) whatever the cause of or reason for change is, it is well beyond anything that we can perceive or understand. Kurt Vonnegut, Jr., offers a typical null explanation of the second variety in *The Sirens of Titan*. Vonnegut suggests that we have no idea at all why we do what we do.

> "There is something you should know about life in the Solar System," he said. "Being chrono-synclastic infundibulated, I've known about it all along. It is, none the less, such a sickening thing that I've thought about it as little as possible.
>
> "The sickening thing is this:
>
> "Everything that every Earthling has ever done has been warped by creatures on a planet one-hundred-and-fifty-thousand light years away. The name of the planet is Tralfamadore.
>
> "How the Tralfamadorians controlled us, I don't know. But I know to what end they controlled us. They controlled us in such a way as to make us deliver a replacement part to a Tralfamadorian messenger who was grounded right here on Titan."[2]

GEOGRAPHIC DETERMINISM

Still another explanation for social change, *geographic determinism*, maintains that social changes follow upon changes in the natural environment. Some historians as well as geographers have adopted this explanation. Renowned British historian Arnold Toynbee, for instance, has found that certain societies have responded to their natural environment by becoming highly industrious. (People in cold climates have had to work harder to survive than those in moderate climates.)

The popular press likewise has not dismissed this explanation. Recently *Time* magazine suggested that 200-year-long "climate cycles" are a major force in social change, and that climate shifts are able to produce a social atmosphere in which "agricultural disasters like Ireland's great potato famine come to be accepted as a natural feature of life."[3]

According to geographic determinism, as the natural environment changes, a social system changes to adapt to the new situation. Thus the potato famine of the 1840s affected Irish society. The new situation caused the people of Ireland to have doubts about their own future and that of their country. Indeed many Irish emigrated to the United States during this period.

MATERIAL DETERMINISM

The explanations offered thus far have not been as widely accepted as the formulation known as *material determinism* (sometimes more narrowly referred to as economic determinism). This doctrine holds that changes in the material aspects of a society's culture act to bring about social changes as well. Most people who accept this interpretation consider economic changes the most significant material changes that occur. The leading exponent of this explanation, Karl Marx, believed that changes in the "mode of production" were always accompanied by changes in social life. Thus the shift from feudalism to capitalism was actually a change from agrarian to industrial production, and this shift resulted in far-reaching social changes affecting religion, family relations, and government institutions. The "source" of such material shifts is not necessarily determined. What is crucial to an understanding of social change is the shift itself.

Although material determinists maintain that changes in material culture always bring social changes in the long run, in the short run a culture lag may develop. According to sociologist William F. Ogburn, originator of the theory, a *culture lag* occurs when significant changes in material culture (inventions), which are often abrupt, are not matched by related and accommodating changes in nonmaterial culture (norms), which are often relatively slow to develop. Ogburn's long and detailed research of numerous inventions indicated that the ensuing cultural adaptations have taken as long as fifty years to develop. Material culture can change much more rapidly than nonmaterial culture.

BIOLOGICAL DETERMINISM

Although material determinism has had a great deal of support among scholars, some have proposed an alternate theory, *biological determin-*

An expanding railroad network (a material change) had important effects on America's nonmaterial culture in the 1800s. And in this century the automobile brought even more rapid change.

ism, as a better explanation of social change. According to this theory, social change has been brought about by the biological evolution of humankind. One sociologist who supported this theory, Vilfredo Pareto (1848–1923), suggested that social elites are determined by biologically inherited "instincts" and natural skills. "Talent" must naturally rise to the top.[4] If a social system does not allow the talented to rise to the top, the system will necessarily become unproductive and will eventually be destroyed.

The most dangerous version of biological determinism links change to race. This version states that changes in human history have been brought about by the development of distinct races. Adolf Hitler's notion of a master race that would rule the world provides one notorious example of this theory.

Norms may change more slowly than material culture. Here an older Tokyo resident rides a modern subway seated in the traditional manner, kneeling with her shoes removed.

CULTURAL DETERMINISM

A final explanation of social change, *cultural determinism*, maintains that changes in nonmaterial culture (norms) are more crucial to social change than are changes in material culture. Max Weber was the foremost advocate of this view. In his work *The Protestant Ethic and the Spirit of Capitalism*, Weber suggested that the basic values of Protestantism as encompassed in the Protestant ethic (thrift, propriety, and hard work) were determining factors in bringing about the Industrial Revolution, which in turn fostered great social change. Thus Weber, while recognizing the importance of an economic base, gave prior importance to nonmaterial factors. His work was a major counter to material determinism.

The Interaction of Variables

Although some of the preceding explanations are clearly more credible than others, most contemporary scholars tend to discount the idea that any single variable—be it material or cultural, biological or geographic—is responsible for social change. Most now consider a number of factors, in varying relationships to each other, as the source or sources of change. They feel that the isolation of any single cause is overly simplistic and misleading.

For instance, the many changes in the structure of the American family during the twentieth century are not traceable to any single cause. Obviously increased mobility and changing residence patterns have served to isolate the nuclear family from relatives. Here, changes in the material culture, such as improved communication and transportation facilities, have had an impact. Shifts in the nonmaterial culture, such as changing ideas about the "role" of women, have also affected family life. Further, increased health care facilities and modern medical knowledge have extended productive years as well as life expectancy. Clearly, in the case of the American family, social change is not the result of any single factor.

Although all variables may play some role in explaining change, sociologists generally agree that some variables explain a wider variety of social change than others. For instance, changes in material and nonmaterial culture explain recent social history better than do changes in the biological structure of humans.

The tremendous technological advances of the past two centuries serve to highlight this point. One hundred and fifty years ago wooden sailing ships and horses, the major forms of transportation, were the vehicles of international and domestic commerce. In that era Jules Verne, who wrote science fiction works filled with ships that could submerge, flying machines, and voyages to the moon in bullet-like projectiles, was considered outlandishly imaginative. The material changes brought about by technology during the twentieth century alone have been truly awesome, matched only by the social changes that have accompanied them. However, the few generations that have lived during this period of great change have altered little biologically. Indeed, most biologists note that there has been relatively little biological change in humans during the past several thousand years.

The rather obvious and compelling conclusion is, of course, that the great shifts in the structure of society over the past century or so are much more the result of material and nonmaterial cultural changes than of biological changes. Even the most imaginative biological determinists, such as Robert Ardrey, do not dispute this conclusion. It may be that we are the descendants of predatory killer apes as Ardrey suggests. It is even possible

An illustration in Jules Verne's science fiction book *From the Earth to the Moon,* considered wildly speculative a hundred years ago.

that our apparent need for war and destruction results from some form of "natural instinct."[5] But even if this admittedly imaginative speculation is accurate, the human ability to wage war is much more dependent upon technology and inventiveness than upon any "instinct" for aggression.

The dominant sociological explanation of change, therefore, emphasizes the importance of culture, although it recognizes that culture is composed of both material aspects (inventions) and nonmaterial aspects (norms). Most of us have dutifully learned the familiar catechism of inventors and their inventions: Thomas A. Edison—the electric light; Alexander Graham Bell—the telephone; Eli Whitney—the cotton gin; and so on. We have been led to believe that a few great individuals have been responsible for cultural innovations; and, no doubt, through their particular genius and hard work, individuals have brought about change.

Two points, however, must be made very clear in terms of individuals and cultural change. First, few if any inventors ever created something that was entirely new. They were dependent on the related works of others and were also products of their own culture and time. (Obviously, the Wright brothers were dependent upon the invention of numerous connecting devices and stress supports simply to hold their plane together. Moreover, the flight of their plane was necessarily preceded by all the discoveries that brought about the internal combustion engine.) Second, many crucial innovations might well have been "invented" numerous times before the date noted in history books, since to have a recognized creation, one must have a receptive audience. For example, a rudimentary printing press might have been invented during the Dark Ages but lost to history; a society in which few could read would have had little use for printed matter. Similarly, the Moog synthesizer could hardly have become known before the music world was in a position to utilize it. Time and place must be right for an invention to receive widespread acceptance. Its worth, its innovativeness, and the honor accorded its inventor are all determined by the society's nonmaterial culture. The inventor of spray underarm deodorant, for example, would receive few accolades in a society that did not find body odors offensive. This process of acceptance or rejection of change by a society and the reasons for such acceptance or rejection are all related to what sociologists call cultural diffusion.

Cultural diffusion refers to the processes that produce cultural similari-

Technology and society were ready to both produce and accept the inventions of Alexander Graham Bell (far left) and Thomas A. Edison (center). Although the Wright brothers are acclaimed as the fathers of the airplane, their achievement was obviously based on the research and inventions of many others. Here is an "airship kite" aloft in 1892.

ties in various societies. Most sociologists and anthropologists distinguish three separate processes. The first is *primary diffusion*, which occurs through migration. For example, many changes in American culture took place when great numbers of immigrants came to the United States at the turn of the century. The second process, called *secondary diffusion*, involves the direct transfer of something (usually material culture) from one society to another. For example, many changes in the cultures of underdeveloped Third World countries have been brought about in recent years through the transfer of machinery from the advanced industrialized nations. The third process is *stimulus diffusion*, which refers to the transfer of ideas. Although such diffusion takes place without direct migration or even the transfer of a particular machine, it often brings great change. For instance, the idea of liberty, equality, and fraternity expounded by the French Revolution of 1789 had a profound effect upon people in other countries.

One should not be left with the impression that a kind of cultural determinism absolutely overwhelms the individual efforts of human beings. We have stressed the importance of culture because most of us are so ingrained with what has come to be known as "the great-man theory of history" that we fail to recognize that all humanity exists within a social context. Great men and women have not made history—George Washington was not solely responsible for the founding of the United States, nor did Joan of Arc create French nationalism. But it would be just as wrong to say

With identification papers clamped between their teeth and carrying all their worldly possessions, these immigrants embarked on a new life in America around 1900. Yet they also brought changes to their new homeland.

that individuals have no influence over history. Individuals can indeed make a difference. Kurt Vonnegut, Jr., speaks of this in *Mother Night*:

> *I saw a huge steam roller,*
> *It blotted out the sun.*
> *The people all lay down, lay down;*
> *They did not try to run.*
> *My love and I, we looked amazed*
> *Upon the gory mystery.*
> *"Lie down, lie down!" the people cried.*
> *"The great machine is history!"*
> *My love and I, we ran away,*
> *The engine did not find us.*
> *We ran up to a mountain top,*
> *Left history far behind us.*
> *Perhaps we should have stayed and died,*
> *But somehow we don't think so.*
> *We went to see where history'd been,*
> *And my, the dead did stink so.*[6]

We need not lie down for history—though many do. Recent political events such as disclosure of the Watergate cover-up through the efforts of diligent reporters suggest that individuals and individual efforts do make a difference. The steamroller of history does not force everyone to lie down.

Change and Individual Adjustment

When Alvin Toffler's book *Future Shock,* describing contemporary social change, was published in 1970, its almost instantaneous success suggested that many Americans were quite concerned with the effects of social change on their own lives. Toffler's basic assumption is that "the future is arriving ahead of schedule." Change, primarily in material culture, now occurs at such an "endlessly accelerating" rate that people are no longer able to cope with it. Toffler captures the essence of "today's accelerative thrust" in a *Teacher's Guide to Future Shock:*

> *Divide the last 50,000 years of man's existence into lifetimes of 62 years each. There have been 800 such lifetimes. Of these, fully 650 were spent in caves. Only during the last 70 lifetimes has it been possible to communicate effectively from one lifetime to the next. Only during the last six lifetimes have masses of men seen a printed word. Only during the last four has anyone used an electric motor. The overwhelming majority of the material goods we use in daily life today have been developed within this, the 800th lifetime. For us the environment is always new — it's increasingly unfamiliar, alien, foreign. It's this "foreignness" that produces future shock.*[7]

Of major concern is the increasing *transience,* or lack of permanence, in everyone's life. There is precious little that Toffler can find which seems to lend any feeling of continuity to contemporary American lives. Cultural foundations have been shaken and sometimes done away with. Previously unquestioned values, such as the absolute worth of hard work, have been called into question. We no longer interact only with people we know. Much of the time we are forced to interact with strangers and machines. That which we knew to be true in our youth is no longer true. Sometimes that which we knew to be true last week is no longer true.

This updated and provocative version of Ogburn's culture lag theory focuses on some very real daily problems of surviving in the "800th lifetime." Transience is a fact of life in our society. One need only ask people how often they move or inquire, "How long have you known your 'best friend'?" to recognize that fact. One might also ask how many births, deaths, divorces, marriages, job promotions, demotions, or layoffs have occurred in my family — or on my block — in the past year or two.[8] The answers are always revealing. We have become, for the most part, "the rootless society," as sociologist and popular social critic Vance Packard put it. One in five American families moves each year!

Aside from coping with continuous uprooting, members of our society must also deal with the possibility of being replaced by, and perhaps ultimately subjugated by, machines. That development has been made possible by the introduction of a new science, *cybernetics*, which studies ways to replace human effort with electronic systems. Many people, including factory workers and office clerks, have already confronted the reality that machines can perform their work much more efficiently, and many more of us will soon face the same situation as computers become increasingly more sophisticated. Occupational groups, social classes, even entire nations will be unable to avoid the change.

Unquestionably the myriad social changes of the "800th lifetime" have been unprecedented. Yet change, particularly on the personal level, has always been similar in that in its extreme form it involves a breakdown of personal and social values and consequently invokes feelings of anxiety and even humiliation. When we are no longer able to cope, when we are out of step or not in tune, when our time has passed, we experience the trauma of social change. There is almost a timeless quality to it, and perhaps this is one of our few remaining constants: social change will always be with us.

The personal defeat that individuals can suffer as a result of social change is movingly portrayed by Franz Kafka in what many consider his best short story, "A Hunger Artist."

> During these last decades the interest in professional fasting has markedly diminished. It used to pay very well to stage such great performances under one's own management, but today that is quite impossible. We live in a different world now. At one time the whole town took a lively interest in the hunger artist; from day to day of his fast the excitement mounted; everybody wanted to see him at least once a day; there were people who bought season tickets for the last few days and sat from morning till night in front of his small barred cage; even in the nighttime there were visiting hours, when the whole effect was heightened by torch flares; one fine day the whole

Change at the personal level is common in contemporary American society. The moving van represents the loss of friends and familiar places and a new physical and social environment.

The position of the elderly in American society can be difficult. The world they knew no longer exists, and their values, like those of the hunger artist, are often out-dated.

cage was set out in the open air, and then it was the children's special treat to see the hunger artist; for their elders he was often just a joke that happened to be in fashion, but the children stood open-mouthed, holding each other's hands for greater security, marveling at him as he sat there pallid in black tights, with his ribs sticking out so prominently, not even on a seat but down among straw on the ground, sometimes giving a courteous nod, answering questions with a constrained smile, or perhaps stretching an arm through the bars so one might feel how thin it was, and then withdrawing deep into himself, paying no attention to anyone or anything, not even to the all important striking of the clock that was the only piece of furniture in his cage, but merely staring into vacancy with half-shut eyes, now and then taking a sip from a tiny glass of water to moisten his lips.[9]

The hunger artist took great pride in his profession, in his ability to discipline his will and body. His greatest regret had always been the time limitations placed on his work. "Experience had proved that for about forty days the interest of the public could be stimulated by a steadily increasing pressure of advertisement, but after that the town began to lose interest."[10] The marketplace dictated that he be limited in his quest for the ultimate fast—he was always stopped. Changes in popular taste were greatly affecting his career.

Why stop fasting at this particular moment, after forty days of it? He had held out for a long time, an illimitably long time; why stop now, when he was in his best fasting form? Why should he be cheated of the fame he would get for fasting longer, for not only being the rec-

ord hunger artist of all time, which presumably he was already, but for beating his own record by a performance beyond human imagination, since he felt there were no limits to his capacity for fasting?[11]

The time finally came when the hunger artist was no longer able to work as an independent. The public was not interested in the art of fasting; many did not have any conception of what it was. Yet by working with a large circus, as a small attraction among the animal cages, he was able to find employment and perhaps a chance at breaking the record fast of forty days, that goal which had so long eluded him. Whereas he was once a hero, cultural change had now relegated him to the outer fringes of the circus.

And all too rarely did it happen that he had a stroke of luck, when some father of a family fetched up before him with his children, pointed a finger at the hunger artist and explained at length what the phenomenon meant, telling stories of earlier years when he himself had watched similar but much more thrilling performances, and the children, still rather uncomprehending, since neither inside nor outside school had they been sufficiently prepared for this lesson — what did they care about fasting? — yet showed by the brightness of their intent eyes that new and better times might be coming. Perhaps, said the hunger artist to himself, many a time, things would be a little better if his cage were set not quite so near the menagerie. That made it too easy for people to make their choice, to say nothing of what he suffered from the stench of the menagerie, the animals' restlessness by night, the carrying past of raw lumps of flesh for the beasts of prey, the roaring at feeding times, which depressed him continually. But he did not dare to lodge a complaint with the management; after all, he had the animals to thank for the troops of people who passed his cage, among whom there might always be one here and there to take an interest in him, and who could tell where they might seclude him if he called attention to his existence and thereby to the fact that, strictly speaking, he was only an impediment on the way to the menagerie.

  A small impediment, to be sure, one that grew steadily less. People grew familiar with the idea that they could not be expected, in times like these, to take an interest in a hunger artist; with this familiarity the verdict went out against him. He might fast as much as he could, and he did so; but nothing could save him now, people passed him by. Just try to explain to anyone the art of fasting! Anyone who has no feelings for it cannot be made to understand it. The fine placards grew dirty and illegible, they were torn down; the little notice board telling the number of days of fast achieved, which at first was changed carefully everyday, had long stayed at the same figure, for after the first few weeks even this small task seemed point-

less to the staff; and so the artist simply fasted on and on, as he had once dreamed of doing, and it was no trouble to him, just as he had always foretold, but no one counted the days, no one, not even the artist himself, knew what records he was already breaking, and his heart grew heavy. And when once in a time some leisurely passer-by stopped, made merry over the old figure on the board and spoke of swindling, that was in its way the stupidest lie ever invented by indifference and inborn malice, since it was not the hunger artist who was cheating, he was working honestly, but the world was cheating him of his reward.

Many more days went by, however, and that too came to an end. An overseer's eye fell on the cage one day and he asked the attendants why this perfectly good stage should be left standing there unused with dirty straw inside it; nobody knew, until one man, helped out by the notice board, remembered about the hunger artist. They poked into the straw with sticks and found him in it. "Are you still fasting?" asked the overseer; "when on earth do you mean to stop?" "Forgive me everybody," whispered the hunger artist; only the overseer, who had his ear to the bars, understood him. "Of course," said the overseer, and tapped his forehead with a finger to let the attendants know what state the man was in, "We forgive you." "I always wanted you to admire my fasting," said the hunger artist. "What a fellow you are," said the overseer, "and why can't you help it?" "Because," said the hunger artist, lifting his head a little and speaking with his lips pursed, as if for a kiss, right into the overseer's ear, so that no syllable might be lost, "because I couldn't find the food I liked. If I had found it, believe me, I should have made no fuss and stuffed myself like you or anyone else." These were his last words, but in his dimming eyes remained the firm though no longer proud persuasion that he was still continuing to fast.

"Well, clear this out now!" said the overseer, and they buried the hunger artist, straw and all. Into the cage they put a young panther. Even the most insensitive felt it refreshing to see this wild creature leaping around the cage that had so long been dreary. The panther was all right. The food he liked was brought him without hesitation by the attendants, he seemed not even to miss his freedom; his noble body furnished almost to the bursting point with all that it needed, seemed to carry freedom around with it too; somewhere in his jaws it seemed to lurk; and the joy of life streamed with such ardent passion from his throat that for the onlookers it was not easy to stand the shock of it. But they braced themselves, crowded round the cage, and did not want to move away.[12]

Even the final words of the hunger artist, a mixture of both pride and apology, were unable to save him from a humiliating death, discarded with the dirty straw. Be it hunger artistry, buggy building, or key punch operating, eventually cultural shifts make the practitioners of these trades superfluous, undesirable, and ultimately dreary. Perhaps, as Toffler suggests, we have come to that final point in cultural progression where we have instantly disposable people.

Chapter Summary

Among the general theoretical explanations offered for understanding social change, geographic, biological, material, and cultural determinism are the most common. Sociologists tend to support the theories of material and cultural determinism because those theories supply the most convincing explanations of recent social changes. Most also agree that there is no single cause of change. Many factors interact to disrupt, alter, destroy, promote, reward, and humiliate both groups and individuals.

There will never be a society that does not experience change. Societies go through periods of slow, almost imperceptible alteration and periods of dramatically accelerating change, yet change itself is always present. Alvin Toffler has commented on the seeming inability of people to cope with the radical changes in society that have occurred during the past century. The great focal point of change, as Toffler sees it, is transience. We are left with fewer and fewer touchstones of civilization—our foundations are disappearing. Indeed, the cybernetic revolution threatens all of us with being replaced by machines.

Some people feel pessimistic about the ability of human beings to cope with the rapid changes of postindustrial society, yet we must keep in mind the fact that change has always been with us. Impermanence has been a constant companion of humanity. It is just that now the transience of groups and individuals is more obvious, affects greater numbers, and occurs at an accelerating pace.

Key Terms for Review

biological determinism, p. 286
cultural determinism, p. 287
cultural diffusion, p. 290
culture lag, p. 286
cybernetics, p. 294

"800th lifetime," p. 293
geographic determinism, p. 285
material determinism, p. 286
null explanation, p. 285
primary diffusion, p. 291

secondary diffusion, p. 291
social change, 283
stimulus diffusion, p. 291

theological explanation, p. 285
transience, p. 293

Suggested Readings

SOCIOLOGICAL

Etzioni, Amitai, and Eva Etzioni. *Social Change: Sources, Patterns, and Consequences.* New York: Holt, Rinehart & Winston, 1964. This book is one of the definitive contemporary treatments of the subject of social change.

Moore, Wilbert E. *Social Change.* Englewood Cliffs, N.J.: Prentice-Hall, 1963. Moore's discussion of the process of change emphasizes the continuous nature of it. Change is ever-present in human social systems.

Ogburn, William F. *Social Change.* New York: Huebsch, 1922. This classic study of social change delineates the theory of culture lag. Though certain aspects of Ogburn's work are now clearly dated (a comment on change itself), his general perspective and the discussion of cultural diffusion remain as benchmarks.

Toffler, Alvin. *Future Shock.* New York: Random House, 1970. Toffler views the accelerating pace of change with dismay. Human beings, according to Toffler, are simply no longer able to control or adjust to change.

LITERARY

Burdick, Eugene, and Harvey Wheeler. *Fail-Safe.* New York: Dell, 1962. Burdick and Wheeler tell of the great faith we have placed in a little, mechanical, black box (fail-safe) and our inability to cope with the machines of war once their imperfections have surfaced. The ultimate and "unthinkable" horror of nuclear exchange is finally made to seem quite possible.

Norris, Frank. *The Octopus.* New York: Bantam, 1958; orig. 1901. This is a classic story of the railroad's impact on the farmers and ranchers of the West. Machines prove victorious as human relationships are torn and destroyed by the oncoming "iron horse."

Waters, Frank. *People of the Valley.* Chicago: Swallow Press, 1969; orig. 1941. The great impact of a dam project on the lives of the agrarian Spanish-speaking peoples of the Sangre de Cristo Mountains is examined. Maria del Valle is the focal character of Waters's story of change, and she brings a marvelous shrewdness and intuition to combat the sometimes overwhelming forces of the government.

IN THIS CHAPTER

Types of Collective Behavior   305

   Crowds   305
   Publics   309
   Crazes and fashions   309
   Social movements   310

Explanations of Collective Behavior   310

   Ignorant mass view   310
   Alienated mass view   311
   Value-added theory   317

Rumor: Communication in Collective Behavior   318

Social Movements   320

   Objectives, programs, and ideologies   320
   Commitment   321
   Stages of development   323
   Kinds of social movements   323

Summary   325

Key Terms for Review   326

Suggested Readings   326

Can crowds and social movements bring about social change?
Do people riot and revolt because they are ignorant or because they are frustrated and deprived?
Do most social movements evolve out of class, racial, or sexual struggles?
How does a social movement keep its members committed to the cause?

13

COLLECTIVE BEHAVIOR AND SOCIAL MOVEMENTS

The person on the street who thinks that the subject matter of sociology is the study of collective behavior is in a sense correct. However, sociologists use the term "collective behavior" in a narrower sense than does the general public. For them *collective behavior* generally means behavior which seems rather unstructured, unstable, and unpredictable. It is behavior that tends to be short-lived, sometimes emotional, and based on considerable personal interaction.* Several examples will help illustrate the sociologist's use of the term.

James Thurber's "The Day the Dam Broke" is a short story about the residents of Columbus, Ohio. It seems that on March 12, 1913, a rumor was spread that the nearby dam had broken. At least 2,000 citizens decided to escape the ravaging waters which were supposed to destroy the town. Thurber recalls the events of the day:

> My memories of what my family and I went through during the 1913 flood in Ohio I would gladly forget. And yet neither the hardships we endured nor the turmoil and confusion we experienced can alter my feeling toward my native state and city. I am having a fine time now and wish Columbus were here, but if anyone ever wished a city was in hell it was during that frightful and perilous afternoon in 1913 when the dam broke, or, to be more exact, when everybody in

---

*For a discussion of sociologists' traditional usage of the term "collective behavior" see Ralph H. Turner and Lewis M. Killian, *Collective Behavior* (Englewood Cliffs, N. J.: Prentice-Hall, 1962), chap. 1. For a critique of this traditional usage see Richard A. Berk, *Collective Behavior* (Dubuque, Iowa: William C. Brown, 1974).

town thought that the dam broke. We were both ennobled and demoralized by the experience. Grandfather especially rose to magnificent heights which can never lose their splendor for me, even though his reactions to the flood were based upon a profound misconception; namely, that Nathan Bedford Forrest's cavalry was the menace we were called upon to face. The only possible means of escape for us was to flee the house, a step which grandfather sternly forbade, brandishing his old army sabre in his hand. "Let the sons —— come!" he roared. Meanwhile hundreds of people were streaming by our house in wild panic, screaming "Go east!, Go east!" We had to stun grandfather with the ironing board. Impeded as we were by the inert form of the old gentleman—he was taller than six feet and weighed almost a hundred and seventy pounds—we were passed, in the first half-mile, by practically everybody else in the city. Had grandfather not come to, at the corner of Parsons Avenue and Town Street, we would unquestionably have been overtaken and engulfed by the roaring waters—that is, if there had been any roaring waters. Later, when the panic had died down and people had gone rather sheepishly back to their homes and their offices, minimizing the distances they had run and offering various reasons for running, the city engineers pointed out that even if the dam had broken, the water level would not have risen more than two additional inches in the West Side. . . .

The fact that we were all as safe as kittens under a cook-stove did not, however, assuage in the least the fine despair and grotesque desperation which seized upon the residents of the East Side when the cry spread like a grass fire that the dam had given way. Some of the most dignified, staid, cynical, and clear-thinking men in town abandoned their wives, stenographers, homes, and offices and ran east. There are few alarms in the world more terrifying than "The dam has broken!" There are few persons capable of stopping to reason when that clarion cry strikes upon their ears, even persons who live in towns no nearer than five hundred miles to a dam.[1]

How can we characterize the actions of Columbus residents? Since most, if not all, had never experienced a crisis of this type, they lacked guidelines as to what was appropriate behavior. Faced with an unstructured, unfamiliar situation, residents had to make a spontaneous decision on what action was necessary. Also, many individuals, particularly "grandfather," seemed somewhat overtaken by their own emotions.

A second example concerns a victory celebration by fans of the Pittsburgh Pirates baseball team during 1971. People celebrating the city's first World Series victory in eleven years turned into an overexuberant mob which engaged in vandalism, looting, and public love-making.

While Pittsburgh city officials denied earlier news reports of rapes and criminal assaults taking place in downtown streets, there was evidence of such "anti-social acts" as the overturning of at least four vehicles including a taxi, the smashing of about 30 store windows and the burning of a police motorcycle. Nearly 100 celebrants of the Pirate victory over Baltimore were arrested. As for eyewitness accounts of lovemaking in the park, the police chief conceded that some people "got a little out of hand."[2]

Some officials observed that even individuals who did not know whether Pittsburgh had won or lost, or even that a game had been played, joined in the excitement. Like the citizens of Columbus, these Pittsburgh residents displayed seemingly spontaneous emotional behavior.

A final illustration concerns the 1970 student riots at Kent State University in Ohio. Prior to the riots, the university had never experienced a major disturbance. In fact, students had been described as politically indifferent or conservative, and the "insurance salesmen of tomorrow."[3] Yet, as a protest to the widening of the war in Southeast Asia, students broke windows, burned the ROTC building, and threw rocks at police. In his book about the riots, *The Killings at Kent State: How Murder Went Unpunished*, journalist I. F. Stone quotes from the Akron *Beacon Journal*, which describes some of the student behavior:

Friday, May 1

    Friday night, the scene of attention shifted to downtown Kent, to an area on N. Water St. called "The Strip," . . .

    Chaz Madonio, the bass player at Big Daddy's, said it all started casually. "It was so hot inside," he said, "the people came outside for fresh air. When they saw the crowd (gathering outside), they decided to stay. When the crowd swelled, they started to get brave."

    Steve Sharoff said he was sitting in Seaver's, the hippie bar, having a beer, when "I heard a crash and a guy came in and said, 'Guys are throwing bottles out there.' I said, 'Wow, that's pretty far out.' "

    Roman Tymchyshyn, a graduate art student, said he was on The Strip about 11:15 P.M. when "I saw people spilling into the street and they closed it off. They were dancing in the streets and shouting 'F—— Agnew' and "1-2-3-4, we don't want your f——ing war.' "

    Patrolman Robert Defluiter of the Kent Police Department said that between 11:27 and 11:41 P.M. he watched young demonstrators, shouting, "Get out of town, pigs!" bombard two police cars with bottles, glasses and beer pitchers.

    "They put three cars across the street in front of J. B.'s (a tavern) and blocked off the street," Defluiter said. "They dragged wood and paper and trash out from behind the buildings and built a bonfire in the street."

    After about 20 policemen arrived at the scene soon after midnight dressed in full riot gear, the demonstrators, both students and nonstudents, started breaking windows. . . .

> Demonstrators took a lawnspreader from the Getz Hardware Store and threw it through the window of the Portage County National Bank. It was the first of more than 50 windows they broke in 15 business places.
>
> A crowd of about 500 hurled rocks and bottles at police and sheriff's deputies, injuring five. . . .
>
> Saturday, May 2
>
> . . . A plainclothes detective for the campus police got down to the ROTC building about 8 P.M. Saturday. He said a crowd of 500 to 700 students had already gathered on the commons . . . someone soaked a rag in the gas tank of a parked motorcycle "and they lit the rag and put this on the curtains and got it going good. The fire started burning up the wall." . . .
>
> The riot squad of the campus police force arrived then, 18 men in gas masks wearing helmets and carrying batons. The students shouted "Pigs! Pigs!" and somebody threw a big firecracker right into the middle of their ranks. "Then the kids started throwing rocks like mad."[4]

The disturbances ended May 4 on a tragic note. Four students were killed as national guardsmen shot into a crowd of demonstrators.

What characteristics do these three examples have in common? First, people were faced with unstructured and unstable situations where past experiences and established norms seemed absent or, at least, sufficiently loose to provide no guide to behavior. Lacking well-defined guidelines, individuals were forced to make on-the-spot decisions about how to react to the situation. Second, the group action in each example was temporary, or short-lived. Third, many individuals behaved in excited and emotional ways. And, fourth, in each case we can assume that a large degree of personal interaction occurred among group members.*

Sociologists examine collective behavior for essentially two reasons. One reason is to understand the conditions which lead to the phenomenon. For example, in regard to the World Series celebration in Pittsburgh, some explained that it was Sunday, and with most services curtailed people were simply bored and looking for excitement. Others explained the incident from an economic perspective. Many steel mills had closed down during the previous summer and unemployment was high, so cheering the local heroes offered a distraction from personal problems and gave the community a renewed sense of pride.

The second reason sociologists study collective behavior is to observe the social change that results from such behavior. For example, the urban riots in Newark, Detroit, Watts, and Tampa in the middle and late 1960s greatly affected society. Paradoxically, urban renewal, welfare aid, and

---

*Berk, *Collective Behavior*, presents many of the same characteristics of "collective behavior."

The urban riots of the 1960s left ghettos in shambles and American society in a state of shock. Here we see (left) police sealing off a riot area in Detroit and (right) a burned out block in Watts.

other social programs were employed to improve ghetto conditions, while police and national guardsmen were given mace, shotguns, rubber bullets, and tear gas for the same purpose. In another example, the student riots at Kent State, Berkeley, Columbia, and other universities during the 1960s and early 1970s effected change, though here too the responses were varied. Many schools established Black, Chicano, and Native American Studies programs; administrators asked students to serve on university committees; state legislators adopted a "get tough" attitude toward "sympathetic and radical" faculty; and many citizens developed a fatalistic attitude toward "irresponsible youth" and the future. Collective behavior can initiate sweeping social change.

Types of Collective Behavior

Even though collective behavior refers to a rather wide range of human conduct, sociologists have classified the action into various types. The more important types deserve discussion.

CROWDS

The illustrations at the beginning of this chapter indicated that a crowd is a prime example of collective behavior. A *crowd* may be defined as a temporary gathering of people at one time and place. In addition, there are different types of crowds.

Sociologist Herbert Blumer discusses four types. The *casual crowd* is an aggregate of onlookers viewing a common event, such as shoppers looking in a department store window. The group has no unity or internal organization and only a momentary existence. In contrast, the *conven-*

New York City's traditional Easter parade (one from the early 1900s is shown here) provides an example of the conventionalized crowd.

tionalized crowd consists of individuals pursuing a mutual goal. Their behavior is considerably more established and regularized. Fans watching a football game and members of a congregation listening to a Sunday sermon are examples. Of course, the relatively few and simple norms and sanctions operating in these groups are quite different. A member of a congregation would hardly jump up from a pew, shake his fist, and boo the minister for a poor sermon, nor would an avid football fan sit placidly with her arms folded as her team was penalized by a "nearsighted" referee. A somewhat uncomplicated type of social organization is guiding behavior, but instability is still present.

Whereas casual and conventionalized crowds do not engage in direct action toward individuals and objects, the *active crowd* does. A lynch mob or soccer fans who square off and battle each other are examples. In the fourth type, the *expressive crowd*, participants gather together for self-stimulation. People who shout, sing, and rejoice at a religious revival and an emotional audience that experiences a "happening" at a rock music festival such as Woodstock are examples. Blumer maintains that expressive crowds usually begin as conventionalized crowds, but as emotions become intense, the social organization guiding member behavior becomes ineffectual. Self-exaltation eventually dominates.[5]

Characteristics of Blumer's four types of crowds overlap in many situations. For example, consider the incident at Sabana Grande, Puerto Rico, on May 25, 1953, when 100,000 people arrived to witness the appearance of the Virgin. The scene is described by Tamotsu Shibutani in *Improvised News: A Sociological Study of Rumor:*

> They had been coming for days—not only from all parts of Puerto Rico, but from Haiti, Cuba, and even as far away as New York. Travel to Sabana Grande was tortuously slow. . . .
>
> About a month before seven children had reported to their teacher that the Virgin had appeared at a well during recess. For a time she reappeared daily. Although interviews revealed some inconsistencies in their accounts, the mass media took up the event with enthusiasm. The mayor of a nearby town had an altar built at the well and organized worshipers into processions. Parents urged the children on, encouraging them to continue their visits with the Virgin. . . .
>
> The pilgrims gathered around the well, which was surrounded on three sides by steep hills. From time to time one of the children would pray, and others followed in unison. The children had indi-

The thousands of rock music fans at the Woodstock festival in 1969 formed an expressive crowd.

cated that the Virgin would appear at 11 A.M., and as the hour approached, tension grew. At 10:45 it started to rain, but the umbrellas that went up were quickly lowered, when word spread that the children had said no umbrellas were to be opened. Various individuals reported seeing miracles: the Virgin appeared silhouetted in the clouds or in rings of color around the sun. People who had been sick for years suddenly felt well. Just after 11 o'clock a cry went up that the Virgin, dressed in black, was walking down the west hill toward the well. Some of the devout were overwhelmed. Investigation revealed that this was just an old woman dressed in black. . . . By 5 P.M. people began departing in droves.

Afterwards considerable disagreement arose over what had happened. Some who themselves had not seen the Virgin believed that the children had; they argued that only the pure and untainted could be so honored. Many who had been doubtful left as believers; they felt that something supernatural must have happened. Even if they had not seen the Virgin, they had spoken to others who claimed they had. Some had come seeking relief from illness, and they felt better. They saw others who claimed to have been cured. Unusual celestial movements were also cited.[6]

The crowd was a conventionalized type in the sense that people were pursuing a common goal, to be present at the appearance of a celestial being, and simple guides to behavior characteristic of religious followers were also operating. Still, the crowd was an expressive type since individuals sought personal religious experience, relief from illness, or confirmation of miracles and the supernatural. Emotion and excitement were present and probably would have dominated the event if, for instance, the identity of the woman in black had not been discovered.

Three crazes that have swept college campuses over the years: goldfish swallowing, phone booth stuffing, and "streaking."

PUBLICS

In contrast to crowds, some collective behavior can emerge even when people are geographically separated. One such collective is a *public*. Individuals define themselves as affected by some issue—such as consumer rights, unemployment, school busing, abortion, Medicare, or ecology—and register their concern. A public seldom has a definite membership; people's interest in an issue can grow and decline as events change. It also has no internal organization. Members of a public will interact with one another on the basis of both fact and emotion to arrive at a position on the issue of concern. Out of such debate may emerge a collective voice, *public opinion*.

In a democratic society public opinion is assumed ideally to affect the decisions and policies of national leaders. However, there is much debate between power elite and pluralist theorists as to whether American citizens represent an audience—a passive and ineffectual group with no influence on key decisions; or a public—a collective whose opinions dictate the direction of society. (See chapter 7 for a discussion of the power elite and pluralist theories of power and decision-making in American society.)

CRAZES AND FASHIONS

A *craze* is another type of collective behavior engaged in by people who may not be in direct contact. It is short-lived, popular, and usually defined by society as bizarre behavior. Students have been particularly prone to this type of collective behavior. In the past they have engaged in such crazes as "streaking" (running naked) across campuses, cramming into phone booths or Volkswagens, and swallowing goldfish.

A *fashion* is also classified by some as collective behavior. It is temporary, appeals to large numbers, and refers to people being "different" in a socially acceptable way. Fashion is current style or custom. Past examples include hot pants, midi and maxi dresses, zoot suits, platform shoes, long sideburns, the shag hairdo, the Ivy League look, dirty white buck shoes, the D.A. hair style, and the Charleston, twist, and calypso dances.

SOCIAL MOVEMENTS

A *social movement* is an extremely important type of collective behavior since it is a concerted and deliberate attempt to bring about social change. The participants usually have a mutual goal or direction and tend to be highly committed to their cause. Christianity, communism, nazism, black civil rights, women's liberation, "Jesus people," world disarmament, and gay liberation are all examples of social movements. It is important to note that social movements usually become more organized over time. For example, the movement for black equality in the United States began in the early 1900s as a collective of unorganized individuals, lacking defined goals and means for success. After many setbacks, this movement became more organized, with leaders, specific goals, and regularized procedures. Eventually, bureaucratic organizations such as the NAACP emerged. Because there are various types of social movements and, more important, because they can frequently change the course of a society and even world history, social movements are discussed in further detail later in this chapter.

Explanations of Collective Behavior

There are various and sometimes contradictory explanations as to what social factors cause collective behavior, particularly crowd behavior. The explanations that sociologists tend to accept today differ markedly from early ones.

IGNORANT MASS VIEW

An early explanation for collective behavior was that such action is a result of the growing power of uneducated, unreasoning, impulsive, and "inferior" people. Such an explanation, which we will call the *ignorant mass view*, was offered by the nineteenth-century French aristocrat Gustave LeBon. During the late 1800s France experienced considerable social change—rapid industrialization and urbanization and loss of tradition.

LeBon wished to preserve the status quo and was dismayed with the political and economic changes of his time. Of most concern to him was the fact that the lower and middle classes were challenging the position of the aristocracy. Mobs were rushing into the streets to make their wishes known.

As LeBon watched the masses engage in riots, he developed a theory of crowd behavior. He contended that the anonymity of individuals in a crowd actually made people act in strange and evil ways. Savage and, according to LeBon, "unconscious motivations" which needed to be gratified emerged. Members acquired a feeling that nothing was impossible. A rapid spread of feelings and sentiments, "contagion," seemed to operate within the collective. And, finally, members were very "suggestible," or easily influenced by others. The masses appeared to be in a hypnotic trance and were easily led. In essence, LeBon was saying that the crowd produces profound and undesirable changes in the thinking of its members.[7]

LeBon's theory is now considered highly prejudiced and outdated. For example, he asserted that all crowd behavior is evil. Such a stance assumes that a crowd is necessarily a bloodthirsty mob. Further, even if all crowds happen to be hostile mobs, whether or not their actions are defined as justified depends on the oberver's viewpoint. Also, as sociologist Richard Berk explains, LeBon's concepts lack clarity and utility in explaining collective action:

> "Contagion" provided no mechanism to explain how crowd behavior ever stops. If people are "suggestible" why don't they just continue to act? Obviously, crowds cease to exist, so somehow contagion is reversed. Further, why doesn't everyone near a crowd become involved? Are some people immune to the "contagion"?[8]

LeBon's ideas, at best, only describe superficial aspects of crowd psychology. And his discussion tells us little about the societal conditions related to collective behavior.

ALIENATED MASS VIEW

In contrast to the ignorant mass view, most sociologists today tend to adopt some version of the *alienated mass view*. This perspective maintains that when members of the lower and middle classes engage in mob action, riots, and social movements, they do so not because of their impulsive savagery, but because of their alienation from society. Contemporary Western societies are highly industrialized and urbanized. Individuals have fewer ties with family, friends, and community; this results in feelings of distrust, loneliness, isolation, and powerlessness. People, seeking remedies to their problems, are thus ready to undertake collective action, which promises to provide solutions.

Social Movements Through Posters

Social movements such as those associated with wars, revolutions, and political campaigns often follow a predictable course, and posters may serve very well to illustrate such a sequence.

A prime factor in social movements is the spread of a generalized belief that a group—ethnic, racial, class, nationality—is responsible for some injustice or state of inequality. Posters both reflect and spread such a belief; for example, the World War I poster at left depicting a brutish German soldier laying waste the land and trodding on innocent victims.

After the "enemy" group is identified, a particular event,

or precipitating factor, often serves to dramatize the injustice or inequality. For instance, in American history we find the slogans Remember the Alamo, Remember the Maine, and (in World War I) Remember Belgium, which referred to Germany's invasion of a neutral country.

Following such a dramatic event, the participants in the movement become mobilized. During this period they must be convinced of their ability to effect change, as in the very specific World War II poster shown at right. Often charismatic leaders emerge during this stage, for example Winston Churchill and Franklin D. Roosevelt (above).

Participants who are not immediately and dramatically involved are made to feel a part of the movement, as in the many posters urging increased production during World War II.

A POSTER WHICH WAS USED FIRST IN 1918 AND WHICH, AMENDED —FOLLOWING GERMANY'S DEFEAT—WAS ALSO FORCEFUL IN 1919

The victory garden and home canning programs promoted by the U.S. government during both world wars drew millions of American civilians into the movement to defeat the common enemy. Ultimately, in social movements of this type, the entire society becomes part of the effort.

In 1973 members of the American Indian Movement occupied Wounded Knee, South Dakota, in protest against government Indian policies and the poverty, unemployment, and inadequate services characteristic of many reservations.

The alienated mass view of collective behavior goes beyond the explanation of citizens set adrift in a large, complex, changing, rootless world, however. It would maintain that the riots in Detroit, Newark, and Tampa during the 1960s were also, in part, reactions to the hardships experienced by the rioters. Poverty, unemployment, inferior housing, and related ghetto conditions were real-life situations which sent many people into the streets.*

A corollary to the alienated mass view, the *frustration-aggression hypothesis* formulated by John Dollard and Neil Miller, can also be used to explain why ghetto residents resort to rioting. This hypothesis maintains that frustrated people resort to aggression as a source of psychological reward.[9] Just as the salesman who fails to sell his product might scream at his wife, so might economically depressed slum dwellers burn buildings and loot stores. The specific sources of frustration may vary from one person to another. Some probably resort to rioting because of *absolute deprivation*, a realization that one lacks the most basic necessities of life—food, a job, adequate housing. Others may riot because of *relative deprivation*, a realization that one's life is unsatisfactory relative to other people or situations. As an individual views others he or she begins to think that life is not improving as quickly as it once was, that others get much more out of life, or that the society has not lived up to its promises. Based on absolute standards the person's life may not be horrendous, but when compared to that of people in other situations, it is defined as bad.

---

*See the *Report of the National Advisory Commission on Civil Disorders* (Washington, D.C.: U.S. Government Printing Office, 1968) for a detailed discussion of the conditions which led to these riots.

VALUE-ADDED THEORY

A third view of the causes of collective behavior, particularly crowd behavior, is Neil Smelser's *value-added theory*, which considers both general societal conditions and more immediate specific events to explain the phenomenon. To understand the view, consider the analogy of the steps involved in making a product, with each step adding to the value of the commodity. For example, an automobile begins as iron ore; the ore is processed into steel; the steel is cut and shaped; and eventually an auto is produced. Raw materials are increasingly transformed and shaped. Collective behavior comes about in a similar manner, in stages. Broad social conditions are transformed and shaped until a specific type of collective action results. The steps that lead up to a specific collective action are as follows:

1. *Structural conduciveness.* Some societies have characteristics which make possible certain kinds of collective behavior. For example, the 1965 riot in Watts, a black suburb of Los Angeles, would not have been possible except for the broad preconditions that American society has a black and a white population and public dissent is tolerated to some extent.
2. *Structural strain.* A society may experience internal contradictions and tensions. For instance, blacks are often discriminated against in our society, yet the ideal of equality is continually espoused.
3. *Growth and spread of a generalized belief.* People define and interpret strains and problems. Given the preceding conditions, residents of Watts came to believe that white police in their community discriminated against blacks and resorted to brutal methods in enforcing the law. White police were thought of as trying to perpetuate white supremacy.
4. *Precipitating factors.* A specific, usually dramatic event takes place which confirms the generalized belief. Such an event occurred in Watts. Police attempted to arrest an intoxicated black driver who had been speeding through Watts. The driver resisted, whereupon the police struck him with a club and shoved him into a squad car. The driver's mother began screaming at the sight of her son's blood, and onlookers cried "police brutality."
5. *Mobilization.* Rumors begin and people are solicited to participate in collective action. In Watts the rumors spread quickly after the arrest incident. Police were said to have viciously beaten the driver and attacked many onlookers. They were also said to have manhandled a pregnant woman. Young black males were recruited to join in action against the police, the establishment, and whites in general. Blacks began stopping cars and buses passing through their neighborhood and beating white passengers. Burning of buildings and looting of stores, usually owned by white merchants, lasted for six days.
6. *Social control.* After the collective action begins, authorities may employ various means to quell the disturbance. Police immediately sealed off Watts after rioting began, and thousands of national guardsmen were

Physical force is sometimes used to quell disturbances. Here national guardsmen move in on rioting students at Kent State University on May 4, 1970. The tragic result—four dead and eleven wounded.

called in to stop the disturbance. The eventual reaction of authorities to the $40 million worth of property damage, thirty-four killings, and days of rioting was legislation designed both to curb injustices against blacks and to suppress forcibly any similar disturbance in the future.[10]

These steps illustrate that collective behavior is an emerging action stemming from several preconditions. The preconditions emphasize societal deprivations, injustices, and strains, and in this sense Smelser's formulation is similar to the alienated mass view. But value-added theory is different in two respects: (1) it focuses on specific as well as general factors which may be related to collective behavior; and (2) it provides a sequence of steps culminating in final action.

Rumor: Communication in Collective Behavior

A rumor has been defined as "communication through which men caught together in an ambiguous situation attempt to construct a meaningful interpretation of it by pooling their intellectual resources." It is not a type of collective behavior but may be thought of as "a form of collective problem-solving."[11] Rumors are often incorrect. For instance, after President John Kennedy was assassinated, it was rumored that Vice-President Johnson suffered a heart attack.

Rumors are not fixed and unchanging but are shaped and reshaped in the communication process. They may change in a number of ways: (1) *leveling* is the tendency for the report to become increasingly shorter and more concise as it is passed to others: (2) *sharpening* is the tendency for individuals to selectively retain and report only a limited number of details; and (3) *assimilation* is the tendency for people to interpret reports in light of their own interests, prejudices, and stereotypes.[12] Some participants may merely listen and pass the message along, but others may interpret the report in light of historical events, doubt the authenticity of the message, or insert ideas as to what should be done.[13]

One rumor usually calls forth another. This *compounding pattern*, the idea that rumors increase in number with a given incident, is an expected consequence of people's seeking explanation and solution to crisis.* As an illustration, after the Japanese navy attacked Pearl Harbor in a surprise air raid on December 7, 1941, literally hundreds of rumors were fabricated to explain how the enemy could have executed the attack with such precision. Tamotsu Shibutani, in *Improvised News*, describes the target and substance of some of the rumors:

> The finger pointed directly at Hawaii's 160,000 residents of Japanese ancestry, and hundreds of rumors arose implicating them. Among the most widespread of these rumors were: a McKinley High School ring was found on the body of a Japanese flier shot down over Honolulu; the water supply had been poisoned by the local Japanese; Japanese plantation workers had cut arrows pointing to Pearl Harbor in the cane fields of Oahu; the local Japanese had been notified of the time of attack by an advertisement in a Honolulu newspaper on December 6; Nisei [Americans of Japanese ancestry] armed with machine guns drove up to the main gate at Pearl Harbor in trucks and as the side panels dropped off shot down marines; automobiles driven by local Japanese blocked the roads from Honolulu to Pearl Harbor; Japanese residents waved their kimonos at the pilots and signaled to them; some local men were dressed in Japanese Army uniforms during the attack. . . .
>
> Rumors of the complicity of local Japanese were immediately denied by military and civilian officials, and the denials were apparently accepted by most Hawaiians. On the mainland, however, the tales persisted; they were disseminated in newspapers and magazines and even incorporated into motion pictures, such as Air Force.[14]

Unfortunately, the rumors that Japanese-Americans were spies and traitors became widely accepted. Eventually the United States government acted on them by imprisoning innocent Japanese-American citizens

---

*The compounding pattern is illustrated in Warren A. Peterson and Noel P. Gist, "Rumor and Public Opinion," *American Journal of Sociology*, 57 (September 1951): 159–167.

in work camps, not just in Hawaii but on the mainland as well. No doubt rumors focus, mobilize, and establish action for individuals faced with ill-defined, confused situations.

Social Movements

Social movements, collectives that attempt to change society, often develop out of class, racial, and sexual struggles.[15] The Russian Revolution, the American Indians' Native American movement, and the women's liberation movement illustrate these types of struggles. In each instance, dissatisfied members of society have come together in an organized, long-term effort to establish and promote a better way of life. In addition, social movements have several other distinguishing characteristics.

OBJECTIVES, PROGRAMS, AND IDEOLOGIES

All social movements have objectives. Marlene Dixon, an active feminist, contends that the women's liberation movement has three objectives.

The three major groups which make up the new women's movement—working women, middle class married women and students—bring very different kinds of interests and objectives to women's liberation. Working women are most concerned with the economic issues of guaranteed employment, fair wages, job discrimination and child care. . . .

Middle class women, oppressed by the psychological mutilation and injustice of institutionalized segregation, discrimination and imposed inferiority, are most sensitive to the dehumanizing consequences of severely limited lives. Usually well educated and capable, these women are rebelling against being forced to trivialize their lives, to live vicariously through husbands and children.

Students, as unmarried middle class girls, have been most sensitized to the sexual exploitation of women. They have experienced the frustration of one-way relationships in which the girl is forced into a "wife" and companion role with none of the supposed benefits of marriage.[16]

Movements also develop programs for change. The feminist movement maintains that females must become educated and aware of their oppression and that radical social change in the economic and occupational structure of society must occur. Dixon continues:

The 1963 civil rights march on Washington. The civil rights movement developed in response to racial discrimination in our society.

Male supremacy, marriage, and the structure of wage labor—each of these aspects of women's oppression has been crucial to the resurgence of the women's struggle. It must be abundantly clear that radical social change must occur before there can be significant improvement in the social position of women. Some form of socialization is the minimum requirement, considering the changes that must come in the institutions of marriage and the family alone.

The heart of the movement, as in all freedom movements, rests in women's knowledge, whether articulated or still only an illness without a name, that they are not inferior—not chicks, nor bunnies, nor quail, nor cows, nor bitches, nor ass, nor meat.[17]

In addition, movements establish an ideology—beliefs, norms, and values to justify their existence and give themselves direction. As systematic doctrines, ideologies claim to represent the interests of large social groups. The Back-to-Africa movement of Marcus Garvey in the 1920s claimed to represent the interests of all black Americans. The women's liberation movement claims to represent the interests of all women—poor black and poor white women, working women exploited in the labor force, middle-class women, and women attending college.[18]

COMMITMENT

Goals, programs for change, and ideologies are all elements of social movements, but also essential to the lifeblood of a movement is member commitment. Slogans, rituals, flags, uniforms, songs, frequent meetings,

Women's liberation, like most social movements, uses demonstrations, symbols, and slogans to inspire dedication in members and gather public support.

manuals, and other objects and practices are used to inspire dedication in members.

Commitment-inspiring objects and practices are used, for example, by TOPS (Taking Off Pounds Sensibly), a social movement concerned with self-improvement. Local chapters within the movement have lighthearted names such as Blubber Busters, Snack Snubbers, and Cheerful Cherubs to promote identification within the group. Weekly sessions are held during which members are weighed. Those members who lose weight are labeled "Tops" and are duly honored with a cardboard heart specifying the number of pounds lost. In contrast, those who gain weight, "Pigs," must wear a bib or pig-shaped label. These symbols encourage dedication to the cause. At a ceremony during each meeting members pledge to be slimmer and to help others eat less. The high point of the year is the national convention, at which Queens and Kings, members who have usually lost over a hundred pounds, are chosen. During the convention, local chapters exchange plans and ideas with the aim of improving the total movement. All these features develop a consciousness among members about their similar plight, beliefs, and goals. The intention is to motivate members to work toward a common cause—a smaller dress or trouser size.[19]

American populism emerged out of class struggle during the 1890s. The movement's political platform was directed to the needs of common people.

STAGES OF DEVELOPMENT

Social movements pass through stages of development. A movement's *incipient phase* is characterized by considerable confusion and disorganization. Goals, ideologies, and programs for change are only vaguely defined. Members are few in number, inexperienced, lacking in resources, and vulnerable to opposing groups. Still, their loyalty to the cause is intense. After a time, the movement enters an *organizational phase*, in which leadership, goals, ideologies, and programs are further defined and elaborated. Close ties and informal interaction among members begin to diminish as the movement becomes more formalized. Finally, the movement enters a *stable phase*, in which internal organization is no longer shifting. The early, charismatic, inspirational leaders are replaced by rational-legal administrators. The movement has evolved into a bureaucratic organization, such as the National Organization for Women or TOPS. The organization's main task then becomes recruitment of converts to the cause.[20]

Some movements fail to make it through these three stages of development. Garvey's Back-to-Africa movement began to fade when followers doubted their leader's proclamation that God was black, and membership quickly dwindled when Garvey was imprisoned for mail fraud. American populism of the 1890s never evolved into a full-blown and enduring national political party. The technocracy movement of the 1930s, which proposed that technical experts run society, never gained public support. And a 1973 American youth movement to publicize the Soviet Union's oppression of novelist Alexander Solzhenitsyn fell flat after the author was exiled from Russia.

KINDS OF SOCIAL MOVEMENTS

There are many different kinds of social movements, distinguishable by the means they use to accomplish their goals. A *power-oriented movement* uses coercive force to reach objectives. Since members of this type of movement stridently assert that goals must be reached, illegitimate means—including assassination and kidnapping of officials, bribery and payoffs, and the destruction of property—may be employed. Revolutionary movements and extremist political parties are examples.

A *persuasion-oriented movement* uses legal means—such as lobbying to change laws and policies; propaganda disseminated through newspapers, books, movies, and other mass media; and formal education—to accomplish its objectives. Unlike those in power-oriented movements, members tend to accept the premise that change is gradual and that it can best be brought about by a nonviolent program. The Right to Life antiabortion movement and women's liberation are examples of persuasion-oriented movements.

When coercion and force are employed to bring about social change, as was the case in the Russian Revolution of 1917 illustrated here, the movement is termed power oriented.

A *participation-oriented movement* is less concerned with changing society than creating a following of dedicated believers. People join to gain orientation, satisfaction, or help from the movement itself. A millennial movement, one that predicts the end of the world, is an illustration. Members join to prepare for the end of this life and to gain favor from a higher being. The Father Divine movement of the 1930s is another instance of a participation-oriented movement. Thousands of lower-class black Americans worshiped the "immortal" Father Divine because he and the movement provided escape, meaning, and status to members during a time of economic crisis. Additional examples are Alcoholics Anonymous and Gamblers Anonymous, which are groups that participants join for self-help.[21]

No social movement lives a self-contained life. Members of the larger society will react to movements. Revolutions are often violently suppressed either by the larger society or by the existing power structure. Some movements — such as satanism, a devil-worshipping religion — are defined by the public as peculiar. A typical reaction by society is ridicule and ostracism. Others — for example the world disarmament movement — are defined as legitimate and respectable by the public. Such movements may meet with widespread public support or public disinterest and only token support.*

Chapter Summary

When sociologists use the term "collective behavior," they mean behavior which seems rather unstructured, unstable, and unpredictable and which tends to be short-lived, sometimes emotional, and based on considerable personal interaction. Sociologists study collective behavior to understand the conditions that lead to the phenomenon and to observe the social change that results from it.

A crowd, a temporary gathering of people at one time and place, is a clear example of collective behavior. Crowds may be unorganized (casual) or somewhat organized (conventionalized). Some crowds direct action toward individuals and objects (active), while others exist for the participants' self-stimulation (expressive). A public consists of people who are geographically separated but exhibit some collective behavior. Additional types of collective behavior are crazes, fashions, and social movements.

There are three views as to the social causes of collective behavior. The ignorant mass view maintains that the masses riot and revolt because they are uneducated, uncivilized savages. The more comprehensive alienated mass view maintains that collective behavior is a result of citizens set adrift in a large, complex, rootless world. This perspective also gives importance to the hardships and frustrations experienced by the masses. Value-added theory is closely related to the alienated mass view, but it examines general and specific causes of collective behavior and provides a sequence of steps culminating in collective action.

As individuals face crises, they interact with one another to solve their common problem. What sometimes results is rumor — unverified communication transmitted by word of mouth. Rumors go through the processes of leveling, sharpening, and assimilation as they are passed to others. Also, one rumor seems to call forth others as people seek explanations and solutions to crises.

Social movements are particularly important kinds of collective behavior since dissatisfied individuals come together in an organized way to

---

*A discussion of societal reactions to social movements is found in Turner and Killian, *Collective Behavior*, pp. 327–330.

bring about social change. Social movements develop out of class, racial, and sexual struggles. For a movement to survive, it must establish objectives, a program for change, an ideology, and a high degree of member commitment. Movements go through stages of development until finally a bureaucratic organization emerges. There are many different types of movements. For instance, we find power-, persuasion-, and participation-oriented types.

The view is sometimes expressed that collective behavior and social change are evil and regressive. The opposite view, that collective behavior and social change are naturally good and progressive, has also been voiced, particularly among participants in various social movements. Both positions are exaggerated and misleading. Crowds, publics, and social movements and the changes that might result from collective action may intensify social problems or assist in their amelioration. The latter is, of course, the more desirable alternative.

Key Terms for Review

absolute deprivation, p. 316
active crowd, p. 306
alienated mass view, p. 311
assimilation, p. 319
casual crowd, p. 305
collective behavior, p. 301
compounding pattern, p. 319
conventionalized crowd, p. 306
craze, p. 309
crowd, p. 305
expressive crowd, p. 306
fashion, p. 310
frustration-agression hypothesis, p. 316
ignorant mass view, p. 310
incipient phase, p. 323

leveling, p. 319
organizational phase, p. 323
participation-oriented movement, p. 324
persuasion-oriented movement, p. 323
power-oriented movement, p. 323
public, p. 309
public opinion, p. 309
relative deprivation, p. 316
rumor, p. 318
sharpening, p. 319
social movement, p. 310
stable phase, p. 323
value-added theory, p. 317

Suggested Readings

SOCIOLOGICAL Berk, Richard A. *Collective Behavior*. Dubuque, Iowa: William C. Brown, 1974. This scholarly but brief and very readable text is excellent for beginning students. The author traces early and recent approaches to collective behavior, particularly crowd behavior.

Brinton, Crane. *The Anatomy of Revolution.* New York: Random House, 1960. The author maintains that revolutions tend to occur under certain social conditions, some of which are governmental financial problems, ineffective efforts at reform, a split in the ranks of the ruling class, class antagonism, and the emergence of a revolutionary myth.

Millett, Kate. *Sexual Politics.* New York: Doubleday, 1970. The author discusses the goals and ideologies of the women's liberation movement. This book had a great impact on stimulating the growth of the movement during the early 1970s.

Roberts, Ron E., and Robert Marsh Kloss. *Social Movements: Between the Balcony and the Barricade.* St. Louis: C. V. Mosby, 1974. This is a humanistic, conflict-oriented discussion of social movements. As the authors discuss the oppressive tendencies of institutions and governments, they provide humane possibilities for change.

Shibutani, Tamotsu. *Improvised News: A Sociological Study of Rumor.* Indianapolis: Bobbs-Merrill, 1966. Fascinating case studies are presented to illustrate rumor formation and processes. The author maintains that individuals continually modifying their outlook when faced with crisis and change.

Stone, I. F. *The Killings at Kent State: How Murder Went Unpunished.* New York: New York Review, 1971. Journalist I. F. Stone presents a vivid picture of events during the Kent State University riots. After reviewing FBI reports, newspaper accounts, and interviews, he concludes that national guardsmen massacred four students without reason. The unfolding story of crowd behavior is a startling exposé.

Toch, Hans. *The Social Psychology of Social Movements.* Indianapolis: Bobbs-Merrill, 1965. The author discusses the predispositions, motivations, frustrations, and dissatisfactions of individuals who join social movements, as well as the careers of members within movements. The book is essentially a psychological evaluation of social movements.

LITERARY

Clark, Walter Van Tilburg. *The Ox-Bow Incident.* New York: Signet, 1960. Clark captures the intense emotion which characterizes an active crowd. The story revolves around a lynching in the Old West.

Dickens, Charles. *A Tale of Two Cities.* New York: Oxford University Press, 1960. Dickens's classic novel about the French Revolution presents a picture of governmental oppression before the revolution and the reign of terror during the revolution. The novel vividly describes the fears and struggles of individuals facing violent change.

Lee, Harper. *To Kill a Mockingbird.* Philadelphia: Lippincott, 1960. LeBon maintained that a mob has great influence on the individual's thinking. It arouses people to act in unpredictable ways. In this novel, the object of action was the lynching of a black man.

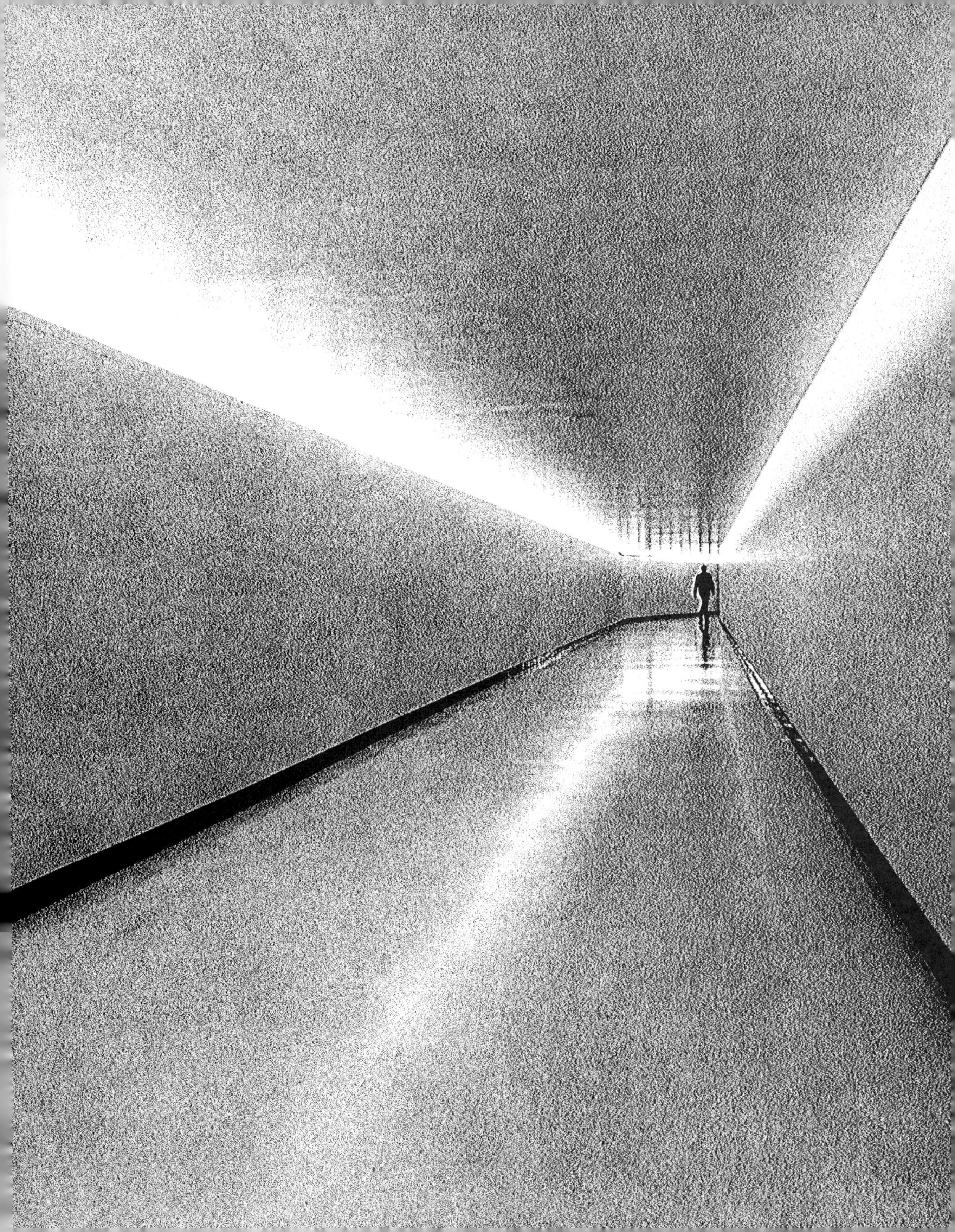

part five

PROBLEMS AND ISSUES

The ultimate test of humanist scholars is whether they can gain understanding and knowledge of troublesome problems and issues. Recall that the major task of humanist sociologists is the alleviation of human problems. Surely we all recognize that what is a problem for one group or individual is not necessarily a problem for others, yet there are problems and issues that many of us who share "the spaceship Earth" have in common. Such topics have long held the interest of sociologists and have served as general organizing subjects for sociological inquiry. We focus here on six problem areas: alienation (chapter 14), race and ethnicity (chapter 15), deviance and crime (chapter 16), leisure and sport (chapter 17), cities and suburbs (chapter 18), and population (chapter 19). In our discussions we attempt both to present some findings of contemporary research and to encourage an understanding of the complexities of the issues investigated.

IN THIS CHAPTER

The Concept of Alienation   331

    Powerlessness   331
    Meaninglessness   334
    Normlessness   335
    Isolation   336
    Self-estrangement   339
    Subjective and objective alienation   339

Social Conditions Related to Alienation   342

Alienated Groups in American Society   344

    Industrial workers   344
    Racial and ethnic minorities   345
    Students   347
    The middle class   349

Summary   351

Key Terms for Review   352

Suggested Readings   352

14

Does "alienation" refer to feelings we hold or to dehumanizing conditions in society?
Does "alienation" mean isolation from others? normlessness? powerlessness? meaninglessness? self-estrangement?
Is industrial growth evil and alien to the individual?
Why would people with good educations and jobs be alienated?

ALIENATION

Although some of us lead happy and satisfying lives, American society also contains many alienated people. Individuals may feel confused and frustrated because of the norms they are forced to obey or the careers they must pursue. Some are disillusioned with social institutions and feel powerless to bring about any change. Others can find no meaning in life. The concept of alienation has played an important role in the thinking of many writers, philosophers, and social scientists and in the mind of the general public. Sociologists are particularly concerned with alienation as a problem affecting many people and as a phenomenon often linked to drug and alcohol abuse, mental illness, suicide, crime, racial turmoil, and political apathy.

In this chapter we will first define the concept of alienation, although this is not an easy task since the term has been used to describe a wide range of human experiences. Second, we will discuss some of the social structures and issues that appear to be related to alienation. And, third, we will examine the alienation experienced by several specific groups.

The Concept of Alienation

As noted, the term "alienation" refers to many human experiences. Sociologist Melvin Seeman, however, has attempted to draw together the many meanings the term has. According to Seeman, alienation may mean powerlessness, meaninglessness, normlessness, isolation, or self-estrangement.

POWERLESSNESS

Alienation is often associated with *powerlessness,* or "the expectancy or probability held by the individual that his own behavior cannot determine the occurrence of the outcomes, or reinforcements, he seeks."[1] Both poets and scholars have dealt with this dimension of alienation. For example, the essence of powerlessness was captured by W. H. Auden in his poem "The Shield of Achilles":

> A crowd of ordinary decent folk
>   Watched from outside and neither moved nor spoke
> As three pale figures were led forth and bound
>   To three posts driven upright in the ground.
>
> The mass and majesty of this world, all
>   That carried weight and always weighs the same,
> Lay in the hand of others; they were small
>   and could not hope for help, and no help came;
>   What their foes liked to do was done;[2]

Karl Marx's discussion of alienation also emphasized the notion of powerlessness. Workers in a capitalist society, according to Marx, are degraded and powerless. They are coerced into an economic system in which they are denied both the possibility and the means of making important decisions. (Refer to chapter 7 for further discussion of Marxist theory.)

Although many of us have occasional feelings of powerlessness, some individuals experience such feelings intensely each day. For example, many of the impoverished immigrants who came to the United States around the turn of the century in search of a better life felt powerless to change their situation. In *The Jungle* Upton Sinclair transports us into the world of Jurgis Rudkis, an immigrant who found that he had no control over his working and living conditions in Chicago during the early 1900s.

> Poor Jurgis was now an outcast and a tramp once more. He was crippled—he was as literally crippled as any wild animal which has lost its claws, or been torn out of its shell. He had been shorn, at one cut, of all those mysterious weapons whereby he had been able to make a living easily and to escape the consequences of his actions. He could no longer command a job when he wanted it; he could no longer steal with impunity—he must take his chances with the common herd. . . .
>
> Jurgis became once more a besieger of factory gates. But never since he had been in Chicago had he stood less chance of getting a job than just then. For one thing, there was the economic crisis, the million or two of men who had been out of work in the spring and summer, and were not yet all back, by any means. And then there was the strike, with seventy thousand men and women all over the country idle for a couple of months—twenty thousand in Chicago, and many of them now seeking work throughout the city. . . .

At the end of about ten days Jurgis had only a few pennies left; and he had not yet found a job—not even a day's work at anything, not a chance to carry a satchel. Once again, as when he had come out of the hospital, he was bound hand and foot, and facing the grisly phantom of starvation. Raw, naked terror possessed him, a maddening passion that would never leave him, and that wore him down more quickly than the actual want of food. He was going to die of hunger! The fiend reached out its scaly arms for him—it touched him, its breath came into his face; and he would cry out for the awfulness of it, he would wake up in the night, shuddering, and bathed in perspiration, and start up and flee. He would walk, begging for work, until he was exhausted; he could not remain still—he would wander on, gaunt and haggard, gazing about him with restless eyes. Everywhere he went, from one end of the vast city to the other, there were hundreds of others like him; everywhere was the sight of plenty—and the merciless hand of authority waving them away. There is one kind of prison where the man is behind bars, and everything that he desires is outside; and there is another kind where the things are behind the bars, and the man is outside.

When he was down to his last quarter, Jurgis learned that before the bakeshop closed at night they sold out what was left at half price, and after that he would go and get two loaves of stale bread for a nickel, and break them up and stuff his pockets with them, munching a bit from time to time. He would not spend a penny save for this; and, after two or three days more, he even became sparing of the bread and would stop and peer into the ashbarrels as he walked along the streets, and now and then rake out a bit of something,

When failure of action through other channels causes feelings of powerlessness, people may resort to protests and demonstrations.

shake it free from dust, and count himself just so many minutes further from the end.

So for several days he had been going about, ravenous all the time, and growing weaker and weaker; and then one morning he had a hideous experience, that almost broke his heart. He was passing down a street lined with warehouses, and a boss offered him a job, and then, after he had started to work, turned him off because he was not strong enough. And he stood by and saw another man put into his place, and then picked up his coat, and walked off, doing all that he could to keep from breaking down and crying like a baby. He was lost! He was doomed! There was no hope for him! But then, with a sudden rush, his fear gave place to rage. He fell into cursing. He would come back there after dark, and he would show that scoundrel whether he was good for anything or not! . . .

So far the weather had been fair, and he had slept out every night in a vacant lot; but now there fell suddenly a shadow of the advancing winter, a chill wind from the north and a driving storm of rain. That day Jurgis bought two drinks for the sake of the shelter, and at night he spent his last two pennies in a "stale-beer dive." This was a place kept by a Negro, who went out and drew off the old dregs of beer that lay in barrels set outside of the saloons; and after he had doctored it with chemicals to make it "fizz," he sold it for two cents a can, the purchase including the privilege of sleeping the night through upon the floor, with a mass of degraded outcasts, men and women.

All these horrors afflicted Jurgis all the more cruelly, because he was always contrasting them with the opportunities he had lost.[3]

Many people today—the elderly, alcoholics, heroin addicts, ghetto dwellers, mental patients, "trapped" housewives, convicts—may experience feelings of powerlessness not unlike those expressed by Jurgis Rudkis.

MEANINGLESSNESS

According to Seeman, alienation can also refer to *meaninglessness*, or an individual's uncertainty about what to believe as he or she searches for meaning in life.[4] In "The Hollow Men" T. S. Eliot draws a bleak picture of humankind, existing without form or substance in a directionless world:

>We are the hollow men
>We are the stuffed men
>Leaning together
>Headpiece filled with straw. Alas!
>Our dried voices, when
>We whisper together
>Are quiet and meaningless

*As wind in dry grass
Or rats' feet over broken glass
In our dry cellar*

*Shape without form, shade without colour,
Paralysed force, gesture without motion;*

*Those who have crossed
With direct eyes, to death's other Kingdom
Remember us—if at all—not as lost
Violent souls, but only
As the hollow men
The stuffed men.*[5]

We can easily understand why many people in a complex society are confused about what values to trust or goals to pursue. For example, Archie Bunker of television's "All in the Family" just cannot make sense of changing attitudes and new life styles. Archie may represent millions who close their eyes to social problems and rapid change so that the meaning they give to life can go unchallenged.

NORMLESSNESS

Alienation is also associated with *normlessness*. Here the individual is faced with an absence of rules and feels "that socially unapproved behaviors are required to achieve given goals."[6]

The hippies of the 1960s, alienated from the goals of American society, developed new ideals and rules to govern their lives.

Isolation, boredom, neglect, and poverty make growing old an alienating experience for many.

Sociologist Robert Merton has discussed how American society encourages normlessness by emphasizing success. According to Merton, although the majority of Americans believe that everyone should achieve wealth, power, and prestige, our society has failed to establish rules for accomplishing these goals. As a result of this anarchic situation, citizens have adopted an attitude of "anything goes."[7]

ISOLATION

A quite common meaning of alienation is *isolation,* or the feeling of being apart or different in some way. According to Seeman, isolated individuals "assign low reward value to goals or beliefs that are typically highly valued in the society."[8] He cites examples of the intellectual, artist, or writer who prefers to detach himself or herself from such popular cultural standards as owning expensive cars, boats, and houses; watching television soap operas; or knowing the weekly football scores.

Seeman's characterization of the isolated individual is limited in scope, however. In a broader sense anyone who lacks close relationships with others and as a result feels alone or apart may be considered isolated. Matthew Arnold illustrates this broader meaning of isolation in his poem "To Marguerite":

> Yes! In the sea of life enisled,
> With echoing straits between us thrown,
> Dotting the shoreless watery wild,
> We mortal millions live alone.[9]

Sherwood Anderson's short story "Hands" dramatizes the individual's separation from others. The main character, Wing Biddlebaum, is a pathetic, nervous, timid, old man who seldom spoke. Although he lived in a small town, he knew hardly anyone.

> Among all the people of Winesburg but one had come close to him. With George Willard, son of Tom Willard, the proprietor of the new Willard House, he had formed something like a friendship. . . .
>
> In the presence of George Willard, Wing Biddlebaum, who for twenty years had been the town mystery, lost something of his timidity, and his shadowy personality, submerged in a sea of doubts, came forth to look at the world.[10]

George, like all the citizens of the town, wondered why Biddlebaum hid his hands. Only after they talked for a while did Biddlebaum's hands eventually emerge, though even then they moved in a mysterious and restless way.

> As for George Willard, he had many times wanted to ask about the hands. At times an almost overwhelming curiosity had taken hold of him. He felt that there must be a reason for their strange activity and their inclination to keep hidden away.[11]

George was correct in sensing a reason because the hiding of the hands symbolized Biddlebaum's self-doubts and loneliness. Biddlebaum had been a victim of a callous and unthinking world during his early years.

> In his youth Wing Biddlebaum had been a school teacher in a town in Pennsylvania. He was not then known as Wing Biddlebaum, but went by the less euphonic name of Adolph Myers. As Adolph Myers he was much loved by the boys of his school.
>
> Adolph Myers was meant by nature to be a teacher of youth. He was one of those rare, little-understood men who rule by a power so gentle that it passes as a lovable weakness. In their feeling for the boys under their charge such men are not unlike the finer sort of women in their love of men. . . .
>
> With the boys of his school, Adolph Myers had walked in the evening or had sat talking until dusk upon the schoolhouse steps lost in a kind of dream. Here and there went his hands, caressing the shoulders of the boys, playing about the tousled heads. . . . In a way the voice and the hands, the stroking of the shoulders and the touching of the hair was a part of the schoolmaster's effort to carry a dream into the young minds. By the caress that was in his fingers he expressed himself. . . . Under the caress of his hands doubt and disbelief went out of the minds of the boys and they began also to dream.

Social isolation takes many forms, sometimes affecting the young and resulting from personal choice and other times affecting the elderly, who may have little choice in the matter.

And then the tragedy. A half-witted boy of the school became enamored by the young master. In his bed at night he imagined unspeakable things and in the morning went forth to tell his dreams as facts. Strange, hideous accusations fell from his loose-hung lips. Through the Pennsylvania town went a shiver. Hidden, shadowy doubts that had been in men's minds concerning Adolph Myers were galvanized into beliefs.

The tragedy did not linger. Trembling lads were jerked out of bed and questioned. "He put his arms about me," said one. "His fingers were always playing in my hair," said another.

One afternoon a man of the town, Henry Bradford, who kept a saloon, came to the schoolhouse door. Calling Adolph Myers into the school yard he began to beat him with his fists. . . .

They had intended to hang the schoolmaster, but something in his figure, so small, white, and pitiful, touched their hearts and they let him escape. . . .

For twenty years Adolph Myers had lived alone in Winesburg. He was but forty but looked sixty-five. . . . Although he did not understand what had happened, he felt that the hands must be to blame. Again and again the fathers of the boys had talked of the hands. "Keep your hands to yourself."[12]

Biddlebaum was thus forced to live in constant withdrawal and isolation because of the false charges of homosexuality. Social isolation is not always so severely imposed, but it can be felt just as intensely by those who find themselves socially apart.

SELF-ESTRANGEMENT

Those individuals who are unable to find self-rewarding activity suffer from a form of alienation known as *self-estrangement*. As Seeman points out, the idea of people finding no intrinsic meaning in work was a central point in Marx's discussion of alienation, and others now maintain that this condition is an essential feature of modern alienation.[13] Examples of people today who might experience such feelings include assembly-line workers who find nothing rewarding about placing a nut on a bolt for eight hours a day other than salary and college students who study not because they desire to learn but because it is necessary to receive a passing grade. In both examples the assumption is that the self-estranged eventually view themselves as alien beings. As sociologist C. Wright Mills noted, "One makes an instrument of himself and is estranged from it also."[14]

SUBJECTIVE AND OBJECTIVE ALIENATION

There is a common thread running through the meanings of alienation we have discussed here. All of them describe an individual's state of mind as he or she interprets events in life. Most sociologists, when they refer to alienation in their writings, have this common denominator in mind; they are concerned with something people internalize and feel—what is called *subjective alienation*.

In addition to seeing alienation as a subjective feeling, sociologists also agree that a person can experience several aspects of alienation simultaneously. It is possible, for example, to feel both isolated from others and powerless to change one's existence, as the character Wing Biddlebaum probably did. Both, of course, are internalized states.

Karl Marx emphasized another concept of alienation. When Marx used the term alienation, he referred not just to individual subjective reactions but also to dehumanizing events and conditions of society, what is called *objective alienation*. Marx believed that the increased division of labor required by capitalism had an objectively alienating effect on all societal members.

It is important to distinguish between objective and subjective alienation because it is possible for an individual to live in a dehumanizing society and never really understand how the larger social conditions are related to his or her personal misery. Such was the case of Willy Loman in Arthur Miller's play *Death of a Salesman*. Willy never realized that he was a victim of the great American dream, which glorifies material success and denigrates those who fail to become "number one." As Arthur Miller's play unfolds, Willy knows that he has failed to reach the top and that "something" caused him to fail, but he never quite grasps that America's values are to blame.

> WILLY: Figure it out. Work a lifetime to pay off a house. You finally own it, and there's nobody to live in it.
> LINDA: Well, dear, life is a casting off. It's always that way.
> WILLY: No, no, some people — some people accomplish something.[15]

Willy becomes increasingly confused and withdraws because he cannot contend with life. Finally, he ends his misery with suicide. At the funeral his family discusses his past.

> HAPPY, deeply angered: He had no right to do that. There was no necessity for it. We would've helped him.
> CHARLEY, grunting: Hmmm.
> BIFF: Come along, Mom.
> LINDA: Why didn't anybody come?
> CHARLEY: It was a very nice funeral.
> LINDA: But where are all the people he knew? Maybe they blame him.
> CHARLEY: Naa. It's a rough world, Linda. They wouldn't blame him.
> LINDA: I can't understand it. At this time especially. First time in thirty-five years we were just about free and clear. He only needed a little salary. He was even finished with the dentist.
> CHARLEY: No man only needs a little salary.
> LINDA: I can't understand it.
> BIFF: There were a lot of nice days. When he'd come home from a trip; or on Sundays, making the stoop; finishing the cellar; putting on the new porch; when he built the extra bathroom; and put up the garage. You know something, Charley, there's more of him in that front stoop than in all the sales he ever made.
> CHARLEY: Yeah. He was a happy man with a batch of cement.
> LINDA: He was so wonderful with his hands.
> BIFF: He had the wrong dreams. All, all, wrong.
> HAPPY, almost ready to fight Biff: Don't say that!
> BIFF: He never knew who he was.
> CHARLEY, stopping Happy's movement and reply. To Biff: Nobody dast blame this man. You don't understand: Willy was a salesman. And for a salesman, there is no rock bottom to the life. He don't put a bolt to a nut, he don't tell you the law or give you medicine. He's a man way out there in the blue, riding on a smile and a shoeshine. And when they start not smiling back — that's an

In Arthur Miller's play *Death of a Salesman*, the character Willy Loman (played here by Lee J. Cobb, center) is a victim of both objective and subjective alienation.

earthquake. And then you get yourself a couple of spots on your hat, and you're finished. Nobody dast blame this man. A salesman is got to dream, boy. It comes with the territory.
BIFF: Charley, the man didn't know who he was.[16]

Subjective alienation and objective alienation are perhaps two sides of the same coin. It cannot be denied that Willy Loman felt genuinely isolated and powerless to cope with his dilemma, and in this sense the concept of subjective alienation best explains his state. But it is also undeniable that social pressure to pursue the false dream of success brought him to this state, so that his situation was also one of objective alienation. Ultimately, alienation has to do with both personal feelings and an indifferent or hostile world.

Social Conditions Related to Alienation

When sociologists study the objective conditions that give rise to alienated states, they may take one of two approaches. The *global approach* concentrates on large, complex, hard-to-define societal conditions to explain the individual's alienation. Three conditions—industrialization, urbanization, and bureaucratization—are frequently linked to increased feelings of powerlessness, normlessness, isolation, and so on.

Before the Industrial Revolution of the late 1700s, Western societies were very different from what they are today. The countryside was dotted with small towns and villages; the main economic institution was agriculture; and people were socialized into a rather homogeneous culture. The craftsman or artisan of the time would design his product, obtain his own raw materials, and, with the help of perhaps an apprentice or two, make his wares and sell directly to the customer. The craftsman took pride in his finished product.

With the growth of technology and industry, life changed greatly. Machines began to replace craftsmen in making products; new production techniques and power sources were discovered; distant trade markets were established; and for the first time money was accumulated for investment in industries. The economic basis of society was radically altered. In addition, the development of factories meant that workers were concentrated in small geographic areas. Strangers of diverse backgrounds who were crowded together in urban areas encountered new problems. Finally, the growth of industry gave rise to the administrative machinery called bureaucracy. It was necessary to follow the principles of fixed rules, established lines of rational-legal authority, and division of labor in order for efficiency to prevail. The entire work process had changed.

Given these rapid changes, many theorists of the day warned that the forces of industrialization, urbanization, and bureaucratization would have evil consequences for the individual. For example, Karl Marx, in *The Economic and Philosophical Manuscripts of 1844*, maintained that capitalism with its accompanying conditions of increased division of labor and exploitation of the worker would create an alienated work force. Workers would be alienated from the product they produced, from the work process in which they participated, from themselves and their own creative potential, and from their fellow workers. Marxist theory concentrated on *economic alienation*, the idea that human misery results from a capitalistic economic system. But Marx also discussed *political alienation* and *religious alienation*, which occur when the institutions of government and religion cooperate with the capitalistic economic institution to prevent individuals from starting a class-based revolution.[17]

Theorists after Marx continued to warn of the evils of industrialization. Emile Durkheim feared that social bonds would weaken and social disorganization occur in industrial society. Whereas individuals in preindustrial societies were tied to the community by similar attitudes and a common morality, an industrial society would throw together people holding dissimilar values. As a result, individuals would be uncertain about what societal rules to follow. Consequently, they would experience anxiety, isolation, and despair. Max Weber expressed concern that bureaucracies would regiment human actions. People would become controlled by and subordinate to the bureaucracy. And Georg Simmel (1858–1918) expressed concern over the alienating effects of urban life. He maintained that the city would cause us to become strangers to one another and to ourselves.[18]

Sociologists today accept many of the explanations put forth by earlier theorists, but some have turned to a new approach to the study of social conditions underlying alienation. The *context-specific approach* concentrates on the more specific conditions in a society that may produce alienation.[19] These can be seen by examining selected social groups. For instance, the study of a particular corporation's rules and policies may show why its employees experience feelings of powerlessness. By focusing on such smaller groups, sociologists hope to better understand the conditions that contribute to alienation—and thus be able to suggest ways of alleviating human suffering.

Early sociologists, such as Georg Simmel, thought that urban society was alienating, causing people to feel isolated and to interact in impersonal and callous ways.

Alienated Groups in American Society

Alienation in American society is a generalized phenomenon, touching people from all walks of life. We will briefly examine the alienation experienced by members of four groups—industrial workers, racial and ethnic minorities, students, and the middle class. Sociological research indicates that the causes and forms of alienation vary somewhat across these groups.

INDUSTRIAL WORKERS

"Alienation from work" is a phrase widely used to describe feelings of dissatisfaction with one's job. When we are dissatisfied with our work, we may be reacting to a number of things: monotony and boredom, insufficient salary, insecurity, inflexible rules, dangerous working conditions, overbearing bosses, lack of freedom in decision-making, lack of opportunity for promotion, and a variety of other conditions.

For the most part sociologists have studied the alienation from work experienced by assembly-line workers. Ely Chinoy, for example, found that automobile assembly-line workers receive few intrinsic rewards, such as a feeling of accomplishment or pride of craftsmanship, from their jobs. Salary and fringe benefits supply the only motivation for these individuals to continue working. He also found that many workers aspire to own their own small businesses, which might indicate that they hope to gain more control over their future working conditions.[20] And Robert Guest found that automobile assembly-line workers see their jobs as repetitive, boring, and meaningless.[21]

Robert Blauner also studied contemporary worker alienation. He examined four industries—printing, automobile manufacturing, textile manufacturing, and chemical production—and found that workers differ considerably in the degree and states of alienation they experience. He maintained that structural factors in the particular industry, such as the degree of mechanization, extent of division of labor, and the general work environment, can increase or reduce alienation.[22] Of course, alienation depends also on the characteristics of individuals. Some of us are more aspiring, self-motivated, and independent than others. These and other personal characteristics influence how we cope with particular work situations.*

Alienation from work can be felt by anyone, from the poorest paid jani-

---

*For another study of alienation among industrial workers see John C. Leggett, *Class, Race, and Labor: Working-Class Consciousness in Detroit* (New York: Oxford University Press, 1968).

The monotony of an assembly-line job is frequently cited as a cause of worker alienation.

tor to the chairman of the board at General Motors. Although the janitor probably thinks those above him love their jobs, this is often not the case. George Miller discovered, for example, that professional scientists and engineers sometimes feel alienated from their jobs. This is particularly true when they are given few opportunities to make decisions or work independently and little recognition for their accomplishments.[23] (Refer to chapter 6 for a discussion of procedures and situations which might reduce alienation in bureaucracies.)

RACIAL AND ETHNIC MINORITIES

There is overwhelming evidence that blacks, Chicanos, Orientals, American Indians, and other racial and ethnic groups have been deprived of the economic, political, and educational opportunities afforded to many others in American society. (Refer to chapter 15 for a discussion of the inequalities minority-group members experience.) This deprivation takes on greater importance when one considers that our society emphasizes the ideals of equal opportunity and fair treatment for all citizens.

The disgust, frustration, and estrangement a minority-group member might feel as a result of living in a dehumanizing world are described in the novel *Invisible Man* by black writer Ralph Ellison. For many years the central character in the novel had tried to live up to the expectations imposed upon him by society. Failing to meet them, he now finds himself estranged from others, so much so that he feels he is "invisible" to the outside world.

> *I am an invisible man. No, I am not a spook like those who haunted Edgar Allan Poe; nor am I one of your Hollywood-movie ectoplasms. I am a man of substance, of flesh and bone, fiber and liquids—and I might even be said to possess a mind. I am invisible, understand, simply because people refuse to see me. Like the bodiless heads you*

These Mexican-Americans seek the equality of opportunity praised but not always provided in our society.

see sometimes in circus sideshows, it is as though I have been surrounded by mirrors of hard, distorting glass. When they approach me they see only my surroundings, themselves, or figments of their imagination—indeed, everything and anything except me.

Nor is my invisibility exactly a matter of biochemical accident to my epidermis. That invisibility to which I refer occurs because of a peculiar disposition of the eyes of those with whom I come in contact. A matter of the construction of their inner eyes, those eyes with which they look through their physical eyes upon reality. I am not complaining, nor am I protesting either. It is sometimes advantageous to be unseen, although it is most often rather wearing on the nerves. Then too, you're constantly being bumped against by those of poor vision. Or again, you often doubt if you really exist. You wonder whether you aren't simply a phantom in other people's minds. Say, a figure in a nightmare which the sleeper tries with all his strength to destroy. It's when you feel like this that, out of resentment, you begin to bump people back. And, let me confess, you feel that way most of the time. You ache with the need to convince yourself that you do exist in the real world, that you're a part of all the sound and anguish, and you strike out with your fists, you curse and you swear to make them recognize you. And, alas, it's seldom successful.

One night I accidentally bumped into a man, and perhaps because of the near darkness he saw me and called me an insulting name. I sprang at him, seized his coat lapels and demanded that he apologize. He was a tall blond man, and as my face came close to his he looked insolently out of his blue eyes and cursed me, his breath hot in my face as he struggled. I pulled his chin down sharp upon the crown of my head, butting him as I had seen the West Indians do, *and I felt his flesh tear and the blood gush out, and I yelled, "Apologize! Apologize!" But he continued to curse and struggle, and I butted him again and again. . . . I got out my knife and prepared to slit his throat, right there beneath the lamplight in the deserted street, holding him by the collar with one hand, and opening the knife with my teeth—when it occurred to me that the man had not seen me, actually; that he, as far as he knew, was in a midst of a walking nightmare! And I stopped the blade, slicing the air as I pushed him away, letting him fall back to the street. I stared at him hard as the lights of a car stabbed through the darkness. He lay there, moaning on the asphalt; a man almost killed by a phantom. . . . I ran away into the dark, laughing so hard I feared I might rupture myself. The next day I saw his picture in the Daily News, beneath a caption stating that he had been "mugged." Poor fool, poor blind fool, I thought with sincere compassion, mugged by an invisible man!*[24]

Minority-group members have expressed their feelings of alienation in several ways. The Mexican-American La Causa movement, the 1965 disturbance in Watts, and the occupation of Wounded Knee in South Dakota are a few of the more publicized ways. Some alienated people are prone to resort to militancy, whereas others become totally apathetic and overwhelmed by feelings of "What's the use of trying." Sociologist Gary Marx found that those American blacks who have a militant orientation and are willing to participate in some form of protest tend to be young, male, more educated than the average black, employed, upwardly mobile, and residents of non-Southern urban areas. He maintains that such blacks, generally more affluent than others of their group, see militancy as a realistic course of action for two reasons: (1) they feel hopeful about the future, and (2) they possess the resources, skills, and positive self-image needed to enable them to challenge existing institutions. In contrast, blacks in the lower class feel there is less possibility of improving their conditions and so tend to be less active in social movements and in initiating civil disturbances.[25]

STUDENTS

Contemporary social scientists have studied student alienation largely because of the strikes and demonstrations which occurred on college campuses during the 1960s. Although the vast majority of students were not activists, a significant number did bring national problems to public attention. The National Commission on the Causes and Prevention of Violence maintained that students protested because they began to recognize the magnitude of poverty in America; the "credibility gap" of the Johnson administration; the excessive power of the military in making political decisions; the deterioration of urban areas; and the failure of government to solve problems effectively.[26]

Universities also came under attack. Students thought they could bring about an immediate change in their role in society by gaining power within their schools. Administrators and faculty were accused of being conservative, bureaucratic, racist, overly concerned with research rather than teaching, and supportive of national military policies.* Arthur Stinchcombe devised the term *expressive alienation* to describe both the attitudes and behaviors of students who reject the values of their school. He contends that students experience expressive alienation when their goals and aspirations are not being satisfied by the orientation, curriculum, and instruction of their school. Such students give little meaning to their school activities and come actively to defy those in control.[27]

Student riots and protests have virtually died since the late 1960s, and the once youthful leaders have largely dropped from public attention. In fact, some of the student leaders now sell insurance, vote for Democrats and Republicans, and pursue formerly scorned middle-class values. Although the decline of student protest could be taken to mean that the society and university have corrected their dehumanizing conditions, this seems unlikely. A more probable explanation is that students now focus their attention on more personal concerns, such as career advancement. As do many groups, students may continue to live an alienated existence, but they no longer express their feelings in ways visible to society.

*For a discussion of student rebellion during the 1960s, see Seymour Martin Lipset, *Rebellion in the University* (Boston: Little, Brown, 1971).

Student protest demonstrations, common in the 1960s, are virtually nonexistent today. But does this mean that college students no longer feel alienated from the larger society?

THE MIDDLE CLASS

Alienation has been tied to the individual's level of expectations. Members of the middle class have come to expect the good life that America has promised them, and when reality does not meet their expectations, many experience relative deprivation. (See chapter 13 for a discussion of relative deprivation.) They may have adequate homes and automobiles yet feel that they deserve more than this. Further, members of the middle class may be losing faith in traditional institutions and values. Political corruption, profiteering by large corporations, the environmental crisis, the inflationary cost spiral, and the failure of leaders and bureaucracies to solve problems have contributed to this loss of faith.

Thus far, there have been few, and no violent, public manifestations of discontent. This may change, however, if discontent and alienation increase. Some speculate that middle-class Americans will become intellectually or even actively revolutionary, but this seems unlikely. (See chapter 7 for a discussion of the potential for class consciousness and class struggle in American society.) Others contend that members of the middle class will continue to operate within the existing economic and political systems in an attempt to bring about change. And still others maintain that middle-class citizens will feel so hopeless that they will simply withdraw, become inactive, and learn to live with their alienation as a natural state of affairs.

Apathy and cynicism in the middle class may possibly reach the proportions felt by Mark Twain in his later years. Twain came to feel "sour" about all of humanity, as this excerpt from his essay "The Lowest Animal" illustrates:

> In all ages the savages of all lands have made the slaughtering of their neighboring brothers and the enslaving of their women and children the common business of their lives.
> Hypocrisy, envy, malice, cruelty, vengefulness, seduction, rape, robbery, swindling, arson, bigamy, adultery, and the oppression and humiliation of the poor and the helpless in all ways have been and still are more or less common among both the civilized and uncivilized peoples of the earth.
> For many centuries "the common brotherhood of man" has been urged—on Sundays—and "patriotism" on Sundays and weekdays both. Yet patriotism contemplates the opposite of a common brotherhood.
> Women's equality with man has never been conceded by any people, ancient or modern, civilized or savage.
> I have been studying the traits and dispositions of the "lower animals" (so-called), and contrasting them with the traits and dispositions of man. I find the result humiliating to me. For it obliges me to renounce my allegiance to the Darwinian theory of the Ascent of Man from the Lower Animals; since it now seems plain to me that theory ought to be vacated in favor of a new and truer one, this new and truer one to be named the Descent of Man from the Higher Animals.
> In proceeding toward this unpleasant conclusion I have not guessed or speculated or conjectured, but have used what is commonly called the scientific method. . . . These experiments convinced me that there is this difference between man and the higher animals: he is avaricious and miserly, they are not.
> In the course of my experiments I convinced myself that among the animals man is the only one that harbors insults and injuries, broods over them, waits till a chance offers, then takes revenge. The passion of revenge is unknown to the higher animals. . . .
> Of all the animals, man is the only one that is cruel. He is the only one that inflicts pain for the pleasure of doing it. It is a trait that is not known to the higher animals. . . .
> The higher animals engage in individual fights, but never in organized masses. Man is the only animal that deals in that atrocity of atrocities, War. . . .
> Man is the only animal that robs his helpless fellow of his country—takes possession of it and drives him out of it or destroys him. Man has done this in all the ages. . . .
> Man is the only Slave. . . .

In truth, man is incurably foolish. Simple things which the other animals easily learn, he is incapable of learning....

One is obliged to concede that in true loftiness of character, Man cannot claim to approach even the meanest of the Higher Animals.[28]

Chapter Summary

All kinds of people feel alienated, and this feeling has been used by social theorists to explain increased drug and alcohol abuse, mental illness, suicide, crime, racial turmoil, and political apathy.

The concept of alienation has been shown to have at least five distinct meanings. Powerlessness is the individual's expectation that he or she cannot determine sought-after outcomes. Meaninglessness refers to a person's uncertainty as to what is significant in life. Normlessness occurs when an individual is faced with an absence of rules and feels that socially unapproved behaviors are necessary to achieve goals. Isolation refers to the absence of close relationships with others and the resulting feeling of being alone or apart. Self-estrangement results when a person fails to find self-rewarding activity.

Although the concept covers a wide range of human experiences, most sociologists agree that alienation refers to an individual's state of mind—subjective alienation. Karl Marx believed that it was also important to take into account objective alienation—the dehumanizing events and conditions of society which give rise to the subjective state. No doubt a complete definition of alienation would consider both the alienated person's inability to cope and the indifferent or hostile world that contributes to this.

Scholars such as Marx, Durkheim, Weber, and Simmel examined large, complex social conditions to explain alienation (the global approach). They discussed industrialization, urbanization, and bureaucratization as forces that increase alienation. Contemporary social scientists, however, are examining more specific conditions in smaller groups which may produce such feelings (the context-specific approach).

Many groups in American society have been studied to ascertain the form of alienation members experience and its causes. Industrial workers often feel alienated from their work. Structural factors in an industry, such as degree of mechanization, extent of division of labor, and general work environment, can increase or reduce such feelings. Racial and ethnic minorities have experienced alienation because of economic, political, and social deprivations. Some have reacted with militancy, while others have become apathetic. During the 1960s students publicly demonstrated their alienation from political and educational institutions. Today, however, student protest has all but died, although students may still feel alienated. Even middle-class Americans appear to be experiencing increased alienation. Many feel relatively deprived, and some may be losing faith in traditional values and institutions. There is some speculation that middle-class citizens may eventually become revolutionary as a result, but more likely alternatives are that they will either operate within established institutions to bring about change or learn to live with their feelings.

From our discussion it is obvious that much of our activity is concerned with coping. While some of us lead happy lives, others are unable to deal with certain aspects of life. The task confronting sociologists is to understand—in order to prevent or change—those conditions which are alienating for specific groups in society.

Key Terms for Review

context-specific approach, p. 343
economic alienation, p. 342
expressive alienation, p. 348
global approach, p. 342
isolation, 336
meaninglessness, p. 334
normlessness, p. 335

objective alienation, p. 339
political alienation, p. 342
powerlessness, p. 331
religious alienation, p. 342
self-estrangement, p. 339
subjective alienation, p. 339

Suggested Readings

SOCIOLOGICAL

Blauner, Robert. *Alienation and Freedom: The Factory Worker and His Industry.* Chicago: University of Chicago Press, 1964. The author rejects the idea that alienation can be studied as a "global" concept. In four industries he found that extent of technology, division of labor, and degree of bureaucratization are factors affecting worker alienation.

Finifter, Ada W., ed. *Alienation and the Social System.* New York: John Wiley, 1972. The readings link alienation to other social concerns. The areas covered include alienation in academia, alienation from work, political alienation, and alienation and social change.

Israel, Joachim. *Alienation: From Marx to Modern Sociology.* Boston: Allyn and Bacon, 1971. The book traces the concept of alienation from Marx to present-day sociologists. A variety of philosopher-scientists are discussed, including Mizruchi, Marcuse, and Fromm. The author considers alienation the result of dehumanizing societal processes and conditions.

Nisbet, Robert A. *The Sociological Tradition.* New York: Basic Books, 1966. According to the author, alienation is one of five ideas which form the nucleus of the sociological tradition. He examines Tocqueville, Marx, Durkheim, Weber, and Simmel for their ideas concerning alienation.

Seeman, Melvin. "On the Meaning of Alienation." *American Sociological Review,* 24 (December 1959): 783–791. Social scientists are said to use the concept of alienation in five ways: powerlessness, meaninglessness, normlessness, isolation, and self-estrangement. Seeman discusses the historical derivation of each usage.

LITERARY

Masters, Edgar Lee. *Spoon River Anthology.* Logan, Iowa: Perfection Form Co., 1914. Alienation can be illustrated well by use of the poetic mode. This collection of poetry is in the form of epitaphs from an Illinois village graveyard. The reader learns of the hypocrisy, discontentment, jealousies, and cruelty of some 250 past residents of the village.

Miller, Arthur. *Death of a Salesman.* New York: Viking, 1949. The main character, Willy Loman, is a tragic one. Like many Americans, he is a wishful dreamer striving to be "number one."

Salinger, J. D. *The Catcher in the Rye.* Boston: Little, Brown, 1951. There is probably some of Holden Caulfield in each of us. He is a sensitive, sad, dejected, confused, and isolated character within a crazy world. Salinger's book is a classic statement on the misery of modern life.

Sykes, Gerald, ed. *Alienation: The Cultural Climate of Modern Man,* vols. I and II. New York: George Braziller, 1964. This is an excellent collection of literary excerpts, essays, and short stories on the topic of alienation. The selections discuss the meaning of alienation as well as some of its victims and survivors. Dostoevsky, Mailer, Sartre, Fitzgerald, Eliot, Gogol, Kafka, Blake, and Lawrence are just a few of the writers represented in the anthology. The editor contends that Herman Melville's *Moby Dick, Pierre,* and *Bartleby the Scrivener* provide the best examples of alienation.

IN THIS CHAPTER

Interracial and Interethnic Contact   359

    Segregation   359
    Stratification   360
    Assimilation   360
    Pluralism   363
    Expulsion   365
    Annihilation   367
    Amalgamation   367

Race Relations Cycles   372

Power and Race Relations   373

    Apartheid in South Africa   373
    Stratification in Hong Kong   376
    Segregation in the United States   378

Causes of Prejudice   378

Prospects   380

Summary   383

Key Terms for Review   383

Suggested Readings   384

How do we decide who belongs to a particular race?
Is the United States the most racist country in the world?
Is it possible that another Hitler may come to power?
What lies ahead in race relations?

15

RACE AND ETHNICITY

If humanity were somehow able to achieve a utopian society and bring to trial all the many ideas that have created human suffering, "race" would be among the major defendants, and one of the charges against it would be fraud. The concept of race is a fraudulent one because distinct races of human beings actually do not exist, at least not in the physical sense. Sociologists and anthropologists have agreed for several decades that the concept of physical races is useless as an explanatory device and that human perception of these so-called "racial" differences is the sole basis for racial groupings.[1]

Contemporary scholars see *race* as a human group that perceives itself and/or is perceived by other groups as different by virtue of presumed innate and immutable physical characteristics.[2] Certainly physical criteria are used in determining racial groupings, but the true basis for determination is perception. In the United States we tend to think there is a sharp distinction between those who are black and those who are white. If an individual has any trace of what are thought of as "black" physical characteristics, the person is classified as black. But the distinction between blacks and whites has been based on other criteria than just physical characteristics. In some towns where families have been known for generations, merely the rumor of black ancestry is sufficient to categorize a person as black. Some individuals perceived as black in a number of small, rural Southern towns would be perceived as white anywhere else in the world. A high percentage of American blacks would be considered mulattoes elsewhere and in some places would be considered white. Table 15–1, on page 356, illustrates the different ways that four societies classify individuals racially according to certain physical characteristics.

TABLE 15–1
Varying Cultural Perceptions of Racial Differences

	Continuum of Physical Characteristics		
Society	Woolly Hair Dark Brown to Brown Skin Broad Facial Features	Either Smooth or Woolly Hair Medium Brown Skin Medium-sized Features	Smooth Hair Light Skin Aquiline Features
United States	Black	Black	White
Mexico	Black or Mixed	Mixed	White
Colombia	Black or Mixed	White	White
Brazil	Black	Mulatto	White

These differences in perception have proved to be a major source of embarrassment for several prominent American academicians. During the early years of the Johnson administration, when national attention was very much focused on integration and the festering problems of urban housing, the newly created Department of Housing and Urban Development (HUD) helped sponsor an international conference on urban housing in Bogotá, Colombia. Upon their return from the conference, several enraptured sociologists eloquently praised the Colombians for having high standards of public housing and virtually no problems with racial tensions. The academics had seen blacks and whites living together in complete harmony in well-cared-for public housing. They were very impressed. Unfortunately, however, perception and ethnocentrism had misled the Americans. To Colombian eyes, only whites were living in public housing projects, for in their country, if an individual has obvious physical traces of white heritage, that person is categorized as white. The "blacks" whom the sociologists saw were not black after all; they were white. Race, like the Cheshire cat in Lewis Carroll's *Alice in Wonderland*, is impossible to grasp, and it leads us into some very strange places which become "curiouser and curiouser."

Ethnicity is somewhat easier to understand than race. As with race, the basis for ethnic categorization rests with human perception. But unlike the situation with race, most people recognize that ethnic identification is based primarily on cultural rather than physical or biological characteristics. An *ethnic group* is a human group that perceives itself and/or is perceived by other groups as different by virtue of presumed cultural characteristics.[3]

The line between what is an ethnic group and what is a racial group is not always distinct. Some groups are perceived to have both racial and ethnic characteristics. Jews, for example, are perceived and perceive themselves both as a race—the highly industrious and extremely bright "Jewish people"; and as an ethnic group—the inheritors of many centuries of tradition and struggle.

RACE AND ETHNICITY / 357

The ambition and industriousness of Jewish immigrants to the United States have been described by numerous writers, including Harry Golden, publisher of *The Carolina Israelite*. In *Only in America* Golden relates the early experiences of his Uncle Koppel.

My Uncle Koppel (K. Berger) was twenty years old when he came to America. The day after his arrival he opened a small butcher shop on Scammel Street, on New York's Lower East Side. For the next three years he opened up his shop at six o'clock in the morning,

The Amish, who live primarily in rural Pennsylvania and Ohio, are an American ethnic group whose life style is clearly distinct from that of the larger society. Here we see a typical community project— a barn raising.

worked till after dark, cooked his meals on a stove in the back of the store, and pushed the meat block up against the front door to sleep. What English he learned he picked up from the truck drivers, who delivered the meat and the poultry. There was nothing unusual about this. There were thousands of immigrants who lived, worked, and died within the confines of a few city blocks. But with Koppel Berger it was to be different, because Uncle Koppel had imagination, courage, ability, and above all, he seemed to know what America was all about.

It was 1904 and all America was singing, "Meet me in St. Louey, Louey, meet me at the Fair . . ." and my immigrant Uncle took the lyrics literally. He arrived in St. Louis, Missouri, with five hundred dollars, a wife, and a vocabulary of about thirty words of broken English. He acquired a lease on a rooming house, which accommodated thirty guests. Again he worked night and day. His wife did the laundry, cleaned the rooms, and made the beds; Uncle Koppel carried the baggage, roomed the guests, kept the accounts, carried the coal, made the hot water, and told his guests that he was an employee so that he could also run all their errands. The St. Louis Fair was a success, and so was Koppel Berger. After two years, he and his wife and infant son returned to New York with a little over eight thousand dollars.

Up on Broadway at 38th Street was the old Hotel Normandie, which was not doing so well under the management of the great prize fighter, the original Kid McCoy (Norman Selby).

With a vocabulary of about seventy-five words of broken English, Uncle Koppel took over the lease on this 250-room hotel in the heart of the theatrical district. Of course, even a genius must have some luck, too, and we must concede that Koppel Berger acquired the Hotel Normandie at exactly the right moment. New York and America were becoming "hotel-minded"; in addition, the theatre was entering upon its greatest era, a "golden age" such as we shall never see again. Between 1907 and 1927, there were literally hundreds and hundreds of road shows and stock companies; burlesque was in all its glory; dozens of opera "extravaganzas" were playing all over the country; vaudeville was at its all-time peak; and on Broadway itself, there were at least one hundred and fifty attractions produced each year.

In those days, "actors" and "actresses" were not particularly welcome at the best hotels. In fact, many New Yorkers will remember the signs on some small hotels and rooming houses, "Actors Accommodated."[4]

The language barrier faced by Uncle Koppel did not prevent him from realizing what many have called "the American Dream." He remained immersed in his own subculture (ethnic group), yet was able to find success in his new homeland.

Interracial and Interethnic Contact

The increased mobility of people during the past several centuries has brought numerous racial and ethnic groups into contact with each other. Such contact has sometimes been beneficial, but often it was filled with conflict. Such interaction between racial and ethnic groups may yield a variety of results (see Figure 15–1), some illustrating the best in humanity and others the worst.

SEGREGATION

Segregation implies a stringent separation between racial or ethnic groups with no group necessarily considered superior. The separation may be largely voluntary as in the case of the Mennonites, a religious sect concentrated, in the United States, mainly in Pennsylvania and Ohio. It may be clearly involuntary as with *apartheid*, the system of racial separation in South Africa. Or segregation may be a combination of the two, as is the current reality for Americans. What we must keep in mind is that true segregation — separate but equal — seldom exists. Such a situation is more often a desire or an expressed ideology. This is most obvious in the case of

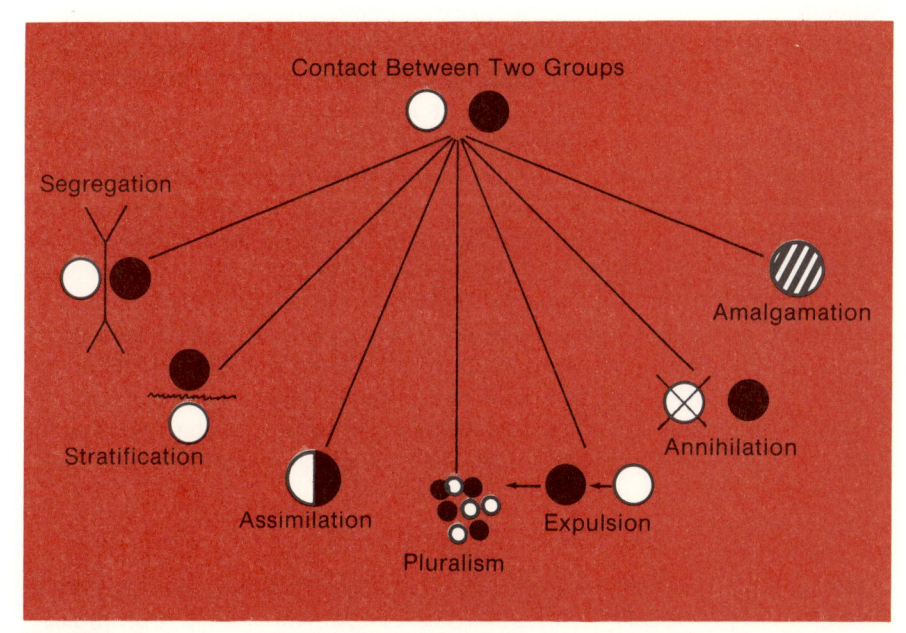

FIGURE 15–1 Seven Possibilities of Interracial and Interethnic Contact

South Africa, where extreme inequalities exist despite the ruling whites' ideology that the system provides for racial separation but equality for all.

STRATIFICATION

Sociologists generally apply the term "stratification" to the divisions of society based on wealth, education, religion, and/or family heritage. (See chapter 7.) But in the context of race and ethnicity, *stratification* means the enforced separation of racial or ethnic groups with one group being clearly dominant. Two examples are the relation of blacks and whites in South Africa and of American Indians and the dominant society in the United States during much of our history.

Like stratification of social classes, stratification by race and ethnicity is supported by an elaborate system of beliefs and ideas. These are usually expressed in the form of racial and ethnic stereotypes—the dumb Pole, the shuffling darkie, the thieving Mexican, the drunken Irishman, and so on. Such stereotypes serve to reinforce the status quo—to justify the unequal distribution of society's rewards, which is the crucial ingredient of stratification. The thinking goes as follows: racial- and ethnic-group members are poor and in unrewarding jobs because they are inherently or culturally flawed. They are naturally ignorant (racial group) or have grown up with sinful habits, such as drinking excessively (ethnic group). They thus possess any number of traits which make them unfit to take a more rewarding place in the social system.

In stratified societies many people in the deprived or exploited group are understandably anxious to remove themselves from such a position. Sometimes the means for achieving this change in status is very clearly specified. In the past, laws of *manumission* codified the means by which slaves could be freed or gain their own freedom, a rare occurrence in the United States but a quite common one in Brazil.

A more common method for gaining the rewards of the dominant group, however, is very simple indeed: one joins the dominant group. Jews change their names and perhaps their occupations; Poles and Hungarians change their names; light-skinned blacks process their hair and move to a new neighborhood. These people attempt to be recognized as members of the privileged racial or ethnic group. The practice, known as *passing*, is very much a part of the racial and ethnic history of the United States and has been associated with virtually every contact between "different" peoples. Indeed, it is estimated that 40,000 to 50,000 American blacks "pass" into the white community annually, and that perhaps 25 percent of supposedly white Americans have black ancestors.[5]

ASSIMILATION

Passing is really a form of *assimilation*, defined as a cultural blending of two or more previously distinct peoples. People who pass take on the cultural characteristics of the dominant group and consciously attempt to become a part of that group.

Immigrants to the United States have often found the process of assimilation difficult. Yet for many there was little choice about leaving their old homeland. In *The American Irish* William Shannon speaks of the forces which caused many people to leave Ireland.

> Irish life in America begins from a sharp and tragic rejection. To "come out" to the new country meant thrusting behind the old, usually forever, unless in a few instances success brought enough money to visit the old country once more. Even then, however, many who could financially afford the return visit to Ireland never made the trip. It would be a journey back in more than one sense, a journey back into the house of their father, into the womb of old memories and long-forgotten sadnesses. To return would be to reconsider the crucial decision that it was no use to reconsider. The pleasures of nostalgia would not be worth the pain.
>
> Why did they leave and what did they seek?
>
> The answer is that most did not leave willingly. They were hurled out, driven by forces larger and more complex than they could fully understand or cope with. They made the decision to go, of course; the responsibility was theirs and they could not deny it (least of all to themselves in the later and the harder years), but the range of choice was narrow. To the question What did they seek? the answer is the same for them as for all men. They sought a door that would open and give them access to hope.[6]

The faces of these immigrants reflect both their hopes and fears upon arrival at Ellis Island in New York Harbor.

Our own "nation of immigrants," although heavily influenced by the cultural heritages of northern Europe and especially the British Isles, is a blend of many cultures. In that sense we are all products of assimilation. The social and psychological difficulties involved in the process, however, are many. A person who has "passed" from one group or culture to another is often beset by feelings of insecurity, remorse, disloyalty, and anxiety, and is, in the phrase of Robert Park, a *marginal man*. That individual is caught between two cultures and is not fully a part of either. Dick Gregory established his national reputation as a comedian with comments on the marginality of American blacks: for instance, the upwardly mobile black woman trying to smuggle a watermelon into her suburban split-level, or the middle-class black man trimming his hedge who is asked by a white neighbor how much he charges for the work. The feelings associated with marginality are very much like those experienced in culture shock (see chapter 3), with the exception that here the feelings of normlessness are experienced within one's own society.

Virtually all members of identifiable minority racial or ethnic groups are members of their particular subculture. Some choose to celebrate their cultural heritage, while others are forced into membership in the subculture by the dominant majority. The crucial point is that most members of a subculture are necessarily marginal. If one is a WASP in the United States, it is possible to spend weeks, months, or even years without having to deal with another culture. But if one is a member of a minority group, such cultural isolation is impossible. Blacks and Chicanos must leave the ghettos and barrios to work; they must exist in several cultures.

Majority-group members often enforce a very rigid code of interaction with minority-group members, and the code is buttressed by a firm belief system. But belief systems can change. John Wain's story of conflicting attitudes between generations, "Down Our Way," amply illustrates shifting belief systems.

> "God made us all different. Don't talk back to your mother," said Mr. Robinson.
>
> "It's not the blacks I mind. They don't know any better," said Mrs. Robinson. "But a man like that, knocking on people's doors and making trouble. There ought to be a law against it."
>
> "I expect there is, come to think of it," said Mr. Robinson. "Appearing in disguise on the public highway."
>
> "Not now," said Arthur Robinson, blowing on his tea. "In olden days, yes. But it wouldn't work today. What with all these wigs and that, and not being able to tell whether it's a girl or a boy till you come right up to 'em—" he expelled a harsh blast of air that sent his tea climbing dangerously high up its white glazed wall. "You'd have to put half the country in prison."
>
> "Good job too," said Mrs. Robinson. She cut her piece of fruitcake into sections, vigorously. "They want teaching a good lesson, some of 'em. Dirty little madams."

"The black fellers have got to live, Mum," said Doris Robinson with her usual stolid defiance.

"Nobody's stopping them," said Mr. Robinson. "They're welcome to live as long as they stay where the good Lord put 'em. But they shouldn't come pouring into a white man's country. That's what I say and I've got the Bible to prove it."

"Some people don't reckon the Bible proves anything," said Doris. "After you, Arthur. I like jam, too."

"They ought to be ashamed, then," said Mrs. Robinson. "Dirty color-blind little madams. They don't care who they're with, so long as it's a man."

"Well, they've got a point," said Doris, attacking the jam.

"Make allowances, Mum," said Arthur. "I expect that's what it feels like when you're twenty-six and haven't got a husband yet."

"Why don't you go and give all your blood to the Red Cross?" queried his sister indifferently.

"I bet you'd go out with a darkie fast enough," said Arthur, disappointed at Doris's calm.

"I would if I like him."[7]

PLURALISM

A fourth possible outcome of interethnic and interracial contact — *pluralism* — is very highly valued by many. In a pluralistic relationship among racial or ethnic groups, none of the groups dominates, there is interaction among and free movement between the groups, and the groups maintain their racial and/or ethnic identity. This seemingly utopian relationship does exist, though understandably it is relatively rare. While there are some elements of racial and ethnic pluralism in the United States, most notably in Hawaii,[8] we could hardly say that we have a pluralistic system; far too much segregation and stratification exists. Switzerland and Fiji offer better examples of pluralistic societies.

Switzerland is a small nation (15,000 square miles — the size of Connecticut and Massachusetts combined) of immense cultural diversity. The major indications of ethnic difference — language and religion — give at least a glimpse of this variety. Two-thirds of the Swiss speak some variety of the German dialect known as Schwyzerdeutsch, while 20 percent speak French and another 10 percent speak Italian. The remainder use a variety of other languages, including 1 percent who speak an obscure ancient language called Romansh. Fifty-eight percent of the population are Protestant and the remainder are Roman Catholic. These ethnic differences have not been reconciled by systems of segregation or stratification or by headlong assimilation. Instead, the Swiss have managed to avoid conflict while continuing to celebrate their differences. They have adopted a clear policy of religious freedom and have approached the potential difficulties inherent in linguistic diversity by designating the three major languages as

Racial and ethnic pluralism is apparent in this photograph of a Honolulu plaza. Hawaii is the only state in the Union in which no racial or ethnic group constitutes a majority. Each of the two largest groups—people of European descent and those of Japanese descent—makes up only about a third of the population.

"official languages." All government documents and pronouncements appear simultaneously in French, German, and Italian. Cultural diversity has become a way of life with the Swiss. They have achieved a relatively stable pluralistic system with a minimum of ethnocentrism; "they have been without peers in putting into practice this rare and difficult pattern of accommodation in ethnic group relations."[9]

The recently independent island nation of Fiji offers an illustration of racial pluralism, which is even more rare than ethnic pluralism. Fijians, who compose 44 percent of the population, and Indians, who constitute 49 percent, each view themselves and the other group as racial groups. Most of us would also perceive them as racial groups. The Fijians are classified as Micronesian. They are quite big, heavy-muscled, large-featured, bushy-haired, and very dark-skinned. The Indians, who were imported from India by the British during the latter part of the nineteenth century to work sugar and cotton crops, are small-featured, smooth-haired, and bronze-skinned. Unlike the interaction of most racial groups, however, the relationship that has been established in Fiji is not one of stratification or segregation. The Indians do tend to live in the "urban" areas, most notably Suva, while the Fijians remain primarily rural. However, neither dominates. The Indians are often better educated and earn a disproportionate share of the national income, but the Fijians own the land. A long-established law forbids anyone but a Fijian from owning land in Fiji.

EXPULSION

A fifth possibility in interracial and interethnic contact, *expulsion*, involves the forceful removal of one group by another. Most of us are able to think of numerous instances of expulsion. Two of the more notorious examples in American history involve Indians and Japanese-Americans.

During the 1830s federal troops removed the prosperous Cherokee Nation from its homeland in the southeastern United States and herded it into what is now Oklahoma. The Cherokees had suffered the misfortune of having gold discovered on their tribal land. Only half the 10,000 tribal members who began the journey known as the "trail of tears" survived it. The final irony and indignity of this expulsion was that the United States government submitted a bill for the cost of the trip to the Cherokee Nation. It was paid.

The forced removal of Issei, Nisei, and Sansei (first-, second-, and third-generation Japanese-Americans) from their communities during World War II is a shameful episode in American history. It was racism in its most virulent form, summed up in the quote from the operation's commanding officer, General J. L. DeWitt: "Once a Jap always a Jap." The "relocation," as it was euphemistically designated, succeeded in removing 120,000

The expulsion of the Cherokee Nation from the Southeast is portrayed in this painting by Robert Lindneux. Only half the Indians who set out on this "trail of tears" survived the long trek.

During World War II all but a few Japanese-Americans were "relocated" in camps such as this one at Manzanar, California.

Japanese-Americans, mainly from the West Coast, to ten camps established in isolated inland areas. The rationale for the removal was "national security," but it had no basis at all in fact. Not one Japanese-American was ever found guilty of sabotage or of "cooperating with the enemy," and the Japanese-American "Go for Broke" division of the American army was one of the most highly decorated ever to serve the nation. What did matter was that the Japanese who "infamously" attacked Pearl Harbor looked very much like some of the people who lived down the street. Japanese-Americans were seen as members of an enemy "race" and were persecuted indiscriminately. Americans of Italian and German ancestry were not harassed in such a way. They were not as identifiable as were Japanese-Americans. They were not a "race."

Nazi Germany's attempt to exterminate European Jews during World War II is a notorious example of a policy of annihilation. Nordhausen (left) and Buchenwald (right) were two of the Nazis' concentration camps.

ANNIHILATION

A sixth possible outcome of interracial and interethnic contact is *annihilation*, in which one group attempts to eliminate another racial or ethnic group. For example, white Americans annihilated a number of Indian tribes during the development of this country. However, it is necessary to look elsewhere for the most pernicious examples.

The island of Tasmania, located off the southern coast of Australia, witnessed the complete annihilation of its Aborigines within 73 years. Between 1803 and 1876 the Tasmanian Aborigines were the target of some of the most ruthless and inhumane treatment ever recorded. They were hunted for sport by many of the European settlers. One enterprising newcomer, in what may be the low point in human interaction, hunted Aborigines, not for sport, but to use them as dog food.[10]

Other better-known attempts at annihilation have been directed at Jews. In 70 A.D. a Roman army under Titus captured and destroyed Jerusalem in what came to be known as the Great Dispersion. More than 1 million Jews were killed. The attempted extermination of Jews by Nazi Germany during World War II, however, is more widely known and was so monstrous that a new word was coined to describe it. Professor Raphael Lemkin of Duke University termed it *genocide:* "a denial of the right of the existence of entire human groups in the same way as homicide is the denial of the right to live for individual human beings."[11] The effectiveness of the Nazi program is undeniable. Of the 10 million Jews who lived in Europe at the start of Hitler's rule, somewhere between 6 and 7 million were killed. The numbers defy adequate comprehension.

AMALGAMATION

Ultimately, the inevitable outcome of interracial and interethnic contact is *amalgamation,* the physical blending of previously distinct groups. This is the "mongrelization" so much feared by the Ku Klux Klan and other similar groups. Much of the world's population has obviously resulted from racial and ethnic amalgamation. Large percentages of the populations of most South American countries are classified as "mixed." Indeed, even such "pure" groups as the Daughters of the American Revolution are a mixture of Anglo and Saxon stock.

What is certain is that if two or more racial or ethnic groups come into contact with each other and remain in contact—if one group is not annihilated or expelled—they will become amalgamated. This prediction raises the interesting question of sequential arrangement: When racial or ethnic groups come into contact, do certain of the seven possible outcomes tend to occur early in the contact and others later? The answer is clearly yes.

Pluralism in American Society

Since the middle of the 1960s there has been a resurgent awareness and assertion of racial and ethnic identity in the United States. Many members of racial and ethnic communities see this rising consciousness of their heritage as a source of strength and identity. To sociologists, it represents a shift toward pluralism and away from assimilation. But whatever one's perception or level of analysis, the fabric of American life is greatly enriched by the existence of numerous racial and ethnic groups.

The variety in our society is most obvious during the holidays and celebrations of the diverse groups—for instance, Chinese New Year festivities (above), religious festivals, such as that of San Gennaro in New York City's Little Italy (above right), and celebrations of differing art forms, such as the Buddhist Dance Festival (right).

Race and ethnicity are also celebrated in parades. Here we see New York City's famous St. Patrick's Day parade, a Puerto Rican Day parade, and a Greek parade.

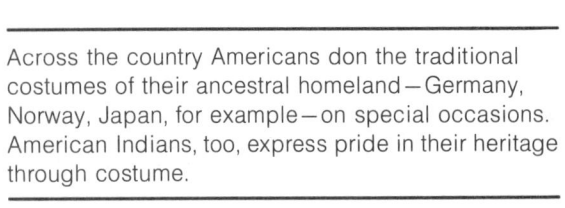

Across the country Americans don the traditional costumes of their ancestral homeland—Germany, Norway, Japan, for example—on special occasions. American Indians, too, express pride in their heritage through costume.

Pride in racial and ethnic identity is also expressed in the daily lives of other American groups, such as blacks, Jews, and Mennonites (below). Indeed, the Mennonites today seem little changed from their ancestors who fled persecution elsewhere to become citizens of the United States. American society has been fed by streams from Europe, Asia, and Africa, and it remains a society of great diversity and heterogeneity.

Race Relations Cycles

A number of scholars have attempted to specify sequences, or *race relations cycles,* which groups pass through after coming into contact with each other. We will discuss a few of the most famous and more lucid attempts. Robert Park commented that "in the relations of races there is a cycle of events which tends everywhere to repeat itself."[12] Park documented five specific stages: contact, competition, accommodation, assimilation, and amalgamation. He believed this cycle to be "progressive and irreversible," and to a great extent Park's theory has remained unchallenged by recent history. A major criticism of Park's work, however, is that it is too abstract.

Others have taken Park's basic cycle and given it more detail. Emory Bogardus painstakingly documented the progress of the many racial and ethnic groups that have been migrants to California. He found that Park's basic assumptions were correct. Clarence Glick found similar support for the inevitability of amalgamation in his observation of European overseas expansion. The relationship between Europeans and colonial peoples tended to move along the lines of Park's cycle.

Another group of observers has commented that the critical issue is not one of particular sequence but of initial relationships. The majority of these scholars are convinced that the most important factor is power. Stanley Lieberson of the University of Wisconsin believed that power is based on technology and noted that since European technology was, at the

Some sociologists have referred to the initial stage of racial or ethnic contact as that of "economic welcome." Such welcome is usually called exploitation. These were the sleeping quarters for immigrant laborers at a construction camp in New York in 1909.

time of expansion, more advanced than that of other civilizations. Europeans tended to dominate.[13] Don Noel has illustrated that both power and the peculiar ethnocentrism of the British were most probably responsible for the development of the system of slavery used in the United States.[14]

Power and Race Relations

What emerges from the numerous studies of interethnic and interracial contact is the virtual certainty that (1) power is a critical factor in determining patterns of interaction, and (2) ethnic and racial relationships move toward amalgamation. The details of how race relations develop in situations of unequal power vary. Three cases—of South Africa, Hong Kong, and the United States—show this clearly.

APARTHEID IN SOUTH AFRICA

South Africa is today probably the most racist and race-conscious nation on earth. The gulf between blacks and whites is enormous, something well beyond what most Americans know. In the United States the median income of the black worker is three-fourths that of the white worker, whereas in South Africa the median black income is only one-twelfth that of the white.

The extreme racism and stratification of South Africa has its origin in the European expansion of the seventeenth century. In 1652 the Dutch East India Company established a supply station for its ships at the Cape of Good Hope. The initial contact between the white Europeans (Dutch) and the black Africans (Hottentot) was characterized primarily by what we would refer to as ethnic interaction. The two groups saw each other as culturally, but not inherently, different, and for the first few years intermarriage was quite acceptable as long as the Hottentot became a Christian. Such acceptance began to fade quickly, however, as color became crucial in the development of slavery. Since slaves were black, the color line had to be firmly drawn. There could be no mixing, socially, between blacks and whites. Racism and apartheid were now beginning to take hold.

As we noted early in the chapter, the concept of race is very much like the Cheshire cat of *Alice in Wonderland*. And much like Alice's experience in Wonderland, life in South Africa, at least from our perspective, is quite absurd. A black suburb of Johannesburg—Soweto—was virtually unknown until the uprising there in 1976. The reason most outsiders had never heard of Soweto, a city of over half a million people, is that it does not really exist. It *really* exists, but like the Cheshire cat, then again it does not. It is not on maps because, although it has been in existence for over half a century, it is considered only temporary. Joseph Lelyveld, a correspondent for *The New York Times* who has spent much time explaining and reporting on South African affairs, succinctly captures the heady rationale for it all:

> Soweto is not a Zulu or Xhosa word standing for something like Harmony or the name of some great black leader. It is simply an amalgam of the words South Western Townships—an appropriate bureaucratic designation for this realization of the relentless bureaucratic idea that whites and blacks must live apart. Officially the government considers Soweto a temporarily unavoidable social aberration in what has now been declared a "white area." Eventually—or so the theory of apartheid, at its most preposterous, holds— the entire black population will melt back into tribal reserves. Thus, when community leaders in Soweto meekly requested the right to own their own homes, a cabinet minister replied, "If we allow freehold rights in Soweto, that would be the anchor for Africans to settle permanently in our midst. That is against Government policy."[15]

Government codification and definition of race make the entire situation even more difficult to understand. It is, as one observer once noted, "like trying to nail jello to a tree," but we will try. There are actually three racial categories in South Africa—blacks, whites, and a category intermediate between the two, coloreds. The government of South Africa established the Registration Act in 1950 for fear that too many black Africans were moving into the colored category and from there into the privileged white group. The Registration Act simply specified that everyone would be registered at birth as belonging to one of the three groups. The only group that is not entirely hereditary is the colored, in which children of mixed parentage may be placed. But such a racial caste system, even with the official sanction of the government, does have its problems from time to time. In 1968 an officially white Cape Town couple had their fourth child, a girl, who, it soon became apparent, was not officially white. She was the couple's daughter, but certainly she would not be able to live with them. The ironic solution to this problem: the daughter could reside with her parents if she were classified a colored house servant.

Given the conditions of official separation and stratification, observers often interpret day-to-day civilities between whites and blacks in South Africa as an indication of a lack of turmoil and racial hostility. Closer and more perceptive examination, however, often reveals very deep antagonisms, as Dan Jacobson suggests in his story "Beggar My Neighbor."

> "Thank you, baas."
> "Thank you, baas."
> They ate the bread in Michael's presence; watching them, he felt a little more kindly disposed towards them. "All right, you can come another day, and there'll be some more bread for you."

"Thank you, baas."

"Thank you, baas."

They came back sooner than Michael had expected them to. He gave them their bread and told them to go. They went off, but again did not wait for the usual five or six days to pass, before approaching him once more. Only two days had passed, yet, here they were with their eternal request—"Stukkie brood, baas?"

Michael said, "Why do you get hungry so quickly now?" But he gave them their bread.

When they appeared in his games and fantasies, Michael no longer rescued them, healed them, casually presented them with kingdoms and motor cars. Now he ordered them about, sent them away on disastrous missions, picked them out to be shot for cowardice in the face of the enemy. And because something similar to these fantasies was easier to enact in the real world than his earlier fantasies, Michael soon was ordering them about unreasonably in fact. He deliberately left them waiting; he sent them away and told them to come back on days when he knew he would be in town; he told them there was no bread in the house. And when he did give them anything, it was bread only now; never old toys or articles of clothing.

So, as the weeks passed, Michael's scorn gave way to impatience and irritation, irritation to anger. And what angered him most was that the two piccanins seemed too stupid to realize what he now felt about them, and instead of coming less frequently, continued to appear more often than ever before. Soon they were coming almost every day, though Michael shouted at them and teased them, left them waiting for hours, and made them do tricks and sing songs for their bread. They did everything he told them to do; but they altogether ignored his instructions as to which days they should come. Invariably, they would be waiting for him, in the shade of one of the trees that grew alongside the main road from school, or standing at the gate behind the house with sand scuffed up about their bare toes.

South Africa's policy of racial segregation extends even to park benches.

They were as silent as before; but more persistent, inexorably persistent. Michael took to walking home by different routes, but they were not to be so easily discouraged. They simply waited at the back gate, and whether he went into the house by the front or the back gate he could not avoid seeing their upright, unmoving figures.

Finally, he told them to go and never come back at all. Often he had been tempted to do this, but some shame or pride had always prevented him from doing it; he had always weakened previously, and named a date, a week or two weeks ahead, when they could come again. But now he shouted at them, "It's finished! No more bread—nothing! Come on, voetsek! *If you come back I'll tell the garden boy to chase you away." . . . The sun seemed to seize the back of his neck as firmly as a hand grasping, and its light was so bright he was aware of it only as a darkness beyond the little stretch of ground he looked down upon. He opened the back gate. Inevitably, as he had known they would be, the two were waiting.*

He did not want to go beyond the gate in his pyjamas and dressing gown, so, shielding his eyes from the glare with one hand, he beckoned them to him with the other. Together, in silence, they rose and crossed the lane. It seemed to take them a long time to come to him, but at last they stood in front of him, with their hands interlinked. Michael stared into their dark faces, and they stared into his.

"What are you waiting for?" he asked.

"For you." First the boy answered; then the girl repeated, "For you."

Michael looked from the one to the other; and he remembered what he had been doing to them in his dreams. Their eyes were black to look into, deep black. Staring forward, Michael understood what he should have understood long before: that they came to him not in hope or appeal or even in reproach, but in hatred. What he felt towards them, they felt towards him; what he had done to them in his dreams, they did to him in theirs.[16]

STRATIFICATION IN HONG KONG

Official race-labeling difficulties plagued the British in Hong Kong during the 1930s. Hong Kong was and to a great extent remains a highly stratified society: the 1 percent of the population that was British lived well above the 98 percent that was Chinese. Such an elevated position was not only figurative. The British lived at the very top of Victoria Peak, 2,000 feet above the rest of Hong Kong, in what is known as the Peak District. All non-British were forbidden to live there by the government of the crown colony.

After being pressed on the question of racism, the government officially

Hong Kong exhibits a contrast of East and West, of modernity and tradition, of poverty and affluence.

responded that race was not the issue; the determining factor in residential patterns was health. In a classic enactment of the old elitist phrase "the unwashed masses," the Chinese were viewed as unclean. They were believed to be carriers of typhus, malaria, and tuberculosis. The Chinese population was incensed. To defuse their anger, the government of Hong Kong, in a move reminiscent of the Nazi government's designation of "honorary Aryans," found one Chinese, a diplomat and businessman, Sir Hong Chow, to be clean—a sort of "honorary clean Chinese." Until after the Japanese invasion of China in World War II, Sir Hong Chow was the only Chinese in Hong Kong adjudged to be clean. Even today the Peak District is dominated by the British, who still compose less than 2 percent of the entire colony's population.

SEGREGATION IN THE UNITED STATES

As in South Africa and Hong Kong, an effort was long made in parts of the United States to keep the dominant whites apart from other racial groups by law. Historically the most stringently enforced statutes, those that carried the severest penalties, were the laws forbidding *miscegenation*, the intermarriage of different races. But these laws varied from state to state in regard to which racial groups could not intermarry.

At one time nineteen states had laws which barred intermarriage. All of these forbade the marriage of blacks and whites; thirteen barred the marriage of whites and "Mongolians" (Orientals), and six banned whites and Indians from marrying. Two states prevented blacks and Indians from marrying, and Oklahoma forbade any intermarriage between "Negroes, Indians, and Mongolians." Some states had very broad laws. Georgia law stated that a white could not marry anyone with "any ascertainable trace of African, West Indian, Asiatic Indian, or Mongolian blood." Others were even more general, forbidding white marriage with anyone with "African or Mongolian heritage." Some states made it illegal for whites to marry *octoroons*, anyone with one-eighth "black blood." For violating such laws one could spend ten years in prison and be fined $2,000. Miscegenation laws were on the books until 1967, when they were finally declared unconstitutional by the United States Supreme Court.

Causes of Prejudice

The song "Carefully Taught" from Rodgers and Hammerstein's musical *South Pacific* gives a valuable lesson in prejudice: you have to be carefully taught to hate people who are different. *Prejudice* refers to a negative attitude toward a racial or ethnic group and all members of that group. Such an attitude is based on superstition and belief systems rather than on any formal testing of reality. Racial and ethnic prejudice is passed on from one generation to the next through socialization, a process that is not always planned. If your family dislikes whites or Indians or Germans or Catholics or whatever, the chances are very high that you too will look askance at such groups.

Like families, some nations are quite prejudiced and others relatively free of the affliction. Although there are many reasons for the development of varying degrees of racial and ethnic prejudice, certain constants

Hitler Youth parading in Berlin. Racial and ethnic prejudices are usually learned at an early age.

are found in all settings.* Individual and family prejudice is very closely linked with self-concept and feelings of worth. It is often a matter of "we" and "they": we are good; they are bad.† The observation has often been made that the only thing poor whites in this country have is their prejudice. That enables poor whites to say to themselves, "At least I'm better than the _____." Another basic reason for prejudice is that of power and economic relationships. This may be clearly seen on the national and international levels. One group or nation has the means to impose its will on another group or nation, to exploit it, and a justifying ideology for such ex-

---

*Fine accounts of the development and functions of prejudice are found in Gordon W. Allport, *The Nature of Prejudice* (New York: Doubleday Anchor, 1958).
†There is a good discussion of this tendency and possible alternatives in Erik H. Erikson, "The Concept of Identity in Race Relations," in *Old Memories, New Moods*, vol. 2 of *Americans from Africa*, ed. Peter I. Rose (Chicago: Aldine, 1970), p. 323.

ploitation is prejudice. *They* (another racial or cultural group) are treated harshly because *they* are stupid or perverted or sick or whatever pejorative labeling happens to appeal to those applying the definition.

Whatever the dominant prejudices are, once they become a part of a culture, they are transmitted and maintained in every possible way, through literature, film, television and radio programs, advertising, records, and word of mouth. Few people in a culture are exempt from these prejudices. National leaders and scholars have at times captured, codified, and lent credence to many of their society's prejudices. Charles Ellwood, author of the leading social problems text of the 1920s, was enthralled with the popular stereotypes of blacks then prevalent and justified the stereotypes by a peculiar brand of geographic determinism:

> *Suffice to say that the African environment of the ancestors of the present negroes of the United States deeply stamped itself upon the innate traits and tendencies of the race. For example, the tropical environment is generally unfavorable to severe bodily labor. Persons who work hard in the tropics are, in other words, apt to be eliminated by natural selection. On the other hand nature furnishes a bountiful supply of food without much labor. Hence the tropical environment of the negro failed to develop in him an energetic nature, but favored the survival of those naturally shiftless and lazy. Again, the extremely high death rate in Africa necessitated a correspondingly high birth rate in order that any race living there might survive; hence, nature fixed in the negro strong sexual propensities in order to secure a high birth rate.*[17]

Prejudice is widespread; its causes are complex; and the means for its perpetuation are many.

Prospects

Beyond commenting that we are slowly and inevitably moving toward amalgamation, predicting patterns of racial and ethnic interaction on the international and domestic scenes is an extremely hazardous business. We do know that ethnocentrism in the form of racial or ethnic prejudice is prevalent in almost all cultures. We also have seen that power is a vital ingredient in race and ethnic relations and is very much related to exploitation. In a culture where racial or ethnic prejudice aids in the exploitation of the weak by the strong, prejudice will be present.

What makes prediction particularly difficult is that although the "irreversible cycle" of Robert Park remains valid, the aberrations and fluctuations of the cycle are sometimes extreme. The devastation that Nazi Ger-

As the reception of many immigrants to this country suggests, racial and ethnic prejudices have not been absent from American society. This drawing shows the "welcome" at times accorded Chinese immigrants in nineteenth-century San Francisco.

many wrought makes this painfully clear. Few would have predicted the disaster wreaked by Germany in World War II. Even commentators with the most brazen hindsight were reluctant to say, "I told you so." Prior to Hitler's rise Germany was seen by many as a showpiece of Western culture. The list of German cultural giants seemed endless—Kant, Beethoven, Einstein, Goethe, Marx, Bach, Mendelssohn. The glories of this culture were greatly dimmed by the horrors discovered in the concentration and extermination camps at Auschwitz, Buchenwald, Dachau, and other places.

Many studies have attempted to understand, to rationalize, to explain the Nazi atrocities. What has finally emerged is the basic truth that "we have met the enemy and he is us." That is, the horrors of racial and ethnic annihilation are not likely to occur without at least the passive participation of good and decent citizens. In the film *Judgment at Nuremburg* the character Ernst Janning was a gifted and highly civilized German judge. He had friends who were Jews; he was not a prejudiced man. Like many good and decent citizens of Germany, Janning slowly changed. What would have been totally repugnant to him in 1933 (when the Nazis first came to power) he found acceptable by 1937; what he could not accept in 1937, he had learned to live with by 1940. Through small steps and occasionally through giant leaps, we are able to rationalize much that violates our personal value system. We do so simply by maintaining that a higher value is at stake. Janning saw Hitler as a figure who would soon pass from the scene. The Nazis' treatment of the Jews was not desirable, but it was a temporary, necessary evil which would allow Germany to survive. The question "Could it happen here?" must be met with an unqualified "Of course."

The main character in Edward Anhalt's screenplay *QB VII* suggests a similar conclusion in recalling the horrors of the Nazi era:

> *The men and women of this jury have played back to us what Europe has learned over the bodies of its millions of dead and what, God willing, the rest of the world will learn before it is too late. That those who hate the bomb and starve other men because they fear the color of their skin because it is different from theirs, or their politics because it is different from theirs, or their religion because it is different from theirs, are evil men. That there is any common meaning to the words "good" and "evil" lies in the difference between such men and ourselves. So long as we allow them to rule nations, to command armies, to minister to sects, we will continue to be their victims. Am I satisfied? It is a word that cannot be used in connection with the issues this trial has touched upon. Because what happened from 1939 to 1945 in Europe is still happening in a half dozen countries of this world. And it will continue to happen so long as evil men remain organized and good and gentle men are deceived and put upon and paralyzed by them. That is the meaning of what has happened here in these courts in this contest.*[18]

In the novel *Meeting the Bear* Lloyd Zimpel paints a scenario of the 1970s in which the United States is torn by open racial warfare. A charismatic and dashing leader known as Brother Black gives rousing and fiery speeches in black communities throughout the nation. People, both black and nonblack, become frightened. The media and a number of politicians interpret sporadic urban gunfire as signaling the outbreak of a racial revolution. Social scientists suggest programs of retraining for the black citizens of the United States. They would go through a kind of "behavior modification." The retraining programs do not work, of course. Black people are quite angry about being rounded up and shipped off to retraining centers, but it does not really matter. What does matter is that "retraining" provides the perfect excuse for good and decent citizens to let loose their deep-seated prejudices. Pretenses of urban renewal are abandoned, and large sections of every major urban area of the country are simply bulldozed and burned out of existence. The relocation camps used for Japanese-Americans during World War II are reopened and expanded.

The line between fiction and reality is difficult to find, and many will argue that we need not rely on the imagination of Lloyd Zimpel to see that we are still the enemy. There are many difficulties of a racial and ethnic nature in this country. Television documentaries have exposed the malnutrition suffered by diverse groups, yet the problem remains. The outrages of some prison systems are also known to many, but they continue. Good and decent people continue to live with these obvious social evils. The rationale is, "What else can we do?"

Racial warfare, however, in the United States, is unlikely although we must recognize that it is possible. Our current celebration of ethnic differences seems to many to be a very healthy and necessary stage in accommodation between racial and ethnic groups. Our system is increasingly pluralistic, but in the long run pluralism will be only a passing stage. Clearly we are moving toward a cultural and physical blend: assimilation and amalgamation.

Chapter Summary

Racial and ethnic boundaries are perceived and defined by humans and have no actual basis in physical reality. This sociological fact becomes obvious when we observe that the same individual would be viewed as a member of one race by one culture and as a member of another race by a second culture.

Of particular interest to sociologists is what occurs when different racial or ethnic groups come into contact with each other. It has been found that seven specific outcomes are possible: segregation, stratification, assimilation, pluralism, expulsion, annihilation, and amalgamation. All of these outcomes have occurred at various times in history.

In addition to noting the possible outcomes of interracial and interethnic contact, sociologists have indicated that such outcomes tend to occur sequentially. They have also found that power is a critical factor in determining patterns of interaction between racial and ethnic groups.

The task of predicting the future of race and ethnic relations either in this country or internationally is extremely difficult. What seems certain is that racial and ethnic groups will be a part of human interaction indefinitely, but that we are moving toward both assimilation and amalgamation.

Key Terms for Review

- amalgamation, p. 367
- annihilation, p. 367
- apartheid, p. 359
- assimilation, p. 360
- ethnic group, p. 356
- expulsion, p. 365
- genocide, p. 367
- manumission, p. 360
- marginal man, p. 362
- miscegenation, p. 378
- octoroon, p. 378
- passing, p. 360
- pluralism, p. 363
- prejudice, p. 378
- race, p. 355
- race relations cycles, p. 372
- segregation, p. 359
- stratification, p. 360

Suggested Readings

SOCIOLOGICAL

Allport, Gordon W. *The Nature of Prejudice*. New York: Doubleday Anchor, 1958; orig. 1954. This now classic investigation of the roots and manifestations of prejudice remains, more than twenty years after its publication, the major source for much contemporary research.

Botkin, B. A., ed. *Lay My Burden Down; A Folk History of Slavery*. Chicago: University of Chicago Press, 1945. The stories of slavery through the eyes of former slaves are presented in this transcription collected through government-sponsored writers' projects of the 1930s. Many readers find the firsthand portrayal of slavery to be both fascinating—because of the nuances of eye-witness accounts—and surprising—because of the often expressed mildness and pleasures of the slave experience.

DuBois, W. E. B. *The Souls of Black Folk*. Greenwich, Conn.: Fawcett, 1960; orig. 1903. This is the most famous collection of essays and stories of the black leader who was both civil rights advocate and sociologist. His often poignant and always gripping writings tell of his early days in America, of the first time he learned he was "different," and of the dual existence that American blacks must live.

Fanon, Frantz. *Black Skin, White Masks*. New York: Grove Press, 1967; orig. 1952. The book is an examination of the psychological and social psychological roots of racism and minority oppression by the black psychiatrist and revolutionary who has become a hero of many young intellectuals. Fanon's own experiences and insights are inextricably joined with his exploration of the minority position.

Lewis, Oscar. *La Vida*. New York: Vintage, 1965. Lewis, a famous cultural anthropologist, examines the Rios family in their journey from San Juan, Puerto Rico, to New York and their continued struggle with the culture of poverty. The author presents contemporary social scientific work in an appealing literary style. His presentation of the Rios family is not only good cultural anthropology and sociology, but fine literature as well.

Liebow, Elliot. *Tally's Corner*. Boston: Little, Brown, 1967. Liebow portrays the lives of the black men who inhabit an actual streetcorner of the urban slums of Washington, D.C. Liebow's observations and sensitive exploration of the marginally employed underclass of the black ghetto are highly regarded. *Tally's Corner* presents a penetrating account of the cultural and structural reasons for the deteriorating lives of the men it describes.

LITERARY

Brown, Claude. *Manchild in the Promised Land*. New York: New American Library, 1965. This essentially autobiographical account of Brown's coming of age in the urban American ghetto is one of the literary masterpieces of the genre. Brown's sensitive perceptions of the contemporary setting are most readable and brutally illuminating.

Kosinski, Jerzy. *The Painted Bird*. Boston: Houghton Mifflin, 1965. Kosinski's series of stories of oppression are often so finely painted that they serve perfectly to illustrate a number of sociological concepts.

Larson, Charles R., ed. *Prejudice*. Chicago: Mentor, 1971. This excellent collection of short stories relates various contexts and instances of racial and ethnic prejudice. Anatole France, Bernard Malamud, Albert Camus, W. E. B. DuBois, and Stephen Crane are among the authors included. The work is not just another reader, but an outstanding collection of fine literature.

Singer, Isaac Bashevis. *A Crown of Feathers and Other Stories*. New York: Farrar, Straus & Giroux, 1970. Singer is a widely read storyteller who has provided both entertainment and insight for many years with his tales of immigrants in their ethnic neighborhoods. This collection is a fair sampling of a marvelous writer.

Thomas, Piri. *Down These Mean Streets*. New York: Signet, 1967. This autobiographical sketch is similar in scope to *Manchild in the Promised Land*. Its setting is the *barrio* of Spanish Harlem. In an appealing and engaging story Thomas recounts his life as a young Puerto Rican who ultimately becomes a convict.

IN THIS CHAPTER

Explanations for Deviant and Criminal Behavior   389
    Pathology   389
    Differential association   390
    Social disorganization   393
    Labeling   394
    Value conflict   395

Deviant Behavior and Several of Its Forms   396
    Prostitution   398
    Homosexuality   400
    Alcoholism   402
    Mental illness   406

Crime and Several of Its Forms   408
    Criminal homicide   409
    White-collar crime   415
    Organized crime   417

Summary   421

Key Terms for Review   422

Suggested Readings   422

Do most homosexuals, alcoholics, and other "deviants" suffer because of their status? Do they want to "get straight"?
Is crime getting worse?
What is deviant? What is normal?
Do most violent crimes occur in slum areas?

16

DEVIANCE AND CRIME

Very often, for the individual who is labeled "deviant," the experience is painful and disorienting, but for those in the "straight" world, the life of the deviant is fascinating to witness. Most people would not care to have "deviants" for their neighbors, but rather enjoy them as subjects for television, movies, novels, and gossip.

Deviance is any behavior that transgresses or is in violation of accepted cultural norms. A *deviant* is anyone who violates a society's or a group's expectations. The types of deviant behavior are numerous—immorality, criminality, "perversion," freakishness, drug addiction, alcoholism, and prostitution are but a few. In *The Town and the City* Jack Kerouac has portrayed the "obvious" deviants in our society:

> Right across the street from here there's an amusement center . . . and there you have, at around four in the morning, the final scenes of disintegrative decay: old drunks, whores, queers, all kinds of characters, hoods, junkies, all the castoffs of bourgeois society milling in there with nothing to do really but just stay there, sheltered from the darkness as it were.[1]

Many of the studies during the 1920s conducted by the "Chicago school" of sociology (see chapter 1) investigated the behavior of deviants—for instance, taxi dancers (women employed by dance halls to dance with customers for a fee), jack-rollers (people who beat and rob [mug] residents of skid-row areas), hobos, and thieves. More recent sociological investigations, often employing the same approach used in the early Chicago studies, indicate a continuing interest in deviant behavior. Massage parlor patrons and employees, swinging couples, homosexuals,

The popularity of certain forms of "deviance" suggests that such behavior is not deviant after all. Yet cultural norms, not popularity, determine what is and what is not deviant behavior.

Most people agree that female impersonators are deviant.

faith healers, and strippers have been the subjects of these more recent investigations. Sociologists have tried to expose the social processes by which deviance is identified, the societal and cultural bases of the phenomenon, and the social-psychological impact of such behavior on the deviants themselves.

It is now generally understood that the same basic processes that produce "normal" behavior also produce deviant behavior. The particulars may vary from one type of deviance to another, but the essential processes of socialization are the same. Prostitutes, for instance, belong to primary groups, interact with others, are subjected to alienating social situations, and participate in various social institutions just as do members of the local Jaycees. Furthermore, contemporary scholars have come to recognize that deviance itself is not a clearly defined category.

Many people whose memories have dimmed with time like to recall the simpler days when it seemed easy to categorize behavior: hookers were hookers, perverts were perverts, criminals were criminals, and all such deviants were alien beings. Now vocal deviant subcultures announce that their behavior is not at all strange, that perhaps it is the "normal" world which is alien. People are also faced with several other equally bothersome considerations. If a criminal is simply one who breaks the law, we are virtually all criminals. The complexities of contemporary living make it most difficult not to break some laws; for example, most people violate traffic laws at one time or another. Furthermore, it has become disturbingly clear that the distance between "normality" and "sickness" is not always great. Daily exposure to news stories of child beatings, rates of alcoholism, Eagle Scouts turned killers, and "normal" people who ultimately are not normal at all has blurred the old lines of identification that made many so complacent.

Despite the increasing difficulty of identifying deviance with assurance, there is still some agreement on the categories of people who deserve the label "deviant." Table 16–1 shows typical responses to the question: Who is deviant?

TABLE 16–1
Most Frequent Responses to the Question
"Who is Deviant?"

Category	Considered Deviant by Respondents (percentage)
Male homosexuals	50
Drug addicts	43
Alcoholics	31
Murderers	25
Prostitutes	24
Lesbians	13
Mentally ill	13
Perverts	12
Politicians	10
Communists	10
Atheists	10
Political extremists	10

SOURCE: F. W. Preston and R. W. Smith, "Attitude Survey," Spring 1976.

Explanations for Deviant and Criminal Behavior

The most common explanations for deviance and crime offered by sociologists are pathology, differential association, social disorganization, labeling, and value conflict.* Each has at one time been the dominant theory on the cause of such behavior, and all continue to find supporters among scholars and students of human interaction.

PATHOLOGY

The earliest and for many people the most satisfying explanation for crime and deviance is pathology. *Social pathology* considers deviant behavior the result of a societal disease, a "sickness" which must be isolated, contained, and treated. *Biological pathology* maintains that deviance and crime result from actual physical illnesses, malfunctions, or deformities.

*For a discussion of several of these perspectives, see Martin S. Weinberg and Earl Rubington, eds., *The Solution to Social Problems* (New York: Oxford University Press, 1973).

In the nineteenth century skull size and shape were thought by many to determine a person's character and thus explain criminal and deviant behavior. This lad's skull is being examined to discover inherent traits.

The theory behind the treatment program of Alcoholics Anonymous (AA) is that alcoholism is both "a physical allergy and a mental compulsion"[2]; that is, that it results from both biological and social pathology. The recent suggestion that males with a record of violent crimes have an extra "male," or Y, chromosome in their genetic make up (XYY) rather than the usual configuration (XY) follows in the tradition of biological pathology made famous by Italian criminologists a century ago. At that time Cesare Lombroso and others thought that head size, slope of forehead, jaw size and protrusion, stature, and other such physical traits were crucial determinants of criminal behavior.

Pathology as an explanation for criminal and deviant behavior continues to be both popular and satisfying for several reasons, none of which is related to the possible validity of the perspective. First, pathological hypotheses are easily grasped. All of us understand physical disease; thus the explanation of sickness, whether physical or societal, is one that is quickly acknowledged. Second, and even more crucial, pathological hypotheses remove the element of culpability: no person or institution is really responsible. A successful and faithful member of the "normal" community confronted with the reality of crime and deviance need not feel responsible for it since such behavior is brought about by some physical or societal malady. For the deviant or criminal the pathological explanation also offers the sustenance of nonresponsibility: I am the victim, not the creator, of my circumstances; I am afflicted with an illness.

DIFFERENTIAL ASSOCIATION

Differential association, first suggested by Edwin Sutherland in the late 1930s, links crime and deviance to the individual's primary or reference groups or subculture: people learn to become criminals or deviants because of an overabundance of associations with criminal or deviant behavior patterns. The main assumptions of this explanation are:

1. Criminal behavior, whether in the form of habitual, professional, organized, or white-collar crime, must be learned.
2. Social interaction and communication are central to the learning process.
3. Criminal behavior is acquired through personal participation in groups, as opposed to simple contact with mass media and formal agencies or institutions.
4. The learning process involves the acquisition of techniques for committing crimes and the formation of new attitudes, motives, drives, and forms of rationalization; criminality evidenced is systematically reinforced.
5. Delinquency occurs because norms favorable to violation of the law exceed norms unfavorable to violation of the law. These definitions, however, are usually reinforced by the group commitments or the relationships which the individual has established.
6. Whether or not an individual will commit criminal acts depends on how much contact he or she has with a group that accepts or approves such acts.

7. All the mechanisms of learning are involved in learning criminal or anti-criminal behavior.
8. Criminal and noncriminal behavior are both expressions of individual or group needs and/or values.[3]

In a similar vein Albert Cohen, in *Delinquent Boys: The Culture of the Gang*, has proposed that delinquent subcultures are very far removed from the culture of the larger society. The gang promotes adventure and adrenaline-producing thrills; that is, it ignores the values of deferred gratification and work while promoting lawlessness and short-run hedonism. The gang thus influences adolescent behavior by providing its own social norms.[4]

Other sociologists have suggested that such delinquent and other criminal behavior may be more appropriately related to *differential opportunity*. The phrase refers to the greater opportunity that certain individuals have, by reason of their social class or racial and ethnic affiliation, to become involved in criminal activities. In *Delinquency and Opportunity* Richard Cloward and Lloyd Ohlin state:

> *If an illegal (criminal) structure is not readily available in a given social location, a criminal subculture is not likely to develop among adolescents. If violence offers a primary channel to higher status in a community, greater participation by juveniles in conflict (violence) will normally occur.*[5]

Delinquent subcultures sometimes have quite formal ways of inducting new members. Charles Dickens's portrayal of Fagin's "school" of crime in *Oliver Twist* provides an example:

> "Well," said the Jew [Fagin], glancing slyly at Oliver, and addressing himself to the Dodger, "I hope you've been at work this morning my dears?"
> "Hard," replied the Dodger.
> "As Nails," added Charley Bates.

Today group norms are considered a major factor in determining behavior patterns, whether criminal or noncriminal. The norms of delinquent subcultures, for instance, are often quite different from those of the larger society.

"Good boys, good boys!" said the Jew. "What have you got, Dodger?"

"A couple of pocket-books," replied the young gentleman.

"Lined?" inquired the Jew, with eagerness.

"Pretty well," replied the Dodger, producing two pocket-books; one green and the other red.

"Not so heavy as they might be," said the Jew, after looking at the insides carefully; "but very neat and nicely made. Ingenious workman, ain't he, Oliver?"

"Very, indeed, sir," said Oliver. At which Mr. Charles Bates laughed uproariously; very much to the amazement of Oliver, who saw nothing to laugh at, in anything that had passed.

"And what have you got, my dear?" said Fagin to Charley Bates.

"Wipes," replied Master Bates; at the same time producing four pocket-handkerchiefs.

"Well," said the Jew, inspecting them closely; "they're very good ones, very. You haven't marked them well, though, Charley; so the marks shall be picked out with a needle, and we'll teach Oliver how to do it. Shall us, Oliver, eh? Ha! ha! ha!"

"If you please, sir," said Oliver.

"You'd like to be able to take pocket-handkerchiefs as easy as Charley Bates, wouldn't you, my dear?" said the Jew.

"Very much, indeed, if you'll teach me, sir," replied Oliver.

Master Bates saw something so exquisitely ludicrous in this reply that he burst into another laugh; which laugh, meeting the coffee he was drinking, and carrying it down some wrong channel, very nearly terminated in his premature suffocation.

"He is so jolly green!" said Charley when he recovered, as an apology to the company for his impolite behavior.

The Dodger said nothing, but he smoothed Oliver's hair over his eyes, and said he'd know better, by-and-by; upon which the old gentleman, observing Oliver's colour mounting, changed the subject by asking whether there had been much of a crowd at the execution that morning? This made him wonder more and more; for it was plain from the replies of the two boys that they had both been there; and Oliver naturally wondered how they could possibly have found time to be so very industrious.

When the breakfast was cleared away, the merry old gentleman and the two boys played at a very curious and uncommon game, which was performed in this way. The merry gentleman, placing a snuff-box in one pocket of his trousers, a note-case in the other, and a watch in his waistcoat pocket, with a guard-chain round his neck, and sticking a mock diamond pin in his shirt; buttoned his coat tight round him, and putting his spectacle-case and handkerchief in his pockets, trotted up and down the room with a stick, in imitation of the manner in which old gentlemen walk about the streets any hour *in the day. Sometimes he stopped at the fire-place, and sometimes at the door, making believe that he was staring with all his might into shop-windows. At such times he would look constantly round him, for fear of thieves, and would keep slapping all his pockets in turn, to see that he hadn't lost anything, in such a very funny and natural manner, that Oliver laughed till the tears ran down his face. All this time, the two boys followed him closely about: getting out of his sight, so nimbly, every time he turned round, that it was impossible to follow their motions. At last, the Dodger trod upon his toes, or ran upon his boot accidentally, while Charley Bates stumbled up against him behind; and in that one moment they took from him, with the most extraordinary rapidity, snuff-box, note-case, watch-guard, chain, shirt-pin, pocket-handkerchief, even the spectacle-case. If the old gentleman felt a hand in any one of his pockets, he cried out where it was; and then the game began all over again.*[6]

The training received by most of today's delinquents is not quite so studied and organized as that of Fagin's school, yet the socialization processes that produce youthful lawbreakers remain very effective.

SOCIAL DISORGANIZATION

A third explanation for criminal and deviant behavior is *social disorganization*. As noted in chapter 4, social disorganization involves a disruption of the normative system. Social disorganization may take the form of culture conflict, normlessness, or a breakdown of the system.

Culture conflict suggests that deviant and criminal behavior results when two normative systems come into contact. Member expectations in one system differ from those in the other, and actions outside the dominant normative system appear deviant. For instance, Eastern European men commonly kiss each other as a form of greeting. Such behavior is outside the normative system in the United States, and anyone practicing it here would most likely be thought of as deviant.

Folk wisdom offers many explanations for crime and deviance which fall under the general title of normlessness: idle hands are the devil's workshop; give a boy a bat and a ball and he'll never cause trouble; he did it because he just didn't have anything better to do. Crime is perceived as resulting from a condition of confusion or an indolent drift, while deviance, almost by definition, results when no norms specify behavior.

Finally, social disorganization can occur when there is a breakdown of the system; that is, when adherence to cultural expectations does not yield the anticipated consequences. You work hard, but receive few rewards; or, as the lyrics of a Country and Western hit once phrased it, "You work your fingers to the bone and what do you get? Bony fingers." If the normative system does not function, an obvious solution to your difficulties is to work outside the system.

LABELING

The explanation of deviant behavior most favored in contemporary sociology is labeling theory, an approach first articulated by Edwin Lemert and later formalized by Howard S. Becker.[7] *Labeling theory* contends that what defines criminal or deviant behavior is not the action itself, but the perception of such action by others or by the actors themselves. Studies utilizing the labeling approach concentrate on (1) the system, group, or individual that affixes the label "criminal" or "deviant" and (2) the consequences for the person so labeled. A crucial variable is the power of the labeler. If an individual or group is not powerful enough effectively to affix the deviant label on a person displaying some out-of-the-ordinary behavior, then no consequences will follow.

Another important aspect of labeling theory concerns the perceptions of individuals whose actions deviate from the norm. While many deviants are forced into such a status by very powerful labelers, for instance, a judge who may sentence them to ten years in the state prison, a more sensitive individual may be horrified and stricken by a raised eyebrow, a frown, or an imagined glance. Kurt Vonnegut, Jr., in *Breakfast of Champions*, depicts such a reaction.

> *Dwayne Hoover told poor Harry LeSabre that the Hawaiian Festival, only a long weekend away, was Harry's golden opportunity to loosen up, to have some fun, to encourage other people to have some fun, too.*
>
> *"Harry," said Dwayne. "I have some news for you: modern science has given us a whole lot of wonderful new colors, with strange exciting names like red! orange! green! and pink!, Harry. We're not stuck anymore with just black, gray, and white! Isn't that good news, Harry? And the State Legislature has just announced that it is no longer a crime to smile during working hours, Harry, and I have the personal promise of the Governor that never again will anybody be sent to the Sexual Offender's Wing of the Adult Correctional Institution for telling a joke!"*
>
> *Harry LeSabre might have weathered all this with only minor damage, if only Harry hadn't been a secret transvestite. On weekends he liked to dress up in women's clothing, and not drab clothing either. Harry and his wife would pull down the window blinds, and Harry would turn into a bird of paradise.*
>
> *Nobody but Harry's wife knew his secret.*
>
> *When Dwayne razzed him about the clothes he wore to work, and then mentioned the Sexual Offender's Wing of the Adult Correctional Institution at Shepherdstown, Harry had to suspect that his secret was out. And it wasn't merely a comical secret, either. Harry could*

be arrested for what he did on weekends. He could be fined up to three thousand dollars and sentenced to as much as five years hard labor in the Sexual Offender's Wing of the Adult Correctional Institution of Shepherdstown. So poor Harry spent a wretched Veterans' Day weekend after that. . . .

Harry and his wife had spent all weekend arguing about whether or not Dwayne suspected that Harry was a transvestite. They concluded that Dwayne had no reason to suspect it. Harry never talked about women's clothes to Dwayne. He had never entered a transvestite beauty contest or done what a lot of transvestites in Midland City did, which was join a big transvestite club over in Cincinnati. He never went into the city's transvestite bar, which was Ye Old Rathskeller, in the basement of the Fairchild Hotel. He had never exchanged Polaroid pictures with any other transvestites, had never subscribed to a transvestite magazine.

Harry and his wife concluded that Dwayne had meant nothing more than what he said, that Harry had better put on some wild clothes for Hawaiian Week, or Dwayne would can him.

So here was the new Harry now, rosy with fear and excitement. He felt uninhibited and beautiful and suddenly free.

He greeted Dwayne with the Hawaiian word which meant both hello and goodbye. "Aloha," he said. . . .

When Dwayne Hoover saw Harry LeSabre, his sales manager, in leaf-green leotards and a grass skirt and all that, he could not believe it. So he made himself not see it. He went into his office which was also cluttered with ukeleles and pineapples.

Harry LeSabre, meanwhile, had been destroyed by Dwayne.

When Harry presented himself to Dwayne so ridiculously, every molecule in his body awaited Dwayne's reaction. Each molecule ceased its business for a moment, put some distance between itself and its neighbors. Each molecule waited to learn whether its galaxy, which was called Harry LeSabre, would or would not be dissolved.

When Dwayne treated Harry as though he were invisible, Harry thought he had revealed himself as a revolting transvestite, and that he was fired on that account.

Harry closed his eyes. He never wanted to open them again. His heart sent this message to his molecules: "For reasons obvious to us all, this galaxy is dissolved!"[8]

VALUE CONFLICT

The theory of value conflict has been a sometimes revolutionary part of varying intellectual traditions for many centuries. Karl Marx was the most influential advocate of the theory, although others such as Georg Simmel and Ludwig Gumplowicz (1838–1910) have also captured large followings. This perspective includes aspects of social disorganization, labeling, and differential association. *Value conflict theory* holds that acts are considered criminal or deviant because they are at variance with a group's values. Also implied and very often stated as a part of the theory is the assumption that what is valued by one group is not valued by another. The ultimate determinant, then, of whether some act is deviant or criminal is the orientation or interest of the group that is offering the definition. In *Soul on Ice* Eldridge Cleaver writes:

> *Which laws get enforced depends on who is in power. If the capitalists are in power, they enforce laws designed to protect their system, their way of life. They have a particular abhorrence for crimes against property, but are prepared to be liberal and show a modicum of compassion for crimes against the person—unless, of course, an instance of the latter is combined with an instance of the former. In such cases, nothing can stop them from throwing the whole book at the offender. For instance, armed robbery with violence to a capitalist, is the very epitome of evil. Ask any banker what he thinks of it.*
>
> *If Communists are in power, they enforce laws designed to protect their system, their way of life. To them, the horror of horrors is the speculator, that man of magic who has mastered the art of getting something with nothing and who in America would be a member in good standing of his local Chamber of Commerce.*
>
> *"The People," however, are nowhere consulted, although everywhere everything is done always in their names and ostensibly for their betterment, while their real-life problems go unsolved. "The people" are a rubber stamp for the crafty and sly. And no problem can be solved without taking the police department and the armed forces into account. Both kings and bookies understand this, as do first ladies and common prostitutes.*[9]

Deviant Behavior and Several of Its Forms

Whatever the major cause of a particular deviant act, the ultimate effect upon individual deviants is realized through perception—their own and that of those around them. As we have seen, interaction among individuals determines what is perceived as real, and in the instance of deviant behavior, perceptions of "reality" can and do vary. To borrow a phrase, there is a confusion of fruits: some people think they are oranges, but they are really apples. Sociologists therefore distinguish between primary and secondary deviants.

Primary deviants are persons who "engage in deviant acts but continue to occupy a conventional status and role" and are able to think of such acts "as a function of a socially acceptable role."[10] Thus, whenever individuals do not perceive themselves as deviants, as playing a deviant role, they remain primary deviants. Yet as soon as they begin to accept a deviant status, and when they are recognized by others as deviants, they become career deviants, or *secondary deviants*.

Table 16-2 shows that the line between primary and secondary deviance, as the condition is called, is not always clear, nor is the acceptance of a deviant role always immediate. A petty bureaucrat who "borrows" from a fund he administers is a primary deviant. It may never occur to him or anyone else that he is a deviant, that he is, in fact, an embezzler. Throughout his career he may use the small monetary resources that he administers as a kind of personal loan fund and never get caught with accounts not matching. But if the auditors arrive unexpectedly and he is discovered, the borrower becomes an embezzler, the primary deviant becomes a secondary deviant. He is now identified by others and ultimately by himself as outside the conventional role of petty bureaucrat.

Such a duality of roles exists in all forms of deviant behavior, and the percentage of deviants who never become secondary deviants is high. There are several reasons for this. Secondary deviance is a role that individuals anticipate being uncomfortable with, that they fear, that others do not accept, or that just does not seem possible. The data from current sociological research suggest fairly unanimously that deviants in our society are often unable or unwilling to accept society's labels for them-

TABLE 16-2
Perception of Primary and Secondary Deviance

Behavior	Societal View	Self-Perception	Perception of Individual by Others	Kind of Deviance
"Borrower" from a fund	Unclear: not criminal in most instances	Nondeviant	Nondeviant	Primary
"Closet" homosexual	Deviant: sometimes in criminal code	Some deviant, some nondeviant	Nondeviant	Primary
Alcoholic	Deviant: specific acts in criminal code	Some deviant, some nondeviant	Some deviant, some nondeviant	Some primary, some secondary
"Drag queen"	Deviant: often in criminal code	Deviant	Deviant	Secondary

selves. A closer examination of several of the obvious forms of deviance should give a more complete understanding of this phenomenon.

PROSTITUTION

The world's "oldest profession" is certainly not currently viewed as its most noble profession. American attitudes toward prostitution are quite different from the views of the ancient Greeks, whose temples of Aphrodite were built and maintained by the earnings of "priestess-prostitutes" charged with ministering to both the spiritual and physical needs of the worshipers.[11] For most people in the United States and most other industrialized nations, the role of prostitute is one of deviance and low status. Although there have been a number of studies of varying aspects of the profession, including investigations by reputable scholars, reliable data are most difficult to obtain.* It is not easy to determine what percentage of "working women" are primary deviants who, for example, view themselves as actresses or models simply "picking up" a little supplementary income.

What does seem clear is that a majority of women who engage in sexual relations for monetary reward do not consider themselves to be "common prostitutes." Within the profession there is a stratification system directly related to the system of rewards. At the pinnacle are high-priced call girls whose clientele pay very well for their services. A call girl may work for others (a high-priced pimp) or be relatively independent. She may or may not be a career, or secondary, deviant. Despite the often imposing income that she commands by being at the zenith of her profession, the high-priced call girl may consider herself an actress, a model, or simply an interesting and witty companion.[12]

As one moves down the status scale of prostitution—passing from the lesser call girls, to the working girls who are part of a "stable" (the prostitutes working for a pimp or madam), and finally to the flagrant streetwalkers who tap on car windows at stoplights—the chances of finding women who have accepted the role of secondary deviance increase, but they still are uncertain.[13] Secretaries and teachers who become "chippies" (amateur prostitutes) as they travel to Las Vegas for the weekend do not consider themselves anything other than secretaries and teachers who earn a little extra money on the side.

Although many women who are paid for sexual services never accept the role of call girl or prostitute, some do. Yet the move may be both subtle and unsettling. One of America's most famous prostitutes, Xaviera Hollander, the "Happy Hooker" of the book by the same name, tells, perhaps

---

*Two of the more notable investigations have been Kingsley Davis, "Prostitution," in R. K. Merton and R. A. Nisbet, eds., *Contemporary Social Problems* (New York: Harcourt Brace Jovanovich, 1971), pp. 262–288; and Alfred C. Kinsey, Wardell B. Pomeroy, and Clyde E. Martin, *Sexual Behavior in the Human Male* (Philadelphia: W. B. Saunders, 1948), pp. 595–604.

with some imagination, of her own initial faltering steps toward the career role:

> Evelyn was witty, urbane, generous—everything Carl and the others were not.
>
> For the next week I spent the days dreaming about the nights. After work each day I would float across the half-block between my office and the Hilton to meet my lover for romantic dinners, movies, Broadway shows, and passion. It was a fantastic relationship, sexual and cerebral, and no wonder I was in love—or thought I was—and showed it in every way.
>
> But Evelyn had another way of demonstrating his feeling for me. A way I have since learned is typical of people of his breeding and background, and, to my horror, he exposed me to it toward the end of the week after a romantic dawn.
>
> I remember vividly the setting for the conversation that was to change the entire course of my straight and simple life. He was leaning back against the pillow, and I was cradled in his arms.
>
> "Xaviera," he began in his slow, Oxford-accented English. "I can never tell you in words just how wonderful you have made this week in New York."
>
> I shuddered at the reminder that today was Friday and on Sunday he would leave. "To show you what you have meant, I have something for you," he went on.
>
> "What is it?" I asked dreamily. I was always on a cloud after we made love.
>
> "Here," he said, and handed me a hundred-dollar bill.
>
> I froze. I was shocked, hurt, and speechless with anger. At least if this was not love on his part he had no right to make it seem like prostitution.
>
> My mother had always told me not to accept money from any man except the man I marry. "If a friend insists on giving you something, ask for flowers or chocolates," was her advice.
>
> "Evelyn," I said when the numbness wore off, "you make me feel like a whore. I don't want your hundred dollars; here it is, please take it back."
>
> He was genuinely surprised, but he still persisted. "Xaviera, I know you are supporting your parents, so take it and at least give it to them." He took an envelope from the drawer, asked me to address it to their home in Holland, put the money inside, got dressed, and went out to mail it. That made me feel better because I did not use the money myself.
>
> Next day Evelyn took me to Saks and bought me $800 worth of dresses, shoes, and handbags and whatever I wanted. And, this, to me, was the really tremendous gesture of a gentleman, and he was the first man who ever bought me anything of value.[14]

A streetwalker plying her trade.

For those who do accept the role of deviant, there is a subculture and accompanying ideology which views prostitution as one of the very few honest occupations in the world. According to this ideology, prostitutes are not a part of the complex hypocrisy of contemporary marriage in which women exchange sex for the privileges of being housed, clothed, and fed. Marriage is seen as a relationship of pay for sex without the honesty of prostitution. The often repeated slogan is that "all women are sitting on a gold mine."[15]

COYOTE (Call Off Your Old Tired Ethics), the recently formed association of prostitutes centered in San Francisco, provides a common forum for prostitutes to articulate their difficulties and to voice the values they hold. By appearing on local and network television talk shows, leaders of COYOTE have forced many to address questions on the status of prostitution. They have also presumably assisted some of their sister practitioners to move from primary to secondary deviance.

HOMOSEXUALITY

Though professional groups such as the American Psychological Association no longer view homosexuality as a psychological problem, homosexuals still face many difficulties in American society and continue to be perceived as deviant by a majority of the population. *Homosexuality* refers to sexual desire or behavior directed toward a person or persons of one's own sex. But the simplicity and conciseness of this standard definition fades upon further inquiry.

First, homosexuality usually refers to male sexual behavior (and we will use it in that sense in this discussion); female homosexuality is specified as *lesbianism*. Second, the problem arises, as it always seems to in examining deviance, of delineating just who is a homosexual. Depending on one's perspective, it is possible to view anywhere from 4 percent to nearly 100 percent of the male population as homosexual. The 4 percent figure refers to those with "genuine inversion"—or exclusive homosexuality—and the 100 percent figure encompasses those with passing and non-acted-upon desires.[16] The most commonly used data are those of Alfred Kinsey and associates, which state that 37 percent of the white male adult population in the United States have engaged in some form of overt homosexual behavior; that 25 percent of the same population have had more than incidental homosexual experience; that 18 percent have had as much homosexual as heterosexual experience; that 10 percent are almost exclusively homosexual in their behavior; and that 4 percent spend their entire lives as homosexuals.[17]

Like other forms of deviant behavior, homosexuality carries with it a stigma that prevents many from recognizing and accepting their deviant roles. Laud Humphreys's now classic study, *Tearoom Trade: Impersonal Sex in Public Places,* suggests that the majority of practicing homosexuals are primary deviants.[18] Humphreys's data are drawn from his own partici-

The gay liberation movement has enabled many homosexuals to accept their deviant role—to move from primary to secondary deviance.

pant-observation studies undertaken in 1966 and 1967. During this period he posed as a "watchqueen," which is a homosexual who serves as a lookout in "tearooms" (public restrooms). Humphreys specified five types of homosexuals: (1) trade homosexuals, (2) ambisexuals, (3) gay guys, (4) closet queens, and (5) adolescent male hustlers.

The "trade homosexuals" composed 38 percent of Humphreys's sample and were described as married or formerly married working-class men, primarily truck drivers and machine operators. Trade homosexuals do not consider themselves deviant and in no way identify with the subculture that openly avows the value of homosexuality. They seek sexual gratification that is more satisfying than masturbation and less expensive than a prostitute.

"Ambisexuals," who constituted 24 percent of the sample, were predominantly middle- and upper-class men who often considered themselves capable of enjoying sexual relations with both men and women. They often perceived their behavior as deviant but would not accept the label "homosexual." They also saw themselves as talented and sensitive, often identifying with famous artists and actors who shared their predilection.

The "gay guys," 14 percent of the sample, are unmarried homosexuals who openly proclaim their deviant behavior. They constitute a larger percentage of the homosexual world than the sample shows since their involvement in the homosexual subculture usually takes them to places other than the clandestine meetings of the tearoom. The gay guys have fully accepted their role and are secondary deviants. Like others in similar positions, they have taken on the supportive ideology of their perspective and are able to cite highly respected individuals who shared their behavior—Socrates, Plato, Michelangelo, Julius Caesar, Walt Whitman, Oscar Wilde, Marcel Proust, Frederick the Great, and Christopher Marlowe, among others. It is this gay subculture that frequents the bars, cafés, and restaurants of such communities as San Francisco's Polk Street.

Ten percent of the tearoom trade were "closet queens," men who engage in homosexual acts and have homosexual feelings but are unable to admit to themselves that they are homosexual. Finally, a small number of "hustlers"—male prostitutes, or "midnight cowboys," who charge for their participation in homosexual behavior—were also observed. They too do not perceive themselves as deviants, merely as wage earners. Their participation is for profit and not for sexual gratification.

As with other forms of deviance, the impact of the label upon the individual may be profound, particularly for a secondary deviant who is attempting to live a life other than that defined by the confining bounds of the homosexual role. Merle Miller, for example, once told of his mother's great relief upon hearing that his latest book would *not* deal with his own world of homosexuality. In this excerpt from an article entitled "What It Means to Be a Homosexual," Miller gives a disturbing and poignant account of his experience at an "enlightened" and urbane gathering:

A little while after the dance began a man whose face had been only vaguely familiar and whose name I would not have remembered if he had not earlier reminded me came up, an idiot grin on his face, his wrists limp, his voice falsetto, and said, "How about letting me have this dance, sweetie?" He said it loud for all to hear. . . . Later, several people apologized for what he had said, but I wondered (who would not?) how many of them had been tempted to say the same thing. Or would say something of the kind after I had gone. Fag, faggot, sissy, queer. A fag is a homosexual gentleman who has just left the room.

The fear of it simply will not go away, though. A man who was once a friend, maybe my best friend, the survivor of five marriages, the father of nine, not too long ago told me that his eldest son was coming to my house on Saturday: "Now please try not to make a pass at him." He laughed. I guess he meant it as a joke: I didn't ask.[19]

ALCOHOLISM

Estimates of the number of alcoholics in the United States range from 5 to 10 million, with most experts favoring the higher figure.[20] Yet obviously most liquor addicts do not apply the label "alcoholic" to themselves. Rather, they see themselves as social drinkers; or, if they have had personal problems and others have suggested that they are problem drinkers, they may describe themselves as heavy drinkers. Alcoholics, like homosexuals, rationalize their behavior by pointing to past creative talents who were heavy drinkers—Edgar Allan Poe, Ernest Hemingway, Jack London, H. L. Mencken, O. Henry, F. Scott Fitzgerald, and many others.[21]

As with other forms of deviance, there is debate over the definition of alcoholism. Alcoholics Anonymous defines it as "a mental compulsion and a physical allergy" but allows anyone into its program who claims the label "alcoholic." There are also highly complex inventories of symptoms used to define the term, and the American Medical Association has laid down certain physically diagnosable criteria.

The stigma of alcoholism prevents most from accepting the label. If one uses the figure (given by the Department of Health, Education, and Welfare) of 9.6 million alcoholics in the United States and compares it with the estimated figure of 800,000 members in the most successful treatment program, Alcoholics Anonymous, it seems that most alcoholics continue to drink. According to AA, most practicing alcoholics disclaim any problem with alcohol despite continuing physical deterioration and the loss of jobs, money, family, and friends.[22] Jack B., a member of AA and a "recovered alcoholic," tells of his final "bottom," the point at which he moved from primary to secondary deviance:

Skid row alcoholics are easily identified, but many problem drinkers do not consider themselves alcoholics and are protected from the deviant label.

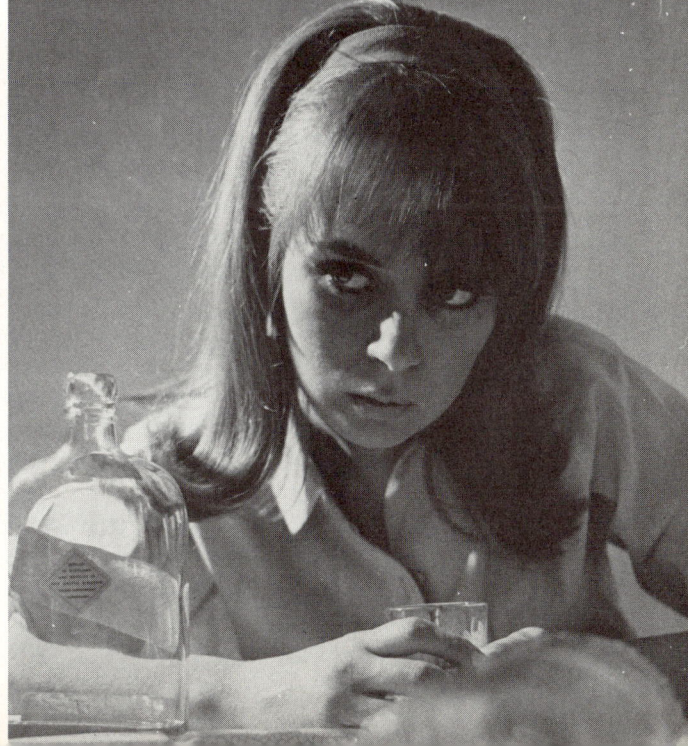

> One morning I went into a bar to take my morning drink, into a filthy bathroom in a Bowery bar. And I took a drink of wine that I had in a bottle. It was 15¢ for a pint. And I had about half a bottle and I'd slept with it like it was a baby and I'd guarded it all night cause I'd need it in the morning. And I took my morning drink and I threw it up, and I threw half my stomach with it. I had hemorrhages of the stomach and I was so weak that I fell down and hooked my chin on the toilet bowl and I said, "My God what now." I watched myself literally running down the toilet bowl and I looked at the bottle in my hand and said, "It's got to be this," because I couldn't blame nothin' else no more and I threw it over my shoulder and I said, "I don't want to live no more, why do I fight?" So I resigned myself to die, don't you see.
>
> I crawled out of that bathroom some seven or eight hours later and I begged somebody to call A.A. for me and they did. And I don't know who it was to this minute, but I remember somebody kept saying in my ear, "Sit down and don't wander away, because I did call em and they're comin'." And I had to sit there and forcibly keep myself sitting because you see the alcoholic sits here, but his mind is there. He don't know where his body is goin' even, following what he's thinkin'. Now I had to be very careful that I was not following a will o' the wisp as an alcoholic does in the condition I was in. And I had to keep there, "they're comin', they're comin', they're comin'." Then I had to reassure myself, "Ya, I did hear it. It wasn't some noise. It wasn't some dream. They're comin'." And I tried to wipe some of the blood off myself and I tried to look like a human being, but how could you. Hair down your neck, no shoes, no socks, no underwear. A pair of filthy pants and a filthy shirt, that's all I owned in this world. Then A.A. came. Now I'd always bragged about being an Irish Catholic and I thought the guy comin' would at least be named Murphy or O'Callahan or somethin'. And my sponsor came through the door and the first thing he said to me was, "My God." And the second thing he said was, "Well, that's all right." He said, "My name is Sam Cohen, and I'm here to help you." He said something that I longed so much to hear. He said, "You come with us Jack and you don't have to drink no more and you'll be all right."[23]

As is illustrated in Jack's description, the acceptance of being an alcoholic is crucial to the recovery program of AA, and this has been attested by sociological studies.[24] Yet the acceptance of the deviant role is not sufficient to guarantee recovery. Indeed, acceptance of the role sometimes reinforces behavior. There is even evidence that some people on skid row who have had no previous drinking problem become alcoholics to meet the deviant role expectations of their residence.[25] Others accept their plight, unable or unwilling to remedy it. Upton Sinclair in "Love's Pilgrimage" recalls his own youth and his father—a hopeless alcoholic:

It was the highway of lost men.

They shivered, and drew their shoulders together as they walked, for it was night, and a cold, sleety rain was falling. The lights from saloons and pawnshops fell upon their faces—faces haggard and gaunt with misery, or bloated with disease. Some stared before them fixedly; some gazed about with furtive and hungry eyes as they shuffled on. Here and there a policeman stood in the shelter, swinging his club and watching them as they passed. Music called to them from dives and dance-halls, and lighted signs and flaring-colored pictures tempted them in entrances of cheap "museums" and theatres; they lingered before these, glad of even a moment's shelter. Overhead the elevated trains pounded by; and from the windows one could see men crowded about the stoves in the rooms of the lodging houses, where the steam from their garments made a blur in the air.

Down the highway walked a lad, about fifteen years of age, pale of face. His overcoat was buttoned tightly about his neck, and his hands thrust into his pockets; he gazed around him swiftly as he walked. He came to this place every now and then, but he never grew used to what he saw.

He eyed the men who passed him; and when he came to a saloon he would push open the door and gaze about. Sometimes he would enter, and hurry through, to peer into the compartments in the back; and then go out again, giving a wide berth to the drinkers, and shrinking from their glances. Once a girl appeared in a doorway, and smiled and nodded to him. Her wanton black eyes haunted him, hinting unimaginable things.

Then, on a corner, he stopped and spoke to a policeman. "Hello!" said the man, and shook his head—"No, not this time." So the boy went on; there were several miles of this highway, and each block of it was the same.

At last, in a dingy bar-room, with saw-dust strewn upon the floor, and the odor of stale beer and tobacco-smoke in the air—here suddenly the boy sprang forward, with a cry: "Father!" And a man who sat with bowed head in a corner gave a start, and lifted a white face and stared at him. The man rose unsteadily to his feet, and staggered to the other; and fell upon his shoulder, sobbing.

The man clung to him, weeping and pouring out the flood of his shame. "I have fallen again. I am lost, my son, I am lost!"

The occupants of the place were watching the scene with dull curiosity; and the boy was trembling like a wild deer trapped. "You must come home."

"You still love me, son?"

"Yes, Father, I still love you. I want to help you. Come with me."

Then the boy would gaze about and ask, "Where is your hat?"

"Hat? I don't know. I have lost it." The boy would see the torn and mud-stained clothing, the poor old pitiful face, eyes bloodshot and swollen; and the skin that once had been rosy was now a ghastly, ashen gray. He would choke back his feelings, and grip his hands to keep himself together.

"Come, Father, take my hat, and let us go."

"No, my son. I don't need any hat. Nothing can hurt me—I am lost! Lost!"

So they would go out again, arm in arm; and while they made their progress up the highway, the man would pour out his remorse, and tell the story of his weeks of horror.

Then, after a mile or so, he would halt.

"My son!"

"What is it, Father?"

"I must have something to drink."

"No, Father!"

"But, my boy, I can't go on! I can't walk! You don't know what I'm suffering!"

"No, Father!"

"I've got the money left—I'm not asking you, I'll come right with you—on my word of honor I will!"

And so they would fight it out—all the way back to the lodging house where they lived, and where the mother sat and wept. And here they would put him to bed, and lock up his clothing to keep him in; and here with drugs and mineral-waters, and perhaps a doctor to help, they would struggle with him, and tend him until he was on his feet again. Then with clothing newly-brushed and face newly-shaven, he would go back to the world of men; and the boy would go back to his dreams.[26]

The "disease concept" of alcoholism is amply illustrated by both the personal recollections of Jack B. and the boyhood memories of Sinclair. Alcoholics very often do not like themselves and have tremendous difficulty maintaining a positive self-image. They struggle with their illness under social conditions that define them as deviants who are personally responsible for their plight. The more recent recognition of alcoholism as a disease will hopefully encourage people such as Jack B. and Sinclair's father to seek help.

MENTAL ILLNESS

The term "mental illness" shares a negative connotation with other terms we use to label deviance. It carries with it an often deadening stigma, one that may sentence the bearer to a life of disgrace and inhuman neglect in the wards of a state mental hospital. And, like the preceding examples of deviance we discussed, it is difficult to define precisely. Depending on the criteria, one finds estimates of mental illness in the United States ranging from 1 to 64 percent.[27] Less than 1 percent of the population is hospitalized for mental disorders, but some researchers feel that almost two-thirds of the population suffer from at least mild emotional upsets and anxieties. As in the case of alcoholism, there is substantial evidence indicating that the basis for some mental disorders is physical. Yet despite this evidence, most people perceive mental illness as something quite apart from a physical disorder. When one is accused of being, "sick in the head," the implied cure is usually not medicinal.

Thomas Szasz, a New York psychiatrist, has suggested that such a position may indeed be correct.[28] He feels that there is no physical basis for most types of mental illness and that those who are labeled "mentally ill" are placed in that category because they are deviant to the point of being unable to operate within acceptable bounds. Mental illness, for Szasz, is primarily the result of the labeling process. People are considered mentally ill if they do not fit in. Whereas once we might have called such people witches, today we refer to them as psychotic. Other scholars strongly disagree with Szasz. They note that relabeling seems to have no effect with many individuals, such as schizophrenics, and that chemical and vitamin imbalances are obviously involved in many types of mental disorder.[29]

Wherever reality lies, and one must suspect that both explanations have validity in a variety of cases, the shift from primary to secondary deviance for the mentally ill is trying and often postponed. Most people who are mentally ill do not accept the label. This is particularly obvious when we note that a study of midtown Manhattan concluded that "marked, severe, and incapacitating" symptoms of mental illness were present in 23.4 percent of the population.[30] Individuals may see themselves as troubled with anxiety, or perhaps charmingly neurotic, but not mentally ill.

Hannah Green, in *I Never Promised You a Rose Garden*, offers a moving portrayal of mental illness in contemporary America. In the following excerpt sixteen-year-old Deborah Blau finally perceives herself to be mentally ill:

> *She was terrified of the Disturbed Ward, from which all pretensions to comfort and normalcy had been removed. Women were sitting bolt upright in their chairs, and sitting and lying on the floor—moaning and mute and raging—and the ward's nurses and attendants had big, hard, muscular bodies. It was somehow terrifying and somehow comforting in a way that was more than the comfort of the finality of being there. Looking out of a window barred and screened like a fencer's mask, she waited to find out why there seemed to be some subtle good about this frightening place.*
>
> *A woman had come up behind her. "You're scared, aren't you?"*
> *"Yes."*
> *"I'm Lee."*

"An attendant or something?"

"Hell no, I'm a psychotic like you. . . . Yes, you are; we all are."

The woman was small, dark-haired, and troubled, but she had looked out of herself far enough to see another's fear, and, being a patient, had all the direct and immediate access that no staff member could attain. She has courage, Deborah thought. I might have belted her one, for all she knew. And Deborah suddenly knew what was good about D ward: no more lying gentility or need to live according to the incomprehensible rules of Earth. When the blindness came, or the hard knots of pain from the nonexistent tumor, or the Pit, no one would say, "What will people think!" "Be ladylike," or "Don't make a fuss!"[31]

It was at this point, at the instant of moving into a full acceptance of secondary deviance, that Deborah found the relief that comes with the support of a deviant subculture. Like the alcoholic who admits his problem and joins AA, or the homosexual who openly enters the gay community, or the prostitute who is comforted by the assertive stance of COYOTE, young and painfully isolated Deborah was no longer alone.

Crime and Several of Its Forms

Unlike the forms of deviance we have discussed, crime is very clearly specified. A *crime* is "a violation of the criminal law for which the individual can be punished through the use of formal sanctions applied by governmental authority."[32]

Still, despite the concise definition, the study of crime does encounter some difficulties. A major problem involves statistics. The *crime rate* indicates the number of reported crimes per 100,000 inhabitants. Despite attempts to create a standardized classification form for reporting crime, significant problems remain.

First, many crimes are never reported to the police. Some suggest that the majority of certain types of crime—rape, for example—go unreported. Second, crime statistics necessarily reflect the orientation of local police. Some police departments are very much concerned with nonviolent crime, such as burglary or larceny, while others concentrate on crimes of violence—assault, rape, and so on. Third, various law enforcement agencies use different techniques for reporting and categorizing types of crimes. Consequently, there is a very sizable unknown in crime rate statistics. Crime may indeed be increasing; however, it is impossible to determine precisely to what extent the statistical rates reflect an actual shift in behavior.

The recent popularity of electronic burglar alarms and protective iron bars is not evidence of a new concern, as this 1875 cartoon, "Burglar-proof," illustrates.

CRIMINAL HOMICIDE

Homicide is the taking of the life of one human being by another. *Murder*, or killing with malice aforethought, is the most extreme form of homicide. Most states recognize a scale of homicide ranging from first-degree murder through justifiable homicide. There are typically three categories of criminal homicide: first-degree murder, second-degree murder, and manslaughter. They are distinguished by the degree of culpability of the perpetrator and punishment varies accordingly. Of the three only manslaughter requires no malice aforethought or premeditation. Excusable homicide refers to accidental killing, and justifiable homicide to killing resulting from duty, such as an execution.[33]

Obviously a good deal of judgment is involved in determining the level of homicide that has occurred. And because there is an obvious victim, homicide is the most accurately and completely reported crime. Likewise the arrest rate for homicide is the highest for any crime, ranging from 75 to 80 percent.

Criminal homicide rates vary by racial and ethnic groups, type of community, and region. A primary determinant seems to be the presence or absence of what some scholars have referred to as a "subculture of violence." Certain groups and regions seem to be characterized by a willingness to resolve differences and problems of personal interaction through violence. Clearly, if a person is ready to use force in an argument and also has a weapon, the chances that a murder will occur are greater than they would be if violence were condemned and weapons unavailable.

Life in slums and poverty areas has long been associated with violence, and murder rates reflect this. Studies in Houston, Texas, and London, England, indicate that murder is predominantly an inner-city crime.[34] Murder has also been linked to race in the United States, but probably because the black population is overrepresented in the urban lower class. Although making up less than 17 percent of the nation's urban population (11 to 13 percent of the population as a whole), blacks recently constituted 62.2 percent of all arrests for criminal homicide. In Cleveland, with a black population of 11 percent, 76 percent of the homicide arrests were of blacks; in Houston, with a black population of 23 percent, 63 percent of the homicide arrests were of blacks.[35]

It should be emphasized that for murder, as for all categories of violent crime, the pattern is clearly intraracial rather than interracial. A major investigation of seventeen metropolitan areas in the United States indicated that 66 percent of criminal homicides involved blacks killing blacks, 24 percent whites killing whites, 6 percent blacks killing whites, and 4 percent whites killing blacks.[36]

Regional differences are also apparent. Data from the South show that Southern homicide rates sometimes range as high as twice those of the rest of the country. Again, the prevailing subculture helps explain the difference. Affronts to one's dignity, whether real or imagined, are often met with violence of a physical nature in the South rather than with the well-placed damaging remark or a lawsuit as they might be handled elsewhere.

Although murder, like other crimes of violence, tends to be urban and lower-class—a fact that seems to reinforce one of the stereotypes held by suburban dwellers—the pattern of "real life" murder that crime statistics reveal does not fit all our preconceptions. Murderers are not unknown fiends skulking through the night; rather, they are usually husbands, wives, relatives, or friends. Over 70 percent of all "willful killings" in the United States are committed by family members or others who are well known by the victims.[37] The fear of violence and the "rising crime rate" that has created a bonanza for the purveyors of locks, iron window gratings, and burglar alarms is not without substance, of course. Yet, if you are going to be murdered, the chances are that the killer will not be a stranger prying open your window after midnight. It is more likely that he or she eats poached eggs or Wheat Chex with you each morning.

It has long been argued that ease in acquiring firearms makes homicide more likely. This cartoon appeared in the British magazine *Punch* in 1882.

MURDER MADE EASY.

Licensed Retailer. "ACONITE, SIR? WE ONLY SELL POISONS TO MEDICAL MEN; BUT ANYTHING IN REVOLVERS AND DYNAMITE"——!!!

One such killer was Chester E. Gillette, who was electrocuted in 1908 for drowning his pregnant lover, Grace Brown. Theodore Dreiser gave a fictionalized account of events surrounding this murder in his classic, *An American Tragedy*. Gillette became Clyde Griffiths, who drowns the pregnant Roberta:

It could be done—it could be done—swiftly and simply, were he now of the mind and heart, or lack of it—with him swimming swiftly away thereafter to freedom—to success—of course—to Sondra and happiness—a new and greater and sweeter life than any he had ever known.
  Yet why was he waiting now?
  What was the matter with him, anyhow?

Bizarre and sensational killings, such as those for which Charles Manson (center) was tried in 1970, are much less common than homicides resulting from family quarrels.

Why was he waiting?

At this cataclysmic moment, and in the face of the utmost, the most urgent need of action, a sudden palsy of the will—of courage—of hate or rage sufficient; and with Roberta from her seat in the stern of the boat gazing at his troubled and then suddenly distorted, fulgurous, yet weak and even unbalanced face—a face of a sudden, instead of angry, ferocious, demoniac—confused and all but meaningless in its registration of a balanced combat between fear (a chemic revulsion against death or murderous brutality that would bring death) and a harried and restless and yet self-repressed desire to do—to do—to do—yet temporarily unbreakable here and now—a static between a powerful compulsion to do and yet not to do.

And in the meantime his eyes—the pupils of the same growing momentarily larger and more lurid; his face and body and hands tense and contracted—the stillness of his position, the balanced immobility of the mood more and more ominous, yet in truth not suggesting a brutal, courageous power to destroy, but the imminence of trance or spasm.

And Roberta, suddenly noticing the strangeness of it all—the something of eerie unreason or physical and mental indetermination so strangely and painfully contrasting with this scene, exclaiming: "Why, Clyde! Clyde! What is it? Whatever is the matter with you anyhow? You look so—so strange—so—so—Why, I never saw you look like this before. What is it?" And suddenly rising, or rather leaning forward, and by crawling along the even keel, attempting to approach him, since he looked as though he was about to fall forward into the boat—or to one side and out into the water. And Clyde, as instantly sensing the profoundness of his own failure, his own cowardice or inadequateness for such an occasion, as instantly yielding to a tide of submerged hate, not only for himself, but Roberta—her power—or that of life to restrain him in this way. And yet fearing to act in any way—being unwilling to—being willing only to say that never, never would he marry her—that never, even should she expose him, would he leave here with her to marry her—that he was in love with Sondra and would cling only to her—and yet not being able to say that even. But angry and confused and glowering. And then, as she drew near him, seeking to take his hand in hers and the camera from him in order to put it in the boat, he flinging out at her, but not even then with any intention to do other than free himself of her—her touch—her pleading—consoling sympathy—her presence forever—God!

Yet (the camera still unconsciously held tight) pushing at her with so much vehemence as not only to strike her lips and nose and chin with it, but to throw her back sidewise toward the left wale which caused the boat to careen to the very water's edge. And then he, stirred by her sharp scream (as much due to the lurch of the boat, as the cut on her nose and lip), rising and reaching half to assist or recapture her and half to apologize for the unintended blow—yet in so doing completely capsizing the boat—himself and Roberta being as instantly thrown into the water. And the left wale of the boat as it turned, striking Roberta on the head as she sank and then rose for the first time, her frantic, contorted face turned to Clyde who by now had righted himself. For she was stunned, horror-struck, unintelligible with pain and fear—her lifelong fear of water and drowning and the blow he had so accidentally and all but unconsciously administered.

"Help! Help!

"Oh, my God, I'm drowning, I'm drowning. Help! Oh, my God!

"Clyde, Clyde!" . . .

". . . Wait—wait—ignore the pity of that appeal. And then—then—But there! Behold. It is over. She is sinking now. You will never, never see her alive any more—ever. And there is your own hat upon the water—as you wished. And upon the boat, clinging to that rowlock a veil belonging to her. Leave it. Will it not show that this was an accident?"

And apart from that, nothing—a few ripples—the peace and solemnity of this wondrous scene. . . ."[38]

The image of murder as a crime unrelated to violent family arguments or lovers' quarrels persists, however. No more chilling a portrait of the impersonal killer has been conceived than that of Rofion Raskolnikov, the main character of Dostoevsky's novel *Crime and Punishment*.

"Good evening, Alëna Ivanovna," he began, as easily as possible, but his voice refused to obey him, and he was broken and trembling, "I have . . . brought you . . . something . . . but hadn't we better come in here . . . to the light? . . ." And without waiting for an invitation, he passed her and went into the room. The old woman hastened after him; her tongue seemed to have been loosened.

"Good Lord! What are you doing? . . . Who are you? What do you want?"

"Excuse me, Alëna Ivanovna . . . You know me . . . Raskolnikov . . . See, I have brought the pledge I promised the other day," and he held it out to her.

The old woman threw a glance at it, but then immediately fixed her eyes on those of her uninvited guest. She looked at him attentively, ill-naturedly, and mistrustfully. A minute or so went by; he even thought he could see a glint of derision in her eyes, as if she had guessed everything. He felt that he was losing his nerve and was frightened, so frightened that he thought if she went on looking at him like that, without a word, for even a minute longer, he would turn tail and run away.

"Why are you looking at me like that, as though you didn't recognize me?" he burst out angrily. "Do you want it, or don't you? I can take it somewhere else; it makes no difference to me."

He had not intended to say this, but it seemed to come of its own accord.

The old woman collected herself, and her visitor's resolute tone seemed to lull her mistrust.

"Why be so hasty, my friend? . . . What is it?" she asked, looking at the packet.

"A silver cigarette case; surely I told you that last time?"

She stretched out her hand.

"But what makes you so pale? And your hands are trembling. Are you ill or something?"

"Fever," he answered abruptly. "You can't help being pale . . . when you haven't anything to eat," he added, hardly able to articulate his words. His strength was failing again. But apparently the answer was plausible enough; the old woman took the packet.

"What is it?" she asked, weighing it in her hand and once again fixing her eyes on Raskolnikov.

"A thing . . . a cigarette case . . . silver . . . look at it."

"It doesn't feel like silver. Lord, what a knot!" Trying to undo the string she turned for light towards the window (all her windows were closed, in spite of the oppressive heat), moved away from him and stood with her back to him. He unbuttoned his coat and freed the axe from the loop, but still kept it concealed, supporting it with his right hand under the garment. His arms seemed to have no strength in them; he felt them growing more and more numb and stiff with *every moment. He was afraid of letting the axe slip and fall. . . . His head was whirling.*

"Why is it all wrapped up like this?" exclaimed the woman sharply and turned towards him.

There was not a moment to lose. He pulled the axe out, swung it up with both hands, hardly conscious of what he was doing, and almost mechanically, without putting any force behind it, let the butt-end fall on her head. His strength seemed to have deserted him, but as soon as the axe descended it all returned to him.

The old woman was, as usual, bare-headed. Her thin fair hair, just turning grey, and thick with grease, was plaited into a rat's tail and fastened into a knot above her nape with a fragment of horn comb. Because she was so short the axe struck her full on the crown of the head. She cried out, but very feebly and sank in a heap to the floor, still with enough strength left to raise both hands to her head. One of them still held the "pledge." Then he struck her again and yet again, with all his strength, always with the blunt side of the axe, and always on the crown of the head. Blood poured out as if from an overturned glass and the body toppled over on its back. He stepped away as it fell, and then stooped to see the face: she was dead. Her wide-open eyes looked ready to start out of their sockets, her forehead was wrinkled and her whole face convulsively distorted.[39]

Although murder as an ultimate form of family or personal argument continues to be the norm in this country, a substantial percentage of criminal homicide involves people who were previously unknown to each other.

WHITE-COLLAR CRIME

The definition of crime as a violation of the criminal law becomes blurred when we examine the concept of white-collar crime first articulated by Edwin H. Sutherland. According to Sutherland, *white-collar crime* refers to violations of the criminal law (though not always stated) by members of the upper-middle or upper classes that are carried out in conjunction with their occupations.[40] For instance, an executive of a food processing company may be endangering the lives of his customers (a crime) by cutting corners in his system of production (not specifically a crime).

Such crimes are seldom as dramatic as the drowning of a pregnant woman or as obvious as a purse-snatching. White-collar crime takes such forms as misrepresenting products through false advertising, restraint of trade, violation of trademarks and patents, padding expense accounts, and various other similar activities. As Sutherland noted, white-collar crimes are socially harmful and, like other more obvious criminal violations, can result in legal prosecution.[41] Still, white-collar crimes are seldom well publicized and even more rarely prosecuted.

According to George Vold, the reason the criminal behavior of the powerful generally goes undetected and unpunished is that the bulk of our legal system is both defined and maintained by those in power.[42] The norms and values of the upper classes are likely to be codified into criminal statutes, while the interests of the lower classes are not similarly protected by legislation. This is very much like the satiric interpretation of the Golden Rule: He who has the gold makes the rules.

Thus armed robbery, a crime against property and the propertied classes, is clearly defined as a violation of law. But informal price fixing, which may cheat the lower and lower-middle classes of millions of dollars, is not so clearly defined as a crime and, when detected, is very difficult to prove in a court of law. The gin-filled lower-class teenager who robs a store at gunpoint is likely to be caught and spend many years in prison; the corporate executive who engages in price fixing will probably not be pursued by authorities or not punished severely if caught.

The detection of widespread white-collar crime in the Nixon administration is a recent illustration of this point. Despite obvious violations of the public trust and numerous instances of criminal practices, few of the major figures in the Watergate scandal have served time in prison, and those few were let off with comparatively light sentences.

Aside from obvious differences of treatment before the law, white-collar criminals are also distinguished from other criminals in another way: whereas murderers, robbers, and other felons often consider themselves secondary deviants, white-collar criminals seldom move beyond primary deviance. One reason for this, according to Simon Dinitz and Walter Reckless, is that white-collar criminals are insulated from the consequences of

The Ervin committee hearing testimony from John Dean about the Watergate affair.

their crimes.⁴³ No one has punished them for their behavior; indeed, they have been rewarded and told they were doing an excellent, aggressive, and innovative job. People who perceive themselves to be honest and straightforward "good citizens" have no reason to suspect that they are criminals.

Donald Cressey gives a similar explanation for a somewhat more clandestine form of white-collar crime. He suggests that white-collar criminals are able to gain reinforcement from their reference group for their activity, but they must be selective in both their perceptions and their choice of role models. Cressey's white-collar offenders are faced with a problem, such as an expensive love affair or major debts, that they are unable to share with those around them. They must get money and must do so in private—they thus become white-collar criminals and selectively rationalize their behavior.⁴⁴

The line between white-collar and other crime is difficult to determine, but the occupational level of the criminal is clearly an important factor. Obviously it is necessary to be in a position of power and trust to be able to commit a white-collar crime. The line between primary and secondary deviance is also difficult to determine. As is the case with other forms of deviance, it is not a given act but the perceptions of the individuals involved that make white-collar criminals primary or secondary deviants.

ORGANIZED CRIME

Francis Ford Coppola's Academy Award winning productions of Mario Puzo's *The Godfather* and *The Godfather Part II* have helped rekindle interest in organized crime in the United States. They have also reinforced the popular image of organized crime as being dominated by sometimes sinister but basically understandable men from Sicily. Puzo's character Michael Corleone has joined Al Capone and Albert Anastasia as representative of the breed. Like many popular stereotypes, that of organized crime is not without some substance, although how much seems to defy verification.

The basis for the contemporary image of organized crime is often traced to the murder in 1890 of New Orleans' superintendent of police, Peter Hennessey. Since Hennessey had been actively pursuing an outlaw gang of Sicilians, the Matranga brothers, the public assumed that the gang was responsible for the superintendent's death. The local press made excellent and salable copy with stories of the secret society of the "Black Hand," or the "Mafia," supposedly an old Sicilian protective society that had been transplanted to the United States. The Italian community, of course, denied the existence of any such organization.⁴⁵ Charges and denials have continued since then.

Many scholars now deny the existence of any real organized crime in this country prior to the 1920s, when Prohibition opened the door for

Al Capone, shown here (left) on his way to federal prison in 1932, was a major figure in organized crime in Chicago during the 1920s. Many believe that organized crime is as extensive today as it was in Capone's time.

bootleggers like Frank Nitti, Al Capone, "Bugs" Moran, and "Lucky" Luciano. A full-scale public investigation of organized crime did not come, however, until the early 1950s, when the Senate Crime Committee under Estes Kefauver was convened. It was Kefauver's committee that popularized the term "Mafia," which was now taken to mean an organized crime syndicate with long traditions in Sicily but operating in the United States as well. In the 1960s another official group, the McClellan Commission, heard testimony from Joseph Valachi, a reputed member of an organized crime syndicate. According to Valachi, the Vito Genovese "family" headed a hierarchy of "families" known as the Cosa Nostra—a multiethnic organization which evolved under Charles "Lucky" Luciano but remained dominated by Italians. Figure 16–1 details the Cosa Nostra structure Valachi described.

Many who study crime in the United States feel that elements of the Mafia and the Cosa Nostra do indeed control much wealth and power in this country.* Others, however, remain unconvinced. They suggest that there has been an embarrassing lack of real evidence. The Kefauver Committee seemed to believe that because law enforcement agents told the committee to expect silence from crime figures (who were supposedly bound by a Mafia code of honor) and because reputed criminal leaders did indeed refuse to testify, that in itself was proof that the Mafia existed. Critics maintain that this is hardly convincing. Evidence from the McClellan Commission is not much better. Some suggest that Valachi had as much claim to knowing the workings of the Cosa Nostra as a pump jockey in an Exxon station would have to know the international dealings of Aramco.

*See, in particular, Donald R. Cressey, *Theft of the Nation: The Structure and Operations of Organized Crime in America* (New York: Harper & Row, 1969); and Denny F. Pace and Jimmie C. Styles, *Organized Crime: Concepts and Control* (Englewood Cliffs, N.J.: Prentice-Hall, 1975).

Harvard sociologist Daniel Bell states that the Mafia and the Cosa Nostra are primarily scapegoats for ineffective law enforcement agencies. "Things" are controlled from "upstairs" by "them"—"them" being a synonym in this instance for "organized crime."[46]

There may indeed be a Mafia, although reality probably lies a bit closer to the suggestion of Ramsey Clark, formerly attorney general of the United States. Clark suggests that crime is organized in regions by specializing

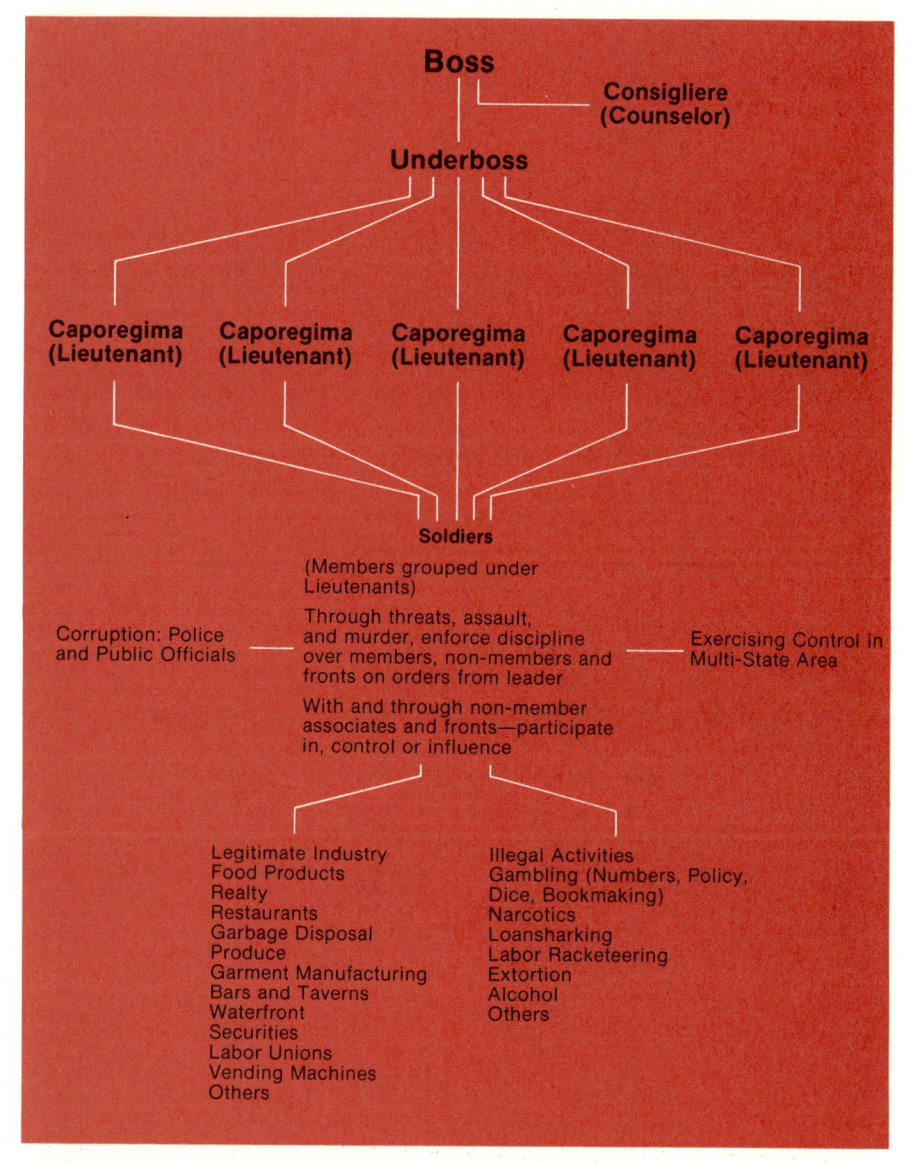

```
                              Boss
                               |————— Consigliere
                               |       (Counselor)
                           Underboss

Caporegima   Caporegima   Caporegima   Caporegima   Caporegima
(Lieutenant) (Lieutenant) (Lieutenant) (Lieutenant) (Lieutenant)

                            Soldiers
                   (Members grouped under
                         Lieutenants)

Corruption: Police     Through threats, assault,      Exercising Control in
and Public Officials   and murder, enforce discipline  Multi-State Area
                       over members, non-members and
                       fronts on orders from leader.

                       With and through non-member
                       associates and fronts—participate
                       in, control or influence

   Legitimate Industry              Illegal Activities
   Food Products                    Gambling (Numbers, Policy,
   Realty                           Dice, Bookmaking)
   Restaurants                      Narcotics
   Garbage Disposal                 Loansharking
   Produce                          Labor Racketeering
   Garment Manufacturing            Extortion
   Bars and Taverns                 Alcohol
   Waterfront                       Others
   Securities
   Labor Unions
   Vending Machines
   Others
```

FIGURE 16–1 The Organization of the Cosa Nostra

SOURCE: *The Challenge of Crime in a Free Society*, Report of the President's Commission on Law Enforcement and Administration of Justice (Washington, D.C.: U.S. Government Printing Office, 1967), p. 194.

gangs rather than through a national network.[47] Whatever the truth, we are very much like blind fishermen describing a whale having touched only a part of it. We just do not know. Comedian Woody Allen's rendition of organized crime may be as accurate as that of any purported underworld figure:

> It is no secret that organized crime in America takes in over forty billion dollars a year. This is quite a profitable sum, especially when one considers that the Mafia spends very little for office supplies. Reliable sources indicate that the Cosa Nostra laid out no more than six thousand dollars last year for personalized stationery, and even less for staples. Furthermore, they have one secretary who does all the typing, and only three small rooms for headquarters, which they share with Fred Persky Dance Studio.
>
> Last year, organized crime was directly responsible for more than one hundred murders, and mafiosi participated indirectly in several hundred more, either by lending the killers carfare or by holding their coats. Other illicit activities engaged in by Cosa Nostra members included gambling, narcotics, prostitution, hijacking, loansharking, and the transportation of a large whitefish across the state line for immoral purposes. The tentacles of this corrupt empire even reach into the government itself. Only a few months ago, two gang lords under federal indictment spent the night at the White House, and the President slept on the sofa.

HISTORY OF ORGANIZED CRIME IN THE UNITED STATES

In 1921, Thomas (The Butcher) Covello and Ciro (The Tailor) Santucci attempted to organize disparate ethnic groups of the underworld and thus take over Chicago. This was foiled when Albert (The Logical Positivist) Corillo assassinated Kid Lipsky by locking him in a closet and sucking all the air out through a straw. Lipsky's brother Mendy (alias Mendy Lewis, alias Mendy Larsen, alias Mendy Alias) avenged Lipsky's murder by abducting Santucci's brother Gaetano (also known as Little Tony, or Rabbi Henry Sharpstein) and returning him several weeks later in twenty-seven separate mason jars. This signalled the beginning of a bloodbath.

Dominick (The Herpetologist) Mione shot Lucky Lorenzo (so nicknamed when a bomb that went off in his hat failed to kill him) outside a bar in Chicago. In return, Corillo and his men traced Mione to Newark and made his head into a wind instrument. At this point, the Vitale gang, ran by Giuseppe Vitale (real name Quincy Baedeker), made their move to take over all bootlegging in Harlem from Irish Larry Doyle—a racketeer so suspicious that he refused to let anybody in New York ever get behind him, and walked down the street constantly pirouetting and spinning around. Doyle was killed when the Squillante Construction Company decided to erect their new offices on the bridge of his nose. Doyle's lieutenant, Little Petey (Big Petey) Ross, now took command; he resisted the Vitale takeover and lured Vitale to an empty midtown garage on the pretext that a costume party was being held there. Unsuspecting, Vitale walked into the garage dressed as a giant mouse, and was instantly riddled with machine-gun bullets. Out of loyalty to their slain chief, Vitale's men immediately defected to Ross. So did Vitale's fiancee, Bea Moretti, a showgirl and star of the hit Broadway musical Say Kaddish, who wound up marrying Ross, although she later sued him for divorce, charging that he once spread an unpleasant ointment on her.

Fearing federal intervention, Vincent Columbraro, the Buttered Toast King, called for a truce. (Columbraro has such tight control over all buttered toast moving in and out of New Jersey that one word from him could ruin breakfast for two-thirds of the nation.) All members of the underworld were summoned to a diner in Perth Amboy, where Columbraro told them that internal warfare must stop and that from then on they had to dress decently and stop slinking around. Letters formerly signed with a black hand would in the future be signed "Best Wishes," and all territory would be divided equally, with New Jersey going to Columbraro's mother. Thus the Mafia, or Cosa Nostra (literally, "my toothpaste" or "our toothpaste"), was born. Two days later, Columbraro got into a nice hot tub to take a bath and has been missing for the past forty-six years.[48]

Chapter Summary

On one level the definitions of deviance and crime are very concise and understandable. Deviance is simply any behavior that transgresses or is in violation of accepted cultural norms, while crime is a violation of the criminal law. On closer examination, however, it becomes obvious that the two categories are not precise at all. The perceptions of both participants and those around them are critical in defining what is and what is not "deviant," while the determination of what constitutes a crime depends very much on one's position in the system of social stratification.

To underscore the importance of perception in the determination of what is deviant, sociologists have distinguished two types of deviants. Primary deviants do not accept their deviant status and are able to think of their acts as a function of a socially acceptable role. Secondary deviants, on the other hand, accept their status and are recognized by others as deviant.

Numerous theories have been suggested to explain deviance and crime. Explanations of social and biological pathology stress that deviance is a physical or societal disease. Differential association theory maintains that the groups with which a person interacts largely determine whether he or she will become deviant. The theory of social disorganization emphasizes that a disruption of a culture's normative system leads to the onset of deviant behavior. Labeling theory contends that there are no specific actions that are in themselves deviant; actions are deviant because they are so labeled by powerful groups or individuals. A variant of this explanation, value conflict theory, maintains that acts are considered deviant because they are at variance with a group's values. Labeling theory and the theory of value conflict are the currently accepted explanations for the majority of deviance and crime.

A brief look at differing forms of deviance and crime—prostitution, homosexuality, alcoholism, mental illness, criminal homicide, white-collar crime, and organized crime—points to two major conclusions. First, many criminals and deviants do not accept their deviant status and thus remain primary deviants. Second, the rather distinct stereotypes that many of us conveniently use to understand the world do not survive even a brief examination.

Key Terms for Review

biological pathology, p. 389
crime, p. 408
crime rate, p. 408
deviance, p. 387
deviant, p. 387
differential association, p. 390
differential opportunity, p. 391
homicide, p. 409
homosexuality, p. 400

labeling theory, p. 394
lesbianism, p. 400
murder, p. 409
primary deviants, p. 396
secondary deviants, p. 397
social disorganization, p. 393
social pathology, p. 389
value conflict theory, p. 396
white-collar crime, p. 415

Suggested Readings

SOCIOLOGICAL Clinard, Marshall B. *Sociology of Deviant Behavior,* 4th ed. New York: Holt, Rinehart & Winston, 1974. This text remains a scholarly and encyclopedic exploration of deviance and crime and is perhaps the most complete text of its kind now in print.

Cressey, Donald R. *Theft of the Nation: The Structure and Operations of Organized Crime in America.* New York: Harper & Row, 1969. This is the most complete

DEVIANCE AND CRIME / 423

and scholarly view of organized crime that has ever been published. Cressey examines available data and concludes that there is indeed such a thing as organized crime in this country.

Schur, Edwin. *Crimes Without Victims.* Englewood Cliffs, N.J.: Prentice-Hall, 1965. Schur's widely read paperback popularized the concept of victimless crime (crime that hurts no one) and examined the relationship between perceptions and public policy. Specifically Schur examines abortion, drug addiction, and homosexuality.

Winick, Charles, and Paul M. Kinsie. *The Lively Commerce.* New York: Signet, 1971. This work is a complete and readable examination of prostitution in the United States. The authors provide a thorough summary of previous research and offer an international and cross-cultural perspective on the "world's oldest profession."

Winslow, Robert W., and Virginia Winslow. *Deviant Reality.* Boston: Allyn and Bacon, 1974. The Winslows' interesting text employs a number of transcribed narratives by secondary deviants to give the reader a firsthand account of "deviant reality." They introduce each narrative with a brief summation of pertinent sociological literature and explanatory hypotheses and follow each presentation with an interesting and insightful discussion of the points presented. *Deviant Reality* examines most popularly recognized forms of crime and deviance.

LITERARY

Green, Hannah. *I Never Promised You a Rose Garden.* New York: Signet, 1964. This sensitive and beautifully written novel is considered by many to be *the* outstanding portrait of mental illness in contemporary America. It takes the reader through the very real torment of being in a mental institution and ends on an optimistic note of compassion.

Kerouac, Jack. *On the Road.* New York: Viking, 1957. This is Kerouac's most remembered novel and presents the frenetic, searching, drug-ridden world of the "beat generation" of the 1950s. Dean Moriarity leads his group in a search for a world of feeling and reality that they never find.

Malamud, Bernard. *A New Life.* New York: Pocket Books, 1973; orig. 1961. S. Levin, a young professor of English, embarks on his academic career in Marathon, Cascadia (Corvallis, Oregon), finding that the boundaries of deviance are not always easily determined.

Sinclair, Upton. *The Cup of Fury.* Great Neck, N.Y.: Channel Press, 1956. Sinclair presents alcoholism as it affected his own family and the lives and families of his many close and talented friends. He offers often brilliant insights into the struggles and rationalizations that destroyed the careers and ultimately the lives of many of our most famous writers and artists.

Vonnegut, Kurt, Jr. *Breakfast of Champions.* New York: Delta, 1973. Vonnegut presents a strange and often depressing view of life in the United States during the 1970s. The main character, Kilgore Trout, a science fiction author, is never quite able to separate the normal from the bizarre. With his usual incredible wit and magnificent phrasing, Vonnegut places one in a world where the line between normalcy and crime and deviance is completely erased.

IN THIS CHAPTER

The Meaning of Leisure   425

The Meaning and Importance of Sport   427

Why Sports Are Popular   429
    The success of sports   429
    The comprehensibility of sports   429
    The mystery and romance of sports   431
    Sports and displacement of aggression   432
    Sports and ethnocentrism   433
    The benefits of sports   436

Sports and Social Mobility   437
    Early loss of income   442
    Loss of public acclaim   442

The Future of Leisure and Sport   444

Summary   446

Key Terms for Review   446

Suggested Readings   447

Will the continuing increase of leisure time bring forth a modern utopia?

Why are sports so popular?

Do people prefer to watch or participate in certain sports because of their class background?

17

LEISURE AND SPORT

The comedian Shelly Berman used to relate the story of the college sophomore who, head stuffed with introductory philosophy, would come home for the holidays with such a perverse sense of the profound that he could make the most lighthearted and festive occasion tedious and boring. At the Thanksgiving feast, he laboriously studied what was before him and intoned, "Ah, a glass of water—but we must consider what is a glass of water and if this is a glass of water." Following a giggle from his younger sister and a kick under the table from his younger brother, he continued his inquiry. "What is the meaning of a glass of water?" Somewhere between the cranberry sauce and the second helping of dressing, his quest for the hidden meaning of a glass of water—to the relief of all—would be abandoned.

Our attempt to explain leisure and sport in this chapter may seem to place us disturbingly close to the pedantic meanderings of the earnest young man. Risking that, we will examine the meanings of leisure and sport and some sociological findings about their pursuit in our culture.

The Meaning of Leisure

Classical Greek interpretations of leisure emphasize peace, quiet, and contemplation. According to one scholar, the Greeks thought of leisure as a pure form of being "in which activity is performed for its own end."[1] In later Christian thought leisure was contemplation of God. This concept dominated Western thought until the Renaissance, when the perception of leisure became more contemporary. Leisure was no longer thought of as a means of enabling the kingdom of God to be present on earth; rather, it was a part of everyday life intertwined with all other aspects of living.[2]

Today we perceive leisure very much in conjunction with its presumed opposite. *Leisure is time free from work.* The definition is necessarily vague and leaves open the question of which activities should be considered work. Just how one would classify all the chores performed during "nonworking" hours, for example, or how one should interpret the "work" of fishing guides is debatable. But the thrust of the definition is clear: leisure is any time unencumbered by the routine of earning enough money to pay the bills. How people use such time largely depends on the values and practices of the class to which they belong.

For years the report cards of elementary school children have contained evaluations of performance in the category "makes good use of leisure time." Good use of leisure time is a value revered by the middle and upper classes in the United States. Free time should not be "wasted" but utilized to (1) develop useful skills and knowledge (such as in handicrafts or hobbies), (2) develop discipline by working toward a clearly defined goal (as in bettering one's performance in sports), (3) sustain health (as by jogging), or (4) increase specialized knowledge (with "intellectual" hobbies such as music and reading). As Benjamin Franklin put it two centuries ago, "Leisure is Time for doing something Useful." The values associated with leisure by the middle and upper classes are closely related to other norms they hold which center around the work ethic. Work and the development of skills are paramount. Leisure, then, is very much a part of work. At the very least it should somehow make one better qualified to pursue work.[3]

Working-class norms, on the other hand, tend to emphasize hedonism in leisure activity. Time free from work is thought of as an escape rather

A nineteenth-century quilting party (far left) illustrates the middle-class "yankee" practice of putting leisure time to productive use. Reading and playing a musical instrument are other examples of "good use of leisure time."

than as a preparation for or sharpening of work-related skills. Gadgets and excitement are important to working-class leisure. Consuming—the new toy, the faster boat or car, the latest thrill—is basic to leisurely pursuits.[4]

Yet whatever the class outlook, leisure today is totally removed from the Greek concept of an activity "performed for its own sake and as an end in itself." Nowhere is the mixture of work and play more apparent than in the primary sphere of leisure activity, sport.

Sport has become a very important part of contemporary American life. As Table 17–1 shows, although the percentage of the consumer dollar spent on recreation has increased only slowly over the years, expenditures on and participation in sports have grown remarkably since 1940. Since many Americans take sports so seriously, the phenomenon deserves close investigation.

TABLE 17–1
Sport and Recreation Growth

	1930	1940	1950	1960	1970
Percent of consumer income spent on recreation	5.6	5.2	5.1	5.3	6.6
Spectator sports (millions of dollars)	NA	98	222	290	516
Outboard Motors (millions of units)	NA	NA	2.8	5.8	7.2

SOURCE: Data from *Information Please Almanac*, ed. Ann Golenpaul (New York: Simon & Schuster, 1976), pp. 875, 876, 63; and Max Kaplan, *Leisure* (New York: Wiley, 1975), pp. 117, 371.

NA—figures not available.

The Meaning and Importance of Sport

The concept sport is a difficult one to define precisely. Many think of the term "sport" as synonymous with the term "game," but there are many games that are not sports and vice versa. For example, few would contend that playing Monopoly is a sport nor would many suggest that prize fighting is a game. Another way to define sport is in terms of physical skill, yet even that does not clearly demarcate sport from nonsport activity. Ballet and modern dance require high levels of physical skill but are usually classified as performing arts.[5] And a nonphysical game like bridge is regularly reported as a sports activity in *Sports Illustrated*, while professional wrestling is more entertainment than sport. Our own inquiry simply assumes that *sport* is something that is defined as such by a culture. Consideration here is limited to those activities normally considered to be sport in the United States.

Sports are extremely popular in this country, though the list of popular sports is surprisingly small. As Table 17–2 shows, only ten were designated "favorite sports" by 3 percent or more of the population. The table also shows that certain class, residence, and sex differences affect the choices of favorites. The availability of private clubs for golf and tennis accounts for the upper-class popularity of those sports, while lower-class cultural tendencies toward physical aggression help to explain the popularity of boxing for that class. The difference in class values is particularly apparent in Table 17–3, which distinguishes between spectator and participant sports. The table indicates that the upper classes prefer participant sports. Although the distinction between spectator and participant preferences is not clear with the middle and lower classes, upper-class emphasis on skill and discipline, as discussed earlier, is quite clear, with only one in three upper-class respondents offering a spectator sport as first choice.

Yet whatever the choice and whatever the social differences, the tables suggest that sports are central to American culture. Three out of every four

Table 17–2

Social Differences in Sports Designated as Favorites by Metropolitan Residents

Favorite Sports	Age	Sex	Residence	Socioeconomic Strata	Percent of Respondents Selecting a Favorite Sport (N = 540)
Football			U–S	M–U–L	24.4
Baseball		M–F		L–M–U	15.4
Golf				U–M–L	11.3
Fishing		M–F			9.6
Swimming	Y–O	F–M	U–S	M–U–L	7.6
Basketball				M–L–U	6.8
Bowling		F–M		L–M–U	6.3
Tennis				U–M–L	3.7
Hunting		M–F			3.7
Boxing		M–F		L–M–U	3.3
Others too diverse to analyze					7.8

SOURCE: Gregory P. Stone, "Some Meanings of American Sport: An Extended View," in *Sociology of Sport: Proceedings of the C.I.C. Symposium on the Sociology of Sport,* ed. Gerald S. Kenyon (Chicago: Athletic Institute, 1969), p. 11.

*Categories of informants making most mentions of any specified activity are listed first, those making fewest mentions are listed last, reading from left to right. In the age category those less than forty years of age are designated "Y," those forty years of age or more are designated "O." In the sex category, men are designated "M" and women "F." In the residence category, "U" designates respondents living in the Minneapolis city limits; "S" those living in the suburbs. In the socioeconomic category, those in the highest category are designated "U," those in the middle, "M," and those in the lowest, "L."

TABLE 17–3
Socioeconomic Differences in the Designation of Spectator or Participant Sports as Favorites by Metropolitan Residents

Favorite Sport	Upper (percent)	Middle (percent)	Lower (percent)	Totals (percent)
Spectator	35.6	57.1	54.7	48.8
Participant	64.4	42.9	45.3	51.2
Totals	100.0 (N = 188)	100.0 (N = 175)	100.0 (N = 172)	100.0 (N = 535)

Socioeconomic Strata

SOURCE: Gregory P. Stone, "Some Meanings of American Sport: An Extended View," in *Sociology of Sport: Proceedings of the C.I.C. Symposium on the Sociology of Sport*, ed. Gerald S. Kenyon (Chicago: Athletic Institute, 1969), p. 10.

American males report discussing sports "frequently" or "very frequently," while almost half the female population, even before the arrival of tennis champion Billy Jean King, reported a similar interest in sports.

Why Sports are Popular

No leisure-time activity can arouse the interest that sports can. The fine arts command a very small audience compared to sports, while the very popular pastime of watching television cannot match the emotional intensity of sports competition. The reasons for this popularity, however, are many and often complex, varying with personal and social circumstances. Sociologists have offered six distinct explanations for the continuing interest of people in sports.

THE SUCCESS OF SPORTS

A major explanation offered for the continuing popularity of sports is disturbingly circular, but valid. In the cliché of the sports idiom, success breeds success. Sports are popular, therefore many people participate in them and identify with them; as a result, many people emulate and idolize sports figures, and, consequently, sports are popular. Football has become practically a national preoccupation because of the snowballing effect of its initial popularity.

THE COMPREHENSIBILITY OF SPORTS

Some sociologists maintain that sports arouse widespread interest because they are easily comprehensible and have fixed rules. The workings

One reason for the popularity of baseball is its comprehensibility. Fans such as these can easily understand the game and also judge the performance of individual players.

of a sport or the expectations of participants in it are far more understandable to the average American than the workings of an opera or the expectations placed upon a mezzo-soprano. And the criteria for performance and excellence in sports are specified as they are not in literature and the fine arts. The whims and fashions of "experts" or critics carry no weight in sports. When the criteria for judging a sport are not set (as in the case of the highly subjective and political world of international figure skating competition) the sport becomes less understood by and accessible to the general public.

For the most part, though, excellence is both obvious and measurable. The skill of the performance is open to public comprehension and scrutiny. The skill of the "born" baseball player, for example, comes through in this description from Bernard Malamud's novel *The Natural*:

> The long rain had turned the grass green and Roy romped in it like a happy calf in its pasture. The Redbirds, probing his armor, belted the ball to him whenever they could, which was often, because Hill was not too happy on the mound, but Roy took everything they aimed at him. He seemed to know the soft, hard, and bumpy places in the field and just how high a ball would bounce on them. From the flags on the stadium roof he noted the way the wind would blow the ball, and he was quick at fishing it out of the tricky undercurrents on the ground. Not sun, shadow, nor smoke-haze bothered him, and when a ball was knocked against the wall he estimated the angle of rebound and speared it as if its course had been plotted on a

chart. He was good at gauging slices and knew when to charge the pill to save time on the throw. Once he put his head down and ran ahead of a shot going into the concrete. Though the crowd rose with a thunderous warning, he caught it with his back to the wall and did a little jig to show he was alive. Everyone laughed in relief, and they liked his long-legged loping and that he resembled an acrobat the way he tumbled and came up with the ball in his glove. . . .

His batting was no less successful. He stood at the plate lean and loose, right-handed with an open stance, knees relaxed and shoulders squared. The bat he held in a curious position, lifted slightly above his head as if he prepared to beat a rattlesnake to death, but it didn't harm his smooth stride into the pitch, nor the easy way he met the ball and slashed it out with a flick of the wrists. The pitchers tried something different every time he came up, sliders, sinkers, knucklers, but he swung and connected, spraying them to all fields. He was, Red Blow said to Pop, a natural.[6]

THE MYSTERY AND ROMANCE OF SPORTS

Sociologists and laypeople alike recognize that sports are popular because they contain a certain element of mystery and romance. Sports and sports heroes are understandable but they are also removed from the ordinary and as such are subject to romanticization. They seem to epitomize to their fans all that is glorious. Followers are generally blind to the flaws and vanity of their sports heroes. The lionization of sports heroes can yield markedly unromantic and disillusioning experiences when they fail to live up to expectations. Sports journalist Roger Kahn recalls his first youthful confrontation with the magnificent Brooklyn Dodgers:

We stood waiting outside the old ball park, Jerry, Lefty and I, tense and chattering in expectancy. The wooden hot dog stand beside the parking alley had closed and the September dusk was dying and we would all be late for dinner. Still, beside the alley outside the old ball park we had to wait.

"I know they park their cars here," Lefty said. Like the young Dylan Thomas, Lefty was scrawny, curly, dirty.

"You sure now?" Jerry said. At twelve, Jerry had grown a Rotary chairman's jowls.

"My sister knows this cop," Lefty said. "The cop told her."

"What are those guys doing in there this long?" Jerry said.

"Playing cards," I said. "My Dad told me after games, the ballplayers play cards. Especially when they lose, like today."

"Let's go home," Jerry said.

"Look," Lefty said. "You want to see a ballplayer? A big-league ballplayer? Or do you want to go back to the house?"

"I'm hungry," Jerry said. "I wish the hot dog stand was open."

"I want to see a big-leaguer," I said. "I've never seen a big-leaguer on a street."

Like all important memories, the day returns in patches of gold. Peanut bags littered the sidewalk and the time could not have been good. 1940. A country riding from Depression into war. A world of Stalin, the Greater East Asia Co-Prosperity Sphere, Dachau. But Lefty's sister had found out where the Dodgers parked their cars, and in that troubled September, twilight glowed.

"Who do you want to see most?" Lefty said.

"Durocher," I said. Leo Durocher. Playing manager. The bald-headed shortstop. An artist at getting rid of the ball quickly. A genius at hustling pool. Fought with Babe Ruth. Didn't matter. Great manager. Leo The Lip.

"I'm for Reiser," Lefty said. Pete Reiser. The kid with all the tomorrows. Hall-room boy. Bats left or right. Throws left or right. Maybe he'll hit 400. Pistol Pete.

"Medwick," Jerry said. Joe Medwick. The big stick. Former batting champion. Then a fast ball crashed into his head. Fighting back now, fighting that fear. Ducky Medwick.

We grabbled in aimless excitement until at length four ballplayers appeared at a narrow gate. They looked about, considering the children. Twenty of us were milling near the cars. The ballplayers broke into quickstep, heads down. They said nothing. They had lost.

Durocher wasn't there, nor Pistol Pete, but with rising shock I recognized Ducky Medwick. The old batting champion was a short, heavyset man, who scowled and sucked a great cigar. He rolled the cigar over his teeth as he walked.

"Mr. Medwick."

No response.

"Mr. Medwick."

He kept walking. The four ballplayers reached the alley and slipped into a large black car with such briskness that they might have been bank robbers.

"Can I have an autograph, Mr. Medwick?" I called through an open window.

"Get away from the car, kid, before we run ya the fuck down." Mr. Medwick had concluded my first colloquy with a major-league ballplayer.[7]

SPORTS AND DISPLACEMENT OF AGGRESSION

A fourth general explanation for the popularity of sports stresses the social usefulness of restrained and channeled competition. Human beings are naturally competitive and live amid alienating and frustrating social

It has become common in recent years to explain the popularity of professional football in terms of violence. Yet violent it is, and many fans gain vicarious pleasure from the aggression on the field.

conditions. Sport is a perfect forum for acting out competitiveness and relieving frustrations. Sociologists refer to the phenomenon of acting out one's competitive drives as the *displacement of aggression.* In this sense sports are seen as a socially useful safety valve. It is better for the Oakland Raiders' defensive backfield to annihilate an opposing flanker than to vent their hostilities in society, and it is better for spectators to displace vicariously their aggressions through the Raiders than to take out frustrations on their families.

SPORTS AND ETHNOCENTRISM

In chapter 2 we defined ethnocentrism as the tendency of people to judge other cultures by the standards of their own. Ethnocentrism may involve national, class, ethnic, and racial prejudice. All these differing forms of prejudice can be manifested in competitive contests. Reputations of schools from the most elite universities to the least aspiring community college are carried forth to fields of battle by the modern "gladiators."

This aspect of sports should not be glibly dismissed as the rather primitive behavior patterns of the unsophisticated. Decades of exploitation, repression, fear, and hope may be concentrated into just a few moments of sports action. In "The Black Boxer: Exclusion and Ascendance," Jack Orr focuses on one such concentrated moment—June 22, 1938.

That was the night the immortal Joe Louis, who had recently become heavyweight champion of the world, explosively knocked out the German challenger, Max Schmeling, in a little over two minutes as 70,000 fans screamed their approval and millions of others hunched excitedly over their radio sets.

434 / PROBLEMS AND ISSUES

The victory of Joe Louis, a black American, over Max Schmeling, the pride of Nazi Germany, in 1938 had both national and racial overtones.

To set the scene for this unforgettable fight, it must be recalled that Louis, who had been fighting professionally for four years and was still only twenty-four, had won every fight of his career—except a previous bout with Schmeling in 1936. At the time of the return match, Adolf Hitler was at the height of his power in Germany and the United States was beginning to be seriously disturbed over his teachings that the Germans were a "master race," destined to rule the world. The Nazis, and Schmeling himself, voiced particular disdain for blacks in general and Joe Louis in particular. Schmeling called him a "black stupid amateur."

Throughout the world the bout took on international and racial implications—American democracy versus Nazism and Aryan supremacy. Schmeling, a powerful puncher and very durable on defense, was favored by the experts. They had seen the German dynamite Joe Louis into submission two years earlier and had not forgotten. They forecast an early knockout of Louis and it was hard for anybody to foresee that they would be wrong.

On that hot night in 1938, Louis was a dedicated and ferocious fighter. At the first bell he dashed from his corner and caught Schmeling with a quick left followed by a punishing right cross. The German went down and the crowd exploded with deafening cheers. He got up, blood trickling from his mouth. Louis hit him again, a left and a right. Schmeling actually whimpered in pain as he went down again. *His face had an anguished look. He tried to get up, but the battle was over. Louis wore an almost disinterested look as the referee counted to ten.*[8]

In this instance, the ethnocentric overtones were both national and racial.

Appeals to nationalism in sports activities are frequently heard. This country's two most physically vigorous presidents, Theodore Roosevelt and Gerald Ford, both strongly endorsed the uplifting and seemingly American aspects of physical competition. In one speech before a Harvard audience, Roosevelt said:

We cannot afford to turn out of college men who shrink from physical effort or from a little physical pain. In any republic courage is a prime necessity for the average citizen if he is to be a good citizen, and he needs physical courage no less than moral courage; the courage that dares as well as the courage that endures, the courage that will fight valiantly alike against the foes of the soul and the foes of the body.

Athletics are good, especially in their rougher forms, because they tend to develop such courage. They are good also because they encourage a true democratic spirit, for in the athletic field the man must be judged, not with reference to outside and accidental attributes, but to that combination of bodily vigor and moral quality which go to make up prowess.[9]

In a similar vein President Ford has defended the value of sports.

The reason I make reference to those winning seasons at Michigan is that we have been asked to swallow a lot of home-cooked psychology in recent years that winning isn't all that important anymore, whether on the athletic field or in any other field, national and international. I don't buy that for a minute. It is not enough to just compete. Winning is very important. Maybe more important than ever.[10]

Although Ford's comments are not so filled with the jingoism of Teddy Roosevelt, his message remains the same: Competition is good. Competition is American!

Political banners of varying camps are borne into the arena by both teams and individual sports figures. The football teams of both Vince Lombardi and Woody Hayes carried with them a large burden of political ideology during the 1960s. Hard work, much diligence, and political conservatism were the ingredients of their success. Similarly, the rock-ribbed Republicans of Green Bay and Columbus loved their championship football teams, the Packers and the Buckeyes. For many followers, the Green Bay victories over the upstart Chiefs and Raiders in the first two Super Bowls and Ohio State's national championship in 1968 were not just pass-

President Theodore Roosevelt, advocate of the "strenuous life."

ing triumphs but political statements—testimonies to a way of life. Such conservatives were not the only sports enthusiasts with standard bearers, of course. Broadway Joe Namath, the first football hero to "wear his hair like a girl," carried the hopes of many "long hairs," flamboyant youth, and rebels.

The sports figure with perhaps the greatest political significance over the past decade has been the brazen, amusing, and charismatic Muhammad Ali. Ali's alliance with the Black Muslims, which he announced immediately after taking the heavyweight boxing championship from Sonny Liston in 1964, repelled many of boxing's followers who had not already been alienated by what they considered his arrogance. The final affront to political moderation came in 1967, when Ali refused to be inducted into the military with the statement, "I ain't got nothing against them Viet Congs."[11] Though his action was upheld by the Supreme Court seven years later, his claim that he should be exempted from military service because of his Muslim ministry evoked great hostility from many. Ali was stripped of the heavyweight championship and prevented from boxing for three and one-half years. As a result he became a hero to some and anathema to others.

THE BENEFITS OF SPORTS

A final hypothesis for the continuing popularity of sports emphasizes the benefits that participants receive. The benefits most often cited range from simple conditioning to true spiritual asceticism.

Many participant sport activities are pursued for their presumed benefits of good health and long life. The tremendous growth in the number of joggers during the past decade is an obvious example. People engage in sports because they want to lead long, vigorous, and healthy lives.

Yet for some, more than simple conditioning is involved. For such people sports activity takes on almost mystical and certainly very Oriental qualities. Like the ancient Greeks, they see leisure activity, and sports in particular, as a form of discipline and pure contemplation. Almost any sport can be used to pursue personal asceticism, though perhaps none so obviously as distance running. Alan Sillitoe, in *The Loneliness of the Long-Distance Runner*, captures something of the spiritually uplifting aspect of sports:

> And this long-distance running lark is the best of all, because it makes me think so good that I learn things even better than when I'm on my bed at night. And apart from that, what with thinking so much while I'm running, I'm getting to be one of the best runners in the Borstal. I can go my five miles round better than anybody else I know.
>
> So as soon as I tell myself I'm the first man ever to be dropped into the world, and as soon as I take that first flying leap out into the frosty grass of an early morning when even birds haven't the heart to whistle, I get to thinking, and that's what I like. I go my rounds in a dream, turning at lane or footpath corners without knowing I'm turning, leaping brooks without knowing they're there, and shouting good morning to the early cow-milker without seeing him. It's a treat, being a long-distance runner, out in the world by yourself with not a soul to make you bad-tempered or tell you what to do or that there's a shop to break and enter a bit back from the next street. Sometimes I think that I've never been so free as during that couple of hours when I'm trotting up the path out of the gates and turning by that bare-faced, big-bellied oak tree at the land end. Everything's dead, not good, because it's dead before coming alive, not dead after being alive. That's how I look at it. Mind you, I often feel frozen stiff at first. I can't feel my hands or feet or flesh at all, like I'm a ghost who wouldn't know the earth was under him if he didn't see it now and again through the mist. But even though some people would call this frost-pain suffering if they wrote about it to their moms in a letter, I don't, because I know that in half an hour I'm going to be warm, that by the time I get to the main road and am turning on to the wheatfield footpath by the bus stop I'm going to feel as hot as a potbellied stove and as happy as a dog with a tin tail.[12]

Sports and Social Mobility

Sports have long been a vehicle for upward mobility in this country. Tales of poverty-ridden youth of various racial and ethnic backgrounds rising above their station to become national heroes are very widespread in our culture. Such stories help validate the dream of an open society, free of racial and ethnic prejudice, where talent and hard work find their reward. The biographies of Jackie Robinson, Joe DiMaggio, and Bob Gibson from baseball; Johnny Unitas, Gale Sayers, and Joe Namath from football; and Bill Russell, Wilt Chamberlain, and John Havlicek from basketball lend support to our belief system. Though often embellished, the stories are generally true. Sports have provided an avenue out of the depths of numbing poverty for many. This was particularly true during the Great Depression of the 1930s, as Roger Kahn relates:

> Come back then to that alley, near the demolished ball park, and consider sport as it was in a complex, darkening, angry world. The athletes, all of them, were Depression men. They had known unemployment, felt hunger, seen breadlines. They had been raised on farms, or in bleak clapboard houses, and the options before them were spare. One could play ball—it was not play, of course, but labor—or failing that, one could look for work. Except there wasn't any work to find.
>
> Cookie Lavagetto, the old third baseman, has talked about what it meant for him to make the major leagues. "My people lived in Oakland," Lavagetto said, "and nobody was working. We couldn't get jobs. The first time I came up in spring training I hit a single and when I got to first base I was so happy, I burst out laughing. Next time I came up the pitcher threw four fast balls at my head. He thought I'd been laughing at him. I couldn't have kept myself from laughing. With that hit, I was taking the whole family off relief."[13]

The folklore regarding the open society of the United States and the many talented youths who rise above poverty to "make it big" is not without its stereotypical counterparts. Indeed, many images exist of those not terrifically bright athletes who are unable to do much more than what is required by their particular athletic specialty. The "dumb jock" football player has never been more humorously presented than in James Thurber's account of the mighty Bolenciecwcz in his essay "University Days."

> Another course that I didn't like, but somehow managed to pass, was economics. I went to that class straight from the botany class, which didn't help me any in understanding either subject. I used to get them mixed up. But not as mixed up as another student in my economics class who came there direct from a physics laboratory. He was a tackle on the football team, named Bolenciecwcz. At that time Ohio State University had one of the best football teams in the country, and Bolenciecwcz was one of its outstanding stars. In order to be eligible to play it was necessary for him to keep up his studies, a very difficult matter, for while he was not dumber than an ox he was

Major league baseball was segregated until Jackie Robinson (right) joined the Brooklyn Dodgers in 1947. Robinson endured much racial prejudice during the early years of integrated baseball.

not any smarter. Most of his professors were lenient and helped him along. None gave him more hints, in answering questions, or asked him simpler ones than the economics professor, a thin, timid man named Bassum. One day when we were on the subject of transportation and distribution, it came to Bolenciecwcz's turn to answer a question. "Name one means of transportation," the professor said to him. No light came into the big tackle's eyes. "Just any means of transportation," said the professor. Bolenciecwcz sat staring at him. "That is," pursued the professor, "any medium, agency, or method of going from one place to another." Bolenciecwcz had the look of a man who is being led into a trap. "You may choose among steam, horse-drawn, or electrically propelled vehicles," said the instructor. "I might suggest that one which we commonly take in making long journeys across land." There was a profound silence in which everybody stirred uneasily, including Bolenciecwcz and Mr. Bassum. Mr. Bassum abruptly broke this silence in an amazing manner. "Choo-choo-choo," he said, in a low voice, and turned instantly scarlet. He glanced appealing around the room. All of us, of course, shared Mr. Bassum's desire that Bolenciecwcz should stay abreast of the class in economics, for the Illinois game, one of the hardest and most important of the season, was only a week off. "Toot, toot, too-toooooooot!" some student with a deep voice moaned, and we all looked encouragingly at Bolenciecwcz. Somebody else gave a fine imitation of a locomotive letting off steam. Mr. Bassum himself rounded off the little show. "Ding, dong, ding, dong," he said, hopefully. Bolenciecwcz was staring at the floor now, trying to think, his great brow furrowed, his huge hands rubbing together, his face red.

"How did you come to college this year, Mr. Bolenciecwcz?" asked the professor. "Chuffa chuffa, chuffa chuffa."

"M'father sent me," said the football player.

"What on?" asked Bassum.

"I git an'lowance," said the tackle, in a low, husky voice, obviously embarrassed.

"No, no," said Bassum. "Name a means of transportation. What did you ride here on?"

"Train," said Bolenciecwcz.

"Quite right," said the professor. "Now, Mr. Nugent, will you tell us—"[14]

The story of Bolenciecwcz is obviously an exaggeration, with a basis in fact in a few cases. In actuality, the same may be said of the belief that sports are a vehicle of upward mobility for a significant number of poor blacks and ethnics. For every DiMaggio and Lavagetto, for every Robinson and Chamberlain, there are thousands of aspiring athletes whose dreams of wealth and fame are never realized. Fewer than one in a thousand high school athletes ever receives a "full ride" scholarship to play college ball, and of the college athletes, fewer than one in several hundred ever becomes an established star. Besides the rather impressive numbers arguing against the climb from poverty via strong legs and arms, there is another flaw in the general belief. Most successful athletes are from middle-class backgrounds.

Boxing is the one sport that has consistently drawn from the lower classes.[15] That sport has been dominated by the succession of racial and ethnic groups that have started at the lower end of the American stratification system, as Table 17-4 shows. As groups become middle class, they become underrepresented in professional boxing.

Boxing has been especially appealing to the "tough guys" of the lower classes. As we discussed earlier, overt aggression is rewarded and expected by members of these classes, while members of the middle and upper classes find such behavior a clear normative violation. But beyond the fact that boxing and social class are related, there is the assumption that "the

TABLE 17-4

Rank Order of Number of Prominent Boxers of Various Ethnic Groups for Certain Years

Year	Rank 1	Rank 2	Rank 3
1909	Irish	German	English
1916	Irish	German	Italian
1928	Jewish	Italian	Irish
1936	Italian	Irish	Jewish
1948	Negro	Italian	Mexican
1970	Negro	Mexican	

SOURCE: Data from *World's Annual Sporting Record* (1910 and 1917); *Everlast Boxing Record* (1929); *Boxing News Record* (1938); and *Ring* (1948, 1949, and 1970), as reported in S. Kirson Weinberg and Henry Arond, "The Occupational Culture of the Boxer," *American Journal of Sociology*, 58 (March 1952): 460–469.

Muhammad Ali, shown here knocking out challenger Richard Dunn in 1976, epitomizes the charismatic sports hero.

hungry fighter" is the best fighter. Like the youthful Cookie Lavagetto who saw baseball as the only means he had for raising his family from poverty, the hungry fighter is presumed willing to take more punishment and be more aggressive. The following comparison between college boxers and professional fighters makes this point clearly:

> *They say that too much education softens a man and that is why the college graduates are not good fighters. They fight emotionally on the gridiron and they fight bravely and well in our wars, but their contributions in our rings have been insignificant. The ring has been described as the refuge of the under-privileged. Out of the downtrodden have come our greatest fighters. . . . An education is an escape, and that is what they are saying when they shake their heads—those who know the fight game—as you mention the name of a college fighter. Once the bell rings, they want their fighters to have no retreat, and a fighter with an education is a fighter who does not have to fight to live and he knows it. . . . Only for the hungry fighter is it a decent gamble.*[16]

Despite the lower-class emphasis, though, boxing too is a poor risk as an avenue for upward mobility. S. Kirson Weinberg and Henry Arond report two studies of mobility in boxing, one viewing career patterns in the late 1930s, the other in the 1950s. The results of these studies are shown in Table 17–5. In both instances professional fighters rarely became nationally known contenders but remained instead poorly paid fringe fighters who fought in local clubs and as preliminary bout contestants.

TABLE 17-5
Boxing Career Patterns*

Year	Local and Preliminary Fighters	National Recognition
1938	92.9%	7.1%
1950	91.2%	8.8%

SOURCE: Compiled from S. Kirson Weinberg and Henry Arond, "The Occupational Culture of the Boxer," *American Journal of Sociology,* 58 (March 1952): 465.

*The number of participants in the 1938 study was 107 and in the 1950 study, 1,831.

EARLY LOSS OF INCOME

Even for those few who do achieve some upward mobility through sports, the chances are that they will not retain their high status for long. Most successful careers in sports are characterized by rapid upward mobility for the athlete, a few years of relatively stable peak performance, then a deterioration of skills with the accompanying lingering decline in performance before the end. The end for athletes comes not at age sixty-five as it does for most of us but near age thirty for professionals and in the early twenties for college athletes unable to continue their performance professionally. Negotiations between owners and players' associations have cushioned the financial fall of retirement considerably for those who spend a number of years in the "big leagues," but such pensions are recent innovations and apply only to a small percentage of major sports participants. For the most part athletes are forced to cope with a sudden, almost total loss of adulation as well as an extremely restricted budget.

LOSS OF PUBLIC ACCLAIM

It would seem, though, that it is not so much downward economic mobility that is so difficult for former athletes to cope with. The most difficult adjustment is finding ways to overcome the loss of admiration (and consequent feelings of self-worth) once so readily forthcoming from admiring fans.

For some, the loss of fame is recaptured in the misty recollection of past glories. In Philip Roth's novel *Goodbye, Columbus,* former basketball player Ron Patimkin could be aided in his recollections through his stereo equipment and his "goodbye, Columbus" album, recording some of the events of his final days at Ohio State.

> *And here comes Ron Patimkin dribbling out. Ron, Number 11, from Short Hills, New Jersey. Big Ron's last game, and it'll be some time before Buckeye fans forget him . . .*
>
> *Big Ron tightened on his bed as the loudspeaker called his name; his ovation must have set the nets to trembling. Then the rest of the players were announced, and then basketball season was over, and*

it was Religious Emphasis Week, the Senior Prom (Billy May blaring at the gymnasium roof), Fraternity Skit Night, E. E. Cummings reading to students (verse, silence, applause); and then, finally, commencement:

"The campus is hushed this day of days. For several thousand young men and women it is a joyous yet a solemn occasion. And for their parents a day of laughter and a day of tears. It is a bright green day, it is June the seventh of the year one thousand nine hundred and fifty-seven and for these young Americans the most stirring day of their lives. For many this will be their last glimpse of the campus, of Columbus, for many many years. Life calls us, and anxiously if not nervously we walk out into the world and away from the pleasures of these ivied walls. But not from its memories. They will be the concomitant, if not the fundament, of our lives. We shall choose husbands and wives, we shall choose jobs and homes, we shall sire children and grandchildren, but we will not forget you, Ohio State. In the years ahead we will carry with us always memories of thee, Ohio State . . ."

Slowly, softly, the OSU band begins the Alma Mater, and then the bells chime that last hour. Soft, very soft, for it is spring.

There was goose flesh on Ron's veiny arms as the Voice continued. "We offer ourselves to you then, world, and come at you in search of Life. And to you, Ohio State, to you Columbus, we say thank you, thank you and goodbye. We will miss you, in the fall, in the winter, in the spring, but some day we shall return. Till then, goodbye, Ohio State, goodbye, red and white, goodbye, Columbus . . . goodbye, Columbus . . . goodbye . . ."

Ron's eyes were closed. The band was upending its last truckload of nostalgia, and I tiptoed from the room, in step with the 2163 members of the Class of '57.[17]

It is this nostalgia, the remembrance of marvelous victories and good fellowship, that is perhaps at the very center of sport's romantic appeal. The poignancy that is often a prime ingredient of this romance is not so clearly focused with Ron Patimkin and Ohio State, nor is it captured by the unstoppable oratory of Howard Cosell. To experience truly the poignancy of retirement let us return to boxing. Journalist Mark Kram has provided an account of one of the most famous and storied corner men in the game, Charley Goldman.

From the sideshow feet to the derby which crowned a head reminiscent of Van Gogh's potato eaters, Charley was right out of central casting. He was the perfect embodiment of the public image of the corner man, a wandering sect that scratched out survival with swab sticks, stopwatches, pails full of humbug, muttlike loyalty and a compulsive attention to detail. [Charley] . . . treated all of his fight-

Sports and hobbies can help change a retirement of boredom and loneliness into one of pleasure and fulfillment.

ers as if they were made of porcelain. His advice was endless: never buy diamonds off anyone on the street; only a sucker git hit with a right hand. At the end of his life at 85, Charley lived alone in one room on the upper West Side of Manhattan. The fixtures of his work were all over that room, Q-Tips, beat-up satchels, old chewed-up mouthpieces with a thin coat of dust. He used to sit there, his gnarled little hands clasped, and speak of Rocky Marciano. "I was the trainer of Rocky Marciano," he liked to say. He was not being boastful. He just wanted to make sure it was part of the record, for that was all he had left. And then one day they found him in his room, dead and wearing an old robe of Rocky's.[18]

Charley had never been the center of attention himself; he had only shared a small portion of the limelight that had shown so brightly on world heavyweight champions. Yet he had been a part of a world he loved, and the nostalgia of his last years illustrates the romantic appeal of that world.

The Future of Leisure and Sport

In all probability, there will be a marked increase in leisure time during the next half century. Further, the growing presence and sophistication of media and communication systems seem to assure that major sports will continue to thrive. If the shift toward more free time is rapid, many social problems may result.

The "instant leisure" which faces many upon retirement today demonstrates this. Unable to cope with the loss of self-esteem that had been supplied by their "useful" life while employed, many retired individuals feel hopelessly lost in the supposed "golden years" of leisure. Even the numerous hobby and sports clubs that are a fixture in middle-class retirement villages are often inadequate pastimes. Jerry Jacobs's study of "Fun City," a retirement community in the West, has exposed the inadequacies of planned leisure as a way of coping with the sudden loss of work that had long given meaning to life.[19]

We seem to be wedded to the work ethic, although we face a future in which work will not be as central to life. Speculation on the social problems that may result has given rise to a growing academic subfield often termed the *sociology of sport and leisure*. There is a rapidly increasing amount of research in this area, much of which is found in Max Kaplan's fine work on leisure.* Perhaps such studies will ultimately help provide us with an alternate "leisure ethic" that will allow us to use our growing time free from work in ways we can value as useful. Then, as Kaplan notes, we can begin to appreciate leisure as "an opportunity to master time—and ourselves."[20]

*See Max Kaplan, *Leisure* (New York: Wiley, 1975).

446 / PROBLEMS AND ISSUES

Chapter Summary

Various cultures have interpreted the term "leisure" differently, but for our purposes it means simply time free from work. Similarly, "sport" is a culturally defined term which in the United States refers to a relatively small list of activities. Classes and subcultures vary in attitudes toward "time free from work," and they differ as well in preferences for a variety of sports. Both leisure time and money spent for recreation and sport have increased greatly over the past half century.

Several explanations have been offered for the growing popularity of sports. Success breeds success is one explanation. Another is that sports are easily understood and participants in them generally know the standards of excellence they must meet. The mystery and romance of sports may also draw people to them. Sports are valued, according to another explanation, because they provide a means for people to discharge their aggressions in ways that are not harmful to society. Somewhat related to this is the hypothesis that sports serve as an outlet for natural ethnocentric tendencies. Finally, some maintain that sports are popular because they offer participants both physical and spiritual benefits.

A review of data relating to the cherished belief in sports as a means of upward mobility suggests that few actually ever attain through sports the goals of fame and wealth to which they aspire. For most participants sports yield no financial rewards, yet dreams of long-term contracts and huge salaries continue to sustain many aspiring champions.

Finally, the future of both leisure and sports activities seems quite positive. Sport as big business will continue, as will the trend toward increased leisure time. The major uncertainty involves cultural adaptations to increased leisure time. At present, studies of retirement villages and the euphemistically described "golden years" of leisure indicate that because we give so little value to time free from work, we may face increased social problems in the future when more free time is available.

Key Terms for Review

displacement of aggression, p. 433
leisure, p. 425

sociology of sport and leisure, p. 445
sport, p. 427

Suggested Readings

SOCIOLOGICAL

De Grazia, Sebastian. *Of Time, Work, and Leisure.* Doubleday, 1962. Garden City, N.Y.: This literate and informative study is the most thorough and profound treatment of leisure that has yet been published. De Grazia examines the historical development of leisure and traces varying philosophic and cultural attitudes toward it.

Edwards, Harry. *The Revolt of the Black Athlete.* New York: Free Press, 1969. This work has established Edwards as the most famous of the sociological investigators currently examining sport. He portrays the life of black athletes in the sports industry of today.

———. *The Sociology of Sport.* Homewood, Ill.: Dorsey Press, 1973. A more scholarly and exhaustive study of sport than the earlier *Revolt,* this work is a critical examination of sport as it currently exists in the United States.

Kaplan, Max. *Leisure.* New York: Wiley, 1975. Kaplan provides a very readable and insightful examination of current thoughts and data pertinent to the "leisure problem." The work is the best available overview of the subject.

Scott, Jack. *The Athletic Revolution.* New York: Free Press, 1971. Many see Scott as the guru and leading intellectual of the "antiestablishment" sport critics. His work places contemporary sport within a historical perspective and is a great aid in understanding the many vested interests that dominate big business sports enterprises.

Talamini, John T., and Charles Hunt Page, eds. *Sport and Society.* Boston: Little, Brown, 1973. This carefully edited anthology contains both academic and journalistic examinations of various aspects of sport. If one must choose a single book to explore the world of sport, this would be the best.

LITERARY

Kahn, Roger. *The Boys of Summer.* New York: Harper & Row, 1972. Kahn is one of the best contemporary sports journalists and his brilliant writing makes this portrait of the great Brooklyn Dodger teams of the 1950s a joy to read. All that is both human and romantic in sports is presented by Kahn as he traces the lives of the old Brooklyn stars after they left the game.

Malamud, Bernard. *The Natural.* New York: Farrar, Straus, 1961. This novel is probably the finest literary effort ever produced dealing with sport. Malamud presents a young "natural" and his spiritual quest in baseball.

IN THIS CHAPTER

Urban Growth   451
  Origins of the modern city   451
  Metropolitan areas and the megalopolis   455

Urban Life   456

Problems of the Central City   462
  Financial strains   463
  Decentralized government   465
  Crime   470
  Pollution   472
  Mass transit   473
  Ghettos   474

Suburbs   477

Summary   483

Key Terms for Review   484

Suggested Readings   484

18

Are cities huge, complex, impersonal monsters that devour the individual, or are they centers of opportunity and civilization which satisfy human aspirations?

Is almost everybody in American society, including farmers, affected by its urban character?

Why do many city dwellers have a "mind your own business" and "don't get involved" attitude?

Is suburbia the land of promise?

CITIES AND SUBURBS

Ever since the appearance of modern, industrial cities, people have wondered whether they are a blessing or a curse. To cultural historian Lewis Mumford, cities today are places where diverse energies collect to produce a higher civilization.

> The diffused rays of many separate beams of life fall into focus, with gains in both social effectiveness and significance. The city is the form and symbol of an integrated social relationship: it is the seat of the temple, the market, the hall of justice, the academy of learning. Here in the city the goods of civilization are multiplied and manifolded; here is where human experience is transformed into viable signs, symbols, patterns of conduct, systems of order.[1]

Poet Carl Sandburg gives an eloquent tribute to Chicago, describing his city as powerful and proud — the epitome of growth and progress.

> Hog Butcher for the World,
> Tool Maker, Stacker of Wheat,
> Player with Railroads and the Nation's Freight Handler;
> Stormy, husky, brawling,
> City of the Big Shoulders:
>
> . . .
>
> Come and show me another city with lifted head singing
>   so proud to be alive and coarse and strong and cunning.
> Flinging magnetic curses amid the toil of piling job
>   on job, here is a tall bold slugger set vivid against
>   the little soft cities;

> *Fierce as a dog with tongue lapping for action, cunning
> as a savage pitted against the wilderness.*[2]

These observers of city life, along with many other individuals, would agree with Walter Lippmann's contention that "a great society is simply a big and complicated urban society."[3]

Yet for every person who feels the power and exaltation of cities, there is probably another who considers cities repulsive. The English Romantic poet Lord Byron found the beauty and silence of nature pleasurable, "but the hum of cities torture."[4] And fellow Romantic Percy Bysshe Shelley agreed that "hell is a city much like London—a populous and smoky city."[5] To people with this outlook, cities are blighted places that stifle and alienate the human spirit and destroy the body with poisonous gases, deafening sounds, and violent crimes. Unfortunately for those with anti-urban feelings, the trend over the last two centuries has been an increasing concentration of people in cities and surrounding areas. This concentration has been most pronounced in Western industrial societies, where urbanization appears to be almost complete. But, as the developing na-

Gin Lane by William Hogarth. Many have viewed city life as bringing out the worst in people—greed, immorality, debauchery, drunkenness, and corruption.

tions of Africa, Asia, and South America become more industrialized, their peoples too will experience the fortunes or misfortunes of city life.

Why and how do cities originate and grow? Does urbanization affect a society's cultural and social life? What are the problems modern cities face? Are there solutions to these problems? These are the major questions we will address in this chapter.

Urban Growth

Before we can discuss urban growth, we must define two terms, "urbanization" and "city." *Urbanization* refers to an increase in the "proportion of population living in urban places" and to "the process by which rural areas become transformed into urban areas."[6] Although the growth of cities almost always means urbanization, this is occasionally not the case. Urbanization requires a shift in population from the countryside to the cities. If the proportion of urban and rural areas in a country stays the same as population grows, then urbanization does not occur. Urbanization must also be distinguished from population density. For example, India has a large population (over 600 million people) and yet a low degree of urbanization. Its citizens live in numerous small villages as well as large cities such as Bombay and Calcutta.

Most people think of a city as a geographical area with official boundaries, a legal name, and a charter. But sociologists use the term somewhat differently. They define a *city* as a community of substantial size and population density wherein residents tend to engage in diverse, specialized activities which are nonagricultural in nature.[7] Sociologists emphasize the organizational and cultural features of cities.

The first cities, which appeared some 5,500 years ago, were quite small and inhabited by people with rural orientations. With a few notable exceptions, such as imperial Rome or seventeenth-century Amsterdam, cities remained much like villages until the 1800s, when both their size and numbers greatly increased. And in the twentieth century urbanization has occurred with revolutionary speed. In 1900 only one society, that of Great Britain, could be properly described as predominantly urban, whereas today all industrial societies are predominantly urban. Within ten to twenty years of this writing the majority of the world's population will live in urban rather than rural places.[8]

ORIGINS OF THE MODERN CITY

Urbanization appears clearly related to a society's evolutionary development. Sociologist Gideon Sjoberg maintains that the modern industrial city appeared only after certain societies had passed through three levels

Rural life, often remembered with nostalgia, is rare in American society today; less than 5 percent of the population is directly involved in farming.

of organization. The first level, which Sjoberg calls *folk society*, contained a small, preliterate, homogeneous population totally concerned with food gathering. This was necessarily a pre-urban society. A second and more complex level of organization, *feudal society*, then evolved. In this stage the society was able to produce some surplus food, which allowed a few individuals to engage in nonagricultural activities. Technology as we think of it today was in its infancy and literacy was limited to only a few. Cities first appeared in the latter part of this evolutionary period. Eventually a third level of organization, *industrial society*, evolved. Because of technological advances, a food surplus could be produced and stored. In this period the society was also characterized by industrialization, an organized and specialized labor force, and widespread literacy. Only at this evolutionary stage could the modern industrial city that we know today emerge.[9]

As Sjoberg notes, the huge, complex cities of today could not have evolved if it were not for several factors. First, a food surplus and the ability to store it allowed a large proportion of the society's members to turn to nonagricultural activities. Second, the Industrial Revolution brought the growth of factories, which lured people from rural regions to work and live together in densely settled areas. In addition, improved transportation and communication facilities—also products of industrialization—made large cities feasible. And, third, mass literacy made possible complex political, administrative, and legal systems, all so necessary for city life. Besides these factors, a rapidly growing world population obviously contributed to the phenomenon of dense concentrations of people.*

*See J. John Palen, *The Urban World* (New York: McGraw-Hill, 1975), Chap. 2, for further discussion of necessary preconditions for the emergence of cities.

There is a limit to urbanization, however, because there is a limit on how many people can leave their rural jobs of food production. Some sociologists maintain that a minimum of 5 to 10 percent of the population must remain on the farm to produce food for the whole society. But even without a continuing influx of people from the countryside, cities will still continue to grow. The world population is mushrooming at alarming rates, and so the already overcrowded city of today may actually double or triple in population in the future. (See chapter 19 for a discussion of the rate of world population growth.) Table 18–1 lists the fifteen largest urban areas in the world, all of which have populations of over 5 million. The population figures are for the entire urban area—the city proper plus neighboring smaller cities, towns, and villages.

The United States now has one of the most urbanized societies in the world. Between 70 and 75 percent of Americans live in urban areas (places of 2,500 inhabitants or more) and slightly less than 5 percent are directly involved in growing food for the society. Figure 18–1 illustrates the shift in rural and urban population between 1890 and 1970. Jobs, conveniences, diverse activities, and entertainment lure people to the city. But even those who remain in the countryside are affected by the larger urban society. Writer Granville Hicks, in "How We Live in America," describes the dominant role the city plays in shaping rural life.

Around our house in upstate New York are lawn and flower gardens and a kitchen garden, but beyond this small area of cultivation the

TABLE 18–1
Population of the World's Largest Urban Areas

Urban Area	Population	Source
New York, U.S.A.*	16,206,841	1970 census
Tokyo, Japan	11,324,417	1973 census
Shanghai, China	10,820,000	1970 estimate
Paris, France	9,250,647	1970 estimate
Mexico City, Mexico	8,589,630	1970 census
Buenos Aires, Argentina	8,352,900	1970 census
Osaka, Japan	7,838,722	1973 census
São Paulo, Brazil	7,693,000	1973 estimate
Peking, China	7,570,000	1970 estimate
London, England	7,418,020	1970 estimate
Moscow, U.S.S.R.	7,300,000	1971 estimate
Los Angeles–Long Beach, U.S.A.	7,032,075	1970 census
Calcutta, India	7,031,382	1971 census
Chicago, U.S.A.	6,978,947	1970 census
Bombay, India	5,970,575	1971 census

SOURCE: *The World Almanac and Book of Facts: 1976* (New York: Newspaper Enterprise Association, 1976), p. 682.

*New York's urban area includes part or all the population of ten New Jersey counties and five New York State counties in addition to the five boroughs of New York City.

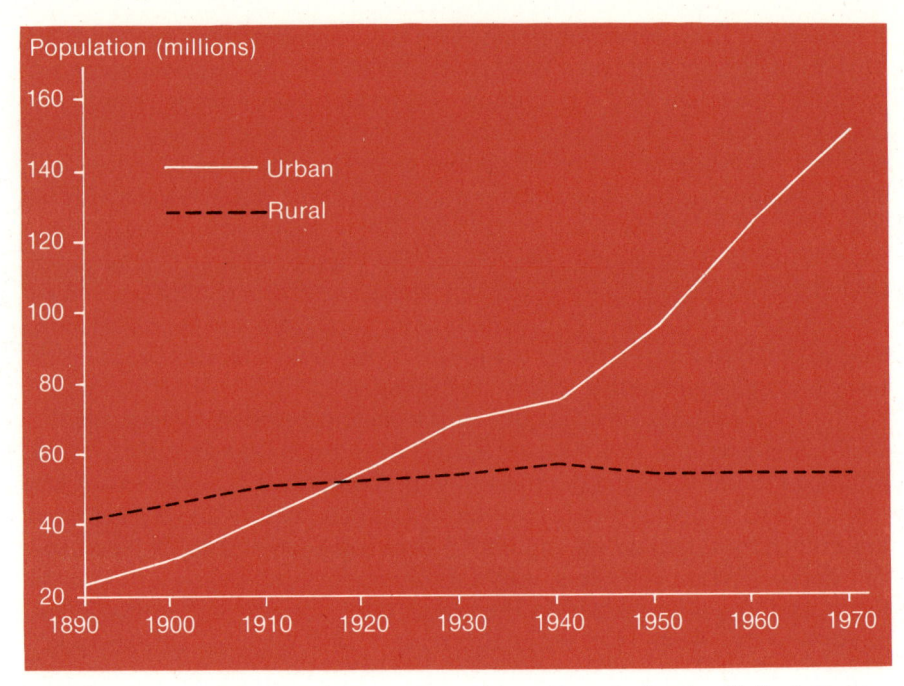

FIGURE 18-1 Urban and Rural Population Growth in the United States, 1890–1970

SOURCE: U.S. Bureau of the Census, *Historical Statistics of the United States, Colonial Times to 1957* (Washington, D.C.: U.S. Government Printing Office, 1960) and *Statistical Abstract of the United States: 1974* (Washington, D.C.: U.S. Government Printing Office, 1974), p. 19.

forest has taken over. Yet this was a farm for more than a hundred years, supporting four generations, and when Roxborough's population was at its peak, in the middle of the 19th century, it was one of hundreds of farms in the town. Today there aren't half a dozen men in the whole of Roxborough who get the major part of their livelihood from farming. We have our kitchen gardens, and some of us have hens, and here and there a family keeps a cow, but most of what we eat comes from the counters and shelves of supermarkets. Our clothing is selected from mail order catalogues or bought in city stores, and the spinning wheels and looms and hatchels of our ancestors are bait for antique dealers. The fuel we burn is delivered in trucks, and wood for the fireplace is hard to come by and almost as dear as in the cities.

These are signs of a two-way revolution. The farming is now done elsewhere, and done with fewer and fewer men and more and more machines, under conditions that often approximate the conditions of the mass production industries. We live in the country, but we live on the produce of California and Texas and Florida and New Jersey, just as we would if we lived in Troy or Albany or New York City. And by and large we make our living out of industry, most of us directly, by working in the factories of the Capital District, most of the others indirectly, by catering to the summer people or serving the needs of the commuters. The small town has been absorbed by the great society. . . .

As anybody can see, rural life more and more closely resembles urban life, and this is true not only for small towns like ours, which has become a semi-suburb, but also for the areas that raise the nation's food. In the dairy country of western New York, in the Corn Belt, in the Wheat Belt, in the fruit-raising sections of California and Florida, farmers not only have thousands of dollars worth of labor-saving machinery in their fields and barns; they have the conveniences and luxuries in their homes. Even in the poorer farm country the automobile and electricity are remaking the pattern of rural life.[10]

METROPOLITAN AREAS AND THE MEGALOPOLIS

Urbanization in the United States has resulted in the formation of *metropolitan areas*—social and economic communities that include several cities plus an urban fringe. The U.S. Bureau of the Census has devised a unit called the *Standard Metropolitan Statistical Area (SMSA)*. The SMSA is a city of at least 50,000 population or a city with a population of at least 25,000 which, with the addition of the population of adjacent areas, has a density of at least 1,000 people per square mile. The adjacent areas must be economically and socially integrated with the city. In the United States in the mid-1970s there are 272 SMSAs, in which over 149 million, or almost three quarters of the population, resides. Incredibly, these SMSAs cover only a small share of the total U.S. land area—about 14 percent.[11] A metropolitan area is more than just a large city. It is a new, complex form of urban area that includes downtowns, ghettos, bedroom and industrial suburbs, and unincorporated urban sprawl.

Particularly in the industrial sections of the United States, metropolitan areas have collided with and overlapped one another to form a massive and continuous urbanized region. This supermetropolitan unit is referred to as a *megalopolis*. In *The Making of the President 1960*. Theodore H. White describes two megalopolises he saw from the air while covering John F. Kennedy's campaign.

From the census one had the impression of a strange new society being formed: a series of metropolitan centers growing and swelling in their suburban girdles until the girdles touched one another, border on border, stretching in giant population belts hundreds of miles long while wilderness rose again on the outside of the girdle . . .

From the air the changes were clearly visible. By day one could see the dust clouds rising in midsummer as the bulldozers tore away at the potato patches of Long Island to clear land for more develop-

ments on the East Coast girdle; and flying out of Los Angeles, one could see again the same dust clouds as the bulldozers tore away at the orange groves of the San Fernando Valley. Late in the fall, flying north from Florida to New York on the Kennedy press plane, I went up to the cockpit to talk to the pilot. It was night as we spoke. It used to be, said the veteran pilot, looking out on lights knotting at all the crossroads far below, it used to be that you could fly visually on a clear night like this. You could pick up Norfolk from the air, then you could recognize Washington, then you could recognize Baltimore, and all the way up to Boston it was that way—one city, then the next. Now, he said, there was just a continuous belt of night light from Newport News north, and you couldn't locate yourself visually; you had to do it by instruments. "There's still a patch of open country you can pick up at night between Hartford and Boston, though," he said.[12]

The megalopolis that runs from the urban fringe of New York City to the suburbs of Washington, D.C., covers ten states and the District of Columbia, contains over 45 million people, and has an overall population density of 2,000 people per square mile. Although smaller in total population and in population density, the West Coast megalopolis stretches from San Diego north to Santa Barbara, and many would contend that it extends all the way to San Francisco. Further, a new such strip of overlapping cities appears to be forming from Chicago to Cleveland.[13]

Urban Life

With the industrial and urban growth of the nineteenth century, sociologists became intensely concerned with how cities affect a person's thinking and behavior. Emile Durkheim maintained that archaic societies are held together by *mechanical solidarity*—social bonds based on the similarity of individuals; while advanced societies are characterized by *organic solidarity*—bonds which develop out of the interdependence of dissimilar individuals. Ferdinand Tönnies described the traditional village or tribe as friendly and cohesive *(Gemeinschaft)* and the large city as impersonal and formal *(Gesellschaft)*. (See chapter 5 for a further discussion of *Gemeinschaft* and *Gesellschaft*.) And Georg Simmel feared that city life threatened the individual's self-identity.

Later American scholars followed in the tradition of these early European theorists. University of Chicago anthropologist Robert Redfield distinguished between two types of society. He characterized one, *folk society*, as small, preliterate, homogeneous, isolated, traditional, and family- and community-centered. In contrast, he saw *urban society* as large, complex, heterogeneous, bureaucratized, impersonal, and constantly changing.[14] Kurt Vonnegut, Jr., once an anthropology major and student and admirer of Redfield, commented on his professor's ideas in an address to the National Institute of Arts and Letters. Vonnegut first presents Redfield's proposition that the essential difference between folk and urban societies can be seen in how members relate to one another — whether they see others as persons or things.

> *Dr. Redfield is dead now. . . . While he lived, he had in his head a lovely dream which he called "The Folk Society." . . .*
>
> *He acknowledged that primitive societies were bewilderingly various. He begged us to admit, though, that all of them had certain characteristics in common. For instance: They were all so small that everybody knew everybody well, and associations lasted for life. The members communicated intimately with one another, and very little with anybody else.*
>
> *The members communicated only by word of mouth. There was no access to the experience and thought of the past, except through memory. The old were treasured for their memories. There was little change. What one man knew and believed was the same as what all men knew and believed. There wasn't much of a division of labor. What one person did was pretty much what another person did. . . .*
>
> *In a folk society, says Dr. Redfield, and I quote him now: . . . behavior is personal, not impersonal. A "person" may be defined as that social object which I feel . . . [will] respond to situations as I do, with all the sentiments and interests which I feel to be my own; a person is myself in another form, his qualities and values are inherent within him, and his significance for me is not merely one of utility. A "thing," on the other hand, is a social object which has no claim upon my sympathies, which responds to me, as I conceive it, mechanically; its value for me exists in so far as it serves my end. In the folk society, all human beings admitted to the society are treated as persons; one does not deal impersonally ("thing fashion") with any other participant in the little world of that society.*[15]

In his rather typically facetious style, Vonnegut then gives his own view that all urbanites, consciously or unconsciously, desire to return to the intimacy of folk society.

> *And I say to you that we are full of chemicals which require us to belong to folk societies, or failing that, to feel lousy all the time. We are chemically engineered to live in folk societies, just as fish are chemically engineered to live in clean water—and there aren't any folk societies for us anymore.*
>
> *How lucky you are to be here today, for I can explain everything. Sigmund Freud admitted that he did not know what women wanted.*

> *I know what they want. Cosmopolitan magazine says they want orgasms, which can only be a partial answer at best. Here is what women really want: They want lives in folk societies, wherein everyone is a friendly relative, and no act or object is without holiness. Chemicals make them want that. Chemicals make us all want that.*
>
> *Chemicals make us furious when we are treated as things rather than persons. . . . The generation gap is an argument between those who believe folk societies are still possible and those who know they aren't.*
>
> *Older persons form clubs and corporations and the like. Those who form them pretend to be interested in this or that narrow aspect of life. Members of the Lions Club pretend to be interested in the cure and prevention of diseases of the eye. They are in fact lonesome Neanderthalers, obeying the First Law of Life, which is this: "Human beings become increasingly contented as they approach the simpleminded, brotherly conditions of a folk society."*[16]

In 1938 sociologist Louis Wirth, also at the University of Chicago, wrote an essay entitled "Urbanism as a Way of Life." This essay examined three factors—large numbers, density, and heterogeneity—and their consequences for urban living. Wirth maintained that when large numbers of people concentrate in a small territory, life becomes more diverse, opportunities arise that are absent in rural areas, and new activities and institutions develop. On the other hand, density makes urbanites unable to interact with everyone they know on a personal basis, and so most relationships tend to be short-lived, superficial, and directed toward utilitarian goals. Indeed, some American cities are so densely populated that hundreds of thousands of people are crammed together. As one example, the Regional Plan Association calculates that a person in midtown Manhattan may encounter some 220,000 people within a ten-minute radius of his or her office.[17] Although not specifically discussed by Wirth, density is also sometimes used to explain urban conflict and violence. Gus Tyler, in an article entitled "Can Anyone Run a City?," cites population density as a major factor contributing to urban unrest.

> *Throughout the developing world, the city is failing badly.*
>
> *What is the universal malady of cities? The disease is density. Where cities foresaw density and planned accordingly, the situation is bad but tolerable. Where exploding populations hit unready urban areas, they are in disaster. Where ethnic and political conflict add further disorder, the disease appears terminal.*
>
> *Some naturalists, in the age of urban crisis, have begun to study density as a disease. Crowded rats grow bigger adrenals, pouring out their juices in fear and fury. Crammed cats go through a "Fascist" transformation, with a "despot" at the top, "pariahs" at the bottom, and a general malaise in the community, where the cats, according*

to P. Leyhausen, "seldom relax, they never look at ease, and there is continuous hissing, growling, and even fighting."

How dense are the cities? . . . If we all lived as crushed as the blacks in Harlem, the total population of America could be squeezed into three of the five boroughs of New York City.[18]

Finally, Wirth claimed that the third factor, heterogeneity, creates in the urbanite a greater tolerance for diverse ideas and cultural patterns.[19]

No doubt Wirth and other sociologists studying urban life during the 1920s and 1930s saw the advantages of cities, but their efforts were clearly directed toward researching and exposing their evil aspects. Mental illness, suicide, delinquency, and other problems were viewed as a natural part of the urban scene, and city dwellers were all pictured as living isolated, lonely, uncertain, and depersonalized lives. Over a century earlier, English essayist Thomas De Quincey reflected similar views when he described his feelings about London.

> *No man ever was left to himself for the first time in the streets, as yet unknown, of London, but he must have been saddened and mortified, perhaps terrified, by the sense of desertion and utter loneliness which belong to his situation. No loneliness can be like that which weighs upon the heart in the centre of faces never-ending, without voice or utterance for him; eyes innumerable, that have "no speculation" in their orbs which he can understand; and hurrying figures of men and women weaving to and fro, with no apparent purposes intelligible to a stranger, seeming like a mask of maniacs, or, oftentimes, like a pageant of phantoms. The great length of the streets in many quarters of London; the continual opening of transient glimpses into other vistas equally far-stretching, going off at right angles to the one which you are traversing; and the murky atmosphere which, settling upon the remoter end of every long avenue, wraps its termination in gloom and uncertainty; all these are circumstances aiding that sense of vastness and illimitable proportions which for ever brood over the aspect of London in its interior.*[20]

Were these theories and descriptions of urban life correct? Contemporary researchers have demonstrated that the city is not as *Gesellschaft* as was once believed, particularly in neighborhoods where residents are bound together by a common racial, ethnic, religious, or social-class background and there is residential stability. The close relationships found in some neighborhoods — possibly an Italian-American section, a black ghetto, or an upper-middle-class suburb — can create a *Gemeinschaft* existence for inhabitants.* On the surface the traditional notion of the impersonal,

---

*Herbert J. Gans, *The Urban Villagers* (New York: Free Press, 1962); Elliot Liebow, *Tally's Corner* (Boston: Little, Brown, 1967); and William H. Whyte, Jr., *The Organization Man* (Garden City, N.Y.: Doubleday, 1956) illustrate the high degree of intimacy and cohesion that can exist in some neighborhoods.

"Ethnic villagers" maintain close in-group ties and have relatively little contact with people outside their neighborhoods.

callous city appears to be refuted. But in defense of early sociologists we should note that they based their conclusions mostly upon observations of the core city—usually a place of extreme diversity, transience, change, and deterioration. What they described was true, but only for particular locations within the city. And when they wrote about the alienation of urbanites they were correct, but again this description applies only to some. The city contains some people who live an alienated existence and others who lead satisfying lives.

Clearly the activities, experiences, and personalities of the city are extremely varied. Sociologist Herbert Gans illustrates the montage-like quality of urban life by identifying five life styles frequently found in the central city. First, there are the "cosmopolites"—artists, writers, musicians, intellectuals, and professionals who have been drawn to the city because of its cultural advantages. Second, the "unmarried or childless" are attracted to the city because it provides entertainment and activity. Their commitment to city life is not great, and they may live there only briefly. Third, "ethnic villagers" are members of ethnic groups who have clustered together to form their own neighborhood. They typically isolate themselves from the rest of the city's population. Fourth, the "deprived" consist of the very poor, the handicapped, and often the nonwhite who tend to populate slum areas. And, fifth, the "trapped" are those people, usually elderly, who are unable to move to new communities and must remain in their neighborhood in spite of its deterioration.[21]

Urban life does foster a sense of aloofness from strangers and chance acquaintances. The city dweller comes into contact with thousands of individuals, some of whom appear to represent perverse and threatening ways of life, and as a result the urbanite avoids involvement. Author Herbert Gold, in his essay "A Dog in Brooklyn, A Girl in Detroit: A Life Among the Humanities," recounts an unfortunate incident that illustrates the "don't get involved" and "not my business" attitude of the urbanite. Gold maintains that people in a small, closely knit community would have behaved differently from the city dwellers he describes.

News item of a few years ago. A young girl and her date are walking along a street in Brooklyn, New York. The girl notices that they are being followed by an enormous Great Dane. The dog is behaving peculiarly, showing its teeth and making restless movements. A moment later, sure enough, the dog, apparently maddened, leaps slavering upon the girl, who is borne to earth beneath its weight. With only an instant's hesitation, the boy jumps on the dog. Its fangs sunk first in one, then in the other, the dog causes the three of them to roll like beasts across the sidewalk.

A crowd gathers at a safe distance to watch. No one interferes. The becalmed curiosity of teevee viewers.

A few moments later a truckdriver, attracted by the crowd, pulls his vehicle over to the curb. This brave man is the only human being stirred personally enough to leave the role of passive spectator. Instantaneously analyzing the situation, he leaps into the struggle—attacking and beating the boy. He has naturally assumed the dog must be protecting an innocent young lady from the unseemly actions of a juvenile delinquent.

In contrast to other inner-city dwellers, the "deprived" and "trapped" have virtually no choice regarding their residence.

> *I recounted this anecdote in the classroom in order to introduce a course which attempted a summary experience of Humanities 610 for a monumental nine credits. There were a number of points to be made about the passivity of the crowd ("don't get involved," "not my business") and the stereotypical reaction of the truckdriver who had been raised to think of man's best friend as not another human being but a dog. In both cases, addicted to entertainment and cliches, the crowd and the trucker could not recognize what was actually happening before their eyes; they responded irrelevantly to the suffering of strangers; they were not a part of the main. This led us to discussion of the notion of "community." In a closely knit society, the people on the street would have known the couple involved and felt a responsibility toward them. In a large city, everyone is a stranger.*[22]

The indifferent, insensitive behavior of many urbanites may be a natural way of coping with a complex and hostile environment. Psychologist Stanley Milgram maintains that the city dweller's aloofness is an adaptive mechanism for dealing with genuine "psychic overload." We might further conjecture that this overload is due to the individual's constantly encountering something new and different, having to share limited space with others, and trying to avoid real or imagined enemies.[23]

Problems of the Central City

America's central cities are in a state of crisis. They are beset by a multitude of problems—rats, unclean water, bankruptcy, slums, violence—and the severity of these problems is increasing. One has only to listen to the 6:00 P.M. news in any major metropolitan area to recognize the calamities besetting cities and their inhabitants. In *The Prisoner of Second Avenue* playwright Neil Simon presents a typical news account originating in the biggest city of all—New York, "The Big Apple."

> *This is Roger Keating and the Six O'Clock Report. . . . New York was hit with its third strike of the week. This time the city employees of thirty-seven New York hospitals walked out at 3 P.M. this afternoon. The Mayor's office has been flooded with calls, as hundreds of patients and elderly sick people have complained of lack of food, clean sheets and medicines. One seventy-nine-year-old patient in Lenox Hill Hospital fell in the corridor, broke his leg and was treated by a seventy-three-year-old patient who had just recovered from a gall-bladder operation. . . . Two of the most cold-blooded robbers in the city's history today made off with four thousand dollars, sto-*

len from the New York City Home for the Blind. Police believe it may have been the same men who got away with thirty-six hundred dollars on Tuesday from the New York Cat and Dog Hospital. . . . Water may be shut off tomorrow, says the New York Commissioner of Health, because of an anonymous phone call made to the bureau this morning, threatening to dump fifty pounds of chemical pollutants in the city's reservoirs. The unidentified caller, after making his threat, concluded with, "It's gonna be dry tomorrow, baby." . . . And from the office of Police Commissioner Murphy, a report that the number of apartment house burglaries has risen seven point two percent in August.[24]

FINANCIAL STRAINS

During 1975 and 1976 New York City found itself in desperate financial straits. It was hundreds of millions of dollars in debt and few solutions were in sight: banks refused the city's loan requests and tax revenues were grossly insufficient to cover the deficit.* Although most American cities do not face a dilemma of this magnitude, many large cities are encountering similar financial strangulation. The reasons are numerous. Cities generally have high crime rates, large numbers of poor people, extensive pollution, major transportation problems, and inadequate housing. As a result enormous sums must be spent on police and fire protection; welfare services; programs to remedy water, noise, and air pollution; mass transportation; and new housing. Yet local tax revenues are often inadequate to support these services. When a city taxes businesses heavily, small concerns may go bankrupt and large industries simply relocate outside the city. And residents, all too frequently the "deprived" and "trapped," have little taxable income.

The central city's economic decay also affects business enterprises. Bernard Malamud, in *The Assistant*, describes the plight of an aging Jewish grocer trying to run his small store in a modern city. The grocer's economic situation had become steadily worse "as the neighborhood had." Poor people had replaced middle-class residents as the neighborhood deteriorated, and it had become harder and harder for the grocer to eke out a living.

> He recalled the bad times he had lived through, but now times were worse than in the past; now they were impossible. His store was always a marginal one, up today, down tomorrow—as the wind blew. Overnight business could go down enough to hurt; yet as a rule it slowly recovered—sometimes it seemed to take forever—went up, not high enough to be really up, only not down. When he had first

---

*For a beginning discussion of New York City's financial plight, see "How New York City Lurched to the Brink," *Time*, June 16, 1975, pp. 16–21. Also many subsequent issues during 1975–1976 dealt with New York City's financial crisis.

A common pattern has been for large stores to move from downtown areas to suburbs, leaving behind a collection of small, run down, "mom and pop" businesses in the central city.

bought the grocery it was all right for the neighborhood; it had got worse as the neighborhood had. Yet even a year ago, staying open seven days a week, sixteen hours a day, he could still eke out a living. What kind of living?—a living; you lived. Now, though he toiled the same hard hours, he was close to bankruptcy, his patience torn. . . .

Last year a broken tailor, a poor man with a sick wife, had locked up his shop and gone away, and from the minute of the store's emptiness Morris had felt a gnawing anxiety. He went with hesitation to Karp, who owned the building, and asked him to please keep out another grocery. In this kind of neighborhood one was more than enough. If another squeezed in they would both starve. Karp answered that the neighborhood was better than Morris gave it credit (for schnapps, thought the grocer), but he promised he would look for another tailor or maybe a shoemaker, to rent to. He said so but the grocer didn't believe him. Yet weeks went by and the store stayed empty. Though Ida pooh-poohed his worries, Morris could not overcome his underlying dread. Then one day, as he daily expected, there appeared a sign in the empty store window, announcing the coming of a new fancy delicatessen and grocery.

Morris ran to Karp. "What did you do to me?"

The liquor dealer said with a one-shouldered shrug, "You saw how long stayed empty the store. Who will pay my taxes? But don't worry," he added, "he'll sell more groceries. Wait, you'll see he'll bring you in customers."

Morris groaned; he knew his fate.[25]

One way that cities might improve their financial position is by annexing surrounding areas, often middle- and upper-middle-class suburbs. This would broaden the tax base and increase revenues. However, most states have laws which inhibit central cities from freely annexing suburbs. Texas, an exception, allows for annexation. As one example, Houston has extended its original political boundaries to include surrounding areas, thereby giving itself a strong financial base.

DECENTRALIZED GOVERNMENT

Faced with failure in solving crises in education, housing, and other areas, some city officials have exclaimed that cities are ungovernable. Gus Tyler notes that some mayors have voluntarily given up their offices.

Can anyone run a city? For scores of candidates who have run for municipal office across the nation this week, the reply obviously is a rhetorical yes. But if we are to judge by the experiences of many mayors whose terms have brought nothing but failure and despair, the answer must be no. "Our association has had a tremendous casualty list in the past year," noted Terry D. Shrunk, mayor of Portland, Oregon, and president of the U.S. Conference of Mayors. "When we went home from Chicago in 1968, we had designated thirty-nine mayors to sit in places of leadership. . . . Today, nearly half of them are either out of office or going out . . . most of them by their own decision not to run again." Since that statement, two of the best mayors in the country—Jerome P. Cavanagh of Detroit and Richard C. Lee of New Haven—have chosen not to run again.

Why do mayors want out? Because, says Mayor Joseph M. Barr of Pittsburgh, "the problems are almost insurmountable. Any mayor who's not frustrated is not thinking." Thomas B. Currigan, former mayor of Denver, having chucked it all in mid-term, says he hopes "to heaven the cities are not ungovernable, [but] there are some frightening aspects that would lead one to at least think along these lines."[26]

A View of the City

Whereas all of America's communities have felt the impact of urbanization, large cities remain different from towns and rural settings, not only in terms of their greater number of people, but also in regard to economic activities, population density and diversity, and the rapidity of change. The environment of a big city produces for its residents a particular set of sights, sounds, and smells—some pleasant and some not.

For example, in contrast to the child growing up in Cedar Rapids, Iowa, or on a wheat farm outside Spokane, Washington, the daily life of children in a large city may mean seeing a policeman on horseback, riding bikes in the park, listening to a noisy jackhammer, feeding the city's wildlife, finding a new (and possibly dangerous) place to play . . .

reading graffiti, having to step over bodies on the sidewalk, seeing workers arrive at a factory, watching some old guys play checkers . . .

visiting an art museum, trying to stay out of certain people's way, listening to an outdoor concert, choking on air pollution, going on a class outing to the zoo . . .

wondering whether a restaurant's food tastes as good as it smells, seeing some guys being frisked, barely being able to see the sky, pitching rocks at a condemned building, looking for a book in an enormous library.

What makes city government so difficult and frustrating? One problem is that most metropolitan areas do not have one single government but many governments that overlap and duplicate one another's efforts. For example, in the St. Louis metropolitan area there are numerous mayors, commissioners, police and fire chiefs, and other public officials because each city, town, and village within the metropolitan area operates as a separate and distinct government unit.

In contrast to this fragmented system, a single, centralized government might be more economical and could better coordinate facilities and services for the total metropolitan area. Wealthy suburbs, however, have typically opposed centralized government. Residents of these suburbs usually want their tax dollars spent on local services, not used to rescue deteriorated parts of the central city. And, as we noted earlier, most state laws do not allow central cities freely to annex surrounding areas. Usually the consent of the state legislature is required, and of course, wealthy suburbs put considerable pressure on legislators to stop any annexation proposals by central cities. In addition, Americans have traditionally valued the right to control the destiny of their own particular community. This cultural value produces strong resistance to centralization.

CRIME

There is a scene in the play *The Prisoner of Second Avenue* that is repeated hundreds of times daily in any large city—an apartment is burglarized. Edna and Mel, the main characters, find it hard to believe that in broad daylight their television, books, clothing, and other valuables were stolen.

> EDNA *You read about it every day. And when it happens to you, you can't believe it.*
>
> MEL *A television I can understand. Liquor I can understand. But shaving cream? Hair spray? How much are they going to get for a roll of dental floss?*
>
> EDNA *They must have been desperate. They took everything they could carry.* (Shakes the book one last time) *They even found my kitchen money.*
>
> MEL *What kitchen money?*
>
> EDNA *I kept my kitchen money in here. Eighty-five dollars.*
>
> MEL *In cash? Why do you keep cash in a book?*
>
> EDNA *So no one will find it! Where else am I gonna keep it?*
>
> MEL *In a jar. In the sugar. Some place they're not going to look.*
>
> EDNA *They looked in the medicine chest, you think they're not going to look in the sugar?*
>
> MEL *Nobody looks in sugar!*
>
> EDNA *Nobody steals dental floss and mouthwash. Only sick people. Only that's who live in the world today. Sick, sick, sick people!*

(She sits, emotionally wrung out. MEL comes over to her and puts his arm on her shoulder, comforting her)

MEL It's all right . . . It's all right, Edna . . . As long as you weren't hurt, that's the important thing.

(He looks through the papers on the table)

EDNA *Can you imagine if I had walked in and found them here? What would I have done, Mel?*

MEL *You were very lucky, Edna. Very lucky.*

EDNA *But what would I have done?*

MEL *What's the difference? You didn't walk in and find them.*

EDNA *But supposing I did? What would I have done?*

MEL *You'd say, "Excuse me," close the door and come back later. What would you do, sit and watch? Why do you ask me such questions? It didn't happen, did it?*

EDNA *It almost happened. If I walked in here five minutes sooner.*

MEL (Walking away from her) *You couldn't have been gone only five minutes . . . It took the Seven Santini Brothers two days to move everything in, three junkies aren't gonna move it all out in five minutes.*[27]

In a fit of rage Mel rushes to the terrace and in desperation screams obscenities to the city because of the destruction it has brought him.

 . . . BASTARDS! . . . YOU DIRTY BASTARDS!

(Suddenly a VOICE, probably from the terrace above, yells down)

VOICE *Shut up, down there! There are children up here!*

MEL (Leans over the terrace wall and yells up) *Don't you yell at me! They took everything! EVERYTHING! They left me with a goddamned pair of pants* and a golf hat!

VOICE *There are children up here! Are you drunk or something?*

MEL *Drunk? Drunk on what? They got my liquor . . . You wanna keep your children, lock 'em up. Don't you tell me you got children up there.*

VOICE *Don't you have any respect for anyone else?*

MEL (Screaming up) *Respect? I got respect for my ass, that's what I got respect for! That's all anybody respects . . .*[28]

The high crime rates characteristic of central cities naturally provoke demands for better police protection. But financially hard-pressed cities are finding it difficult to meet these demands. As noted earlier, most metropolitan areas contain many separate police departments. They vary in size, training programs, equipment, record-keeping, facilities, and attitudes. Given this diversity and overlap, efficient and coordinated law enforcement is difficult to achieve, and the partial solution of consolidating efforts has occurred in only a few places.

Industry is clearly a major source of pollution; industrial areas like this one in Detroit are a problem nationwide.

POLLUTION

Urban governments are also expected to provide pure water, clean air, and adequate sewage disposal for residents, but many city dwellers must survive in an extremely polluted environment. Over 6,000 of the nation's public water supplies, serving some 58 million people, do not meet Public Health Service drinking water standards; each year the 50 million rats in America's cities bite 45,000 people, mostly children; and since 1940 automobiles have caused an annual increase in the atmosphere of 4 percent carbon monoxide, 3.3 percent hydrocarbons, and 4.8 percent nitrogen oxide.[29] Author Robert Abernathy vividly describes the sights, sounds, and smells of a polluted city in his short story "Single Combat."

> Late cloudless afternoon lay like a blanket on the city. Above the squat grimy structures close at hand, the great buildings soared, flashing with windows. Above all, smoke smudges drifted, lazy in the smothering calm. In the streets traffic growled past, shedding gasoline fumes and the smell of heated asphalt. The alley stank; the city stank; even the swift river stank.
>
> Head back, eyes narrowed against reflected sunlight, he snuffed its air that was rank with memory.
>
> The stench of many summers . . . Get up, I smell gas. No, it's the wind from across the river. The refineries there. Well, it's making the baby choke. Can't we do something?
>
> The everlasting cough and rumble, the voice of the city . . . Goddamn trucks, going by all night. Can't sleep for them. If I could just get some sleep. . . .

The raucous voices, the jeers, the blows, brutality of life trapped in a steel and cement jungle.[30]

The pollution created by a city does not necessarily confine itself to that location. Some 10 million people living between Detroit and Buffalo are provided with water from Lake Erie, yet sewage and industrial wastes from many municipalities in this area are dumped directly into the lake. And, although Phoenix already has an air pollution problem of its own making, the problem is compounded by drifting smog from Los Angeles.

Unfortunately, cleaning up pollution is an enormous task—one that cities cannot accomplish alone. They lack the money, regulatory power, and expertise required to correct a problem of such dimensions. Clearly the federal government will have to assume a prominent role in pollution control.*

MASS TRANSIT

Cities have been faced with the problems of unsightly freeways, traffic jams, and inadequate parking facilities—all of which are a result of Americans' obsession with the automobile. Such problems will not be corrected until attractive and efficient forms of mass transportation are established. At present, almost no city has mass transit services that can compete with automobiles. Current mass transit facilities are criticized for inconveniently located stations, poor routes, unreliable service, crowding, lack of comfort, unclean facilities, and threats to personal safety. As a result, most people prefer to drive their own cars.

Some ways for cities to make immediate improvements in their mass transit systems have been suggested, such as reserving certain street lanes for buses to speed service and using computers to improve scheduling. Another proposal suggests establishing a cheap rental service for low-powered vehicles for short trips within the city. But major solutions to urban transportation problems will require new ideas and concentrated effort at all government levels. The monorail, dial-a-bus, minibus, high-speed subway, and moving sidewalk might be economically and technically efficient and attractive enough to lure Americans out of their automobiles.

Urban centers are expected to provide a wide range of services, not only to their own residents but to all those who come into the city. Among the services we have not discussed are fire protection, safe and adequate housing, parks and recreation centers, and elementary and secondary schools. (See chapter 10 for a discussion of education problems in slum schools.) Of utmost importance in solving the urban "service crisis" is a

---

*For an informative discussion of the crises arising from water and air pollution, see Aber Wolman, "The Metabolism of Cities," in *Cities: A Scientific American Book* (New York: Alfred A. Knopf, 1969), pp. 156–174.

In 1976 Los Angeles instituted its "Diamond Lane Express" plan, which reserved the far left lane of selected freeways for car pools and buses to encourage use of group or mass transportation. But most people continued driving their own cars to and from work, and the experiment's future is in doubt.

more widespread awareness that services provided by the city also benefit nonresidents.*

GHETTOS

The term "ghetto" originally meant that section of the medieval European city officially designated for Jews. In the United States, however, *ghetto* has come to mean a central-city area densely populated by impoverished and isolated individuals, particularly blacks. Although not all live in ghettos or are impoverished, about three-fourths of all black Americans now live in metropolitan areas, and other 60 percent live in central cities.[31] Figure 18-2 illustrates the changing composition of metropolitan population inside and outside central cities.

Ghettos, which have been known by other names—"Tin Can Alley," "Goat Alley," "Buzzard's Alley," and "Bronzeville," for instance—contain the worst of the central cities' problems. In *Dark Ghetto: Dilemmas of Social Power*, Kenneth Clark, American intellectual and then director of the Social Dynamics Research Institute of the City College of the City University of New York, reports statements by ghetto residents about their daily life. Their comments reveal lives marred by unemployment, poverty, violence, and alienation.

> They are raising the rents so high, like that, with a job, the menial jobs that we have or get, the money we will receive—we won't be able to pay the rent! So where we going to go? They are pushing us further, and further, and further—out of Harlem.
>
> —Man, age 31

*For an overall discussion of the "service challenge" facing cities, see John C. Bollens and Henry J. Schmondt, *The Metropolis: Its People, Politics, and Economic Life* (New York: Harper & Row, 1975), Chap. 7.

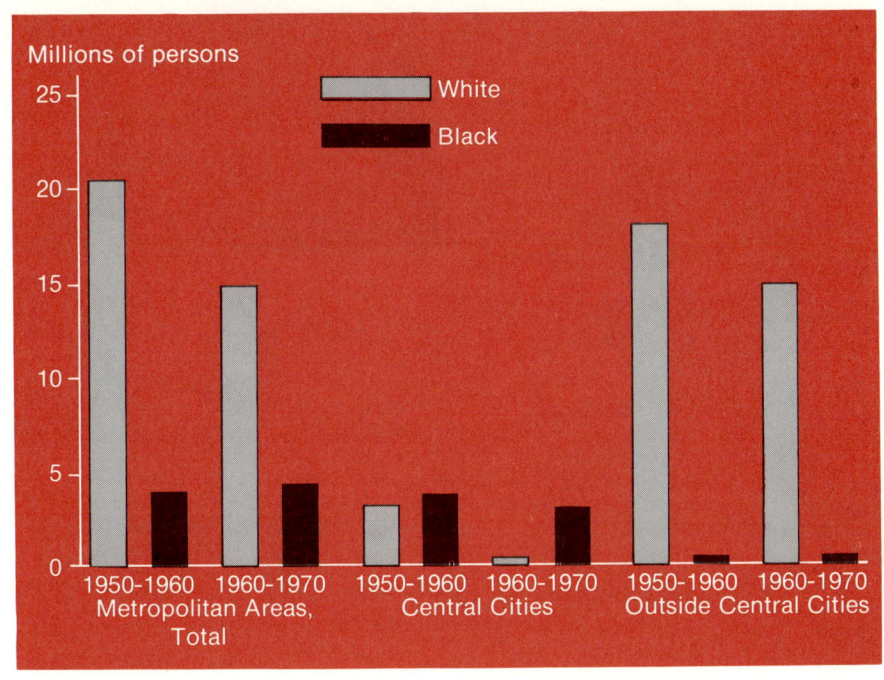

Figure 18–2 Population Changes in Urban Areas in the United States, 1950–1970

SOURCE: U.S. Bureau of the Census, *Statistical Abstract of the United States; 1974* (Washington, D.C.: U.S. Government Printing Office, 1974), p. 4.

If you could get onto the ninth floor of the Tombs [prison], you would see for yourself. They are lying there like dogs, vomiting and what not, over one another. It is awful. It smells like a pigpen up there. If you look, you'll see nothing but Spanish. And the black man. You'll seldom see a white man. When you do, he is from a very poor group. They are 20 years old, looking like they were 40.

—Drug addict, male,
age about 37

. . .

Well, the gang, they look for trouble, and then if they can't find no trouble, find something they can do, find something they can play around. Go in the park, find a bum, hit him in the face, pee in his face, kick him down, then chase him, grab him and throw him over the fence.

—Boy, age 15

. . .

We don't want any bloodshed if we can help it, but if there has to be a little bloodletting, well and good. But this is only the beginning—

Slum clearance projects sometimes leave residents with no place to live. Even when new housing is made available, slum dwellers may resist moving if this means higher rents or leaving the familiarity of their old neighborhood.

what happened here today. Our next big step is the Harlem Police Department—we want black captains and we're going to have them. I've been fighting for dozens of years here in Harlem, where the so-called leaders play—Uncle Tom—play politics and let the people starve. You have district leaders here that draw a big fat salary. You can't hardly walk the street for trash. You have captains here—district captains and what not—all kinds of leaders here in Harlem. You never see them until election.

—Woman, age about 30[32]

Selections from the diary of a Puerto Rican woman, published in the *New York Herald Tribune*, also reveal the daily crises of living in a cold, rat-infested flat in a ghetto. When she wrote these entries, the woman had four children, was separated from her husband, and on welfare.

Wednesday, Feb. 5: I got up at 6:45. The first thing to do was light the oven. The boiler was broke so not getting the heat. All the tenants got together bought the oil. We give $7.50 for each tenant. But the boiler old and many things we don't know about the pipes, so one of the men next door who used to be superintendent is trying to fix. I make the breakfast for the three children who go to school. . . . Miss Christine Washington stick her head in at 7:30 and say she go to work. I used to live on ground floor and she was all the time trying to get me move to third floor next door to her because this place vacant and the junkies use it and she scared the junkies break the wall to get into her place and steal everything because she live alone and go to work.

I'm glad I come up here to live because the rats so big downstairs. We all say the "rats is big as cats." I had a baseball bat for the rats. It's lucky me and the children never got bit. The children go to school and I clean the house and empty the pan in the bathroom that catches the water dripping from pipe in the big hole in the ceiling. You have to carry umbrella to the bathroom sometimes. I go to the laundry place this afternoon and I wash again on Saturday because I change my kids clothes every day because I don't want them dirty to attract the rats. . . .

After I go out to a rent strike meeting at night, I come home and the women tell me that five policemen came and broke down the door of the vacant apartment of the ground floor where we have meetings for the tenants in our building. They come looking for something—maybe junkies, but we got nothing in there only paper and some chairs and tables. They knocked them all over. The women heard the policemen laughing. When I come up to my place the children already in bed and I bathe myself and then I go to bed and read the newspaper until 11:30.

Thursday, Feb. 6: I wake up at six o'clock and I went to the kitchen to heat a bottle for my baby. When I put the light on the kitchen I yelled so loud that I don't know if I disturbed the neighbors. There was a big rat coming out from the garbage pail. He looks like a cat. I ran to my room, I called my daughter Carmen to go to the kitchen to see if the coast was clear. She's not scared of the rats. So I could go back to the kitchen to heat the bottle for my baby. Then I left the baby with a friend and went downtown.[33]

Other negative aspects of ghetto life are high rates of infant and maternal mortality, deficient diets, lack of medical care and insurance, inadequate garbage collection, schools where little education takes place, and exploitation by white merchants who own ghetto stores but live outside the neighborhood. Not surprisingly, ghetto residents feel intense bitterness and resentment toward the larger society and white society in particular.*

Suburbs

Suburbs in the United States have been growing faster than central cities for some fifty years. Only 17 percent of the population lived in suburbs in 1920, but 37 percent of the population were suburbanites in 1970.[34] There are several reasons for this movement. First, some have moved to suburbs to escape the crowdedness, deterioration, crime, loneliness, and rapid

---

*A good discussion of problems in the ghetto can be found in the *Report of the National Advisory Commission on Civil Disorders* (Washington, D.C.: U.S. Government Printing Office, 1968), part II, chap. VI.

pace of the big city. In "Life in the New Suburbia" Ralph Martin presents the advantages he sees to suburban living.

> *People who lived for years in apartment houses without ever really knowing their neighbors come here and start living Dale Carnegie. For newcomers it sometimes becomes overwhelming. You come home from work to find your neighbor (whom you hadn't yet met) had put your milk in her refrigerator so the sun wouldn't spoil it. If you don't have a car, neighbors with cars are always asking your wife, "I'm going shopping. Do you want to come along?"*
>
> *Before you can ask somebody for the neighbor's lawnmower, he usually volunteers it. One woman left her faucet running and came back to a flooded kitchen, but six neighbors were already mopping it up. If your car gets stuck here, don't worry, the next car that comes along will stop to help. When polio victim Norman Modell came out of the hospital and needed some strong arms to support him while he tried to walk again, he had all the volunteers he needed.*
>
> *Perhaps all this explains why Mrs. Edwin Niles said, "For the first time since I left Fordyce, Arkansas, I really feel at home."*
>
> *There's a small-town friendliness at the Village Greens (there are three so far, more coming up fast). Modernly styled, the Green is the shopping center for each area—and something more. People are always stopping to talk to each other there. Nobody rushes.*[35]

Second, economic advantages have drawn some to suburbia. Housing is often cheaper than in urban areas because land is less expensive, and down payments on new homes are frequently lower. In addition, taxes are usually lower in suburbs while services tend to be better—wide streets, community parks, well-equipped schools.

Third, overall population growth has encouraged movement to the suburbs. Urban housing, particularly in the northeastern part of the country, has frequently been inadequate to absorb large population increases. The post–World War II "baby boom" in particular put intense pressures on city housing, contributing to the tremendous postwar growth of suburbs.

The desire to own a home, enjoy a relaxed social life with neighbors, and shop in ease and comfort are among the reasons for the exodus of inner-city residents to suburbs.

And, fourth, American families have traditionally shown a preference for owning their own homes and property. Suburbs offer this possibility no matter how similar and stacked together some suburban tract houses may appear to be.

Intellectuals have frequently expressed disdain for the suburban way of life. The typical suburb is pictured as a cultural wasteland filled with ranch-style houses, well-kept lawns, swimming pools, and station wagons. And suburbanites are seen as dull and unimaginative people concerned mainly with displaying their wealth and moving another rung up the ladder of success. Critics contend that suburban life is devoted to consumption, as shown by an overconcern with gadgets like lawn edgers and gas-operated barbecues. They argue that cocktail parties, country clubs, bridge clubs, neighbors, scout troops, and "togetherness" in general produce unthinking conformity and stifle individuality. Finally, some see suburbia as housing only white, middle- and upper-class, narrow, conforming, ultraconservative people.

Phyllis McGinley, in her book *A Short Walk from the Station*, challenges this view of suburbia. She maintains that suburbs offer a life of privacy, individuality, and freedom.

> Spruce Manor has become a sort of symbol to writers and reporters familiar only with its name or trivial aspects. It has become a symbol of all that is middle class in the worst sense, of settled-downness or rootlessness, according to what the writer is trying to prove; of smug and prosperous mediocrity or — even, in more lurid novels, of lechery at the country club and Sunday morning hangovers.
>
> To condemn Suburbia has long been a literary cliche, anyhow. I have yet to read a book in which the suburban life was pictured as the good life or the commuter as a sympathetic figure. He is nearly as much a stock character as the old stage Irishman: the man who "spends his life riding to and from his wife," the eternal Babbitt who knows all about Buicks and nothing about Picasso, whose sanctuary is the club locker room, whose ideas spring ready-made from the illiberal newspapers. His wife plays politics at the P.T.A. and keeps up

with the Joneses. Or—if the scene is more gilded and less respectable—the commuter is the high-powered advertising executive with a station wagon and an eye for the ladies, his wife a restless baggage given to too many cocktails in the afternoon.

These cliches I challenge. I have lived in the country, I have lived in the city. I have lived in an average Middle Western small town. But for the best eleven years of my life I have lived in Suburbia and I like it.

"Compromise!" cried our friends when we came here from an expensive, inconvenient, moderately fashionable tenement in Manhattan. It was the period in our lives when everyone was moving somewhere. Farther uptown, farther downtown, across town to Sutton Place, to a half-dozen rural acres in Connecticut or New Jersey or even Vermont. But no one in our rather rarefied little group was thinking of moving to the suburbs except us. They were aghast that we could find anything appealing in the thought of a middle-class house on a middle-class street in a middle-class village full of middle-class people. That we were tired of town and hoped for children, that we couldn't afford both a city apartment and a farm, they put down as feeble excuses. To this day they cannot understand us. You see, they read the books. They even write them.

Compromise? Of course we compromise. But compromise, if not the spice of life, is its solidity. It is what makes nations great and marriages happy and Spruce Manor the pleasant place it is. As for its being middle-class, what is wrong with acknowledging one's roots? And how free of the city's noise, of its ubiquitous doormen, of the soot on the window sill and the radio in the next apartment. We have released ourselves from the seasonal hegira to the mountains or the seashore. We have only one address, one house to keep supplied with paring knives and blankets. We are free from the snows that block the countryman's roads in winter and his electricity which always goes off in a thunderstorm. I do not insist that we are typical. There is nothing really typical about any of our friends and neighbors here, and therein lies my point. The true suburbanite needs to conform less than anyone else; much less than the gentleman farmer with his remodeled salt-box or than the determined cliff dweller with his necessity for living at the right address. In Spruce Manor all addresses are right. And since we are fairly numerous here, we need not fall back on the people nearest us for total companionship. There is not here, as in a small city away from truly urban centers, some particular family whose codes must be ours. And we could not keep up with the Joneses even if we wanted to, for we know many Joneses and they are all quite different people leading the most various lives.[36]

Most sociologists would agree with McGinley that critics of suburbia often condemn a myth, but they would also note that she describes only one type of suburb. The fact is that there are diverse types—some old and others new, some small and others large, some bedroom communities for the central city and others industrial centers, some growing and others stagnant, some upper-class and others poor. The New York metropolitan area, for example, contains 800,000 suburban poor. Reporter Ralph Blumenthal has described the life of the suburban poor, a life which departs dramatically from the usual notion of the affluent suburbanite.

> *A Westchester housewife sat one evening recently in her sour-smelling, $50-a-month tenement flat where a washline was stretched above the kitchen sink.*
>
> *"People talk about the rich, rich suburbs," she said. "Let 'em come up here."*
>
> *For her and her family, living on Ferris Avenue in White Plains, amid a suburban area known for its affluence, and for about 180,000 other families in thirteen counties ringing New York City, life in the suburbs has nothing to do with back yard barbecues, antique shows, sailboat races, or country club socials.*
>
> *They are the suburban poor, and they number 800,000. They face many of the same problems faced by the urban poor. Indeed, antipoverty officials say, the effort to reduce poverty is more difficult to win in some ways in the suburbs than in the city. "We're fighting not even a holding action because of the limited resources we get," said Adrian Cabral, executive director of Nassau County's antipoverty agency, the Economic Opportunity Commission.*[37]

In brief, the "suburban myth" fails to recognize the diversity of suburbs and their inhabitants.* A suburbanite may be bent on a life of togetherness, conservatism, conformity, and racism, or quite the opposite. And even if it could be demonstrated that most suburbanites fit the stereotyped negative image, is suburbia to blame? Is it a causal factor or merely a result of American cultural values?

Turning greater attention to suburban problems, we see that these communities are increasingly facing many of the same problems of financing, government, and services confronting central cities. Suburbanites are feeling the burden of higher taxes to support their schools, hire more police, and build more roads. In suburbs as well as central cities, mass transit is needed. Reporter David Andelman discusses the traffic jams and sprawling parking lots at suburban shopping centers.

> *To Arthur Freed, Westchester's chief highway engineer, "Christmas is really 25 per cent of the year."*
>
> *The reason is traffic—mind-rotting, stagnating, frustrating, engine-overheating traffic jams that clog every major artery and scores*

---

*For a discussion of the "suburban myth," see Dennis H. Wrong, "Suburbs and Myths of Suburbia," in *Readings in Introductory Sociology*, eds. Dennis H. Wrong and Harry L. Gracey (New York: Macmillan, 1969), pp. 358–364.

of two-lane downtown roads, sending elaborate computer-coordinated traffic control systems into total chaos.

"Once upon a time Christmas came on December 25," said Mr. Freed, "Now we get our major traffic escalation in mid-October and it lasts through January, when people are returning things."

But the real reason is the automobile and the suburban mentality of not just one car in every garage, but a car in every garage for each family member older than 16. And it has many of the nation's top planning and highway experts more concerned than ever.

One evening last October, Vic Carney, director of the New Jersey State Safety Council, looked out of the window of his Chicago-to-New York jet liner and knew he was nearing home:

"It was the nightly traffic jam at the Willowbrook shopping center in Yonkers, more than 30,000 cars a day roll through the parking fields—when they can roll. Others less fortunate sit in traffic jams that back up on the northbound Major Deegan Expressway as far as 225th Street in the Bronx."[38]

Furthermore crime is increasing in suburbia. Andelman maintains that the suburb no longer offers an escape from violence and theft since many types of crimes, particularly burglaries, have become common there.

The crime wave of the nineteen-sixties that sent New Yorkers scurrying to the protection of fortified apartments, or the safety of the suburbs, in the nineteen-seventies has begun to follow the moving population, with a new pattern of fear emerging in the suburban areas that used to be called havens. . . .

According to the Uniform Crime Report compiled by the Federal Bureau of Investigation, the total number of crimes in the first nine months of 1971, compared with the same period in 1970, rose nearly three times as fast in the suburban areas as in cities with populations over one million—11 per cent, compared with 4 per cent. Overall, crime in the suburbs rose nearly twice as fast as in the nation as a whole. . . .

One of the most common patterns recently emerging is that of the "commuter burglar," described in this way by one suburban New Jersey police official:

Working in pairs, they drive out from New York City or Newark, drop off the Garden State Parkway into a residential development and cruise until they find a house that appears to be empty. While one drives around the block, the second rings the doorbell.

If the homeowner answers, the thief asks directions to a fictitious address. If no one answers, he finds a rear door or window, smashes it in and quickly goes through the house, picking up small appliances, cameras, money or jewelry, leaving when his confederate returns in the car. . . .

Lately, this new breed of burglar has become even more brazen, frequently driving up in a delivery van to cart away heavy items such as color television sets and expensive high-fidelity equipment, which are abundant in the affluent suburbs. Delivery trucks are so common in suburban areas that they are scarcely noticed.

"I had one case of a television repairman who entered houses, picked up money or occasionally jewelry, then left in his van," said Chief Mellon. "But we could never catch him in a house with the money, and half of the calls were legitimate. We finally just told him strenuously to get lost. That was the only way we could handle it."[39]

Americans will probably continue their exodus to suburbs, but the life they confront may be much like that in the central city they are trying to escape.

Chapter Summary

Urbanization has occurred at astounding speed in this century. Soon the majority of the world's population will live in urban areas. The first cities appeared some 5,500 years ago and resembled small villages. Eventually the modern industrial city emerged, the result of several factors: (1) a food surplus and storage facilities, (2) industrialization accompanied by improved transportation and communication systems, (3) mass literacy, and (4) world population growth. Urbanization cannot go on indefinitely since a small share of the population, 5 to 10 percent, must remain on farms to produce food. City growth, however, can continue as the world population continues to mushroom.

Durkheim, Tönnies, Simmel, and other early sociologists were especially concerned with the evil and alienating aspects of urban life. This tradition was carried forth by the "Chicago School" sociologists of the 1920s and 1930s. Contemporary sociologists conclude that, indeed, some aspects of the city are alienating to individuals, but other aspects are not. The city is a montage of diverse neighborhoods, experiences, and personalities.

Central cities in the United States are in a state of crisis. Most are experiencing financial strangulation as costs for services climb and tax revenues decline. Urban government is plagued by the fact that metropolitan areas usually contain hundreds of governmental divisions. Cities are expected to provide many services, such as police and fire protection, clean water and air, proper sewage disposal, mass transportation, adequate housing, good schools, and parks and recreation. Yet central cities are finding it increasingly difficult to meet these demands. Finally, ghettos are a major problem. Unemployment, poverty, disease, inadequate schooling, crime, and hostility characterize these deteriorated, isolated sections of the city.

Suburbs continue to grow at a faster rate than central cities. People move to suburbia to escape the city, to reap economic advantages, to find a smaller concentration of people, and to own their own home and property. The notion that all suburbanites are affluent, status seeking, narrow minded, conforming, ultraconservative, and bent on a life of togetherness is a myth. There are diverse types of suburbs ranging from the poor to the wealthy and from the bedroom community to the industrial center. Suburbs are increasingly facing many of the same problems as central cities.

Officials at higher levels of government as well as many American citizens have failed to realize that urban problems are not local but national problems. Our society will soon have to decide whether it wishes to abandon cities, tolerate them with their existing problems, or help them.

Key Terms for Review

city, p. 451
feudal society, p. 452
folk society, p. 452, 456
ghetto, p. 474
industrial society, p. 452
mechanical solidarity, p. 456
megalopolis, p. 455

metropolitan areas, p. 455
organic solidarity, p. 456
Standard Metropolitan Statistical Area (SMSA), p. 455
urbanization, p. 451
urban society, p. 456

Suggested Readings

SOCIOLOGICAL

Banfield, Edward. *The Unheavenly City: The Nature and Future of Our Urban Crisis.* Boston: Little, Brown, 1970. Cities do have problems, but still they are healthy and attractive to people. Banfield defends this controversial view on the grounds that people are largely expecting too much from their cities. City conditions are really not worsening all that much.

Clark, Kenneth B. *Dark Ghetto: Dilemmas of Social Power.* New York: Harper & Row, 1965. The book is an informative diagnosis of the educational, political, and economic problems facing black people who live in ghettos. The author maintains that complete integration of ghetto residents into the larger society is possible only through wide-ranging reforms.

Jacobs, Jane. *The Death and Life of Great American Cities.* New York: Random House, 1961. According to the author American cities are in a state of crisis and decay, and urban renewal is failing. She presents an excellent discussion of city life and what cities could become.

Palen, J. John. *The Urban World.* New York: McGraw-Hill, 1975. This introductory book covers such topics as the emergence and history of cities, the nature of urbanism and urbanization in the United States, the urbanization of Third World countries, and the planning and future of cities.

Scientific American. *Cities: A Scientific American Book.* New York: Alfred A. Knopf, 1969. This excellent collection of articles was compiled by the editors of *Scientific American* for beginning students of urban sociology. The selections by Kingsley Davis, Gideon Sjoberg, and Hans Blumenfeld are quite informative and comprehensive.

Thomlinson, Ralph. *Urban Structure: The Social and Spatial Character of Cities.* New York: Random House, 1969. This general text is organized around the notion of urban ecology—the study of spatial distribution of people and their activities within and around cities. The discussion on metropolitan planning and the future of cities is quite good.

Walton, John and Donald E. Carns. *Cities in Change: Studies on the Urban Condition.* Boston: Allyn and Bacon, 1973. The editors include informative and interesting articles on urbanization, urban life styles, urban politics, and the future of cities.

Wirth, Louis. "Urbanism as a Way of Life." *American Journal of Sociology,* 44 (July 1938): 1–24. This article summarized much of the thinking and research of the Chicago School about the city. Wirth examines the effects on urban life of large numbers of people and population heterogeneity and diversity.

LITERARY

Abernathy, Robert. "Single Combat." In *Sociology Through Science Fiction.* John W. Milstead, Martin Harry Greenberg, Joseph D. Olander, and Patricia Warrick, eds. New York: St. Martin's Press, 1974. Abernathy paints a dramatic picture of an individual pitted against the filth, corruption, and overwhelming size of the city. The character's attempt to destroy the city is symbolic of the traditional view that cities are inherently alien to humans.

Gold, Herbert. "A Dog in Brooklyn, A Girl in Detroit: A Life Among the Humanities." In *The Age of Happy Problems.* New York: Dial Press, 1962. The author discusses the psychology of living in a city. "Mind your own business" and "don't get involved" dominate thinking; meanwhile muggings, rape, and other calamities for people continue to occur.

Sandburg, Carl. *The Complete Poems of Carl Sandburg.* New York: Harcourt Brace Jovanovich, 1969. Poetry sensitizes readers to thoughts and emotions. Sandburg's "Chicago Poems" show us the neighborhoods and characters of one city.

Sartre, Jean-Paul. "New York, The Colonial City," and "American Cities." In *Literary and Philosophical Essays.* New York: Criterion Books, 1955. The two selections are concerned with Sartre's views on city life. In the first, the more interesting and readable, he discusses his initial hatred of New York City and the eventual transformation of his attitude. He comes to view the city as strong, nonoppressive, and freeing of the human spirit.

Simon, Neil. *The Prisoner of Second Avenue.* New York: Random House, 1972. This warm and humorous play concerns a couple's struggle to survive in New York City. They endure in spite of noise, crowdedness, crime, and unemployment. The story is a telling commentary on complex urban society.

IN THIS CHAPTER

The Population Debate   489

    Malthus: recognition of the problem   489
    The neo-Malthusian position   490
    The Marxist position   492
    The Optimists' position   493

Demographic Data and Terminology   494

    Fecundity measurement   495
    Infant mortality measurement   497
    Morbidity measurement   497
    Mortality measurement   497

The Demographic Transition   500

Future Growth   501

Summary   506

Key Terms for Review   506

Suggested Readings   507

Is there currently a "population explosion"?
Will technology be able to provide for the ever increasing number of people in the world?
How will world population grow in the future?

POPULATION

Demography is the study of human populations, focusing on changes in size, density, and distribution. Traditionally, demographers have been concerned primarily with quantitative and statistical measurements. They speak of birth and death rates, sex ratios, infant mortality rates, and other statistical indices. Ultimately, however, all demographic measurement concerns population and its growth or decline.

The widely publicized "population explosion" of recent years has aroused great interest in demography. Population experts Kingsley Davis and Paul R. Ehrlich are widely quoted in the media and frequently asked to appear on television "talk shows." Much discussion is naturally concerned with statistical data. Yet as we have noted many times, statistics give only a partial view of any problem. Paul Ehrlich, in *The Population Bomb*, gives a personal reaction to overpopulation.

I have understood the population explosion intellectually for a long time. I came to understand it emotionally one stinking hot night in Delhi a couple of years ago. My wife and daughter and I were returning to our hotel in an ancient taxi. The seats were hopping with fleas. The only functional gear was third. As we crawled through the city, we entered a crowded slum area. The temperature was well over 100, and the air was a haze of dust and smoke. The streets seemed alive with people. People eating, people washing, people sleeping. People visiting, arguing, and screaming. People thrusting their hands through the taxi window, begging. People defecating and urinating. People clinging to buses. People herding animals. People, people, people, people. As we moved slowly through the mob, hand horn squawking, the dust, noise, heat, and cooking fires gave the scene a hellish aspect. Would we ever get to our hotel? All three of us were, frankly, frightened. It seemed that anything could happen—but, of course, nothing did. Old India hands will laugh at

A street in Bombay. Population pressures are most obvious in densely crowded cities of the Third World.

our reaction. We were just some overprivileged tourists, unaccustomed to the sights and sounds of India. Perhaps, but since that night I've known the feel of overpopulation.[1]

Though one may indeed "feel" overpopulation, demography remains primarily quantitative and statistical. One recently popular method for measuring and projecting population growth is readily understandable and quite impressive. It is concerned with *doubling time*, the time it takes a given population to double. It is estimated that it took a million years for the world's population to double from 2.5 to 5 million by the year 6000 B.C. It then took about 8,000 years—with a doubling time of around 1,000 years—for population to reach 500 million by A.D. 1650. World population growth has continued to accelerate since then, with population reaching 1 billion by 1850—a doubling time of 200 years—and 2 billion by 1930—a doubling time of 80 years.[2] The doubling time for world population is now about 35 years.[3] Taking that very innocent statistic and projecting a continuing doubling time for eight centuries, we find that in the twenty-eighth century there will be 500 individuals for each square yard of the land surface of the earth!

The Population Debate

Recent discussions and arguments about the population explosion, and ways of dealing with overpopulation, have become part of a political-ideological debate between the have and have-not countries. The problem is real enough. Many people are starving today, and the earth's resources undeniably finite. At some point there will be—and some claim there already are—too many people, that is, more than our planet can support. Current argument centers on what constitutes "too many" people.

MALTHUS: RECOGNITION OF THE PROBLEM

For thousands of years the world's population grew very slowly. For centuries more, vast tracts of virgin land awaited a growing population. If there was concern about increasing numbers of people, it was because emerging nation-states did not want their populations surpassed by those of their rivals. Population growth was considered a national asset.

The Industrial Revolution, which brought with it the growth of large

The current population debate began with Thomas Malthus's observations of crowded slum conditions in industrializing England.

urban slums, ultimately made observation of population crowding unavoidable. In 1798 Thomas R. Malthus (1766–1834) authored the most famous demographic essay ever written, *An Essay on the Principle of Population*.[4] In it Malthus set forth many of the assumptions of current discussions about population growth. He noted that members of the English working class tended to have more children than they could afford to maintain, creating human misery. And he argued that if this trend continued, population growth would eventually be brought under control by a rising death rate.

A less emotional assumption of Malthus's argument remains a basic tenet of the demographic portfolio: human procreation takes place geometrically (two, four, eight, sixteen, thirty-two, etc.), while gains in human support materials such as food and housing take place arithmetically (one, two, three, four, five, etc.). To avoid the starvation and rising death rate that he saw as inevitable, Malthus proposed increased social awareness and growing individual responsibility. Marriage should take place later in life, and individuals should practice frugality and sexual continence. Malthus dismissed birth control methods as contrary to tenets of the Church of England and supportive of moral depravity.

THE NEO-MALTHUSIAN POSITION

Although they no longer disdain birth control, many current commentators and demographers are accurately described as neo-Malthusians. Robert S. McNamara, president of the World Bank and former United States secretary of defense, has suggested that the World Bank should give financial and technical aid only to nations with official family planning programs. Like other contemporary followers of Malthus, McNamara sees international problems as being linked directly to overpopulation.[5] In his view, unless major steps are taken to increase the use of family planning, the malnutrition, poverty, and lethargy that now mark much of the world's population will soon become starvation, violence, and a spreading breakdown of social systems.

Organizations such as the Population Council and the International Planned Parenthood Federation also clearly follow in the tradition of Malthus, while other proponents of population control have further refined the argument. Paul Ehrlich, a leading spokesman for what has come to be known as the "ecology movement," departs from the geometric-arithmetic tenets of the Malthusian catechism to suggest that much of the difficulty is ideological. He sees population growth as the result of irrational assumptions on the part of much of the world that growth is good. Like McNamara, Ehrlich favors nonsupport of nations that do not develop effective birth control programs.

Another well-known demographer, Kingsley Davis, is also basically a Malthusian pessimist. He agrees that population growth must be brought under control but views current policies as ineffective, a conclusion supported by ample evidence. He suggests a number of broader, more encompassing strategies, including the following:

1. Strengthening the factors that lead people to postpone or avoid marriage and to downgrade reproduction
2. Rewarding nonfamilial life styles by eliminating the disadvantages of being single, divorced, or widowed
3. Restricting tax exemptions for parents, paid maternity leaves, and family allowances
4. Terminating grants of public housing based on family size and fellowships to married students
5. Ceasing to penalize those who seek harmless forms of nonreproductive sexual expression
6. Shifting concern about population problems from ministries of health to ministries of economics and education
7. Directing efforts toward giving the average person (especially women) a rational basis for redefining the family and finding some exit from poverty through personal improvement and gainful employment[6]

Neo-Malthusians contend that only a series of sometimes drastic changes will avoid a world of terror and starvation which may well arrive in the near future. Without such changes, food riots and increasing oppression in major population centers may well be only twenty-five years away. Such a city was portrayed in the MGM movie *Soylent Green*, which was based on the novel *Make Room! Make Room!* Though not a city of the Third World, the New York of *Soylent Green* is precisely what many of the neo-Malthusians fear.

New York City trembled on the brink of disaster. Every locked warehouse was a nucleus of dissent, surrounded by crowds who were hungry and afraid and searching for someone to blame. Their anger incited them to riot, and the food riots turned to water riots and then to looting, wherever this was possible. The police fought back, only the thinnest of barriers between angry protest and bloody chaos.

Indonesian women learning about IUDs (left), and Indian men attending a class on family planning (right). Unfortunately voluntary birth control programs have been largely unsuccessful in these and other Third World countries.

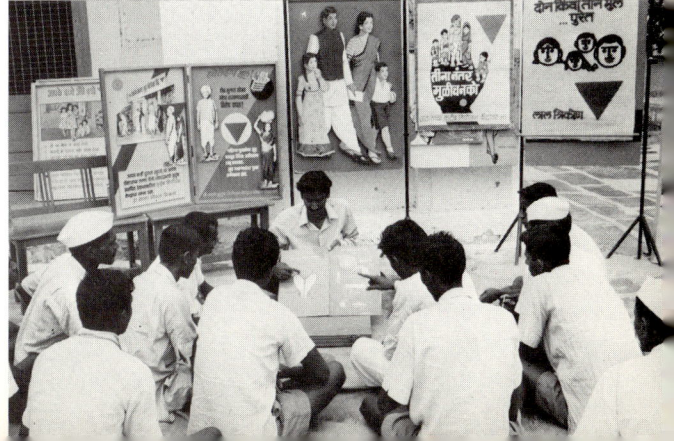

> At first night sticks and weighted clubs stopped the trouble, and when this failed gas dispersed the crowds. The tension grew, since the people who fled only reassembled again in a different place. The solid jets of water from the riot trucks stopped them easily when they tried to break into the Welfare stations, but there were not enough trucks, nor was there more water to be had once they had pumped dry their tanks. The Health Department had forbidden the use of river water: it would have been like spraying poison. The little water that was available was badly needed for the fires that were springing up throughout the city. With the streets blocked in many places the fire-fighting equipment could not get through and the trucks were forced to make long detours. Some of the fires were spreading and by noon all of the equipment had been committed and was in use.
>
> The first gun was fired a few minutes past twelve, by a Welfare Department guard who killed a man who had broken open a window of the Tompkins Square food depot and had tried to climb in. This was the first but not the last shot fired — nor was it the last person to be killed.
>
> Flying wire sealed off some of the trouble areas, but there was only a limited supply of it. When it ran out the copters fluttered helplessly over the surging streets and acted as aerial observation posts for the police, finding the places where reserves were sorely needed. It was a fruitless labor because there were no reserves, everyone was in the front line.[7]

THE MARXIST POSITION

The population debate is not, of course, one-sided. Some scholars and national leaders argue that there is really no "population explosion" — that population growth is simply unwanted by certain countries and individuals for a variety of ideological reasons. The most quoted early opponent of Malthus is Karl Marx, who found Malthus to be a hopeless apologist for the bourgeoisie. According to Marx, Malthus's preaching about morality and frugality was little more than an expression of middle-class values and religion. The poor were living in poverty not because they failed to exercise sexual restraint, but because they were callously exploited by the bourgeoisie. Given access to the means of production, according to Marx, the working class would soon move from poverty to relative affluence.

With few exceptions the official stance of the communist countries is within the Marxian tradition. They recognize many difficulties inherent in unlimited population growth; but their ideology and official pronouncements assert that most discussion of population control in the West is set forth by ruling elites that wish to protect their own narrow interests. Several populous communist nations, including the Soviet Union and the People's Republic of China, have undertaken varying forms of birth control. Programs in China have sometimes been quite rigorous, though not particularly effective. At one point in the early 1960s, Chinese policy involved assigning husbands and wives to separate work farms. It would seem the leadership of these nations is aware of certain problems that accompany rapid population growth, but at the same time is genuinely skeptical about the motives of massive Western family planning efforts.

THE OPTIMISTS' POSITION

Another general position in the great population debate falls in neither the Malthusian nor the Marxist tradition; it is that of the believers, or the optimists. For some, such as Herman Kahn and the researchers and futurists of the famous research "think tank," the Hudson Institute, population growth poses no real problem. Technology will carry us forward to a new day of plenty. For such scientific optimists the future holds the following:

1. New techniques for improving the environment and energy supplies
2. A significant expansion in agriculture and industry
3. Far greater productivity through cybernation
4. Cheap, convenient, and reliable methods of birth control
5. Medical breakthroughs, including genetic control and substitutes for human organs
6. Inexpensive and ultrarapid transportation
7. More varied and effective forms of education, using computers, video communications, and programed dreams
8. New and persuasive means for surveillance, monitoring, and control of individuals and organizations
9. Artificial moons for lighting large areas at night
10. Breakthroughs in personal convenience, such as individual, low-altitude flying platforms and pocket telephones[8]

Neo-Malthusians find such optimism misplaced if not hopelessly naive. They point to the recent failures of the much publicized *green revolution*—the many new strains of plants and the varieties of more effective fertilizers and herbicides that were expected to increase food production significantly. Proponents of the green revolution had hoped for much greater success than has resulted. Genetic weaknesses in some of the new plant strains, increased costs of fertilizers, and depletion of much of the world's marine food supply have greatly dulled the impact of the "revolution."

Another optimist is demographer Donald Bogue, who maintains that growing concern about overpopulation and spreading birth control programs will succeed in bringing the world's population growth rate to near zero by the year 2000. He suggests that recent data indicate that people in all nations are changing their attitudes toward family size and family planning. Bogue feels that such attitude changes will be reflected very quickly in a falling growth rate of world population:

The much heralded "green revolution" which was expected to bring greatly increased crops has passed by many Third World nations. Here a Colombian sharecropper tills the soil in a centuries-old manner.

> *The trend of the worldwide movement toward fertility control has already reached a state where declines in death rates are being surpassed by declines in birth rates. Because progress in death control is slackening and progress in birth control is accelerating, the world has already entered a situation where the pace of population growth has begun to slacken. The exact time at which this "switch-over" took place cannot be known exactly, but we estimate it to have occurred about 1965. From 1965 onward, therefore, the rate of world population growth may be expected to decline with each passing year. The rate of growth will slacken at such a pace that it will be zero or near zero at about the year 2000, so that population growth will not be regarded as a major social problem except in isolated and small "retarded" areas.*[9]

It is extremely difficult to foresee what will actually occur. The debate over population—are there actually too many people—has long been intertwined with conflicting ideologies. In the past few hundred years thinkers such as Malthus and Marx and their followers have perceived the situation in a variety of ways.

Demographic Data and Terminology

In order to understand better the population debate, let us examine some of the measurements, data, and indices that are part of a demographer's presentation. We should begin by noting that demographers typically distinguish between underdeveloped countries, or *UDCs* (such as Mauritania) and developed countries, or *DCs* (such as Sweden). Paul Ehrlich suggests that a more appropriate name for the UDCs would be "hungry." Whatever the label, UDCs are characterized by subsistence agricultural systems, exceedingly low income levels, and high rates of population growth and illiteracy. In contrast, DCs are highly industrialized and have efficient and extremely productive agricultural systems and relatively high levels of literacy and income.[10] Having noted this distinction, we shall examine demographic factors in relation to the lives of two individuals—one born in an underdeveloped and one in a developed country.

FECUNDITY MEASUREMENT

The first crucial factor in the lives of our two individuals will be *fecundity*, or the physiological ability to reproduce. Quite obviously, a number of biological factors determine fecundity, but demographers generally designate the ages fifteen through forty-four as the "child-bearing years." They determine a country's *fertility rate* by calculating the number of births per year per 1,000 women in the 15–44 age bracket. Most sociologists agree that the fertility rate is a more useful statistic than the *birth rate*, which indicates the number of births annually per 1,000 people. A country composed almost entirely of very old and very young people could have a low birth rate but a relatively high fertility rate. The females in the 15–44 age bracket may bear many children—a crucial factor in determining the growth potential of a given population. Returning to our two individuals, we see that if they were standing somewhere in the cosmos waiting to be born, the one in line for the developed country would have a much longer wait. As Figure 19–1 indicates, the birth rate is often three times as great in underdeveloped countries as it is in developed countries.

Rapid population increases in many underdeveloped countries make economic growth extremely difficult. These Zambian children face a life of poverty and hardship.

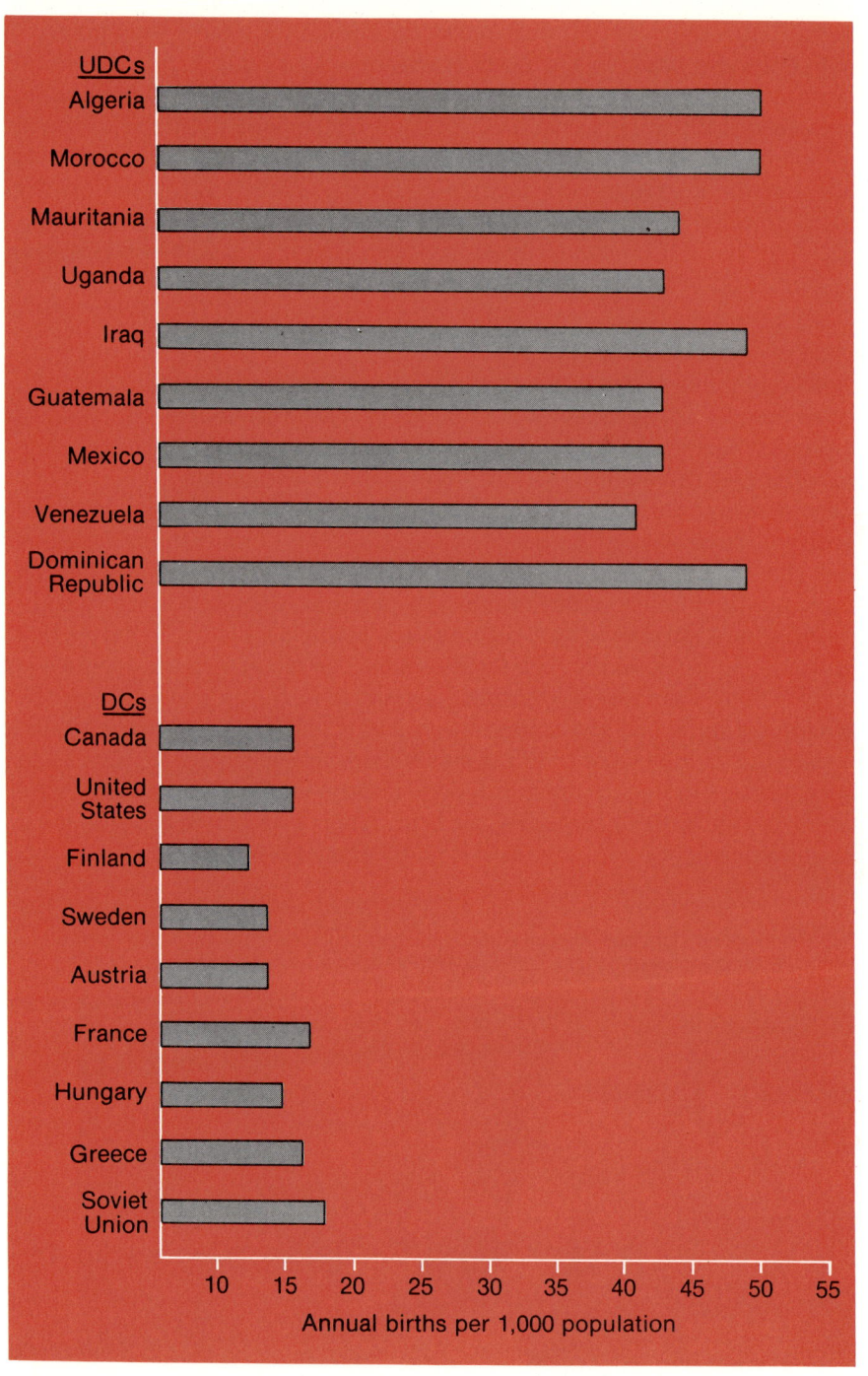

FIGURE 19-1 Birth Rates for Selected Underdeveloped and Developed Countries
SOURCE: Data are from the *1973 World Population Data Sheet*.

INFANT MORTALITY MEASUREMENT

Although the wait to be born may be longer for the individual destined for the developed country, the chances for survival are much greater. The next index used by demographers in determining population growth is the *infant mortality rate*. This rate measures on an annual basis the number of children per 1,000 live births who die during their first year of life. Again, differences between UDCs and DCs are obvious, as shown in Figure 19-2.

MORBIDITY MEASUREMENT

Demographers also study the incidence of illness and disability in various countries. Illness and disability rates are indicators of *morbidity*. Data for morbidity are most often presented in one of two ways: (1) a *prevalence rate* gives the number of people per unit of population (usually 100,000) diagnosed as having a specific affliction in any given period; (2) the more useful *incidence rate* states the number of people per unit of population (again, usually 100,000) who are newly diagnosed as having a particular affliction during a specified time. A nation might have a high prevalence rate for a disease even though a vaccine had been developed to prevent it. For example, the United States still has a significant prevalence rate for polio (people living who suffer from the affliction), but since the discovery of polio vaccine in the 1950s, there has been a sharp decrease in the incidence rate.

Morbidity measurements must necessarily be based on diagnosed illnesses and clearly apparent disabilities since the distinction between health and illness is never completely clear. In any event, our friend in the UDC is much less likely to lead a healthy life than his counterpart in the DC. Most morbidity indicators are higher for underdeveloped countries than for developed countries.[11]

MORTALITY MEASUREMENT

Other demographic indicators fall under the heading measurements of *mortality*. The *death rate* indicates the number of deaths per 1,000 population in a given year; like its opposite, the birth rate, it is a fairly crude index. The more refined and illuminating statistic for mortality is *life expectancy*, which states the average life span of individuals born into a given population. Figure 19-3 presents life expectancy figures for inhabitants of developed and underdeveloped countries.

In reviewing the basic demographic indicators, it is obvious that our

498 / PROBLEMS AND ISSUES

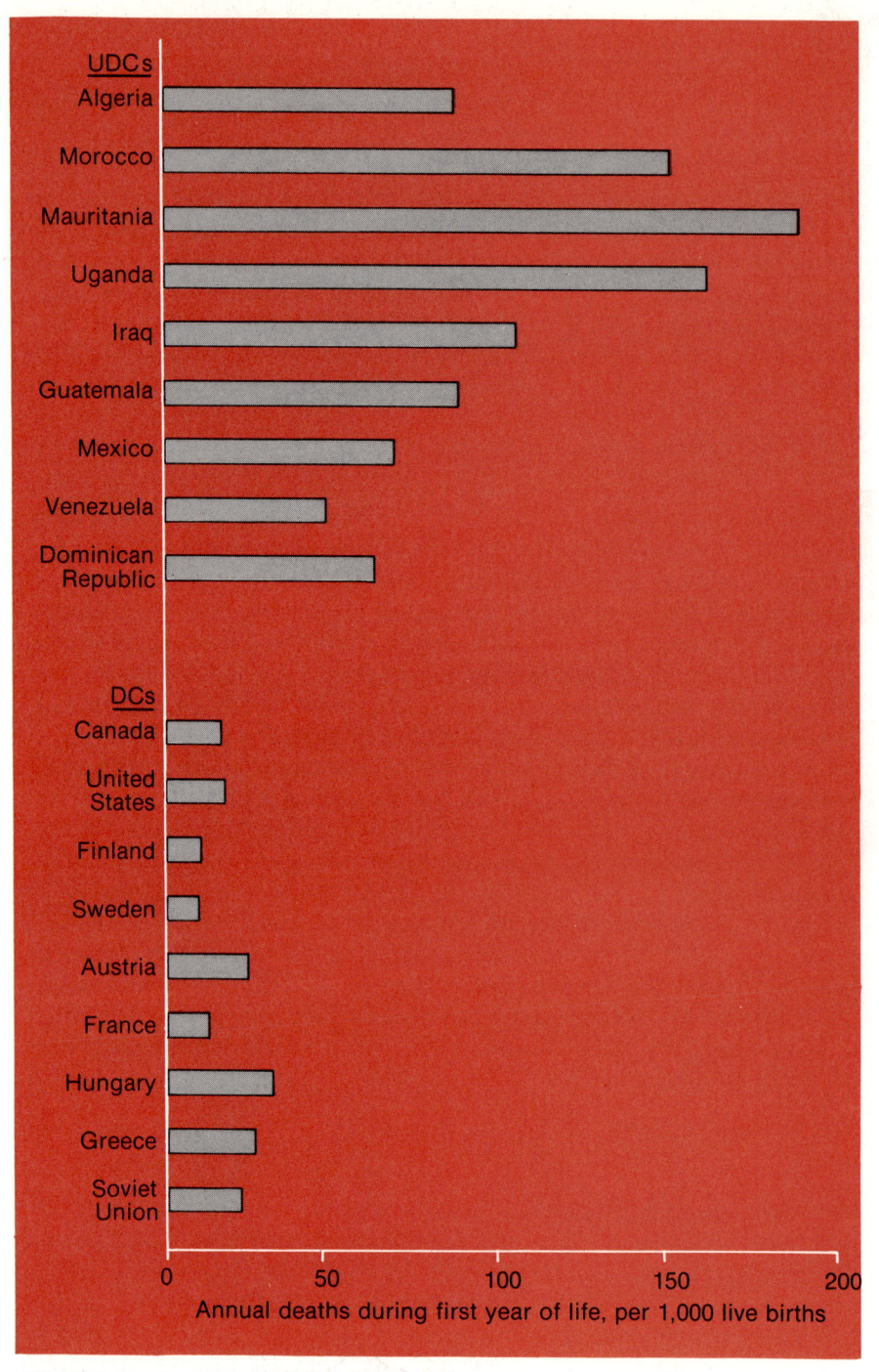

FIGURE 19-2 Infant Mortality Rates for Selected Underdeveloped and Developed Countries

SOURCE: Data are from the *1973 World Population Data Sheet*.

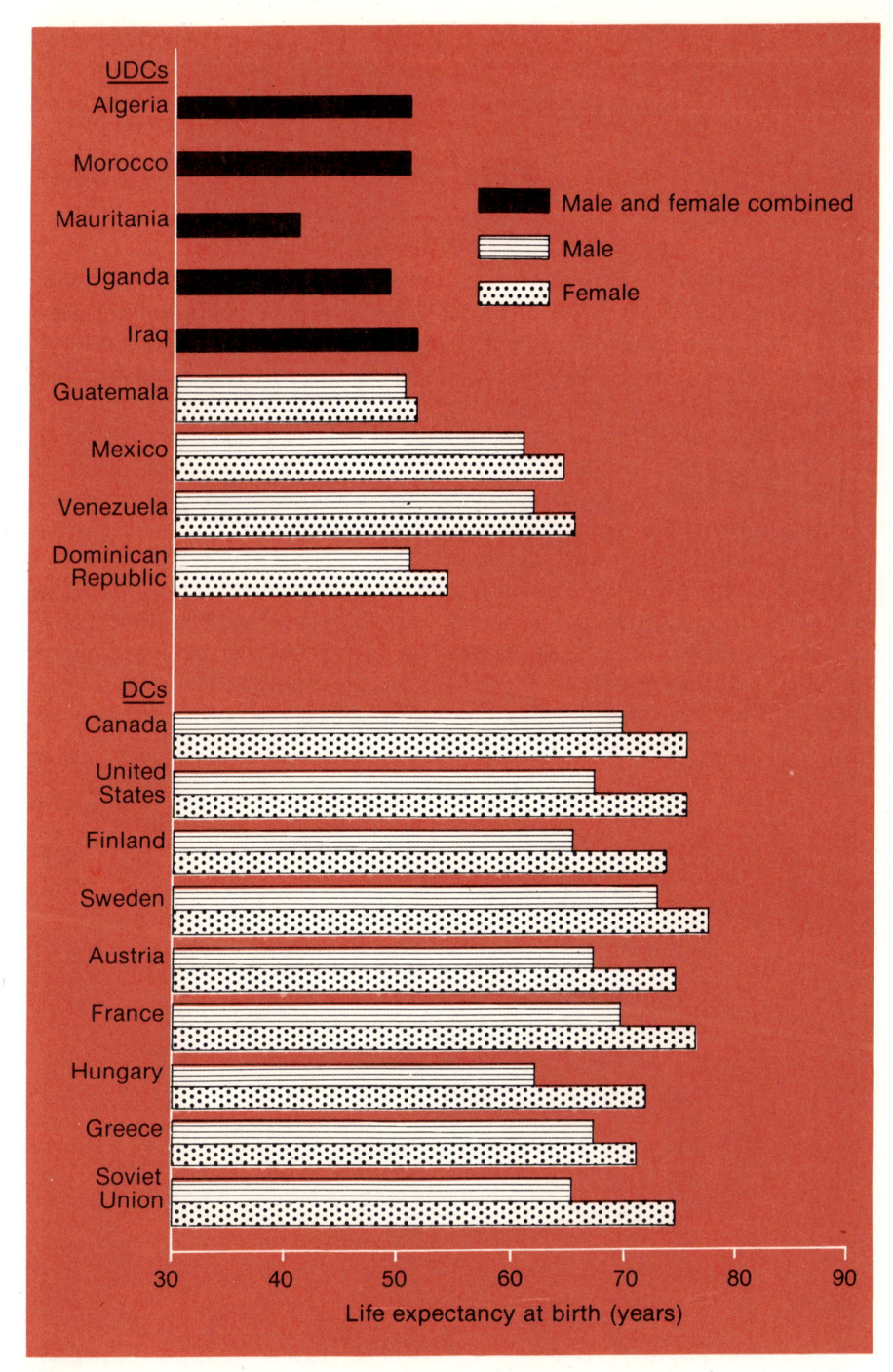

Figure 19–3 Life Expectancy Rates for Selected Underdeveloped and Developed Countries

SOURCE: Data are from the *1973 World Population Data Sheet*.

friend in the developed country is much more likely to enjoy a long, healthy life than is his counterpart living in the underdeveloped country.

The Demographic Transition

The major theoretical explanation for the rapid world population growth during the past century is the theory of *demographic transition*. First proposed during the 1930s, the theory maintains that three broadly defined stages of development determine the population growth of a society. (1) Preindustrial societies have very low growth rates as the result of a balance of high mortality and fertility rates. (2) Transitional societies have high growth rates as the result of lowered mortality rates but continuing high fertility rates. And (3) industrialized societies have low or static population growth as the result of low rates of both mortality and fertility. Figure 19–4 illustrates the demographic transition.

The theory is basically a variation of cultural lag. The introduction of medical technology reduces a society's mortality rate, yet traditional cultural norms affecting birth rates are slow to change. For example, large numbers of children are usually considered desirable in societies where infant mortality is high—two or three children out of five or six can be

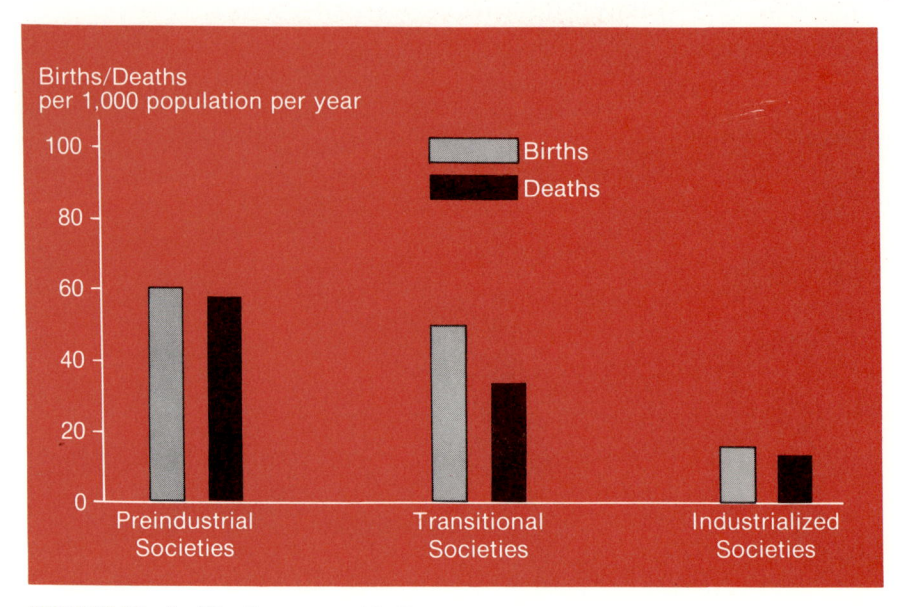

FIGURE 19–4 The Demographic Transition
SOURCE: Data are from the *1973 World Population Data Sheet*.

expected to survive to adulthood. With improved medical facilities, all the children may survive, but the traditional desire to produce many children may continue, at least for a while, despite the changed circumstances. The result is a high rate of population growth in transitional societies.

Although the theory of demographic transition remains widely accepted as an explanation for population growth, it is a somewhat simplified distillation of many variables. Today social change is often much more rapid than it was during the nineteenth and early twentieth centuries. The transitional period may be very short. The most important contemporary variable not specifically noted in the general theory, however, involves technology and its uses in promoting birth control—improved methods, better means of distribution, and mass propaganda. Societies are increasingly able to control their birth rates, and the possibilities of such control become greater each year.

Future Growth

Projecting population growth is a much less certain exercise than many charts and diagrams would lead one to believe. As Figure 19–5 indicates, world population growth has accelerated, and by the year 2000 total population could well be near 7 billion. The major difficulty with such a prediction is that we cannot always calculate the effect of many important factors. The projection in Figure 19–5 assumes a slight decrease in world fertility, but extreme changes in government birth control policies could drastically alter the picture.

In the eighteenth century Jonathan Swift, saddened and dismayed by the plight of the Irish, offered "A Modest Proposal" for dealing with the problem, one that would clearly have caused a radical shift in the country's growth rate.

> *It is a melancholly Object to those, who walk through this great Town or travel in the Country; when they see the* Streets, *the* Roads *and* Cabbin-doors *crowded with* Beggars *of the Female Sex, followed by three, four, or six Children, all in Rags, and importuning every Passenger for an Alms. These* Mothers, *instead of being able to work for their honest Livelyhood, are forced to employ all their Time in stroling to beg Sustenance for their helpless Infants; who, as they grow up, either turn Thieves for want of Work; or leave their dear Native Country, to fight for the Pretender in* Spain, *or sell themselves to the* Barbadoes.
>
> *I think it is agreed by all Parties, that this prodigious number of Children in the Arms, or on the Backs, or at the Heels of their Mothers, and frequently of their Fathers, is in the present deplorable state*

of the Kingdom, a very great additional Grievance; and therefore, whoever could find out a fair, cheap, and easy Method of making these Children sound and useful Members of the Commonwealth, would deserve so well of the Publick, as to have his Statue set up for a Preserver of the Nation.

But my Intention is very far from being confined to provide only for the Children of professed Beggars: It is of a much greater Extent, and shall take in the whole Number of Infants at a certain Age, who are born of Parents in effect as little able to support them, as those who demand our Charity in the Streets.

As to my own Part, having turned my Thoughts, for many Years, upon this important Subject, and maturely weighed the several Schemes of other Projectors, I have always found them grossly mistaken in their Computation. It is true, a Child, just dropt from its Dam, may be supported by her Milk, for a Solar Year with little other Nourishment; at most not above the Value of two Shillings; which the Mother may certainly get, or the Value in Scraps, by her lawful Occupation of Begging: and it is exactly at one Year old that I propose to provide for them in such a manner, as, instead of being a Charge upon their Parents, or the Parish, or wanting Food and Raiment for the rest of their Lives; they shall, on the contrary, contribute to the Feeding and partly to the Cloathing, of many Thousands. . . .

I have been assured by a very knowing American of my Acquaintance in London, that a young healthy Child, well nursed is, at a Year old, a most delicious, nourishing and wholesome Food, whether Stewed, Roasted, Baked, or Boiled; and I make no doubt that it will equally serve in a Fricasie, or Ragoust.

I do therefore humbly offer it to publick Consideration, that of the Hundred and Twenty Thousand Children, already computed, Twenty thousand may be reserved for Breed; whereof only one Fourth Part to be Males; which is more than we allow to Sheep, black Cattle, or Swine; and my Reason is, that these Children are seldom the Fruits of Marriage, a Circumstance not much regarded by our Savages; therefore, one Male will be sufficient to serve four Females. That the remaining Hundred thousand, may, at a Year old be offered in Sale to the Persons of Quality and Fortune, through the Kingdom; always advising the Mother to let them suck plentifully in the last Month, so as to render them plump, and fat for a good Table. A Child will make two Dishes at an Entertainment for Friends; and when the Family dines alone, the fore or hind Quarter will make a reasonable Dish; and seasoned with a little Pepper or Salt, will be very good Boiled on the fourth Day, especially in Winter.

I have reckoned upon a Medium, that a Child just born will weigh Twelve Pounds; and in a solar Year, if tolerably nursed, increaseth to 28 Pounds.

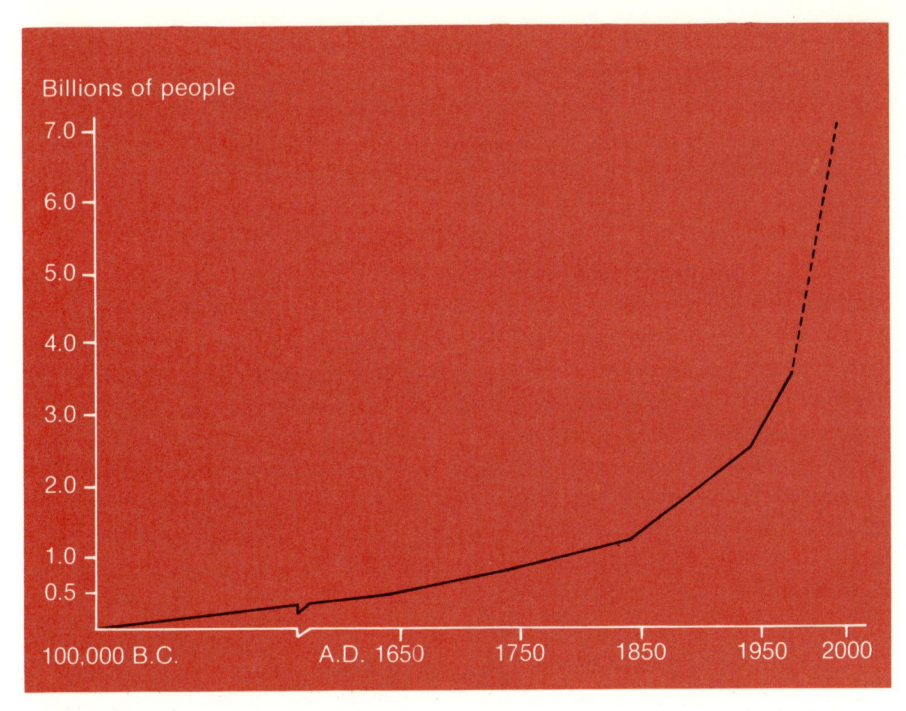

FIGURE 19-5 Population Growth
SOURCE: Data are from William Petersen, *Population* (New York: Macmillan, 1975), pp. 8-10.

I grant this Food will be somewhat dear, and therefore very proper for Landlords; who, as they have already devoured most of the Parents, seem to have the best Title to the Children.

Infant's Flesh will be in Season throughout the Year; but more plentiful in March, and a little before and after; for we are told by a grave Author [Rabelais], an eminent French Physician, that Fish being a prolifick Dyet, there are more Children born in Roman Catholick Countries about Nine Months after Lent, the Markets will be more glutted than usual; because the Number of Popish Infants, is, at least, three to one in this Kingdom; and therefore it will have one other Collateral advantage; by lessening the Number of Papists among us.

I have already computed the Charge of nursing a Beggar's Child (in which List I reckon all Cottagers, Labourers, and Four fifths of the Farmers) to be about two Shillings per Annum, Rags included; and I believe no Gentleman would repine to give Ten Shillings for the Carcase of a good fat Child; which, as I have said, will make four Dishes of excellent nutritive meat, when he hath only some particular Friend, or his own Family, to dine with him. Thus the Squire will learn to be a good Landlord, and grow popular among his Tenants;

the Mother will have Eight Shillings net Profit, and be fit for Work till she produceth another Child.

Those who are more thrifty (as I must confess the Times require) may flay the Carcase; the Skin of which, artificially dressed, will make admirable Gloves for Ladies, and Summer Boots for fine Gentlemen.[12]

Swift's "proposal" was, of course, a biting satirical comment on the society of his day. And it remains unlikely that government edict will resolve population dilemmas in such a manner. More recent projections of government demographic programs, however, seem frighteningly close to reality. Under government auspices individuals deemed to have hereditary defects have been sterilized. The shift from government sterilization programs for "mental and physical defectives" to general sterilization programs for the entire population of a country may be very small indeed. Population pressures may quite possibly usher the Demographic Institute into the government bureaucracy, as Anthony Burgess projects in his futuristic novel *The Wanting Seed*.

This was the day before the night when the knives of official disappointment struck.

Beatrice-Joanna Foxe snuffled a bereaved mother's grief as the little corpse, in its yellow plastic casket, was handed over to the two men from the Ministry of Agriculture (Phosphorus Reclamation Department). They were cheerful creatures, coal-faced and with shining dentures, and one of them sang a song which had recently become popular. Much burbled on the television by epicene willowy youths, it sounded incongruous coming from this virile West Indian deep bass throat. Macabre, too.

> My adorable Fred:
>   He's so, so sweet,
> From the crown of his head
>   To the soles of his feet.
>   He's my meat.

The name of the tiny cadaver had been not Fred but Roger. Beatrice-Joanna sobbed, but the man went on singing, having no feeling of his business, custom having made it in him a property of easiness.

"There we are, then," said Dr Acheson heartily, a fat gelding of an Anglo-Saxon. "Another dollop of phosphorus pentoxide for dear old Mother Earth. Rather less than half a kilo, I'd say. Still, every little helps." The singer had now become a whistler. Whistling, he nodded, handing over a receipt. "And if you'll just step into my office, Mrs Foxe," smiled Dr Acheson, "I'll give you your copy of the death

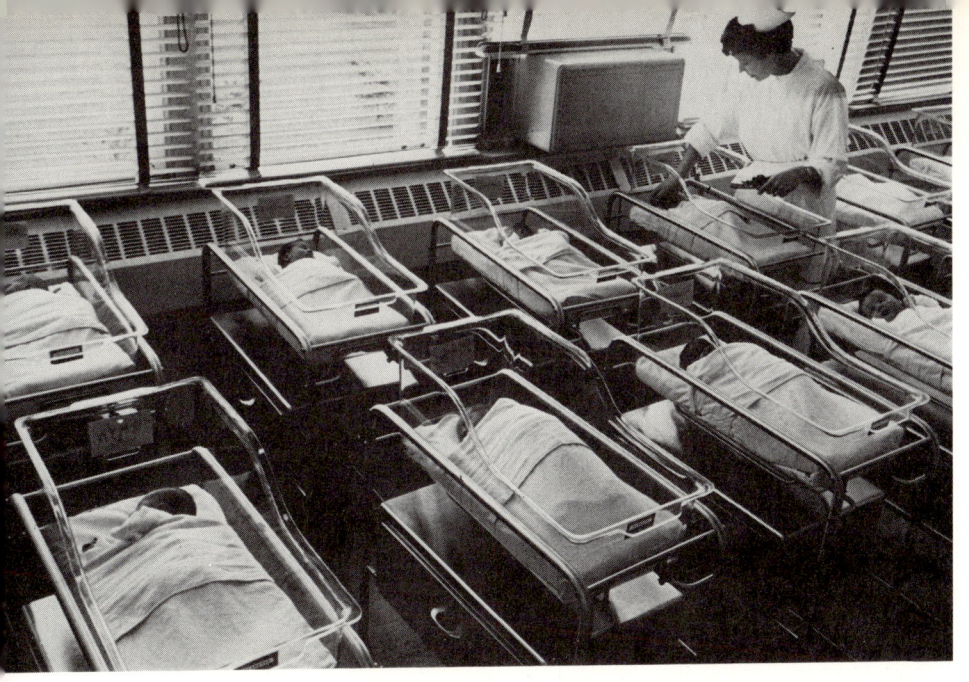

Many contend that birth rates must be lowered or else death rates will rise.

certificate. Take it to the Ministry of Infertility, and they'll pay you your condolence. In cash."

"All I want," she sniffed, "is my son back again."

"You'll get over that," said Dr Acheson cheerfully. "Everyone does." He watched benevolently the two black men carry the casket down the corridor towards the lift. Twenty-one storeys below, their van waited. "And think," he added. "Think of this in national terms, in global terms. One mouth less to feed. One more half-kilo of phosphorus pentoxide to nourish the earth. In a sense, you know, Mrs Foxe, you'll be getting your son back again." . . .

. . . Up there, at least twenty storeys high, on the facade of the Demographic Institute, stood a bas-relief circle with a straight line tangential to it. It symbolized the wished-for conquest of the population problem: that tangent, instead of stretching from everlasting, equalled in length the circumference of the circle. Stasis. A balance of global population and global food supply. Her brain approved, but her body, the body of a bereaved mother, shouted no, no. It all meant a denial of so many things; life, in the name of reason, was being blasphemed against.[13]

It is, of course, impossible to project exactly the future growth of world population. What is clear is that world population growth rates have been accelerating. Reaction to these growth rates has been mixed, but measures nearly as extreme as those noted by Swift and Burgess have been discussed with increasing frequency and are considered by some to be ever more plausible.

Chapter Summary

Demography is the study of human populations, especially changes in their size, density, and distribution. It is concerned with how these changes occur and the problems that may result. Recently much public and governmental attention has focused on what many refer to as the "population explosion" of this century. Obviously there are physical limits to the number of human beings that can live on the planet Earth, but disagreement remains over how many people constitute "too many."

Spokesmen in the tradition of Thomas Malthus are convinced that the world is already overpopulated and that immediate and perhaps drastic efforts are needed to limit further expansion. Other commentators, more in the tradition of Karl Marx, view the "population problem" as resulting more from exploitation than from too many people. A third group, the optimists, believe that technology can keep pace with and thus help support a growing world population.

Demographers use a number of statistical measurements to describe specific characteristics of given populations. They are able to calculate birth and fertility rates, infant mortality rates, and death rates, as well as levels of morbidity and life expectancy. Such statistics allow them to make projections about the future growth of populations. By examining current rates of fertility and mortality and combining them with general theories, such as that of the demographic transition, it is possible to predict the world's population at given future intervals. Quantitative projections, however, are unable to account for possible dramatic shifts in a culture's norms and values, shifts that could significantly affect its birth rate. Nor do they allow for the possibility that future governments may become much more active in population control, strongly affecting future growth.

Key Terms for Review

birth rate, p. 495
DC, p. 494
death rate, p. 497
demographic transition, p. 500
demography, p. 487
doubling time, p. 488
fecundity, p. 495
fertility rate, p. 495
green revolution, p. 493

incidence rate, p. 497
infant mortality rate, p. 497
life expectancy, p. 497
Malthus, p. 490
morbidity, p. 497
mortality, p. 497
prevalence rate, p. 497
UDC, p. 494

Suggested Readings

SOCIOLOGICAL

Ehrlich, Paul R., and Anne H. Ehrlich. *Population, Resources, Environment.* San Francisco: Freeman, 1972. This is a scholarly yet very readable presentation of worldwide demographic concerns, data, and issues. More thorough and complete than Paul Ehrlich's popular *Population Bomb,* this work is a fine introduction to the study of population.

Hernández, José. *People, Power, and Policy: A New View of Population.* Palo Alto, Calif.: National Press Books, 1974. Hernández offers a very lucid and insightful discussion of population problems and many related questions of a political nature. This work is more complete and less Malthusian than the Ehrlichs' study.

Petersen, William. *Population.* New York: Macmillan, 1975. Petersen's comprehensive treatment of demographic theory and data makes this a leading work in the field.

LITERARY

Burgess, Anthony. *The Wanting Seed.* New York: Norton, 1962. Burgess offers a chilling futuristic account of a world faced with extreme population problems. Population pressures are met with the responses of bureaucratic entities such as the Global Agricultural Authority and the Demographic Institute.

Farmer, Philip Jose. *The Fabulous Riverboat.* New York: Berkley, 1971. This recent addition to Farmer's riverworld novels provides a science fiction view of population shifts in a world in which death seems to be unknown. The long displayed imagination of Farmer yields an incredible tale.

Harrison, Harry. *Make Room! Make Room!* New York: Berkley, 1973. This science fiction view of life in New York City with a population of 35 million was made into the movie *Soylent Green* by MGM. Harrison's work is both fascinating and horrifying. The possibilities are well within the imaginable future.

Vonnegut, Kurt, Jr. "Welcome to the Monkey House." In *Welcome to the Monkey House.* New York: Dell, 1970. Vonnegut's short story shows another variation of possible cultural changes in response to population pressures. Vonnegut continues the long tradition of Swift and Burgess with the addition of suicide parlors.

IN THIS CHAPTER

Basic Assumptions   509

Predictions and Scenarios   512
    Increasing culture lag   512
    More social control   515

Methods of Social Control   517
    Behavior modification   517
    Electronic surveillance   520
    Centralized data systems   522

A Ray of Sunshine   523

Key Terms for Review   525

Suggested Readings   525

Is it now possible to predict the future?
What will society be like in the year 2000?
How might technology be used in future social systems?

EPILOGUE THE FUTURE

Speculators, dreamers, utopian idealists, sorcerers, and bookies — among others — spend much of their time looking toward some distant moment when the price of gold will make them immensely wealthy, when perfect romance will bloom, when there will be everlasting peace, or, in the case of bookies, when all the point spreads are perfect. All of us, in fact, have an interest in the future, but we are only marginally able to affect it and often even less able to predict it. Variances in human behavior are sometimes incredible, and we are faced with the seeming randomness of change. Yet if we make certain basic assumptions about the universe and human interaction and delineate alternate variables, we can then state reasonable projections about the future. Writers and scholars who make such assumptions and projections are called *futurists*.

Basic Assumptions

The first assumption essential for predicting the future is that both human interaction and the surrounding universe show some stability and order. Admittedly this is quite an assumption, but most of us make it. Whether we are sociologists or low-temperature physicists, conflict or consensus theorists, high school cheerleaders or cellists in a symphony orchestra, most of us assume the world has stability and order. Although anyone acquainted with basic physics realizes that all matter is unstable and in motion, most of this movement is not perceptible, and we therefore do not have to deal with it — a most fortunate situation, as Bertrand Russell suggests in *The ABC of Relativity:*

510 / EPILOGUE

Most objects on the earth's surface are fairly persistent and nearly stationary from a terrestrial point of view. If this were not the case, the idea of going on a journey would not seem so definite as it does. If you want to travel from King's Cross to Edinburgh, you know that you will find King's Cross where it has always been, that the railway line will take the course that it did when you last made the journey, and that Waverley Station in Edinburgh will not have walked up to the Castle. You therefore say and think that you have travelled to Edinburgh, not that Edinburgh has travelled to you, though the latter statement would be just as accurate. The success of this common-sense point of view depends on a number of things which are really of the nature of luck. Suppose all the houses in London were perpetually moving about, like a swarm of bees; suppose railways moved and changed their shapes like avalanches; and finally suppose that material objects were perpetually being formed and dissolved like clouds. There is nothing impossible in these suppositions. But obviously what we call a journey to Edinburgh would have no meaning in such a world. You would begin, no doubt, by asking the taxi-driver: 'Where is King's Cross this morning?' At the station you would have to ask a similar question about Edinburgh, but the booking-office clerk would reply: 'What part of Edinburgh do you mean, sir? Prince's Street has gone to Glasgow, the Castle has moved up into the Highlands, and Waverley Station is under water in the middle of the Firth of Forth'. And on the journey the stations would not be

Many cartoonists have speculated about life in the future, often predicting a less than perfect world.

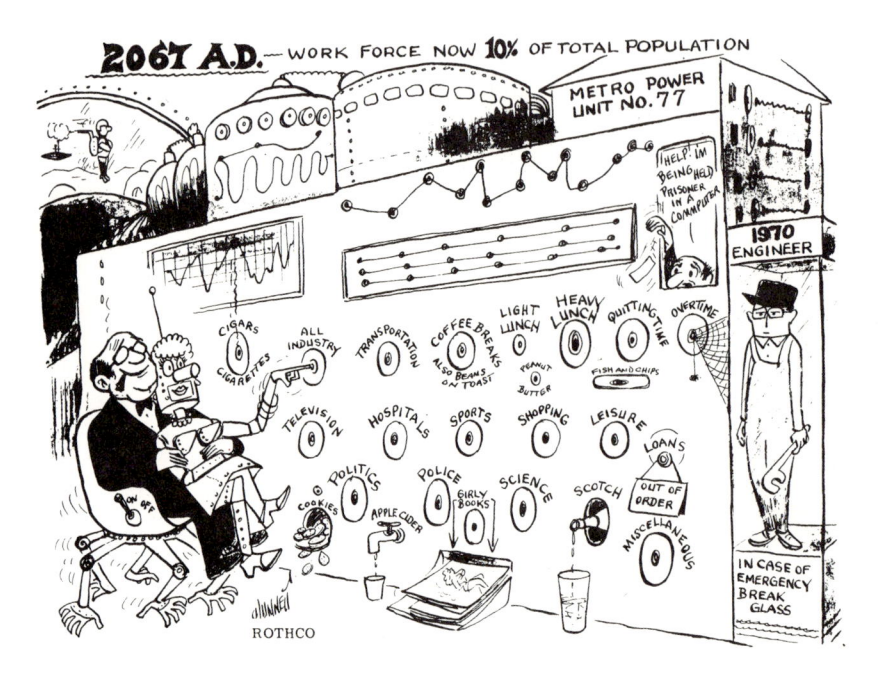

staying quiet, but some would be travelling north, some south, some east, some west, perhaps much faster than the train. Under these conditions you could not say where you were at any moment. Indeed the whole notion that one is always in some definite 'place' is due to the fortunate immobility of most of the large objects on the earth's surface. The idea of 'place' is only a rough practical approximation: there is nothing logically necessary about it, and it cannot be made precise.

If we were not much larger than an electron, we should not have this impression of stability, which is only due to the grossness of our senses. King's Cross, which to us looks solid, would be too vast to be conceived except by a few eccentric mathematicians. The bits of it that we could see would consist of little tiny points of matter, never coming into contact with each other, but perpetually whizzing round each other in an inconceivably rapid ballet-dance. The world of our experience would be quite as mad as the one in which the different parts of Edinburgh go for walks in different directions. If— to take the opposite extreme — you were as large as the sun and lived as long, with a corresponding slowness of perception, you would again find a higgledy-piggledy universe without permanence — stars and planets would come and go like morning mists, and nothing would remain in a fixed position relatively to anything else. The notion of comparative stability which forms part of our ordinary outlook is thus due to the fact that we are about the size we are, and live on a planet of which the surface is not very hot.[1]

"WE'VE JUST FORMED OUR FIRST UNION"

"WHAT I DON'T LIKE IS YOUR IMPERSONAL ATTITUDE, DOCTOR."

In rationally looking toward some future point, we must also assume that societal relationships and the earth itself will remain recognizable from the perspective of our current knowledge. If we attempted to describe the earth after the sun had become a super nova or to portray a complex society lacking any normative system, we would be fantasizing rather than predicting. Though the line between fantasy and reasonable prediction is often elusive, we shall try to remain aware of it.

Predictions and Scenarios

The striking advances in computer technology during the past decade or so have enabled social scientists to compile vast amounts of data to simulate possible future alternatives. Their reasoning process is inductive, moving from what is now known through varying possibilities into alternate futures. The popular term for this type of prophesying is *scenario*, a series of scenes that portray future events. High-level bureaucrats are constantly asking for scenarios on any number of subjects—from possible results of the proliferation of nuclear weapons to the projected impact of the growing plastics industry on bathroom fixtures. Here we will discuss scenarios of the broader variety.

INCREASING CULTURE LAG

It seems reasonable to predict that the disruptiveness of rapid social change that has been a major subject of sociological inquiry will continue as technological innovation causes increasing culture lag. The indicators of "societal illnesses"—such as suicide, divorce, alcoholism, and drug abuse—have been discussed and analyzed by everyone from television talk-show panelists and academicians to taxi drivers and shoe shiners. Essentially, such social disruptions result from the individual's inability to cope with everyday life. Often people feel unable to endure the uncertainties, indignities, and travails of their existence, so they attempt to escape.

Some turn to drugs because the world seems easier to face when their minds are affected by chemical alteration. Others feel that self-induced chemical change is unnecessary; their reality is sufficiently altered without the use of drugs. People of the latter type may be labeled crazy and institutionalized or simply considered eccentric, as was the Countess, the heroine of Jean Giraudoux's play *The Madwoman of Chaillot*. The Countess undeniably alters reality rather grandly, but she is most certainly able to cope with the everyday slurs and indignities of social change.

COUNTESS   *To be alive is to be fortunate, Roderick. Of course, in the morning, when you first awake, it does not always seem so very* gay. When you take your hair out of the drawer, and your teeth out of the glass, you are apt to feel a little out of place in this world. Especially if you've just been dreaming that you're a little girl on a pony looking for strawberries in the woods. But all you need to feel the call of life once more is a letter in your mail giving you your schedule for the day—your mending, your shopping, that letter to your grandmother that you never seem to get around to. And so, when you've washed your face in rosewater, and powdered it—not with this awful rice-powder they sell nowadays, which does nothing for the skin, but with a cake of pure white starch—and put on your pins, your rings, your brooches, bracelets, earrings, and pearls—in short, when you are dressed for your morning coffee—and have had a good look at yourself—not in the glass, naturally—it lies—but in the side of the brass gong that once belonged to Admiral Courbet—then, Roderick, then you're armed, you're strong, you're ready—you can begin again.

(Pierre is listening now intently. There are tears in his eyes)

PIERRE Oh, Madame . . . ! Oh, Madame . . . !

COUNTESS After that, everything is pure delight. First the morning paper. Not, of course, these current sheets full of lies and vulgarity. I always read the Gaulois, the issue of March 22, 1903. It's by far the best. It has some delightful scandal, some excellent fashion notes, and, of course, the last-minute bulletin on the death of Leonide Leblanc. She used to live next door, poor woman, and when I learn of her death every morning, it gives me quite a shock. I'd gladly lend you my copy, but it's in tatters.

SERGEANT Couldn't we find him a copy in some library?

COUNTESS I doubt it. And so, when you've taken your fruit salts—not in water, naturally—no matter what they say, it's water that gives you gas—but with a bit of spiced cake—then in sunlight or rain, Chaillot calls. It is time to dress for your morning walk. This takes much longer, of course—without a maid, impossible to do it under an hour, what with your corset, corset-cover, and drawers all of which lace or button in the back. I asked Madame Lanvin, a while ago, to fit the drawers with zippers. She was quite charming, but she declined. She thought it would spoil the style.

(The Deaf Mute comes in)

WAITER I know a place where they put zippers on anything.

(The Ragpicker enters)

COUNTESS I think Lanvin knows best. But I really manage very well, Martial. What I do now is, I lace them up in front, then twist them around to the back. It's quite simple, really. Then you choose a lorgnette, and then the usual fruitless search for the feather boa that the prospector stole—I know it was he: he didn't dare look me in the eye—and then all you need is a rubber band to slip around your parasol—I lost the catch the day I struck the cat that was stalking the pigeon—it was worth it—ah, that day I earned my wages!

THE RAGPICKER Countess, if you can use it, I found a nice umbrella catch the other day with a cat's eye in it.

COUNTESS Thank you, Ragpicker. They say these eyes sometimes come to life and fill with tears. I'd be afraid . . .

PIERRE Go on, Madame, go on . . .

COUNTESS Ah! So life is beginning to interest you, is it? You see how beautiful it is?

PIERRE What a fool I've been!

COUNTESS Then, Roderick, I begin my rounds. I have my cats to feed, my dogs to pet, my plants to water. I have to see what the evil ones are up to in the district—those who hate people, those who hate plants, those who hate animals. I watch them sneaking off in the morning to put on their disguises—to the baths, to the beauty parlors, to the barbers. But they can't deceive me. And when they come out again with blonde hair and false whiskers, to pull up my flowers and poison my dogs, I'm there, and I'm ready. All you have to do to break their power is to cut across their path from the left. That isn't always easy. Vice moves swiftly. But I have a good long stride and I generally manage.[2]

A major technological leap separates this New York banker from his predecessor who wore a visor and carefully made all notations with a quill pen.

For the Countess, being able to "cut across their path from the left" is, no doubt, an effective means of coping. Yet when an entire society evidences a kind of mass distortion of reality, the coping mechanism may lead to the sort of perverted logic George Orwell presented in *1984* as the three slogans of the Party:

>   *WAR IS PEACE*
>   *FREEDOM IS SLAVERY*
>   *IGNORANCE IS STRENGTH.*[3]

Some scholars have suggested that a similar distorted logic has already begun to take hold in industrialized nations, where problems are often whisked away by a journey into a fantasy land in which evil is no longer perceived to be evil but virtue. Herbert Marcuse comments on such deadly whimsy:

> *Setting the pace and style of politics, the power of imagination far exceeds Alice in Wonderland in the manipulation of words, turning sense into nonsense and nonsense into sense.*
>
> *The formerly antagonistic realms merge on technical and political grounds—magic and science, life and death, joy and misery. Beauty reveals its terror as highly classified nuclear plants and laboratories become "Industrial Parks" in pleasing surroundings; Civil Defense Headquarters display a "deluxe fallout-shelter" with wall-to-wall carpeting ("soft"), lounge chairs, television, and Scrabble, "designed as a combination family room during peacetime (sic!) and family-fallout shelter should war break out." If the horror of such realizations does not penetrate into consciousness, if it is readily taken for granted, it is because these achievements are (a) perfectly rational in terms of the existing order, (b) tokens of human ingenuity and power beyond the traditional limits of imagination.*
>
> *The obscene merger of aesthetics and reality refutes the philosophies which oppose "poetic" imagination to scientific and empirical Reason. Technological progress is accompanied by a progressive rationalization and even realization of the imaginary. The archetypes of horror as well as of joy, of war as well as of peace lose their catastrophic character. Their appearance in the daily life of the individuals is no longer that of irrational forces—their modern avatars are elements of technological domination, and subject to it.*[4]

MORE SOCIAL CONTROL

A second prediction follows from the first. As people become less and less able to cope with their environment, new technology will enable certain groups and individuals to exercise increasingly sophisticated methods of social control. But what forms will such control take and where will they lead? Are we heading toward *utopia*—a society in which some form of

There have been a number of attempts in the past to establish utopian communities. The Oneida community, founded in the 1840s in upstate New York, provides an interesting example. Adult members pooled their resources and labor and considered themselves all married to one another. Children were reared and educated communally with few ties to their biological parents. Here we see women at work in the community's business office and bakery.

ideal system has been established—or toward *dystopia,* which represents the opposite? Many gifted thinkers have envisioned utopian societies in the future, while others have suggested the coming of dystopian social systems. Table 20-1 lists works representing each viewpoint. Writers have portrayed future dystopian societies as both warnings and predictions. If society continues in its current direction, say the dystopian writers, then we may ultimately evolve an evil and degrading system.

Although it is impossible to project precisely what social systems will exist a hundred years from now, current trends and technological developments indicate that we are moving toward more social control.

TABLE 20-1
Utopian and Dystopian Statements

Work	Author and Date
UTOPIAN	
The Republic	Plato (circa 380 B.C.)
Utopia	Sir Thomas More (1516)
The New Atlantis	Francis Bacon (1627)
Walden	Henry David Thoreau (1854)
A Modern Utopia	H. G. Wells (1905)
The City of the Sun	Tommaso Campanella (1923)
Walden Two	B. F. Skinner (1948)
DYSTOPIAN	
Erewhon	Samuel Butler (1872)
Looking Backward	Edward Bellamy (1888)
Brave New World	Aldous Huxley (1932)
Animal Farm	George Orwell (1946)
1984	George Orwell (1949)
Fahrenheit 451	Ray Bradbury (1953)
Fail-Safe	Eugene Burdick and Harvey Wheeler (1962)

Methods of Social Control

How might social control be increased in the future? We already have glimpses of some of the methods and technology that may be employed to "engineer" society.

BEHAVIOR MODIFICATION

Present psychological techniques of behavior modification are both sophisticated and highly effective. Although many less refined methods have been utilized for years by advertising agencies—and we have dutifully purchased an impressive array of deodorants and breakfast cereals—more polished approaches have now been adopted by institutions.

An early and impressive use of behavior modification was made by the North Koreans during the Korean War. Since they were the enemy, we defined their actions as "brainwashing." Yet our own system of social control soon began to utilize very similar methods. By 1962 a detailed program of brainwashing (now called behavior modification) was being offered to prison administrators. During a national conference that year chaired by the director of the Federal Bureau of Prisons, MIT psychology professor Edgar H. Schein discussed some of the techniques:

> *In order to produce marked change of behavior and/or attitudes, it is necessary to weaken, undermine, or remove the supports to the old patterns of behavior and old attitudes. Because most of the supports are the face-to-face confirmation of present behavior which are provided by those with whom close emotional ties exist, it is often necessary to break these emotional ties. This can be done by removing the individual physically and preventing any communication with those he cares about, or by proving to him that those whom he respects are not worthy of it, and indeed, should actively be mistrusted. If at the same time, the total environment inflexibly provides rewards and punishments only in terms of the new human contacts around which to build up relationships, it is highly likely that the desired new behavior and attitudes will be learned.*[5]

Such methods of behavior modification are sometimes coupled with drug therapy. "Difficult" prisoners, "mentally ill" patients, and "hyperactive" students have been the recipients of these techniques for a number of years. Powerful depressants such as Trilafon, Mellaril, and Prolixin have been widely utilized to "calm" or "pacify" prisoners and mental patients, while the superdepressant Acetine, which severely inhibits the respiratory and cardiovascular systems, has been somewhat selectively used. Acetine, which "makes the subjects feel as if they are dying," is particularly useful in "aversion therapy," a method that forces association of negative behavior or past misdeeds with the use of the drug.[6] Very simply, if you continue to think or act in a "negative" way, you will be made to feel as if you are going to die. Acetine is used in both prisons and mental hospitals.

By now it should be painfully clear that in the world of drug therapy and behavior modification, distinctions between present realities and fictional future dystopias are quite difficult to find. Surely the world of the Trilafon dispensers is not far removed from that of the Director of Hatcheries and Conditioning in Aldous Huxley's *Brave New World*.

> "And this," said the Director opening the door, "is the Fertilizing Room."
>
> Bent over their instruments, three hundred Fertilizers were plunged, as the Director of Hatcheries and Conditioning entered the room, in the scarcely breathing silence, the absent-minded, soliloquizing hum or whistle, of absorbed concentration. A troop of newly arrived students, very young, pink and callow, followed nervously, rather abjectly, at the Director's heels. Each of them carried a notebook, in which, whenever the great man spoke, he desperately scribbled. Straight from the horse's mouth. It was a rare privilege. The D. H. C. for Central London always made a point of personally conducting his new students round the various departments.
>
> "Just to give you a general idea," he would explain to them. For of course some sort of general idea they must have, if they were to do their work intelligently—though as little of one, if they were to be good and happy members of society, as possible. For particulars, as everyone knows, make for virtue and happiness; generalities are intellectually necessary evils. Not philosophers but fret-sawyers and stamp collectors compose the backbone of society.
>
> "To-morrow," he would add, smiling at them with a slightly menacing geniality, "you'll be settling down to serious work. You won't have time for generalities. Meanwhile . . ."
>
> Meanwhile, it was a privilege. Straight from the horse's mouth into the notebook. The boys scribbled like mad.
>
> Tall and rather thin but upright, the Director advanced into the room. He had a long chin and big rather prominent teeth, just covered, when he was not talking, by his full, floridly curved lips. Old, young? Thirty? Fifty? Fifty-five? It was hard to say. And anyhow the question didn't arise; in this year of stability, A. F. 632, it didn't occur to you to ask it.
>
> "I shall begin at the beginning," said the D. H. C. and the more zealous students recorded his intention in their notebooks: Begin at the beginning. "These," he waved his hand, "are the incubators."

Behavior modification programs in prisons offer rewards for performance considered "desirable." Here inmates line up to receive their high school equivalency diplomas at a prison graduation ceremony.

And opening an insulated door he showed them racks upon racks of numbered test-tubes. "The week's supply of ova. Kept," he explained, "at blood heat; whereas the male gametes," and here he opened another door, "they have to be kept at thirty-five instead of thirty-seven. Full blood heat sterilizes." Rams wrapped in theremogene beget no lambs.

Still leaning against the incubators he gave them, while the pencils scurried illegibly across the pages, a brief description of the modern fertilizing process; he spoke first, of course, of its surgical introduction—"the operation undergone voluntarily for the good of Society, not to mention the fact that it carries a bonus amounting to six months' salary"; continued with some account of the technique for preserving the excised ovary alive and actively developing; passed on to a consideration of optimum temperature, salinity, viscosity; referred to the liquor in which the detached and ripened eggs were kept; and, leading his charges to the work tables, actually showed them how this liquor was drawn off from the test-tubes; how it was let out drop by drop onto the specially warmed slides of the microscopes; how the eggs which it contained were inspected for abnormalities, counted and transferred to a porous receptacle; how (and he now took them to watch the operation) this receptacle was immersed in a warm bouillon containing free-swimming spermatozoa—at a minimum concentration of one hundred thousand per cubic centimetre, he insisted; and how, after ten minutes, the container was lifted out of the liquor and its contents re-examined; how, if any of the eggs remained unfertilized, it was again immersed, and, if necessary, yet again; how the fertilized ova went back to the incubators; where the Alphas and Betas remained until definitely bottled; while the Gammas, Deltas and Epsilons were brought out again, after only thirty-six hours, to undergo Bokanovsky's Process.

"Bokanovsky's Process," repeated the Director, and the students underlined the words in their little notebooks.[7]

A further buttress of the forces of behavior modification is the fact that many influential groups do not consider such control an assault on human dignity. For them the techniques present a fantastic opportunity to elevate humanity, to relieve suffering. The world they envision may seem to many not far removed from Huxley's, yet they perceive it as utopian. In his futurist novel *Walden Two*, the most famous of the behaviorist theorists, B. F. Skinner, describes such a utopian society:

> The living quarters and daily schedules of the older children furnished a particularly good example of behavioral engineering. At first sight they seemed wholly casual, almost haphazard, but as Frazier pointed out their significant features and the consequences of each, I began to make out a comprehensive, almost Machiavellian design.
>
> The children passed smoothly from one age group to another, following a natural process of growth and avoiding the abrupt changes of the home-and-school system. The arrangements were such that each child emulated children slightly older than himself and hence derived motives and patterns for much of his early education without adult aid.
>
> The control of the physical and social environment, of which Frazier had made so much, was progressively relaxed — or, to be more exact, the control was transferred from the authorities to the child himself and to the other members of his group. After spending most of the first year in an air-conditioned cubicle, and the second and third mainly in an air-conditioned room with a minimum of clothing and bedding, the three- or four-year-old was introduced to regular clothes and given the care of a small standard cot in a dormitory. The beds of the five- and six-year-olds were grouped by threes and fours in a series of alcoves furnished like rooms and treated as such by the children. Groups of three or four seven-year-olds occupied small rooms together, and this practice was continued, with frequent change of roommates, until the children were about thirteen, at which time they took temporary rooms in the adult building, usually in pairs. At marriage, or whenever the individual chose, he could participate in building a larger room for himself or refurnishing an old room which might be available.[8]

ELECTRONIC SURVEILLANCE

A second area in which technology is rapidly bridging the distance between the present and some possible future dystopia is that of the burgeoning electronics industry. The sophistication of today's electronic surveillance equipment is awesome. In *1984* George Orwell speculated on a society in which Big Brother was constantly and everywhere monitoring individuals:

> "You're hurt?" he said.
> "It's nothing. My arm. It'll be all right in a second."
> She spoke as though her heart were fluttering. She had certainly turned very pale.
> "You haven't broken anything?"
> "No, I'm all right. It hurt for a moment, that's all."
> She held out her free hand to him, and he helped her up. She had regained some of her color, and appeared very much better.
> "It's nothing," she repeated shortly. "I only gave my wrist a bit of a bang. Thanks, comrade!"
> And with that she walked on in the direction in which she had been going, as briskly as though it had really been nothing. The whole incident could not have taken as much as half a minute. Not to let one's feelings appear in one's face was a habit that had acquired the status of an instinct, and in any case they had been standing straight in front of a telescreen when the thing happened. Nevertheless it had been very difficult not to betray a momentary surprise, for in the two or three seconds while he was helping her up the girl had slipped something into his hand. There was no question that she had done it intentionally. It was something small and flat. As he passed through the lavatory door he transferred it to his pocket and felt it with the tips of his fingers. It was a scrap of paper folded into a square.
> While he stood at the urinal he managed, with a little more fingering, to get it unfolded. Obviously there must be a message of some kind written on it. For a moment he was tempted to take it into one of the water closets and read it at once. But that would be shocking folly, as he well knew. There was no place where you could be more certain that the telescreens were watched continuously.[9]

Orwell's speculations now seem almost tame; the Orwellian telescreen has already been exceeded. Unobtrusive electronic monitoring of individuals is both commonplace and highly sophisticated. Miniature body and room transmitters (bugs) are relatively inexpensive and are able to transmit strong voice signals for a distance of six city blocks. Law enforcement officials are pleased with the Wackenhut "Bloodhound," a device that can track a matchbook-sized transmitter for a distance of ten miles in populated areas. When the transmitter is attached clandestinely to a car, the possibilities for undetected surveillance are obvious. Rooms can be wired (bugged) with a highly sensitive penny-sized microphone for a cost of less than $40.[10] Our movements in stores and on an increasing number of city streets are observed through closed-circuit television.

Yet even more impressive are the radio-telemetry devices now available. Their suggested use is for control and monitoring of parolees. One, the Behavior-Transmitter-Reinforcer (BTR), is attached to the parolee's belt and wrist. Not only does the BTR monitor the activity and location of

Modern electronic surveillance equipment is easily hidden. This radio transmitter device fits into the heel of a man's shoe.

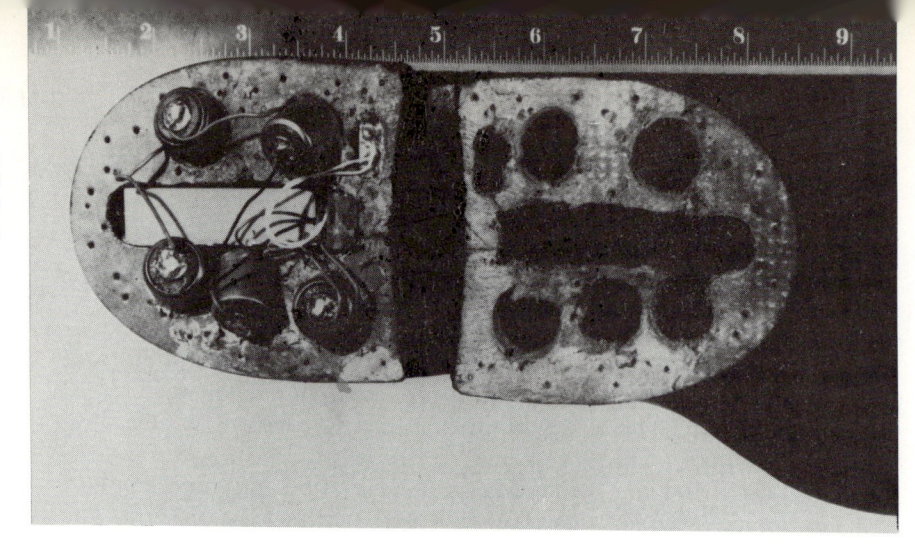

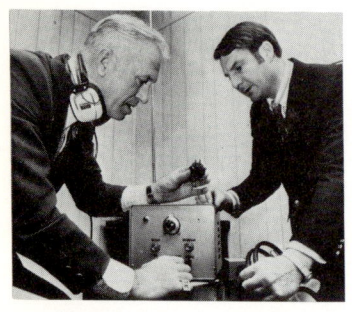

Finding "bugs" has become a multimillion dollar business. Here two specialists in locating electronic listening devices display an ordinary-looking electrical wall plug—which in fact contains a small microphone.

the wearer, it is able to "avert unsuitable activity" by transmitting electronic impulses (shocks) to induce pain. An even more advanced device may be surgically implanted within the individual who is to be observed. Some of us, of course, find such equipment frightening, an indication that dystopian fears have materialized. Others, though, are convinced that the implantation of monitoring devices is simply a scientific advancement with many possible benefits for society. Criminologists Barton L. Ingraham and Gerald W. Smith have discussed these benefits:

> The envisioned system of telemetric control while offering many possible advantages to offenders over present penal measures also has several possible benefits for society. Society, through such systems, exercises control over behavior it defines as deviant, thus insuring its own protection. The offender, by returning to the community, can help support his dependents and share in the overall tax burden. The offender is also in a better position to make meaningful restitution. Because the control system works on conditioning principles, the offender is habituated into non-deviant behavior patterns—thus perhaps decreasing the probability of recidivism and, once the initial cost of development is absorbed, a telemetric control system might provide substantial economic advantage compared to rather costly correctional programs. All in all, the development of such a system could prove tremendously beneficial for society.[11]

CENTRALIZED DATA SYSTEMS

A final area of current technology which seems to be bringing reality rapidly nearer the imagined dystopias is that of the giant computers and centralized data banks. The extent and abuse of such record keeping has become apparent since the early 1970s. Although Congress has repeatedly voted against creation of a national data bank, federal and state agencies have managed to create vast systems of centralized data. Under the banner of varying acronyms such as SEARCH (Systems for Electronic Analysis and Retrieval of Criminal Histories), massive data banks have been assembled. The FBI, the Department of Defense, the Internal Revenue Service, the Central Intelligence Agency, and the Treasury have all been accused of abusing such systems. TRW Credit Data Corporation, one of the giants of the credit industry, has stored in its computer in Anaheim, California, information on over 60 million American consumers.[12]

Again, the similarities to many fictional dystopias are obvious, as is the seemingly impossible task of controlling the controllers. Senator Sam J. Ervin, folk hero of the 1973–1974 Watergate investigations, has expressed his dismay at the growth of this technology and noted the implications:

> The new technology has made it literally impossible for a man to start again in our society. It has removed the quality of mercy from our institutions by making it impossible to forget, to understand, to tolerate. . . . The undisputed and unlimited possession of the resources to build and operate data banks on individuals, and to make decisions about people with the aid of computers and electronic data systems, is fast securing to executive branch officials a political power which the authors of the Constitution never meant any one group of men to have over all others.[13]

A Ray of Sunshine

We do not wish to close on an entirely pessimistic note. The future *is* an unknown, and perhaps predictions of increased repression through more sophisticated technology will prove to be inaccurate. As we have noted, some futurists are greatly heartened by all the new technology. Herman Kahn, director of the Hudson Institute, is filled with marvelous tales of future technological wonders.

Another optimistic futurist is Charles A. Reich, whose views were presented in *The Greening of America*.

> Neither lawful procedures nor politics-and-power can succeed against the Corporate State. Neither can prevent the steady advance of authoritarian rule. If the new consciousness sticks to these tactics, it will throw itself away on an ideology that fails to take account of its real power. The power is not the power of manipulating procedures or the power of politics or street fighting, but the power of new values and a new way of life.
>
> For the road to a new society is there nonetheless. Consciousness is capable of changing and of destroying the Corporate State, without violence, without seizure of political power, without overthrow

Information on millions of American citizens is stored on computer tape.

of any existing group of people. The new generation, by experimenting with action at the level of consciousness, has shown the way to the one method of change that will work in today's post-industrial society: changing consciousness. It is only by change in individual lives that we can seize power from the State.

Can this really work? Have we not said that the Corporate State is subject to no controls whatever, even by a majority of the people? And isn't there evidence of this in the continuance into 1970 of the Vietnam War, which was already so unpopular years earlier that President Johnson was forced to retire, and both candidates promised peace? Moreover, almost all New Left theorists, from Marcuse on down, agree that no revolution is possible in the United States at the present time. And many people believe that if anything happens, it will be a right-wing reaction that will smash whatever there is of the New Left. In the light of all of this, what power can we expect a new consciousness to have? How, after all we have said about the invulnerable power of the Corporate State, could change possibly be so simple?[14]

What answer does Reich have for us? It is, of course, that consciousness raising (to the third level) will be the liberating force. "For culture controls the economic and political machine, not vice versa."[15]

Perhaps this is a ray of sunshine. Surely we all can hope, but as sociologists we suggest that the preponderance of evidence leads to a very different conclusion. Technological changes seem to precede, if not control, culture change, suggesting that Reich's "consciousness three" may be a will-o'-the-wisp. Of course, people may chose to ignore the evidence if they wish. For those who are content to pin their hopes for society on the dream of technological liberation or revolution through consciousness raising, we end this book with a valediction from Kurt Vonnegut, Jr.: "Lots of luck, boys and girls."[16]

Key Terms for Review

dystopia, p. 516
futurist, p. 509
scenario, p. 512
utopia, p. 515

Suggested Readings

SOCIOLOGICAL

Bell, Daniel, ed. *Toward the Year 2000: Work in Progress.* Boston: Beacon Press, 1968. This collection of materials edited by Bell was produced for the American Academy's Commission on the Year 2000. The work contains a variety of perspectives on what the future will be like.

Lundberg, George. *Can Science Save Us?* New York: David McKay, 1961. Lundberg's classic statement of faith in progress and the scientific method remains a strong testament to positivism. Science, says Lundberg, is the great hope for humanity.

Marcuse, Herbert. *One-Dimensional Man.* Boston: Beacon Press, 1964. Marcuse, a Marxist philosopher, offers a penetrating perspective on the interaction among technology, ideology, and perception. His work is widely read and respected.

LITERARY

Huxley, Aldous. *Brave New World.* New York: Bantam, 1968; orig. 1932. Huxley's famous dystopia seems only a small step away from much of the technology and ideology of the present-day industrialized world. Members of Huxley's society are highly programed and often drugged, but at least a few retain some hope for the future.

Orwell, George. *1984.* New York: Harcourt, Brace, & World, 1949. Like *Brave New World,* Orwell's dystopia relies on sophisticated technology to maintain social control. Unlike Huxley, however, Orwell also uses many aspects of normative pressure to explain the future tyranny.

Skinner, B. F. *Walden Two.* New York: Macmillan, 1969. Though offered as a utopian view, Skinner's articulate presentation of the future possibilities of behavior modification is considered by many to be a dismal outlook.

NOTES
GLOSSARY
CREDITS
INDEXES

NOTES

CHAPTER ONE

[1] *The Positive Philosophy of Auguste Comte*, 3 vols., trans. and cond. Harriet Martineau (London: Bell, 1896).

[2] William Graham Sumner, *What Social Classes Owe to Each Other* (Caldwell, Idaho: Caxton Printers, 1963; orig. 1883), p. 19.

[3] Lester Frank Ward, *Applied Sociology* (Boston: Ginn, 1906), p. 331.

[4] Robert M. MacIver, *Society* (New York: Holt, Rinehart & Winston, 1937), pp. 476–477.

[5] Max Weber, *The Theory of Social and Economic Organization*, trans. A. M. Henderson and Talcott Parsons (New York: Oxford University Press, 1947).

[6] Charles Horton Cooley, *Social Organization: A Study of the Larger Mind* (New York: Schocken, 1962), p. 7.

[7] Robert A. Nisbet, "Sociology as an Art Form," *Pacific Sociological Review*, 5 (1962): 67.

[8] C. Wright Mills, *The Sociological Imagination* (New York: Oxford University Press, 1959), p. 182.

[9] Feodor Dostoevsky, *Crime and Punishment*, trans. Coulson, ed. George Gibian (New York: Norton, 1964), p. 9.

CHAPTER TWO

[1] George Herbert Mead, *Mind, Self, and Society* (Chicago: University of Chicago Press, 1934).

[2] Peter Farb, "Man at the Mercy of His Language," in *Man's Rise to Civilization as Shown by the Indians of North America from Primeval Times to the Coming of the Industrial State* (New York: E. P. Dutton, 1968), p. 237.

[3] William Graham Sumner, *Folkways* (Boston: Ginn, 1906), p. 438.

[4] Jerzy Kosinski, *The Painted Bird* (Boston: Houghton Mifflin, 1965), p. 129.

[5] Sumner, *Folkways*, p. 13.

[6] John F. Cuber, *Sociology: A Synopsis of Principles* (New York: Appleton-Century-Crofts, 1968), p. 115.

[7] Horace Miner, "Body Ritual Among the Nacirema," *American Anthropologist*, 58 (June 1956): 503–505.

[8] E. M. Forster, "The Mosque," in *A Passage to India* (New York: Harcourt Brace Jovanovich, 1952), pp. 18–19.

[10] Plato, *The Republic*, trans. Francis MacDonald Cornford (New York and London: Oxford University Press, 1964), pp. 200–201.

[11] Claude Brown, *Manchild in the Promised Land* (New York: Macmillan, 1965, pp. 89–90.

[12] Joseph S. Himes, *The Study of Sociology* (Glenview, Ill.: Scott, Foresman, 1968), p. 83.

CHAPTER THREE

[1] Samuel Langhorne Clemens, "English as She Is Taught," in *The Complete Essays of Mark Twain*, ed. Charles Neider (Garden City, N.Y.: Doubleday, 1963), pp. 38–46.

[2] Samuel Langhorne Clemens, "What Is Man?" in *The Complete Essays of Mark Twain*, p. 360.

[3] Shirley Jackson, "The Lottery," in *The Best Short Stories of the Modern Age*, ed. Douglas Angus (Greenwich, Conn.: Fawcett, 1965), pp. 313, 315–317.

[4] Ernest Hemingway, "Fathers and Sons," in *The Short Stories of Ernest Hemingway* (New York: Scribner's, 1966), pp. 489–490, 496.

[5] Samuel Langhorne Clemens, "Disgraceful Persecution of a Boy," in *The Complete Essays of Mark Twain*, pp. 7–9.

[6] B. F. Skinner, *Walden Two* (New York: Macmillan, 1948).

[7] Aldous Huxley, *Brave New World* (New York: Bantam, 1960), pp. 14–15.

[8] Jean Piaget, *The Moral Judgment of the Child* (New York: Free Press, 1965).

[9] Joost A. M. Meerloo, *Conversation and Communication* (New York: International Universities Press, 1952).

[10] James M. McCrimmon, *Writing with a Purpose* (Boston: Houghton Mifflin, 1973), p. 56.

[11] Charles Horton Cooley, *Human Nature and Social Order* (New York: Schocken, 1964), p. 184.

[12] Samuel Langhorne Clemens, "What Is Man?" in *The Complete Essays of Mark Twain*, p. 344.

[13] Sherwood Anderson, "I'm a Fool," in *Literature:*

Structure, Sound, and Sense, ed. Laurence Perrine (New York: Harcourt Brace Jovanovich, 1970), pp. 71, 76–78.

[14]George Herbert Mead, Mind, Self, and Society (Chicago: University of Chicago Press, 1934), p. 135.

[15]James Weldon Johnson, The Autobiography of an Ex-Coloured Man (New York: Alfred A. Knopf, 1966), pp. 16–19.

[16]Urie Bronfenbrenner, Two Worlds of Childhood: U.S. and U.S.S.R. (New York: Russell Sage Foundation, 1970).

[17]"The Last Soldier," Time, February 7, 1972, pp. 41–42.

[18]"The POW's: What a Difference a Year Makes," Newsweek, February 25, 1974, pp. 68–70.

CHAPTER FOUR

[1]Jerome H. Woolpy, "The Social Organization of Wolves," Natural History, 77 (1968): 46, 51.

[2]Richard Q. Wells, Manners, Culture, and Dress of the Best American Society (Springfield, Mass.: King, Richardson, 1890), pp. 118, 225–226, 271–272, 281.

[3]Virginia Woolf, "The New Dress," in A Haunted House and Other Short Stories (New York: Harcourt Brace Jovanovich, 1944), pp. 47–48.

[4]Herman Melville, White Jacket (Boston: L. C. Page, 1892), pp. 23–30.

[5]Ralph Linton, The Study of a Man (New York: Appleton-Century-Crofts, 1936), chap. 8.

[6]Frederick Douglass, "Letter to Thomas Auld," in Dark Symphony: Negro Literature in America, ed. James A. Emanuel and Theodore L. Gross (New York: Free Press, 1968), pp. 20–24.

[7]Robert K. Merton, Social Theory and Social Structure (New York: Free Press, 1968), p. 423.

[8]Joseph Heller, Catch-22 (New York: Dell, 1967), pp. 16, 69.

[9]Anne Sinclair Mehdevi, "A Persian Courtship," in Modern American Essays, ed. Sylvia Z. Brodkin and Elizabeth J. Pearson (New York: Globe, 1967), pp. 217, 219.

[10]Ibid., pp. 220–222.

[11]Philip Roth, "Defender of the Faith," in Goodbye Columbus and Five Short Stories (New York: Modern Library, 1959), pp. 178–180.

[12]Kai T. Erikson, Wayward Puritans: A Study in the Sociology of Deviance (New York: John Wiley, 1966), pp. 6–7.

[13]Emile Durkheim, The Division of Labor in Society, trans. George Simpson (Glencoe, Ill.: Free Press, 1933).

[14]Stephen Crane, The Red Badge of Courage: An Episode of the American Civil War (New York: Modern Library, 1925), pp. 56–60.

CHAPTER FIVE

[1]George Orwell, "A Hanging," in Shooting an Elephant and Other Essays (New York: Harcourt Brace Jovanovich, 1950), pp. 15–16.

[2]Sinclair Lewis, "Young Man Axelbrod," in Selected Short Stories of Sinclair Lewis (Garden City, N.Y.: Doubleday, 1935), p. 282.

[3]Ibid., p. 285.

[4]Ibid., p. 287.

[5]James Thurber, "The Lover and His Lass," in Further Fables for Our Time (New York: Simon & Schuster, 1956), pp. 36–38.

[6]Ibid., p. 39.

[7]Frank O'Connor, "My Oedipus Complex," in The Stories of Frank O'Connor (New York: Alfred A. Knopf, 1950), pp. 5–6.

[8]Ibid., p. 13.

[9]Ibid., pp. 14–15.

[10]F. Scott Fitzgerald, "The Ice Palace," in The Stories of F. Scott Fitzgerald (New York: Scribner's, 1951), p. 66.

[11]Ibid., pp. 76, 80–81.

[12]Charles Horton Cooley, Social Organization: A Study of the Larger Mind (New York: Schocken, 1962); orig. 1909.

[13]Alfred Kazin, "Brownsville Kitchen," in A Walker in the City (New York: Harcourt Brace Jovanovich, 1951).

[14]Edward Field, "A Bill to My Father," in Stand Up, Friend, With Me (New York: Grove Press, 1963), p. 28.

[15]Ferdinand Tönnies, Gemeinschaft and Gesellschaft, trans. and ed. C. P. Loomis as Community and Society (New York: Harper & Row, 1963).

[16]Oscar Lewis, "In New York You Get Swallowed by a Horse," in Modern American Essays, ed. Sylvia Z. Brodkin and Elizabeth J. Pearson (New York: Globe, 1967), pp. 192–194, 198.

[17]John Donne, Devotions, 1623, XVII.

CHAPTER SIX

[1]Donavid, J. D., "The Bureaucracy Lives," Dun's, 99 (1972): 96.

[2]Amitai Etzioni, *Modern Organizations* (Englewood Cliffs, N. J.: Prentice-Hall, 1964), p. 1.

[3]Much of the discussion here is based on Etzioni, *Modern Organizations*, p. 3.

[4]H. H. Gerth and C. Wright Mills, eds., *From Max Weber: Essays in Sociology* (New York: Oxford University Press, 1958), pp. 196–244.

[5]Peter M. Blau and W. Richard Scott, *Formal Organizations: A Comparative Approach* (San Francisco: Chandler, 1962).

[6]Amitai Etzioni, *Complex Organizations* (New York: Free Press, 1961), pp. 3–22.

[7]Elton Mayo, *The Human Problems of an Industrial Civilization* (New York: Macmillan, 1933); and F. J. Roethlisberger and William J. Dickson, *Management and the Worker* (Cambridge, Mass.: Harvard University Press, 1939).

[8]Erving Goffman, *Asylums* (Garden City, N.Y.: Doubleday, 1961), pp. 256–257.

[9]Ibid., p. 260.

[10]Ibid., pp. 264, 263.

[11]Ibid., p. 267.

[12]Joseph S. Berliner, *Factory and the Manager in the U.S.S.R.* (Cambridge, Mass.: Harvard University Press, 1957), p. 240.

[13]Matthew P. Dumont, "Down the Bureaucracy," *Transaction*, 7 (1970): 10–14.

[14]Roethlisberger and Dickson, *Management and the Worker*, p. 552.

[15]Etzioni, *Modern Organizations*, p. 10.

[16]Robert K. Merton, *Social Theory and Social Structure* (New York: Free Press, 1968), p. 253.

[17]C. Northcote Parkinson, *Parkinson's Law* (Boston: Houghton Mifflin, 1957).

[18]Franz Kafka, *The Castle* (New York: Alfred A. Knopf, 1956), p. 84.

[19]Robert Michels, *Political Parties* (New York: Free Press, 1949).

[20]Blau and Scott, *Formal Organizations*, pp. 245–246.

[21]Robert K. Merton, "Bureaucratic Structure and Personality," *Social Forces*, 18 (1940): 560–568.

[22]Kurt Vonnegut, Jr., *The Sirens of Titan* (New York: Delacorte, 1959), p. 79.

[23]Honoré de Balzac, "Les Employés," in *The Novels of Balzac*, trans. James Waring (Philadelphia: Gebbie, 1899), pp. 305, 314.

[24]Blau and Scott, *Formal Organizations*, pp. 242–244.

[25]Kafka, *The Castle*, pp. 81–82.

[26]Robert Townsend, *Up the Organization* (New York: Alfred A. Knopf, 1970), pp. 137–138.

[27]Robert N. McMurry, "The Case for Benevolent Autocracy," *Harvard Business Review*, 36 (1958): 82–90.

[28]Philip Selznick, *TVA and the Grass Roots* (Berkeley: University of California Press, 1949), p. 13.

[29]Dumont, "Down the Bureaucracy," p. 14.

CHAPTER SEVEN

[1]Charles Dickens, "The Streets—Night," in *Charles Dickens' Best Stories*, ed. Morton Zabel (Garden City, N.Y.: Hanover House, 1959), pp. 39–40.

[2]William M. Thackeray, "Sketches and Travels in London," *The Complete Works of Wm. M. Thackeray* (New York: George D. Sproul, 1899), vol. 4, pp. 113–114.

[3]George Orwell, *The Road to Wigan Pier* (New York: Harcourt, Brace, 1958), pp. 156–160.

[4]John Marshall Harlan, Dissenting Opinion, *Plessy v. Ferguson*, 163 U.S. 537, 539 (1896).

[5]Mark Twain, "What Paul Bourget Thinks of Us," 1899.

[6]Kurt B. Mayer and Walter Buckley, *Class and Society* (New York: Random House, 1970), pp. 30–33.

[7]C. Wright Mills, *The Marxists* (New York: Dell, 1962), p. 90.

[8]Orwell, *The Road to Wigan Pier*, pp. 153–156.

[9]Max Weber, "Class, Status and Party," in *Class, Status, and Power*, ed. Reinhard Bendix and Seymour Martin Lipset (New York: Free Press, 1966), pp. 21–28.

[10]F. Scott Fitzgerald, "The Diamond as Big as the Ritz," in *Stories of F. Scott Fitzgerald* (New York: Scribner's, 1951), pp. 12–13, 15.

[11]Ibid., p. 7.

[12]Ibid., p. 10.

[13]Kingsley Davis and Wilbert E. Moore, "Some Principles of Stratification," *American Sociological Review*, 10 (April 1945): 243.

[14]Melvin M. Tumin, "Some Principles of Stratification: A Critical Analysis," *American Sociological Review*, 18 (August 1953): 390.

[15]Ibid., pp. 387–393.

[16]Dickens, "London Recreations," in *Charles Dickens' Best Stories*, p. 50.

[17]This discussion is based on Pitrim A. Sorokin,

Social and Cultural Mobility (New York: Free Press, 1959), pp. 133–163.

[18]U.S. Bureau of the Census, *Current Population Reports*, Series P-60, No. 80, October 4, 1971, Table 14.

[19]U.S. Bureau of the Census, *Current Population Reports*, Series P-60, No. 77, May 7, 1971.

[20]U.S. Bureau of the Census, *Current Population Reports*, Series P-20, No. 80, October 4, 1971.

[21]William Saroyan, "Being Refined," *Playboy*, May 1965, p. 113.

[22]David Riesman, *The Lonely Crowd* (New York: Doubleday Anchor, 1953).

[23]C. Wright Mills, *The Power Elite* (New York: Oxford University Press, 1956).

[24]Peter M. Blau and Otis Dudley Duncan, *The American Occupational Structure* (New York: John Wiley, 1967), pp. 402–442, and Joseph A. Kahl, *The American Class Structure* (New York: Holt, Rinehart & Winston, 1965), p. 272.

[25]Seymour Martin Lipset and Hans L. Zetterberg, "Social Mobility in Industrial Societies," in *Organizational Issues in Industrial Society*, ed. Jon M. Shepard (Englewood Cliffs, N.J.: Prentice-Hall, 1972), pp. 64–80.

[26]Blau and Duncan, *American Occupational Structure*, pp. 401–402.

[27]Herbert J. Gans, *The Urban Villagers* (New York: Free Press, 1962).

[28]David Matza, "The Disreputable Poor," in *Class, Status, and Power*, Bendix and Lipset, eds., pp. 289–302.

[29]John Steinbeck, *The Grapes of Wrath* (New York: Bantam, 1969), p. 165.

[30]Matthew Arnold, "Equality," *Mixed Essays* (1879).

CHAPTER EIGHT

[1]Ambrose Bierce, *The Devil's Dictionary* (Mount Vernon, N.Y.: Peter Pauper Press, 1958), p. 39.

[2]George Peter Murdock, *Social Structure* (New York: Macmillan, 1949).

[3]"Polygamy in the Desert," *Time*, May 19, 1975, p. 74.

[4]Chin P'ng Mei, *The Adventurous History of Hsi Men and His Six Wives* (New York: Putnam's, 1954); also found in Lewis A. Coser, ed., *Sociology Through Literature* (Englewood Cliffs, N.J.: Prentice-Hall, 1972), p. 538.

[5]Ibid., pp. 358–364.

[6]Kathleen Gough, "Is the Family Universal? — The Nayar Case," in Norman W. Bell and Ezra F. Vogel, eds., *A Modern Introduction to the Family* (New York: Free Press, 1960), pp. 76–92.

[7]Meyer F. Nimkoff and Russell Middleton, "Types of Family and Types of Economy," *American Journal of Sociology*, 66 (1960): 215–225.

[8]Henry Miller, *Black Spring* (New York: Grove Press, 1963), pp. 103–110.

[9]Ibid., pp.

[10]Murdock, *Social Structure*, p. 12.

[11]Simone de Beauvoir, *Memoirs of a Dutiful Daughter*, Trans. James Kirkup (Cleveland: World Publishing, 1959), pp. 111–112, 114–115.

[12]Oscar Wilde, *The Importance of Being Earnest*, in *The Plays of Oscar Wilde* (New York: Modern Library, 1932), pp. 66–68.

[13]Martin Luther, *Table Talk*, 1569.

[14]Robert Louis Stevenson, *Virginibus Puerisque*, 1881.

[15]Women's Bureau, "Highlights of Women's Employment and Education" and "Twenty Facts on Women Workers" (Washington, D.C.: U.S. Department of Labor, 1974).

[16]Ibid.

[17]Dean D. Knudson, "The Declining Status of Women: Popular Myths and the Failure of Func-

[18]Ovid, *The Art of Love and The Loves*, trans. Rolfe Humphries (Bloomington: Indiana University Press, 1957), Book 3, II, pp. 255–279.

[19]Anne Richardson Roiphe, *Up the Sandbox* (New York: Simon & Schuster, 1970), pp. 152–154.

[20]Harry Mark Petrakis, "Dark Eyes," in *The Waves of Night and Other Stories* (New York: David McKay, 1969), pp. 173, 174–175, 177–178.

[21]Urie Bronfenbrenner, *Two Worlds of Childhood: U.S. and U.S.S.R.* (New York: Russell Sage Foundation, 1970).

[22]John Scanzoni, "A Social System's Analysis of Dissolved and Existing Marriages," *Journal of Marriage and the Family*, 30 (August 1968): 452–461.

[23]Saul Bellow, *Seize the Day* (New York: Viking, 1961), pp. 111–115.

[24]Bennett Berger, Bruce Hackett, and R. Mervyn Millar, "The Communal Family," *The Family Coordinator*, 21 (1972): 419–427.

[25]This discussion is adapted from James W. Ramey, "Emerging Patterns of Innovative Behavior in

Marriage," *The Family Coordinator*, 21 (1972): 435–456.

CHAPTER NINE

[1] U.S. Bureau of the Census, *Current Population Reports*, 1973, Series P-20, no. 79.

[2] Ambrose Bierce, *The Enlarged Devil's Dictionary*, ed. Ernest J. Hopkins (Garden City, N.Y.: Doubleday, 1967), p. 241.

[3] James Thurber, "The Owl Who Was God," in *The Thurber Carnival* (New York: Dell, 1962), pp. 298–299.

[4] Emile Durkheim, *The Elementary Forms of the Religious Life*, trans. Joseph Ward Swain (New York: Free Press, 1965; orig. 1915), p. 62.

[5] Ibid., p. 52

[6] Kingsley Davis, *Human Society* (New York: Macmillan, 1948), p. 529.

[7] Ibid.

[8] Karl Marx, "Critique of Hegel" (1844), quoted in Bertell Ollman, *Alienation* (Cambridge, Eng.: Cambridge University Press, 1971), p. 47.

[9] Anthony Haden-Guest, "The Wit and Wisdom of the Rich," *Playboy*, January 1975, p. 202.

[10] This is a quote from a former slave, recorded in B. A. Botkin, ed., *Lay My Burden Down* (Chicago: University of Chicago Press, 1945), p. 25.

[11] Arna Bontemps, *The Black Experience*, ed. Francis E. Kearns (New York: Viking, 1970), pp. x–xi.

[12] Nat Turner, *The Confessions of Nat Turner as Told to Thomas R. Gray*, in *Old Memories, New Moods*, ed. Peter Rose (New York: Atherton Press, 1970), pp. 82–83.

[13] Sinclair Lewis, *Elmer Gantry* (New York: Harcourt, Brace, 1927), p. 359.

[14] Charlotte Bronte, *Jane Eyre* (New York: Dutton, 1908), pp. 35–36.

[15] Davis, *Human Society*, p. 533.

[16] Frederick W. Preston, "A Grounded Re-examination of Alcoholics Anonymous," paper presented at annual meetings of the Pacific Sociological Association, Victoria, B.C., 1975.

[17] Thomas F. O'Dea, *The Sociology of Religion* (Englewood Cliffs, N.J.: Prentice-Hall, 1966), p. 14.

[18] Davis, *Human Society*, p. 533.

[19] Hans Reichenbach, *The Rise of Scientific Philosophy* (Berkeley: University of California Press, 1951).

[20] Irving Stone, "The Scopes Evolution Case," from "Clarence Darrow for the Defense," in *Great Trials of Famous Lawyers*, ed. Brant House (New York: Ace, 1962), pp. 44–46.

[21] Samuel Langhorne Clemens, "Little Bessie Would Assist Providence," in *American Poetry and Prose*, ed. Norman Foerster (Boston: Houghton Mifflin, 1957), pp. 1048–1049.

[22] Max Weber, *The Protestant Ethic and the Spirit of Capitalism* (London: Allen and Unwin, 1930; orig. 1904).

[23] This church-sect dichotomy is based on one presented by Liston Pope in *Millhands and Preachers* (New Haven, Conn.: Yale University Press, 1942), pp. 122–124.

[24] Lewis, *Elmer Gantry*, p. 378.

[25] James Mooney, *The Ghost-dance Religion and the Sioux Outbreak of 1890* (Chicago: University of Chicago Press, 1965).

[26] George Spindler, "Personality and Peyotism in Menomini Indian Acculturation," *Psychiatry*, 15 (1952): 155.

[27] Rone E. Roberts and Robert Marsh Kloss, *Social Movements* (St. Louis: C. V. Mosby, 1974), pp. 42–43.

[28] Douglas Hill et al., *Witchcraft, Magic and the Supernatural* (London: Octopus, 1974), pp. 20, 150.

CHAPTER TEN

[1] Samuel Langhorne Clemens, *Pudd'nhead Wilson*, Pudd'nhead Wilson's Calendar, Chapter 1, 1894.

[2] Enrollment, expenditures, and educational attainment statistics were taken from the U.S. Bureau of the Census, *Statistical Abstract of the United States: 1974* (Washington, D.C.: U.S. Government Printing Office, 1974), tables 172, 173, and 187.

[3] Joseph C. Pattison, "How to Write an 'F' Paper," in *Insight: A Rhetorical Reader*, ed. Emil Hurtik (Philadelphia: Lippincott, 1970), pp. 198–199.

[4] James Herndon, *How to Survive in Your Native Land* (New York: Simon & Schuster, 1971), pp. 93–94.

[5] Robert K. Merton, *Social Theory and Social Structure* (New York: Free Press, 1968), chap. XIII.

[6] U.S. Bureau of the Census, *Current Population Reports*, 1974, Series P-60, no. 92.

[7] James Bryant Conant, *Annual Report to the Board of Overseers*, Harvard University, January 11, 1943.

[8]Richard Hofstadter, *Anti-Intellectualism in American Life* (New York: Alfred A. Knopf, 1963).

[9]Max Weber, *The Protestant Ethic and the Spirit of Capitalism* (London: Allen and Unwin, 1930; orig. 1904).

[10]Bel Kaufman, *Up the Down Staircase* (Englewood Cliffs, N.J.: Prentice-Hall, 1964), pp. 45, 91, 137.

[11]Ibid., pp. 77, 108, 112, 114, 134, 177, 178, 180, 265.

[12]Ibid., p. 203.

[13]Jacques Barzun, *Teacher in America* (Boston: Little, Brown, 1945), pp. 6–8.

[14]Ibid., pp. 257–259.

[15]Jules Henry, *Culture Against Man* (New York: Random House, 1963), pp. 284, 286, 288.

[16]Charles E. Silberman, *Crisis in the Classroom* (New York: Random House, 1970), p. 524.

[17]Robert D. Reischauer, Robert W. Hartman, and Daniel J. Sullivan, *Reforming School Finances* (Washington, D.C.: Brookings Institution, 1973).

[18]"Estimated Public School Expenditures, 1974, and Personal Income, 1973, By States," *The U.S. Fact Book: The American Almanac for 1973* (New York: Grosset & Dunlap, 1975), no. 214, p. 130.

[19]Jonathan Kozol, *Death at an Early Age* (New York: Bantam, 1970), pp. 162–164.

[20]Jonathan Kozol, *Free Schools* (New York: Bantam, 1972), pp. 10–11, 43–44.

[21]This discussion was adapted from information in Lawrence S. Wrightsman, *Social Psychology in the Seventies* (Monterey, Calif.: Brooks/Cole, 1972), chap. 8.

[22]"Taking the Chitling Test," *Newsweek*, July 15, 1968, pp. 51–52.

[23]Kozol, *Death at an Early Age*, pp. 2–3.

[24]Malcolm X, *The Autobiography of Malcolm X* (New York: Grove Press, 1964), pp. 36–37.

[25]Kaufman, *Up the Down Staircase*, p. 14.

[26]Ibid., pp. 17–18.

CHAPTER ELEVEN

[1]Ambrose Bierce, *The Enlarged Devil's Dictionary*, ed. Ernest J. Hopkins (Garden City, N.Y.: Doubleday, 1967), p. 222.

[2]Merle Miller, *Plain Speaking* (New York: Berkley, 1974), p. 188.

[3]Bierce, *Enlarged Devil's Dictionary*, p. 222.

[4]Kurt Vonnegut, Jr., *Slaughterhouse-Five* (New York: Dell, 1974), pp. 8–9.

[5]Karl Marx and Frederick Engels, *Manifesto of the Communist Party* (New York: International, 1948; orig. 1848), p. 9.

[6]Benjamin Disraeli, Speech of 1838, in Morris E. Speare, *The Political Novel* (New York: Russell and Russell, 1966), p. 55.

[7]Max Weber, *The Theory of Social and Economic Organization*, ed. Talcott Parsons (New York: Free Press, 1964), p. 152.

[8]G. A. Almond, J. S. Coleman, et al., *The Politics of the Developing Areas* (Princeton, N.J.: Princeton University Press, 1960); and Seymour Martin Lipset, *Political Man* (Garden City, N.Y.: Doubleday, 1960).

[9]Daniel Lerner, *The Passing of Traditional Society* (New York: Free Press, 1964).

[10]Ibid., pp. 57–58.

[11]Irving Louis Horowitz, *Three Worlds of Development* (New York: Oxford University Press, 1966).

[12]*Encyclopedia of Sociology* (Guilford, Conn.: Dushkin, 1974), p. 62.

[13]Aimé Césaire, *Cahier d'un retour au pays natal* (Paris: Présence Africaine, 1956) p. 56.

[14]Charles Dickens, *A Tale of Two Cities* (New York: Macmillan, 1962), p. 330.

[15]Milovan Djilas, *The Imperfect Society* (New York: Harcourt Brace Jovanovich, 1969).

[16]Robert Penn Warren, *All the King's Men* (New York: Bantam, 1973), pp. 191–192.

[17]John Kenneth Galbraith, *The New Industrial State* (Boston: Houghton Mifflin, 1967).

[18]Eugene Burdick and Harvey Wheeler, *Fail-Safe* (New York: Dell, 1963), pp. 166–168.

[19]Fred J. Cook, *The Warfare State* (New York: Collier, 1964), pp. 40–41.

[20]See Anatol Rapoport, "Chicken a la Kahn," *The Virginia Quarterly Review* (Summer 1965): 370–389.

[21]Frederick C. Crews, *The Pooh Perplex* (New York: E. P. Dutton, 1965), pp. 23–25.

CHAPTER TWELVE

[1]Mary Baker Eddy, *Science and Health with Key to the Scriptures* (Boston: Trustees of the Will of Mary Baker Eddy, 1934; orig. 1875), p. 1.

[2]Kurt Vonnegut, Jr., *The Sirens of Titan* (New York: Dell, 1973), pp. 296–297.

[3]*Time*, November 11, 1974, p. 80.

[4]Vilfredo Pareto, *Mind and Society* (New York: Harcourt, Brace & World, 1935).

[5]Robert Ardrey, *African Genesis* (New York: Dell, 1967).
[6]Kurt Vonnegut, Jr., *Mother Night* (New York: Dell, 1974), p. 95.
[7]Alvin Toffler, *Teacher's Guide to Future Shock* (New York: Bantam, 1974), p. 5.
[8]Ibid.
[9]Franz Kafka, "A Hunger Artist," in *The Penal Colony; Stories and Short Pieces*, trans. Willa and Edwin Muir (New York: Schocken, 1948), pp. 243–244.
[10]Ibid., p. 244.
[11]Ibid., p. 253.
[12]Ibid., pp. 254–256.

CHAPTER THIRTEEN

[1]James Thurber, "The Day the Dam Broke," in *The Thurber Carnival* (New York: Dell, 1945), pp. 221–222.
[2]"Behaviorists Ask: Why Did Pittsburgh Fans Go Berserk?" *Seattle Times*, October 24, 1971, p. 17.
[3]I. F. Stone, *The Killings at Kent State: How Murder Went Unpunished* (New York: New York Review, 1971), pp. 34–35.
[4]Ibid., pp. 107–110, 112.
[5]Herbert Blumer, "Elementary Collective Groupings," in *New Outline of the Principles of Sociology*, ed. Alfred McClung Lee (New York: Barnes & Noble, 1951), pp. 178–180.
[6]Tamotsu Shibutani, *Improvised News: A Sociological Study of Rumor* (Indianapolis: Bobbs-Merrill, 1966), pp. 114–116.
[7]Gustave LeBon, *The Crowd: A Study of the Popular Mind* (New York: Viking, 1960).
[8]Richard A. Berk, *Collective Behavior* (Dubuque, Iowa: William C. Brown, 1974), p. 25.
[9]John Dollard and Neil E. Miller, *Personality and Psychotherapy* (New York: McGraw-Hill, 1950).
[10]Neil J. Smelser, *Theory of Collective Behavior* (New York: Free Press, 1962).
[11]Shibutani, *Improvised News*, p. 17.
[12]Gordon W. Allport and Leo Postman, *The Psychology of Rumor* (New York: Holt, Rinehart & Winston, 1947).
[13]Shibutani, *Improvised News*, p. 15.
[14]Ibid., pp. 133–134.
[15]Ron E. Roberts and Robert Marsh Kloss, *Social Movements: Between the Balcony and the Barricade* (St. Louis: C. V. Mosby, 1974), p. 11.
[16]Marlene Dixon, "Why Women's Liberation," in *Divided We Stand*, editors of *Ramparts* (San Francisco: Canfield Press, 1970), p. 33.
[17]Ibid., p. 38.
[18]Ibid., p. 32.
[19]Discussion taken from Hans Toch, *The Social Psychology of Social Movements* (Indianapolis: Bobbs-Merrill, 1965), pp. 72–75.
[20]C. Wendell King, *Social Movements in the United States* (New York: Random House, 1956), pp. 41–49.
[21]This discussion of power-, persuasion-, and participation-oriented movements is taken from Ralph H. Turner and Lewis M. Killian, *Collective Behavior* (Englewood Cliffs, N.J.: Prentice-Hall, 1962), chaps. 16–19.

CHAPTER FOURTEEN

[1]Melvin Seeman, "On the Meaning of Alienation," *American Sociological Review*, 24 (December 1959): 784.
[2]W. H. Auden, "The Shield of Achilles," in *The Shield of Achilles* (New York: Random House, 1955), p. 36.
[3]Upton Sinclair, *The Jungle* (New York: New American Library, 1905), pp. 276–279.
[4]Seeman, "On the Meaning of Alienation," pp. 786–787.
[5]T. S. Eliot, "The Hollow Men," in *T. S. Eliot: Collected Poems, 1909–1935* (New York: Harcourt, Brace & World, 1958), p. 101.
[6]Seeman, "On the Meaning of Alienation," p. 788.
[7]Robert K. Merton, *Social Theory and Social Structure* (New York: Free Press, 1968), chap. VI and VII.
[8]Seeman, "On the Meaning of Alienation," p. 789.
[9]Matthew Arnold, "To Marguerite," in *Victorian Poetry and Poetics*, ed. Walter E. Houghton and G. Robert Stange (Boston: Houghton Mifflin, 1968), p. 444.
[10]Sherwood Anderson, "Hands," in *The Portable Sherwood Anderson*, ed. Horace Gregory (New York: Viking, 1972), pp. 47–48.
[11]Ibid., p. 49.
[12]Ibid., pp. 51–52.
[13]Seeman, "On the Meaning of Alienation," p. 790.
[14]C. Wright Mills, *White Collar* (New York: Oxford University Press, 1951), p. 188.
[15]Arthur Miller, *Death of a Salesman* (New York: Viking, 1967), p. 15.
[16]Ibid., pp. 137–138.

[17] Karl Marx, *The Economic and Philosophical Manuscripts of 1844,* ed. Dirk Strivik, trans. Martin Milligan (New York: International Publishers, 1964); and Joachim Israel, *Alienation: From Marx to Modern Sociology* (Boston: Allyn and Bacon, 1971), pp. 32–50.

[18] Robert A. Nisbet, *The Sociological Tradition* (New York: Basic Books, 1966), pp. 264–312.

[19] Ronald W. Smith, "A Context-Specific Approach to Alienation," presented at Pacific Sociological Association meetings, March 1974.

[20] Ely Chinoy, "The Tradition of Opportunity and the Aspirations of Automobile Workers," *American Journal of Sociology,* 57 (1951–1952): 453–459.

[21] Robert Guest, "Men and Machines: An Assembly Line Worker Looks at His Job," *Personnel,* 31 (1955): 496–503.

[22] Robert Blauner, *Alienation and Freedom: The Factory Worker and His Industry* (Chicago: University of Chicago Press, 1964).

[23] George A. Miller, "Professionals in Bureaucracy: Alienation Among Industrial Scientists and Engineers," *American Sociological Review,* 32 (1967): 755–768.

[24] Ralph Ellison, *Invisible Man* (New York: Vintage, 1952), pp. 3–4.

[25] Gary T. Marx, "The Social Context of Militancy," in *Protest and Prejudice* (New York: Harper & Row, 1967), pp. 49–79.

[26] "Students Protest," *AAUP Bulletin,* (Autumn 1969): 309–326.

[27] Arthur Stinchcombe, *Rebellion in a High School* (Chicago: Quadrangle, 1964).

[28] Mark Twain, "The Lowest Animal," in *Letters from the Earth,* ed. Bernard DeVoto (Greenwich, Conn.: Fawcett, 1967), pp. 176–181.

CHAPTER FIFTEEN

[1] Frederick W. Preston, "The Development of Race in American Sociology; Further Explorations in the Sociology of Knowledge," presented at the annual meetings of the Pacific Sociological Association, San Jose, California, March 1974.

[2] Pierre L. van den Berghe, *Race and Racism: A Comparative Perspective* (New York: John Wiley, 1967).

[3] Ibid.

[4] Harry Golden, *Only in America* (New York: Permabooks, 1958, pp. 47–48.

[5] Brewton Berry, *Race and Ethnic Relations* (Boston: Houghton Mifflin, 1965), p. 391.

[6] William Shannon, *The American Irish* (New York: Macmillan, 1964), p. 25.

[7] John Wain, "Down Our Way," in *Death of the Hind Legs and Other Stories* (New York: Cushman, 1966).

[8] Andrew W. Lind, *Hawaii's People,* 3rd ed. (Honolulu: University of Hawaii Press, 1967).

[9] Berry, *Race and Ethnic Relations,* p. 228.

[10] Arnold Toynbee, *The Study of History* (London: Oxford University Press, 1934), vol. 1, p. 465.

[11] *New York Times,* November 17, 1946.

[12] Robert E. Park, "Our Racial Frontier on the Pacific," *Survey Graphic,* 9 (May 1926): 196.

[13] Stanley Lieberson, "A Societal Theory of Race and Ethnic Relations," *American Sociological Review,* 26 (1961): 902–910.

[14] See Donald Noel, "A Theory of the Origin of Ethnic Stratification," *Social Problems,* 16 (Fall 1968): 157–172.

[15] Joseph Lelyveld in introduction to *House of Bondage,* by Ernest Cole and Thomas Flaherty (New York: Random House, 1967).

[16] Dan Jacobson, "Beggar My Neighbor," in *Through the Wilderness and Other Stories* (New York: Macmillan, 1968).

[17] Charles A. Ellwood, *Sociology and Modern Social Problems,* 4th ed. (New York: American Book Company, 1927), p. 249.

[18] Edward Anhalt, screenplay of *QB VII,* in *Los Angeles Times,* November 31, 1975, p. 27.

CHAPTER SIXTEEN

[1] Jack Kerouac, *The Town and the City* (New York: Grosset and Dunlap, 1950), pp. 369–370.

[2] Frederick W. Preston, "A Grounded Re-examination of Alcoholics Anonymous," paper presented at the annual meetings of the Pacific Sociological Association, Victoria, British Columbia, Canada, 1975.

[3] Edwin H. Sutherland, *Principles of Criminology* (Philadelphia: Lippincott, 1947), pp. 6–7.

[4] Albert K. Cohen, *Delinquent Boys: The Culture of the Gang* (Glencoe, Ill.: Free Press, 1955).

[5] Richard A. Cloward and Lloyd E. Ohlin, *Delinquency and Opportunity: A Theory of Delinquent Gangs* (New York: Free Press, 1960), p. 150.

[6] Charles Dickens, *The Adventures of Oliver Twist* (London: Oxford University Press, 1966), pp. 60–62.

[7] Howard S. Becker, *Outsiders: Studies in the Sociology of Deviance* (Glencoe, Ill.: Free Press, 1963).

[8] Kurt Vonnegut, Jr., *Breakfast of Champions* (New York: Delta, 1973), pp. 48–49, 100–101, 112–113.

[9] Eldridge Cleaver, *Soul on Ice* (New York: Dell, 1970, pp. 121–122.

[10] Marshall B. Clinard, *Sociology of Deviant Behavior*, 4th ed. (New York: Holt, Rinehart & Winston, 1974), p. 180.

[11] Arnold W. Green, *Social Problems: Arena of Conflict* (New York: McGraw-Hill, 1975), pp. 4–5.

[12] Charles Winick and Paul M. Kinsie, *The Lively Commerce* (New York: New American Library, 1972), p. 33.

[13] Clinard, *Sociology of Deviant Behavior*, p. 518.

[14] Xaviera Hollander, with Robin Moore and Yvonne Dunleavy, *The Happy Hooker* (New York: Dell, 1972), pp. 74–75.

[15] Robert Linder, "Homosexuality and the Contemporary Scene," in Hendrix Ruitenbeck, ed., *The Problem of Homosexuality in Modern Society* (New York: E. P. Dutton, 1963), p. 61.

[16] Alfred C. Kinsey, Wardell B. Pomeroy, and Clyde E. Martin, *Sexual Behavior in the Human Male* (Philadelphia: W. B. Saunders, 1948).

[17] Ibid.

[18] Laud Humphreys, *Tearoom Trade: Impersonal Sex in Public Places* (Chicago: Aldine, 1970).

[19] Merle Miller, "What It Means to Be a Homosexual," *New York Times Magazine*, January 17, 1971, p. 57.

[20] Robert Strauss, "Alcohol and Alcoholism," in Robert K. Merton and Robert A. Nisbet, eds., *Contemporary Social Problems* (New York: Harcourt Brace Jovanovich, 1971), p. 256; and Alan P. Bates and Joseph Julian, *Sociology* (Boston: Houghton Mifflin, 1975), p. 295.

[21] Upton Sinclair, *The Cup of Fury* (Great Neck, N.Y.: Channel Press, 1956).

[22] Preston, "A Grounded Re-examination of Alcoholics Anonymous."

[23] Jack B., talk before the Annual Palm Springs Conference of Alcoholics Anonymous, 1972.

[24] Harrison M. Trice and Paul M. Roman, "Delabeling, Relabeling, and Alcoholics Anonymous," *Social Problems*, 17 (Spring 1970): 538–546.

[25] Howard M. Bahr, *Skid Row* (New York: Oxford University Press, 1973).

[26] Upton Sinclair, *The Cup of Fury*, pp. 19–22.

[27] Bruce P. Dohrenwend and Barbara Snell Dohrenwend, *Social Status and Psychological Disorder* (New York: Wiley-Interscience, 1969).

[28] Thomas S. Szasz, *The Myth of Mental Illness* (New York: Paul B. Hoeber, 1961).

[29] David Mechanic, *Mental Health and Social Policy* (Englewood Cliffs, N.J.: Prentice-Hall, 1969).

[30] Leo Srole et al., *Mental Health in the Metropolis: The Manhattan Midtown Study* (New York: McGraw-Hill, 1962) pp. 29–30.

[31] Hannah Green, *I Never Promised You a Rose Garden* (New York: Signet, 1964), pp. 53–54.

[32] Gresham Sykes, in *Encyclopedia of Sociology* (Guilford, Conn.: Dushkin, 1974), p. 62.

[33] Robert W. Winslow and Virginia Winslow, *Deviant Reality* (Boston: Allyn and Bacon, 1974), p. 315.

[34] Clinard, *Sociology of Deviant Behavior*, p. 297.

[35] Robert C. Bensing and Oliver Schroeder, Jr., *Homicide in an Urban Community* (Springfield, Ill.: Charles C Thomas, 1960); and Henry A. Bullock, "Urban Homicide in Theory and Fact," *Journal of Criminal Law, Criminology, and Police Science*, 45 (January–February 1955): 565–575.

[36] *Crimes and Violence*, Staff Report to the National Commission on the Causes and Prevention of Violence, Donald J. Mulvihill and Melvin M. Tumin, with Lynn A. Curtis (Washington, D.C.: U.S. Government Printing Office, 1969), vol. 11, p. 209.

[37] *The Challenge of Crime in a Free Society*, President's Commission on Law Enforcement and Administration of Justice (Washington, D.C.: U.S. Government Printing Office, 1968), p. 18.

[38] Theodore Dreiser, *An American Tragedy* (Cleveland: World Publishing, 1948), pp. 530–532.

[39] Feodor Dostoevsky, *Crime and Punishment*, trans. Coulson, ed. George Gibian (New York: Norton, 1964), pp. 72–74.

[40] Edwin H. Sutherland, *White-Collar Crime* (New York: Holt, Rinehart & Winston, 1961).

[41] Ibid.

[42] George B. Vold, *Theoretical Criminology* (New York: Oxford University Press, 1958).

[43] Walter Reckless, Simon Dinitz, and Barbara Kay, "The Self Component in Potential Delinquency and Potential Nondelinquency," *American Sociological Review*, 22 (October 1957): 566–570.

[44] Donald R. Cressey, *Other People's Money* (Glencoe, Ill.: Free Press, 1953).

[45] Winslow and Winslow, *Deviant Reality*, p. 60.

[46] Daniel Bell, *The End of Ideology* (New York: Free Press, 1965).

[47]Ramsey Clark, *Crime in America* (New York: Pocket Books, 1970).
[48]Woody Allen, *Getting Even* (New York: Warner, 1972), pp. 16–18.

CHAPTER SEVENTEEN

[1]Sebastian de Grazia, *Of Time, Work, and Leisure* (Garden City, N.Y.: Doubleday), p. 15.
[2]Ibid., pp. 28–33.
[3]*Report on the Fifth Working Conference on Social Stratification and Social Mobility*, International Sociological Association, 1960.
[4]Ibid.
[5]Charles Hunt Page, "Sports and 'Sport,' The Problem of Selection," in *Sport and Society*, eds. John T. Talamini and Charles Hunt Page (Boston: Little, Brown, 1973), pp. 38–39.
[6]Bernard Malamud, *The Natural* (New York: Farrar, Straus, 1961), pp. 66–67.
[7]Roger Kahn, "Where Have All the Heroes Gone?" *Esquire*, October 1974, p. 141.
[8]Jack Orr, "The Black Boxer: Exclusion and Ascendance," in *Sport and Society*, pp. 240–241.
[9]Theodore Roosevelt, speech at the Harvard Union on February 23, 1907.
[10]Gerald R. Ford, "In Defense of the Competitive Urge," *Sports Illustrated*, July 6, 1974, p. 17.
[11]Muhammad Ali, "Return of the Big Bopper," *Sports Illustrated*, December 23, 1974, p. 87.
[12]Alan Sillitoe, *The Loneliness of the Long-Distance Runner* (New York: Signet, 1959), pp. 10–11.
[13]——— Kahn, "Where Have All the Heroes Gone?" p. 142.
[14]James Thurber, "University Days," in *The Thurber Carnival* (New York: Dell, 1962), pp. 255–256.
[15]S. Kirson Weinberg and Henry Arond, "The Occupational Culture of the Boxer," *American Journal of Sociology*, 58 (March 1952): 460–469.
[16]*Ring*, July 1950, p. 45, quoted in Weinberg and Arond, "The Occupational Culture of the Boxer."
[17]Philip Roth, *Goodbye, Columbus* (New York: Bantam, 1973), pp. 74–75.
[18]Mark Kram, "The One-Minute Angels," *Sports Illustrated*, February 17, 1975, pp. 34, 42.
[19]Jerry Jacobs, *Fun City: An Ethnographic Study of a Retirement Community* (New York: Holt, Rinehart & Winston, 1974).
[20]Max Kaplan, *Leisure* (New York: Wiley, 1975), p. 413.

CHAPTER EIGHTEEN

[1]Lewis Mumford, *The Culture of Cities* (New York: Harcourt Brace, 1938), p. 3.
[2]Carl Sandburg, "Chicago," in *The Complete Poems of Carl Sandburg* (New York: Harcourt Brace Jovanovich, 1969), p. 3.
[3]Walter Lippmann, Address, International Press Institute Assembly (London: May 27, 1965).
[4]George Noel Gordon, Lord Byron, *Childe Harold's Pilgrimage*, 1816, Canto III, St. 72.
[5]Percy Bysshe Shelley, *Peter Bell the Third*, 1819, Part III, St. 1.
[6]J. John Palen, *The Urban World* (New York: McGraw-Hill, 1975), p. 6.
[7]Gideon Sjoberg, "The Origin and Evolution of Cities," in *Cities: A Scientific American Book* (New York: Alfred A. Knopf, 1969), p. 27.
[8]Discussion adapted from Kingsley Davis, "The Urbanization of the Human Population," in *Cities: A Scientific American Book*, pp. 4–5.
[9]Sjoberg, "The Origin and Evolution of Cities," pp. 25–27. The author did not title his third level of organization, but the label of "modern industrial society" aptly describes this evolutionary period.
[10]Granville Hicks, "How We Live in America," *Commentary*, 16 (December 1958): 505–506.
[11]*The U.S. Fact Book: 1976* (New York: Grosset and Dunlap, 1976), pp. 884–885.
[12]Theodore H. White, *The Making of the President 1960* (New York: Atheneum, 1961), pp. 217–218.
[13]Palen, *The Urban World*, pp. 102–103.
[14]Robert Redfield, *Tepoztlan, A Mexican Village* (Chicago: University of Chicago Press, 1930).
[15]Kurt Vonnegut, Jr., "Address to the National Institute of Arts and Letters, 1971," in *Wampeters, Foma, and Granfalloons: Opinions* (New York: Delacorte, 1974), pp. 177–178.
[16]Ibid., pp. 178–179.
[17]Stanley Milgram, "The Experience of Living in Cities," *Science*, 167 (March 13, 1970): 1461.
[18]Gus Tyler, "Can Anyone Run a City?" *Saturday Review*, November 8, 1969, pp. 22–23.
[19]Louis Wirth, "Urbanism as a Way of Life," *American Journal of Sociology*, 44 (July 1938): 1–24.
[20]Thomas De Quincey, *The Collected Writings of Thomas De Quincey, Volume I*, ed. David Masson (Edinburgh: Adam and Charles Black, 1889), p. 182.
[21]Herbert J. Gans, "Urbanism and Suburbanism as Ways of Life: A Re-evaluation of Definitions," in

Human Behavior and Social Processes, ed. Arnold M. Rose (Boston: Houghton Mifflin, 1962), pp. 629–633.

[22]Herbert Gold, "A Dog in Brooklyn, A Girl in Detroit: A Life Among the Humanities," in *The Age of Happy Problems* (New York: Dial Press, 1962), pp. 120–121.

[23]Milgram, "The Experience of Living in Cities," pp. 1461–1468.

[24]Neil Simon, *The Prisoner of Second Avenue* (New York: Random House, 1972), p. 18.

[25]Bernard Malamud, *The Assistant* (New York: Dell, 1947), pp. 10–11.

[26]Tyler, "Can Anyone Run a City?" p. 22.

[27]Simon, *The Prisoner of Second Avenue*, pp. 24–25.

[28]Ibid., pp. 33–34.

[29]Information taken from the U.S. Department of Health, Education, and Welfare, Public Health Service, *Environmental Health Planning* (Washington, D.C.: U.S. Government Printing Office, 1971), pub. no. 2120; U.S. Department of Health, Education, and Welfare, Health Services and Mental Health Administration, *Urban Rat Control* (Washington, D.C.: U.S. Government Printing Office, 1971); and U.S. Environmental Protection Agency, *The National Air Monitoring Program: Air Quality and Emissions Trends, Annual Report*, Vol. 1 (Washington, D.C.: U.S. Government Printing Office, 1973).

[30]Robert Abernathy, "Single Combat," in *Sociology Through Science Fiction*, eds. John W. Milstead, Martin Harry Greenberg, Joseph D. Olander, and Patricia Warrick (New York: St. Martin's Press, 1974), pp. 404–405.

[31]*The U.S. Fact Book: 1976*, p. 28.

[32]Kenneth B. Clark, *Dark Ghetto: Dilemmas of Social Power* (New York: Harper & Row, 1965), pp. 1–5, 8.

[33]Francis Sugure, "Diary of a Rent Striker," *New York Herald Tribune*, February 16, 1964, p. 28.

[34]U.S. Bureau of the Census, "Trends in Social and Economic Conditions in Metropolitan and Nonmetropolitan Areas," *Current Population Reports* (Washington, D.C.: U.S. Government Printing Office, 1970), Series P-23, No. 33.

[35]Ralph G. Martin, "Life in the New Suburbia," *New York Times Magazine*, January 15, 1950; and in *Suburbia in Transition*, eds. Louis H. Masotti and Jeffrey H. Hadden (New York: New Viewpoints, 1974), pp. 17–18.

[36]Phyllis McGinley, "Suburbia of Thee I Sing," in *A Short Walk from the Station* (New York: Viking, 1952), pp. 11–14.

[37]Ralph Blumenthal, "800,000 Suburban Poor Suffer Amid Environment of Affluence," *New York Times*, May 26, 1968; and in *Suburbia in Transition*, p. 212.

[38]David A. Andelman, "Planners Worried by Suburban Auto Glut," *New York Times*, January 3, 1972; and in *Suburbia in Transition*, pp. 192–193.

[39]David A. Andelman, "The Crime Wave Spreading to the Suburbs," *New York Times*, January 30, 1972; and in *Suburbia in Transition*, pp. 196–198.

CHAPTER NINETEEN

[1]Paul R. Ehrlich, *The Population Bomb* (New York: Ballantine, 1968), pp. 15–16.

[2]Ibid., p. 18.

[3]William Petersen, *Population* (New York: Macmillan, 1975), p. 10.

[4]Thomas R. Malthus, *An Essay on the Principle of Population*, 7th ed. (London: Reeves and Turner, 1872).

[5]José Hernández, *People, Power, and Policy: A New View of Population* (Palo Alto, Calif.: National Press Books, 1974), p. 154.

[6]Kingsley Davis, as summarized in Hernández, *People, Power, and Policy*, p. 158.

[7]Harry Harrison, *Make Room! Make Room!* (New York: Berkley, 1973), pp. 151–152.

[8]Herman Kahn, as quoted in Hernández, *People, Power, and Policy*, p. 162.

[9]Donald J. Bogue, "The End of the Population Explosion," in *Social Problems: The Contemporary Debates*, ed. John B. Williamson, Jerry F. Boren, and Linda Evans (Boston: Little, Brown, 1974), p. 239.

[10]Paul R. Ehrlich and Anne H. Ehrlich, *Population, Resources, Environment* (San Francisco: Freeman, 1972), p. 2.

[11]Petersen, *Population*, pp. 236–237.

[12]Jonathan Swift, from "A Modest Proposal for Preventing the Children of Poor People in Ireland from being a Burden to Their Parents or Country; and for Making Them Beneficial to Their Publick" (Dublin: S. Harding, 1729), pp. 1–5.

[13]Anthony Burgess, *The Wanting Seed* (New York: Norton, 1962), pp. 3–4.

EPILOGUE

[1] Bertrand Russell, *The ABC of Relativity* (London: Ruskin House, 1958; orig. 1925), pp. 11–12.

[2] Jean Giraudoux, *The Madwoman of Chaillot*, in Haskell Block and Robert Shedd, eds., *Masters of Modern Drama* (New York: Random House, 1964), p. 740.

[3] George Orwell, *1984* (New York: Harcourt, Brace, & World, 1949), p. 7.

[4] Herbert Marcuse, *One-Dimensional Man* (Boston: Beacon Press, 1964), p. 248.

[5] Edgar H. Schein, "Man Against Man: Brainwashing," *Correctional Psychiatry and Journal of Social Therapy*, 2 (1962): 91–92.

[6] Richard Quinney, *Criminology* (Boston: Little, Brown, 1975), p. 250.

[7] Aldous Huxley, *Brave New World* (New York: Bantam, 1968; orig. 1932), pp. 1–3.

[8] B. F. Skinner, *Walden Two* (New York: Macmillan, 1969; orig. 1948), pp. 116–117.

[9] Orwell, *1984*, p. 89.

[10] Information from the Intelligence Division, Las Vegas Metropolitan Police, 1976.

[11] Barton L. Ingraham and Gerald W. Smith, "The Use of Electronics in the Observation and Control of Human Behavior and Its Possible Use in Rehabilitation and Parole," *Issues in Criminology*, 7 (Fall 1972): 43.

[12] Anthony Fortuno, Administrator, TRW Credit Data Corporation, September 1975, interview with F. W. Preston, Las Vegas.

[13] Senator Samuel J. Ervin, Jr., as quoted in Joseph C. Goulden, "Tooling Up for Repression: The Cops Hit the Jackpot," *The Nation*, 211 (November 23, 1970): 520–533.

[14] Charles A. Reich, *The Greening of America* (New York: Random House, 1970), p. 304.

[15] Ibid., p. 306.

[16] Kurt Vonnegut, Jr., "Address to the National Institute of Arts and Letters, 1971," in *Wampeters, Foma, and Granfalloons: Opinions* (New York: Delacorte, 1974) p. 180.

GLOSSARY

absolute deprivation an individual's realization that he or she lacks the most basic necessities of life—food, clothing, and shelter.

academic knowledge education in the fine arts, humanities, earth sciences, and social sciences intended to prepare the individual for thinking and reasoning about the world.

achieved statuses statuses individuals attain through their own choice and effort.

active crowd Herbert Blumer's term for an excited and angered crowd that directs action toward individuals and/or objects.

age-grading the religious function of noting specific times in the individual's maturation process.

agents of socialization sources of information, such as parents, teachers, and the mass media, which transmit to the individual the ways of the larger culture or smaller social groups.

aggregate a collection of people lacking an organized pattern of interaction and a consciousness of kind.

alienated mass view the theory that collective behavior is a result of citizens' genuine dissatisfaction with their life situations.

amalgamation the physical and biological blending of previously distinct groups.

annihilation the actual elimination of one racial or ethnic group by another.

anomie Emile Durkheim's concept that described a society in which norms had broken down and were no longer effective in guiding behavior.

anti-intellectualism the belief that people with too much schooling are impractical dreamers and are not to be trusted.

apartheid the system of rigorous racial separation practiced in South Africa.

ascribed statuses statuses, such as sex, place of birth, and age, assigned to us by society and which we cannot change.

assimilation the cultural blending of two or more previously distinct peoples. When used to describe rumor formation, the term refers to the tendency of people to interpret reports in light of their own interests and prejudices.

associational norms norms unique to smaller, more defined groups in society.

associational statuses statuses known and reacted to only within smaller, more defined groups in society.

associationism the psychological principle that the individual has the ability to associate certain kinds of behavior with particular rewards or punishments.

authority the legitimate right to give commands with the expectation that such commands will be followed.

banana republic a disparaging term for an underdeveloped nation that is heavily dependent upon a single industry.

benevolent autocracy a kind of leadership that makes the important decisions affecting an organization, but gives the appearance of allowing organization members a role in management.

bilateral descent the passage of descent privileges through both the male and female lines.

bilocal residence the practice of having a newly married couple live with either the husband's or the wife's parents.

biological determinism the theory, supported by Vilfredo Pareto and others, that social change has been brought about by the biological evolution of humankind.

biological pathology as used in criminology, the belief that crime and deviance result from an individual's physical illnesses, malfunctions, or deformities.

birth rate the number of births per 1,000 inhabitants in a given year.

bourgeoisie in Marxian theory, the social class which owns the means of production and exploits the working class.

bureaucracy a type of formal administrative structure used by an organization to achieve its goals.

bureaucratic personality Robert Merton's term for a person who is overly concerned with vocational security, excessively methodical, more concerned with rules than organizational goals, and unimaginative in solving problems.

business concern a type of organization, such as General Motors, designed to benefit the owners.

busing transporting students from one neighborhood to another in order to achieve racial balance and equality in educational opportunity.

buttress function the religious function of providing emotional support for individuals during times of personal and societal crisis.

caste system a rigid stratification system in which parentage determines one's caste (stratum) and virtually no social mobility is possible.

casual crowd Herbert Blumer's term for an aggregate of onlookers viewing a common event. The crowd has only a momentary existence and no internal organization.

category a collection of people such as all alcoholics or all Southerners, who share a particular attribute.

cenogamy a type of polygamy in which several men and several women form a marriage relationship with one another.

charismatic authority Max Weber's term for the ability of certain leaders to command because of their personal qualities.

church a religious organization distinguished from a sect by its affluence, system of beliefs supportive to the community, and bureaucratic set-up.

city a community of substantial size and population density wherein residents tend to engage in diverse, specialized activities which are nonagricultural in nature.

class consciousness awareness by members within a social class of their common economic situation and their role and destiny in society.

class-for-itself Karl Marx's term for a class whose members are aware of their common economic situation and are willing to take class action to realize their destiny.

classical administration a school of thought concerned with administrative principles and practices within organizations. Its proponents tend to focus on formal aspects of an organization and rational decision-making.

class-in-itself Karl Marx's term for an aggregate of individuals thrown into a common economic situation within society but unaware of that situation.

class system a stratification system based on personal achievement. The economic gap between its strata (social classes) is generally smaller than that between different castes or estates.

closed group a group, such as an exclusive country club, that has narrowly defined and strictly enforced criteria for membership.

closed society a society with little or no vertical social mobility.

coercive-alienative organization an organization, such as a prison, that utilizes coercion or force to control its members' actions and that consequently often alienates members.

cognitive theory the psychological theory that focuses on how a person perceives, thinks, and chooses. Jean Piaget, a cognitive theorist, found that children of different ages vary in their ability to think and reason abstractly.

collective behavior behavior which seems rather unstructured, unstable, and unpredictable and which tends to be short-lived, sometimes emotional, and based on considerable personal interaction.

commonwealth organization a type of organization, such as the U.S. Department of Health, Education and Welfare, designed to benefit the public.

communal norms widely recognized rules, such as saying "thank you" for a favor, which are followed by almost everyone in a society.

communal statuses statuses, such as age and sex, that are visibly known and reacted to by everyone in society.

commune usually a small community of artists, religious worshipers, ex-drug users, or political idealists who disassociate themselves from the larger society and share duties and resources.

compensatory education additional academic preparation provided lower-class children in programs such as Head Start.

compounding pattern the tendency of one rumor to call forth another.

conflict theory the theory, associated with Karl

Marx and more contemporary sociologists such as C. Wright Mills, which considers members of society in a constant struggle for economic, political, and social rewards. Capitalists are seen as exploiters and the masses are either unaware of and/or dissatisfied with their disadvantaged position.

consciousness of kind Franklin Giddings's term for a feeling held by group members that they are bound together by common traits, views, or situations.

consensus theory a model which proposes that society is established by and exists in a state of consensus or agreement. Consensus and balance are the normal state of affairs.

context-specific approach the sociological approach which suggests examining the smaller or more specific contexts and issues in society that may produce such phenomena as alienation and power.

conventionalized crowd Herbert Blumer's term for a group of people who gather together to pursue a mutual goal and who behave according to established norms.

cooptation absorption of devisive elements into the leadership or policy-determining structure of an organization to avert threats to the organization's stability or existence. (Selznick)

core self The idea that the person has a single, unchanging, coherent view of the self.

coup d'état sudden and forcible seizure of power by a political faction in defiance of normal constitutional processes.

craze a short-lived, popular type of collective behavior usually defined as bizarre by most people.

crime a violation of the criminal law for which the individual can be punished through the use of formal sanctions applied by governmental authority. (Sykes)

crime rate the number of reported crimes per 100,000 inhabitants.

criminal any person who violates a criminal law.

crowd a temporary collection of people gathered together at one time and place.

cult a closed subculture whose practices and membership are secret. A cult often participates in the practice of the supernatural.

cultural determinism the view that behavior is a direct reflection of that culture to which an individual is exposed.

cultural diffusion the processes other than invention which produce cultural similarities in various societies.

cultural relativism the idea that actions and beliefs should be judged within the context of the culture in which they exist.

cultural universals forms of behavior, such as marriage, cooking, and mourning, thought common to all cultures.

culture explicit and implicit patterns of and for behavior that are acquired and transmitted by symbols and that constitute the distinctive achievements of human groups, including their embodiment in artifacts.

culture lag William F. Ogburn's theory of social change which holds that discontinuities in change are brought on by the fact that changes in the material culture (inventions) are often rather abrupt while the related and accommodating changes in the nonmaterial culture (norms) are often relatively slow in developing.

culture shock the disorientation and confusion felt in varying degrees by everyone who moves from one culture to another; the inability to adjust immediately to the tremendous differences in viewpoints and behavior that often exist between cultures.

cumulative deficit theory the educational theory that children who fail to learn culturally acceptable language have increasingly impaired cognitive ability to the extent that they can never catch up.

customs social norms that carry with them less intense feelings than mores and that meet with less severe condemnations if violated.

cybernetics the science which studies ways to replace human effort with electronic machines.

DC the abbreviation for developed country.

death rate the number of deaths per 1,000 inhabitants in a given year.

definition of the situation W. I. Thomas's concept that reality must be understood in terms of an individual's perception and interpretation; that is, reality varies from individual to individual and situation to situation.

demographic transition the theory that population growth occurs in major stages. In preindustrial societies there are high fertility and low mortality rates, in transitional societies there are high fertility but lowered mortality rates, and in industrialized societies there are low rates of both fertility and mortality.

demography the study of population changes and problems, and the manner in which such changes and problems occur.

development lag theory the educational theory which maintains that lower-class children have a retarded language, but with time and effort their language can be made to conform to middle-class standards.

deviance any behavior that transgresses or violates accepted cultural norms.

deviant an individual who violates a society's or a group's expectations.

difference theory the educational theory which maintains that individuals from different social classes and racial groups use the dialects learned in their subcultures and that the larger society should refrain from attempting to change these different language patterns.

differential association Edwin H. Sutherland's theory that individuals learn to become criminals or deviants because of an overabundance of associations with criminal or deviant behavior patterns.

differential opportunity the idea that an individual's chances for engaging in criminal or deviant behavior are greatly affected by his or her social class and racial and ethnic affiliation.

displacement of aggression term derived from psychoanalytic psychology which suggests that hostility is often transferred from one object to another. In sports the term is used to denote the channeling of competitive energy and hostility into sports activities.

diviners practitioners of the art and science of scrying who claim they are able to perceive the future.

dominant majority a large social group that possesses a high degree of economic, political, and social power.

doubling time the projected time it takes a given population to double in size.

dysfunctional behavior behavior that tends to undermine or destroy a social system.

dystopia a hypothetical society which, contrary to a utopia, degrades human existence.

economic alienation Karl Marx's idea that human misery is the result of capitalism.

economic order Max Weber's term for the way a society stratifies its members according to their possession of goods and opportunities for income.

eight-hundredth lifetime Alvin Toffler's term for contemporary culture, derived by dividing the length of human life on earth (50,000 years) by an average lifetime of 62 years. Toffler believes that in this 800th lifetime of humanity, we are all suffering from culture shock.

elite group a small social group that is very powerful in terms of economic, political, and social power.

endogamy marriage within a group specified by society as acceptable.

equalitarian family a family in which both husband and wife share responsibility and power in making decisions.

estate system a type of stratification system, once found in feudal societies, in which a person's social position depends upon his or her relationship to an agricultural economy. Ascriptive criteria are emphasized, and little social mobility is possible.

ethnic group a human group, such as Mexican-Americans or the Jewish people, that defines itself and/or is defined by other groups as different by virtue of certain cultural characteristics.

ethnocentrism the tendency of persons to judge other cultures by the standards of judgment prevailing in their own.

eufunctional behavior behavior that tends to promote or maintain a social system.

exogamy marriage outside a group specified by a society as acceptable.

explanation function the religious function of making intelligible what is commonly thought of as beyond ordinary understanding.

expressive alienation a term describing not only the attitudinal state of an alienated person, but also the individual's actions (protest, drug addiction, etc.) that may reflect his or her alienation.

expressive crowd Herbert Blumer's term for an excited group whose main purpose is self-stimulation and expression of feelings.

expulsion the forceful removal of one ethnic or racial group by another.

extended family a kinship group, sometimes called a "consanguine unit," consisting of a nuclear family plus other various relatives all sharing the same household.

false consciousness Karl Marx's term for the consciousness of a disenfranchised group that tends to support the status quo.

family a social group, consisting of members related either through blood ties or marriage and who also are bound together by legal, moral, and economic rights and duties.

family of orientation the family group into which we are born and in which we are raised.

family of procreation the family group established when a person marries and has children.

fashion a current style or custom—usually pertaining to dress, hair style, or dance—which is temporary and appealing to many people.

fecundity the human's physiological potential to reproduce.

fertility rate the number of births per 1,000 women in the 15–44 age bracket.

feudal society a type of society, existing in Europe from the ninth to the fifteenth centuries, which was agriculturally based and composed of three major groups—nobility, clergy, and peasantry.

folk society Robert Redfield's term for a small, preliterate, homogeneous, isolated, traditional, family- and community-centered society.

folkways social norms that are of relatively little importance when compared to mores and that govern such behavior as styles of dress and speech. The term is sometimes used interchangeably with customs.

formal structure preplanned and written-down aspects of an organization—such as handbooks of policy and procedure, constitutions, and charts showing the chain-of-command—that attempt to dictate the actions of organizational members.

frustration-aggression hypothesis John Dollard and Neil Miller's theory that frustrated people resort to aggression as a source of psychological reward.

functional theory the theory which asserts that social patterns are best understood in terms of the functions they serve for a given society. In regard to stratification, functional theory maintains that stratification is necessary since it ensures that the most important positions in society are filled by the most qualified people.

futurist a writer or scholar who is interested in and makes projections about the future.

game see **imitation**.

Gemeinschaft Ferdinand Tönnies's term for a society wherein members share common traditions and values.

generalized other George Mead's term for the individual's overall impression of what others expect from him or her.

genocide the denial of the right to existence of an entire human group.

geographic determinism the theory that social change is related to shifts in geographic features.

Gesellschaft Ferdinand Tönnies's term for a society wherein members share few traditions and pursue private interests rather than community interests.

gesture a form of nonverbal behavior, such as smiling or shaking a fist, that conveys meaning to others.

ghetto a central-city area densely populated by impoverished and isolated individuals.

Ghost Dance a nativistic and revivalistic movement of northern Plains Indians toward the end of the nineteenth century. Followers believed that whites would be destroyed and the world would be populated by lost buffalo herds and ghosts of the dead.

global approach the sociological approach which favors examining the large, complex, and ill-defined societal conditions that may produce such phenomena as alienation and power.

GNP an abbreviation for gross national product, or all the goods and services produced by a political state within a specified period of time.

goal displacement the substitution within an organization of an illegitimate goal for a goal it was created to fulfill.

green revolution the increased ability of the world to feed growing populations because of the many new strains of plants, fertilizers, and herbicides.

group a collection of people who interact in an organized fashion and share a consciousness of kind.

hedonism the doctrine that humans seek pleasure, satisfaction, and rewards and avoid pain and punishment in their actions.

homicide the taking of the life of one human being by another.

homosexuality sexual desire or behavior toward a member of one's own sex. The term usually refers to male sexual behavior.

horizontal group a group, such as a social club or friendship group, which largely consists of members from the same social class.

horizontal social mobility movement of an individual or group from one position to another in society which does not involve a shift into a higher or lower stratum.

humanism the tradition which holds that human beings can and should solve human problems, that humans should never be treated as objects, and that human life is distinct from all other forms of existence.

human relations a school of thought focusing largely on the informal structure of an organization. Workers are assumed to be responsible and valuable assets in decision-making, and their involvement in the organization is thought to increase morale and efficiency.

"I" George Mead's term for that part of the self composed of spontaneous drives and desires. Its counterpart is called **"me,"** which represents the social aspects of the self as it takes into consideration the expectations of others.

ideal norms norms which a community prefers or says that it prefers to follow, but which are sometimes ignored in actual practice.

ideology the beliefs, norms, and values used by a group to justify its existence and direction.

ignorant mass view Gustave LeBon's theory that collective behavior is a result of uneducated, unreasoning, impulsive, and inferior people.

imitation George Mead's term for the first stage in the self's development in which the child simply copies others. In the second, or **play,** stage, the child plays at roles. In the third, or **game,** stage, the child is able to understand the expectations of many roles simultaneously.

incest sexual intercourse between persons who are closely related, such as parent and child.

incidence rate the number of people per unit of population who are "newly" diagnosed as having a given affliction or disease during a specified time period.

incipient phase the stage of a social movement characterized by confusion and disorganization. It is followed by the **organizational phase**—when leadership, goals, ideologies, and programs are defined and elaborated—and then by the **stable phase,** during which the movement evolves into a bureaucratic organization with rational-legal administrators.

industrial society a society characterized by a high degree of urbanization, technology, industrialization, an organized and specialized labor force, and literacy.

infant mortality rate the number of children who die during their first year of life for every 1,000 live births.

informal structure the network of personal relationships that emerges spontaneously within an organization. The informal structure may help, hinder, or have no effect on accomplishment of official organizational goals.

in-group a group with which an individual identifies and to which he or she gives allegiance.

instincts biologically inherited and fixed behavior patterns.

institution an established, relatively enduring, and organized set of procedures which enables a society to solve its major problems. For example, family, religion, and education are institutions.

intergenerational mobility the movement of an adult individual into a social class different from that of his or her parents.

involuntary group a group that an individual is forced to join or is automatically a member of without personal choice.

GLOSSARY / 545

iron law of oligarchy Robert Michels's theory that in all organizations leadership becomes concentrated among only a few who are solely concerned with their own self-interests.

isolation a form of alienation that occurs when an individual lacks confiding relationships with others and as a result feels alone or apart.

knowledge that which can be grasped intellectually, as a fact.

labeling theory the theory that assigning a deviant status to a person affects his or her self-image and the way others then interact with that individual.

language a set of verbal symbols which enables human beings to communicate. Because language allows people to conceive of abstractions, to think about the future, and to view themselves as objects it distinguishes human beings from other forms of life.

leisure time free from work, or time not needed for practical pursuits.

lesbianism sexual desire or behavior directed at a female by another female.

leveling the tendency for a rumor to become increasingly shorter and more concise as it is passed on to others.

life expectancy the average life span of individuals born into a given population.

looking-glass self Charles Horton Cooley's notion that the self is a reflection of those with whom the individual comes in contact. A self-image develops as we imagine what others think about us.

Macht Max Weber's term for power, defined as the probability that one actor within a social relationship will be in a position to carry out his own will despite resistance.

Mafia an organized crime syndicate with long traditions and controls based in Sicily.

Malthusian a follower of or anything pertaining to the ideas of T. R. Malthus, who suggested that while human reproduction rate grows geometrically (two, four, eight), food and housing grow arithmetically (one, two, three).

manumission codified means by which slaves could be freed or gain their own freedom.

marginal man Robert Park's term for an individual who, after moving from one culture to another, is often beset by feelings of insecurity, remorse, disloyalty, and anxiety. A marginal man is not fully part of either the old culture or the new.

marriage a socially approved sexual and economic relationship between male and female.

material culture the embodiments of nonmaterial culture; the artifacts of a people, such as buildings, books, paintings, and the like.

material determinism the theory that social change is brought about by changes in the material culture (inventions).

matriarchal family a family in which the female has the most power in decision-making.

matrilineal descent passage of descent privileges through the female line.

matrilocal residence the newlywed practice of living with the wife's parents.

"me" see "I."

meaninglessness a form of alienation that results when an individual is uncertain of what to believe as he or she searches for meaning in life.

mechanical solidarity Emile Durkheim's term for the social bonds which develop among people in a homogeneous society.

megalopolis a massive urban region, such as the one extending from New York City to Washington, D.C., composed of overlapping metropolitan areas.

metropolitan area a social and economic community that includes several cities plus an urban fringe.

millennial movement a social movement, usually religious in character, that predicts the end of the world.

minority a small social group that possesses relatively little economic, political, and social power.

miscegenation the intermarriage of members of different races.

monogamy the marriage practice that allows each adult only one mate at a time.

morbidity the amount of disease and sickness in a population.

mores the strongest social norms, which relate to the basic moral judgments of a society.

mortality that which pertains to death or the rate of death.

murder homicide with malice aforethought.

mutual-benefit organization a type of organization, such as a labor union, designed to benefit its members.

nativistic movement a social movement, such as the movements of Plains Indians in the United States toward the close of the nineteenth century, which attempts to restore a "native" social order.

negative reinforcement as used in reinforcement theory, punishments that may subsequently extinguish certain kinds of behaviors.

neolocal residence the newlywed practice of establishing a household apart from that of both the husband's and wife's parents.

nonmaterial culture the ideas, beliefs, norms, and values of a people.

norm a rule, established by a group, that governs behavior in a social situation.

normative-moral organization an organization, such as a church, that utilizes ideology, symbols, and leaders to control its members' actions and whose members' involvement consequently becomes one of commitment or devotion.

normlessness a form of alienation that results when an individual, faced with an absence of rules, believes unapproved behaviors are required to achieve goals.

nuclear family a kinship group, sometimes called a "conjugal unit," composed of a husband, wife, and dependent children, all probably living together.

null explanation the theory that either there is no cause of or reason for change or that whatever the cause or reason, it is well beyond what we can perceive or understand.

objective alienation the dehumanizing events and conditions that exist in society.

objective class Karl Marx's term for an aggregate of individuals who occupy a common economic situation in society.

octoroon an individual with one-eighth "black blood." Whites were once forbidden to marry such individuals by the laws of certain Southern states.

open group a group that has few criteria for membership.

open marriage a nontraditional family pattern based on complete equality between husband and wife in regard to economic support, household chores, and child care. Both partners are free to look outside the family for intellectual, emotional, and sexual expression.

open society a society in which a substantial amount of vertical social mobility is possible.

open-systems theory the theory that all organizations must import needed resources from the outside environment and adapt to changing external conditions to survive.

organic solidarity Emile Durkheim's term for the practical bonds which develop among people in a heterogeneous society.

organization a group deliberately formed to achieve a specific goal or set of goals through a formalized set of rules and procedures. An organization is also known by such terms as formal organization, complex organization, or association.

organizational phase see **incipient phase.**

out-group a group with which an individual does not identify and to which he or she feels no loyalty.

participation-oriented movement a social movement relatively unconcerned about changing society that attempts to create a following of dedicated believers. Members join to gain orientation or help from the movement.

passing living or being known as a member of a racial or ethnic group that is more privileged than one's own.

patriarchal family a family in which the male has the most power in decision-making.

patrilineal descent passage of descent privileges through the male line.

patrilocal residence the newlywed practice of living with the husband's parents.

persuasion-oriented movement a social movement in which members use legal and nonviolent means to accomplish objectives.

Peyote cult a Plains Indian movement noted for its use of the peyote button cactus. The movement grew from the Indian defeat at Wounded Knee and proposed accommodation and peace rather than strife with whites.

Play see **imitation.**

pluralism a relationship in which no one racial or

ethnic group in a society is dominant, in which there is interaction among and free movement between the groups, and in which groups maintain their separate identities.

pluralist theory the theory which, contrary to power elite theory, maintains that power in American society is equally distributed among many diverse veto groups.

political alienation Karl Marx's idea that government is an extension of capitalism and an oppressor of workers.

political order Max Weber's term for how society stratifies its members according to the power they possess within society.

political sociology the study of the nature of power and its relationship to the decision-making process, the political socialization of both social classes and leadership groups, and the power relationships that constitute political entities.

polyandry a type of polygamy in which one woman is married to two or more males at the same time.

polygamy the marriage practice that allows an adult to have several mates at one time.

polygyny a type of polygamy in which one male is married to two or more females at the same time.

positive reinforcement as used in reinforcement theory, those rewards that may subsequently create certain kinds of behavior.

postindustrial socioeconomic system a system that has moved from a production-centered to a service-centered economy.

power the ability of groups or individuals to assert themselves—sometimes, but not always—in opposition to the desires of others.

power elite theory C. Wright Mills's theory which, contrary to pluralist theory, maintains that a small group of politicians, businessmen, and military leaders dominates the major aspects of American life.

powerlessness a form of alienation that results when a person feels he or she cannot control the outcomes he or she seeks.

power-oriented movement a social movement in which members use coercion and often illegitimate means to reach their objective.

prescriptive norms norms that require that a specific action be done.

prevalence rate the number of people per unit of population diagnosed as having a specific affliction during a given time.

priestly function the religious function of supporting the status quo and curbing deviance within a given society.

primary deviant a person who engages in deviant acts but who continues to occupy a socially acceptable role. The person does not think of himself or herself as deviant, and others consider that person respectable.

primary diffusion the transfer of culture through migration.

primary group Charles Horton Cooley's term for a group wherein members develop close, personal, intimate, and enduring relationships.

primary socialization the individual's early and essential preparation for life, which usually includes learning proper eating habits, toilet training, hygienic practices, and basic norms regarding sharing, politeness, and honesty.

profane a characteristic of beliefs and objects which are deemed unworthy of reverence by a religion.

professional-bureaucratic dilemma the dilemma which results from the conflict between principles that govern bureaucracies and those that govern professional workers.

proletariat in Marxian theory, the social class in capitalist society composed of workers who become conscious of their common plight.

prophetic function the religious function of criticizing the values and norms of a society.

proscriptive norms norms that prohibit specific actions.

prostitution engaging in sexual relations for monetary rewards.

Protestant ethic Max Weber's term for the Calvinist idea that thrift and hard work are beneficial both for the individual and society.

public a geographically separated group of people who define themselves as affected by some issue, such as consumer rights, and who through discussion register their concern.

public opinion the collective voice of a substantial number of people on some social issue.

race a human group that defines itself and/or is

defined by other groups as different by virtue of innate and immutable physical characteristics.

race relations cycle any one of a number of sequences that may ensue when racial or ethnic groups come in contact. Race relations cycles have been proposed by a variety of scholars and range from the general to the specific.

rational-legal authority Max Weber's term for authority based on formal and efficient rules to accomplish organizational goals.

real norms norms actually followed by a group and which may depart from what is preferred.

reference group a group that provides an individual with his or her basic beliefs and standards of conduct and serves as a model for evaluation of self as well as others.

reinforcement theory the theory that humans are conditioned to act in certain ways according to the rewards and punishments that are applied.

relations of production Karl Marx's term for the way work is organized in capitalist society, characterized by an extreme division of labor and an exploitation of workers.

relative deprivation a realization that one's life is unsatisfactory, based not on absolute standards but on what others enjoy or on what has been promised.

religion a unified system of beliefs and practices relative to sacred things, uniting into a single moral community all those who adhere to those beliefs and practices. (Durkheim)

religious alienation Karl Marx's notion that religion is an extension of capitalistic thinking and a hindrance to a class-based revolution of the masses.

remunerative-calculative organization an organization, such as a business, that utilizes wages and other rewards to control members' actions and whose members' involvement is consequently of low intensity and based on calculation.

replication duplication of a previous study or experiment.

repressive socialization a method whereby punishment is stressed and two-way communication between socializer and socialized is discouraged.

resocialization the process of giving up a previous way of life and internalizing a new set of expectations. For example, prisoners of war face resocialization when they return to a changed society.

revivalistic movement a social movement, often religious in character, that attempts to recapture an earlier era of lost strength.

revolution a nonlegitimate social movement which attempts to institute far-reaching and sometimes cataclysmic social change by seizing political power.

role the expectations and performance of an individual occupying a particular status. Role as "expectations" refers to the rights, duties, and obligations an individual has while occupying a status; role as "performance" refers to how the individual actually behaves while occupying a status.

role conflict the problem that arises for the individual when he or she occupies one status for which there are two or more opposing sets of expectations or when he or she occupies two or more statuses that have opposing expectations.

role distance the lack of commitment a person feels for a status he or she occupies.

role set the individual's repertoire of performances toward a variety of others while he or she occupies a given status.

routine change the normal slow change that takes place over relatively long periods of time.

rumor the communication through which people caught together in an ambiguous situation attempt to construct a meaningful interpretation of it by pooling their intellectual resources. (Shibutani)

sacred a characteristic of beliefs and objects which are deemed worthy of reverence by a religion.

sanctions rewards or punishments used by a group to reinforce established norms.

Sapir–Whorf hypothesis the theory, proposed by Benjamin Whorf and Edward Sapir, that language determines what individuals are able to see and do.

scenario a popular term for an outline or a series of scenes in which future events are described and enacted.

scrying a form of the supernatural, such as reading palms or tea leaves, that purports to enable a practitioner to see or perceive the past and/or the future.

secondary deviant a person identified by others and ultimately by himself or herself as a deviant.

secondary diffusion the direct transfer of something (usually, material culture such as machinery) from one society to another.

secondary group a group wherein individuals interact on an impersonal, superficial, and utilitarian basis.

secondary socialization the individual's more abstract knowledge of life, learned after childhood.

sect a religious organization distinct from a church in that it is on the cultural fringes of a community and in opposition to community norms. It is characterized by poverty, evangelical preaching, a nonprofessional ministry, and an emphasis on emotional experience.

segregation stringent separation between racial or ethnic groups with no one group necessarily assuming superiority.

self as learned through interaction, an individual's awareness of and attitudes toward his or her own psychological and physiological characteristics.

self-estrangement alienation that results when an individual is unable to find self-rewarding activity.

self-fulfilling prophecy according to Robert Merton, an initially false belief that evokes behavior which eventually causes the belief to come true.

self-identity function the religious function of conferring on individuals an understanding of their place in the universe.

serial monogamy the marriage practice of an individual's marrying one, two, or more times during his or her lifetime.

service organization a type of organization, such as a mental health clinic, designed to benefit its clients.

sharpening the tendency for individuals selectively to retain and report only a limited number of details of a rumor.

significant symbols the symbolic interactionist term for those symbols which arouse the experiences and responses in one person that another person intends.

situational selves the various identities that a person derives from specific situations and audiences.

SMSA (Standard Metropolitan Statistical Area) a city of at least 50,000 population or a city with a population of at least 25,000 which, with the addition of the population of contiguous places, has a density of at least 1,000 people per square mile. The adjacent areas must be economically and socially integrated with the city.

social change a significant shift in the material and nonmaterial culture of a society.

social class a stratum within a class system which consists of people who are usually similar in income, ownership of property, education, and occupational prestige.

social disorganization a situation that arises when group norms, sanctions, status, and role expectations are absent or so severely disrupted that individual behavior is no longer effectively controlled. Social disorganization has been used as an explanation for increased crime and deviance.

socialization the learning process by which an individual internalizes culture and becomes an active participant in society.

social movement an important type of collective behavior marked by a concerted and deliberate attempt to bring about social change in society.

social order Max Weber's term for how a society stratifies its members according to the social esteem and honor given them by others.

social organization the order and patterning that humans exhibit in their behavior as they interact with one another.

social pathology the theory that crime and deviance are societal diseases and must be isolated, contained, and treated.

social strata the various levels within a stratification system. A single stratum consists of individuals who share particular characteristics, such as educational attainment or level of wealth.

social stratification a system of institutionalized social inequality based on important material and symbolic differences in a society, such as differences in wealth, religion, or family heritage.

society a more or less self-perpetuating group, of all ages and both sexes, which shares a culture and resides within the boundaries of a political state.

sociology the study of human beings within their social contexts; the study of human interrelationships.

sorcerers persons who engage in supernatural practices and are said to be able to control the future.

sport a culturally defined activity or experience, usually requiring physical exertion, that gives recreation and a way to use leisure time.

stable phase *see* **incipient phase.**

status the position and rank that a person holds within a particular group.

status inconsistency the situation that arises when there is some disparity among the factors that determine a person's rank in society (occupation, education, income, etc.). For example, an unemployed Ph.D. would be said to experience status inconsistency.

stereotype a preconceived idea, shared by in-group members, that all members of an out-group are alike in some characteristic. The characteristic may be negative or positive.

stimulus diffusion the transfer of ideas from one society to another without direct migration.

stratification with respect to racial and ethnic relations, the enforced separation of racial or ethnic groups, with one group assuming dominant political and economic power.

style of life a pattern of living, including type of occupation, club memberships, recreational activities, and ownership of material objects, that is characteristic of a particular social stratum.

subculture a group whose folkways and mores differ significantly from those of the rest of society.

subjective alienation the individual's subjective or felt negative reactions to the events of life.

subjective class Karl Marx's term for an aggregate of individuals who experience a common economic situation and who also have a class consciousness.

subjugated mass a large social group that nevertheless possesses little economic, political, and social power.

superstition an irrationally based belief.

swinging the practice of two or more married couples mutually deciding to exchange sexual partners or engage in group sex.

symbol the symbolic interactionist term for something that stands for something else and has learned meaning and value for people.

symbolic interactionism the theory which holds that humans are symbol-manipulating and capable of creative behavior.

sympathetic introspection Charles Horton Cooley's term for a method of gaining sociological knowledge by achieving intimate contact with various persons in order to understand their way of life better.

taking the role of the other perceiving oneself or some aspect of the world from the point of view of another.

technocrat a narrowly knowledgeable "expert" whose skill and knowledge are defined as important to the governmental decision-making process.

theological explanation the theory that all social change comes about because of divine intervention in human affairs.

totalitarianism a system of government that maintains surveillance and control over virtually all aspects of social life.

traditional authority Max Weber's term for authority based on custom or tradition.

transience the condition of modern-day life marked by the lack of permanence in social relations.

UDC an abbreviation for underdeveloped country.

understanding personal knowledge; awareness at a "gut level."

urbanization an increase in the proportion of population living in urban places and the process by which rural areas become transformed into urban areas. (Palen)

urban society Robert Redfield's term describing a large, complex, heterogeneous, bureaucratized, impersonal, and quickly changing society.

utopia a hypothetical society which, contrary to a dystopia, embodies an ideal and perfect social order.

value-added theory Neil Smelser's series of steps that describe how broad social conditions are eventually transformed and shaped until a specific collective-behavior event (mob or riot) results.

value conflict theory the hypothesis that acts are considered criminal or deviant because they are at variance with a group's values.

verstehen Max Weber's term for the almost intuitive process by which a person achieves understanding.

vertical group a group, such as Italian-Americans, that contains upper-, middle-, and lower-class members.

vertical social mobility movement of an individual or group into either a higher or lower stratum in society. It is sometimes simply referred to as "social mobility."

vocational training instruction which centers on specialized skills and on-the-job experience so as to train a person for a particular job.

voluntary group a group that people join by their own choice.

white-collar crime violations of criminal law by members of the upper-middle and upper classes carried out in conjunction with their occupations. Examples include price-fixing and padding expense accounts.

ACKNOWLEDGMENTS AND COPYRIGHTS (continued from page iv)

From *A Passage to India* by E. M. Forster, copyright 1924 by Harcourt Brace Jovanovich, Inc.; renewed, 1952 by E. M. Forster. Passage from pp. 18–19. Reprinted by permission of the publishers and Edward Arnold Ltd.

Reprinted with permission of Macmillan Publishing Co., Inc. from *Manchild in the Promised Land* by Claude Brown. Copyright © Claude Brown 1965. By permission Jonathan Cape, Ltd.

Excerpt from "The Lottery" from *The Lottery* by Shirley Jackson. Reprinted with the permission of Farrar, Straus & Giroux, Inc. Copyright 1948, 1949 by Shirley Jackson, copyright renewed 1976, 1977 by Laurence Hyman, Barry Hyman, Mrs. Sarah Webster, and Mrs. Joanne Schnurer; "The Lottery" originally appeared in *The New Yorker*.

Excerpt from "Fathers and Sons" is reprinted by permission of Charles Scribner's Sons and Jonathan Cape, Ltd. from *Winner Take Nothing* by Ernest Hemingway. Copyright 1933 Charles Scribner's Sons.

Abridged from pp. 242–243, 245, 249, 251 "English As She is Taught" and excerpt from p. 43 in *What is Man?* by The Mark Twain Company. By permission of Harper & Row, Publishers, Inc. Abridged from pp. 126–128 "Disgraceful Persecution of a Boy" in *Sketches New and Old* by Samuel L. Clemens. By permission of Harper & Row, Publishers, Inc.

Abridged from pp. 23–25 in *Brave New World* by Aldous Huxley. Copyright 1932, 1960 by Aldous Huxley. Reprinted by permission of Harper & Row, Publishers, Inc. and by Chatto & Windus Ltd.

Excerpt from "I'm A Fool" by Sherwood Anderson published in *The Dial*. Reprinted by permission of Harold Ober Associates Incorporated. Copyright © 1922 by Dial Publishing Company, Inc. Renewed 1949 by Eleanor Copenhaver Anderson.

Permission to reprint excerpts from *The Autobiography of an Ex-Coloured Man* by James Weldon Johnson, copyright 1933, granted by Alfred A. Knopf, Inc.

Excerpted, with permission, from *The Social Organization of Wolves* by Jerome H. Woolpy, *Natural History* Magazine, May, 1968. Copyright © The American Museum of Natural History, 1968.

Excerpt from *Catch 22* by Joseph Heller, Copyright © 1955, 1961 by Joseph Heller. Reprinted by permission of SIMON & SCHUSTER, INC., Joseph Heller and Jonathan Cape Ltd.

Excerpts from "A Persian Courtship" by Anne Sinclair Mehdevi from *Persian Folk and Fairy Tales*, 1965. Reprinted with the permission of Alfred A. Knopf, Inc.

Selections from *Goodbye Columbus* by Philip Roth reprinted with the permission of Houghton Mifflin Company, copyright 1959.

Excerpt from *Wayward Puritans* by Kai Erikson, Copyright © John Wiley & Sons, 1966. Reprinted by permission of John Wiley & Sons, Inc.

Excerpt from *University Days*, Copyright © 1933, 1961 James Thurber. From *University Days*, in MY LIFE AND HARD TIMES, published by Harper & Row, New York. Originally printed in *The New Yorker*. Permission to reprint from *Vintage Thurber* © 1963 Hamish Hamilton, London.

Excerpts from "My Oedipus Complex" from *The Stories of Frank O'Connor* by Frank O'Connor, published in 1952 by Alfred A. Knopf, Inc. and reprinted by permission of A. D. Peters Ltd.

Excerpt from "The Ice Palace" by F. Scott Fitzgerald. Reprinted by permission of Charles Scribner's Sons from "The Ice Palace" from FLAPPERS AND PHILOSOPHERS by F. Scott Fitzgerald. Copyright 1920 Curtis Publishing Co.; renewal copyright 1948 by Zelda Fitzgerald. Reprinted by permission of The Bodley Head from "The Ice Palace" from THE BODLEY HEAD SCOTT FITZGERALD Volume 5.

Extracts from A WALKER IN THE CITY, copyright, 1951, by Alfred Kazin. Reprinted by permission of Harcourt Brace Jovanovich, Inc.

Selections from *Stand Up Friend With Me* by Edward Field. Reprinted by permission of Grove Press, Inc. Copyright © 1963 by Edward Field.

Excerpt from "In New York you get swallowed by a Horse" by Oscar Lewis, published in *Commentary* Nov. 1964. Reprinted by permission of Harold Ober Associates Inc. © 1964 by Oscar Lewis.

Excerpts from *Asylums* by Erving Goffman. Copyright © 1961 by Erving Goffman. Reprinted by permission of Doubleday & Company, Inc.

Excerpts from pp. 84 and 81–82 of THE CASTLE by Franz Kafka, trans. by Edwin and Willa Muir, published 1954 by Alfred A. Knopf, Inc., and reprinted with the permission of Martin Secker & Warburg Ltd.

Excerpt from pp. 137–138 of "People" from UP THE ORGANIZATION by Robert C. Townsend, published 1970 by Alfred A. Knopf, Inc., and reprinted with the permission of Michael Joseph Ltd.

From THE ROAD TO WIGAN PIER by George Orwell. Reprinted by permission of Harcourt Brace Jovanovich, Mrs. Sonia Brownell Orwell, and Secker & Warburg.

Excerpts from "The Diamond as Big as the Ritz" by F. Scott Fitzgerald from TALES OF THE JAZZ AGE. Reprinted by permission of Charles Scribner's Sons from "The Diamond as Big as the Ritz" (copyright 1922 Smart Set Company, Inc.) which first appeared in *Smart Set*, from TALES OF THE JAZZ AGE by F. Scott Fitzgerald, and with the permission of The Bodley Head.

From THE GRAPES OF WRATH by John Steinbeck. Copyright 1939, renewed © 1967 by John Steinbeck. Reprinted by permission of The Viking Press and McIntosh & Otis.

Excerpts from "Being Refined" by William Saroyan which originally appeared in PLAYBOY Magazine; copyright © 1965 by Playboy. By permission of the author.

Table from "Occupational Prestige in the United States 1925–1964" by Robert W. Hodge, Paul M. Siegel, and Peter H. Rossi in *American Journal of Sociology* 70(Nov. 1964):286–302. Copyright by The University of Chicago Press.

Excerpt from *The Adventurous History of Hsi Men and His Six Wives*. Reprinted by permission of G. P. Putnam's Sons and The Bodley Head from Chin P'ing Mei, translated by Bernard Miall. Copyright 1939, renewed 1967, by G. P. Putnam's Sons.

Excerpt from BLACK SPRING by Henry Miller. Reprinted by permission of Grove Press, Inc. and by Agence Hoffman. Copyright 1963 by Grove Press, Inc.

Simone de Beauvoir, *Memoirs of a Dutiful Daughter* (New York: Harper & Row, 1974), pp. 111–112, 114–115. Reprinted by permission of the publisher and by Librairie Gallimard. Copyright © 1958 by Librairie Gallimard. Translation © 1959 by The World Publishing Company.

From Ovid, THE ART OF LOVE, translated by Rolfe Humphries. Copyright © 1957 by Indiana University Press. Reprinted by permission of the publisher.

Excerpt from UP THE SANDBOX by Anne Richardson Roiphe, pp. 152–154. Copyright © 1970 by Anne Richardson Roiphe. Reprinted by permission of SIMON & SCHUSTER, INC. and by Martin Secker & Warburg Ltd.

Copyright © 1969 by Harry Mark Petrakis. From the book THE WAVES OF NIGHT AND OTHER STORIES, published by David McKay Company, Inc. Reprinted by permission of the publisher and Toni Strassman.

Excerpt from SEIZE THE DAY by Saul Bellow. Copyright © 1956 by Saul Bellow. Reprinted by permission of the Viking Press and by Russell & Volkening.

Selection from "The Owl Who Was God." Copyright © 1940 James Thurber. Copyright 1968 Helen Thurber. From FABLES FOR OUR TIME, published by Harper & Row, New York. Originally printed in *The New Yorker*. By permission of Hamish Hamilton, Ltd.

From THE BLACK EXPERIENCE edited by Francis E. Kearns. Copyright © 1970 by Francis E. Kearns. Foreward Copyright © 1970 by The Viking Press, Inc. Reprinted by permission of The Viking Press.

Excerpts for ELMER GANTRY by Sinclair Lewis, copyright, 1927, by Harcourt Brace Jovanovich, Inc.; renewed, 1955, by Michael Lewis. Reprinted by permission of Harcourt Brace Jovanovich, Inc. and by Jonathan Cape Ltd.

Excerpt from *Clarence Darrow For The Defense* by Irving Stone. Copyright 1941 by Irving Stone. Reprinted by permission of Doubleday & Company, Inc.

Excerpt from "Little Bessie Would Assist Providence" in MARK TWAIN'S FABLES OF MAN edited by John S. Tuckey. Copyright © 1972 by The Mark Twain Company; reprinted by permission of the University of California Press.

ACKNOWLEDGMENTS AND COPYRIGHTS / 555

Reprinted by permission of Yale University Press from MILLHANDS & PREACHERS by Liston Pope. Copyright © 1942 by Yale University Press.

From Gallup Opinion Index, *Religion in America*, 1971. Report no. 70, April 1971, p. 57. Reprinted by permission.

The chart entitled "Sex, Use of Alcohol, Tobacco, and Drugs Before and After" from the article entitled "Jesus People" by James T. Richardson and Robert B. Simmonds; the chart entitled "Political Self-Characterization Before and After Joining Christ Commune" from the article entitled "Jesus People" by Mary White Harder, James T. Richardson and Robert B. Simmons. Copyright © 1972 Ziff-Davis Publishing Company. REPRINTED BY PERMISSION OF PSYCHOLOGY TODAY MAGAZINE.

"How to Write an 'F' Paper" by Joseph C. Pattison from the October 1973 *College English*. Copyright © 1963 by the National Council of Teachers of English. Reprinted by permission of the publisher and the author.

Selection from HOW TO SURVIVE IN YOUR NATIVE LAND by James Herndon, pp. 93–94. Copyright © 1971 by James Herndon. Reprinted by permission of SIMON & SCHUSTER, INC. and Bartold Fles.

From the book UP THE DOWN STAIRCASE by Bel Kaufman. © 1964 by Bel Kaufman. Published by Prentice-Hall, Inc., Englewood Cliffs, New Jersey and by McIntosh & Otis, Inc.

From *Teacher in America* by Jacques Barzun, by permission of Little, Brown and Co., in association with the Atlantic Monthly Press. Copyright 1944, 1945 by Jacques Barzun.

Excerpts from *Culture Against Man*, by Jules Henry, copyright 1963, by permission of Random House, Inc.

Selections from pp. 162–164 and 2–3 of DEATH AT AN EARLY AGE and pp. 10–11 and 43–44 FREE SCHOOLS by Jonathan Kozol. Reprinted by permission of Houghton Mifflin Company and by Penguin Books Ltd. Copyright © 1967 and © 1972 by Jonathan Kozol.

From *The Autobiography of Malcolm X* by Malcolm X with the assistance of Alex Haley. Reprinted by permission of GROVE PRESS, INC. and the Hutchinson Publishing Group Ltd. Copyright © 1964 by Alex Haley and Malcolm X. Copyright © 1965 by Alex Haley and Betty Shabazz.

From ALL THE KING'S MEN, copyright 1946, 1974, by Robert Penn Warren. Reprinted by permission of Harcourt Brace Jovanovich, Inc. and by Martin Secker & Warburg Ltd.

From FAIL-SAFE by Eugene Burdick and Harvey Wheeler. Copyright © 1962 by Burdick and Wheeler. Used with permission of McGraw-Hill Book Company.

From *The Pooh Perplex* by Frederick C. Crews. Copyright © 1963 by Frederick C. Crews. Reprinted by permission of the publishers, E. P. Dutton & Co., Inc. and by George Weidenfeld & Nicolson Ltd.

Excerpt from MOTHER NIGHT by Kurt Vonnegut Jr. Copyright © 1961, 1966 by Kurt Vonnegut Jr. Used with the permission of DELACORTE PRESS/SEYMOUR LAWRENCE and DONALD C. FARBER for KURT VONNEGUT JR.

Reprinted by permission of Schocken Books Inc. from THE PENAL COLONY by Franz Kafka. Copyright © 1948 by Schocken Books Inc. Copyright renewed © 1976 by Schocken Books Inc.

Excerpt from *The Lover and His Lass*. Copyright © 1956 James Thurber. From FURTHER FABLES FOR OUR TIME, published by Simon & Schuster, New York. Originally printed in *The New Yorker*. By permission of Hamish Hamilton, Ltd.

Excerpt from a book by J. F. Stone. Reprinted with permission from *The New York Review of Books*. Copyright © 1971 J. F. Stone.

From IMPROVISED NEWS by Tamotsu Shibutani, copyright © 1966 by The Bobbs-Merrill Company, Inc., reprinted by permission of the publisher.

From "Why Women's Liberation" by Marlene Dixon, Dec. 1969. Copyright (1969) by Ramparts Magazine, Inc. Reprinted by permission.

Lines from "The Shield of Achilles" of COLLECTED SHORTER POEMS 1927–1957, by W. H. Auden, published by Random House, 1975.

From "The Hollow Men" in COLLECTED POEMS, 1909–1962 by T. S. Eliot, copyright 1936 by Harcourt Brace Jovanovich, Inc.; copyright 1963, 1964 by T. S. Eliot. Reprinted by permission of the publishers and by Faber and Faber.

From WINESBURG, OHIO by Sherwood Anderson. Copyright 1919 by B. W. Huebsch, Inc., Copy-

556 / ACKNOWLEDGMENTS AND COPYRIGHTS

right 1947 by Eleanor Copenhaver Anderson. Reprinted by permission of The Viking Press and by Jonathan Cape Ltd.

From DEATH OF A SALESMAN by Arthur Miller. Copyright 1949 by Arthur Miller. Reprinted by permission of The Viking Press and by International Creative Management.

Excerpts from "Prologue" of *The Invisible Man* by Ralph Ellison, published 1951 by Random House, Inc.

Abridgement of "The Lowest Animal" (pp. 222–228) in MARK TWAIN: LETTERS FROM THE EARTH, Edited by Bernard DeVoto. Copyright © 1962 by The Mark Twain Co. By permission of Harper & Row, Publishers, Inc.

Excerpt from "Uncle Koppel" by Harry Golden, Copyright © 1958, 1957, 1956, 1955, 1954, 1953, 1951, 1949, 1948, 1944 by Harry Golden from ONLY IN AMERICA by Harry Golden, published by The World Publishing Co., with permission of Thomas Y. Crowell Co., Inc.

"Begger My Neighbour." Reprinted with permission of Macmillan Publishing Co., Inc. and George Weidenfeld & Nicolson Ltd. from *Through the Wilderness and Other Stories* by Dan Jacobson. © Dan Jacobson 1962, 1968. Originally published in *The New Yorker* as "A Gift too Late."

"Address to the National Institute of Arts and Letters, 1971." Excerpted from WAMPTERS, FOMA & GRANFALLOONS By Kurt Vonnegut Jr. Copyright © 1974 By Kurt Vonnegut Jr. Reprinted with the permission of DELACORTE PRESS/SEYMOUR LAWRENCE and Donald C. Farber for Kurt Vonnegut Jr.

Excerpted from *The Happy Hooker* by Robin Moore, Xaviera Hollander, and Yvonne Dunleavy. Copyright © 1972 by Robin Moore and Xaviera Hollander. Reprinted by permission of Dell Publishing Co., Inc.

Excerpt from "What It Means to Be a Homosexual" by Merle Miller, *New York Times Magazine* January 17, 1971. © 1972 by The New York Times Company. Reprinted by permission.

From I NEVER PROMISED YOU A ROSE GARDEN by Hannah Green (Joanne Greenberg). Copyright © 1964 by Hannah Green. Reprinted by permission of Holt, Rinehart and Winston, Publishers and by William Morris Agency.

Excerpt from *American Tragedy* by Theodore Dreiser, Copyright © 1925 by Horace Liveright, Inc., 1926 by Theodore Dreiser, 1953 by Helen Dreiser from AN AMERICAN TRAGEDY by Theodore Dreiser, published by The World Publishing Co., with permission of Thomas Y. Crowell Co., Inc. and by Harold J. Dies.

Excerpt from *Crime and Punishment,* translated by Coulson, edited by George Gibian, published by W. W. Norton, 1964. Reprinted by permission of the publisher and Oxford University Press.

Excerpt from *Getting Even* by Woody Allen, published by Random House, 1971. Reprinted by permission of the publisher and by Rollins & Joffe, Inc.

From Gregory P. Stone, "Some Meanings of American Sport: An Extended View," in *Sociology of Sport: Proceedings of the C.I.C. Symposium on the Sociology of Sport,* Gerald S. Kenyon, ed., 1969, p. 11. Chicago: Athletic Institute. Reprinted with permission of The Athletic Institute, © 1969.

Excerpts from THE ASSISTANT and THE NATURAL by Bernard Malamud. Copyright 1957 and 1961. Reprinted by permission of Farrar, Straus & Giroux, Inc.

Adapted by permission of SPORTS ILLUSTRATED, Mark Kram, "The One-Minute Angels" February 17, 1975 pp. 34, 42 © Time Inc 1975.

From Jack Orr, "The Black Boxer: Exclusion and Ascendance," in Talamini and Page. Permission by Sayre Publishing Inc., New York. © 1969 by Sayre Publishing Inc., New York.

From *The Loneliness of the Long Distance Runner* by Alan Sillitoe. Reprinted with the permission of W. H. Allen & Co. Ltd.

Excerpts from Roger Kahn "Where Have All Our Heroes Gone." Reprinted with permission of Wallace, Aitken & Sheil, Inc. First published in *Esquire* magazine. Copyright © 1974 by Roger Kahn.

From "The Occupational Culture of the Boxer," by S. Kirsten Weinberg and Henry Arond, *American Journal of Sociology* 58 (March 1952), Table 1. Permission granted by The University of Chicago Press.

Excerpt from GOODBYE, COLUMBUS by Philip Roth. Copyright © 1959. Reprinted by permission of Houghton Mifflin Company.

Table of "Population of World's Largest Urban Areas" from *The World Almanac and Book of Facts,*

ACKNOWLEDGMENTS AND COPYRIGHTS / 557

1974 edition; Copyright © Newspaper Enterprise Association, New York 1973.

Excerpt from "How We Live in America" by Granville Hicks. Reprinted from *Commentary,* by permission; copyright © 1953 by the American Jewish Committee.

Excerpted from THE MAKING OF THE PRESIDENT 1960 by Theodore H. White. Copyright © 1961 by Atheneum House, Inc. Reprinted by permission of Atheneum Publishers and by Jonathan Cape Ltd.

Excerpts from BREAKFAST OF CHAMPIONS By Kurt Vonnegut Jr. Copyright © 1973 by Kurt Vonnegut Jr. Reprinted with the permission of DELACORTE PRESS/SEYMOUR LAWRENCE and by Donald C. Farber for Kurt Vonnegut Jr.

Excerpt from "Can Anyone Run a City" by Gus Tyler in the *Saturday Review* (November 8, 1969). Reprinted by permission of the publisher.

Excerpt from "A Dog in Brooklyn, A Girl in Detroit: A Life Among the Humanities" from the book THE AGE OF HAPPY PROBLEMS by Herbert Gold. Copyright © 1962 by Herbert Gold. Reprinted with the permission of THE DIAL PRESS and by James Brown Associates, Inc.

Excerpt from *The Prisoner of Second Avenue* by Neil Simon, published 1972 by Random House, Inc.

Excerpt from *Dark Ghetto: Dilemmas of Social Power* by Kenneth B. Clark, 1965. Reprinted by permission of Harper & Row, Publishers, Inc.

From "Diary of a Rent Striker" by Francis Sugure *New York Herald Tribune,* Feb. 16, 1964, p. 28. Reprinted by permission.

Excerpt from "Life in the New Suburbia" by Ralph G. Martin *New York Times Magazine,* January 15, 1950. © 1950 by The New York Times Company. Reprinted by permission.

From THE PROVINCE OF THE HEART by Phyllis McGinley. Copyright 1949 by Phyllis McGinley. Reprinted by permission of The Viking Press.

Excerpt from "800,000 Suburban Poor Suffer Amid Environment of Affluence" by Ralph Blumenthal *New York Times,* May 26, 1968. © 1968 by The New York Times Company. Reprinted by permission.

Excerpt from "Planners Worried by Suburban Auto Glut" by David A. Andelman *New York Times,* January 3, 1972. © 1972 by The New York Times Company. Reprinted by permission.

Excerpt from *Make Room! Make Room!* by Harry Harrison, published by Doubleday & Company, Inc., 1973.

Reprinted from THE WANTING SEED by Anthony Burgess. By permission of W. W. Norton & Company, Inc. and by Peter Janson Smith. Copyright © 1962 by Anthony Burgess.

Excerpt from THE ABC OF RELATIVITY by Bertrand Russell, published in 1969 by New American Library, and reprinted with permission of George Allen & Unwin Ltd.

Excerpt from *The Madwoman of Chaillot* by Jean Giraudoux. Reprinted by permission of International Creative Management. Copyright © 1947, by Maurice Valency, under the title "La Folle de Chaillot" by Jean Giraudoux, English version by Maurice Valency. Copyright renewed 1974.

Excerpt from "Man Against Man: Brainwashing" by Edgar H. Shein *Corrective and Social Psychiatry* (formerly Corrective Psychiatry and Journal of Social Therapy), 122 North Cooper, Olathe, Kansas 66061. Copyright 1962, and published by Martin Psychiatric Research Foundation Inc., 122 North Cooper, Olathe, Kansas 66061.

Excerpts from pp. 2–4 in BRAVE NEW WORLD (Harper hardbound edition) by Aldous Huxley. Copyright 1932, 1960 by Aldous Huxley. By permission of Harper & Row, Publishers and by Chatto & Windus Ltd.

Excerpt from WALDEN TWO by B. F. Skinner published by Macmillan Publishing Co., Inc. Copyright © 1960. Reprinted by permission of the publisher.

Excerpt from NINETEEN EIGHTY-FOUR by George Orwell. Harcourt Brace Jovanovich, Inc. Copyright 1949 by Harcourt Brace Jovanovich, Inc. Reprinted by permission of the publisher, Brandt & Brandt, A. M. Heath & Company Ltd., Mrs. Sonia Brownell Orwell, and Secker & Warburg.

Excerpts from *The Greening of America* by Charles A. Reich, published by Random House, Inc., 1970.

558 / PHOTO CREDITS

PHOTOGRAPHS

Kubota, Magnum, 4; Glenn, Magnum, 4; Miller, DPI, 5; Culver, 6; Bernheim, Woodfin Camp, 6; Owens, Magnum, 9; Forsyth, Monkmeyer, 9; Rogers, Monkmeyer, 10; Wells, DPI, 10; Corlett, DPI, 11; Roualt, Georges, Plate 12 from *Miserere:* "It is hard to live . . . ," 1922. Etching, aquatint, drypoint and roulette over heliogravure. Plate 18⅞ × 14⁹⁄₁₆". Collection, Museum of Modern Art, New York. Gift of the Artist, 12; Daumier, "The Third Class Carriage," Metropolitan Museum of Art. Bequest of Mrs. H. O. Havemeyer, 1929. The H. O. Havemeyer Collection., 12; Hachey, DPI, 16; Zucker, Photo Researchers, 20; Monroe, DPI, 20; Wells, DPI, 21; Tower Newsphoto, EPA, 24; Greenberg, DPI, 24; Seitz, Magnum, 24; Elinor S. Beckwith, 27; Keler, EPA, 32; Culver, 33; Fujihira, Monkmeyer, 35; Rockefeller, Magnum. 36; Cartier-Bresson, Magnum, 37; Bischof, Magnum, 37; Yaeger, DPI, 42; DeLatour, DPI, 45; Jensen, Monkmeyer, 47; Heron, Woodfin Camp, 47; Elinor S. Beckwith, 47; The Jacob A. Riis Collection, Museum of the City of New York, 48; Park, Monkmeyer, 51; Rogers, Monkmeyer, 54; Bernheim, Woodfin Camp, 57; Frick Art Reference Library, 59; Uzzle, Magnum, 59; Manos, Magnum, 59; Forsyth, Monkmeyer, 60; Monroe, DPI, 64; Tzovaras, EPA, 69 (both); "Touring in the Country," Metropolitan Museum of Art, 71; Culver, 72; Rogers, Monkmeyer, 73; "The Sargent Family," gift of Edgar William and Bernice Chrysler Garcisch, 1953. The National Gallery of Art, 75; Conklin, Monkmeyer, 76; Wide World, 78; Barbey, Magnum, 81; Wide World, 90; Borea, Photo Researchers, 97; Wide World, 97; Owens, Magnum, 99 (both); Wide World, 101; Heron, Monkmeyer, 102; Freer, Rapho/Photo Researchers, 104; Burri, Magnum, 108; Culver, 110; Tooker, George, "The Subway," Whitney Museum of American Art, 111; Wide World, 118; Erwitt, Magnum, 121; Wide World, 121; Zimbel, Monkmeyer, 121; Uzzle, Magnum, 121; Elinor S. Beckwith, 121; Wide World, 121; Mannheim, DPI, 123; Leo, DPI, 126; Lane, Photo Researchers, 126; Capa, Magnum, 128; Kraus, DPI, 129; Malloch, Magnum, 130; Davidson, Magnum, 133; Copley, John Singleton, "Mrs. Metcalf Bowler," National Gallery of Art, Gift of Louise Alida Livingston, 1968, 140; Brown, 141; Bettmann, 144; Falk, Monkmeyer, 144; NYPLPC, 145; "A View of the Buildings of Yale College at New Haven," Yale University Library, 149; Forsyth, DPI, 152; Frank, DPI, 154; Martin, DPI, 158; Monroe, DPI, 158; Bijur, Monkmeyer, 158; Culver, 163; Koch, Rapho/Photo Researchers, 173; Mezey, DPI, 173; Bettmann, 174; Henle, Monkmeyer, 178; Wood, Grant, "American Gothic," Courtesy Art Institute of Chicago, Friends of America Art Collection, 180; Bernstein, EPA, 181; Chwatxky, EPA, 182; Kubota, Magnum, 195; Conklin, Monkmeyer, 195; Cartier-Bresson, Magnum, 188; Goddess Chicomecoatl, volcanic stone, 15 century, Mexico, Aztec, The Brooklyn Museum, A. Augustus Healy Fund, 207 (top); Vishnu, copper, gilt and gems, Nepal, 9 century AD(?), The Brooklyn Museum, gift of Frederick B. Pratt, 207 (bottom); Samardge, DPI, 208; Warren, Photo Researchers, 208; Bullaty-Lomeo, Rapho/Photo Researchers, 210; Monroe, DPI, 212; Lukas, 215; Monkmeyer, 215; Wide World, 215; Svinin, Paul Petrovich, Russian, 1787–1839; "A Philadelphia Anabaptist immersion during a storm." Watercolor on paper, H.7, W.9¾". The Metropolitan Museum of Art, Rogers Fund, 1942, 221; Roberts, Rapho/Photo Researchers, 221; Wood, Photo Researchers, 222; Tower Newsphoto, EPA, 227; EPA, 227; Gatewood, Magnum, 227; Wide World, 228; Strickler, Monkmeyer, 234; Monroe, DPI; Bettman, 237; Vivienne, DPI, 238; Van Bucher, Photo Researchers, 241; Bettmann, 243, Shackman, Monkmeyer, 243; Bettmann, 244; Rogers, Monkmeyer, 247; Bernstein, EPA, 247; Bettmann, 251; Karp, Rapho/Photo Researchers, 251; "House of Lords," plate 52 from *Microcosm of London,* vol. II, T. Rowlandson & A. Pugin. Metropolitan Museum of Art, Harris Brisbane Dick Fund, 1917, 263; Culver, 265; Bernheim, Woodfin Camp, 266; Vecchio, DPI, 266; Frank, DPI, 266; Wide World, 268; Snark International, EPA, 269; Wide World, 271, 273, 275; Culver, 284, 287 (both); Guthrie, EPA, 287; Culver, 289; AT&T, 290; Culver, 290, 291, 292; Elinor S. Beckwith, 294; Eagan, Woodfin Camp, 295; Wide World, 305 (both); Culver, 306; Wolman, Woodfin Camp, 307; Wide World, 308–318; Budnik, Woodfin Camp, 321; Brody, EPA, 322; Anderson, Woodfin Camp, 322; Kansas State Historical Society, Topeka, 322; Wide World, 324; Anderson, Woodfin Camp, 333; Wide World, 355; Eagan, Woodfin Camp, 336; Wide World, 338 (both); Culver, 341; Eagan, Woodfin Camp, 343; Kraus, DPI, 345; Sachs, EPA, 345; Cartier-Bresson, Magnum, 346; Wide World, 348; Strickler, Monkmeyer, 348; Strickler, Monkmeyer, 351; Culver, 361; Camera Hawaii, DPI, 364; Woolaroc Museum, 365; Wide World, 366–7; International

Museum of Photography, George Eastman House, 372; Conklin, Monkmeyer, 375 (both); Miller, DPI, 377; Wide World, 379; Culver, 379; Wide World, 388; Stone, EPA, 388; Culver, 390; Wide World, 391 (both); Glinn, Magnum, 399; Anspach, EPA, 401; Monroe, DPI, 403; Young, DPI, 403; Culver, 409–411; Wide World, 412; NC News/EPA, 416; Wide World, 418; "The Quilting Party," artist unknown, third quarter nineteenth century, oil on composition board, 19⅜ × 26⅛". Abby Aldrich Rockefeller Folk Art Collection, Williamsburg, Va., 426; Greenberg, DPI, 426; Mezey, DPI, 426; Wide World, 430–434; Theodore Roosevelt Collection, Harvard College Library, 436; Wide World, 439–444; Luttenberg, EPA, 445; EPA, 450; Herman, DPI, 452; Lukas, EPA, 460; Anspach, EPA, 460; Anspach, EPA, 461; Hamilton, EPA, 464; Sachs, EPA, 472; Wide World, 474; Laure, Woodfin Camp, 474; Brody, EPA, 478; Sabarise, DPI, 479; Forsyth, Monkmeyer, 479; Krishna, DPI, 489; EPA, 489; UN, 491 (both); Propix, Monkmeyer, 494; Bernheim, Woodfin Camp, 495 (both); Coplan, DPI, 505; Dunnett, Rothco, 510; Dunnett, Rothco, 511 (left); Ross, Rothco, 511 (right); Druskis, EPA, 514; Culver, 516 (all); Wide World, 519–522 (all); Druskis, EPA, 524.

PART OPENERS

Hachey, DPI, 16; Monroe, DPI, 64; Coplan, DPI, 168; Wide World, 280; Uzzle, Magnum, 328.

PHOTO ESSAYS

Ethnocentrism and Our Daily Rituals

Uzzle, Magnum, 28 (tl); Mares, Monkmeyer, 28 (tr); Miller, Magnum, 28 (cl); Burri, Magnum, 28 (b); Attaway, Monkmeyer, 29 (tl); Cuvler, 29 (tr); WHO, Monkmeyer, 29 (cl); Fujihira, Monkmeyer, 29 (cr, br); "La Toilette," Mary Cassatt, ca. 1892, dry point and aquatint, Brooklyn Museum, 30 (tl); Culver, 30 (tr); Cartier-Bresson, Magnum, 30 (cr); Mares, Monkmeyer, 30 (br); Queen and Hairdresser, Limestone relief. Egypt. Dynasty XI, about 2030BC, Brooklyn Museum, Charles Edwin Wilbour Fund, 31 (tl); EPA, 31 (tr); Vivienne, DPI, 31 (cr); Turnley, EPA, 31 (c); Culver, 31 (br).

Face-to-Face Interaction

Rogers, Monkmeyer, 86 (tl); Cartier-Bresson, Magnum, 86 (tr); Sachs, EPA, 86 (cl); Wide World, 86 (cr); Hopker, Woodfin Camp, 87 (tl); Shackman, Monkmeyer, 87 (tr); Reeberg, DPI, 87 (cl); Rogers, Monkmeyer, 87 (cr,br); Wide World, 88 (tl); Tzovoras, EPA, 88 (tc); Reininger, DPI, 88 (tr); Adelman, Magnum, 88 (bl); Anspach, EPA, 88 (br); Lowenthal, EPA, 89 (t); Wide World, 89 (cl); Anspach, EPA, 89 (cr); Monroe, DPI, 89 (bl); Faller, Monkmeyer, 89 (br).

Changing Sex Roles

Heyman, Magnum, 196 (tl); Lacey, DPI, 196 (tr); Glinn, Magnum, 196 (br); Mannheim, DPI, 196 (rc); Kraus, DPI, 196 (rb); Ross, Photo Researchers, 197 (tl); Heyman, Magnum, 197 (tr); Mezey, DPI, 197 (cr); Forsyth, Monkmeyer, 197 (c); Wide World, 197 (bl); Suva, DPI, 198 (t); Reininger, DPI, 198 (lc); Heyman, Magnum, 198 (rc); Malloch, Magnum, 198 (b); Ellis, Rapho/Photo Researchers, 199 (tl); Roberts, Rapho/Photo Researchers, 199 (tr); Forsyth, Monkmeyer, 199 (cl); Lukas, EPA, 199 (cr); McLaren, Rapho/Photo Researchers, 199 (b).

Social Movements Through Posters

Wide World, 312 (t); Culver, 312 (both); Wide World, 313–314 (all); Culver, 315 (tl); Wide World, 315 (tr,b).

Pluralism in American Society

Reininger, DPI, 368 (tl); Wide World, 368 (tr); Vecchio, DPI, 368 (c); Korn, DPI, 368 (br); Rogers, Monkmeyer, 369 (tr); Wide World, 369 (c); Korn, DPI, 369 (b); Capa, Magnum, 370 (tl); Brody, EPA, 370 (tr); Reeberg, DPI, 370 (c); Cartier-Bresson, Magnum, 370 (br); Rogers, Monkmeyer, 371 (t); Merrim, Monkmeyer, 371 (c); Chester, Monkmeyer, 371 (b);

A View of the City

Lukas, EPA, 466 (tl); Elinor S. Beckwith, 466 (tr); Mezey, DPI, 466 (c); Hays, Monkmeyer, 466 (bl); Rogers, Monkmeyer, 466 (br); Martin, DPI, 467 (t); Gordon, DPI, 467 (c); Rogers, Monkmeyer, 467 (bl); Elinor S. Beckwith, 467 (br); Conklin, Monkmeyer, 468 (tl); Anderson, Woodfin Camp, 468 (tr); Kagan, Monkmeyer, 468 (cl); Borea, EPA, 468 (cr); Lukas, EPA, 468 (b); Elinor S. Beckwith, 469 (tl); Moser, DPI, 469 (tc); Hays, Monkmeyer, 469 (tr); Thompson, Woodfin Camp, 469 (cr); Yeomans, Woodfin Camp, 469 (br).

NAME INDEX

Abernathy, Robert, 472–473
Alger, Horatio, 162
Allen, Woody, 420–421
Allport, Gordon W., 379n
Almond, Gabriel A., 265
Anastasia, Albert, 417
Andelman, David, 481–483
Anderson, Sherwood, 54–55, 337–339
Anhalt, Edward, 382
Ardrey, Robert, 288–289
Arnold, Matthew, 336
Arond, Henry, 441
Auden, W. H., 332

Bacon, Francis, 6–7
Balzac, Honoré de, 128
Barzun, Jacques, 242, 244
Beauvoir, Simone de, 181–183
Becker, Howard S., 394
Bell, Alexander Graham, 289, 290
Bell, Daniel, 419
Bellow, Saul, 192–194
Berk, Richard, 311
Bierce, Ambrose, 172, 205, 261
Blau, Peter M., 127
Blauner, Robert, 344
Blumenthal, Ralph, 481
Blumer, Herbert, 305–306
Bogardus, Emory, 372
Bogue, Donald, 493–494
Bontemps, Arna, 209–211
Bronfenbrenner, Urie, 58–59, 191–192
Bronte, Charlotte, 213
Brown, Claude, 35–36
Bryan, William Jennings, 215–217
Burdick, Eugene, 273–274
Burgess, Anthony, 504–505
Byron, George Gordon, Lord, 450

Capone, Al, 417, 418
Carroll, Lewis, 356
Castaneda, Carlos, 223
Césaire, Aimé, 268–269

Chavez, Cesar, 211
Chinoy, Ely, 344
Churchill, Winston, 33–34
Clark, Kenneth, 474–476
Clark, Ramsey, 419–420
Cleaver, Eldridge, 396
Clemens, Samuel L., *see* Twain, Mark
Cloward, Richard, 391
Cohen, Albert, 391
Comte, Auguste, 6, 7
Conant, James Bryant, 237–238
Cook, Fred, 274–275
Cooley, Charles Horton, 10–11, 53–54, 107
Coppola, Francis Ford, 417
Crane, Stephen, 85, 90–91
Cressey, Donald, 417
Crews, Frederick, 276–277
Cullen, Countee, 209–211

Dahl, Robert, 265
Darrow, Clarence, 215–217
Davis, Kingsley, 151, 152, 207, 213, 214, 490–491
De Quincey, Thomas, 459
DeWitt, J. L., 365
Dickens, Charles, 139–140, 153–155, 269–270, 391–393
Dinitz, Simon, 416
Disraeli, Benjamin, 264
Dixon, Marlene, 320–321
Djilas, Milovan, 270
Dollard, John, 316
Dostoevsky, Feodor, 13–14, 413–415
Douglass, Frederick, 76–77
Dove, Adrian, 251
Dreiser, Theodore, 411–413
Dumont, Matthew, 135
Durkheim, Emile, 85, 207, 219, 220, 343, 456

Edison, Thomas A., 289, 290
Ehrlich, Paul, 487–488, 490, 494
Eisenhower, Dwight D., 34
Eliot, T. S., 334–335
Ellison, Ralph, 345–347

561

NAME INDEX

Ellwood, Charles, 380
Engels, Friedrich, 263
Erikson, Erik H., 379n
Erikson, Kai T., 84–85
Ervin, Sam J., 523
Etzioni, Amitai, 118

Farb, Peter, 21–22
Field, Edward, 109
Fitzgerald, F. Scott, 106–107, 149–150
Ford, Gerald, 435
Ford, Henry, 127, 284
Forster, E. M., 32–33
Franklin, Benjamin, 426

Gandhi, Mohandas, 211
Gans, Herbert, 162, 460
Garvey, Marcus, 321, 323
Genovese, Vito, 418
Giraudoux, Jean, 512–514
Glick, Clarence, 372
Goethe, Johann Wolfgang von, 7
Goffman, Erving, 122–124
Gold, Herbert, 461–462
Golden, Harry, 357–358
Green, Hannah, 407–408
Gregory, Dick, 362
Guest, Robert, 344
Gumplowicz, Ludwig, 395

Harlan, John Marshall, 142
Heller, Joseph, 79–80
Hemingway, Ernest, 46–47
Hennessey, Peter, 417
Henry, Jules, 245
Herbert, A. P., 19
Herndon, James, 234–235
Hicks, Granville, 453–455
Hitler, Adolf, 268, 287, 381
Hobbes, Thomas, 7
Hollander, Xaviera, 398–399
Horowitz, Irving Louis, 267
Hume, David, 7
Humphreys, Laud, 400–401
Huxley, Aldous, 50–52, 518–519

Ingraham, Barton L., 522

Jackson, Shirley, 43–44
Jacobs, Jerry, 445
Jacobson, Dan, 374–376
Jesus of Nazareth, 211, 222–223
Joan of Arc, 211, 291
Johnson, James Weldon, 56–57
Johnson, Lyndon B., 264, 267, 318, 347, 356

Kafka, Franz, 126, 130–131, 294–298
Kahn, Herman, 276, 493, 523
Kahn, Roger, 431–432, 438
Kaplan, Max, 445
Kaufman, Bel, 239–241, 255–256
Kazin, Alfred, 108–109
Kefauver, Estes, 418
Kennedy, John F., 267, 318
Kerouac, Jack, 387
King, Coretta, 214
King, Martin Luther, Jr., 211, 214
Kinsey, Alfred, 400
Kosinsky, Jerzy, 23–24
Kozol, Jonathan, 247–250, 252–253
Kram, Mark, 443–444

LeBon, Gustave, 310–311
Leek, Sybil, 226–227
Lelyveld, Joseph, 373–374
Lemert, Edwin, 394
Lemkin, Raphael, 367
Lerner, Daniel, 265
Lewis, Oscar, 110–112
Lewis, Sinclair, 98–99, 212, 222–223
Lieberson, Stanley, 372–373
Lippmann, Walter, 450
Lipset, Seymour M., 162, 265, 267
Locke, John, 7
Lombroso, Cesare, 390
Long, Huey, 270, 271
Louis, Joe, 433–435
Luciano, "Lucky," 418
Lundberg, George A., 8
Luther, Martin, 185

McGinley, Phyllis, 479–480
MacIver, Robert M., 8, 9
McNamara, Robert S., 490
Malamud, Bernard, 430–431, 463–465, 491–492

NAME INDEX / 563

Malcolm X, 253–255
Malthus, Thomas R., 489–490, 492
Marcuse, Herbert, 515
Martin, Ralph, 478
Marx, Gary, 347
Marx, Karl, 140, 146–147, 163, 209, 219, 220, 263–264, 275, 286, 332, 339, 342, 395, 492
Matza, David, 162
Mayo, Elton, 122
Mead, George Herbert, 20, 53, 55–56
Mehdevi, Anne Sinclair, 80, 82
Mei, Chin P'ng, 173–175
Melville, Herman, 74–76
Merton, Robert, 127, 336
Michels, Robert, 126–127
Milgram, Stanley, 462
Miller, Arthur, 339–341
Miller, George, 345
Miller, Henry, 177–179
Miller, Merle, 402
Miller, Neil, 316
Mills, C. Wright, 13, 161, 339
Miner, Horace, 25–27
Moore, Wilbert E., 151, 152
Moran, "Bugs," 418
More, Sir Thomas, 211
Morgan, J. P., 209
Muhammad Ali, 436
Murdock, George Peter, 172

Namath, Joe, 436
Nisbet, Robert A., 11–12
Nitti, Frank, 418
Nixon, Richard M., 261, 264, 265, 267, 416
Noel, Don, 373

O'Connor, Frank, 103–105
O'Dea, Thomas, 214
Ogburn, William F., 286, 293
Ohlin, Lloyd, 391
Orwell, George, 95, 140–142, 147–148, 515, 520–521
Ovid, 187–188

Packard, Vance, 293
Pareto, Vilfredo, 287
Park, Robert, 362, 372, 380

Parkinson, C. N., 126
Pattison, Joseph C., 232–233
Petrakis, Harry Mark, 190–191
Piaget, Jean, 52
Polsky, Nelson, 265
Pope, Liston, 220–222
Puzo, Mario, 417

Reckless, Walter, 416–417
Redfield, Robert, 456–457
Reich, Charles A., 523–524
Reichenbach, Hans, 214
Rockefeller, John D., 209
Roiphe, Anne Richardson, 188–189
Roosevelt, Theodore, 435
Roth, Philip, 82–83, 442–443
Russell, Bertrand, 509–511

Sandburg, Carl, 449–450
Sapir, Edward, 21
Saroyan, William, 157–158
Schein, Edgar H., 517
Scopes, John T., 215
Scott, W. Richard, 127
Seeman, Melvin, 331, 336, 339
Shakespeare, William, 78
Shannon, William, 361
Shelley, Percy Bysshe, 450
Shibutani, Tamotsu, 307–308, 319
Silberman, Charles E., 246
Sillitoe, Alan, 437
Simmel, Georg, 343, 395, 456
Simon, Neil, 462–463, 470–471
Sinclair, Upton, 332–334, 404–406
Sjoberg, Gideon, 451–452
Skinner, B. F., 50, 520
Small, Albion W., 8
Smelser, Neil, 317–318
Smith, Gerald W., 522
Solzhenitsyn, Alexander, 323
Spencer, Herbert, 7
Steinbeck, John, 163–164
Stevenson, Robert Louis, 185
Stinchcombe, Arthur, 348
Stone, I. F., 303–304
Stone, Irving, 215–217
Sumner, William Graham, 7, 23, 25
Sutherland, Edwin H., 390–391, 415

NAME INDEX

Swift, Jonathan, 501–504
Szasz, Thomas, 407

Thackeray, William Makepeace, 140
Thomas, W. I., 8
Thoreau, Henry David, 67
Thorndike, E. L., 49
Thurber, James, 102–103, 206, 301–302, 438–440
Toffler, Alvin, 293, 298
Tönnies, Ferdinand, 110, 456
Townsend, Robert, 132–133
Toynbee, Arnold, 286
Truman, Harry S, 126, 261
Tumin, Melvin M., 152–153
Turner, Nat, 211
Twain, Mark, 41–43, 48–49, 54, 143, 217–219, 231, 350–351
Tweed, William M., 264, 265
Tyler, Gus, 458–459, 465

Valachi, Joseph, 418
Verne, Jules, 288
Vold, George, 416
Voltaire, François Marie Arouet, 7

Vonnegut, Kurt, Jr., 128, 262–263, 285, 292, 394–395, 457–458, 525

Wain, John, 362–363
Ward, Lester Frank, 7–8
Warren, Robert Penn, 270–271
Washington, George, 291
Weber, Max, 10, 119–120, 147–149, 220, 238, 264–265, 287, 343
Weinberg, S. Kirson, 441
Wheeler, Harvey, 273–274
White, Theodore H., 455–456
Whitney, Eli, 289
Whorf, Benjamin Lee, 20–21
Wirth, Louis, 458, 459
Woolf, Virginia, 72
Woolpy, Jerome, 68
Wright, Orville and Wilbur, 290

Young, Brigham, 173

Zetterberg, Hans, 162
Zimpel, Lloyd, 382

SUBJECT INDEX

academic knowledge, 243
administration, classical, 132
aggregate, 96–97
aggression, displacement of, in sports, 432–433
Alcoholics Anonymous, 213, 324, 390, 403, 404
alcoholism, 402–406
   biological pathology of, 390
alienated mass view, 311, 316
alienation, 331–353
   and bureaucracy, 120, 342, 343
   context-specific approach to, 343
   economic, political, and religious, 342
   global approach to, 342
   in groups, 344–351
   and industrialization, 342–345
   and isolation, 336–339
   in Marxism, 146, 332, 339, 342
   meaning of, 331
   and meaninglessness, 334–335
   and normlessness, 335–336
   and powerlessness, 331–334
   in racial and ethnic minorities, 345–347
   and self-estrangement, 339
   subjective and objective, 339–341
   and urbanization, 342, 343, 459–460
amalgamation, racial and ethnic, 367, 380, 383
ambisexuals, 401
American Indian Movement, 223, 316
American Indians, see Indians, American
Amish, 357
Anglican church, 214
animal behavior
   human behavior compared with, 8, 20
   social organization of wolves, 68
annihilation of racial groups, 367
anti-intellectualism, 238
apartheid, 359–360, 373–376
Asian-Americans, racial intermarriage forbidden, 378
assimilation of racial or ethnic groups, 360–363, 383
associationism, 50
astrology, 226, 227
athletes, social mobility, 438–442
atomic weapons, see nuclear weapons

authority
   in bureaucracy, 119–120
   charismatic, 120
   definition of, 265
   in politics, 264–265
   rational-legal, 120, 342
   traditional, 120
autocracy, benevolent, 133
automobiles, 284
aversion therapy, 518

Back-to-Africa movement, 321, 323
Baptists, 101, 224, 225
behavior
   collective, 301–320
   human and animal compared, 8, 20
   in reinforcement theory, 49–50
behavior modification, 517–520
Behavior-Transmitter-Reinforcer (BTR), 521–522
benevolent autocracy, 133
bilateral descent, 177
bilocal residence, 176
biological determinism in social change, 286–287
biological drives, 46
biological traits and culture, 44–46
birth control in population control, 490, 501
birth rate, 495–496, 500
Black Hand, 417
blacks
   alienation, 345–347
   assimilation, 362–363
   in central cities and urban areas, 474
   homicide rates, 410
   militant, 347
   passing into white community, 360
   as race, 355–356
   in schools, inequality, 246–251
   social movements, 310, 321, 323
   in South Africa, see South Africa
   in sports, 433–434, 436, 440
bourgeoisie, 146–147
boxing, 440–442
brainwashing, 517

SUBJECT INDEX

bureaucracy, 117–137
  adaptation to environment, 134
  and alienation, 120, 342, 343
  authority in, 119–120
  changing, 134–135
  communication in, 128–131
  definition and characteristics of, 119–120
  formal control in, 127
  goal displacement in, 125–127
  goals and employee needs, 125
  in government, 124–125, 135
  human relations in, 132
  member participation in, 131–134
  and organizations, 118–122
  professional-bureaucratic dilemma, 127
  in schools, 255–257
bureaucratic personality, 127–128
business concerns, 120, 122

capitalism
  Marxist view of, 146–147
  and Protestant ethic, 220
caste system, 143–144
category, 96–97
Catholic church, 214, 220, 224–225
cenogamy, 172
Central America, banana industry, 266–267
centralized data systems, 522–523
Cherokee Indians, expulsion, 365
Chicanos, 101, 345, 347, 362
child molestation, 72
child-rearing
  family in, 191–192
  socialization methods in, 58, 191–192
children, family relationships, 180, 185
Chile, overthrow of Allende's government, 272
China, People's Republic of, population control, 493
church, sect compared with, 220–222
cities, 449–477
  crime in, 410, 470–471
  definition of, 451
  financial difficulties, 463–465
  ghettos, 474–477
  government, 465, 470
  indifference to strangers in, 461–462
  life in, 456–462
  life styles in, classified, 460–461
  mass transit, 473–474
  modern, origins of, 451–453
  pollution in, 472–473
  problems of, 462–477
  world's largest, population, 453
civil rights movement, 321
class, *see* social class
class consciousness, 146, 147, 163–164
class-for-itself, 146
class-in-itself, 146
class struggle, 146
climate and social change, 286
closed society, 155
cognitive theory of socialization, 52
collective behavior, 301–320
  alienated mass view of, 311, 316
  crazes and fashions, 309–310
  crowds, 305–308
  ignorant mass view of, 310–311
  publics, 309
  rumor in, 307–308, 318–320
  value-added theory of, 317–318
  see also social movements
colleges and universities
  income of graduates, 237
  research in, 236
  riots and demonstrations in, 133, 303–305, 347–348
  statistics on, 231, 232
Colombia, racial distinctions in, 356
communes, 194, 200
communication
  in bureaucracy, 128–131
  symbolic interactionism in, 52–53
computers, 522–523
confirmation ceremony, 214
conflict theory
  of politics, 262–264
  of stratification, 151–153
Congregationalists, 224
consciousness
  false, 275–276
  of kind, 96
consensus theory of politics, 262–264
Constitution of the United States, 142
cooptation, 133
core self, 57
corporations, multinational, 272
Cosa Nostra, 418–419
coup d'état, 268

crazes, 309
crime, 408–421
  in cities, 410, 470–471
  definition of, 408
  differential association in, 390–393
  homicide, 409–415
  organized, 417–421
  pathology of, 389–390
  physical traits of criminals, 390
  and social disorganization, 393
  in suburbs, 482–483
  value conflict in, 395–396
  white-collar, 415–417
crime rate, 408, 410
crowds, 305–308
  active, 306
  alienated mass view of, 311, 316
  casual, 305–306
  conventionalized, 306, 308
  expressive, 306, 308
  ignorant mass view of, 310–311
  value-added theory of behavior, 317–318
cults, 227
cultural determinism, 44, 287, 291–292
cultural diffusion, 290–291
  primary, 291
  secondary, 291
  stimulus, 291
cultural relativism, 34–36
cultural transmission, 20–22
cultural universals, 37
culture, 19–39
  definition of, 19
  education in transmission of, 232–234
  and language, 20–22
  material, 19
  nonmaterial, 19, 22–25
culture lag, 286, 293
  in future, 512
  and population growth, 500–501
culture shock, 32
customs, 24–25
cybernetics, 294

death rate, 497
definition of the situation, 8
demographic transition, 500–501
demography, 487, 494–500

deprivation
  absolute, 316
  relative, 316, 349
Detroit, riots, 305, 316
developed countries (DCs), 494–495
  population statistics, 495–500
developing countries, *see* underdeveloped countries
deviance, 84–85, 90–91, 387–408
  differential association in, 390–393
  labeling in, 394–395
  pathology of, 389–390
  primary and secondary, 396–398
  and social disorganization, 393
  types of, 387–389
  value conflict in, 395–396
differential association in crime and deviance, 390–393
differential opportunity, 391
Disciples of Christ, 224
diviners, 226
divorce, 192–194
dominant majority, 101
drug therapy in behavior modification, 517–518
Dutch in South Africa, 373
dysfunctional, 33–34
dystopia, 516, 518, 520, 522–523

ecology movement, 490
economic determinism, 220, 286
economic inequality, 155–157
economic order, 147
  and religion, 220
economics
  and politics in developing nations, 265–267
  postindustrial system, 272–277
education, 231–259
  academic knowledge vs. vocational training, 243
  American values in, 237–239
  compensatory, 255
  competition in, 238
  conformity in, 238–239
  conservatism vs. social change in, 245–246
  criticism of, 238
  culture transmitted by, 232–234
  for elite and masses, 243–245
  functions of, 231–237
  goals of, 242–246
  problems of, 239–242

and research, 236
in socialization, 49
and social mobility, 236–237
statistics on, 231, 232
testing and evaluation of students, 234–236
see also colleges and universities; schools; students
800th lifetime, 293, 294
electronic surveillance, 520–522
elite
in biological determinism, 287
economic, 156
education for, 243–245
power, 161
elite group, 101
empiricism, 6–7
endogamy, 175–76
Episcopalians, 101, 224, 225
equalitarian family, 176
Eskimos, 25
language, 21–22
estate system, feudal, 144–145
ethnic groups, 100, 356–358
amalgamation, 367, 380, 383
assimilation, 360–363, 383
and Catholic church, 224
definition of, 356
pluralism, 363–365
prejudice against, 378–380
segregation, 359
stratification, 360
ethnic interaction, 359–373, 380–383
ethnocentrism, 25–27, 32–34, 380
and sport, 433–436
eufunctional, 33
evolution, teaching, Scopes trial on, 215
exogamy, 176
expulsion of racial groups, 365–366

false consciousness, 275–276
family, 171–203
affection and companionship in, 185
childbearing in, 180
child-rearing methods, 191–192
descent privileges, 176–177
economic problems, 190–191
equalitarian, 176
extended, 177–179
functions of, 179–185

matriarchal, 176
nontraditional patterns, 194–195, 200
nuclear, 177
of orientation, 171
patriarchal, 176
as primary group, 107–109
problems, 185–201
of procreation, 171
residence patterns, 176
sexual activity regulated in, 180–181
social change in, 288
socialization in, 181–183
status conferred in, 183–185
variations in patterns, 171–172
see also marriage; parents
fashions, 310
Father Divine movement, 324
fecundity, 495
fertility rate, 495, 500
feudal society, 452
estate system, 144–145
Fiji, racial pluralism, 364–365
folk society, 452, 456–457
folkways, 24–25, 33, 34
in 1890s, 70–71
food production
green revolution, 493
and urbanization, 452–455
fortunetelling, 226
French Revolution, 269, 291
frustration-aggression hypothesis, 316
functional theory of stratification, 151, 153
future, 509–525
predictions, scenarios of, 512–516
social control in, 515–523
future shock, 293
futurists, 509

Gamblers Anonymous, 324
games in development of self, 56
gangs of delinquents, 391
gay liberation movement, 401
Gemeinschaft, 110, 112, 456, 459
generalized other, 56
genocide, 367
geographic determinism in social change, 285–286
Germany, Hitler's regime, see Nazis
Gesellschaft, 110–112, 456, 459
ghettos, 474–477

Ghost Dance, 223
government
    bureaucracy in, 124–125, 135
    capitalist, Marxist interpretation, 147
green revolution, 493
groups, 95–115
    alienation in, 344–351
    closed, 99
    definition of, 96–97
    ethnic, see ethnic groups
    in-groups and out-groups, 102–106
    involuntary, 98
    large and small, 100
    majority, 101
    minority, 101, 345–347
    open, 99
    as organizations, 112–113
    primary, 107–109
    reference, 106–107
    secondary, 109–110
    vertical and horizontal, 100–101
    voluntary, 98–99

Hawaii, racial and ethnic pluralism, 363
Head Start, 5, 255
hedonism, 49
hippies, 24, 335
homicide, 409–115
homosexuality, 400–402
Hong Kong, racial stratification, 376–377
Housing and Urban Development, Department of, 356
humanism, 12–13, 20

I, 55
ideology, 276–277
    in social movements, 321
imitation in development of self, 55
immigration of ethnic groups, 356–358, 361–362
incest, 181
India, caste system, 143–144
Indians, American, 100, 345
    annihilation, 367
    expulsion of Cherokees, 365
    Ghost Dance, 223
    Peyote cult, 223
    protest movements, 316, 320, 347
    racial intermarriage forbidden, 378

stratification, 360
industrialization and alienation, 342–345
Industrial Revolution, 120, 452, 489–490
industrial society, 452
infant mortality rate, 497, 498, 500–501
in-groups, 102–106
instincts, 45
institutions, nature and definition of, 169
intelligence tests, 234–236
International Telephone and Telegraph, 272
introspection, sympathetic, 10–11
inventions, 289–290
IQ, student evaluation by, 235–236
Ireland, potato famine, 286
Irish-Americans, immigration, 361
iron law of oligarchy, 127
isolation and alienation, 336–339

Japan, social change in, 283
Japanese in World War II, 319–320
Japanese-Americans interned in World War II, 365–366
Jesus movement, 24, 224–226
Jews, 224–225
    bar mitzvah, 214
    Great Dispersion, 367
    Nazi extermination of, 367, 380–382
    as race and ethnic group, 356, 360

Kefauver Committee on crime, 418
Kent State University, students killed, 303–305, 318
knowledge
    academic, 243
    and understanding, 10–11

labeling
    in deviance, 394–395
    in mental illness, 407
La Causa movement, 347
language
    and culture, 20–22
    cumulative deficit theory, 252
    developmental lag theory, 251–252
    development in schools, 251–252
    difference theory, 252
    Sapir-Whorf hypothesis, 20–22
    symbols in, 52–53

SUBJECT INDEX

leadership
   charismatic, 120, 223
   in religion, 222
leisure, 425–427, 444–445
lesbianism, 400
life expectancy, 497, 499
looking-glass self, 53–54

McClellan Commission on crime, 418
Macht, 264
Mafia, 417–419
magic, 227
majority, dominant, 101
majority groups, 101
Malthusian theory of population, 489–490, 492
manslaughter, 409
manumission, 360
marginal man, 362
marriage, 172–176, 185
   and divorce, 192–194
   miscegenation (racial intermarriage), 378
   open, 194–195, 200
   sexual activity in, 180–181
   swinging (changing partners), 195, 200
   working women, married, 186–187
Marxism
   alienation in, 146, 332, 339, 342
   conflict theory in, 263–264
   and population control, 492–493
   social classes in, 146–147
material culture, 19
material determinism in social change, 286
matriarchal family, 176
matrilineal descent, 177
matrilocal residence, 176
me, 55, 56
meaninglessness and alienation, 334–335
mechanical solidarity, 456
megalopolis, 455–456
Mennonites, 359
mental illness, 406–408
Methodists, 224, 225
metropolitan areas, 455
middle class, alienation in, 349–351
   see also social class
Middle East, economic growth, 265
military forces
   prisoners, returning, 60–61
   repressive socialization in, 58

minority groups, 101
   alienation, 345–347
   majority-group interaction with, 362
   see also ethnic groups; racial groups
miscegenation, 378
mobility
   intergenerational, 162
   social, 153–155, 162–163, 437–444
monogamy, 172
   serial, 172
morbidity measurement, incidence rate and prevalence rate, 497
mores, 23–24, 33, 34
Mormons, 173
mortality rates, 500
   measurement, 497
murder, 409–415
mutual-benefit organizations, 120

Nacirema, body ritual, 25–27
National Organization for Women, 323
Native American movement, 320
nativistic movements, American Indian, 223
Nazis, 268, 380–382
   Jews exterminated by, 367, 380–382
neolocal residence, 176
neo-Malthusians, 490–491, 493
Newark, riots, 316
New York City, finances, 463
nonmaterial culture, 19, 22–25
normal, definition of, 22
normative, definition of, 22
normlessness and alienation, 335–336
norms, 22–25, 32, 46, 70–74, 83
   associational, 73
   communal, 73
   and deviance, 388, 390, 391, 393
   ideal and real, 73
   prescriptive, 72–73
   proscriptive, 72–73
   in social change, 286, 287
   violation of, in politics, 265
nuclear warfare, threat of, 272–276
nuclear weapons, 272–275

occupations
   intergenerational mobility in, 162
   prestige ratings, 158–160

octoroons, 378
Oneida community, 516
open marriage, 194–195, 200
open society, 155
open-systems theory, 134
organic solidarity, 456
organizations
    adaptation to environment, 134
    and bureaucracy, 118–122
    business concerns, 120, 122
    coercive alienative, 122
    commonwealth, 122
    communication in, 128–131
    definition of, 119
    formal structure, 120, 122
    groups as, 112–113
    informal structure, 122–125
    member participation in, 131–134
    mutual-benefit, 120
    normative-moral, 122
    remunerative-calculative, 122
    service, 122
out-groups, 102–106

parents
    as agents of culture, 46
    socialization techniques, 58–59
    in Soviet Union and United States compared, 58–59
participant observation, 11
pathology of crime and deviance, biological and social, 389–390
patriarchal family, 176
patrilineal descent, 176–177
patrilocal residence, 176
Peace Corps, 5
Pearl Harbor, Japanese attack, 319
Peyote cult, 223
Pittsburgh, World Series victory, 302–303, 304
Planned Parenthood Federation, 490
play in development of self, 55–56
pleasure in reinforcement theory, 49
pluralism, racial or ethnic, 363–365
pluralist theory, power in, 161
political order, 147, 148–149
political sociology, 261
politics, 261–271
    change in, 267–271
    conflict and consensus theories of, 262–264
    definition of, 261
    and economics in developing nations, 265–267
pollution in cities, 472–473
polyandry, 172
polygamy, 172
polygyny, 172–173
population, 487–506
    demographic transition theory, 500–501
    doubling time, 488
    future growth, 501–505
    Malthus's theory, 489–490, 492
    Marxist position on, 492–493
    measurements and data, 494–500
    neo-Malthusian position on, 490–491, 493
    world's largest urban areas, 453
    zero growth rate, 493–494
population control
    birth control in, 490, 501
    economic strategies for, 490–491
    optimists' position on, 493–494
Population Council, 490
population explosion, 487–489
populism, 322, 323
postindustrial socioeconomic system, 272–277
poverty, 156–157
    and crimes of violence, 410
    in suburbs, 481
power
    definitions of, 264–265
    political, 264–265
    and race relations, 372–373, 380
power elite, 161
power inequality, 161
powerlessness and alienation, 331–334
prejudice, racial or ethnic, 378–380
Presbyterians, 224
professional-bureaucratic dilemma, 127
Prohibition and organized crime, 417–418
proletariat, 146–147
prostitution, 398–400
Protestant ethic, 220, 238
Protestantism, 220, 224–225
public opinion, 309
publics, 309
Puerto Ricans in New York, 111–112
punishment in socialization, 58

race
    concept of, 355

cultural perception of differences, 355–356
  master, 287
race prejudice, 378–380
race relations
  cycles, 372–373
  and power, 372–373, 380
racial groups
  amalgamation, 367, 380, 383
  annihilation, 367
  assimilation, 360–363, 383
  intermarriage (miscegenation), 378
  murder related to, 410
  pluralism, 363–365
  segregation, 359–360, 378
  stratification, 360, 376–377
recreation, family in, 180
  see also sport
reference groups, 106–107
reinforcement
  negative, 50
  positive, 50
reinforcement theory of socialization, 49–52
religion, 205–229
  age-grading function, 214
  buttress function, 214
  churches as groups, 100–101
  definitions of, 205–207
  explanation function, 214–219
  in family, 180
  priestly function, 208–211, 223
  prophetic function, 211, 223
  self-identity function, 212–213
  and social class, 100–101, 223–225
  and social organization, 219–223
  and social status, 220–222
  theological explanation of social change, 285
replication, 11
research in universities, 236
resocialization, 60–61
retirement and leisure, 445
revivalist movements, American Indian, 223
revolutions, 268–270
  in Marxism, 147
  power-oriented, 323–325
Right to Life movement, 323
riots, urban, in 1960s, 304–305, 316–318
rites of passage, bar mitzvah and confirmation, 214
role, 78–83
  as expectation, 78–79, 83
  of others, taking, 10, 55–56
  as performance, 79
  sex, changing, 186–190
role conflict, 80
role distance, 79
role set, 79
rumor, 307–308, 318–320
  assimilation in, 319
  compounding in, 319
  leveling in, 319
  sharpening in, 319
rural areas and urban areas, population changes, 451, 453–455

Sabana Grande, appearance of the Virgin, 306–308
sacred, definition of, 207
sanctions, 22–23, 70–74, 83
  in socialization, 58
Sapir-Whorf hypothesis, 20–22
scenario of future, 512
schools
  bureaucracy in, 255–257
  busing, 255
  economic support for, 246–249
  equalizing opportunity in, 255
  goals of, 242–246
  language development in, 251–252
  private and public, enrollment and expenditures, 247–249
  problems, 239–242
  racial and economic inequality, 246–251
  and social class, 243–255
  statistics on, 231
  teacher-student status differences, 252–255
scrying, 226
sect, church compared with, 220–222
segregation, racial or ethnic, 359–360, 378
self, 53–57
  core, 57
  "I" and "me," 55, 56
  looking-glass, 53–54
  situational, 57
  three stages of development, 55–56
self-identity in religion, 212–213
sex roles, changing, 186–190
sexual activity
  in family, regulation of, 180–181
  nontraditional patterns, 194–195, 200
Shintoism, 283
situational selves, 57

slavery, 373
  manumission in, 360
social change, 283–299
  biological determinism in, 286–287
  cultural determinism in, 287, 291–292
  definition of, 283
  geographic determinism in, 285–286
  and individual adjustment, 293–298
  material determinism in, 286
  null explanation of, 285
  technology in, 288–290
  theological explanation of, 285
  variables in, 288–292
social class, 145–150
  definition of, 146
  and education, 243–255
  Marxian interpretation of, 146–147
  objective and subjective, 146
  and occupational improvement, 162
  prestige groups, 160
  rags-to-riches belief, 162
  and religion, 223–225
  in United States, 142, 143
  upper-class attitude toward lower class, 140–142
  upper-middle, 148
social control in future, 515–523
social disorganization, 85, 91
  in crime and deviance, 393
socialization, 41–63
  agents of, 46
  cognitive theory, 52
  in family, 181–183, 191–192
  as learning, 41–43
  meaning of, 41–49
  participatory, 58
  primary, 46
  reinforcement theory, 49–52
  repressive, 58
  resocialization, 60–61
  secondary, 47–49
  symbolic interactionism, 52–57
social mobility, 153–155
  horizontal, 153
  and sports, 437–444
  vertical, 153, 155, 162–163
social movements, 310, 320–325
  commitment to, 321–322
  objectives, programs, and ideologies, 320–321
  participation-oriented, 324
persuasion-oriented, 323

phases of, incipient, organizational, and stable, 323
  power-oriented, 323
social order, 147
social organization, 67–93
  definition of, 68–70
  and religion, 219–223
social strata, 143
social stratification, *see* stratification
social structure, 69
society
  definition of, 19
  types of, and urban growth, 456–457
sociology, 3–15
  as art, 9–12
  Chicago school of, 8, 387
  definition of, 6
  meaning and origins of, 5–7
  political, 261
  as science, 7–9, 11–12
  of sport and leisure, 445
sorcerers, 226
South Africa
  apartheid, 359–360, 373–376
  blacks in, 101, 373–374
  coloreds in, 374
  racial stratification, 143
Soviet Union
  child-rearing in, 58–59
  Communist party membership in, 143
  nuclear weapons, 272
  population control, 492–493
  Revolution of 1917, 270, 320, 324
  totalitarianism, 267–268
Soweto, 373–374
sport, 427–446
  displacement of aggression in, 432–433
  ethnocentrism in, 433–436
  popularity of, 428–437
  and social mobility, 437–444
  socioeconomic effects on preferences, 428–429
Standard Metropolitan Statistical Area (SMSA), 455
status, 74–77, 83
  achieved, 76
  ascribed, 76
  associational, 77
  communal, 77
  definition of, 74
  in family, 183–185

574 / SUBJECT INDEX

occupational prestige, 158–160
  and political order, 148–149
  prestige groups, 160
  and religion, 220–222
  and social order, 147–148
  teacher-student differences in schools, 252–255
status inconsistency, 158
status inequality, 157–161
stereotypes, 105–106
  racial and ethnic, 360, 380
stratification, 139–167
  caste system, 143–144
  class, see social class
  conflict theory of, 151–153
  definition of, 143
  economic inequality, 155–157
  economic, social, and political orders, 147–149
  estate system, 144–145
  functional theory of, 151, 153
  power inequality, 161
racial or ethnic, 360, 376–377
  status inequality, 157–161
students
  alienation, 347–348
  changes in, 257
  crazes and fashions, 309–310
  protests and demonstrations, 133, 303–305, 347–348
Students for a Democratic Society, 246
subculture, 24
  and deviance, 388, 390–391
  differential association in, 390–393
  homosexual, 401–402
  of prostitution, 400
  racial or ethnic, 362
  of violence, 410
subjugated mass, 101
suburbs, 477–483
  annexed to cities for tax purposes, 465
  crime in, 482–483
  life in, 478–481
  population movement to, 477–479
  poverty in, 481
  traffic in, 481–482
superstition, 205, 214, 227
swinging, 195, 200
Switzerland, ethnic pluralism, 363–364
symbolic interactionism, 52–57
symbols, 52–53
  significant, 53
sympathetic introspection, 10–11

talent
  in biological determinism, 287
  and social stratification, 151, 152
Tampa, riot, 316
Tasmania, Aborigines exterminated, 367
teachers, 239–241, 251–257
  and students, status differences, 252–255
technocracy movement, 323
technocrats, 272
technology
  in future, 512, 520–525
  machines replacing human beings, 294
  and population, 493, 500–501
  and social change, 288–290
Third World
  cultural diffusion in, 291
  politics and economics in, 265–267
TOPS (Taking Off Pounds Sensibly), 322, 323
totalitarianism, 267–268
transience, 293–294
transportation
  mass transit in cities, 473–474
  suburban traffic, 481–482

underdeveloped countries (UDCs), 494–495
  politics and economics in, 265–267
  population statistics, 495–500
understanding and knowledge, 10–11
Unitarians, 101, 224
universities, see colleges and universities
urban areas
  population changes, 475
  and rural areas, population movements, 451, 453–455
  world's largest, population, 453
  see also cities
urbanization, 451, 453
  and alienation, 342, 343, 459–460
urban society, 451, 456–457
utopia, 515–516, 520

value-added theory, 317–318
value conflict in crime and deviance, 395–396

verstehen, 10
Vietnam War
 popular disapproval of, 33–34
 prisoners, returning, 61
 protests against, 303–305
VISTA, 5
vocational training, 243

war
 in conflict theory, 262–264
 as natural instinct, 289
 nuclear, threat of, 272–276
 and technology, 289
Watergate affair, 261, 265, 292, 416
Watts, Los Angeles, riots, 305, 317–318, 347
wealth
 distribution of, 155–156
 and religion, 209

White Anglo-Saxon Protestants (WASPs), 101
white-collar crime, 415–417
witchcraft, 226–227
women
 careers after marriage, 60, 186
 sex roles, changing, 186–190
 status, 76
 working, 60, 186–187
women's liberation, 189, 320–321, 323
women's rights, 186
Woodstock festival, 306
work
 and alienation, 339, 342, 344–345
 in Protestant ethic, 220, 238
World War II, 43, 283
 Japanese veteran, 60–61
 popular support for, 33–34
Wounded Knee, Indian protest movement, 316, 347